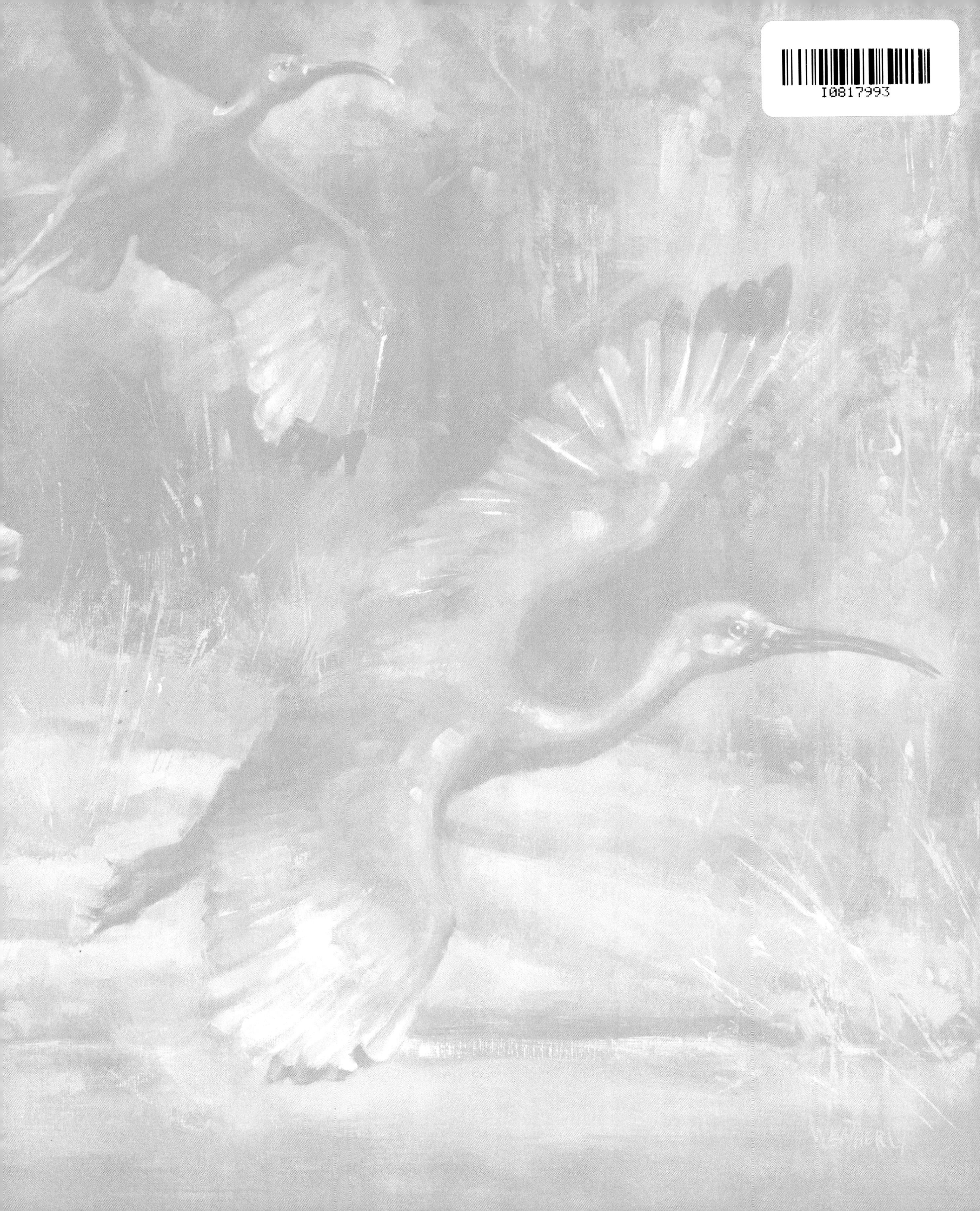
I0817993

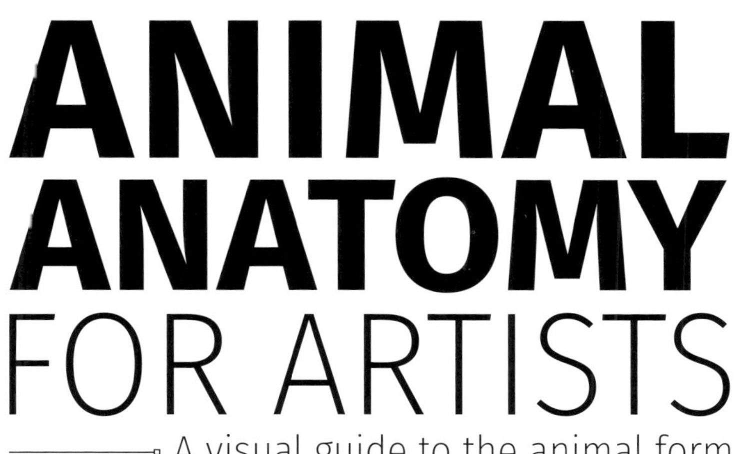

3dtotalPublishing

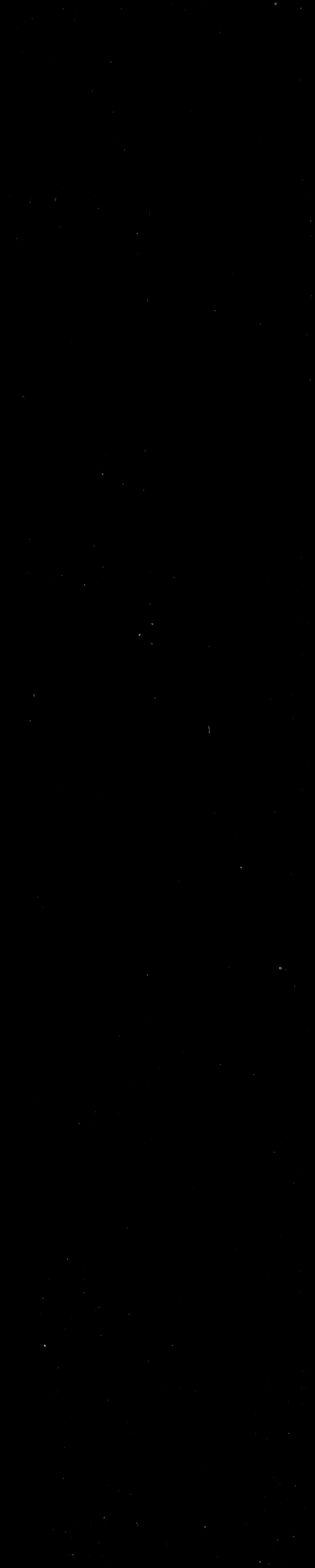

ANIMAL ANATOMY FOR ARTISTS

A visual guide to the animal form

3dtotalPublishing

3dtotal Publishing

Correspondence: **publishing@3dtotal.com**
Website: **store.3dtotal.com**

First published in the United Kingdom, 2025, by 3dtotal Publishing.

Address: 3dtotal.com Ltd, 29 Foregate Street, Worcester, WR1 1DS, United Kingdom.

Hard cover ISBN: 978-1-915992-00-0

Printed and bound in China by C&C Offset Printing Co., Ltd

Visit **store.3dtotal.com** for a complete list of available book titles.

Editor: Philippa Barker
Designer: Fiona Tarbet
Lead Editor: Samantha Rigby
Lead Designer: Joseph Cartwright
Studio Manager: Simon Morse
Managing Director: Tom Greenway

Front cover images
Clockwise starting top left:
Photograph © Tom Friedel / Agami.nl;
Photograph © Caroline Piek/ Agami.nl;
Artwork © Shannon Beaumont;
Photograph © Vincent Legrand / Agami.nl;
Photograph © Aurélien Audevard/ Agami.nl;
Artwork © Joe Weatherly

Back cover images and endpapers
Artwork © Joe Weatherly

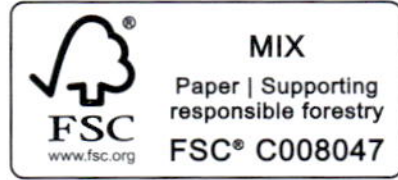

50%
of net profits donated
TO CHARITY

In 2022, 3dtotal Publishing became successful enough to make a pledge to donate **50% of its net profits to charity**. This continues to be possible due to the incredible support from all our customers, employees, and partners. At the time of printing, we have donated over $1.62 million (USD) to charity.

We focus our giving on three charitable areas: **environmental**, **humanitarian**, and **animal welfare**. We use organizations such as Effective Altruism and Founders Pledge to guide who we help within these causes. Some ways of doing good are over 100 times more effective than others, so donating this way hugely increases the impact of our contributions.

See **3dtotal.com/charity** for full details.

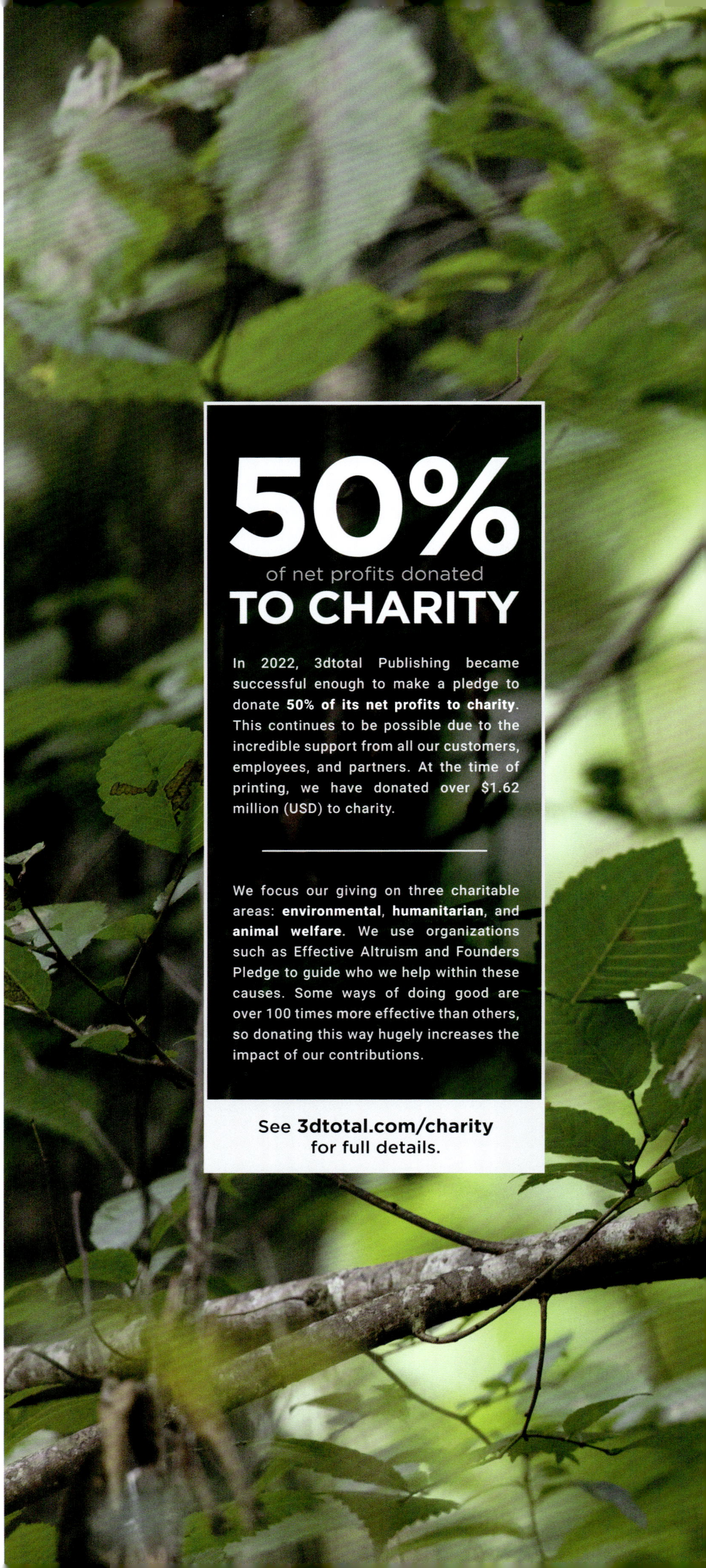

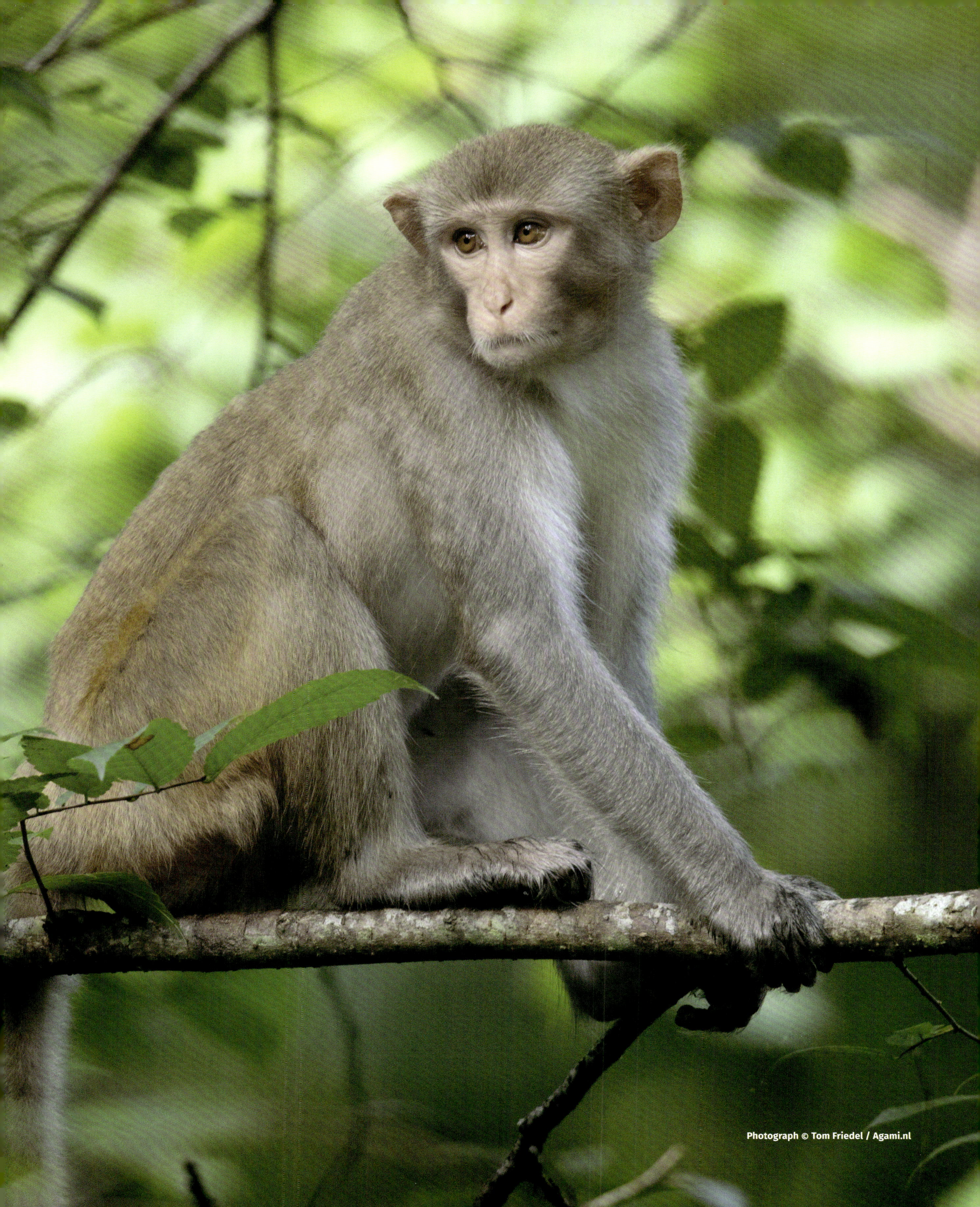

Photograph © Tom Friedel / Agami.nl

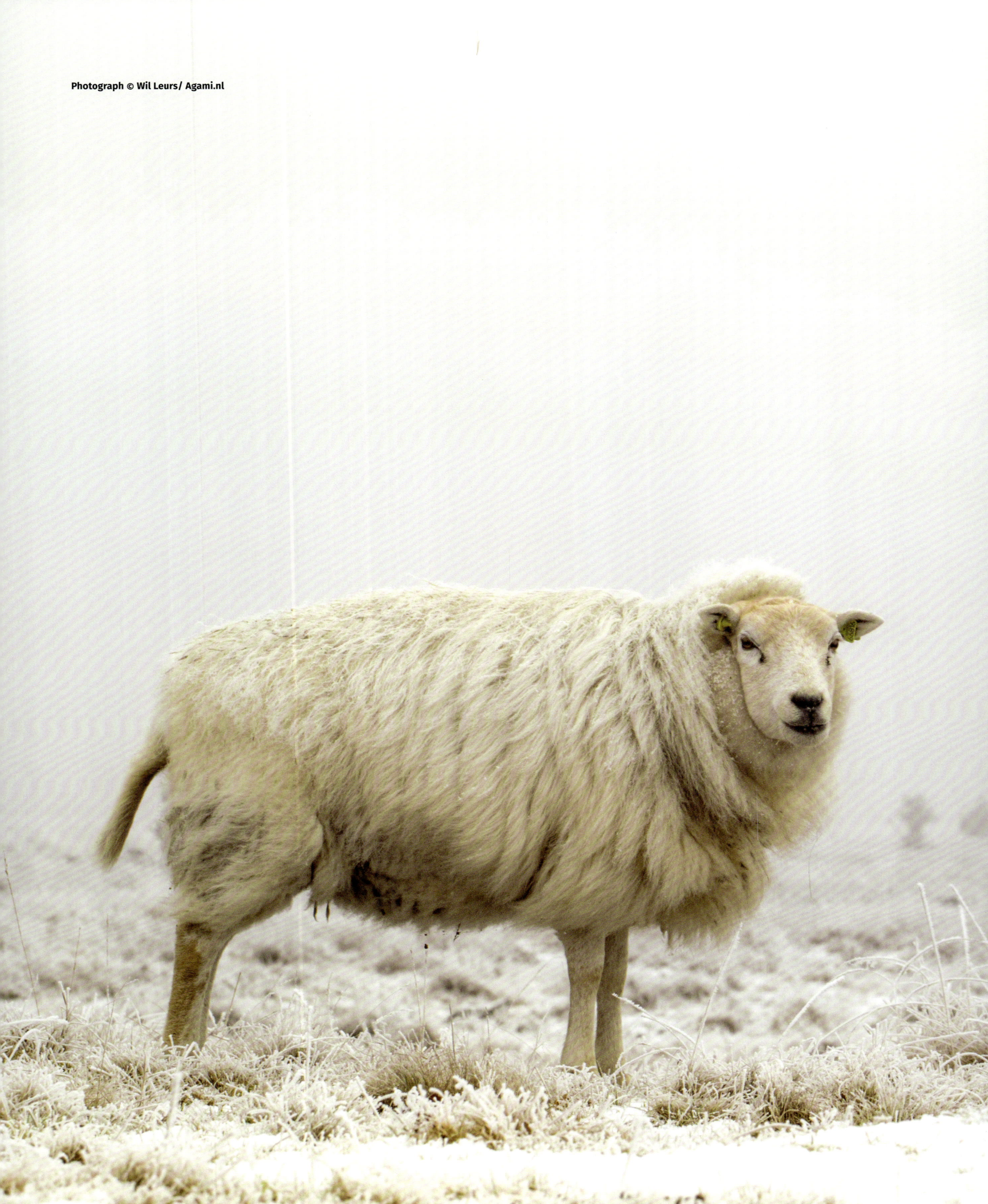

Contents

Foreword

By Marshall Vandruff

Artist & teacher
marshallart.com

If you are reading this, I assume you care about animals and how to draw them, including from the imagination. If you are a beginner, that can be a challenge, and that's why this book is designed for you.

For me, it took fifteen frustrating years. In my teens, I wanted to draw like the artists and animators I loved, inventing creatures that looked convincing without needing to copy an existing image. I had no clue how. I asked my college teachers who had master's degrees in drawing: 'How do you invent creatures from your imagination like that?' But none of them knew. I was baffled until I learned that they were victims of an educational system that had abandoned classic drawing and, as much as I loved them, they were passing on their victimhood to me.

I dropped out of college to pursue a career in illustration and, with my limited knowledge, started making a living. At the age of twenty-six I received an invitation from one of those beloved former instructors to teach a class in illustration. I took it. I figured what better place to learn to draw than in the classrooms where I didn't? Over the next forty years, I developed courses on human and animal anatomy at colleges and art schools. Learning by teaching, I saw students grow into professionals, surpass me in skill, and even become superstars.

LEARNING TO DRAW & INVENT

The simplest way to draw convincingly is to copy what we see, but that gets tiresome if we want to invent, which takes three skills. I'll explain them briefly, then elaborate.

The first skill is to know what we're drawing. Ignorance has its charm, but it doesn't last long. With animal drawing we need to know animal anatomy. That is the first skill.

But anatomy is not enough. Veterinarians who are familiar with an animal's every nerve and fibre will not necessarily be able to draw an animal any better than a cartoonist. An artist needs a kind of visual language. This second skill is form: putting an animal into perspective so it looks less like a paper cut-out and more like a solid body.

Once an artist has these two skills, they can draw realistic animals from imagination, but they may look, as Joe Weatherly puts it, 'like taxidermy'. That leads to our third skill: gesture. This has to do with creating animals that seem alive, granted that they are. Let's look at these three skills in more detail.

OBSERVATION: LEARN ANATOMY

We can't draw what we don't know. While animals are made of bones and flesh, skin, fur, scales, and even exoskeletons, let's limit our study to the basic structures that human bodies have in common with mammals, birds, and reptiles: bones and muscles. We start with bones. This may seem strange, considering that muscles create bigger forms, but there is a reason to study bones first – they don't change shape, and they create big proportions. The muscles and flesh fill in gaps, but they change shape when they move. A lion has the same anatomy in its forepaws as the human hand, but shaped differently. That is proportion. A hoofed animal walks on toenail and fingernail, and though you never mistake a hoof for an extended finger, they have much in common. That is anatomy and proportion. Horses, deer, cats, bears, and dog breeds have their own proportions based on bones that stay constant and flesh that compresses, bulges, pinches, pulls, and even responds to gravity. This is why artists study bones and muscles. They make up the bulk of animal form.

If learning about bones and muscles feels intimidating, let me remind you that there are only about as many bones to learn as there are letters in the English alphabet. Fewer if you are cartooning. More if you are seeking sophisticated mastery. However, you can master the proportions of the major bones of any animal in a month or three if you go at it with interest.

Muscles take a bit more work because they are shapeshifters. Nevertheless, if you know where they start (origins) and where they end (insertions), you know enough to learn their varied shapes, which depend on the positions of the bones they pull. Though we could learn a hundred muscles that make up an animal, we don't need to. We learn them in groups, and this is a major lesson for how to learn anatomy: simplify!

Who can know each and every part of an animal? And what good would this knowledge do? A drawing is always simpler than reality, and every artist invents their own ways to simplify. They may prefer long or short legs, wide or narrow haunches, deep or shallow snouts. They may reduce their ideal creature into shapes and formulas. They may stick to those choices or deviate from them dramatically with every drawing. Anatomy is a science, yet for artists, it invites opinion.

But no matter how decisively an artist chooses proportions, they still have the problem of how to present bodies on paper that appear to aim towards us, turn away, or overlap parts as if they exist in three-dimensional space. That carries us into the second skill: simplifying anatomy into three dimensions. ▸▸

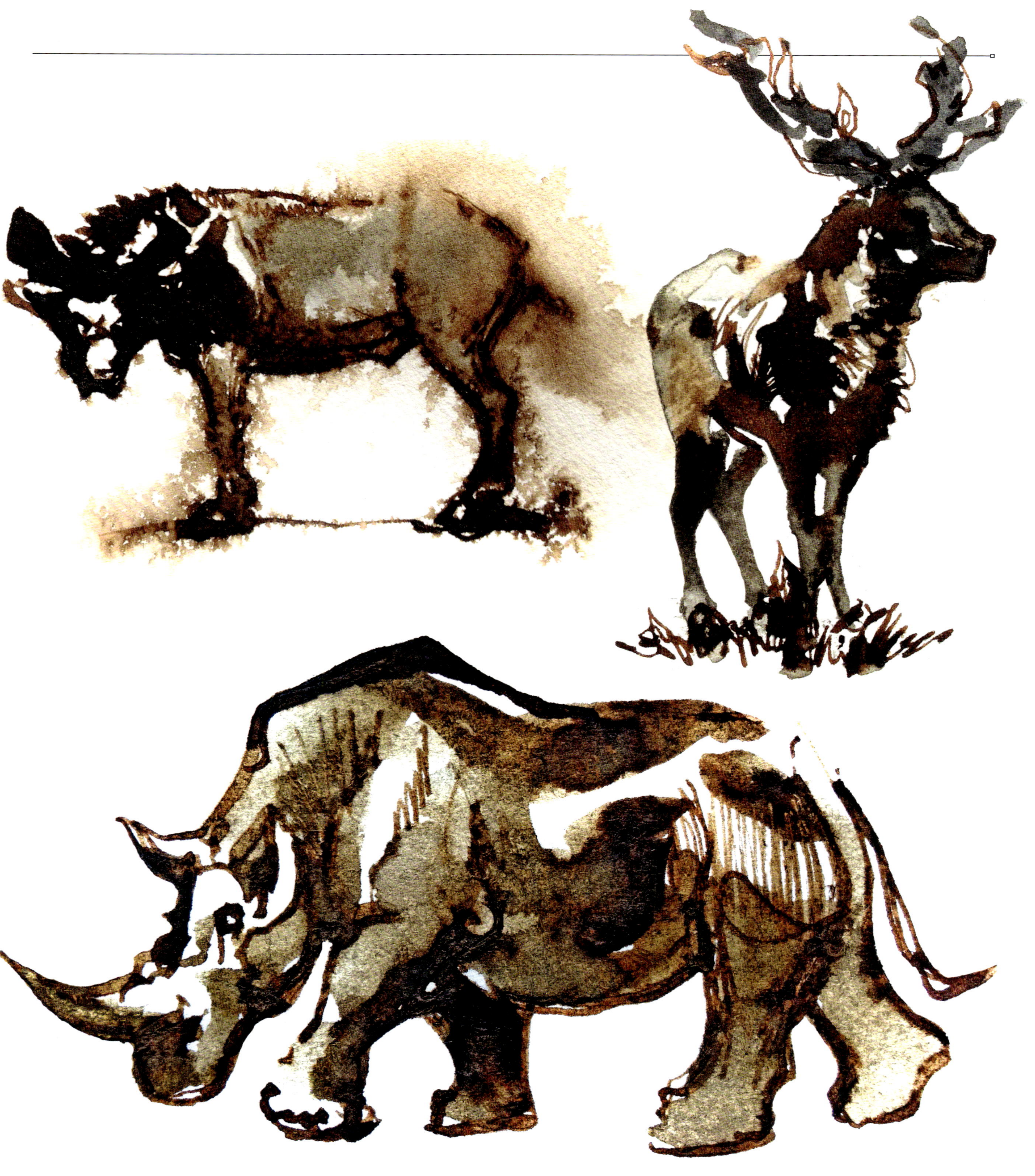

All artwork © Marshall Vandruff

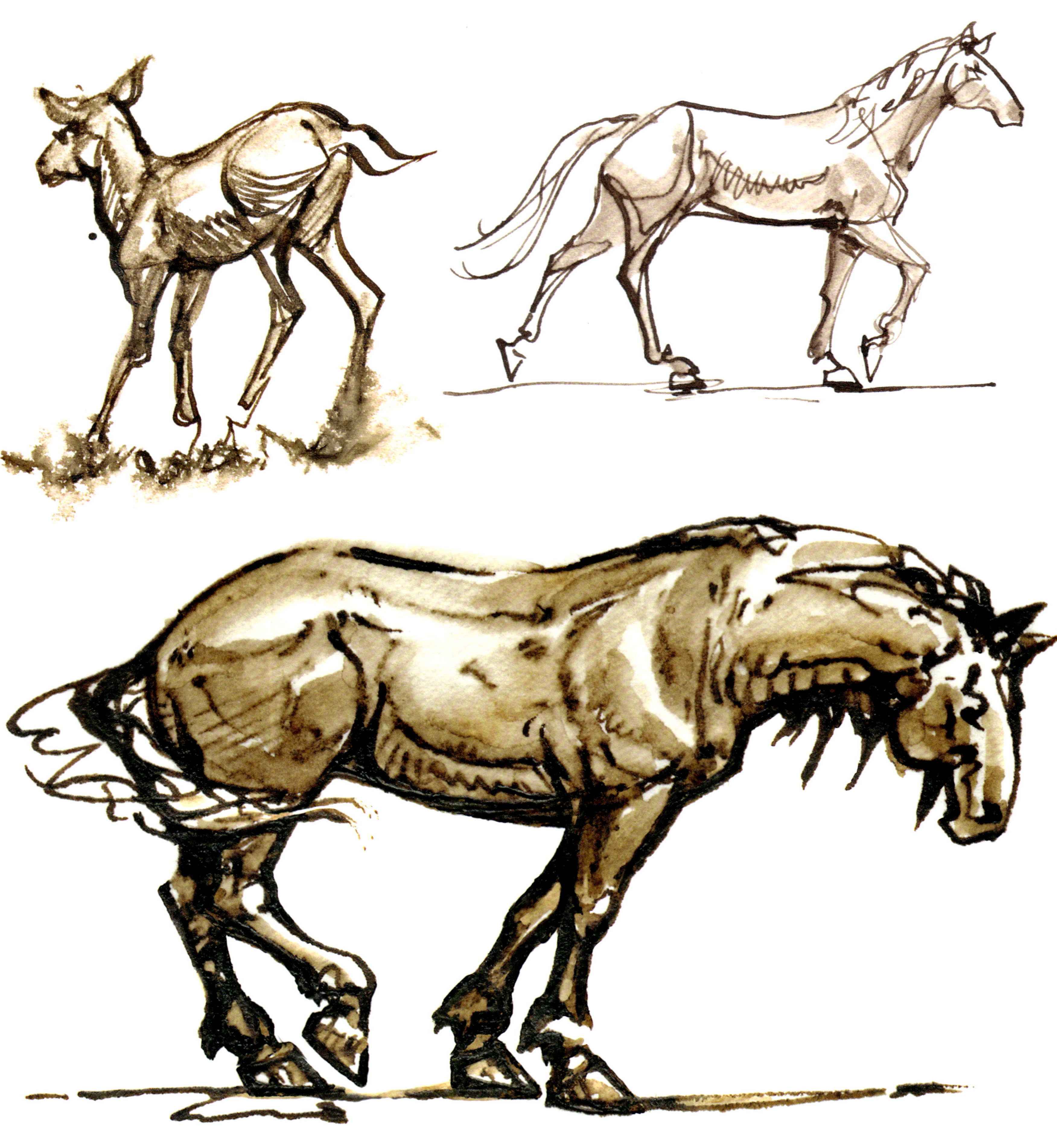

INVENTION: LEARN FORMS

Form describes three-dimensional volumes such as cones, blocks, cylinders, and spheres. For centuries, professional artists learned everything about forms. In college, I learned nothing about them.

During my first year of teaching, I took a workshop with the illustrator Drew Struzan. He told our small group of professionals that we 'didn't have a clue how to draw'. It bruised egos, but not mine. I felt glad for his honesty. He explained that the knowledge of how to draw convincing creatures from imagination has been around for 600 years. He demonstrated this to me by drawing an elk in a different position from its photo reference as easily and quickly as speaking, and with a 'thickness' to the body that made me gasp. He claimed that he used the same skills as masters like Michelangelo, and that I too would do well to learn those skills.

The big secret was to apply perspective to torsos and limbs, heads and features, clothing and hair, or anything else, industrial or organic. I barely understood, but I believed. Unfortunately, students seeking this wisdom from universities often don't find it. It has been neglected for over sixty years. In the 21st century, the internet began offering this instruction to anyone seeking it. We went from a drought to a flood of resources, not all of them good, but at least classic drawing skill is no longer the secret knowledge it was during my years of training.

I first learned it from Robert Beverly Hale's video lectures, recorded in the 1970s at The Art Students League of New York. He demonstrated how the old masters invented their beautifully drawn bodies by encasing them within simplified forms. Ambitious to learn from a teacher who demonstrated line by line, I watched those demos over and over on my four-inch camper TV and was thrilled to finally understand it.

When I showed the videos to my university students, they were less enthralled. Granted, technical knowledge is seldom exciting to artistic types, and form does not at first seem artistic. One student complained: 'I don't want to draw animals made out of boxes and cylinders!' They didn't understand that those boxes and cylinders are the basis for inventing bodies, the way musical scales are the basis for inventing chords and melodic phrases. Hale pointed out that the choice of how to treat body parts – animal or human – as blocks, barrels, or beach balls is an artistic choice. We can choose well or poorly. We can create chunky, masculine styles, or flowing, feminine styles, or surprising combinations of the two, and we can do this with our choices of forms.

But that is advanced. First, we must learn the forms. And just because we now have easy access to the knowledge does not mean that the knowledge is easy. It takes a year or two of serious work to turn anatomy into form, then turn the forms around in space. Learning how an animal looks in 3D is the secret of cartoonists and animators who invent creatures from the imagination and make them look realistic. It does not, however, guarantee an exciting drawing. Therefore, our third and final skill...

GESTURE: BEYOND TAXIDERMY

Our third challenge may be the most misunderstood of all drawing skills. Dictionaries define 'gesture' as a movement of the body, usually to express an emotion. Kimon Nicolaïdes (again, at The Art Students League) popularized the term in the early 20th century. He assigned students to draw hundreds of rapid drawings, rehearsing within their own sensations the feelings their subject feels in a particular position. In his book, *The Natural Way to Draw*, he explains, pitches, preaches, and admonishes students to *empathize* with what they draw.

The lesson here is not what the animal is made of, nor even how it occupies space. It is to sense its physical experience of weight, wind, wetness, elasticity, stiffness, and so on, as well as its emotional experiences, such as fear, aggression, boredom, or friskiness. Without an awareness, or even resonance, of those feelings in the artist, there is no hope of ever getting the subject's 'life' into the drawing.

This is not about realistic anatomy or form. This is about credible actions that come from emotional impulses, and convincing positions that respond to physical pressures. It is the skill of animators who bring their drawings to life, not as marionettes moved by an outside force, but as characters with inner motivations, standing strong, chasing, fighting, resting ... as individual personalities in tactile worlds.

Gesture is a complex term. It leads to opinions and debates. One reason is that an artist's own gestural quality comes into play. Artists can draw with flowing, choppy, rhythmic, meandering, organized, wild, minimal, stiff, spirited, solemn, or syrupy lines. Just as a musical performer interprets a song in their own style, so an artist draws lines in their own style, from their own impulses. In this case, it's not only the animal but the drawing itself that we call gestural (or not). If you keep this distinction in mind, it will keep your mind on drawing rather than debating.

Anatomy and form are less about opinion and more about correct understanding. Gesture, however, is hard to describe as 'correct'. It is less about knowledge and more about practice. It has something to do with graceful lines, but not necessarily. It has something to do with ease of drawing, but not always. It has mostly to do with what the subject is doing, and one way towards mastering it is to study motion. Study animation. Study great masters of gesture like Heinrich Kley. Study the drawings in this book! You hold in your hands a collection of valuable knowledge from Joe Weatherly and Shannon Beaumont that will lead you to a final secret about how to master gesture. Ingrain anatomy and form so deeply into your subconscious that you can forget about them and empathize with the animal you draw as if it were your own body, not forcing your lines but expressing them with your own rhythms and melodies, your own moods and opinions, your own grace and power.

No artist reaches that level without work. Anatomy, form, and gesture are difficult, but they are works of choice. I hope this foreword encourages you to understand them and that this book helps you to master and use them in your own work. ◇

Introduction

By Joe Weatherly

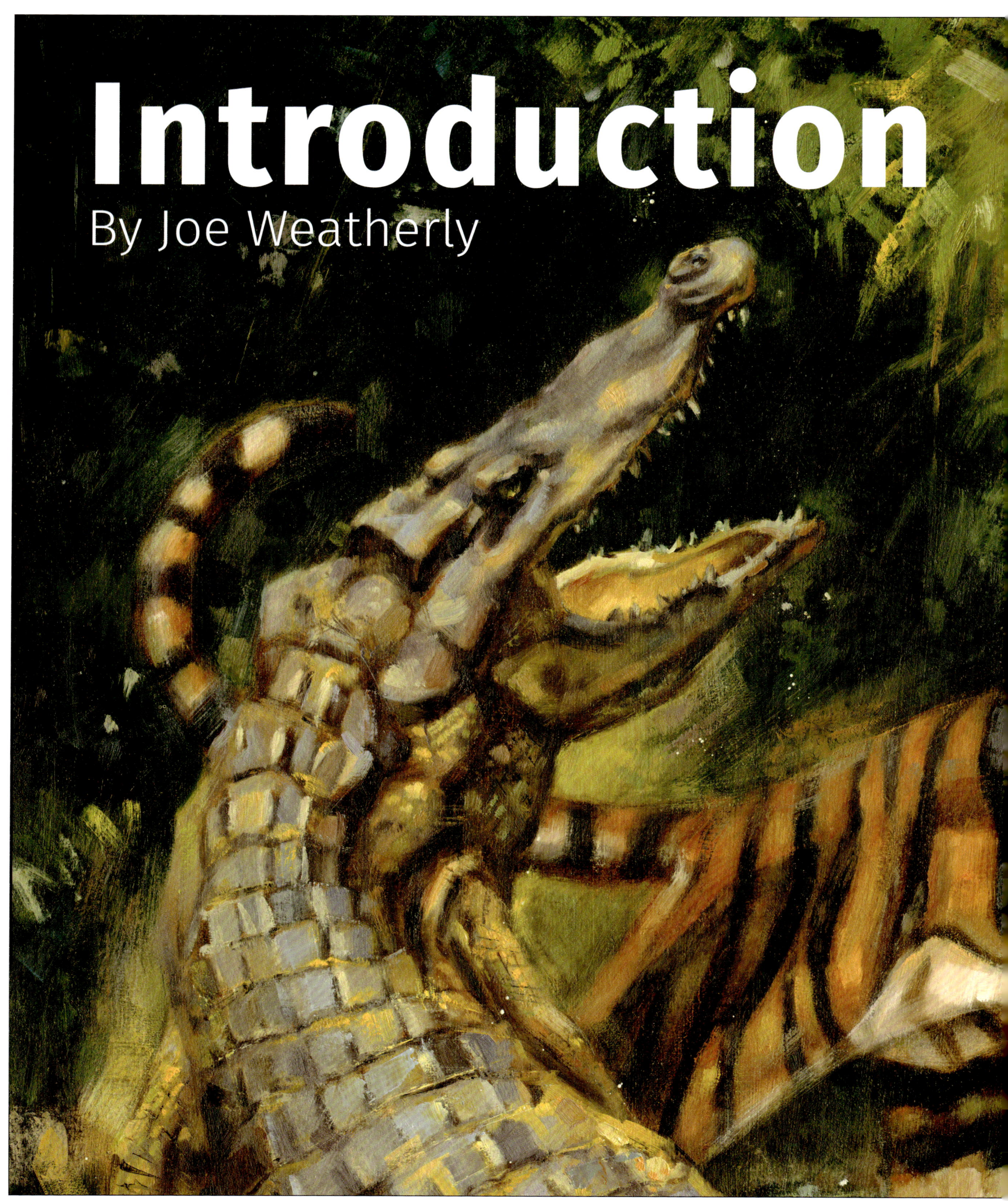

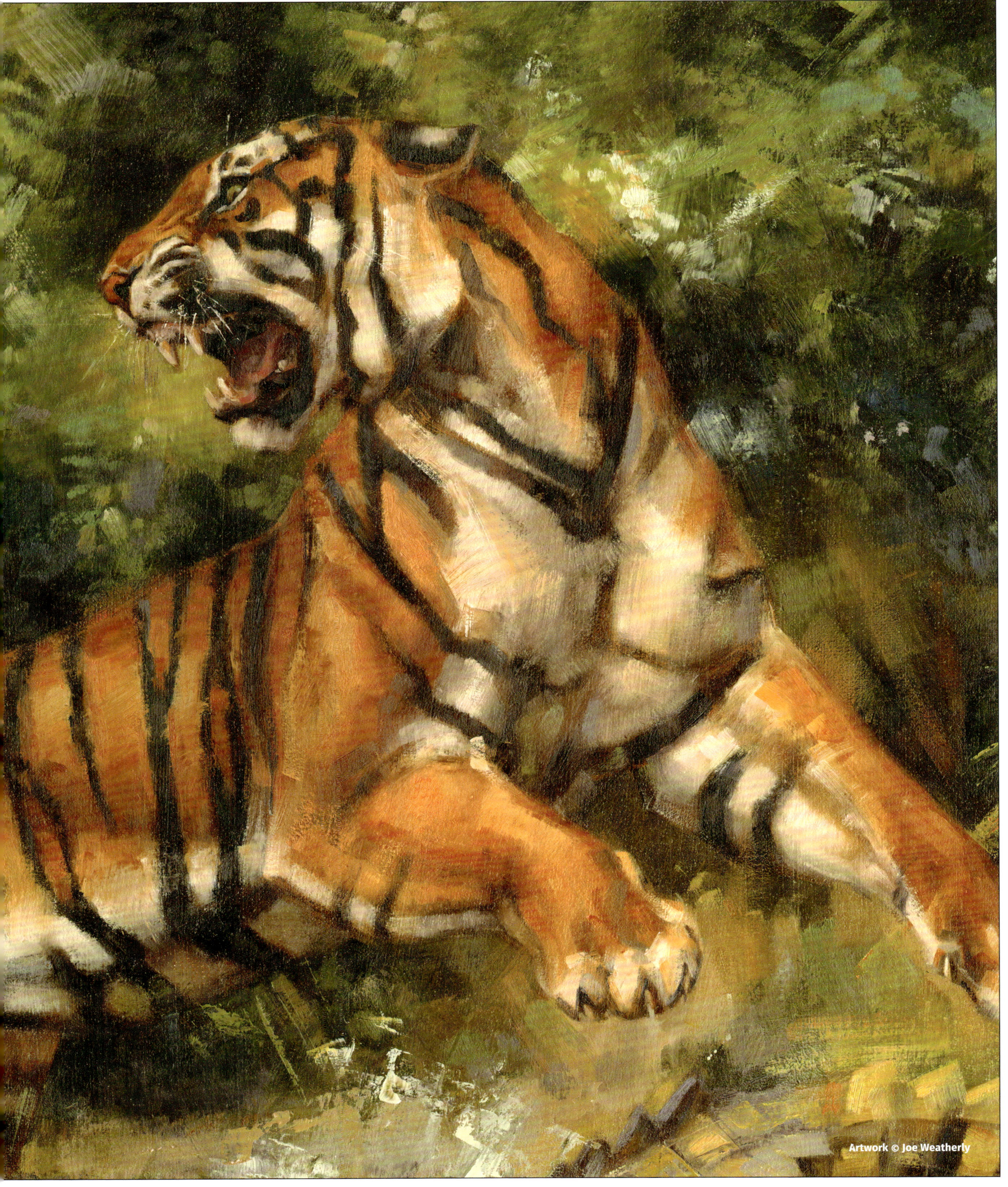

Artwork © Joe Weatherly

Animal drawing is a unique form of art expression, but it is not shrouded in mystery. It requires the same interest and effort that, for example, a figure artist would put forth. Interest and tenacity go a long way towards achieving success in making believable drawings. Anatomical knowledge will help you develop drawings that are both convincing and authoritative.

The study of the artistic anatomy of animals is crucial to any artist who wants to advance their drawing, painting, and sculpting of these subjects. An artist can draw animals without knowledge of their skeletons and muscles, but obtaining such knowledge will allow for drawings that are much better informed and drawn more rapidly and surely.

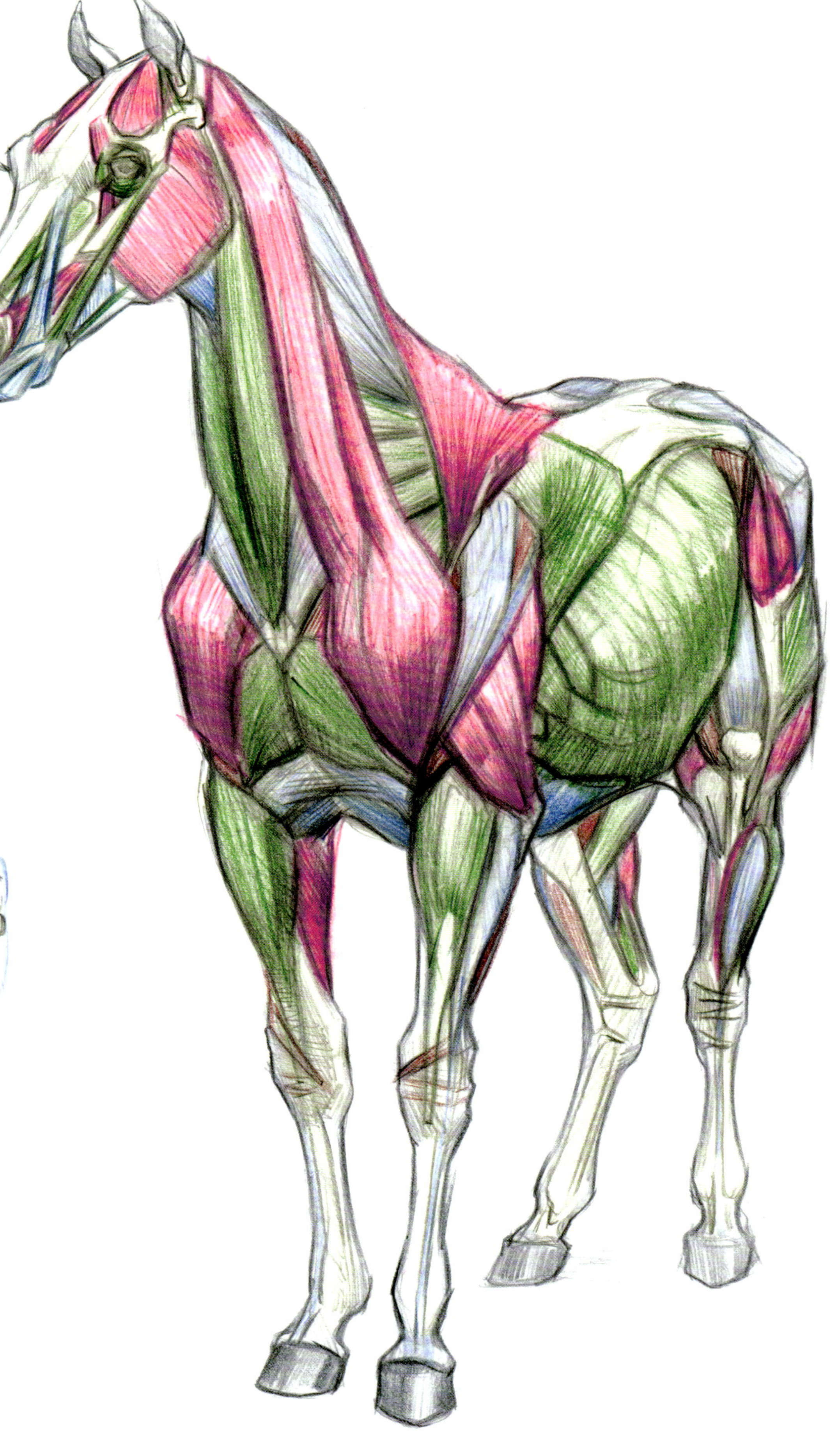

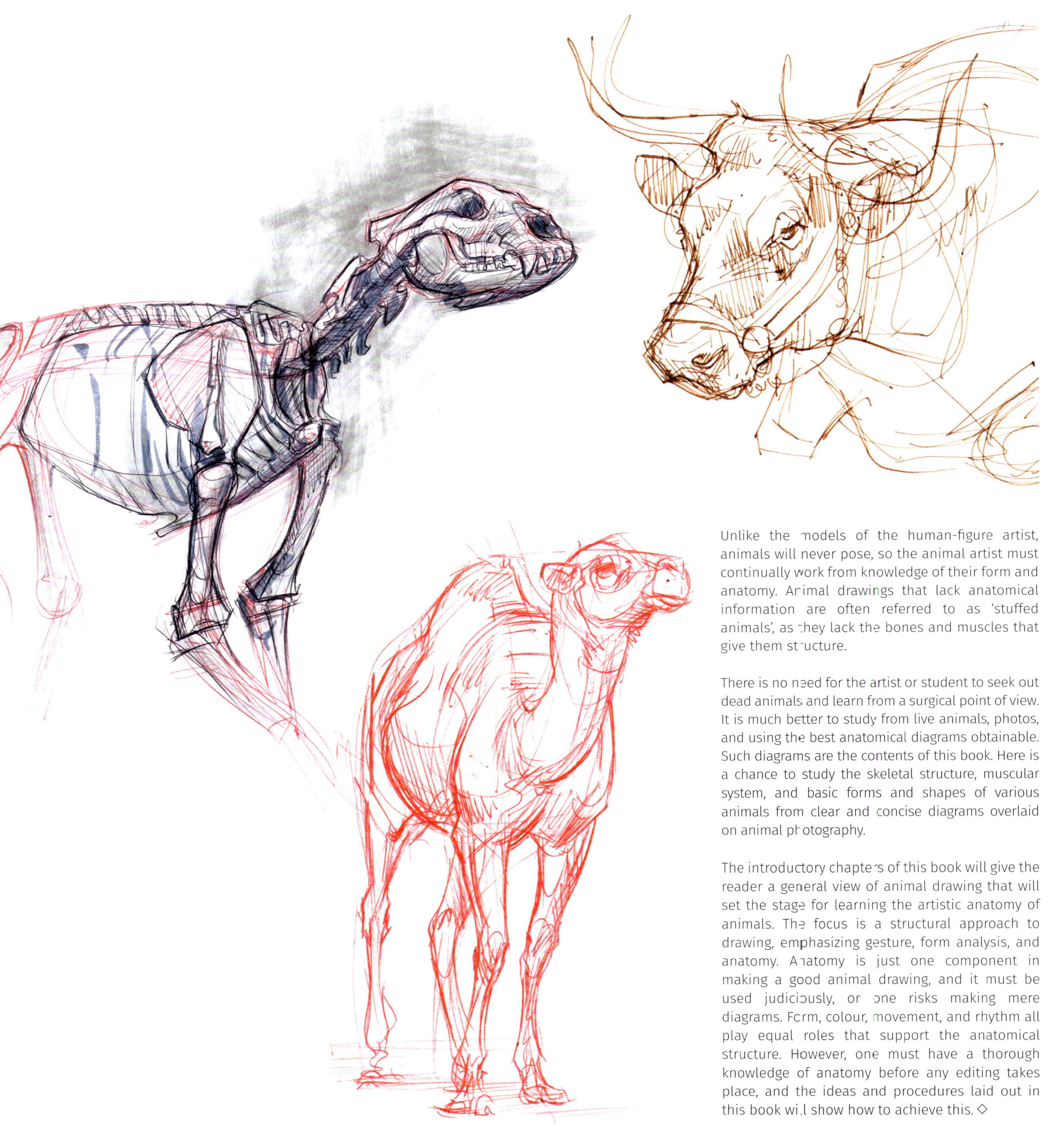

Unlike the models of the human-figure artist, animals will never pose, so the animal artist must continually work from knowledge of their form and anatomy. Animal drawings that lack anatomical information are often referred to as 'stuffed animals', as they lack the bones and muscles that give them structure.

There is no need for the artist or student to seek out dead animals and learn from a surgical point of view. It is much better to study from live animals, photos, and using the best anatomical diagrams obtainable. Such diagrams are the contents of this book. Here is a chance to study the skeletal structure, muscular system, and basic forms and shapes of various animals from clear and concise diagrams overlaid on animal photography.

The introductory chapters of this book will give the reader a general view of animal drawing that will set the stage for learning the artistic anatomy of animals. The focus is a structural approach to drawing, emphasizing gesture, form analysis, and anatomy. Anatomy is just one component in making a good animal drawing, and it must be used judiciously, or one risks making mere diagrams. Form, colour, movement, and rhythm all play equal roles that support the anatomical structure. However, one must have a thorough knowledge of anatomy before any editing takes place, and the ideas and procedures laid out in this book will show how to achieve this. ◇

The Drawing Process

The drawing process can be broken down into three steps. The first, **getting the 'action' or gesture**, refers to capturing the movement or pose of your subject. This should be done with light, loose, and gestural strokes. Establishing the action also helps in determining the rhythms and general proportions, which can be adjusted as you progress. Starting with forms as though you are building a mannequin will result in a stiff drawing. It is better to establish a gesture that you can build on top of with basic geometric forms. The 'action' can also be thought of as the animal's underlying structure.

Constructing the forms is the next step and entails going over the initial lay-in (gesture) by hanging basic geometric forms on top. Drawing only forms with no underlying action will result in a stiff drawing. Instead, you should aim to build up the drawing using a variety of forms. Box forms will reveal where the plane changes occur, and ellipses and cylinders provide easy ways to establish depth and perspective.

Finally, **fleshing the drawing out** or making it organic involves analysing the form to create a sound, realistic-looking drawing. Much of this part of the process comes from practice. The more you draw animals, the easier it will become to draw directly and construct very lightly. Drawing the initial lay-in gesturally, followed by drawing organic forms directly on top, is the goal at a certain point. However, if you skip the learning process of construction, the drawings will lack the knowledge needed for believable work. ◇

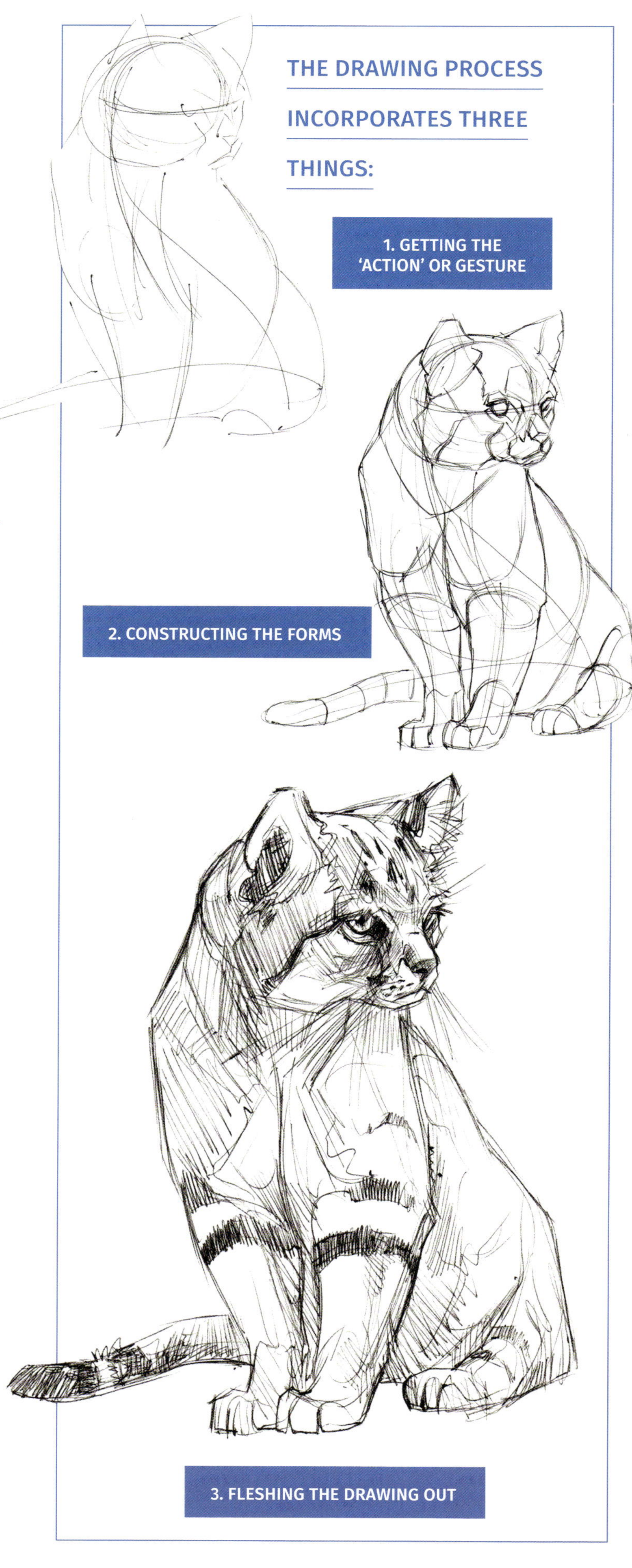

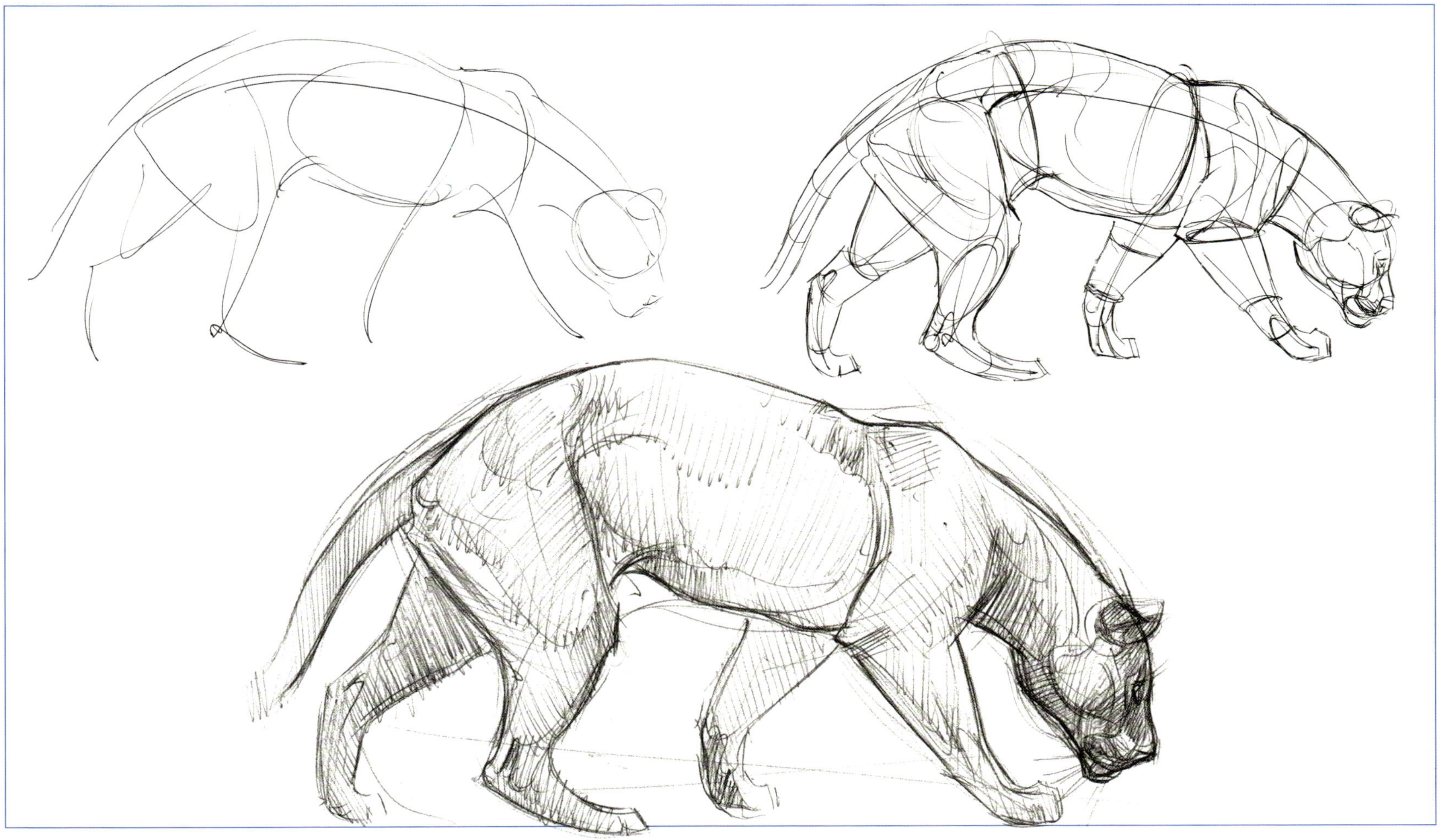

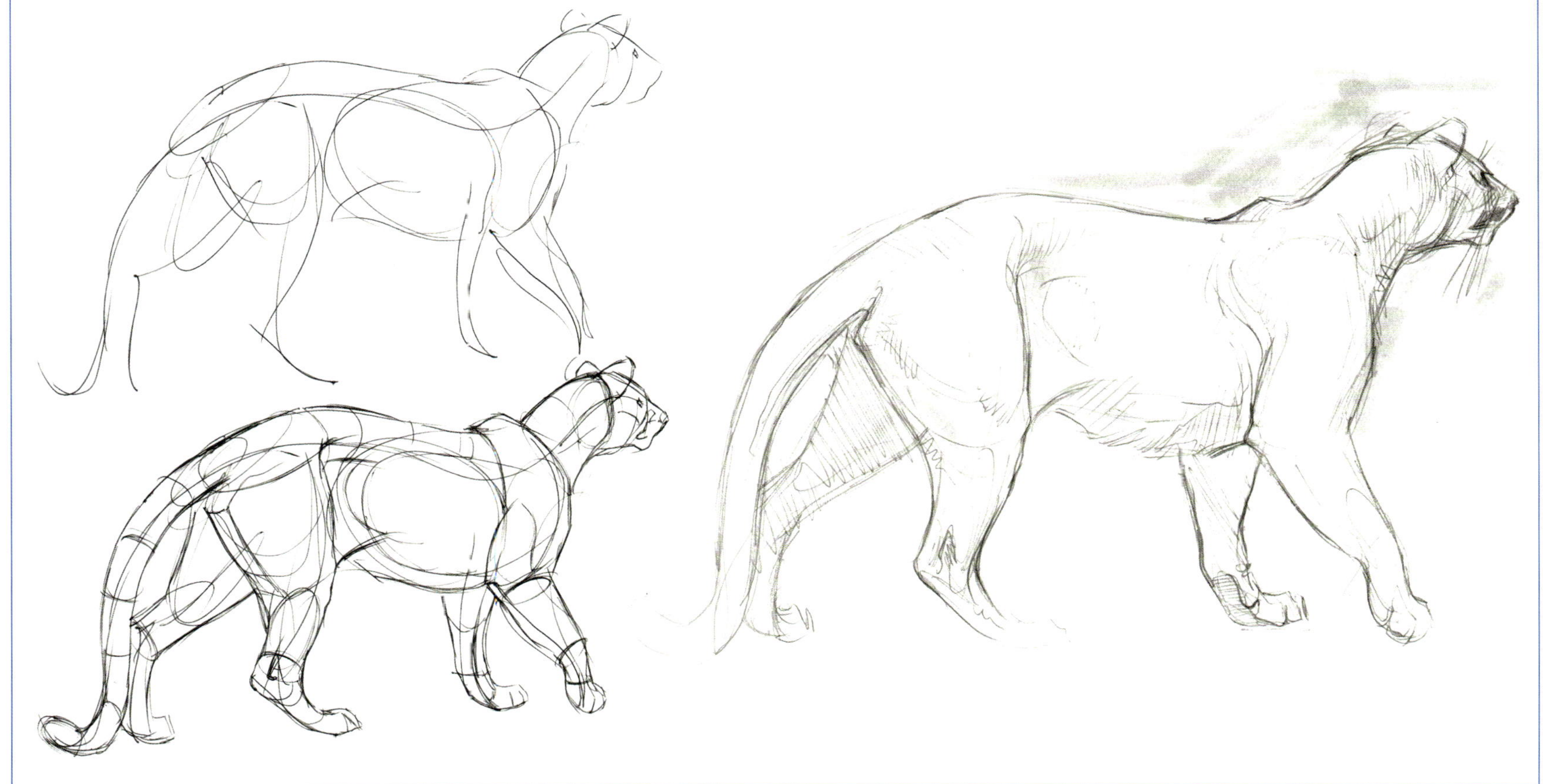

Gesture

Gesture drawing is the first priority in learning to draw animals because it teaches you how to capture the essence of what your subject is doing. A gesture drawing can be a work of art on its own or a great way to 'lay in' a drawing. If you lightly sketch a gesture before you develop a drawing, the subject will have a much better chance of retaining its life and character.

When attempting a gesture drawing, capturing what your subject is *doing* is far more critical than details and development. There are no set rules for approaching a gesture drawing, but they should be done quickly (thirty seconds to three minutes) and composed of long, sweeping, and rhythmical lines that weave in and out of each other to portray what the subject is doing.

Starting with one long 'line of action' is a common way to begin a gesture. The spine is often used for this, as it is the life force of the animal's body, but any body part can be a point of departure. Try to avoid too much construction at this stage and focus on putting down lines that quickly tell the story and portray the movement of your subject. As you scribble through the animal's forms, keep your pen on the paper and feel the action as you draw them. Work from your shoulder more than your wrist to lay down lines with more rhythm and fluidity.

Getting started: An excellent way to start a gesture drawing is to keep things simple and direct. The attitude of the fore and hind limbs can be drawn as single, rhythmical lines that represent what the bones are doing on the inside of the legs and their relative lengths. Draw many such stick-figure animals using gesture to convey their essence before adding more mass or anatomy.

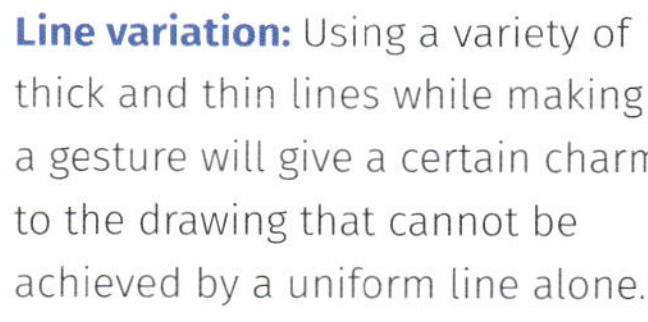

Line variation: Using a variety of thick and thin lines while making a gesture will give a certain charm to the drawing that cannot be achieved by a uniform line alone.

Capture the action: Capturing what your subject is doing is more important than technical excellence or exactitude in gesture drawing.

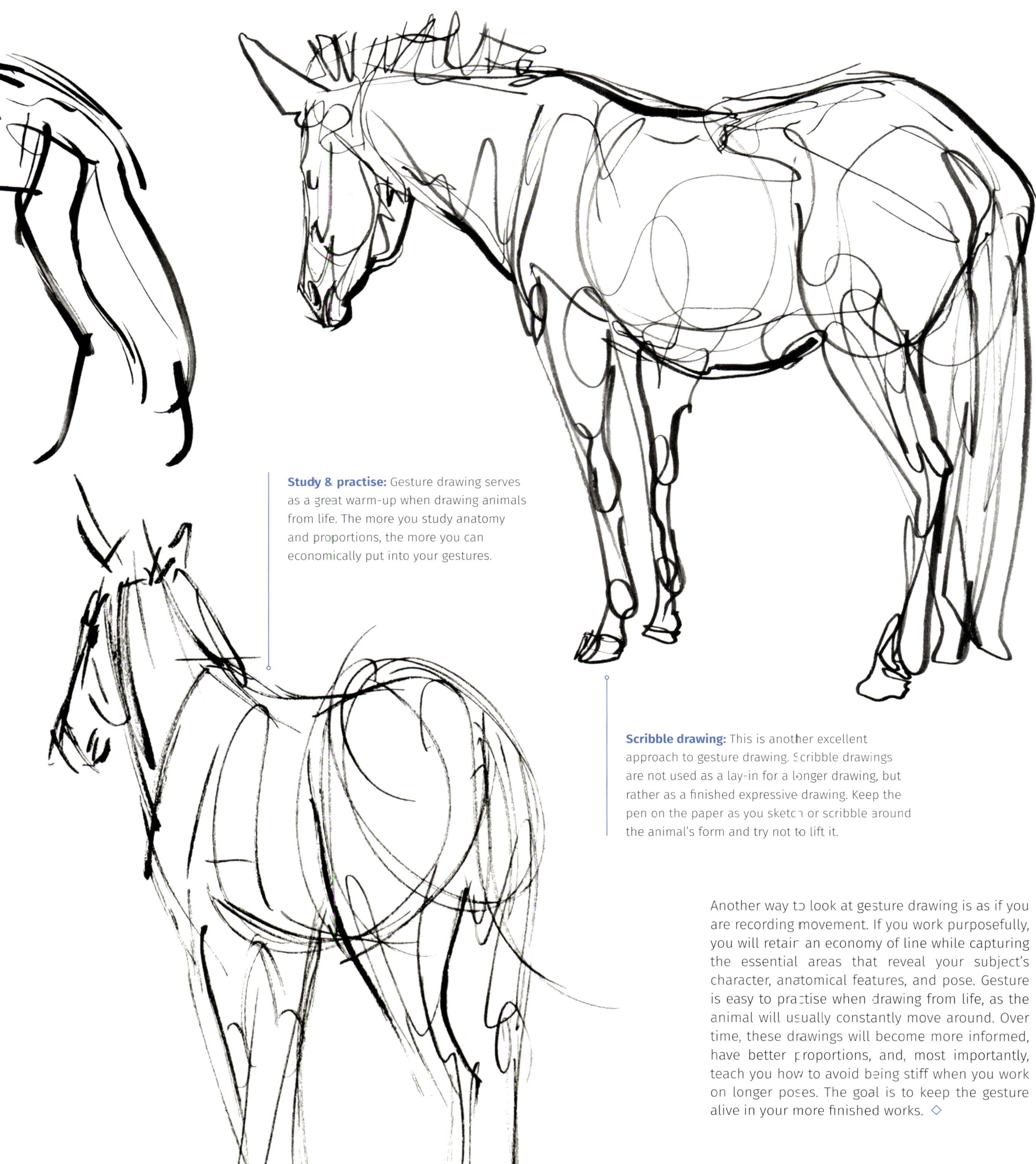

Study & practise: Gesture drawing serves as a great warm-up when drawing animals from life. The more you study anatomy and proportions, the more you can economically put into your gestures.

Scribble drawing: This is another excellent approach to gesture drawing. Scribble drawings are not used as a lay-in for a longer drawing, but rather as a finished expressive drawing. Keep the pen on the paper as you sketch or scribble around the animal's form and try not to lift it.

Another way to look at gesture drawing is as if you are recording movement. If you work purposefully, you will retain an economy of line while capturing the essential areas that reveal your subject's character, anatomical features, and pose. Gesture is easy to practise when drawing from life, as the animal will usually constantly move around. Over time, these drawings will become more informed, have better proportions, and, most importantly, teach you how to avoid being stiff when you work on longer poses. The goal is to keep the gesture alive in your more finished works. ◇

Drawing from the inside out

'Drawing from the inside out' means starting with a gesture sketch or simple stick figure, rather than drawing the outlines of your subject first. It is the key to creating a solid or three-dimensional look. When a drawing is laid in using outer lines, it becomes a two-dimensional consideration. If three-dimensional form is the look and feel desired, then drawing the inside lines first is the way to achieve it.

This approach works particularly well for anatomy drawings because the initial gesture lines act as the skeletal mass upon which to build the forms (volumes) of the body. The concept is similar to building a house, where the visible elements are built upon a solid framework that keeps the house standing. If a drawing is made using an outline only, it is flat and lacks the necessary structure to build upon. Drawing from the inside out also allows you to work out the subject's pose before moving too far into the development of your image. ◇

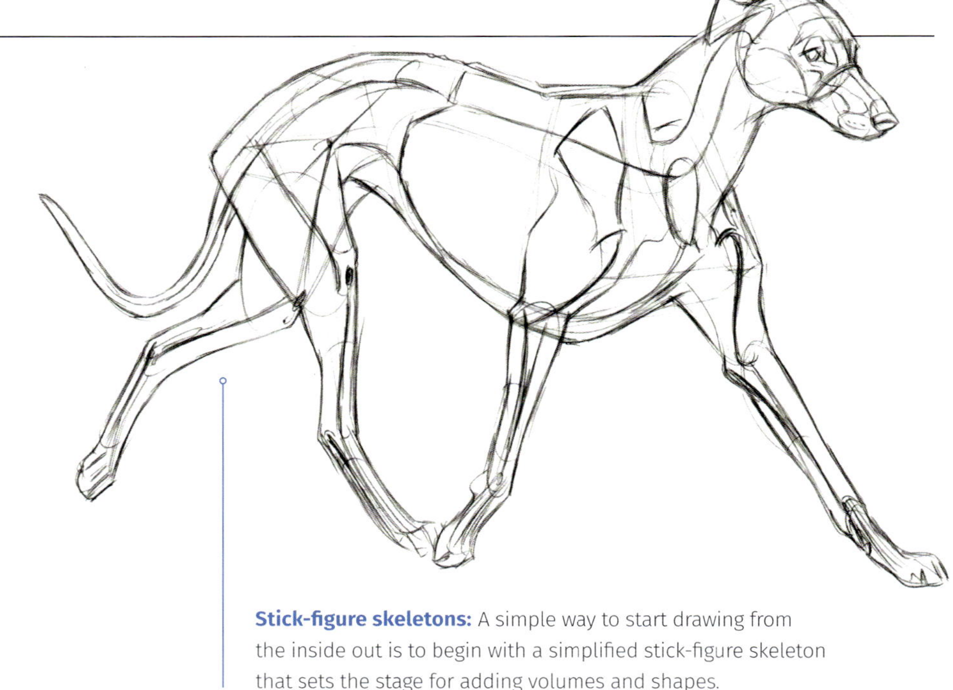

Stick-figure skeletons: A simple way to start drawing from the inside out is to begin with a simplified stick-figure skeleton that sets the stage for adding volumes and shapes.

Thinking lines: Any inside 'thinking' lines or tones can be considered drawing from the inside out. These include things such as bony landmarks, how forms fit and wedge into each other, ellipses, initial gesture lines, and muscle masses and shapes.

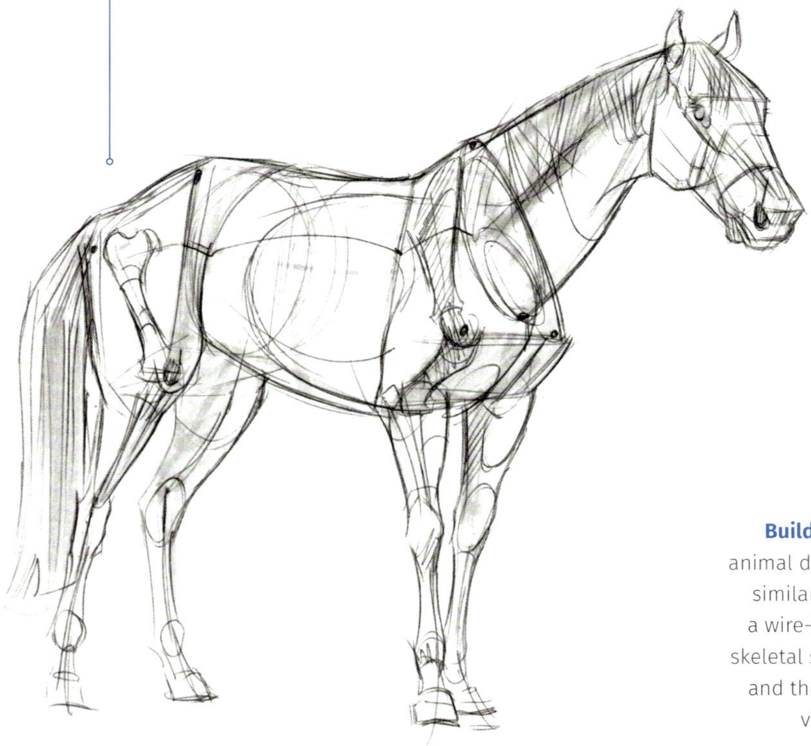

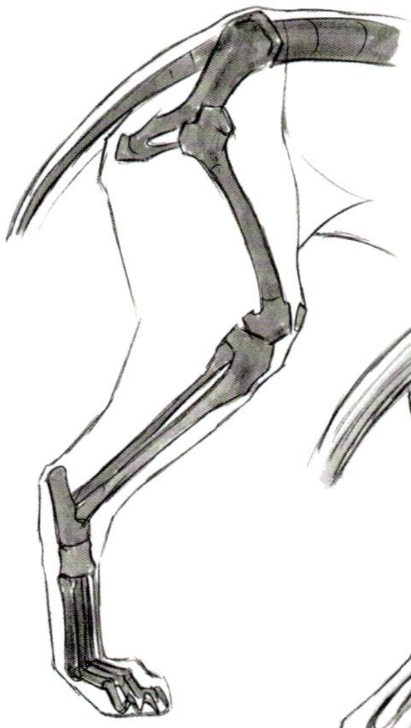

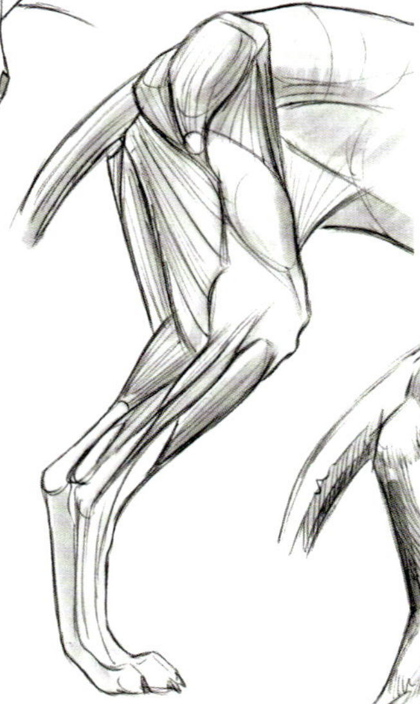

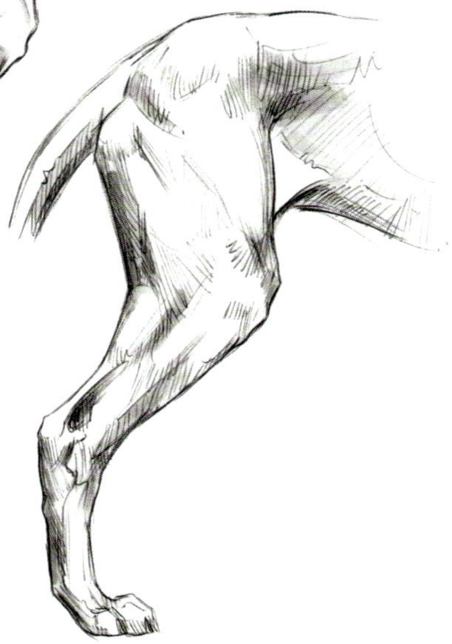

Building up: These three sketches show how an animal drawing can be built up from the inside out, similar to how a sculptor works by adding clay to a wire-frame armature. The first sketch shows the skeletal structure, the second the muscle structure, and the final drawing the outer layer or skin, with visible muscle masses and bony landmarks.

What you know & what you see

Drawing animals from life normally involves working with moving subjects, unless they are sleeping, and requires a specific approach that drawing a posed, stationary model does not. Since animals are moving, we must learn to draw what we *know* more than what we *see*. However, we should still capture elements of what we see so that the drawings do not look formulaic.

To create believable animal drawings, the artist must memorize forms, anatomy, shapes, and proportions that enable them to draw a moving subject. At the same time, the artist must look up, critically analyse what they are seeing, and try to bring this into the mix. It becomes a blend of drawing what you know and what you see. To draw what you know, you must learn enough about anatomy, form, character, and proportions to build a believable drawing. This can be achieved by studying anatomy from books and learning to simplify complex anatomical forms into basic shapes that can be easily located and memorized. This approach to drawing will allow the artist to use photos smartly, only taking the essentials and not slavishly copying them. ◇

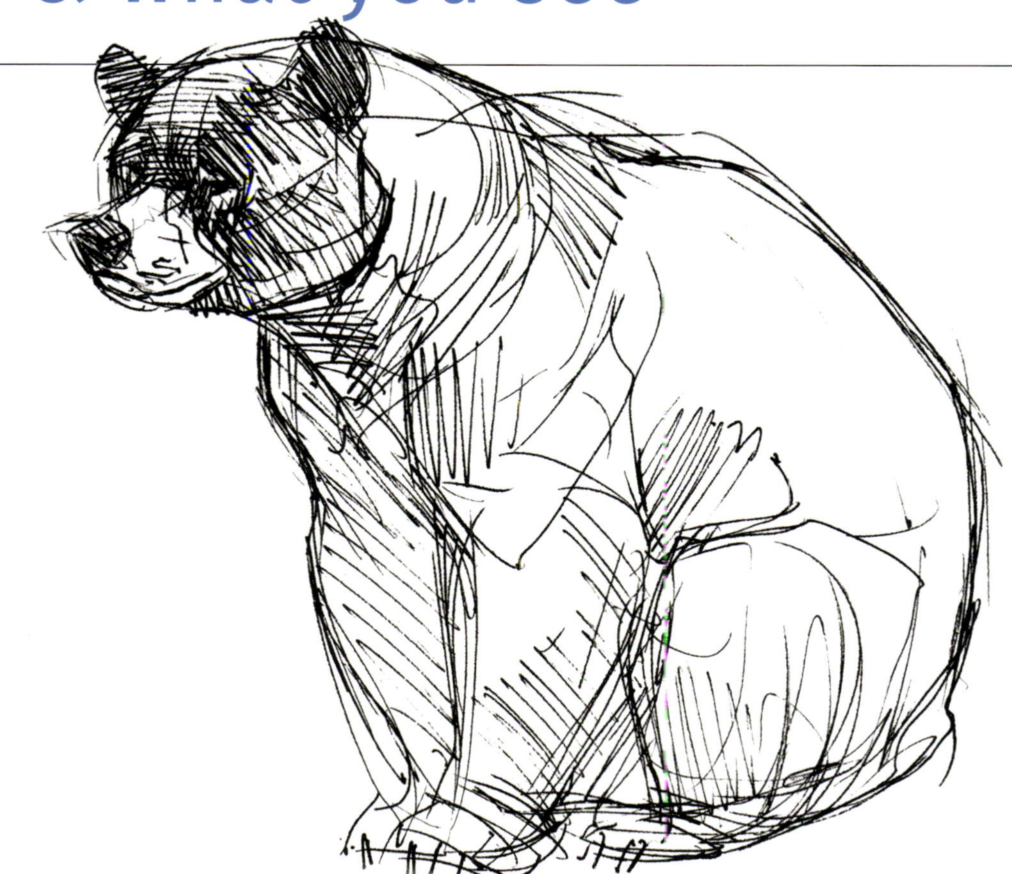

Drawing from life and memory: This sketch was drawn from life while observing a bear in a zoo. This bear stayed still for the most part (although its head moved a lot), allowing me to draw what I saw. However, elements of things memorized after studying and drawing bears for some time also factored into the equation to finish the drawing.

Moving subjects: In this example, the animal was moving around, making it a challenge to draw entirely based on what could see. Instead, I pulled from my own sound knowledge of a bear's anatomy, while also studying the shapes and movement of the subject in front of me.

Rhythm & posing

Rhythm is essential to drawing with flow and interest. Long lines that are either straight or curved, and weave in and out of each other, are considered rhythmic. To convey the grace and flow of a pose, you can use rhythm to lay the drawing in and retain the fluidity until it's finished.

When drawing an animal, decide upon a pose and lay it in using curved rhythmic lines, straight lines, or a combination of the two. Once you establish what your subject is doing (getting the action), be mindful of where the weight is. Animals put stress and strain on their limbs just as humans do and therefore they should be drawn in a way that expresses weight shift and change. For example, if the forearm takes the weight during a walking pose, the shoulder blade rises upward, and if the leg is released, the shoulder blade lowers. Another anatomical area to adjust is the pelvis, which tilts from side to side as the animal shifts its weight.

Symmetry in drawing can be considered monotonous and stiff. When drawing an animal, feel free to change things around so that at least one leg (if not more) is different. If the legs are the same on both sides, this is called 'twinning' and creates a dull, symmetrical image. Not every pose needs to be dynamic, but even a subtle reclining pose will look better if the limbs are not twinned. Using rhythm and composing poses that avoid perfect symmetry in the limbs will create sound, meaningful drawings. ◇

Straights vs. curves: Rhythm is an integral part of the entire drawing process. Lines should weave in and out of each other to create flowing, graceful areas. Note that 'straights vs. curves' is also used on this elephant. For example, the front of the foreleg is curved compared to the back of the foreleg, which is straighter.

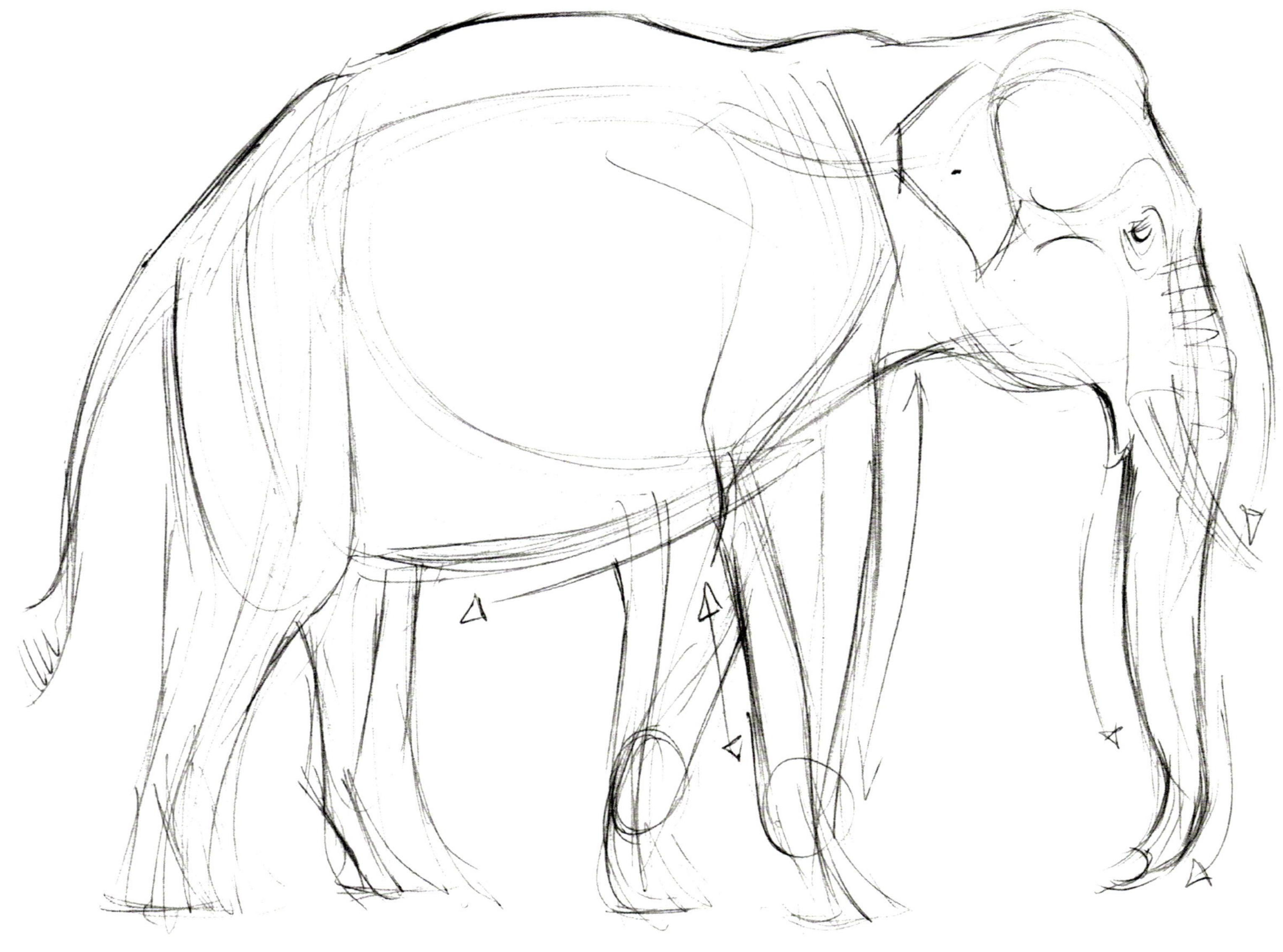

Combination: Lay-in drawings using either curved or straight action lines, or a combination of the two.

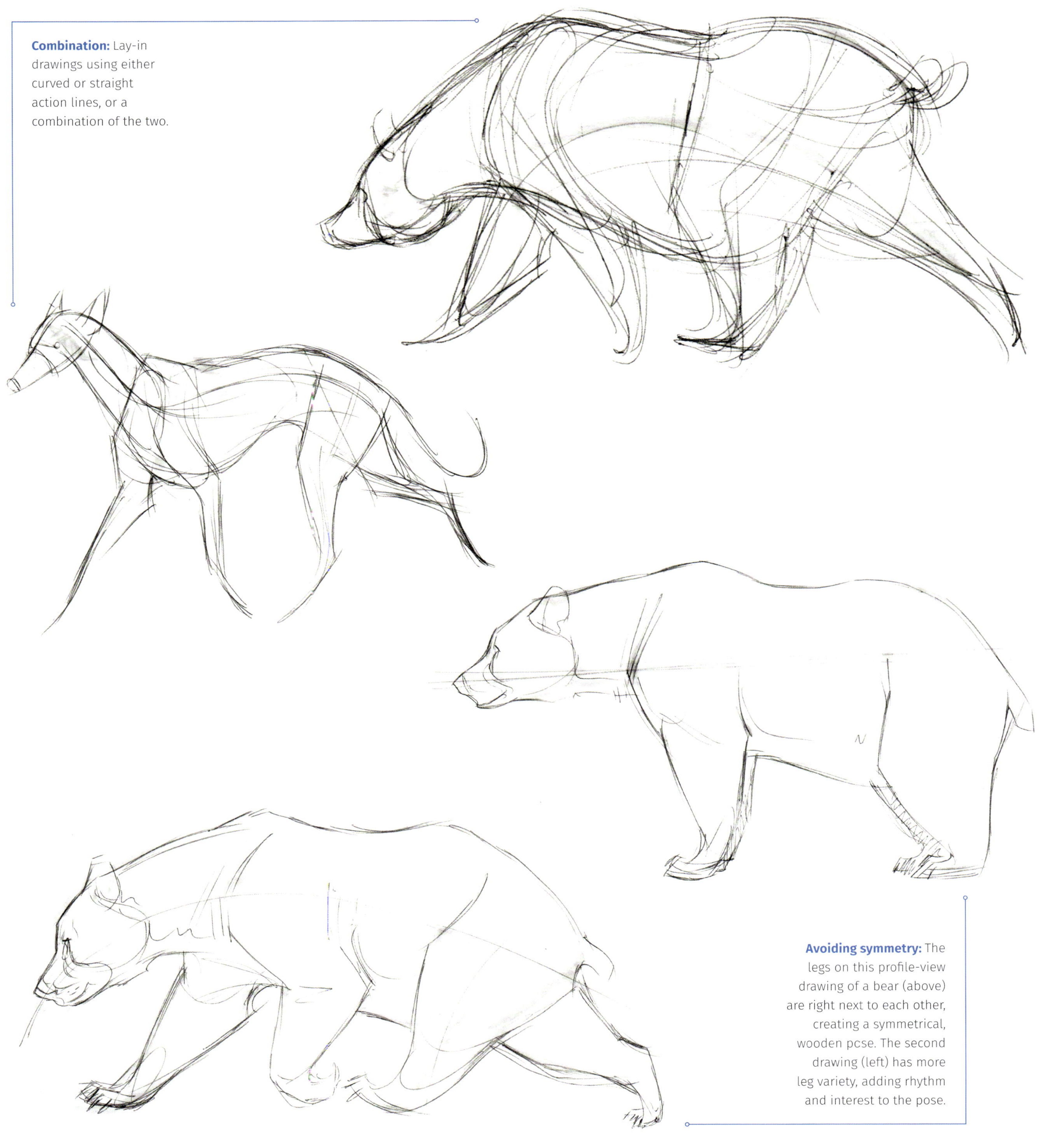

Avoiding symmetry: The legs on this profile-view drawing of a bear (above) are right next to each other, creating a symmetrical, wooden pose. The second drawing (left) has more leg variety, adding rhythm and interest to the pose.

Construction

Construction is a method of drawing animals using simplified forms. Linear construction involves the use of lines to create shapes and forms that appear transparent and have no tonal value, showing the thinking process of the artist. This can include basic two-dimensional shapes, in addition to cylindrical and box forms and planes, plus techniques such as cross-contour lines, to create three-dimensionality. Combining a variety of forms and the use of foreshortening are also key skills needed to construct animals at different angles. If linear construction is well stated and understood, adding tone later will be simple. The plane changes that develop while constructing are the clues to where light or shade will go.

Shapes are two-dimensional and can be used with or developed into forms that give a three-dimensional illusion on a flat surface (paper, tablet, or canvas). These forms have tops, ends, sides, and bottoms called planes. Planes capture light and shade. Forms – such as a box/cube, cylinder, sphere, and ovoid form – can be used to construct and solidly draw any animal (or anything else).

Learning construction is a simple way to develop an animal drawing and sets the stage for constructive anatomy. One of the best reasons to learn how to construct is that it's of tremendous help when drawing from imagination and from life – both what you know and what you see. If you memorize an animal's simple forms, then you can more easily come up with poses from imagination and complete a drawing of a moving subject. Constructive drawing is also a way to tackle perspective and foreshortening. Overall, it provides a sound method of drawing, which, if understood, gives artists a straightforward way to draw animals convincingly. ◇

Begin with gesture: Always start with a gesture as a foundational lay-in upon which to hang the forms, rather than starting to build with just the forms. The gesture captures the attitude of the pose and helps with proportions, but it is also the life force under construction and keeps the drawing fluid. Starting the drawing with forms before the gesture will create a rigid mannequin look.

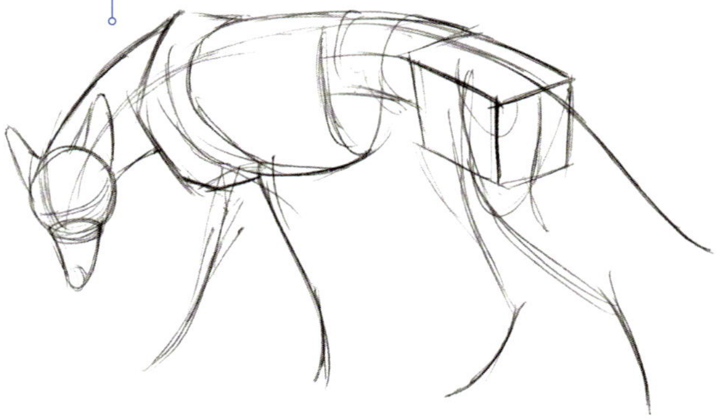

Simple forms: In this drawing, the forms are boiled down to the simplest terms to represent the main parts of the dog's body: the head and neck, shoulders, torso, pelvis, tail, forelegs, and hind limbs. When starting out, it is essential to view the body in terms of these simple forms and recognize the fundamental masses. Once control is gained over the simple forms and they are drawn correctly, it will be simple to draw the details over them.

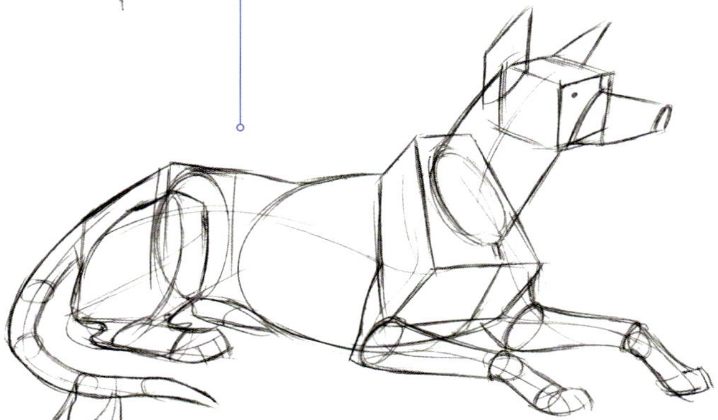

Three-dimensional form: Form has three dimensions and occupies space, as opposed to shapes that are two-dimensional and flat. It is helpful to think of the forms as something solid, such as sculpture, in order to capture the structural look.

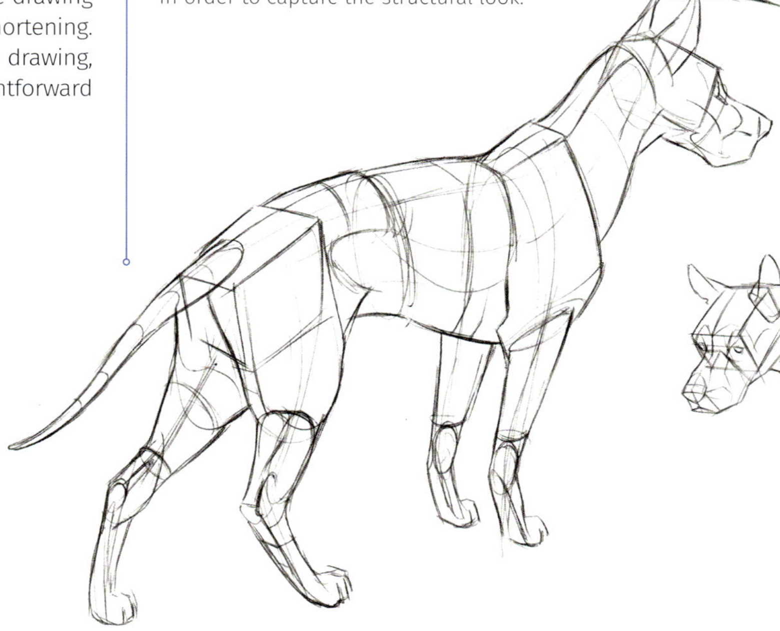

Adding features and contour lines: Construction can get more elaborate by including forms for features and anatomical components, and using more cross-contour lines and corners of forms to find the plane changes.

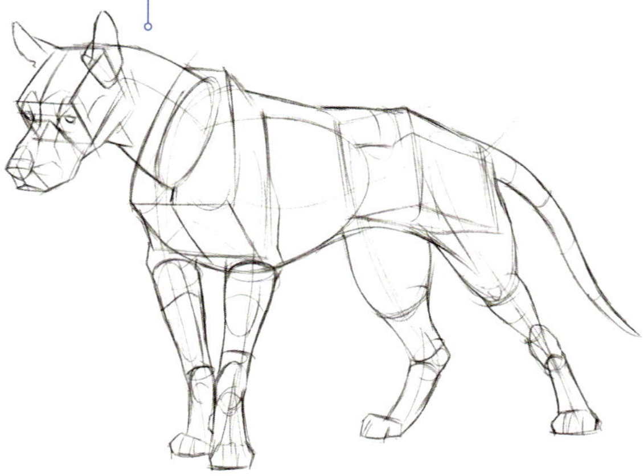

Basic shapes

Shapes are two-dimensional – having only height and width, but no depth – and are useful in the design language of animals. Examples of elementary shapes include circles, squares, vertical and horizontal rectangles, and triangles. When depth is added to elementary shapes, they become forms; for example, a square becomes a box. Using shapes when drawing animals is easiest with profile or straight-on front and back views, but can also be mixed with using forms to complete poses that are in perspective. ▸▸

Two-dimensional shapes: These are basic shapes that have height and width, but no depth.

Simple rectangles: Shapes are typically used for drawings in profile view rather than three-quarter view. This donkey is largely made up of a series of rectangles, and these shapes, even though flat, are the gateway to learning form and anatomy. For example, many animals have a rectangular trunk. Notice also the rectangular box that tilts downwards for the horse's pelvis. Other components, such as the shoulder blade and sections of the legs, can all be created from a rectangle.

Modifying shapes: While still in profile, this drawing shows a more organic approach to drawing using shapes. The shapes are all modified to the body parts they represent.

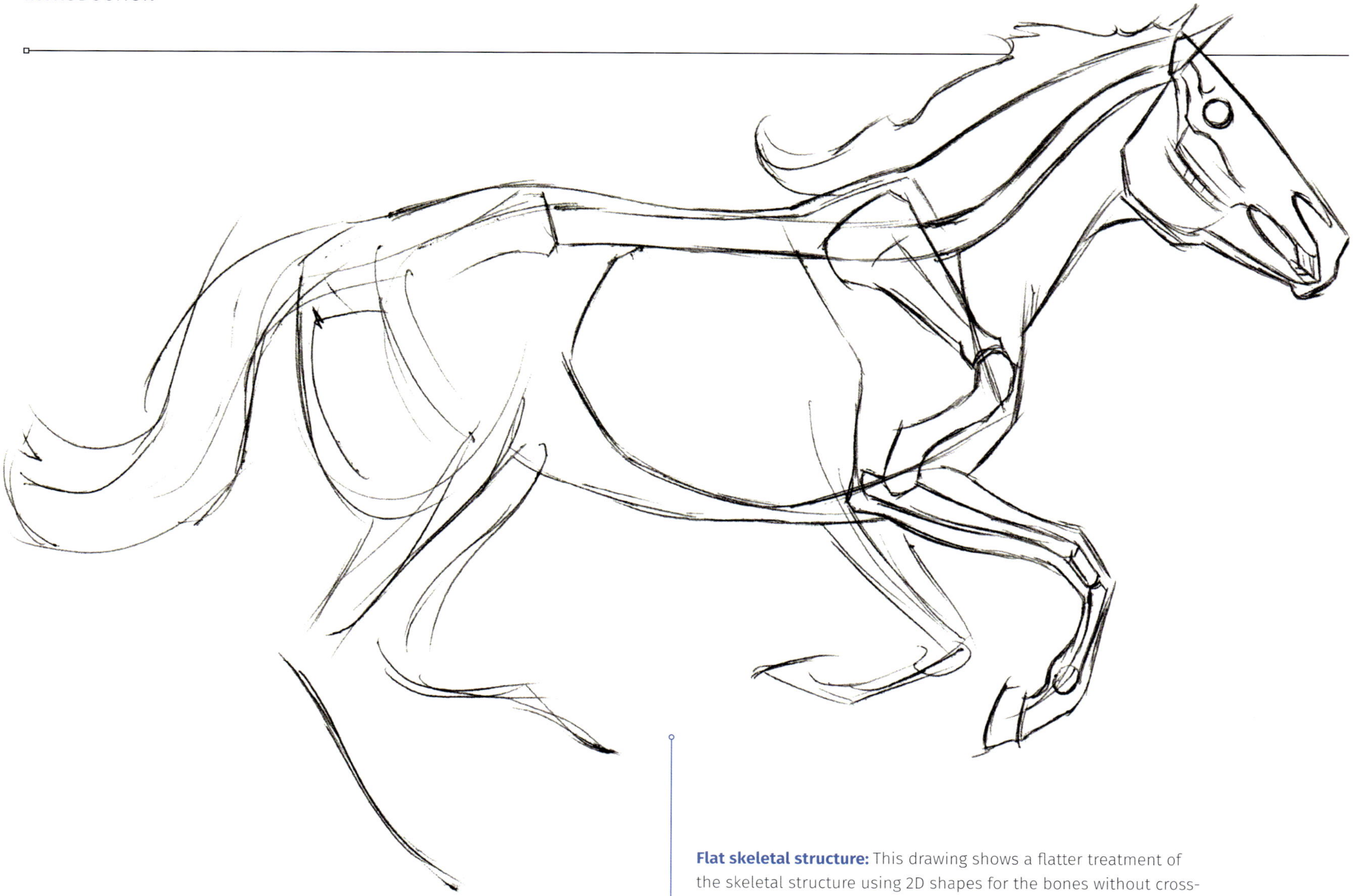

Flat skeletal structure: This drawing shows a flatter treatment of the skeletal structure using 2D shapes for the bones without cross-contour lines to expose the form. This is a good exercise for getting bone placement and proportions correct. Note how the unfinished drawing is being developed over the initial gestural lay-in.

Rhythm lines: Use rhythm lines to tie shapes together.

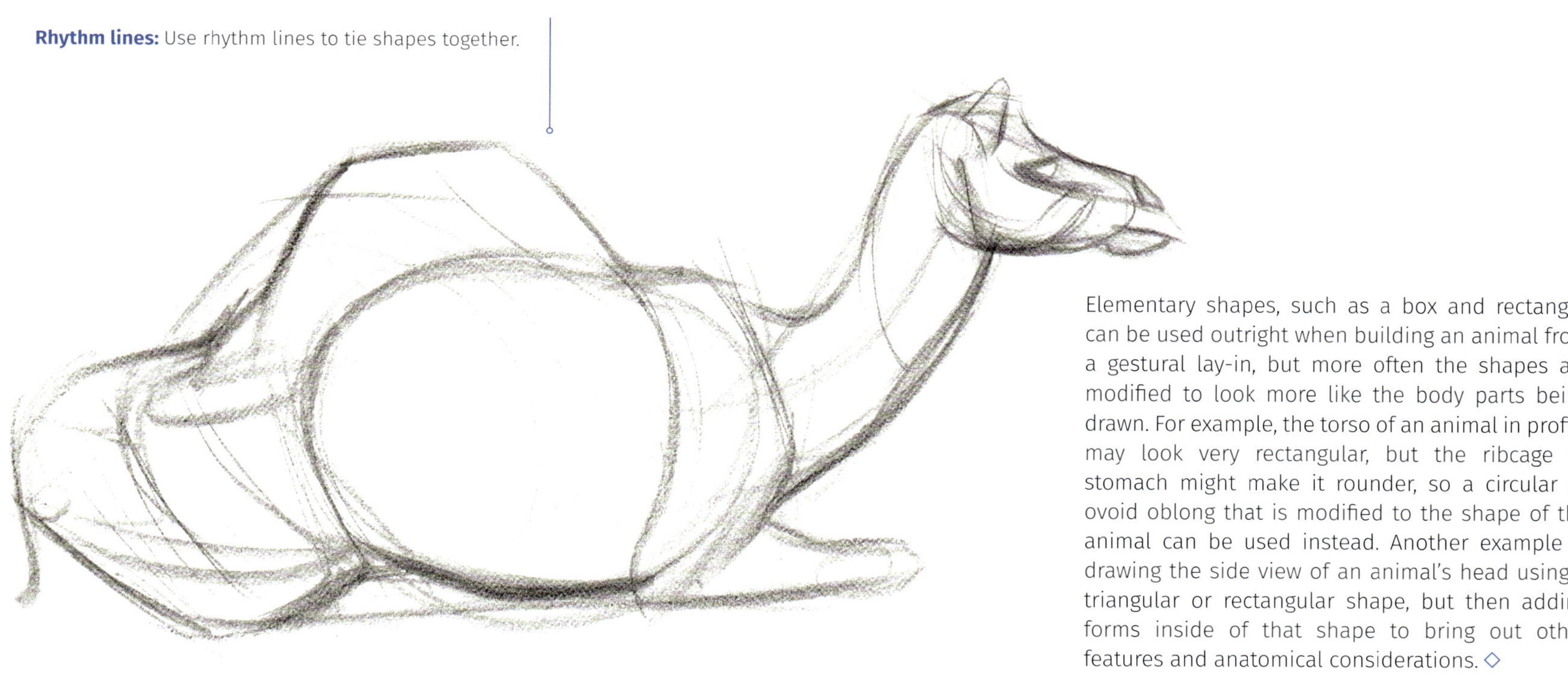

Elementary shapes, such as a box and rectangle, can be used outright when building an animal from a gestural lay-in, but more often the shapes are modified to look more like the body parts being drawn. For example, the torso of an animal in profile may look very rectangular, but the ribcage or stomach might make it rounder, so a circular or ovoid oblong that is modified to the shape of the animal can be used instead. Another example is drawing the side view of an animal's head using a triangular or rectangular shape, but then adding forms inside of that shape to bring out other features and anatomical considerations. ◇

Ellipses, cylinders & cross contour

ELLIPSES

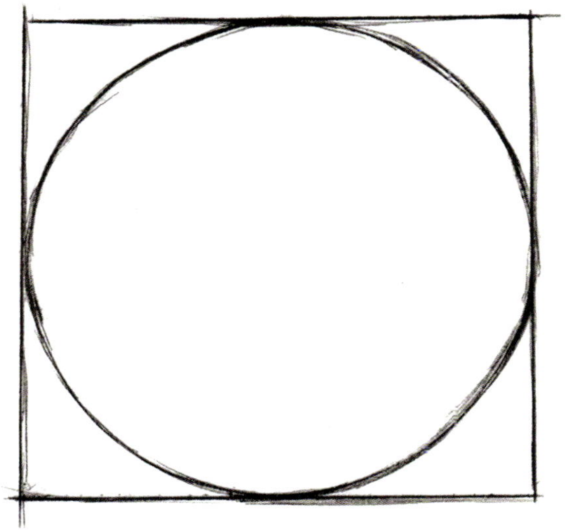

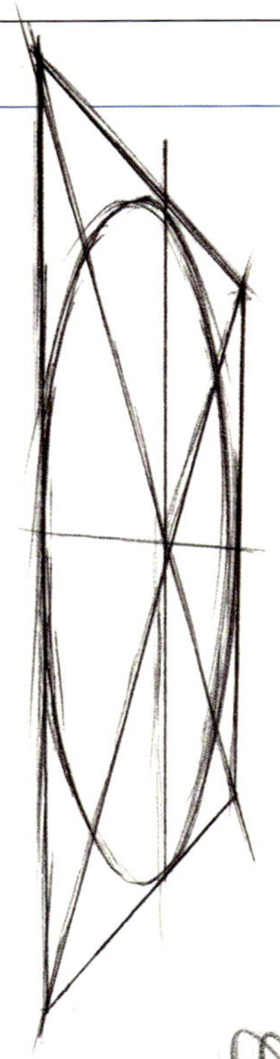

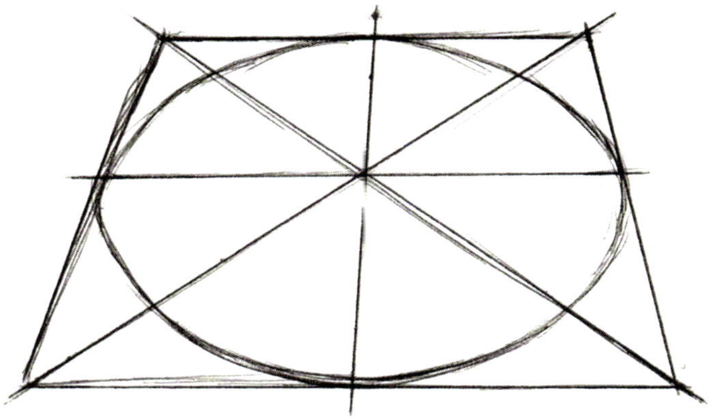

Simple shapes: A true square can surround a true circle, and when this is tilted or foreshortened, the result is an ellipse. The centre of the box and circle can be found by drawing diagonal lines through the corners.

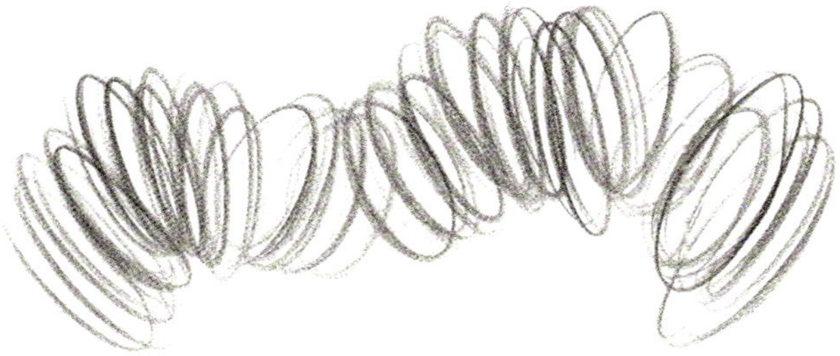

Organic ellipses: A looser, freehand approach to drawing ellipses is more practical when sketching organic forms. Practice drawing from your shoulder and try to press down when the ellipse is closer to the viewer, and 'ghost' it or lightly stroke it when it is further away.

An **ellipse** is a circle drawn in perspective. When drawing animals, ellipses can aid construction by showing how to draw through and around forms. Plus, they make good cylinders and cones. Ellipses should be drawn freehand with loose free-swinging strokes. Drawing from the shoulder as opposed to the wrist will help with this. Mechanically drawing ellipses often results in stiff forms.

The viewer's eye level will determine the openness or flatness of the ellipses. A precise ellipse can be drawn by placing it inside a rectangle and finding the four equal quadrants along its major and minor axis lines. However, when you are drawing a moving animal, this is hardly practical. Drawing 'ellipse animals' is far more helpful and employs the freehand method of wrapping ellipses around all the body parts. ◇

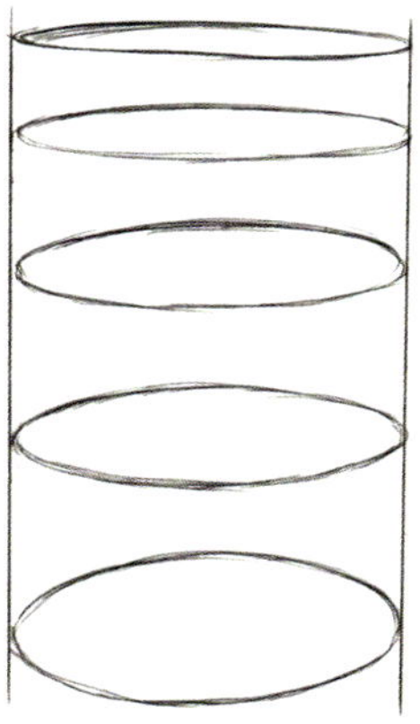

Different angles: Note how the ellipses open as they come down from the top (eye level).

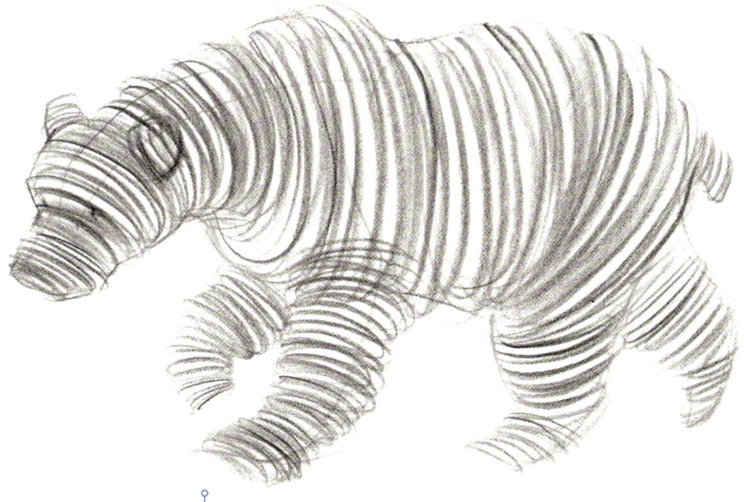

'Ellipse animals': These are a fun way to learn how ellipses turn the form. The idea is not to achieve anatomical accuracy, but to wrap the ellipses around the forms freely.

CYLINDERS

Simple **cylinders** will have an inner two-dimensional axis line running through them and a three-dimensional axis going around them (the ellipse). These cylinders can be used for almost any body part, especially forelegs and hind legs. Cylinders can be modified to show the form and anatomy of the subject. ◇

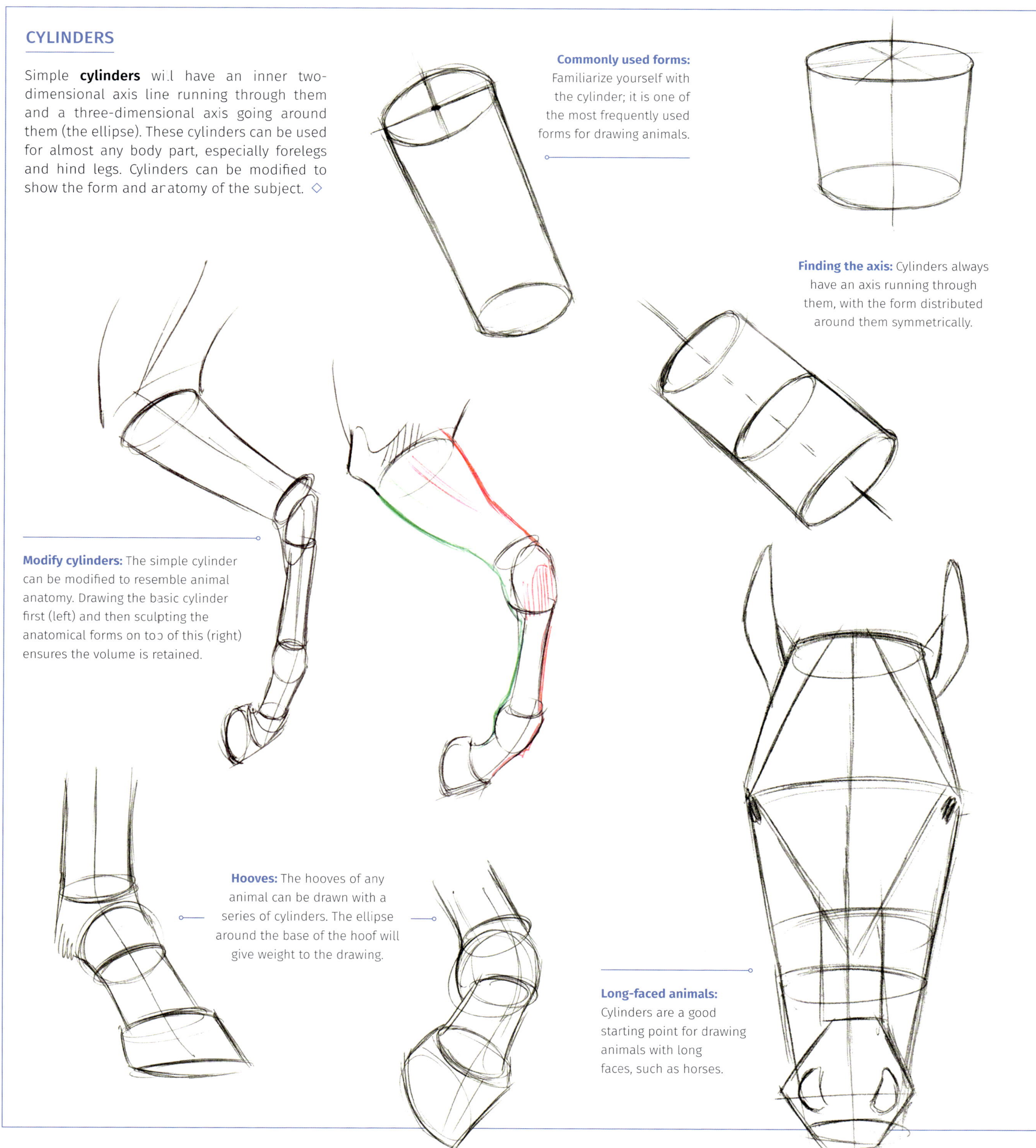

Commonly used forms: Familiarize yourself with the cylinder; it is one of the most frequently used forms for drawing animals.

Finding the axis: Cylinders always have an axis running through them, with the form distributed around them symmetrically.

Modify cylinders: The simple cylinder can be modified to resemble animal anatomy. Drawing the basic cylinder first (left) and then sculpting the anatomical forms on top of this (right) ensures the volume is retained.

Hooves: The hooves of any animal can be drawn with a series of cylinders. The ellipse around the base of the hoof will give weight to the drawing.

Long-faced animals: Cylinders are a good starting point for drawing animals with long faces, such as horses.

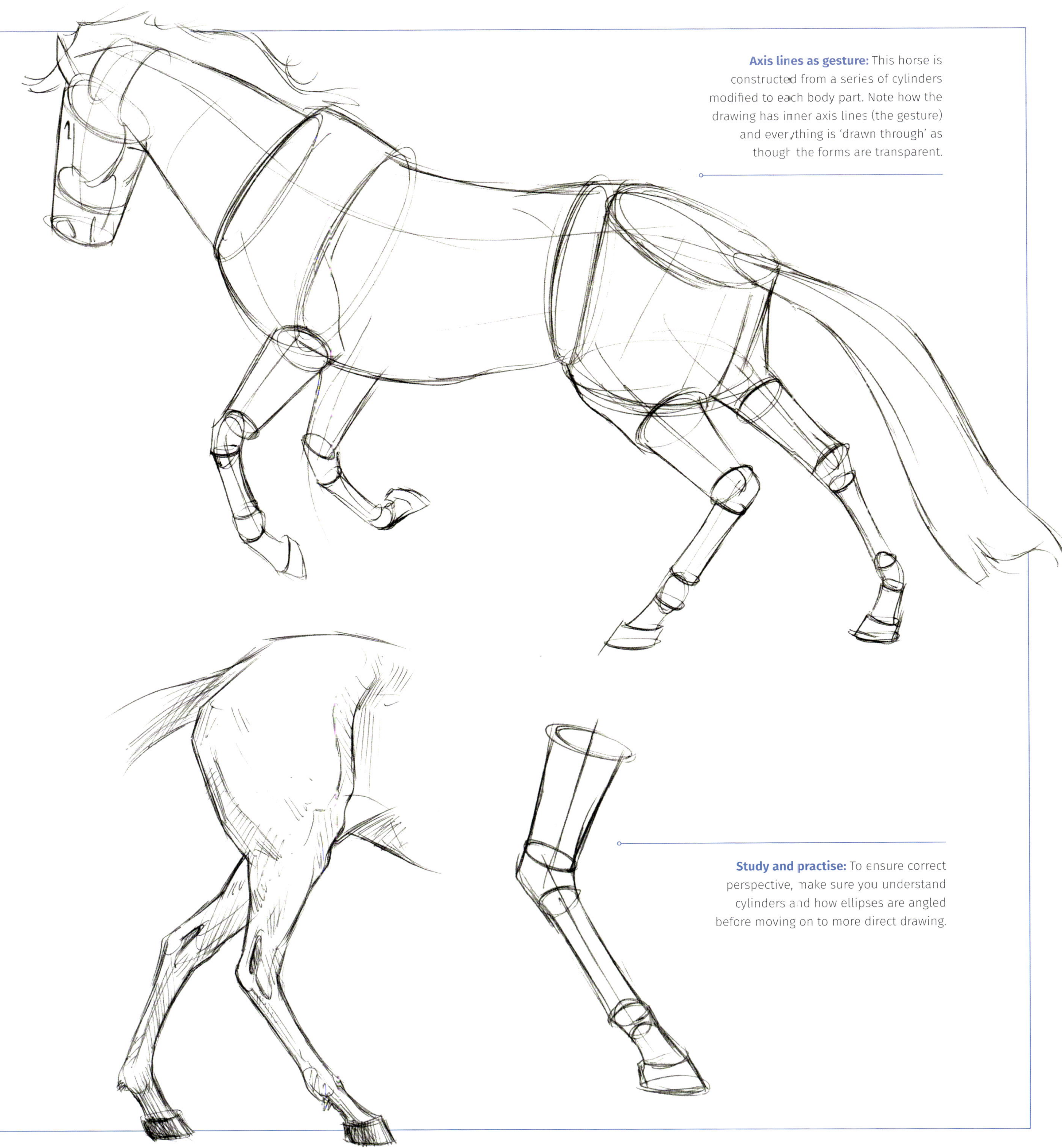

Axis lines as gesture: This horse is constructed from a series of cylinders modified to each body part. Note how the drawing has inner axis lines (the gesture) and everything is 'drawn through' as though the forms are transparent.

Study and practise: To ensure correct perspective, make sure you understand cylinders and how ellipses are angled before moving on to more direct drawing.

CROSS-CONTOUR LINES

Cross-contour drawing refers to putting lines around sections of the forms or shapes (often elliptical) to reveal their three-dimensional qualities. ◇

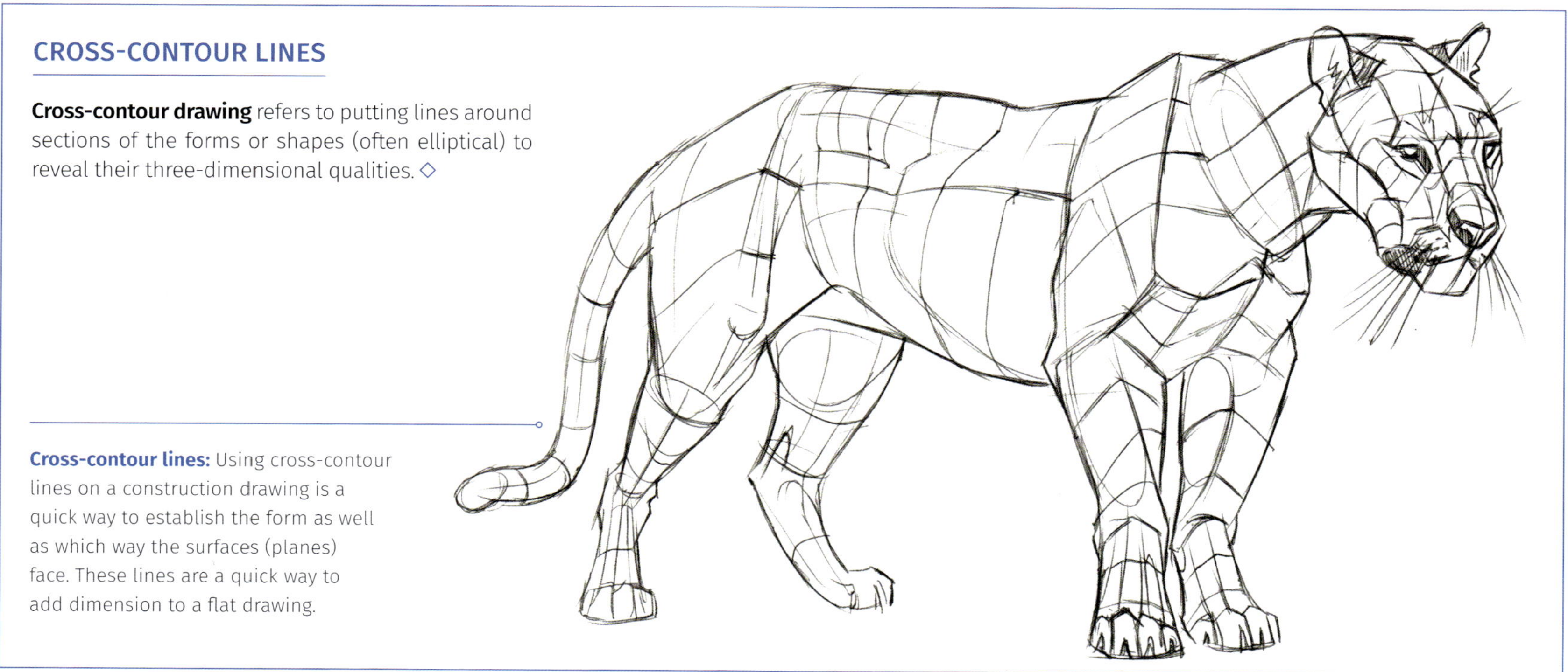

Cross-contour lines: Using cross-contour lines on a construction drawing is a quick way to establish the form as well as which way the surfaces (planes) face. These lines are a quick way to add dimension to a flat drawing.

Theory in practice: In the drawing below, note where cylinders are indicated for various body parts. The jaguar's pattern (rosettes) need to be drawn in perspective to wrap around the form. Thinking of the rosettes as ellipses that wrap around the various body parts will make this much more manageable.

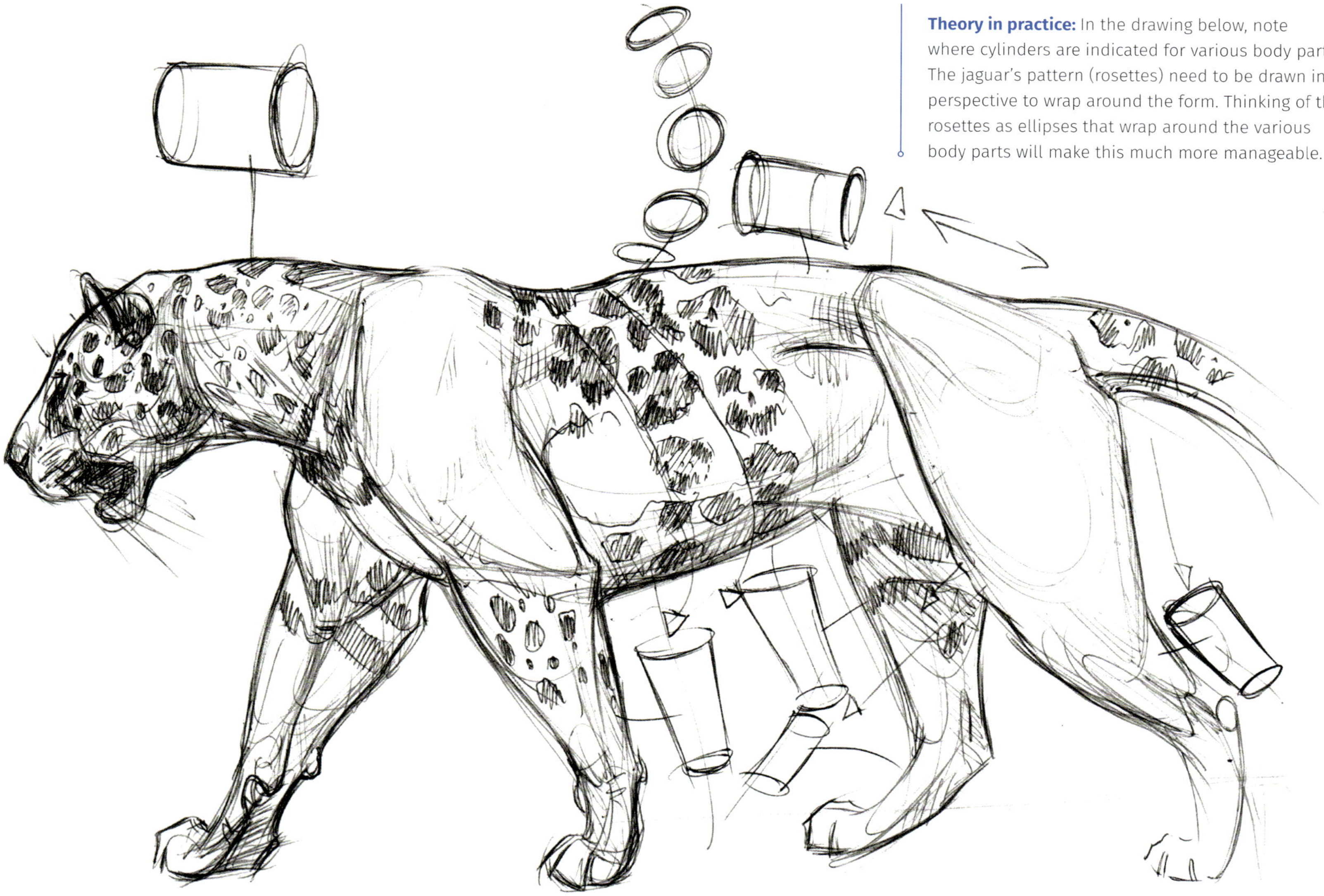

Box forms & planes

The box (also called a cube) comes from the square, but unlike the square, the cube has height, width, *and* depth. The box has four sides with a top and bottom, and learning to draw it is important because it reveals fundamental theories of perspective. Forms that are angular and have flat sides belong to the square forms, and this includes boxes and rectangular boxes as well as cylinders, which have tops, bottoms, and sides to become octagonal forms.

Animals can be built entirely of box-like forms, or boxes can be used for specific body parts, such as the pelvis or head. Boxes show the corners of the form and are the foundation for correctly portraying the plane changes. Planes can be broken up after advancing from the initial blocking-in stage. Box forms are useful for clarifying which way the surfaces face, as well as for figuring out the organization of light and shade. ▸▸

Boxes/cubes: Advancing from the square is the box (or cube) with height, width, and depth. A box showing a corner is in two-point perspective and is often used to figure out three-quarter views.

Finding the corners: The corners of the form can be found using cross-contour lines drawn from one edge to another. This is particularly important when modelling form because the corners typically indicate an anatomical mass or landmark.

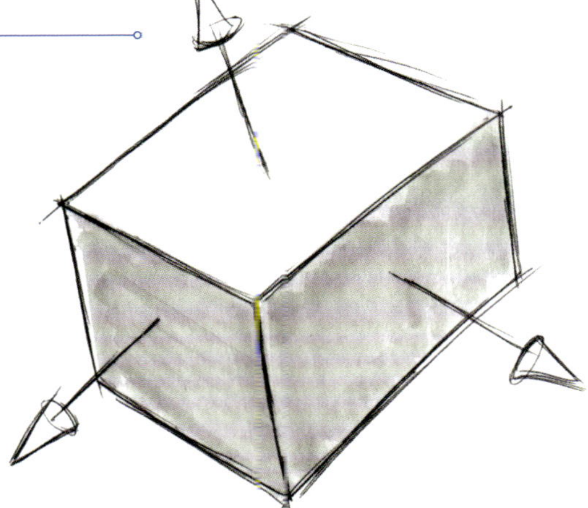

Plane changes: The box shows us which way the surface faces and is an easy way to figure out plane changes.

Freehand boxes: Practise sketching lots of boxes freely, without using a ruler, so that laying them in becomes second nature. Like all other forms, the box has an axis running through it, with space evenly distributed around it.

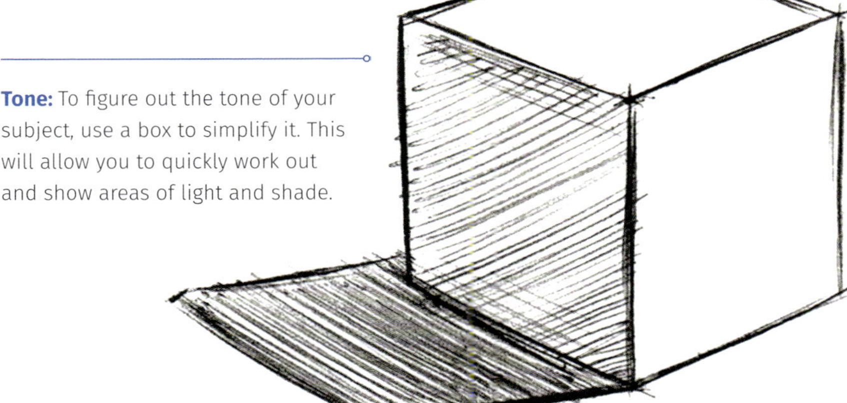

Tone: To figure out the tone of your subject, use a box to simplify it. This will allow you to quickly work out and show areas of light and shade.

Box-like cylinders: A cylinder can be box-like and show plane changes, which makes it octagonal.

Any animal can be put 'into' a box to figure out their perspective. Heads can also be drawn inside boxes, with parallel lines sketched to indicate how the features line up. In addition, the flat square or rectangle can be used to figure out an animal's proportions, as most animals in profile fit into these shapes.

Box forms are, without a doubt, some of the most essential forms to master. They should be drawn frequently using a ruler as well as freehand. ◇

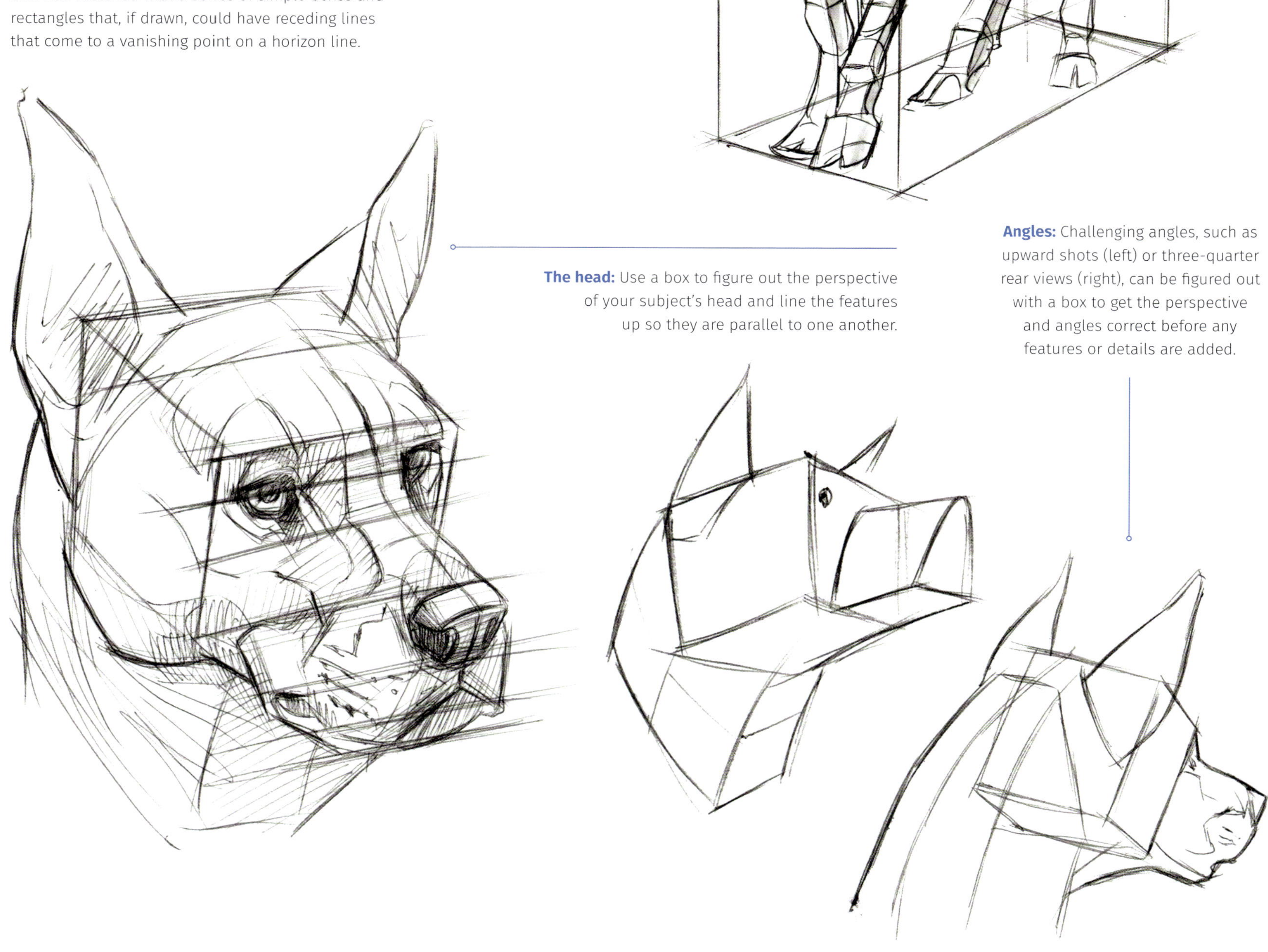

Box perspective: Putting the animal in a box will help you to determine the perspective. The head and neck will often stick out of this box. Note how the cow was sketched with a series of simple boxes and rectangles that, if drawn, could have receding lines that come to a vanishing point on a horizon line.

The head: Use a box to figure out the perspective of your subject's head and line the features up so they are parallel to one another.

Angles: Challenging angles, such as upward shots (left) or three-quarter rear views (right), can be figured out with a box to get the perspective and angles correct before any features or details are added.

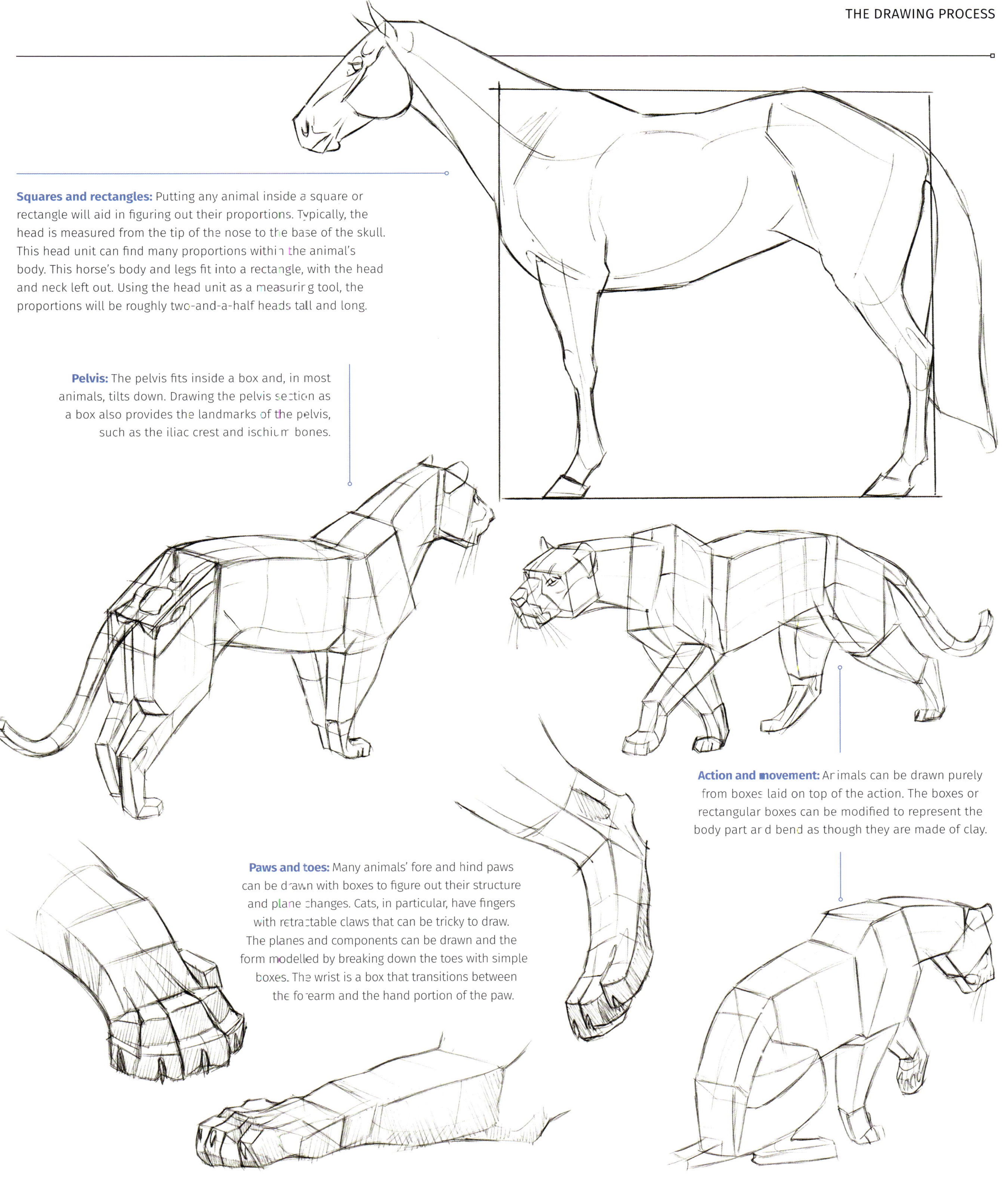

Squares and rectangles: Putting any animal inside a square or rectangle will aid in figuring out their proportions. Typically, the head is measured from the tip of the nose to the base of the skull. This head unit can find many proportions within the animal's body. This horse's body and legs fit into a rectangle, with the head and neck left out. Using the head unit as a measuring tool, the proportions will be roughly two-and-a-half heads tall and long.

Pelvis: The pelvis fits inside a box and, in most animals, tilts down. Drawing the pelvis section as a box also provides the landmarks of the pelvis, such as the iliac crest and ischium bones.

Action and movement: Animals can be drawn purely from boxes laid on top of the action. The boxes or rectangular boxes can be modified to represent the body part and bend as though they are made of clay.

Paws and toes: Many animals' fore and hind paws can be drawn with boxes to figure out their structure and plane changes. Cats, in particular, have fingers with retractable claws that can be tricky to draw. The planes and components can be drawn and the form modelled by breaking down the toes with simple boxes. The wrist is a box that transitions between the forearm and the hand portion of the paw.

Combining forms & using coordinates

COMBINING FORMS

Combining forms is the most common way to construct animals because different angles can require specific volumes. For example, a box may often be the most obvious choice for the hindquarters, but a cylinder might be a better option depending on the angle. If a body part is particularly angular – such as a wrist, elbow, or pelvis – a box-like form is often a good choice, whereas a sphere or cylinder may work better for a rounder body part, such as a ribcage or cranial mass. Forms can also be combined and morphed into each other, such as a cylindrical mass for the arm that becomes box-like at the wrist, where the body is more angular and has obvious plane changes. ◇

Combining forms to fit the angle: Using various forms to construct an animal offers the advantage of choosing ones that fit the body part for that given angle or perspective. In this drawing, a combination of box-like forms, cylinders, and ovoid shapes make up the majority of the forms.

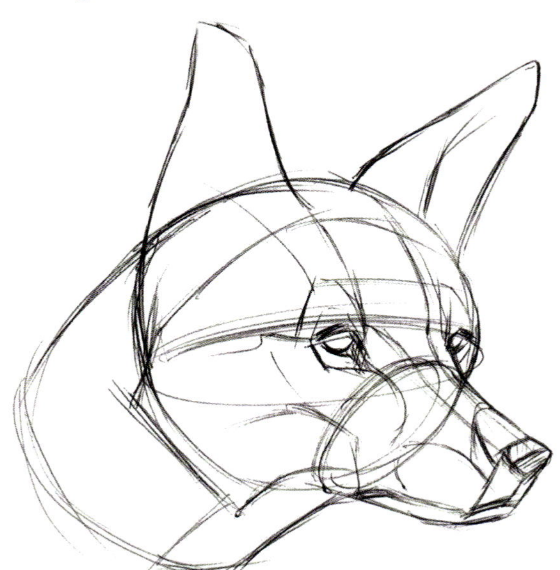

Fusing forms to construct the head: In this coyote head drawing, a sphere is used for the cranial mass and a cylinder with planes for the snout. The elliptical changes in the sphere help to keep the features in alignment.

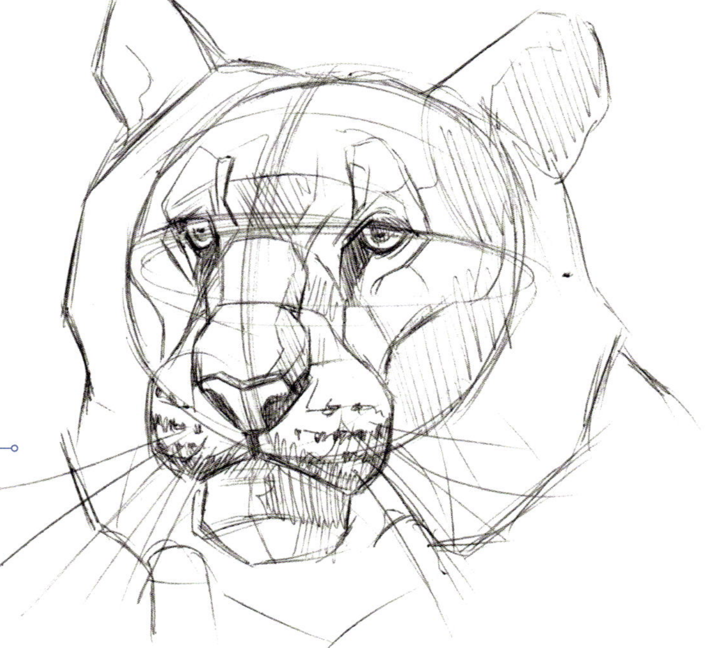

Combining round and straight lines: A sphere is used for this tiger's cranial mass. The spheres are repeated as forms of the muzzle and whisker bed. Subtle straights or angles are added all over the head and features to keep the drawing from becoming too round, which can detract from the natural-looking forms.

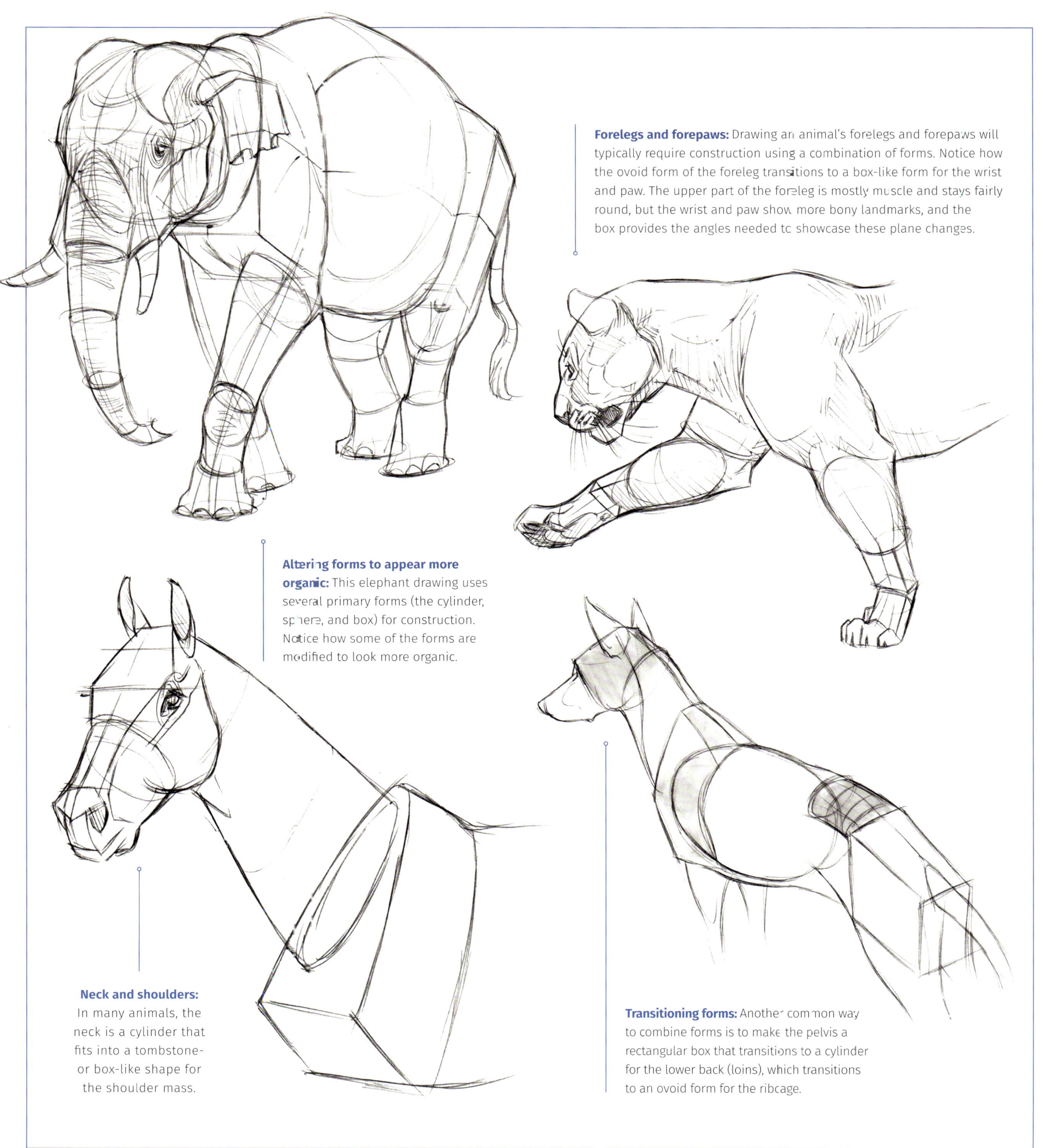

Forelegs and forepaws: Drawing an animal's forelegs and forepaws will typically require construction using a combination of forms. Notice how the ovoid form of the foreleg transitions to a box-like form for the wrist and paw. The upper part of the foreleg is mostly muscle and stays fairly round, but the wrist and paw show more bony landmarks, and the box provides the angles needed to showcase these plane changes.

Altering forms to appear more organic: This elephant drawing uses several primary forms (the cylinder, sphere, and box) for construction. Notice how some of the forms are modified to look more organic.

Neck and shoulders: In many animals, the neck is a cylinder that fits into a tombstone- or box-like shape for the shoulder mass.

Transitioning forms: Another common way to combine forms is to make the pelvis a rectangular box that transitions to a cylinder for the lower back (loins), which transitions to an ovoid form for the ribcage.

COORDINATES

Almost any form can be used to construct animals, and most of the time, it's just a matter of personal preference. Any difficult or complex subject is easier to draw by analysing and reducing each section down to its basic forms. The coordinates of a form are composed of the two-dimensional axis, three-dimensional axis, and surface direction.

Take a cylinder, for example; it has a two-dimensional axis running through the middle that shows the direction or tilt of the form in space, and the mass is distributed evenly around this axis. The three-dimensional axis is the ellipse or cross-contour lines showing the cylinder's depth and sculptural qualities. A final coordinate shows the way the surface faces, which is usually where the centre line is drawn. ◇

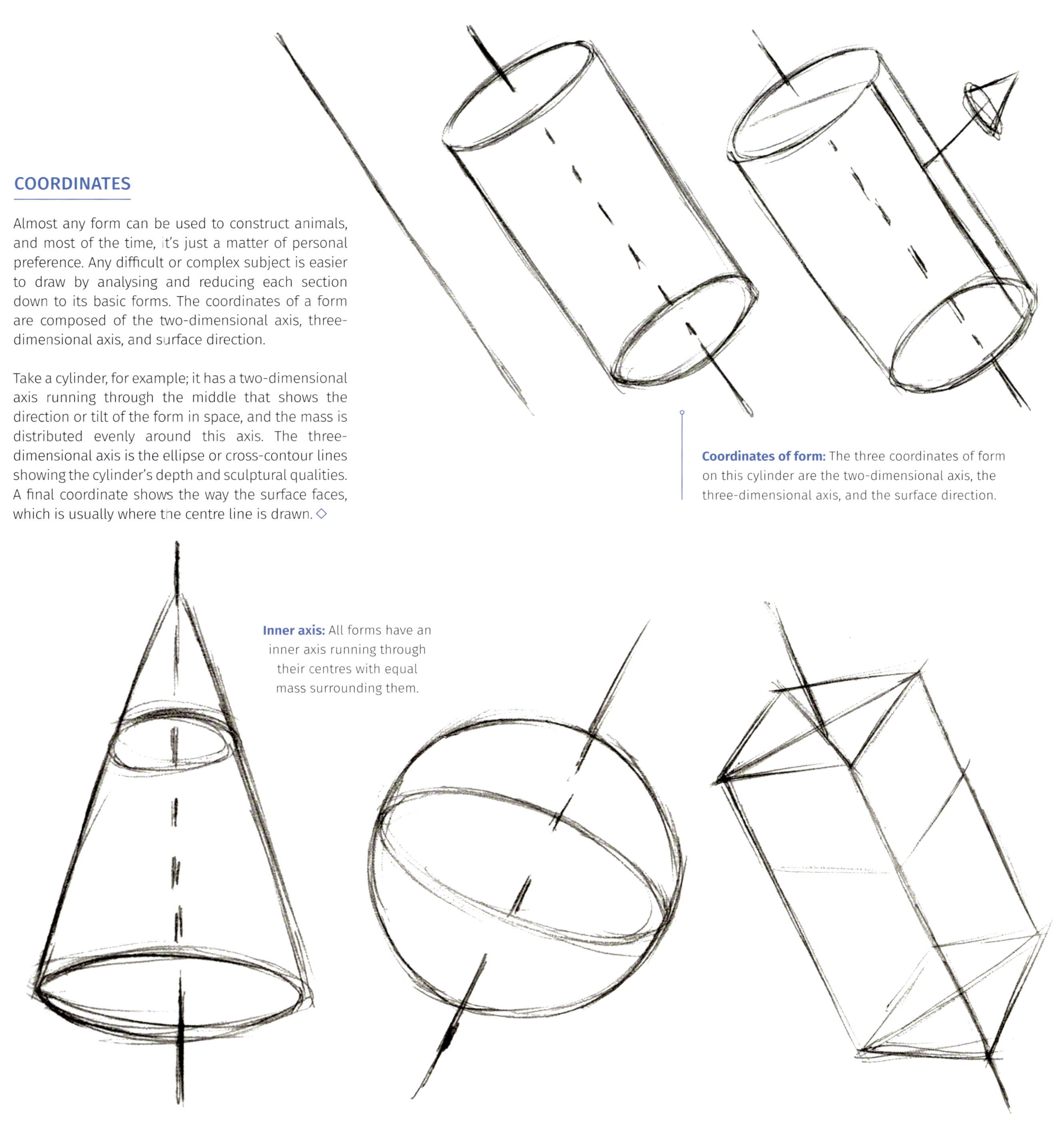

Coordinates of form: The three coordinates of form on this cylinder are the two-dimensional axis, the three-dimensional axis, and the surface direction.

Inner axis: All forms have an inner axis running through their centres with equal mass surrounding them.

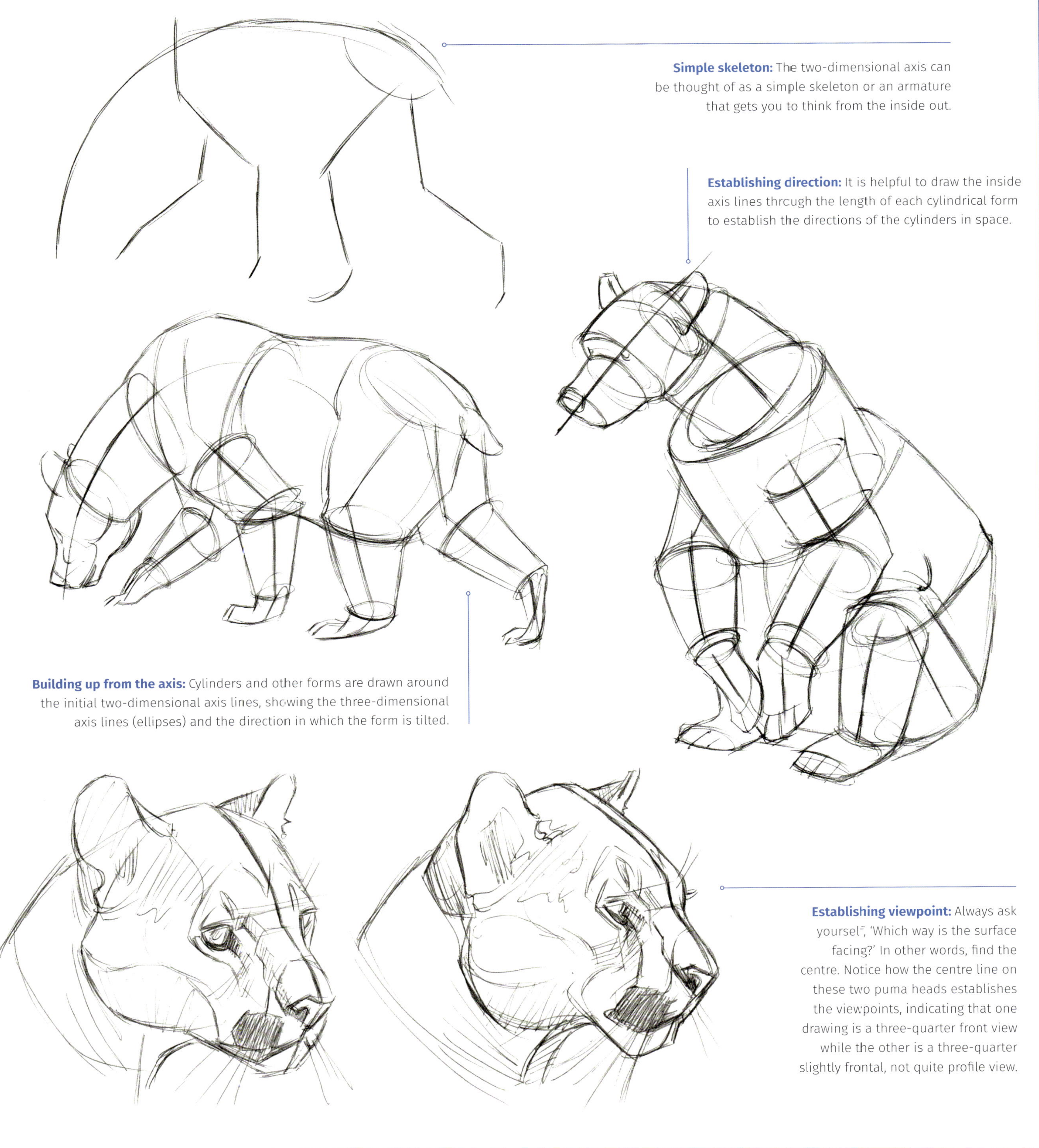

Simple skeleton: The two-dimensional axis can be thought of as a simple skeleton or an armature that gets you to think from the inside out.

Establishing direction: It is helpful to draw the inside axis lines through the length of each cylindrical form to establish the directions of the cylinders in space.

Building up from the axis: Cylinders and other forms are drawn around the initial two-dimensional axis lines, showing the three-dimensional axis lines (ellipses) and the direction in which the form is tilted.

Establishing viewpoint: Always ask yourself, 'Which way is the surface facing?' In other words, find the centre. Notice how the centre line on these two puma heads establishes the viewpoints, indicating that one drawing is a three-quarter front view while the other is a three-quarter slightly frontal, not quite profile view.

Draw-through & foreshortening

DRAW-THROUGH

To draw using construction, you must think of your subjects not just as outlines, but as transparent (or made of glass) with parts within the outlines. The outlines are then made up of these parts. Drawing 'through' allows the artist to understand and position volumes in relation to one another. More accurate forms can be developed by drawing hidden edges and contours of the subject, and a convincing feeling of the third dimension can be established.

An animal's body is often made up of a series of modified cylinders that, if drawn through at the critical connection points, allow the proportions and foreshortening to be easily controlled, even if the animal is in action. Drawing through is a thinking process for planning how forms fit together and relate to one another. It's not an end product. Over time, you will learn which lines to leave in or out and which ones to emphasize to show greater significance and weight. ◇

Transparent forms: Draw 'through' as though your subjects are made of glass. Notice the far-side front hoof on this zebra is mainly behind the other foreleg; however, it is still drawn all the way because doing so makes the rest of that arm appear proportionate.

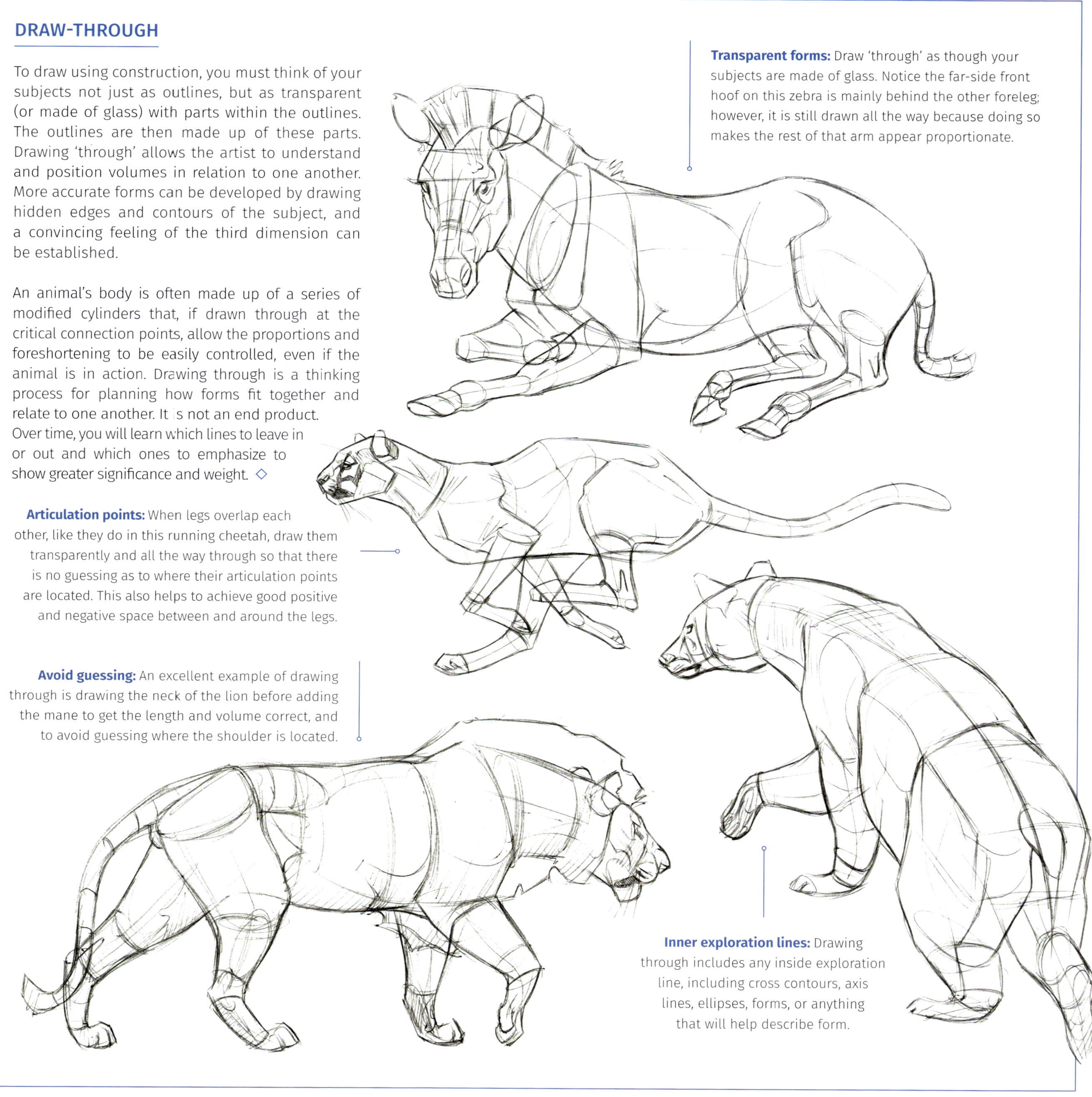

Articulation points: When legs overlap each other, like they do in this running cheetah, draw them transparently and all the way through so that there is no guessing as to where their articulation points are located. This also helps to achieve good positive and negative space between and around the legs.

Avoid guessing: An excellent example of drawing through is drawing the neck of the lion before adding the mane to get the length and volume correct, and to avoid guessing where the shoulder is located.

Inner exploration lines: Drawing through includes any inside exploration line, including cross contours, axis lines, ellipses, forms, or anything that will help describe form.

FORESHORTENING

Foreshortening is drawing an object tipped towards or away from the viewer, or objects that recede away from or advance towards the viewer. As forms recede back in space, they appear smaller and change shape. A cylinder is a good example. When foreshortened, the sides become shorter, and the ellipses open up as the foreshortening is increased. To construct a pose where parts of the body recede from the eye or advance towards it, use basic forms on top of the gesture to figure out the foreshortening and perspective. ◇

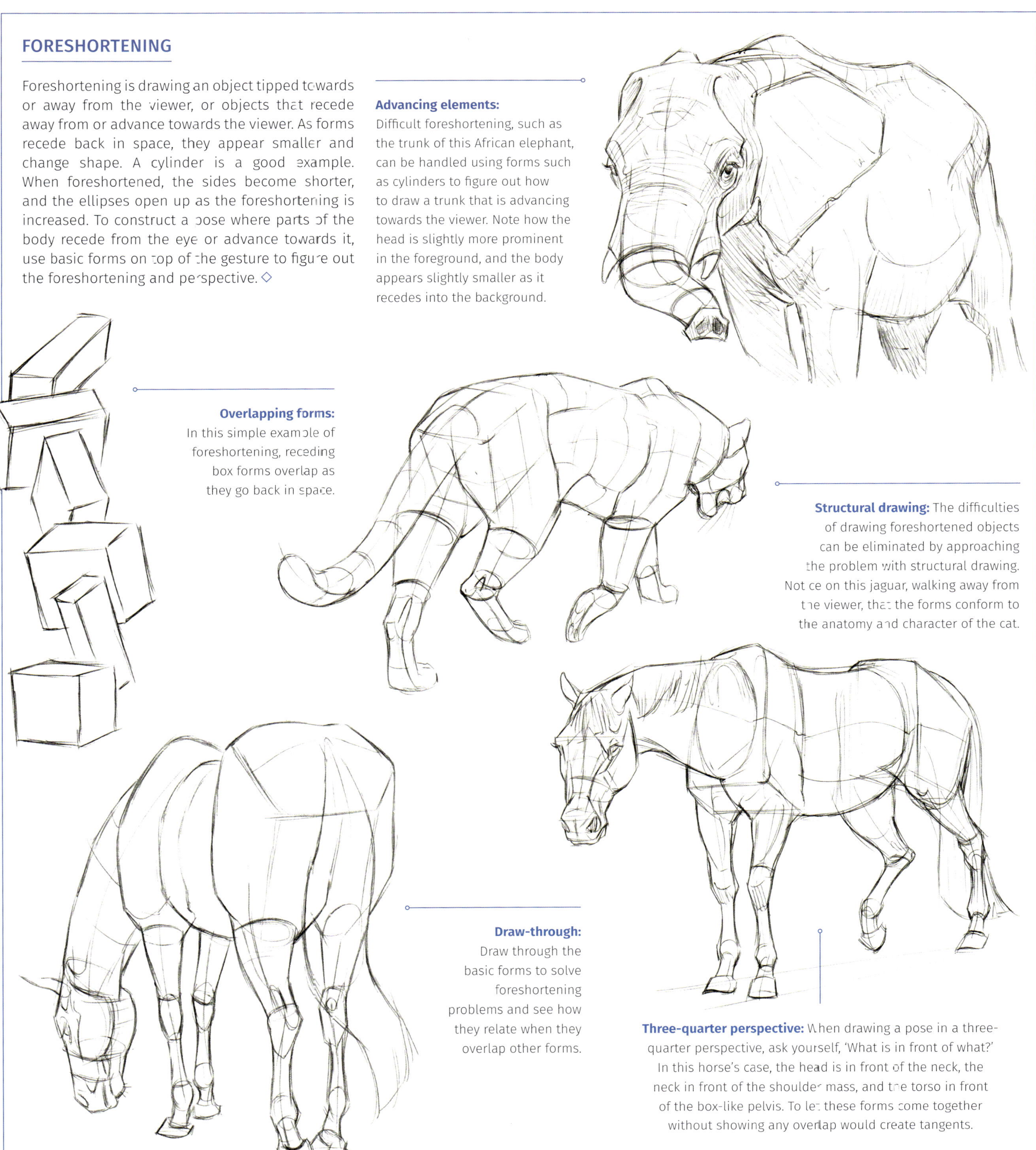

Advancing elements: Difficult foreshortening, such as the trunk of this African elephant, can be handled using forms such as cylinders to figure out how to draw a trunk that is advancing towards the viewer. Note how the head is slightly more prominent in the foreground, and the body appears slightly smaller as it recedes into the background.

Overlapping forms: In this simple example of foreshortening, receding box forms overlap as they go back in space.

Structural drawing: The difficulties of drawing foreshortened objects can be eliminated by approaching the problem with structural drawing. Notice on this jaguar, walking away from the viewer, that the forms conform to the anatomy and character of the cat.

Draw-through: Draw through the basic forms to solve foreshortening problems and see how they relate when they overlap other forms.

Three-quarter perspective: When drawing a pose in a three-quarter perspective, ask yourself, 'What is in front of what?' In this horse's case, the head is in front of the neck, the neck in front of the shoulder mass, and the torso in front of the box-like pelvis. To let these forms come together without showing any overlap would create tangents.

Basic approach

A tried-and-true method for creating a sound, believable drawing involves depicting the gesture, constructing the forms, and finally fleshing it all out to make it look natural and organic. The first step is to draw the gesture, which freely and quickly captures the essence of the pose or what the animal is doing. Focus on getting the flow of the animal's position rather than how it is made. A gesture drawing that will serve as a lay-in to a developed drawing should be kept light, so that the lines or tones will not compete with the construction forms or final details when you draw over it.

Another way of doing this is to lay in the gesture, place new paper over that drawing (tracing paper or using a lightbox), and draw the forms on top. However, if you are using a sketchbook at a zoo to draw from life, it's better to develop and finish one drawing in layers right on top of each other.

The next step is to feel out and build up the basic forms over the gesture. This construction part gives the drawing a sculptural or three-dimensional look. Remember to draw all the forms through to the other side like they are made of glass. ▸▸

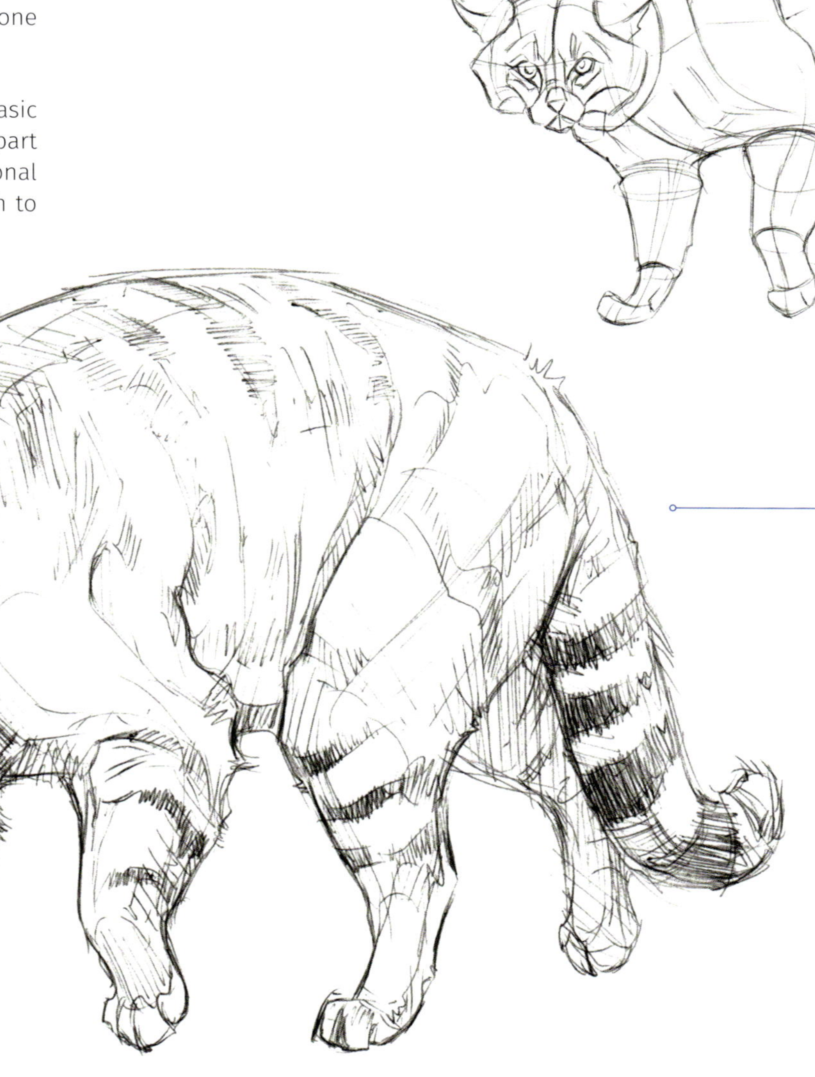

Three stages: The basic approach consists of three stages: capturing the action (gesture), constructing the forms, and fleshing everything out (developing the parts).

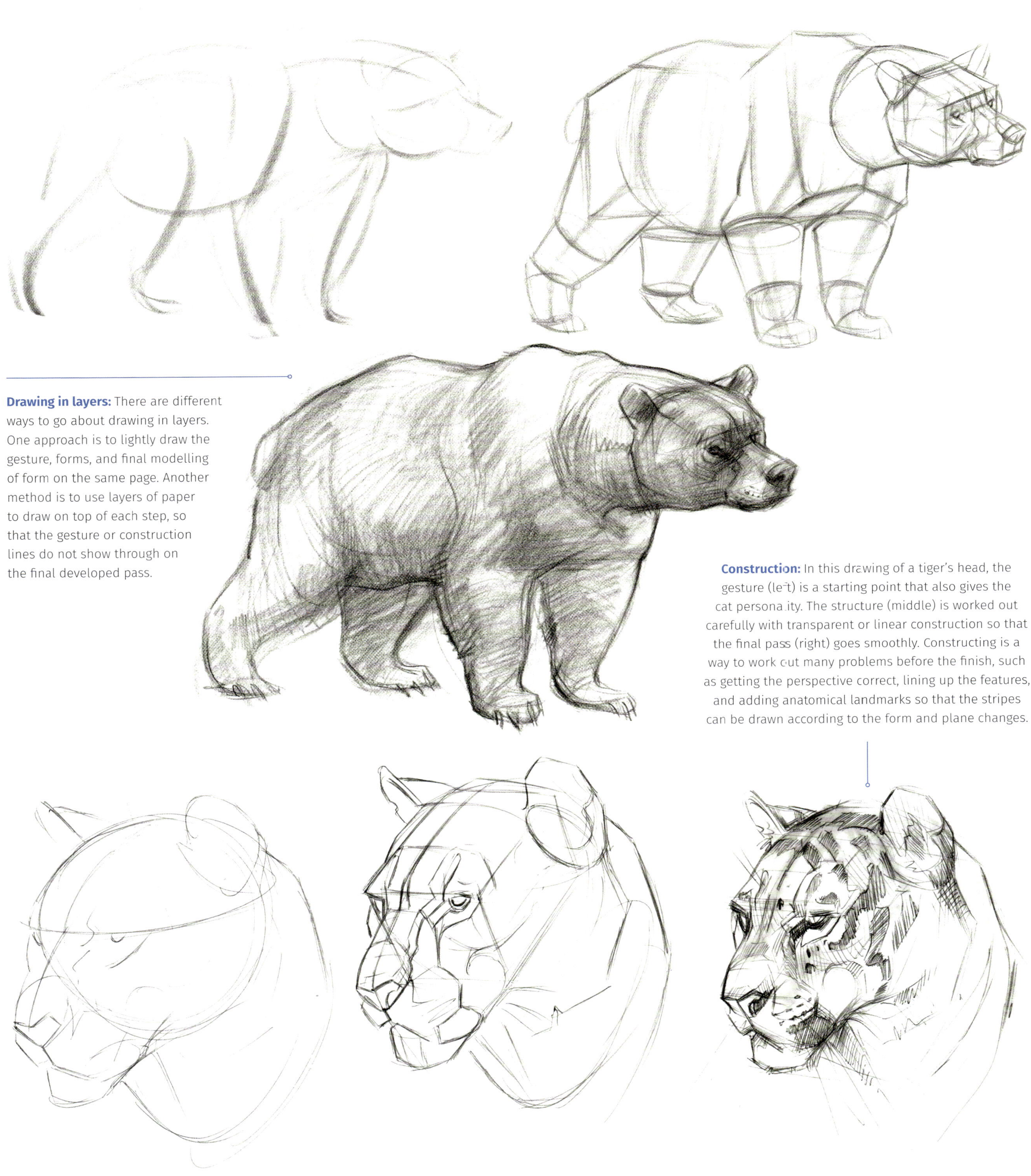

Drawing in layers: There are different ways to go about drawing in layers. One approach is to lightly draw the gesture, forms, and final modelling of form on the same page. Another method is to use layers of paper to draw on top of each step, so that the gesture or construction lines do not show through on the final developed pass.

Construction: In this drawing of a tiger's head, the gesture (left) is a starting point that also gives the cat personality. The structure (middle) is worked out carefully with transparent or linear construction so that the final pass (right) goes smoothly. Constructing is a way to work out many problems before the finish, such as getting the perspective correct, lining up the features, and adding anatomical landmarks so that the stripes can be drawn according to the form and plane changes.

The final step is to 'animalize' the basic forms and make them organic. This 'form analysis' stage means fleshing out the forms and adding elements that make them look natural, such as muscle, bone, plane changes, light and shade, and pattern. How much detail goes into the drawing is a personal choice and comes from much trial and error. Too much rendering can kill a drawing, so to keep the drawing fresh, with a lot of personality, we must learn to pick and choose what to put into a drawing and what to leave out.

This approach is similar to building a house. First, the framework is assembled (the gesture); next, the house is built to be structurally sound (the construction); and finally, the details and finishes are put on (making things organic). ◇

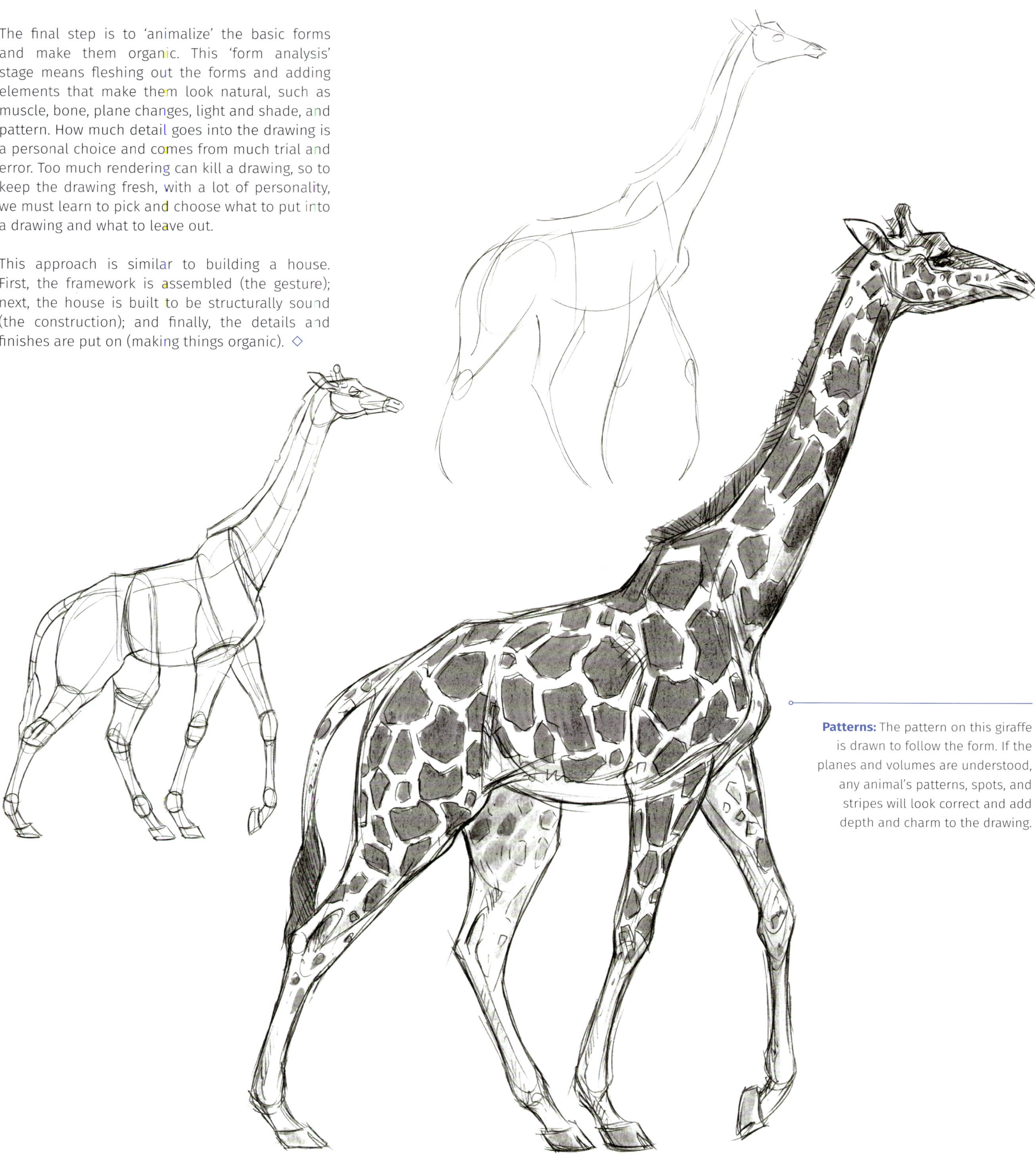

Patterns: The pattern on this giraffe is drawn to follow the form. If the planes and volumes are understood, any animal's patterns, spots, and stripes will look correct and add depth and charm to the drawing.

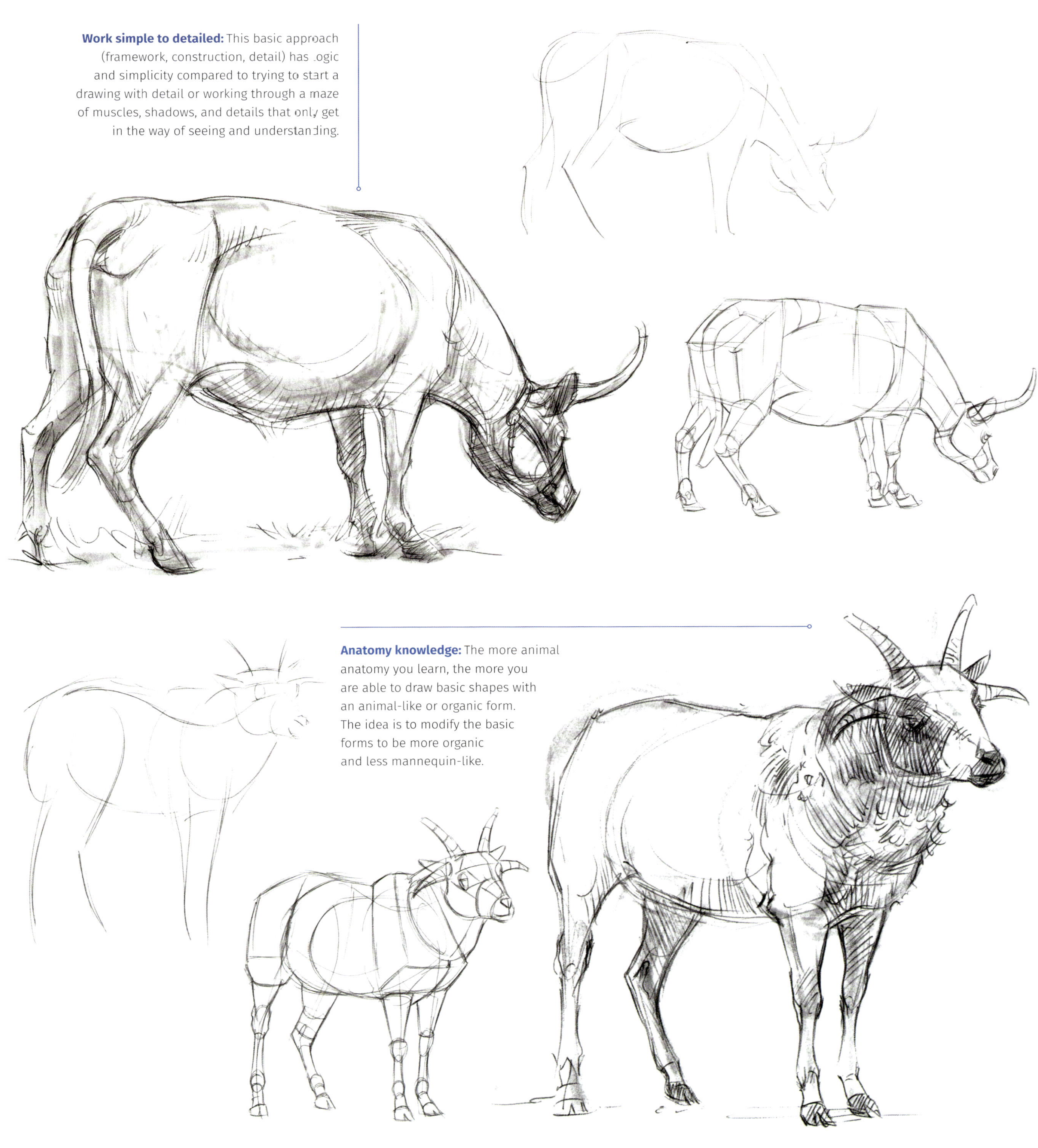

Work simple to detailed: This basic approach (framework, construction, detail) has logic and simplicity compared to trying to start a drawing with detail or working through a maze of muscles, shadows, and details that only get in the way of seeing and understanding.

Anatomy knowledge: The more animal anatomy you learn, the more you are able to draw basic shapes with an animal-like or organic form. The idea is to modify the basic forms to be more organic and less mannequin-like.

Drawing from the imagination

Drawing from the imagination is one of the ultimate goals of animal drawing. When you are sketching moving animals in a life-drawing situation, you are drawing both what you see *and* what you know. The 'what you know' part is drawing from memory and imagination.

After starting by sketching a gesture pose, the next step is to develop the drawing, but you will often find that the animal walks away or somehow moves its body. You can then continue the drawing from your imagination, using anything you have memorized and know to finish it. For this reason, training the visual imagination is more important in animal drawing, where you have moving subjects, than in figure drawing, where the model is posed and holding still for various amounts of time.

Another essential reason to be able to draw from imagination is when working on many forms of illustration, animation, concept art, and entertainment art. In these situations you are often expected to draw animals, which means you need to know how to develop the pose, forms, and character from memory.

Finally, drawing from imagination greatly helps with fine art, such as painting and sculpture. Paintings can be entirely composed from the imagination. If you can't find the body positions you want from reference, you make them up, pulling from your knowledge of form and anatomy. So, in situations like this, drawing what you know, *not* what you see, becomes imperative. ◇

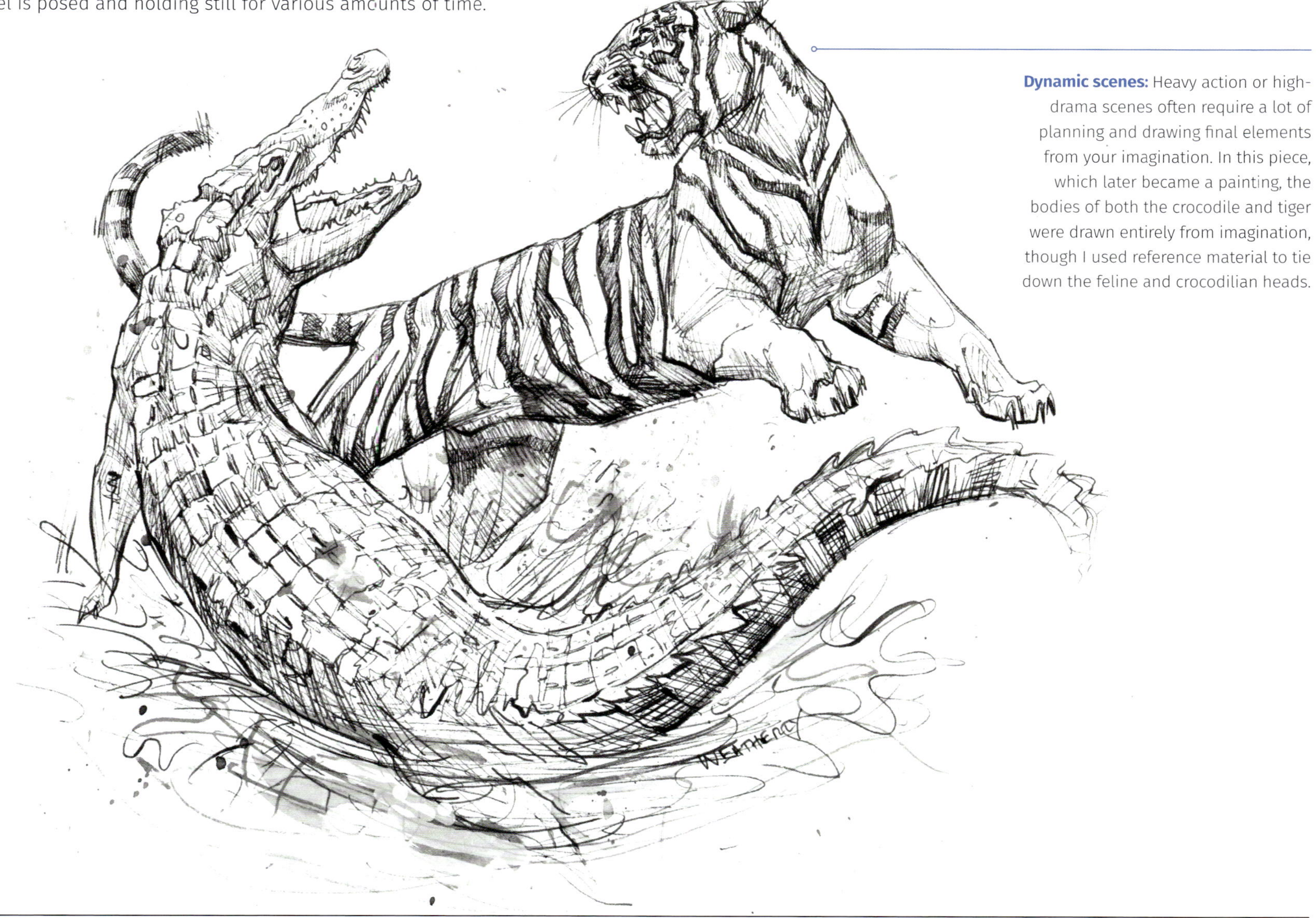

Dynamic scenes: Heavy action or high-drama scenes often require a lot of planning and drawing final elements from your imagination. In this piece, which later became a painting, the bodies of both the crocodile and tiger were drawn entirely from imagination, though I used reference material to tie down the feline and crocodilian heads.

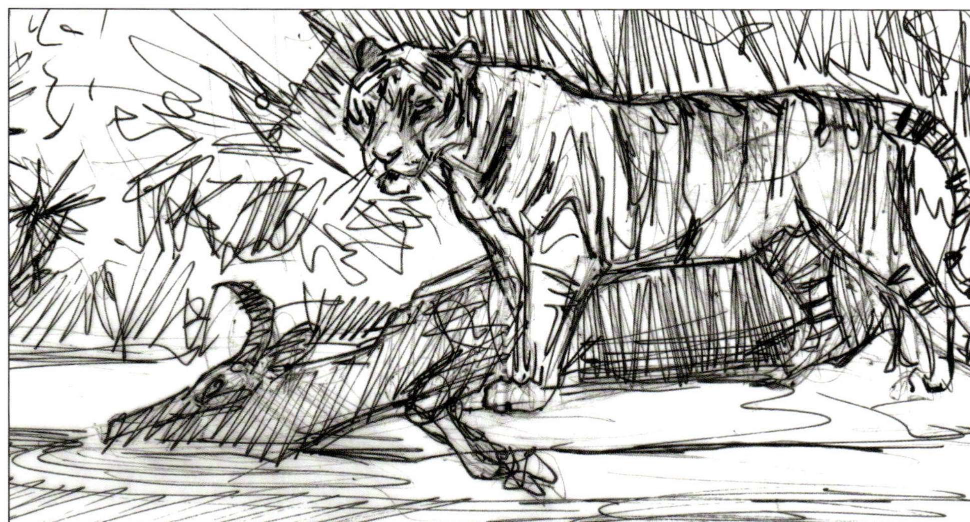

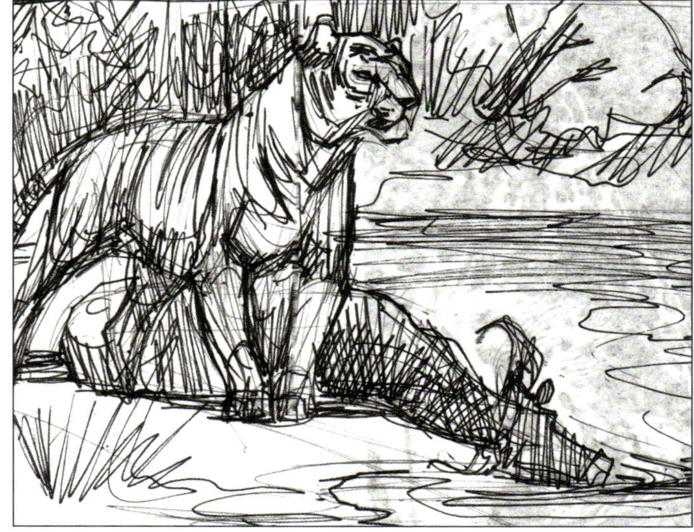

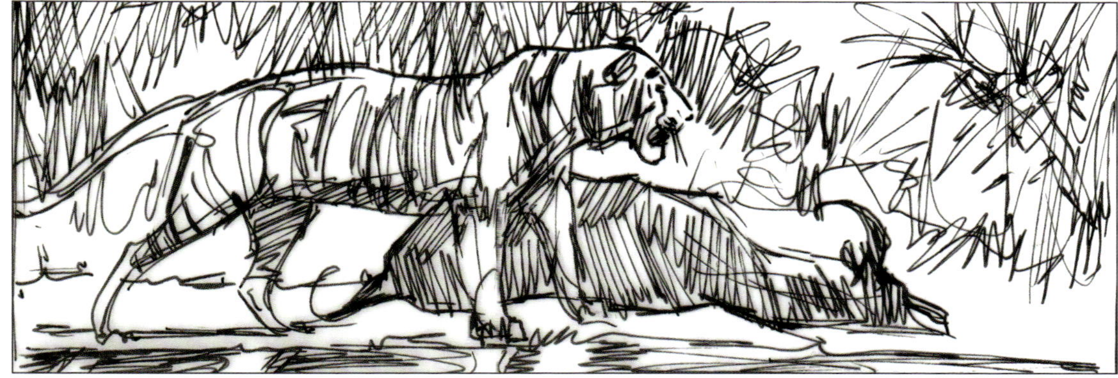

Building scenes: Here is an example of how animal drawings can be used to create a scene, which can be made in any medium. Start by sketching small thumbnails using gesture and only your imagination, with no reference, to come up with ideas. Here, I wanted to depict a scene with a tiger standing over its prey: a gaur. Once a composition is decided upon, use a combination of reference and imagination to create the developed drawing (that can then be transferred to a canvas). Here, I drew the gaur entirely from imagination, while the tiger was a blend of reference and memory.

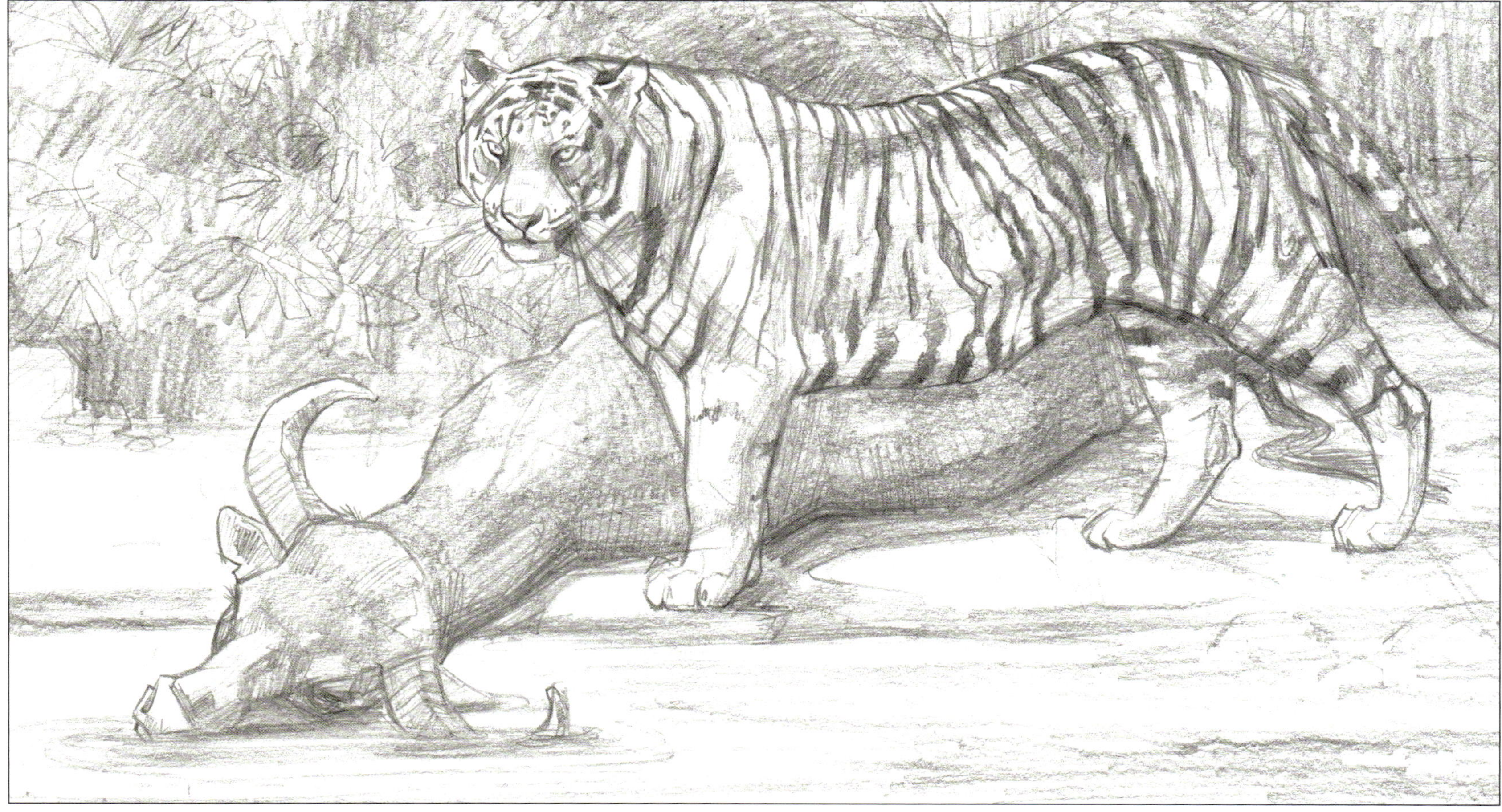

Drawing from life

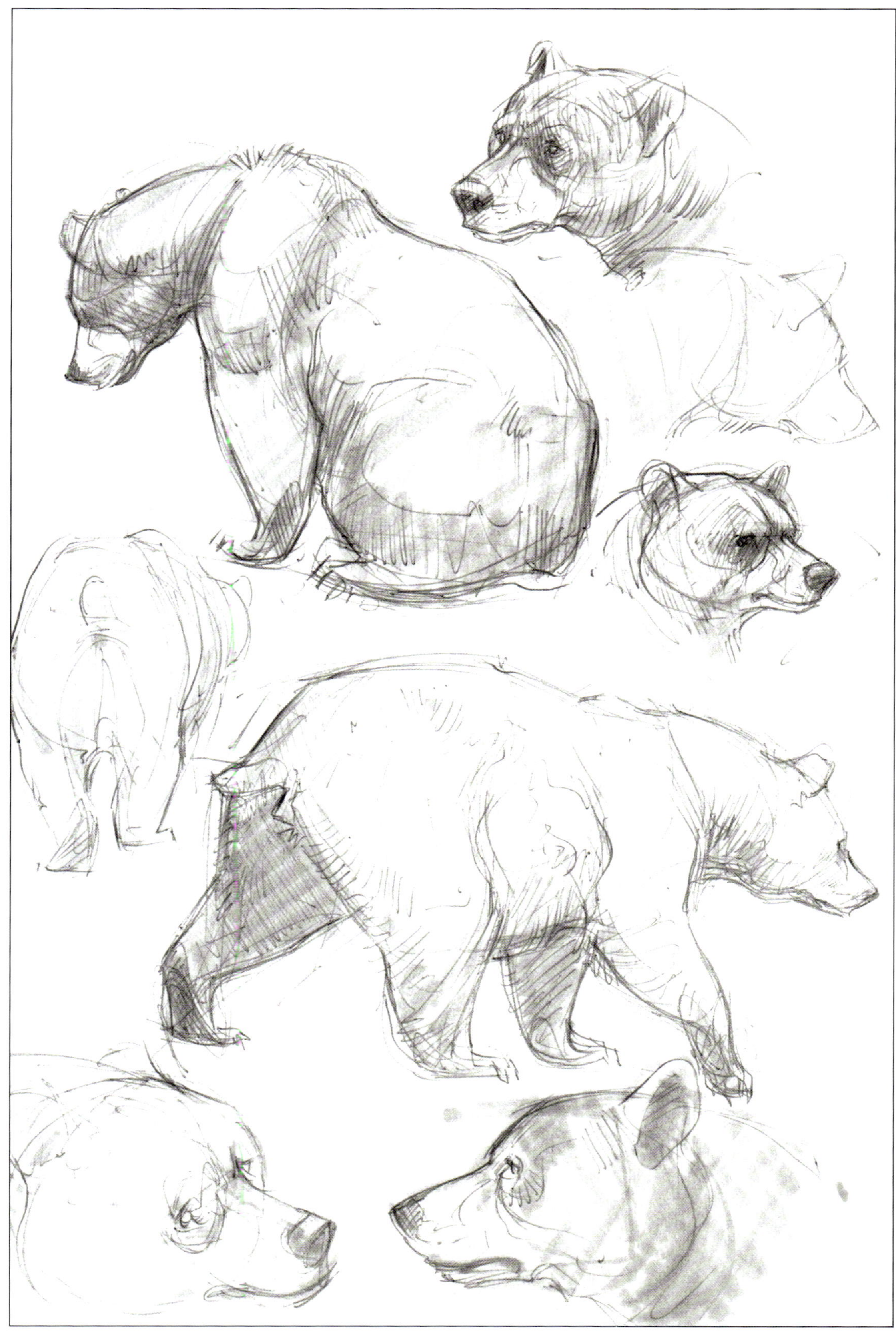

Drawing from life is a vital part of learning to draw animals, or anything at all! When you draw an animal from life, your eyes are able to see around the forms, instead of looking at an image where everything is flattened from the monocular vision of the camera. Life drawing allows you to observe things that cannot be observed from reference photos, such as how three-dimensional the forms are. Also, there is no distortion, which can happen with photography. Cameras can distort proportions, colour, and values, plus they can flatten things out. However, if you have paid your dues and have been drawing from life for some time, using photos to draw from will be advantageous because you will already be familiar with drawing principles such as gesture, form, and anatomy.

Drawing from life is an ongoing training for the artist. Whether once a week or twice a month, make it a regular practice to go to a zoo, equestrian centre, farm, or anywhere with animals to draw for an hour or two. If you have pets, or access to them, these also make good subjects to draw from life. Then, when you create studio art, illustration, painting, or anything requiring you to use photos to accurately capture an animal, you will find what you produce is much more informed. The more you get into the sketchbook habit, the easier drawing from life will become. ◇

Gestural sketching: Drawing from life is a relatively quick process. I like to lay in various gestures, and then develop the ones that show potential. While drawing at the bear exhibit at a local zoo, I focused on developing one head, then concentrated on the rhythm for the rest of the drawings, keeping them quick and gestural.

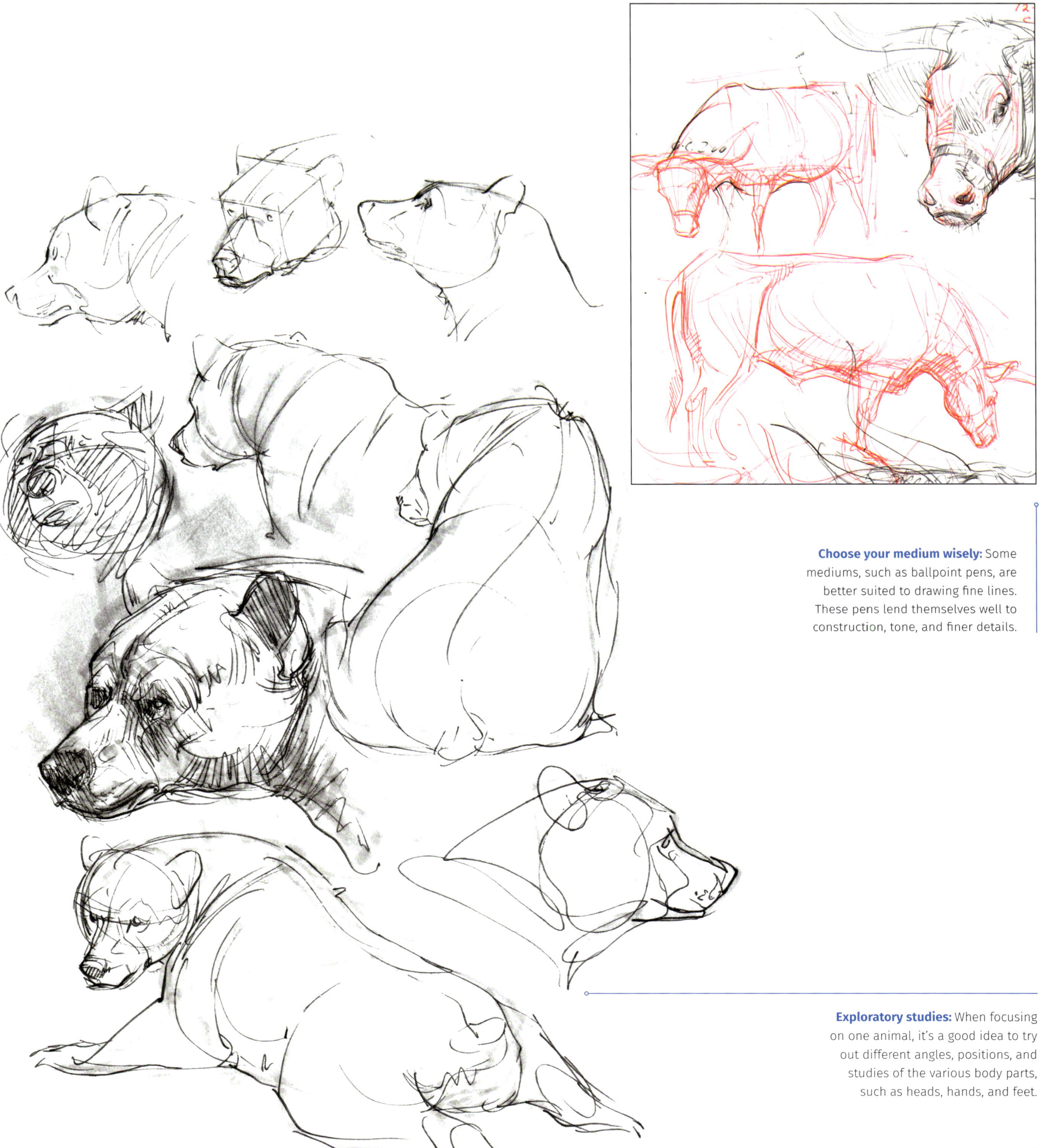

Choose your medium wisely: Some mediums, such as ballpoint pens, are better suited to drawing fine lines. These pens lend themselves well to construction, tone, and finer details.

Exploratory studies: When focusing on one animal, it's a good idea to try out different angles, positions, and studies of the various body parts, such as heads, hands, and feet.

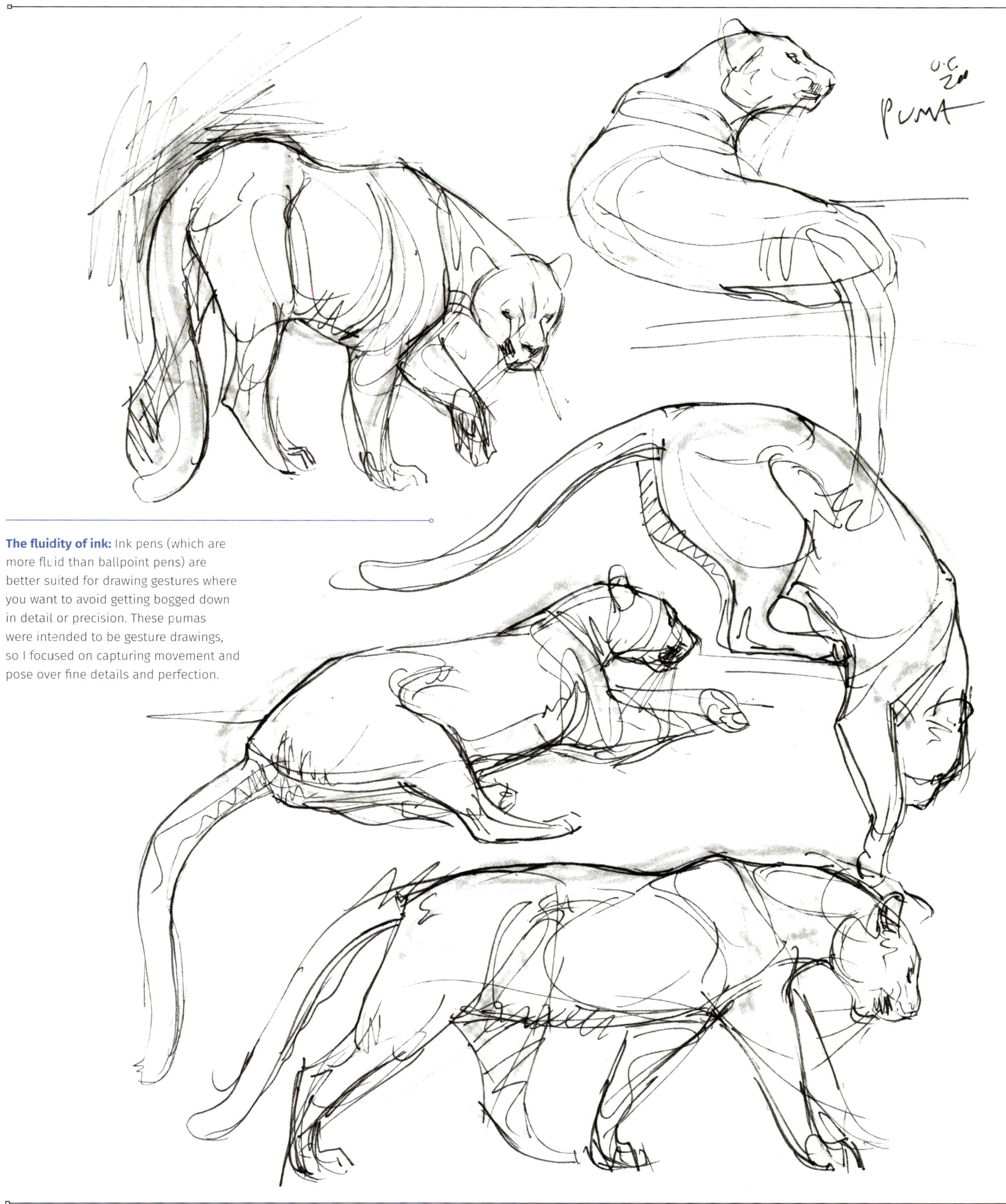

The fluidity of ink: Ink pens (which are more fluid than ballpoint pens) are better suited for drawing gestures where you want to avoid getting bogged down in detail or precision. These pumas were intended to be gesture drawings, so I focused on capturing movement and pose over fine details and perfection.

Keeping a sketchbook

One habit that artists and art students should continually practise is keeping a sketchbook. The best way to become good at drawing is to draw, and keeping a sketchbook is a great way to get pen or pencil mileage. The more you practise drawing, the more you will develop your dexterity using a pen or pencil. Each time you draw an animal, your skill will develop and improve.

Sketchbooks can be taken to zoos to draw animals straight from life, but they are also good for doing homework such as studying, working out ideas for animal compositions, and just about anything related to animal art. When first starting a sketchbook, you may think your drawings appear weak, but with time and practice you will learn to be quite proficient at observational drawing, as well as drawing from your imagination. When working from live animals that are constantly moving, make many starts and you will find the finishes will take care of themselves.

Sketchbooks come in various different sizes and types of paper. A spiral-bound sketchbook is good for drawing at the zoo as you can flip the pages over, which makes it easier to set the book on the railings of the enclosures. Take it everywhere with you to develop your sketchbook practice – you will soon fill it with animals. ◇

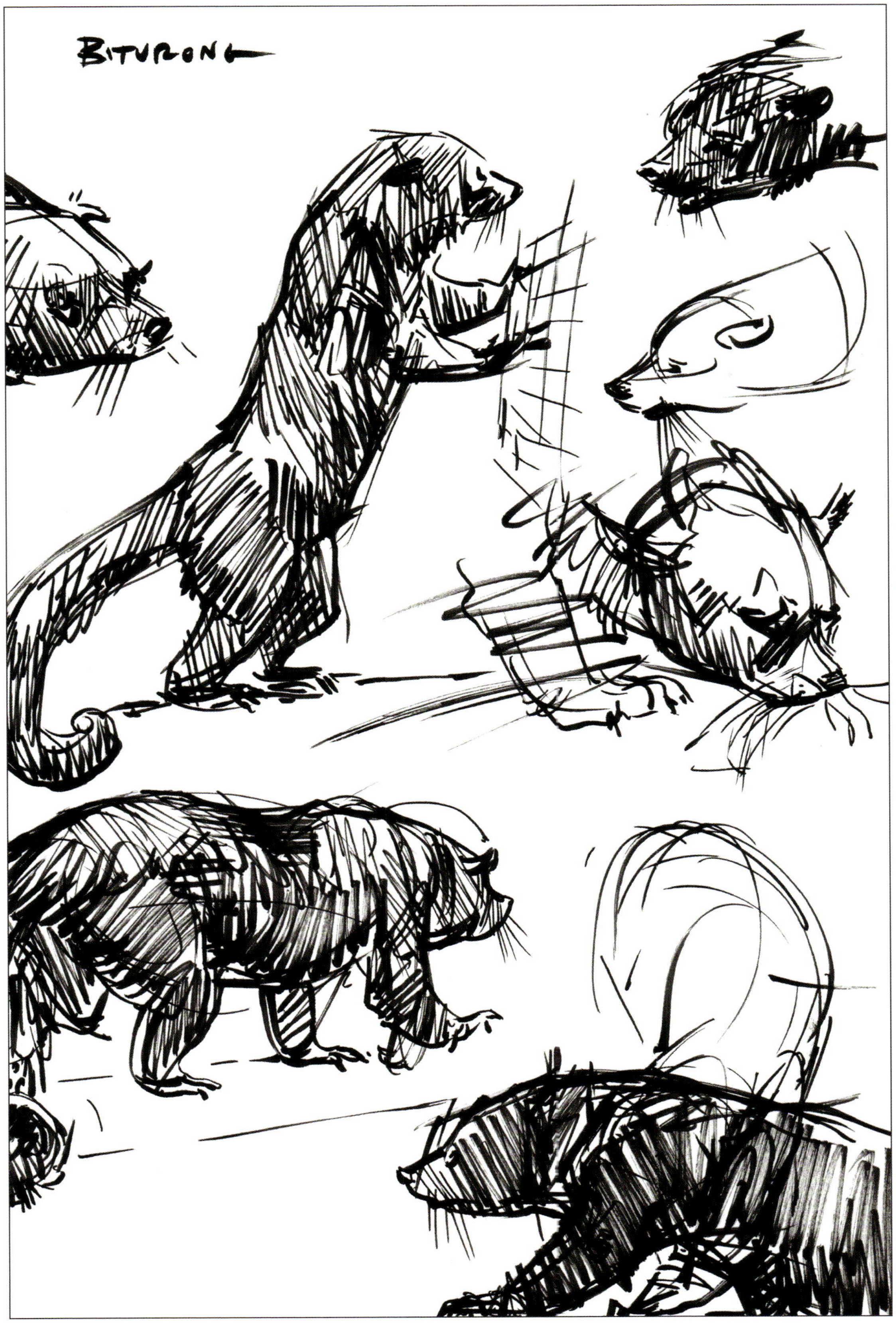

Sketching fast-moving animals: When drawing fast-moving animals, such as binturongs, it's normal to repeatedly start and stop until you find a pose that's worth developing. Using a black brush pen will encourage you to draw directly with no intention of erasing, preventing the drawing from becoming too precise.

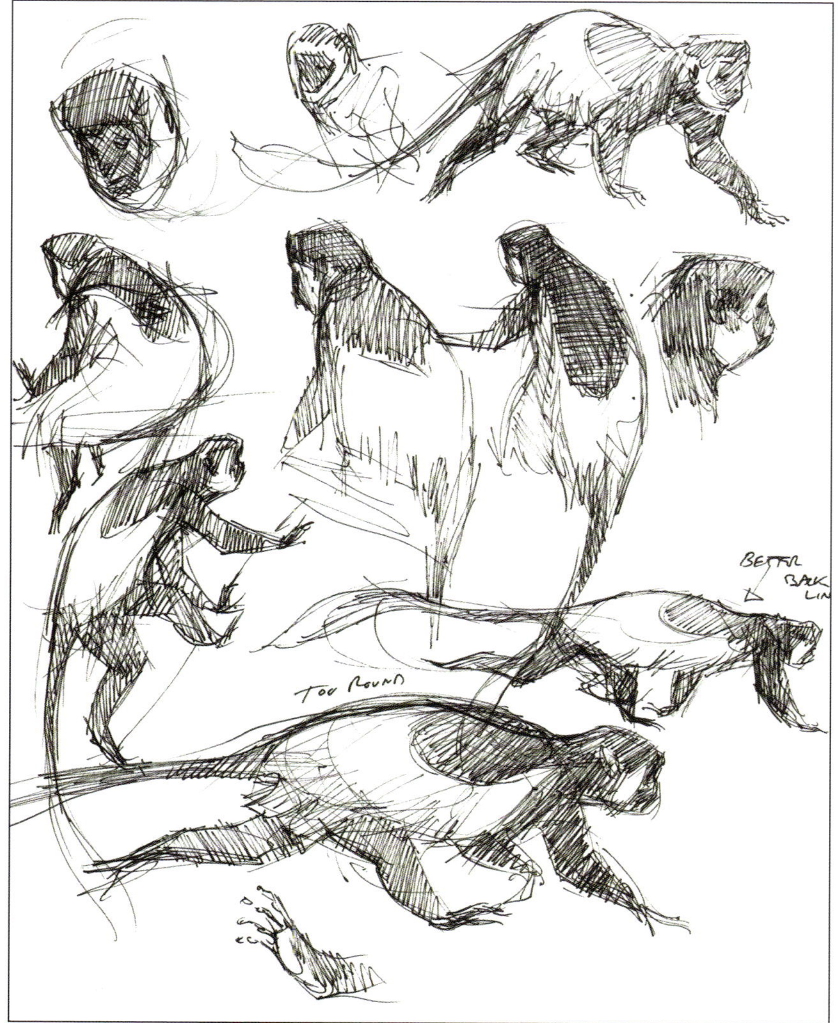

Memorizing basic shapes: Monkeys are fast and drawing them can be frustrating, but each time will become increasingly easier if you have learned and memorized the basic shapes that make up their bodies, plus characteristics such as their long tails or expressive faces.

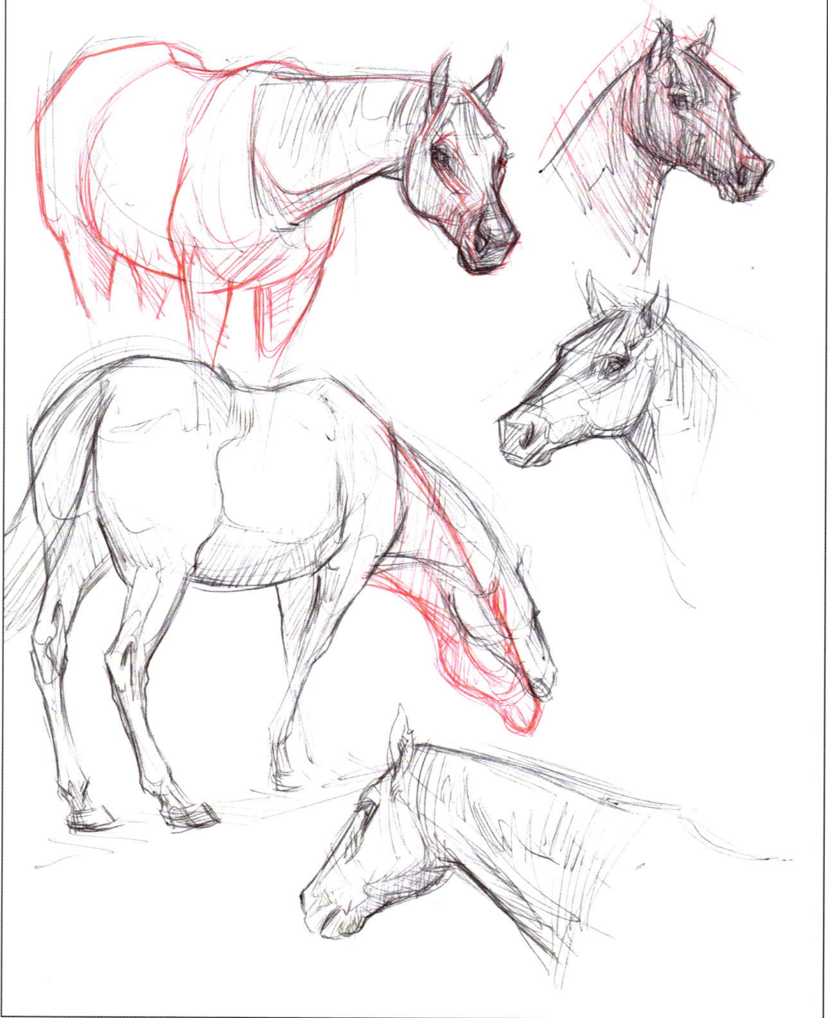

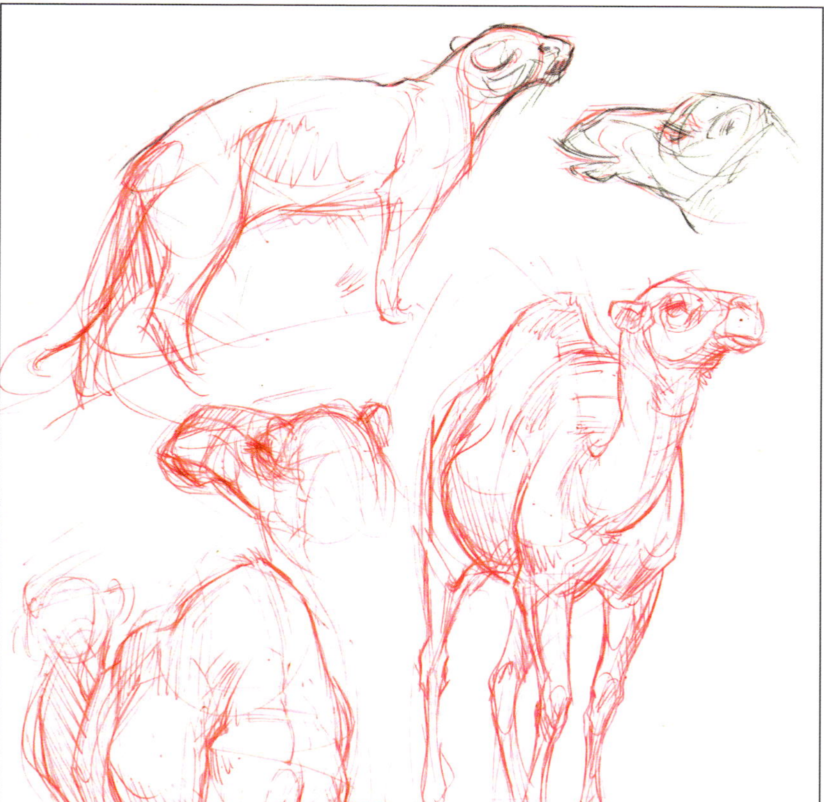

Drawing slow animals: Animals that move slower, such as camels, are the ideal subjects for drawing at a zoo. Once the initial action or first movement or pose of the animal is laid in, then developing that pose is the goal. You can keep looking up to observe the animal at various angles, but drawing from memory is equally as important.

Learn and explore: Keeping a sketchbook is often about learning and exploring, rather than getting everything correct. For example, if a change needs to be made in a neck or head, I will draw right over the original neck or head to try out another angle.

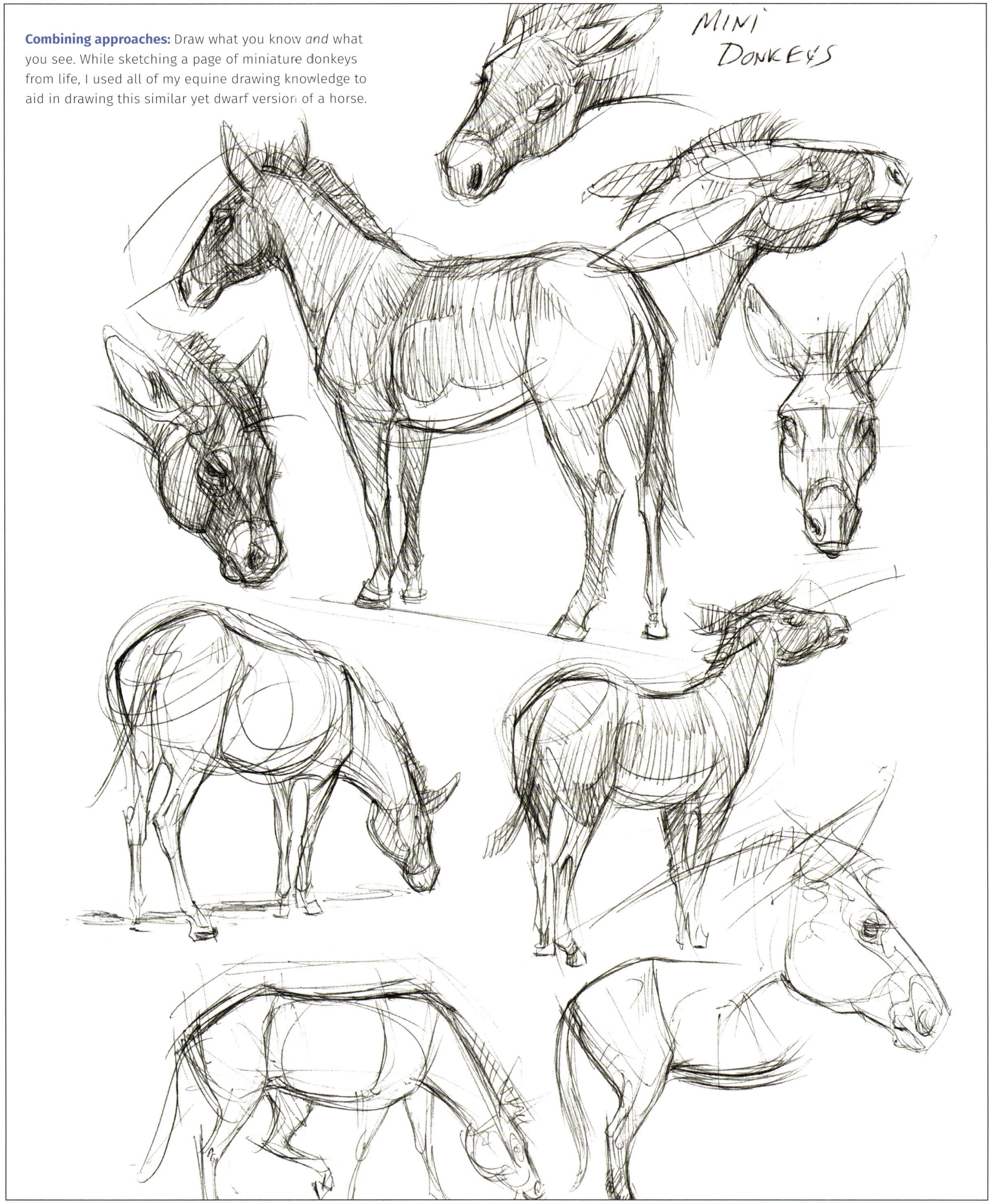

Combining approaches: Draw what you know *and* what you see. While sketching a page of miniature donkeys from life, I used all of my equine drawing knowledge to aid in drawing this similar yet dwarf version of a horse.

Drawing tools

Animals can be drawn with any medium. I prefer using pens to draw animals when working in a sketchbook, especially when drawing from life at a zoo. Pen is a direct medium that does not allow for erasing. Using ink teaches you to think before you put a stroke down and draw with direct accuracy, as you only get a couple of passes to get it correct.

It's advisable to bring several types of ink pens to draw with. Some pens are easy to use, such as ballpoint, which is considered the 'pencil of pens' due to its soft lines that can be built up, making constructing easy. Runnier or wetter pens, such as fountain pens and brush pens, are excellent for direct drawing where you try to get everything correct on the first pass. They are also good for gesture drawing, which by its very nature should be fast and direct.

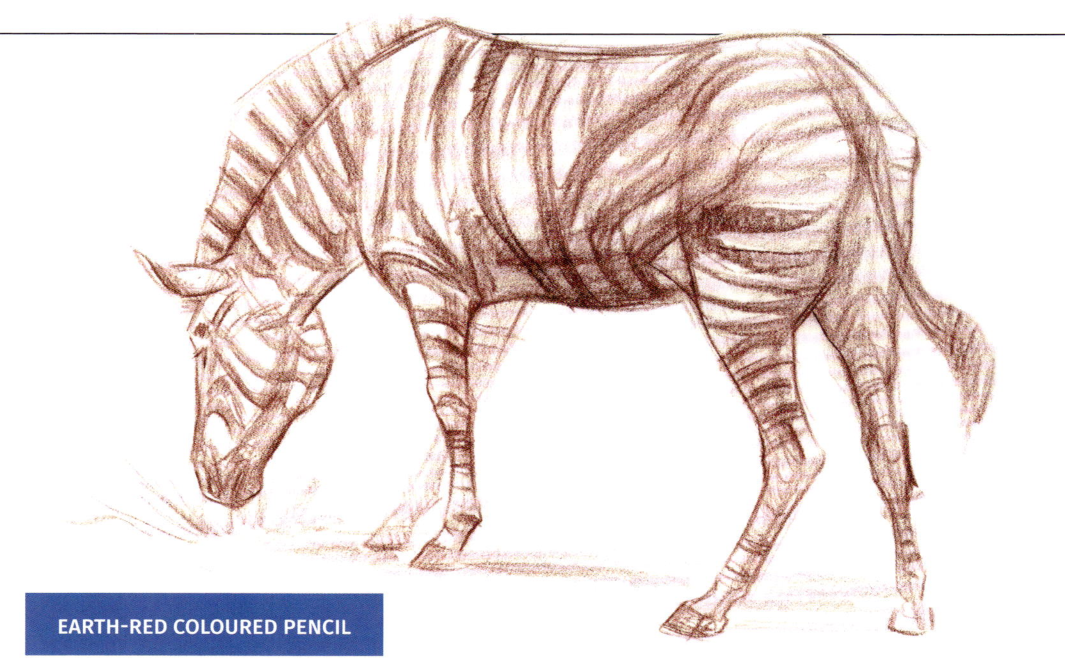

EARTH-RED COLOURED PENCIL

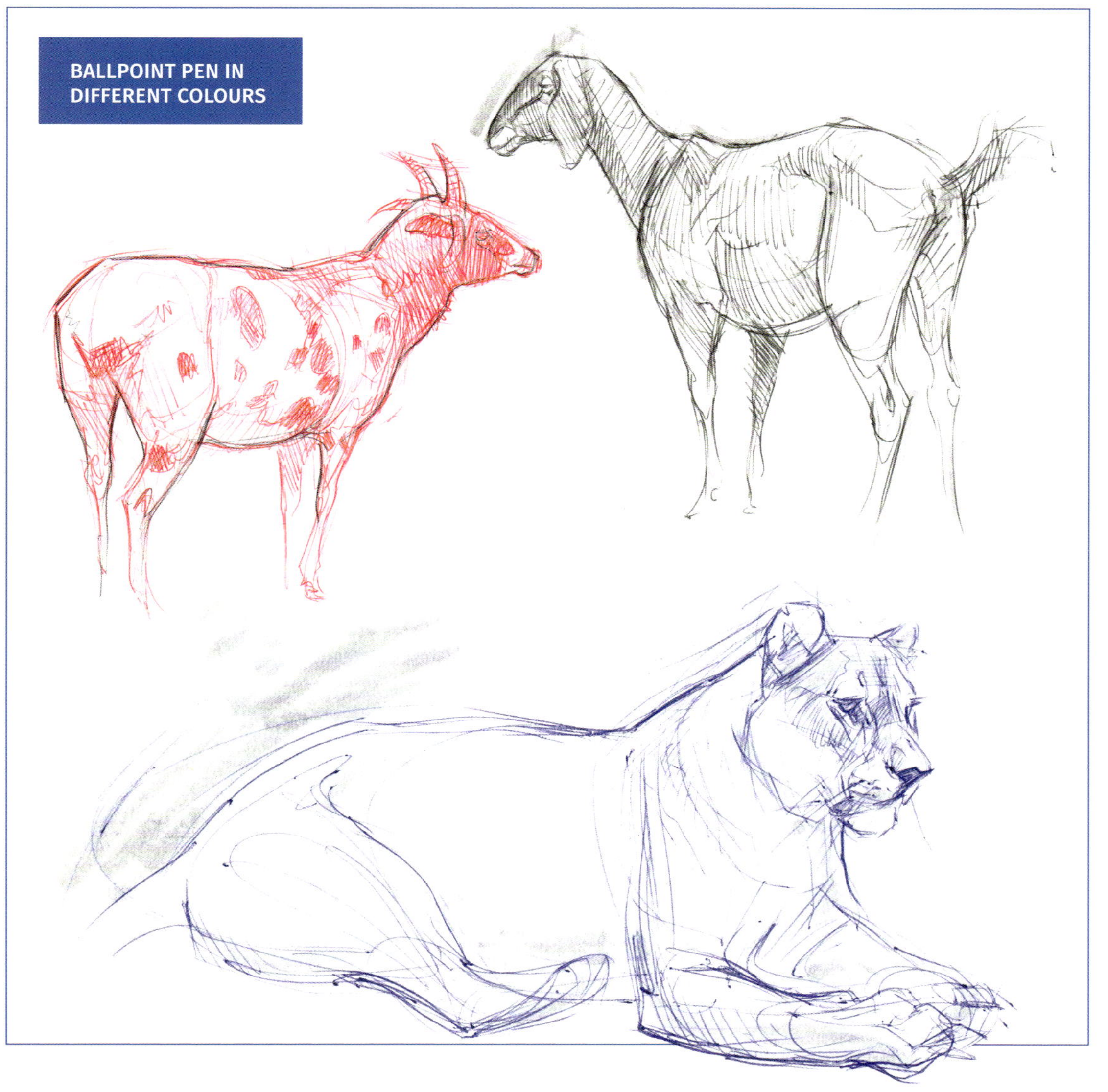

BALLPOINT PEN IN DIFFERENT COLOURS

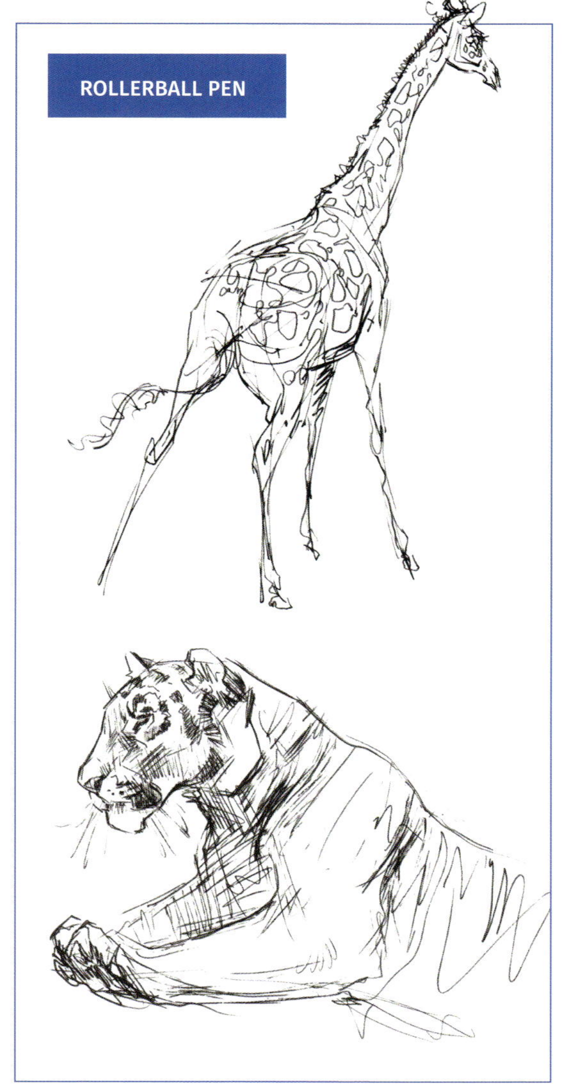

ROLLERBALL PEN

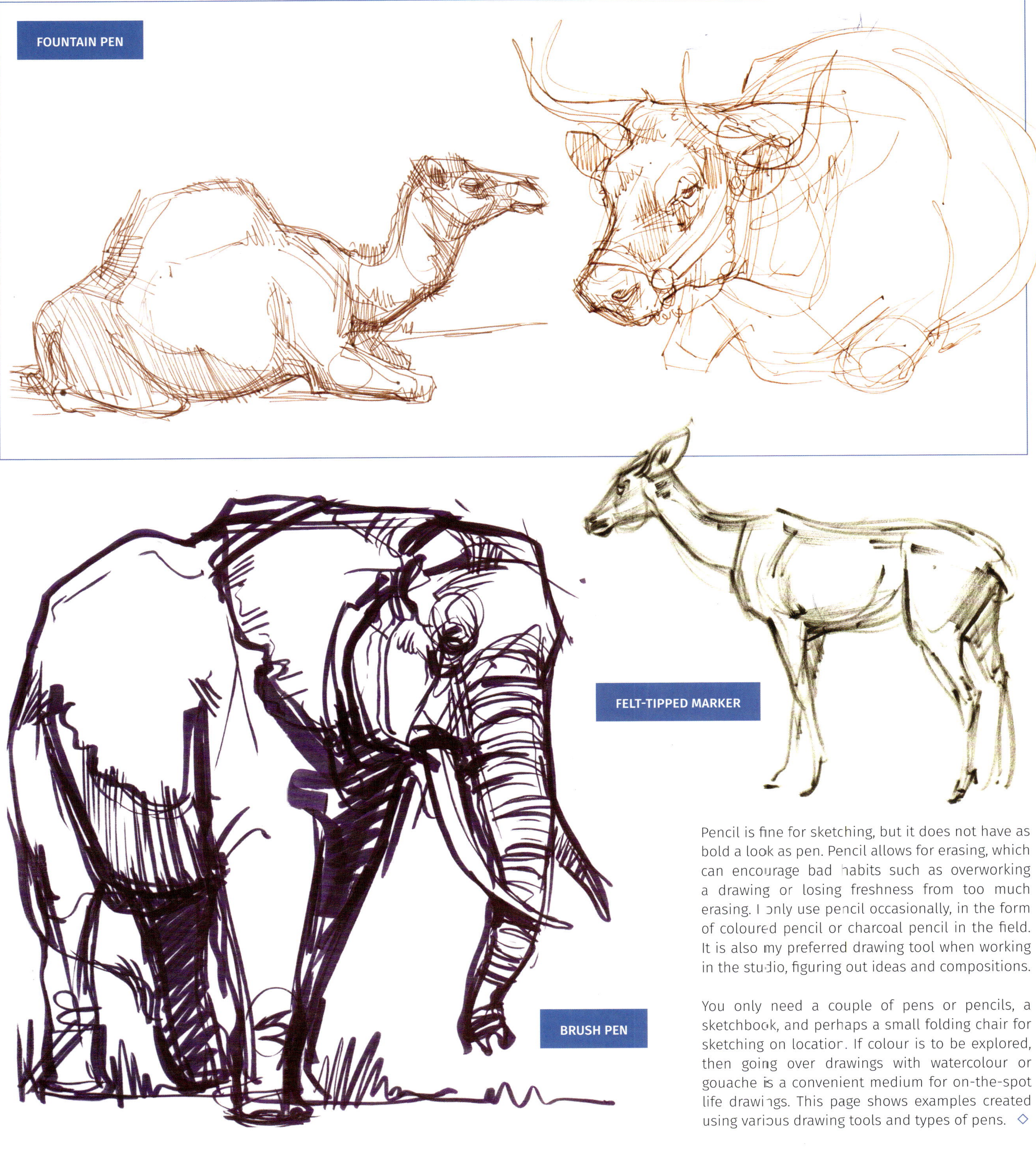

Pencil is fine for sketching, but it does not have as bold a look as pen. Pencil allows for erasing, which can encourage bad habits such as overworking a drawing or losing freshness from too much erasing. I only use pencil occasionally, in the form of coloured pencil or charcoal pencil in the field. It is also my preferred drawing tool when working in the studio, figuring out ideas and compositions.

You only need a couple of pens or pencils, a sketchbook, and perhaps a small folding chair for sketching on location. If colour is to be explored, then going over drawings with watercolour or gouache is a convenient medium for on-the-spot life drawings. This page shows examples created using various drawing tools and types of pens. ◇

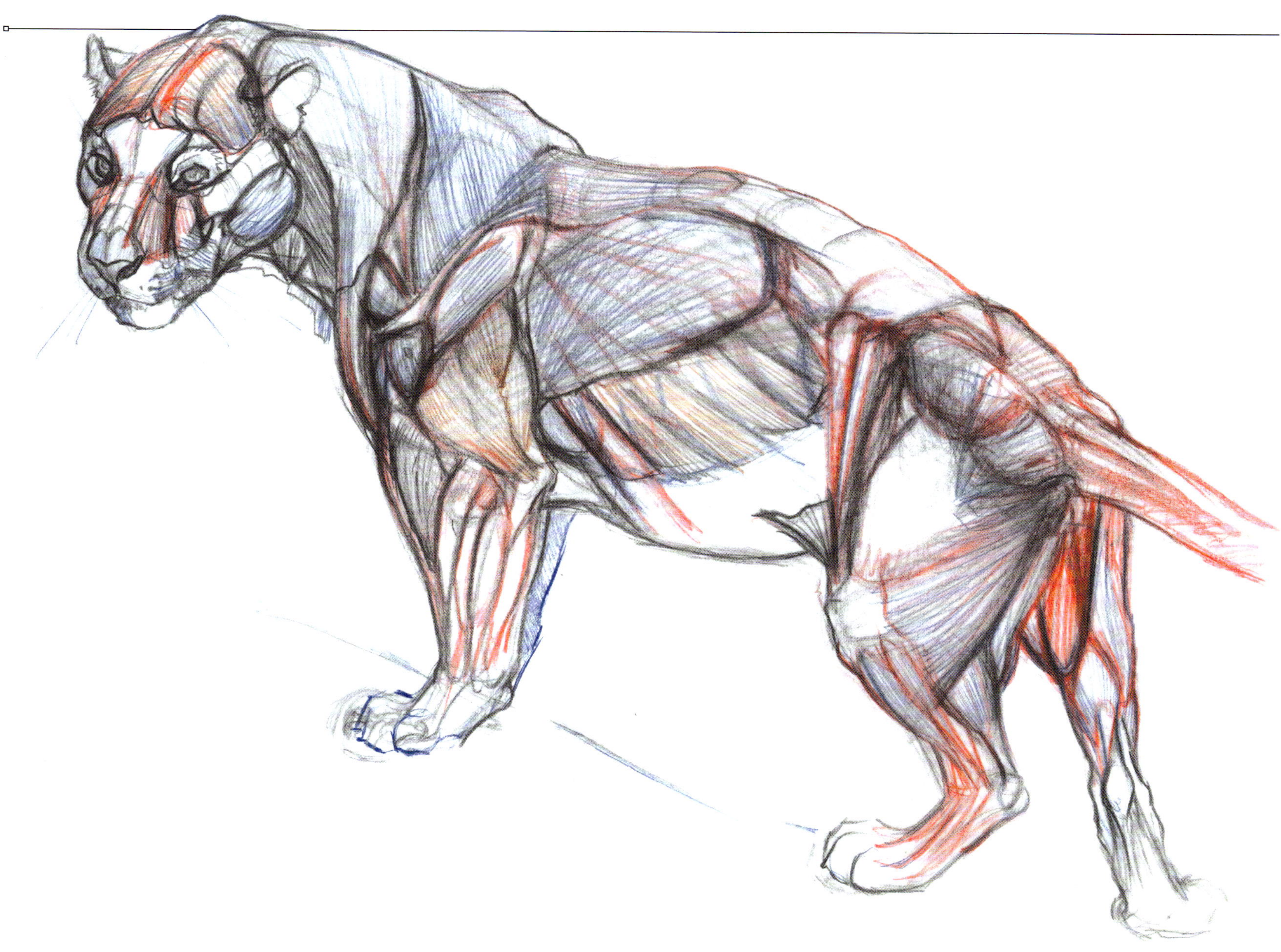

Anatomy Basics

To draw animals convincingly and avoid drawing 'stuffed animals', the artist must have a certain amount of anatomical knowledge. The amount of anatomical knowledge an artist needs will depend on what kind of art they are making, but obtaining a basic understanding of the skeleton, muscles, and action is necessary for most artists.

Artists study 'artistic anatomy' and not medical anatomy. Learning the complete details and functions of every muscle, bone, and tendon in the animal body is not necessary or desirable. However, you should know enough to be able to pick and choose what to put into the drawing, to avoid making a scientific diagram with too many details that will destroy the form. Making diagrams for the sake of learning anatomy is necessary, but their focus should be on gesture, form, and action. This 'constructive' anatomy is what the artist studies to understand the architecture and structure of the animal form. Artistic anatomy consists of the bones, which form the foundation of the animal; the muscles, which, when contracted, move the framework or skeleton; and the action, which consists of drawing the muscles according to their function and movement. The bones are the first priority as they govern the proportions. The bony landmarks, hollows, ridges, lumps, bumps, and swellings are all caused by the underlying structure of muscles and bones, and only a thorough knowledge of them can explain the outward appearance of the form.

You will be able to draw better from memory as you improve your understanding of anatomy. Drawing from imagination is extremely important when drawing from life, since animals move around, and we are forced to make up the missing information. ◇

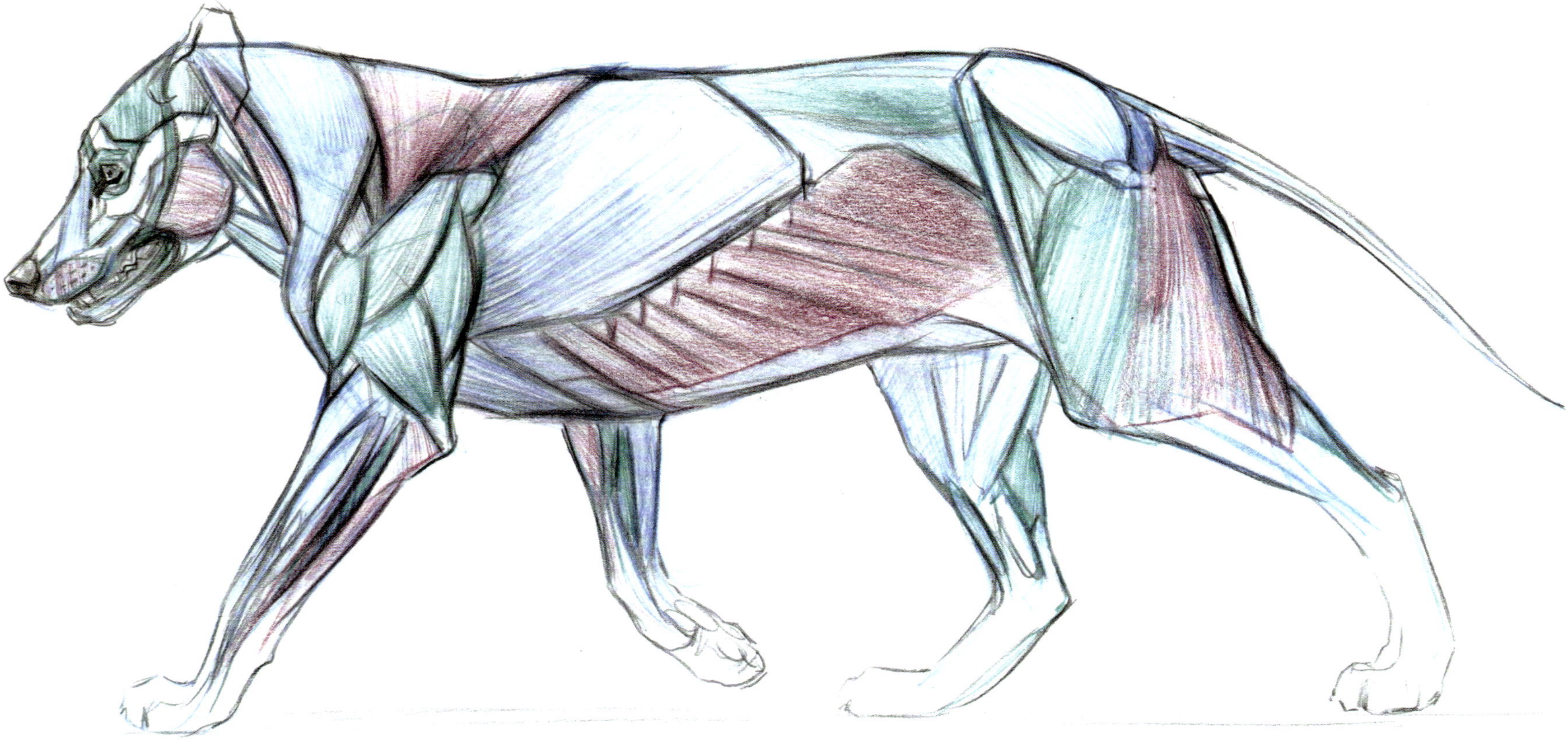

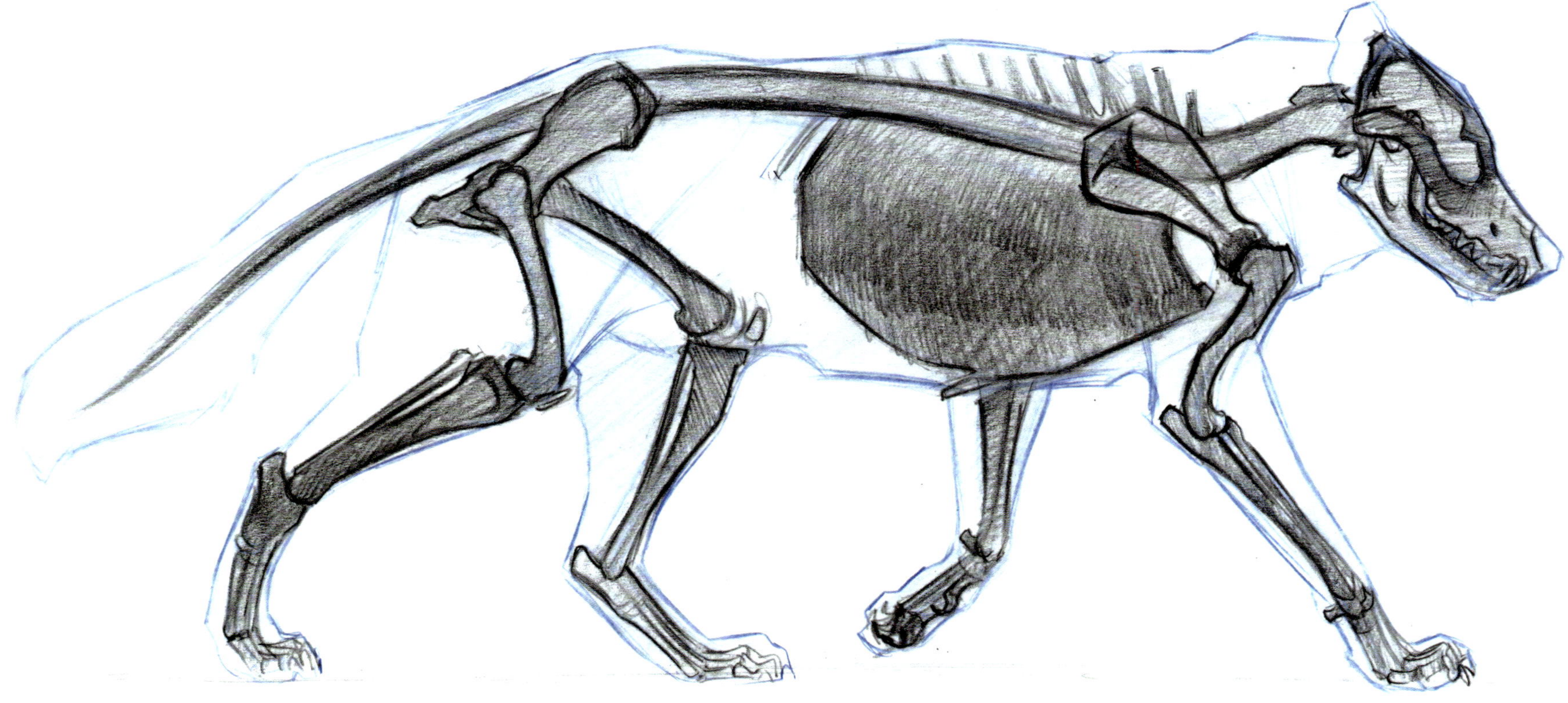

Simplified skeletal structure

Understanding the skeleton of an animal is the priority when learning anatomy. The skeleton is the framework to which muscles are attached, the armature that the muscles move, and the key to getting good proportions. Rendering detailed bones is not required with construction, but rather, drawing them in a structural and simplified way. The simplified skeleton uses volumes such as cylinders, box forms, and ovoid or spherical forms to build the framework.

An artist may choose to draw a skeleton at a museum and describe it gesturally, or with all of the copious details, such as all the ribs or the exact number of vertebrae. When drawing an animal, what will usually help the most is to simplify the bones, as they are buried inside the body and we don't see them. The spine can be treated as a long cylinder with ellipses drawn in, using cross contour to describe the various changes in vertebrae. The bones that project on top of the ribcage can be a flat shape, grouping together all of the bones into one form. The ribcage is essentially an egg-like shape with top, side, and bottom planes indicated on it. ◇

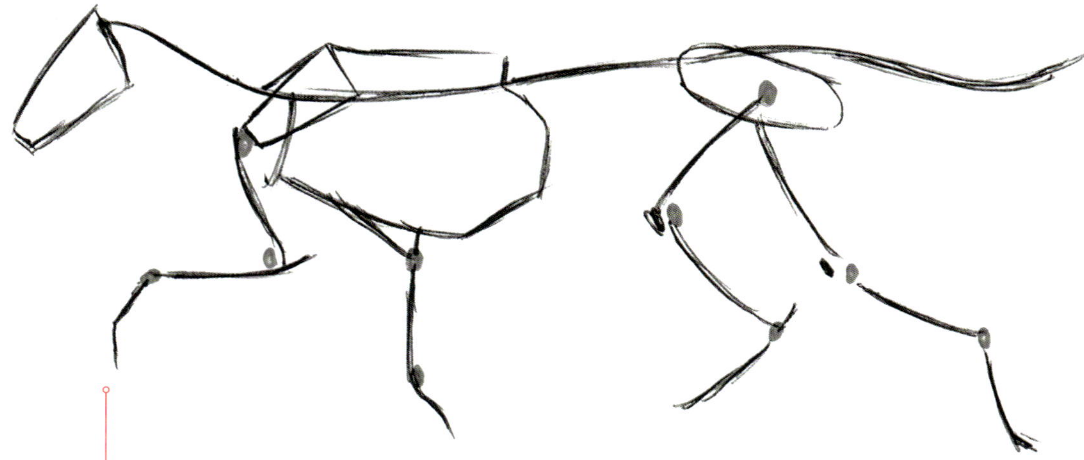

Stick-figure skeleton: The stick-figure skeleton is the simplest skeleton you can draw. With very little time invested, the arrangement and general proportions of the bones can be drawn with fundamental lines. The dots indicate pivot points at the joints where bones move. If any animal motion is desired, these pivot points must be learned, but this can be done within the stick-figure skeleton.

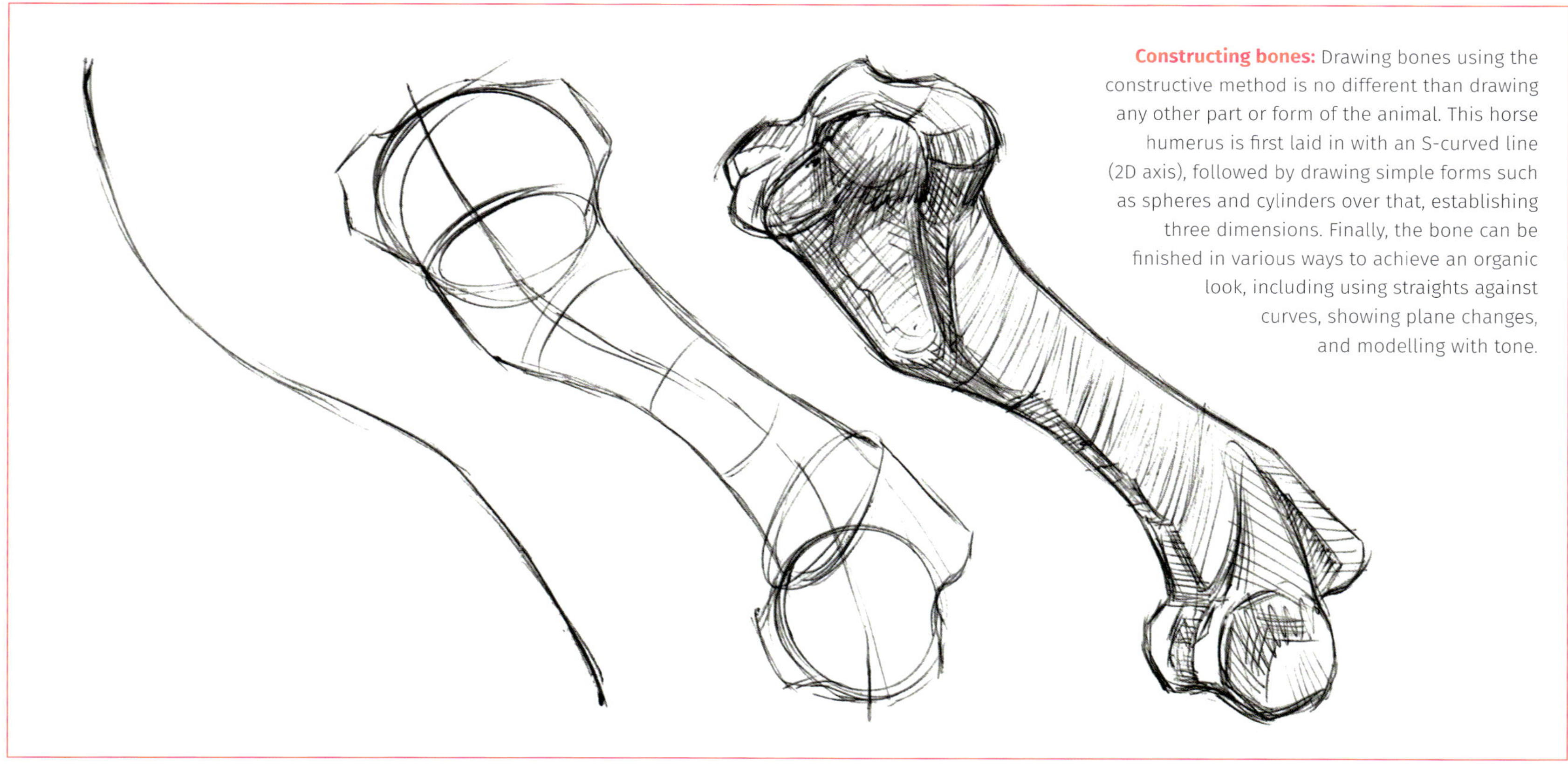

Constructing bones: Drawing bones using the constructive method is no different than drawing any other part or form of the animal. This horse humerus is first laid in with an S-curved line (2D axis), followed by drawing simple forms such as spheres and cylinders over that, establishing three dimensions. Finally, the bone can be finished in various ways to achieve an organic look, including using straights against curves, showing plane changes, and modelling with tone.

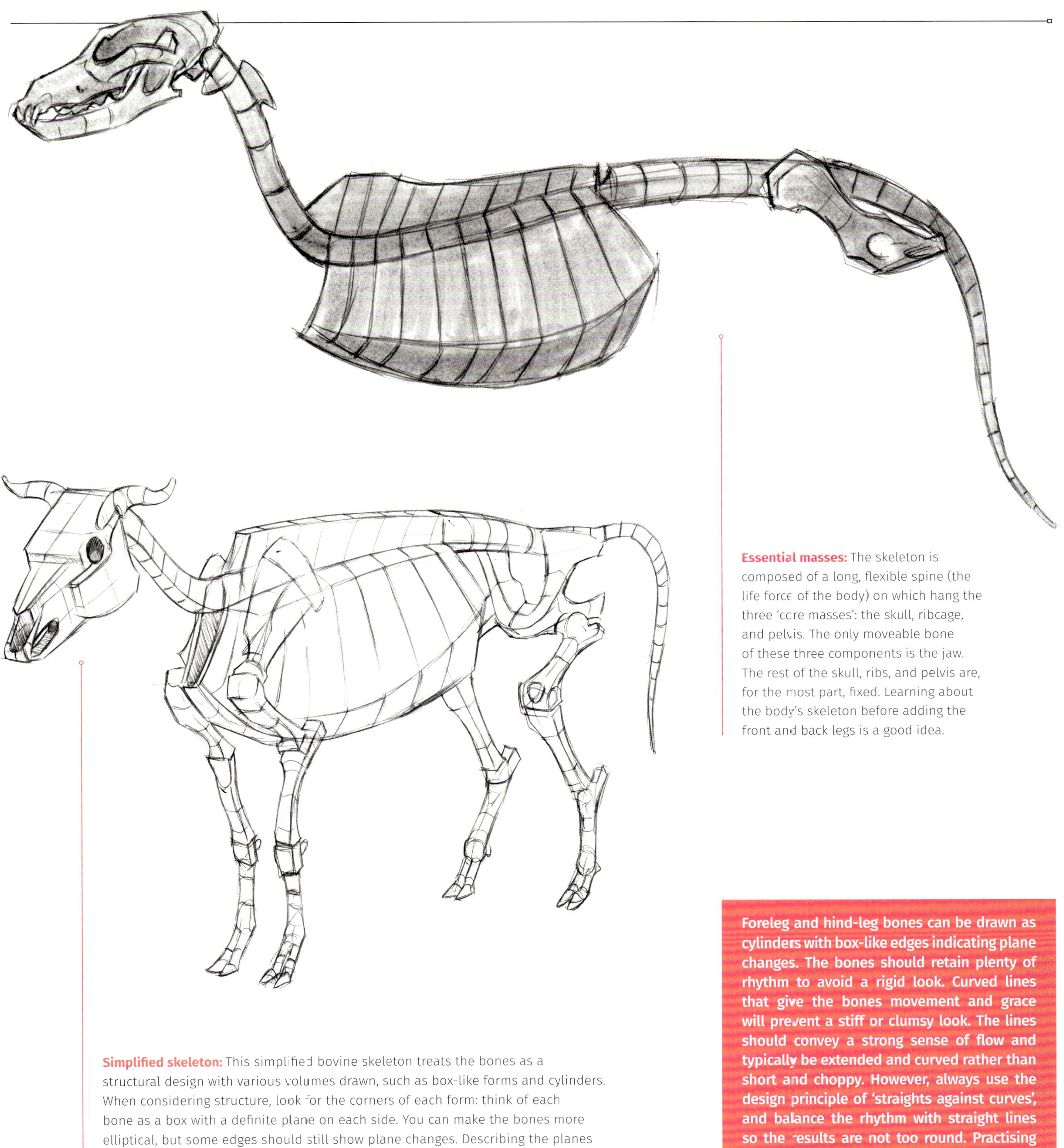

Essential masses: The skeleton is composed of a long, flexible spine (the life force of the body) on which hang the three 'core masses': the skull, ribcage, and pelvis. The only moveable bone of these three components is the jaw. The rest of the skull, ribs, and pelvis are, for the most part, fixed. Learning about the body's skeleton before adding the front and back legs is a good idea.

Simplified skeleton: This simplified bovine skeleton treats the bones as a structural design with various volumes drawn, such as box-like forms and cylinders. When considering structure, look for the corners of each form: think of each bone as a box with a definite plane on each side. You can make the bones more elliptical, but some edges should still show plane changes. Describing the planes is key to the good modelling and value shifts that will bring substance to the subject. It is helpful to put cross-contour lines on the bones while learning where the corners of the form protrude. This method will get you thinking sculpturally.

Foreleg and hind-leg bones can be drawn as cylinders with box-like edges indicating plane changes. The bones should retain plenty of rhythm to avoid a rigid look. Curved lines that give the bones movement and grace will prevent a stiff or clumsy look. The lines should convey a strong sense of flow and typically be extended and curved rather than short and choppy. However, always use the design principle of 'straights against curves', and balance the rhythm with straight lines so the results are not too round. Practising a lot of gesture drawing is a sure way to add rhythm and flow to your work.

Animals are all variants of one another. If you learn one animal well, you can learn others more easily. An excellent way to learn about many animals is to study four groups: equine, canine, bovine, and feline. Each group is representative of many similar types. For example, learning two carnivore groups (canine and feline) will teach the structure of many other carnivores. Learning two herbivores (equine and bovine) will allow understanding of many similar plant-eating animals.

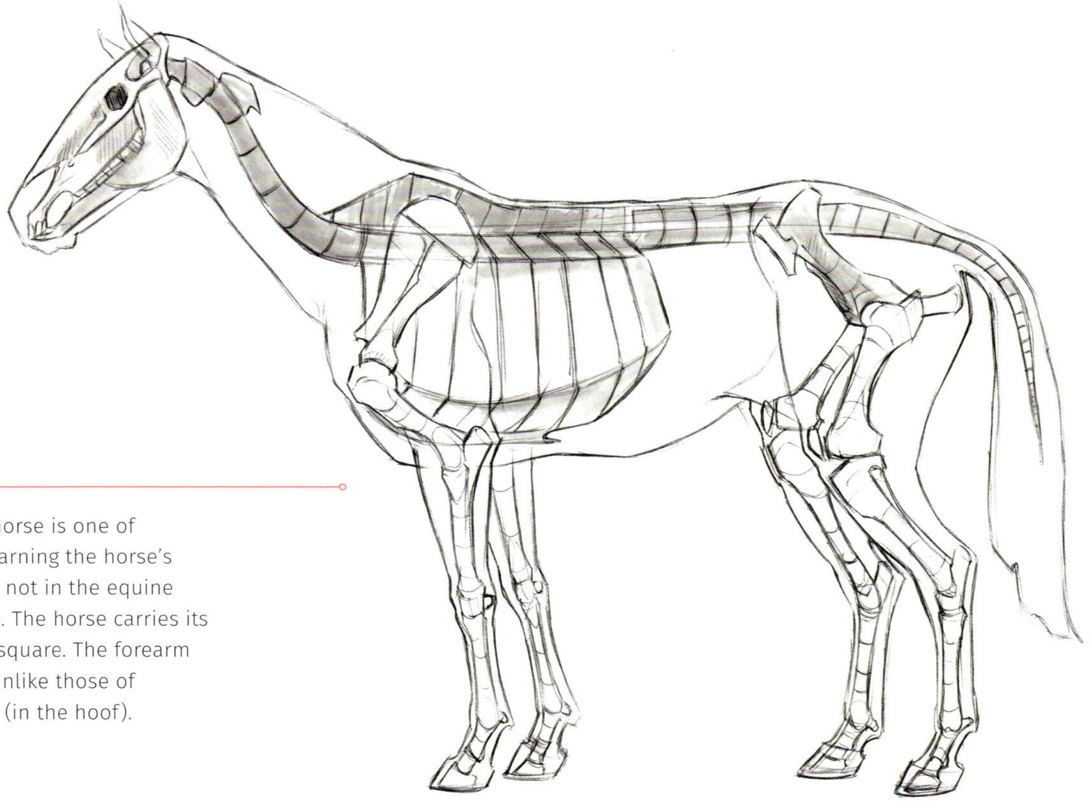

Horse skeleton: Part of the equine family, the horse is one of the most easily accessible animals to study. Learning the horse's skeletal structure will apply to other ungulates not in the equine family, such as giraffes, okapi, deer, and moose. The horse carries its head upright and has a body that fits inside a square. The forearm and lower back-leg bones are fused together, unlike those of carnivores. The horse walks on one single digit (in the hoof).

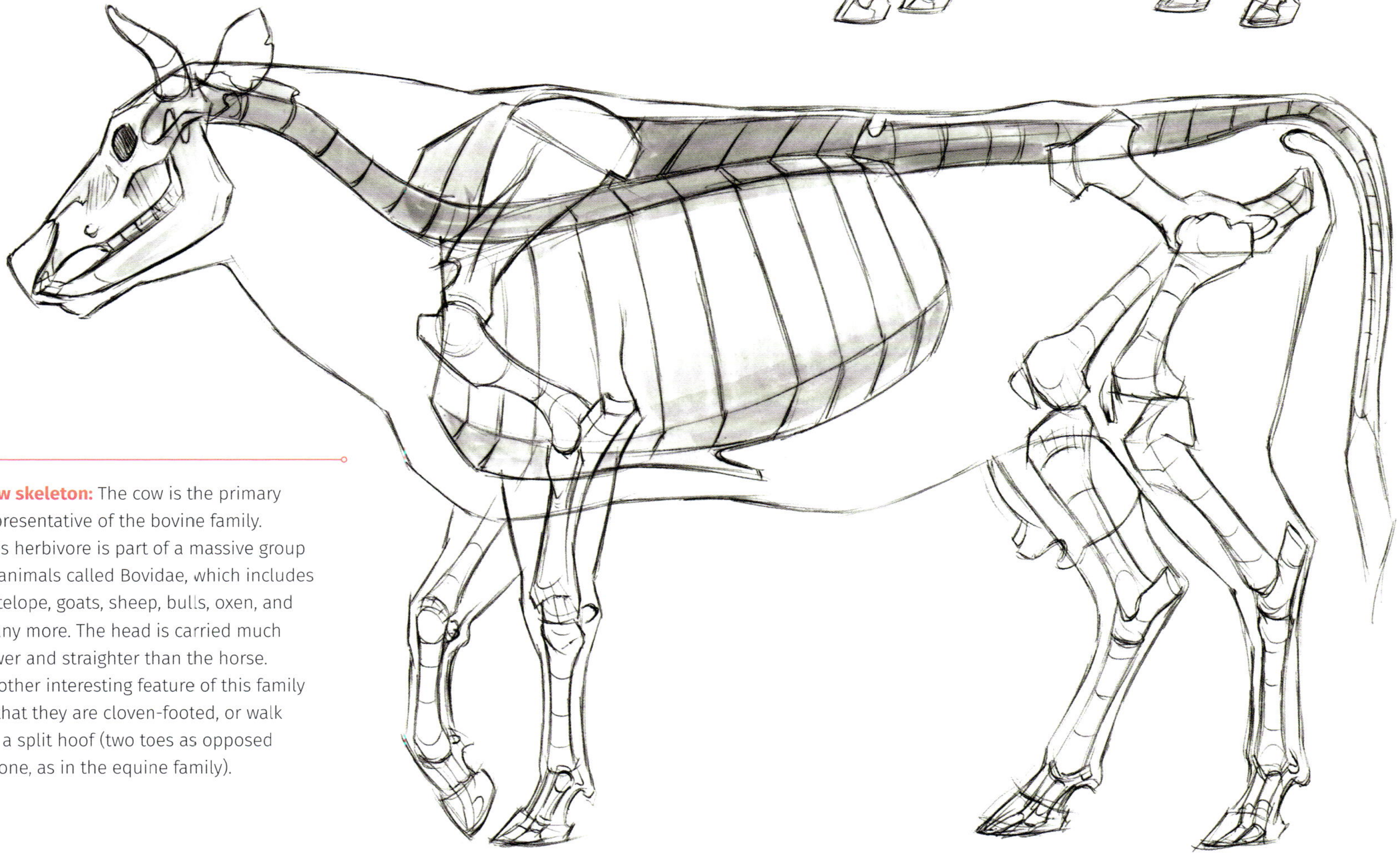

Cow skeleton: The cow is the primary representative of the bovine family. This herbivore is part of a massive group of animals called Bovidae, which includes antelope, goats, sheep, bulls, oxen, and many more. The head is carried much lower and straighter than the horse. Another interesting feature of this family is that they are cloven-footed, or walk on a split hoof (two toes as opposed to one, as in the equine family).

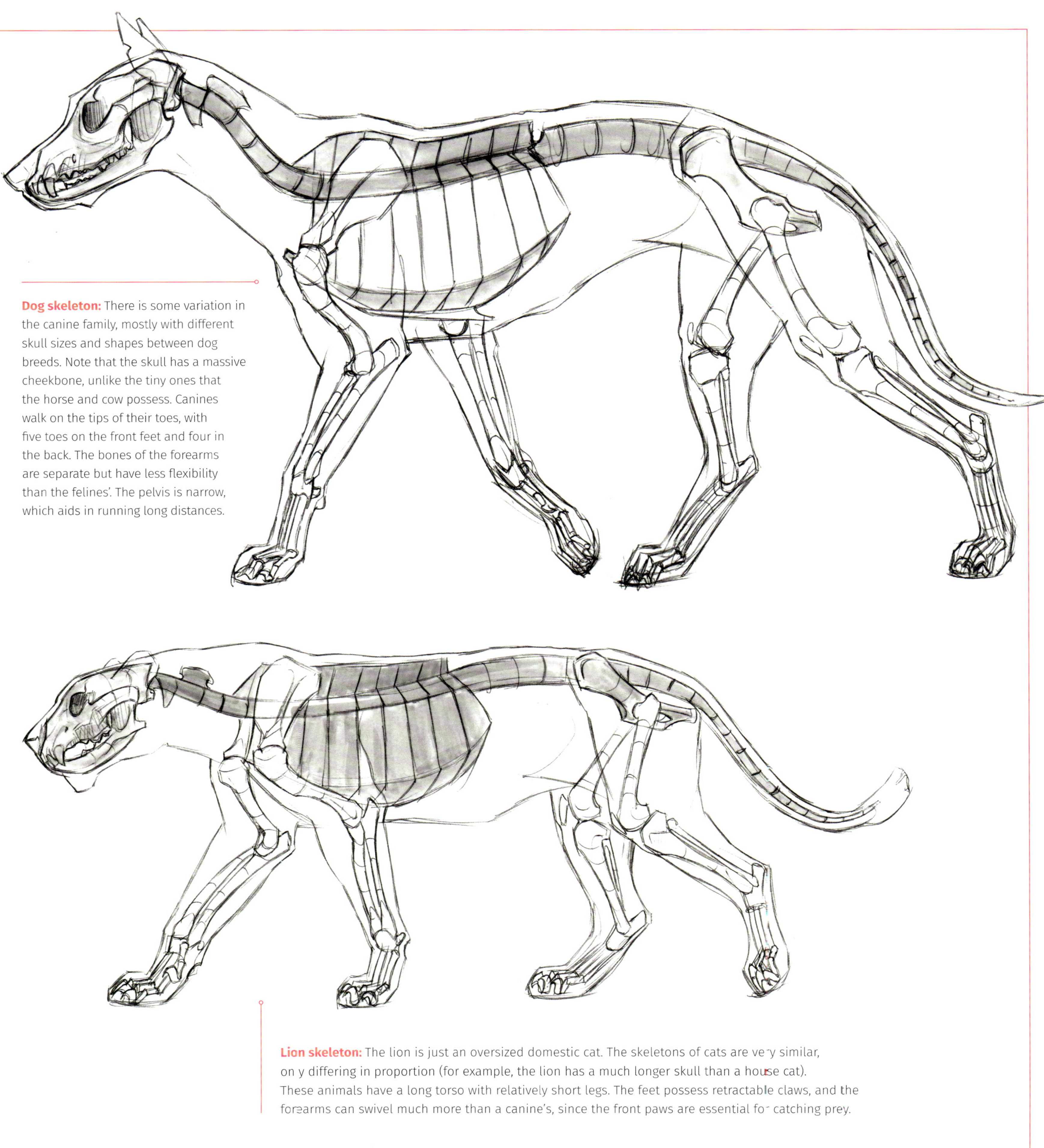

Dog skeleton: There is some variation in the canine family, mostly with different skull sizes and shapes between dog breeds. Note that the skull has a massive cheekbone, unlike the tiny ones that the horse and cow possess. Canines walk on the tips of their toes, with five toes on the front feet and four in the back. The bones of the forearms are separate but have less flexibility than the felines'. The pelvis is narrow, which aids in running long distances.

Lion skeleton: The lion is just an oversized domestic cat. The skeletons of cats are very similar, only differing in proportion (for example, the lion has a much longer skull than a house cat). These animals have a long torso with relatively short legs. The feet possess retractable claws, and the forearms can swivel much more than a canine's, since the front paws are essential for catching prey.

Simplified musculature

While the skeleton is a priority when studying animal anatomy, the muscles are essential, too. They are the forms that go over the bones and are the means to their propulsion. The muscles that influence the surface appearance of the body are called superficial muscles, which are what the artist studies the most. Deep-layer muscles are usually not seen, although they can influence the surface form.

There are different ways to study the musculature, such as drawing over the skeleton or the forms. The drawings in this section are simplified, with no details; each muscle has been boiled down to a form that can be easily located and memorized. Still, these are diagrams, not artistic drawings, of the animal's appearance without all of its skin, fur, and pattern.

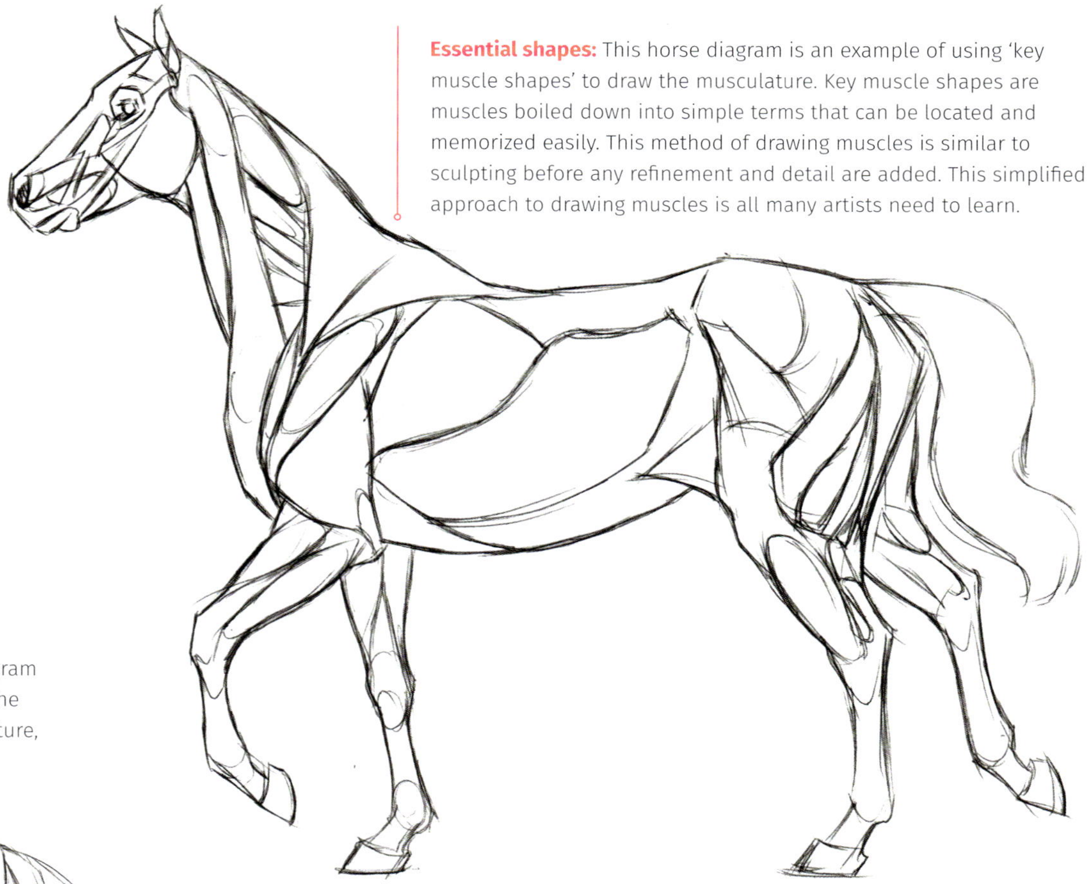

Essential shapes: This horse diagram is an example of using 'key muscle shapes' to draw the musculature. Key muscle shapes are muscles boiled down into simple terms that can be located and memorized easily. This method of drawing muscles is similar to sculpting before any refinement and detail are added. This simplified approach to drawing muscles is all many artists need to learn.

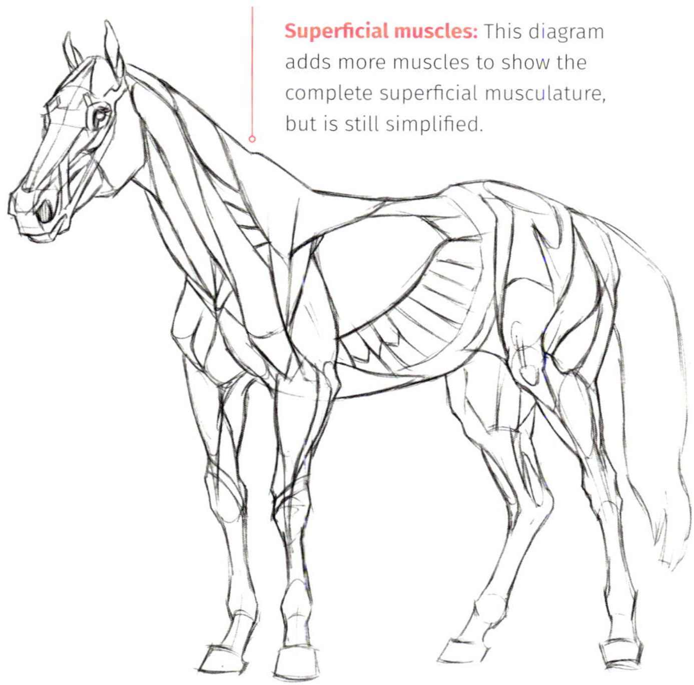

Superficial muscles: This diagram adds more muscles to show the complete superficial musculature, but is still simplified.

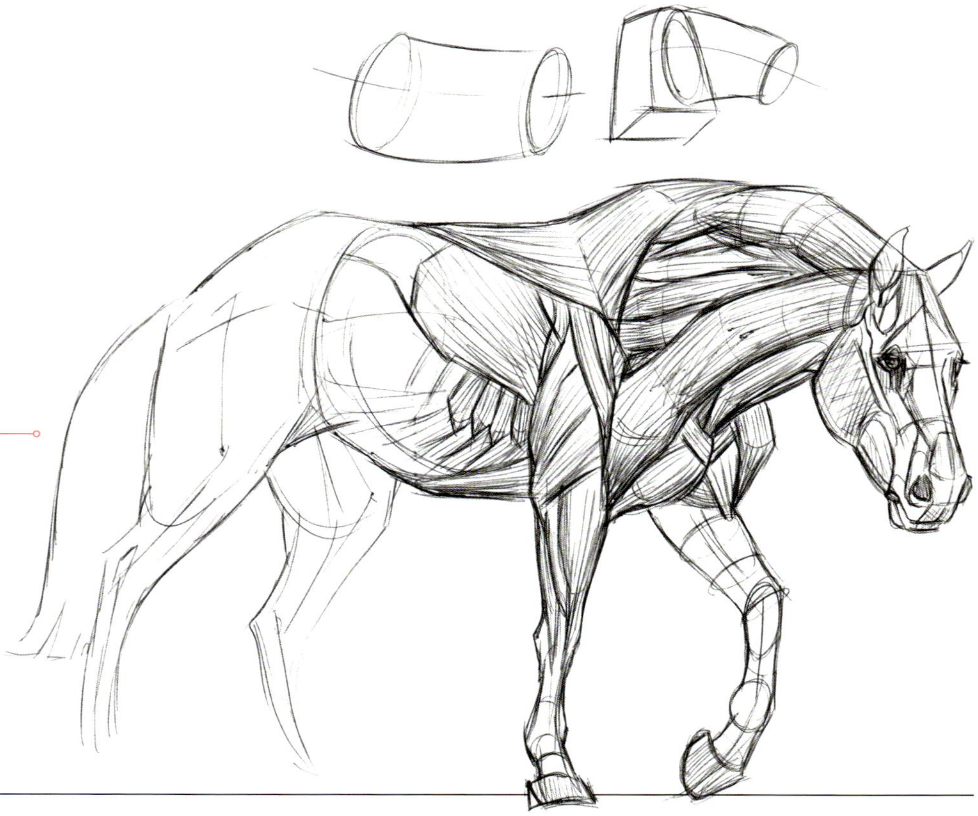

Tone & texture: Another approach to drawing muscles is to model the form with muscle striations and tone. When drawing muscles, one can draw over the skeleton to study the origin and insertion points, which is quite helpful. Alternatively, the muscles can be drawn directly over the underlying forms, as in this drawing. Parts of the draft horse have been left undone to show the initial gestural lay-in and volumes over which the muscles are drawn.

Simplified musculature: The four main animal groups discussed in the previous section are here again, drawn with simplified musculature. Note the similarities in musculature between the two herbivores (equine and bovine) and the two carnivores (canine and feline). Studying these diagrams will show how similar the muscles are in most animals. Shape design is essential when drawing muscles, for simplicity and design considerations.

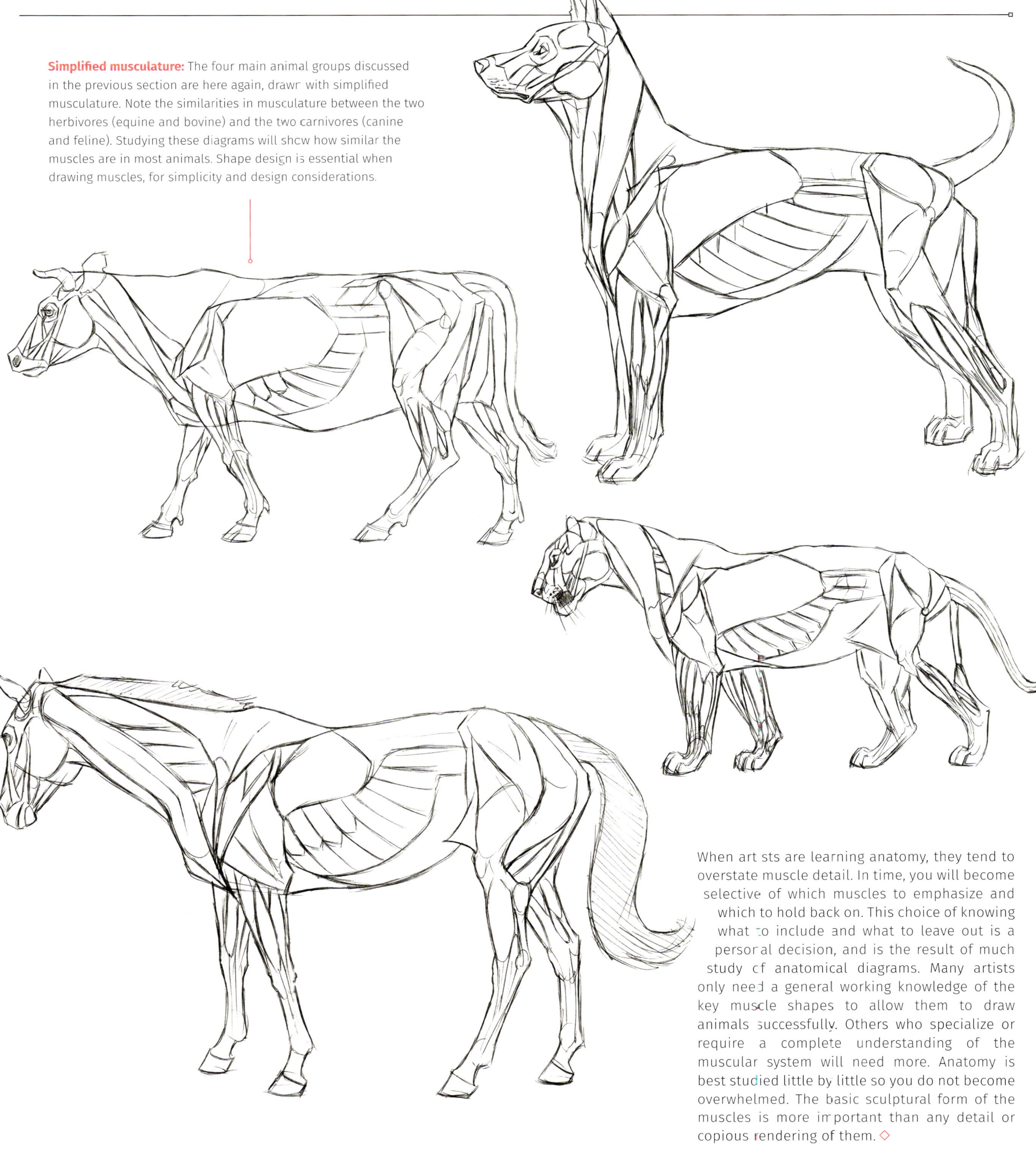

When artists are learning anatomy, they tend to overstate muscle detail. In time, you will become selective of which muscles to emphasize and which to hold back on. This choice of knowing what to include and what to leave out is a personal decision, and is the result of much study of anatomical diagrams. Many artists only need a general working knowledge of the key muscle shapes to allow them to draw animals successfully. Others who specialize or require a complete understanding of the muscular system will need more. Anatomy is best studied little by little so you do not become overwhelmed. The basic sculptural form of the muscles is more important than any detail or copious rendering of them. ◇

Proportions & surface anatomy

The best way to learn proportions is to study the skeleton. Knowing the approximate length of individual bones is a great way to draw profile views, foreshortened views, and any angle, for that matter. However, another way to learn proportions is to put the animal in a box or rectangle and use the head length to measure the animal's height and width. This box technique is suitable for profiles and when exact measurements are needed, but as soon as the animal moves or is foreshortened, that all goes out the window. Guesswork is needed then, and knowing the bone lengths will make the process of getting proportions much easier.

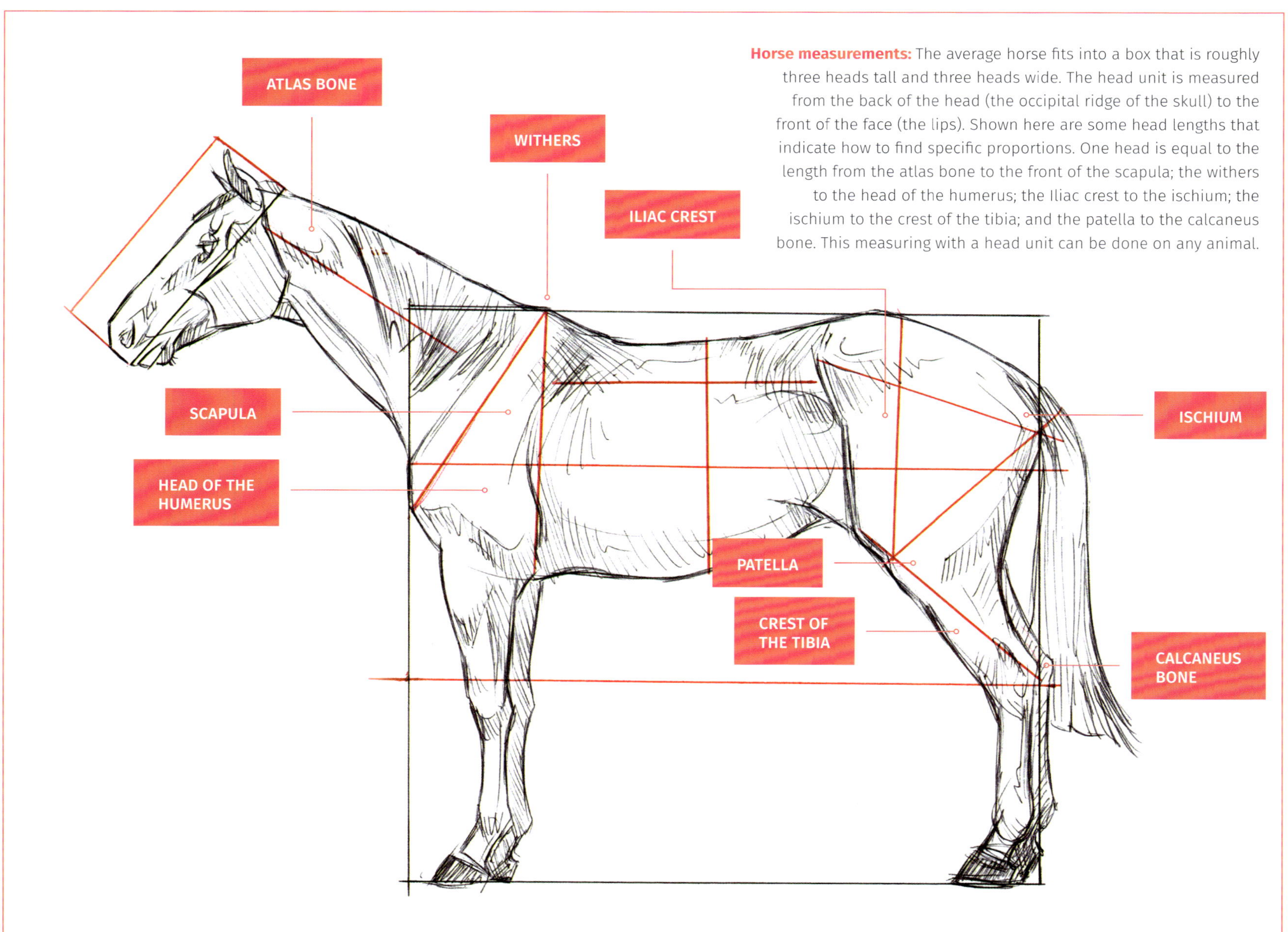

Horse measurements: The average horse fits into a box that is roughly three heads tall and three heads wide. The head unit is measured from the back of the head (the occipital ridge of the skull) to the front of the face (the lips). Shown here are some head lengths that indicate how to find specific proportions. One head is equal to the length from the atlas bone to the front of the scapula; the withers to the head of the humerus; the Iliac crest to the ischium; the ischium to the crest of the tibia; and the patella to the calcaneus bone. This measuring with a head unit can be done on any animal.

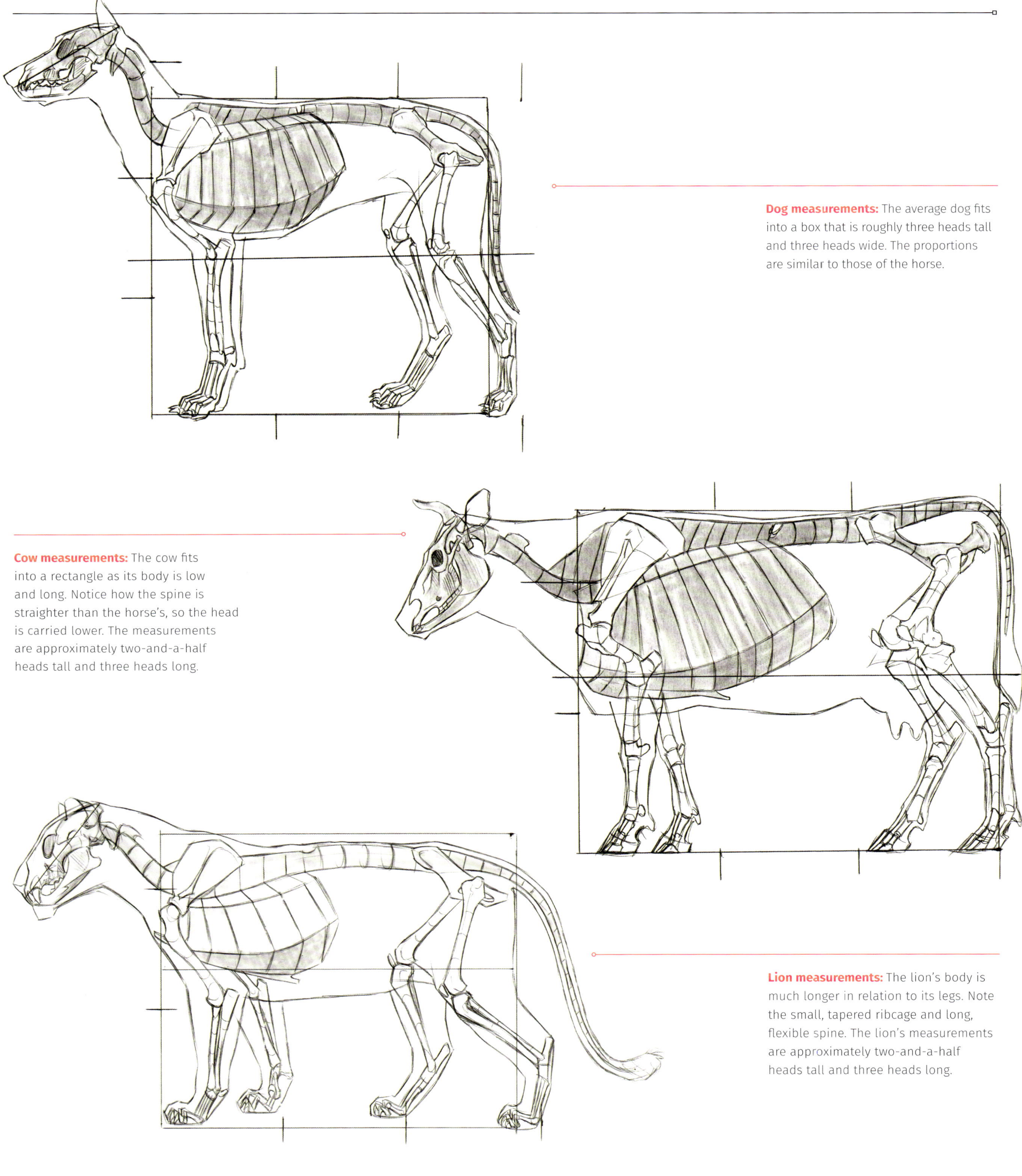

Dog measurements: The average dog fits into a box that is roughly three heads tall and three heads wide. The proportions are similar to those of the horse.

Cow measurements: The cow fits into a rectangle as its body is low and long. Notice how the spine is straighter than the horse's, so the head is carried lower. The measurements are approximately two-and-a-half heads tall and three heads long.

Lion measurements: The lion's body is much longer in relation to its legs. Note the small, tapered ribcage and long, flexible spine. The lion's measurements are approximately two-and-a-half heads tall and three heads long.

Surface anatomy models the muscles and bones that determine the appearance of the surface form. The bones are the straight forms and the muscles are the curves. Bony landmarks are where bones come to the surface, lying just under the skin and determining the surface form. It is essential to recognize and emphasize these underlying anatomical indications while holding back and not showing too much, otherwise your artistic drawing will resemble a diagram. ◇

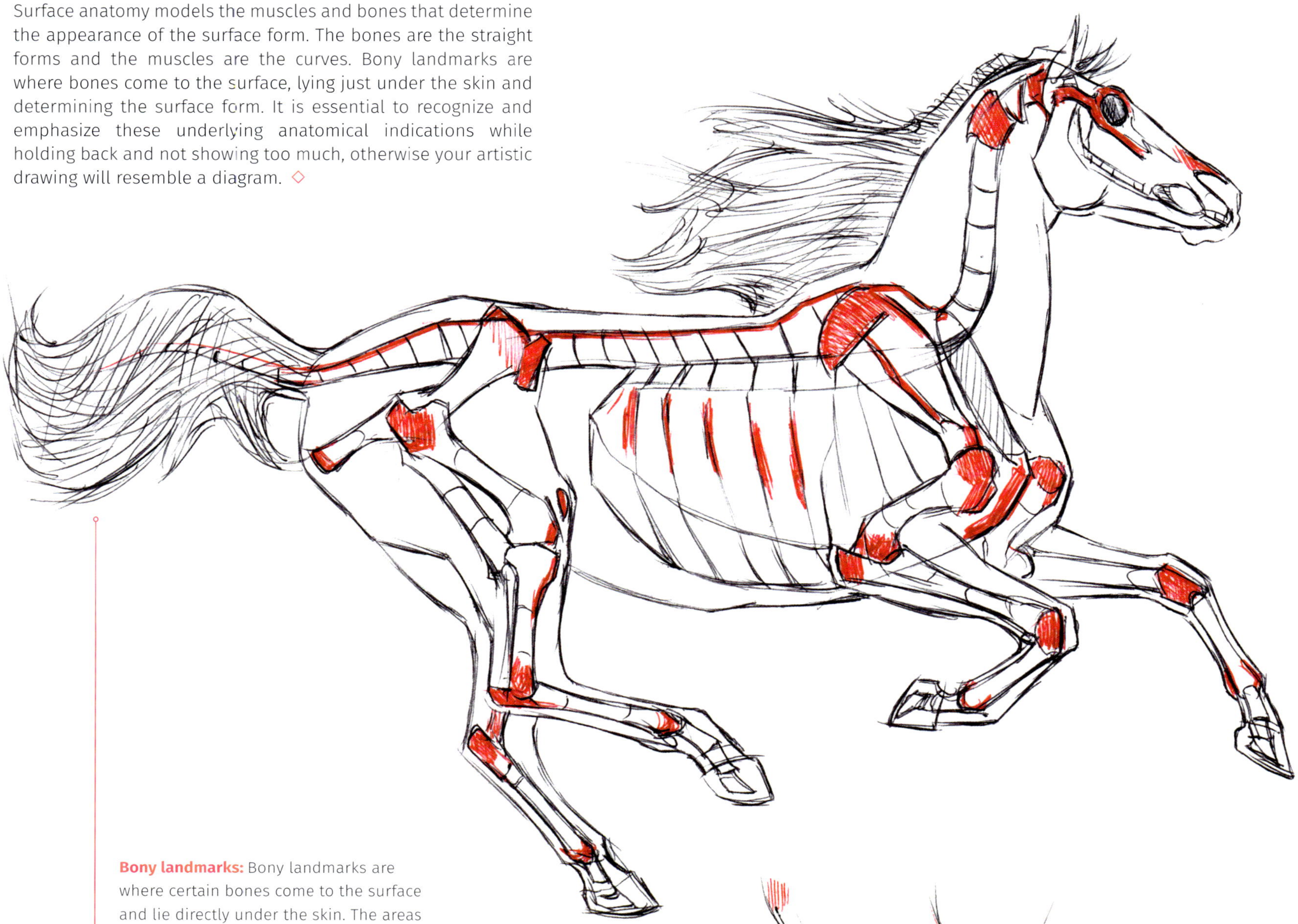

Bony landmarks: Bony landmarks are where certain bones come to the surface and lie directly under the skin. The areas marked in red on this horse's skeleton are the prominent bony landmarks for most mammals and humans.

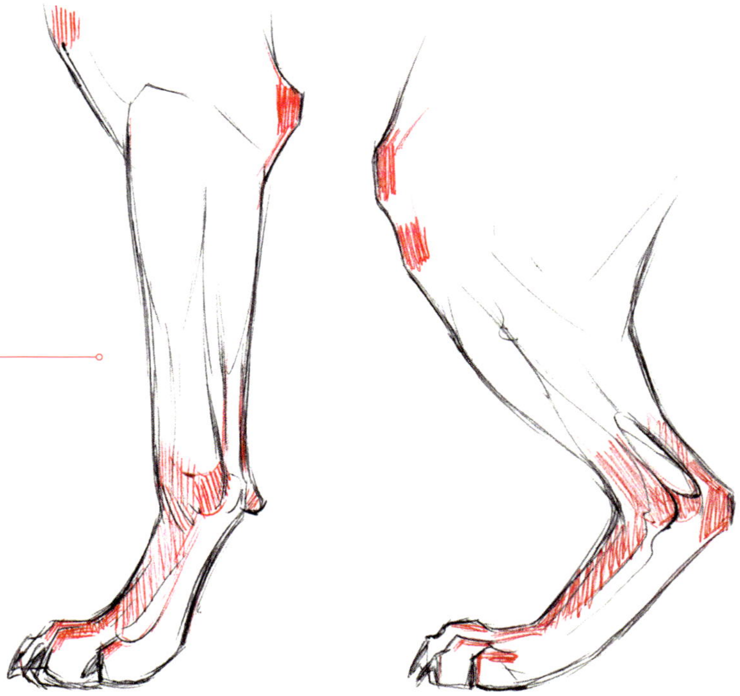

Leg landmarks: Bony landmarks of the fore and hind limbs are the elbows, knees, wrists, tops of the front and hind paws, crests of the tibias, Achilles tendons, and heel bones.

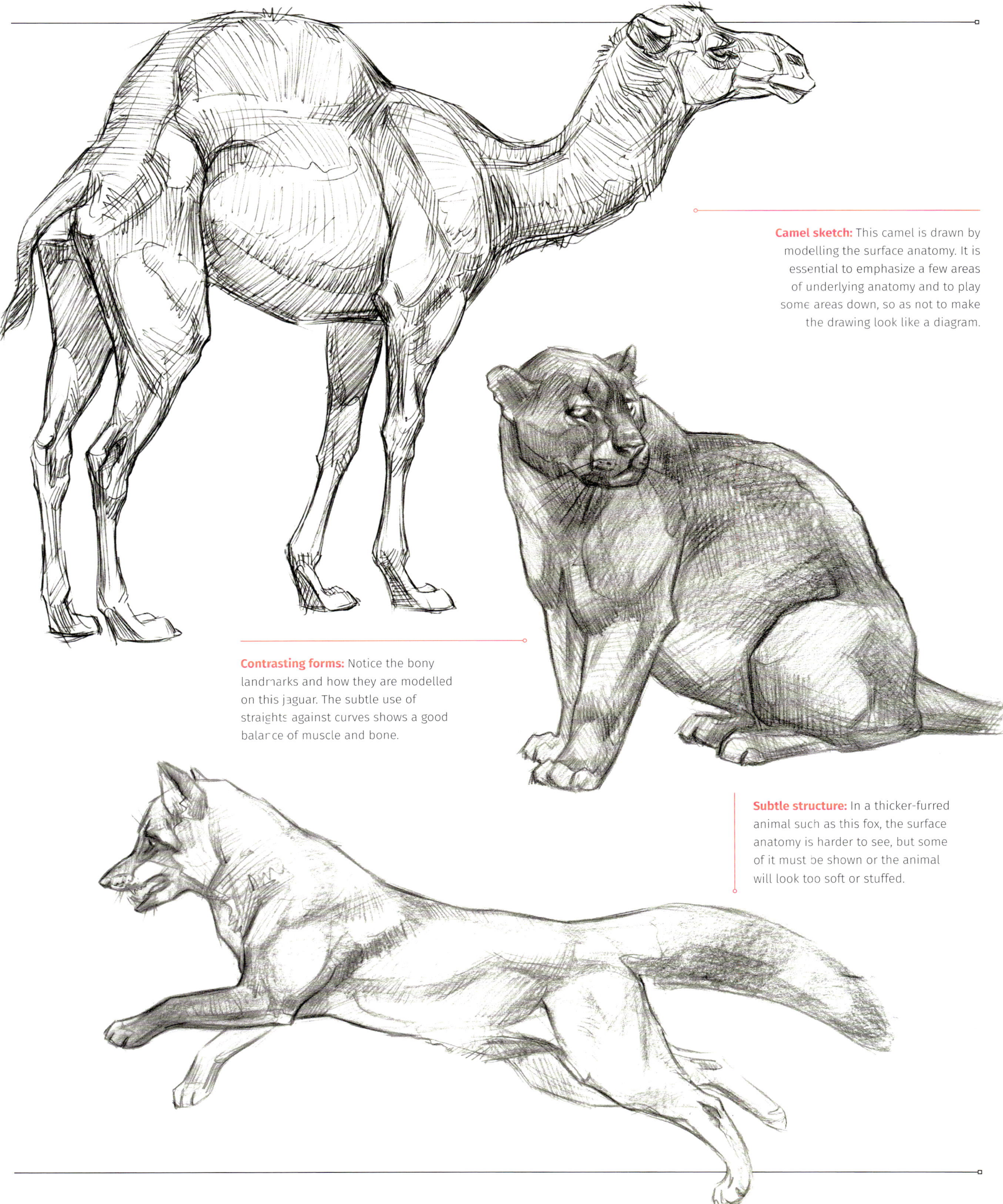

Camel sketch: This camel is drawn by modelling the surface anatomy. It is essential to emphasize a few areas of underlying anatomy and to play some areas down, so as not to make the drawing look like a diagram.

Contrasting forms: Notice the bony landmarks and how they are modelled on this jaguar. The subtle use of straights against curves shows a good balance of muscle and bone.

Subtle structure: In a thicker-furred animal such as this fox, the surface anatomy is harder to see, but some of it must be shown or the animal will look too soft or stuffed.

The simplified head

Knowing the skull is the best way to draw a solid head, as its bones more directly influence the head's outward shape than the bones of the rest of the body. The head resembles the skull since its muscles are thin, and most bones come to the surface (bony landmarks). The cheekbone (zygomatic arch), top of the head, and jaw are particularly prominent on animals' heads. The only moveable bone in the skull is the lower jaw (mandible).

Construction of the head can begin before knowledge of the skull is understood, by using forms such as spheres and boxes. The features should be studied individually. Carnivores have their eyes facing forward to aid in predation; herbivores have eyes on the sides to have a wider field of vision to detect predators. Eyes should be drawn as globular forms with lids wrapping around them, instead of flat shapes. The simpler the eyes are drawn, the better, as they quickly get overly detailed.

Noses are varied in animals, as are mouths. Canines have a round, cylindrical nose; cats have a triangular-shaped nose with a prominent undercut. The nose and mouth on horses are quite flexible, whereas in bovines, the nose and mouth are rigid and shaped differently. Ears, too, are quite different. Dogs have many types of ears, some of which are erect, while others hang down and are pendulous. Cats have erect ears that can fold back, the same as horses do. Cows and most bovines have ears that are cylindrical at the base and open up like flowers at the top. Remember to keep the features parallel to one another so they are in proper perspective.

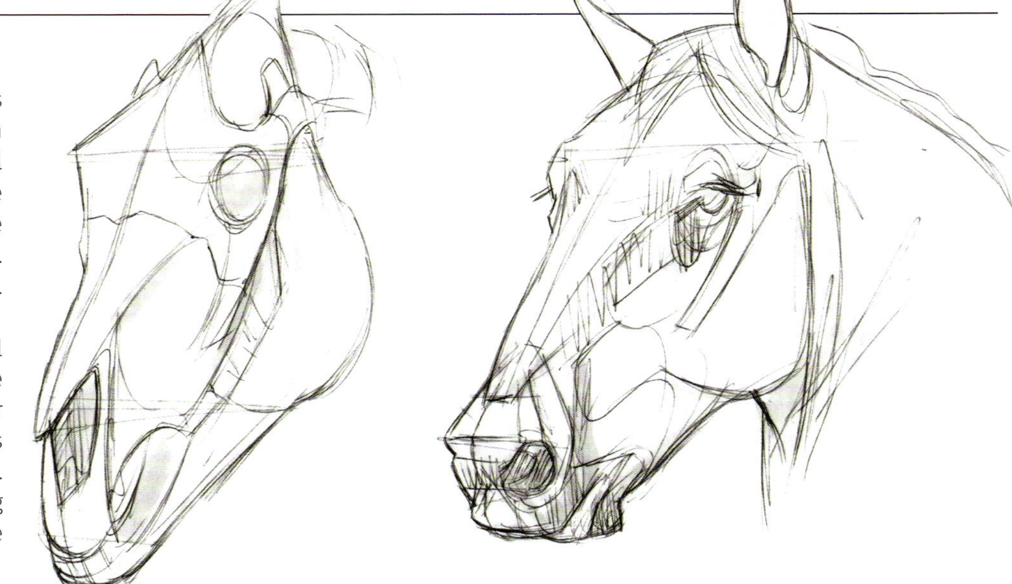

Horse head: Note how the skull dictates the shape of the horse's head and face. Knowing the skull is the secret to a good head drawing.

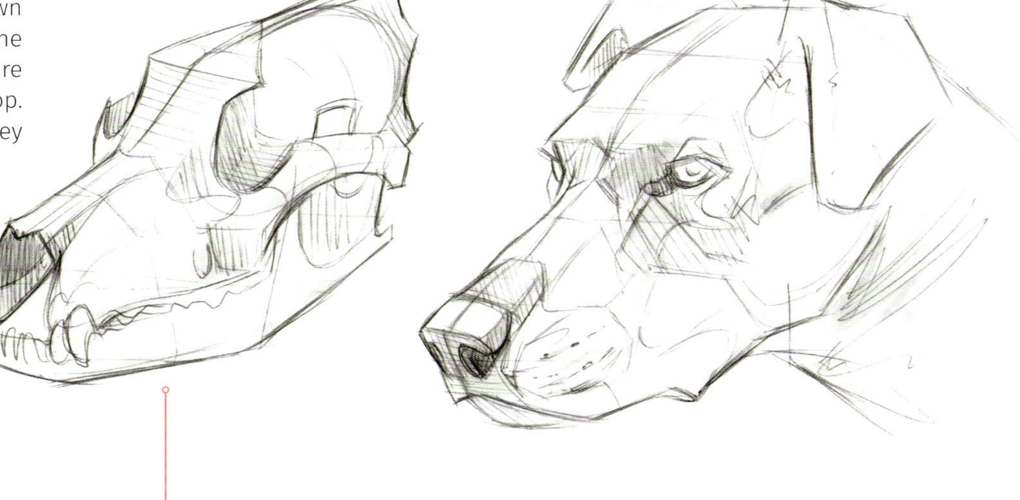

Dog head: In this comparison between the canine skull and fleshed-out head, notice how the bony landmarks such as the cheekbones, jaw, and nasal bone are prominent in the dog.

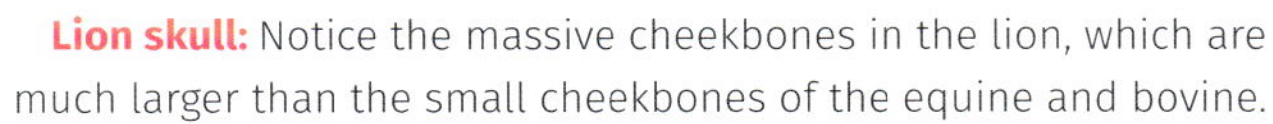

Lion skull: Notice the massive cheekbones in the lion, which are much larger than the small cheekbones of the equine and bovine.

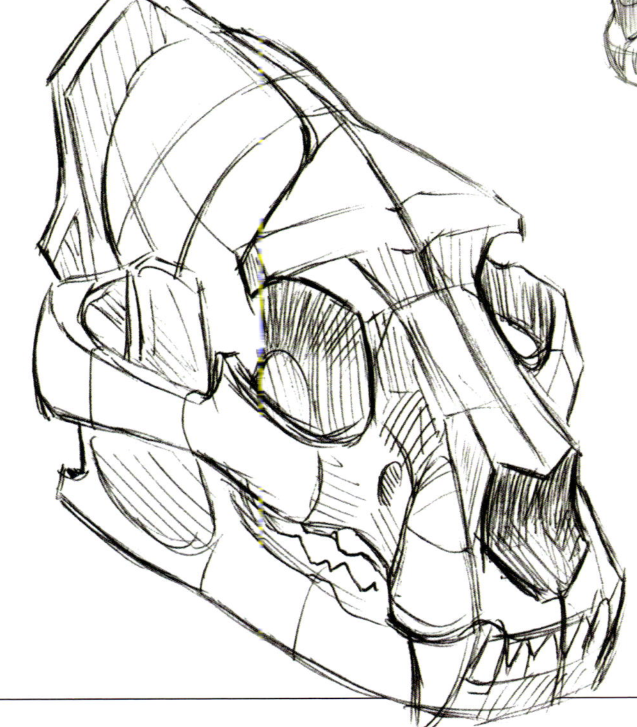

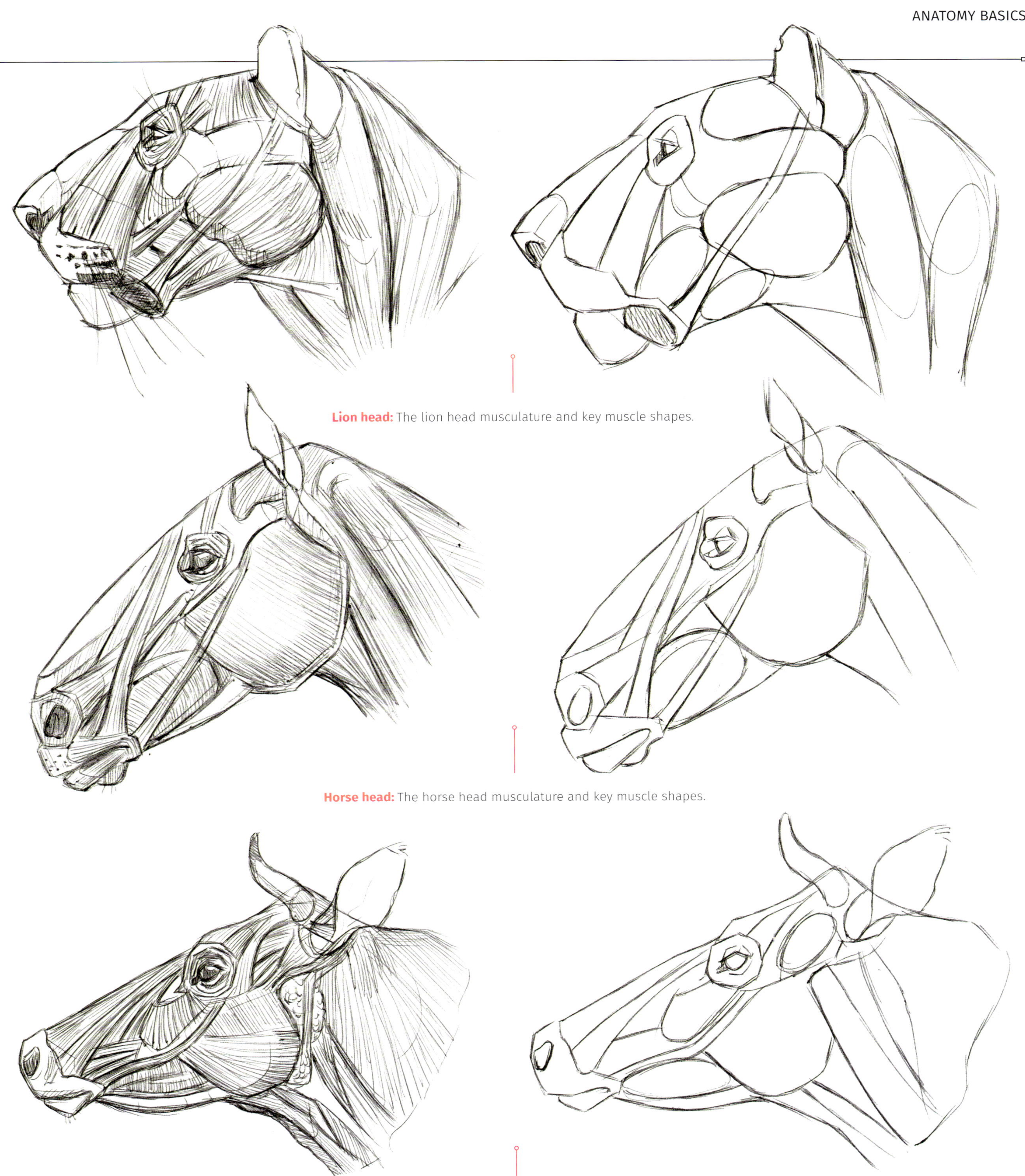

Lion head: The lion head musculature and key muscle shapes.

Horse head: The horse head musculature and key muscle shapes.

Cow head: The cow head musculature and key muscle shapes.

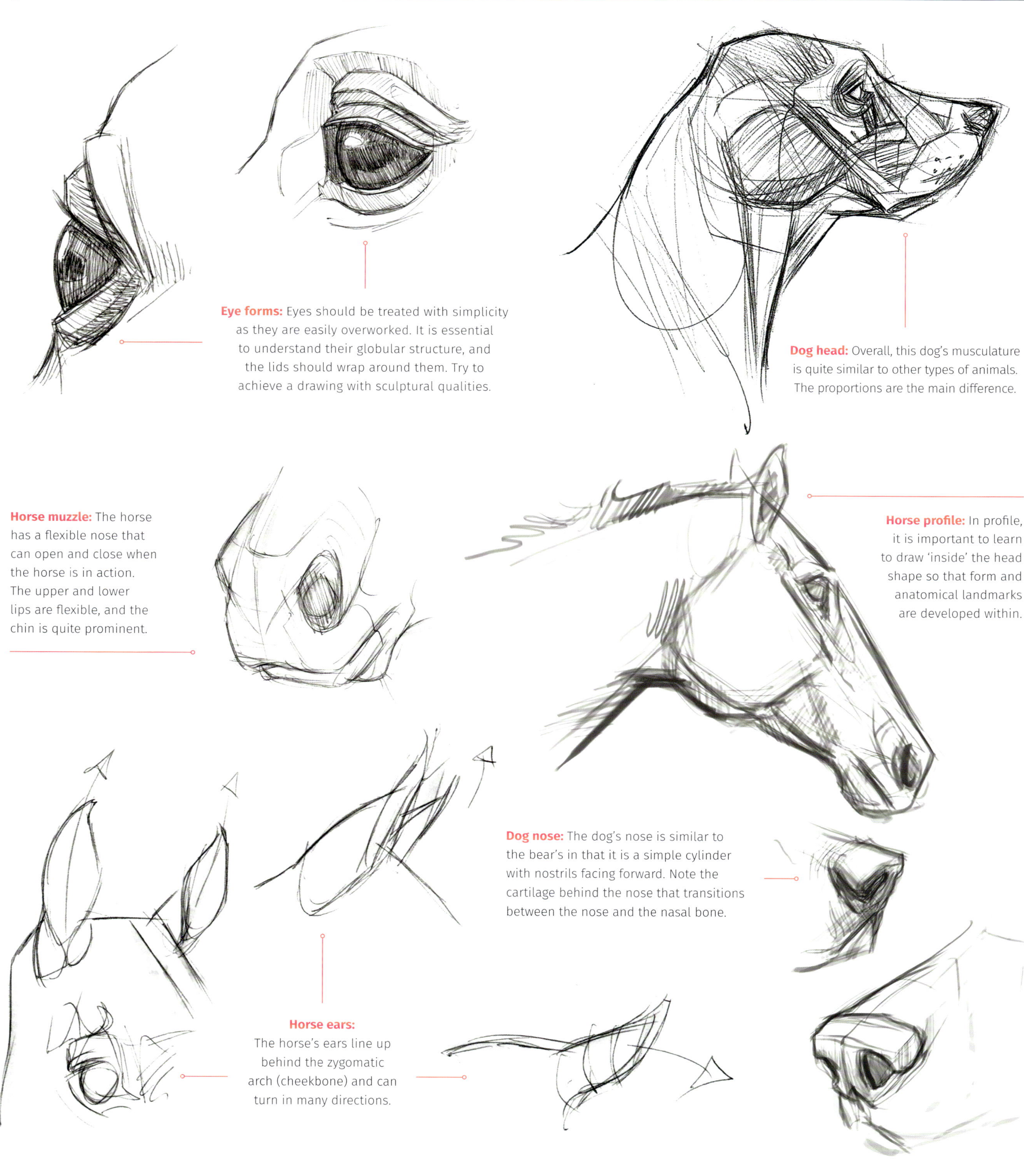

Eye forms: Eyes should be treated with simplicity as they are easily overworked. It is essential to understand their globular structure, and the lids should wrap around them. Try to achieve a drawing with sculptural qualities.

Dog head: Overall, this dog's musculature is quite similar to other types of animals. The proportions are the main difference.

Horse muzzle: The horse has a flexible nose that can open and close when the horse is in action. The upper and lower lips are flexible, and the chin is quite prominent.

Horse profile: In profile, it is important to learn to draw 'inside' the head shape so that form and anatomical landmarks are developed within.

Dog nose: The dog's nose is similar to the bear's in that it is a simple cylinder with nostrils facing forward. Note the cartilage behind the nose that transitions between the nose and the nasal bone.

Horse ears: The horse's ears line up behind the zygomatic arch (cheekbone) and can turn in many directions.

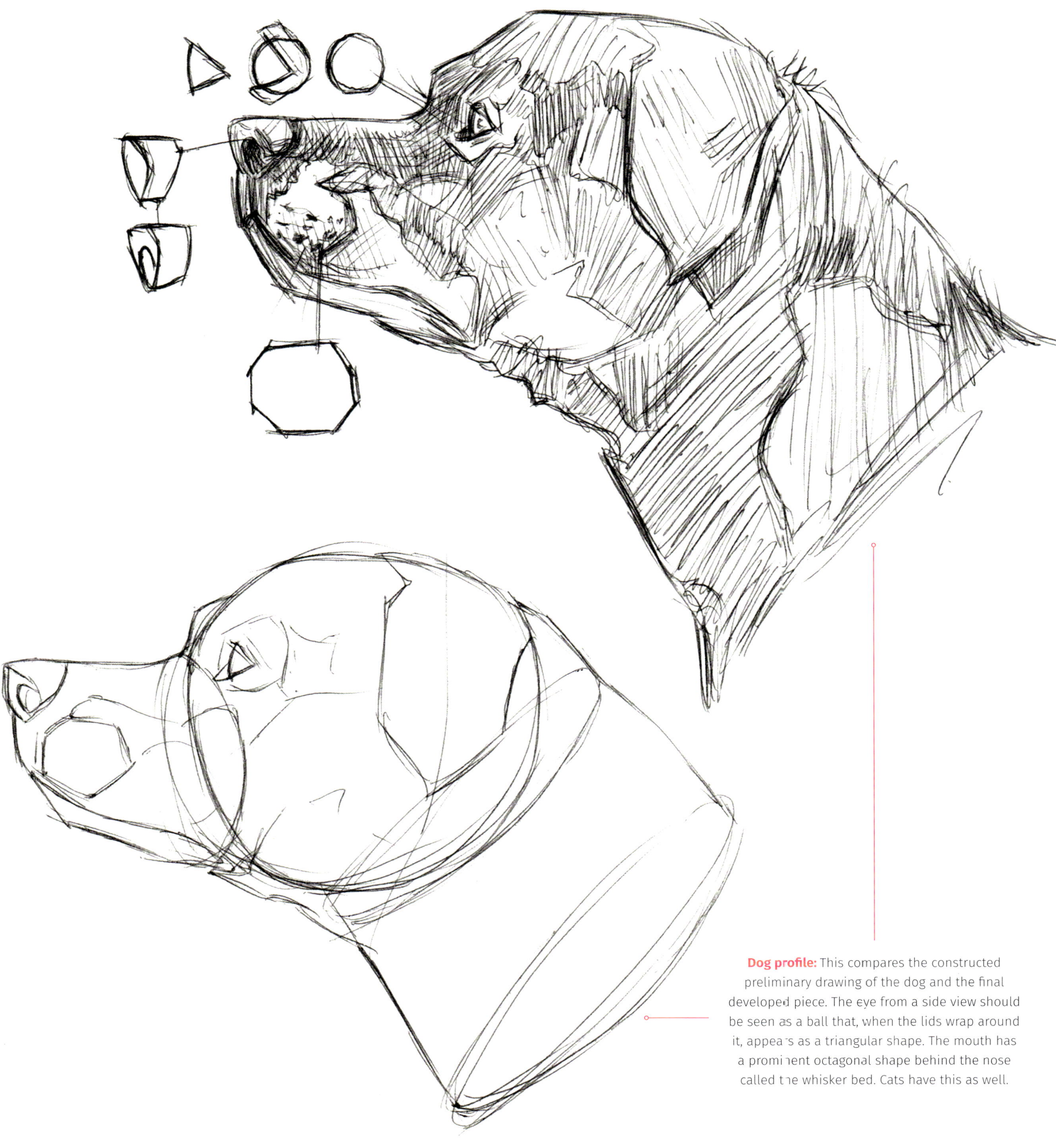

Dog profile: This compares the constructed preliminary drawing of the dog and the final developed piece. The eye from a side view should be seen as a ball that, when the lids wrap around it, appears as a triangular shape. The mouth has a prominent octagonal shape behind the nose called the whisker bed. Cats have this as well.

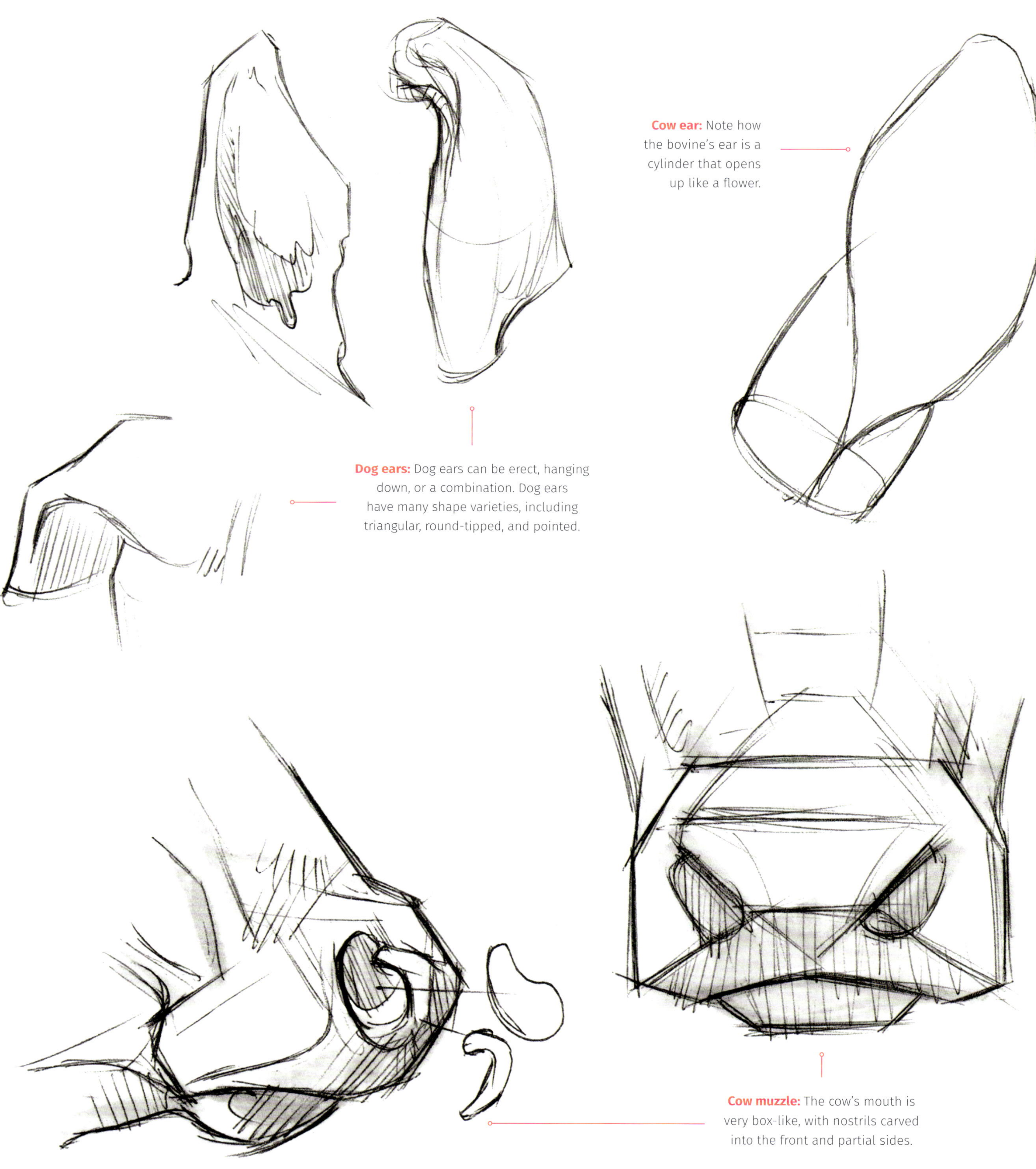
Cow ear: Note how the bovine's ear is a cylinder that opens up like a flower.
Dog ears: Dog ears can be erect, hanging down, or a combination. Dog ears have many shape varieties, including triangular, round-tipped, and pointed.
Cow muzzle: The cow's mouth is very box-like, with nostrils carved into the front and partial sides.

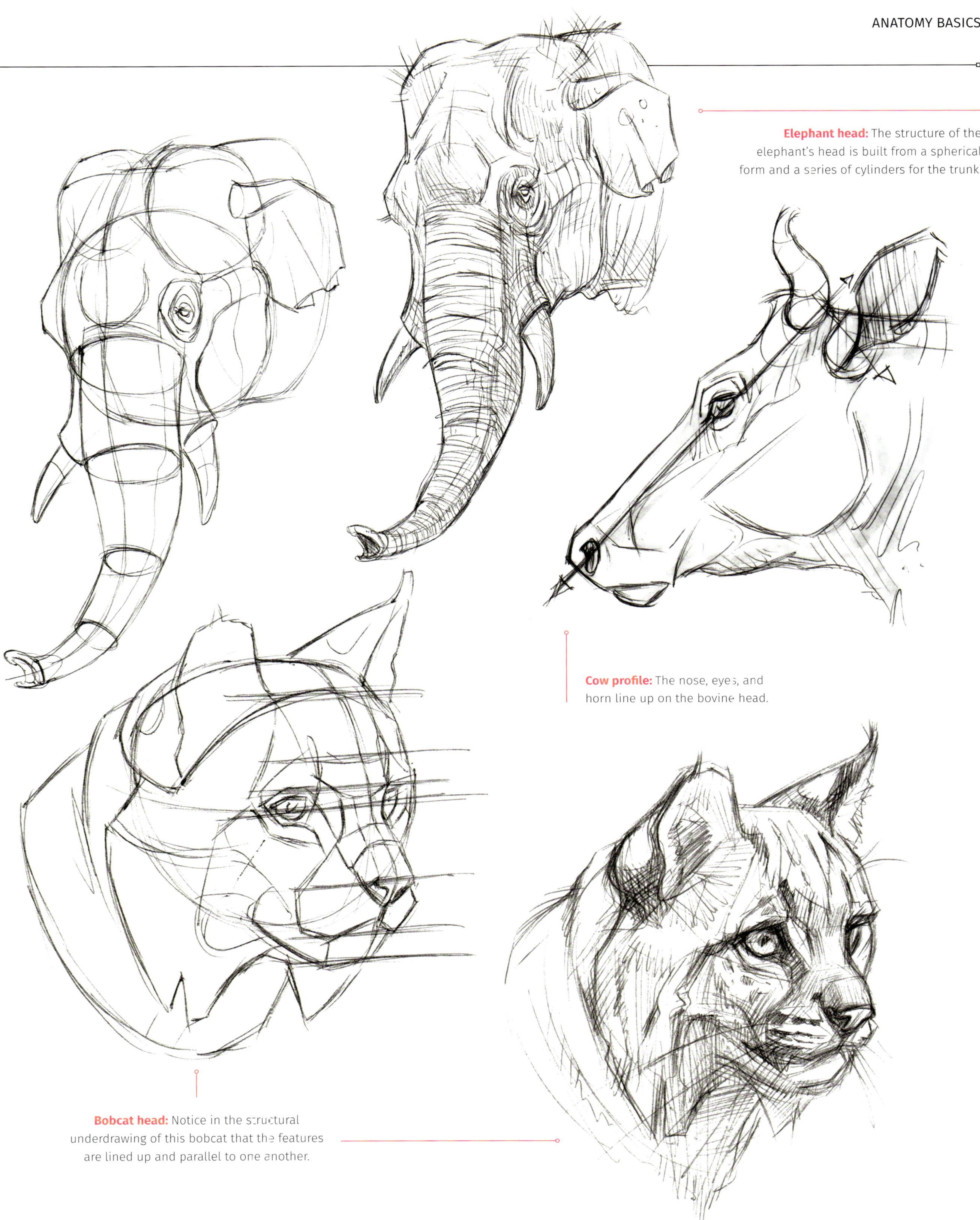

Elephant head: The structure of the elephant's head is built from a spherical form and a series of cylinders for the trunk.

Cow profile: The nose, eyes, and horn line up on the bovine head.

Bobcat head: Notice in the structural underdrawing of this bobcat that the features are lined up and parallel to one another.

The simplified neck & torso

The neck is a modified cylinder that fits into the shoulder mass. Look for the straights and curves that make up the neck, as these subtleties give individual character and a more precise look to the drawn animal. In some animals, such as the horse, the neck is higher in the back and lower in the front. The neck of a camel and other antelopes is a series of curves and straights that present a kinked look. The neck muscles are similar in most animals and can be seen as surface anatomy.

The torso (or trunk) is the body's largest mass, where the ribcage takes up most of the volume. Carnivores will have a floating rib, although this is rarely drawn for simplification reasons. The distance between the last rib and the crest of the ilium can be long or short, depending on the animal's hunting habits. The shoulder can be learned while studying the torso, or it can be omitted and studied during the study of the foreleg. Similarly, the pelvis can be included in the torso study or learned while researching the hind limb. To simplify the torso, use cylinders and boxes to establish the central mass before adding on to it with planes and details. ◇

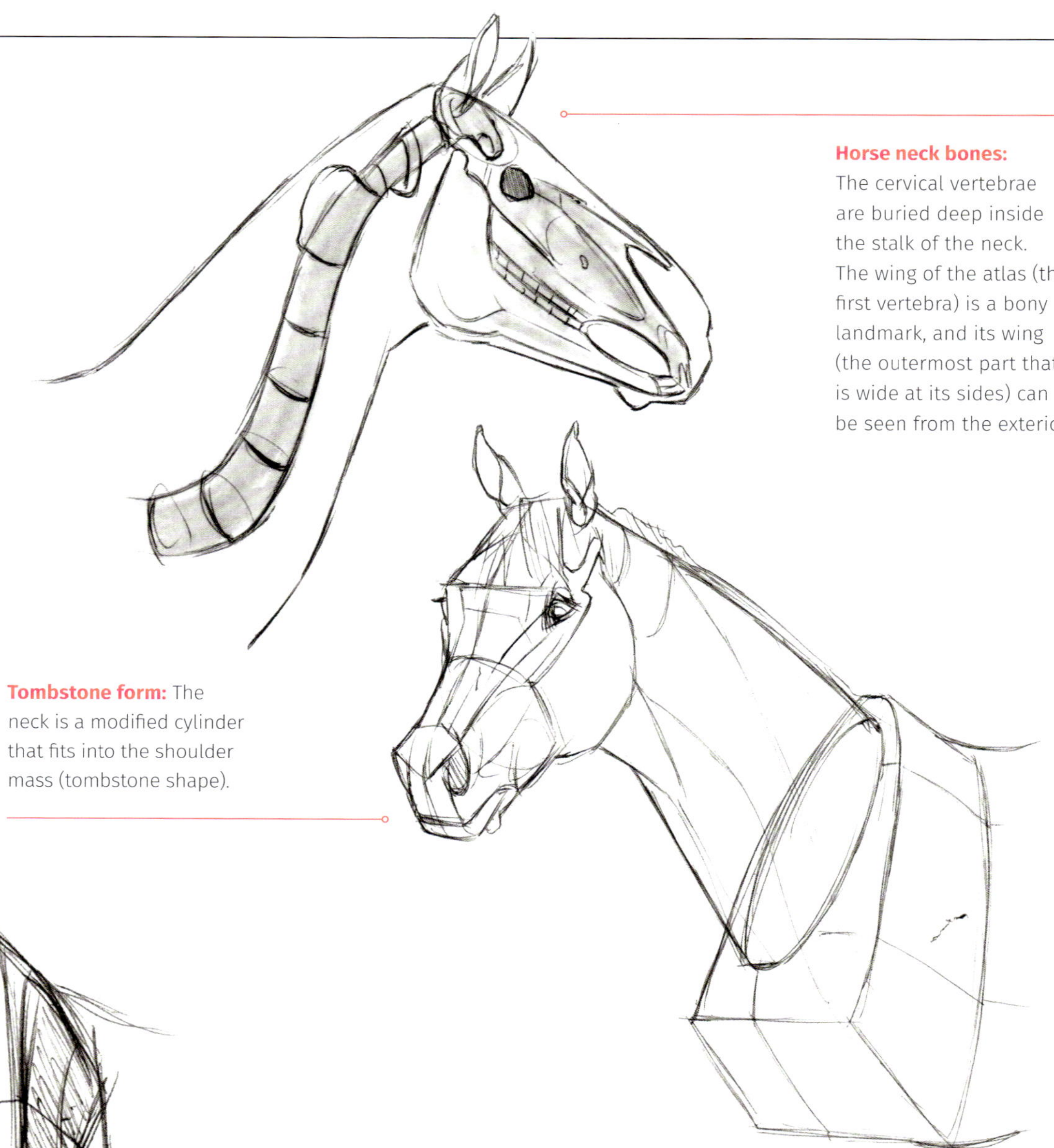

Horse neck bones: The cervical vertebrae are buried deep inside the stalk of the neck. The wing of the atlas (the first vertebra) is a bony landmark, and its wing (the outermost part that is wide at its sides) can be seen from the exterior.

Tombstone form: The neck is a modified cylinder that fits into the shoulder mass (tombstone shape).

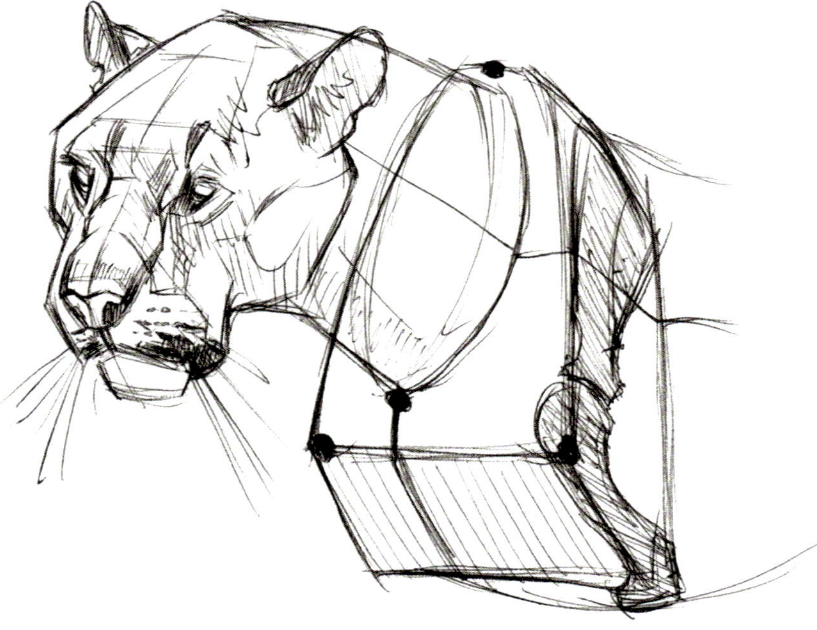

Joining neck to body: Some landmarks help with proportions and reveal where certain bones go inside the tombstone. The apex (top) of the shape represents the apex of the withers (the high point just past the neck). The central part of the lower neck indicates the sternum, which, if followed straight down, shows the keel of the sternum. The two outermost black dots represent the point of the shoulder, where the head of the humerus sits. The tombstone's side plane represents the area in which the scapula sits.

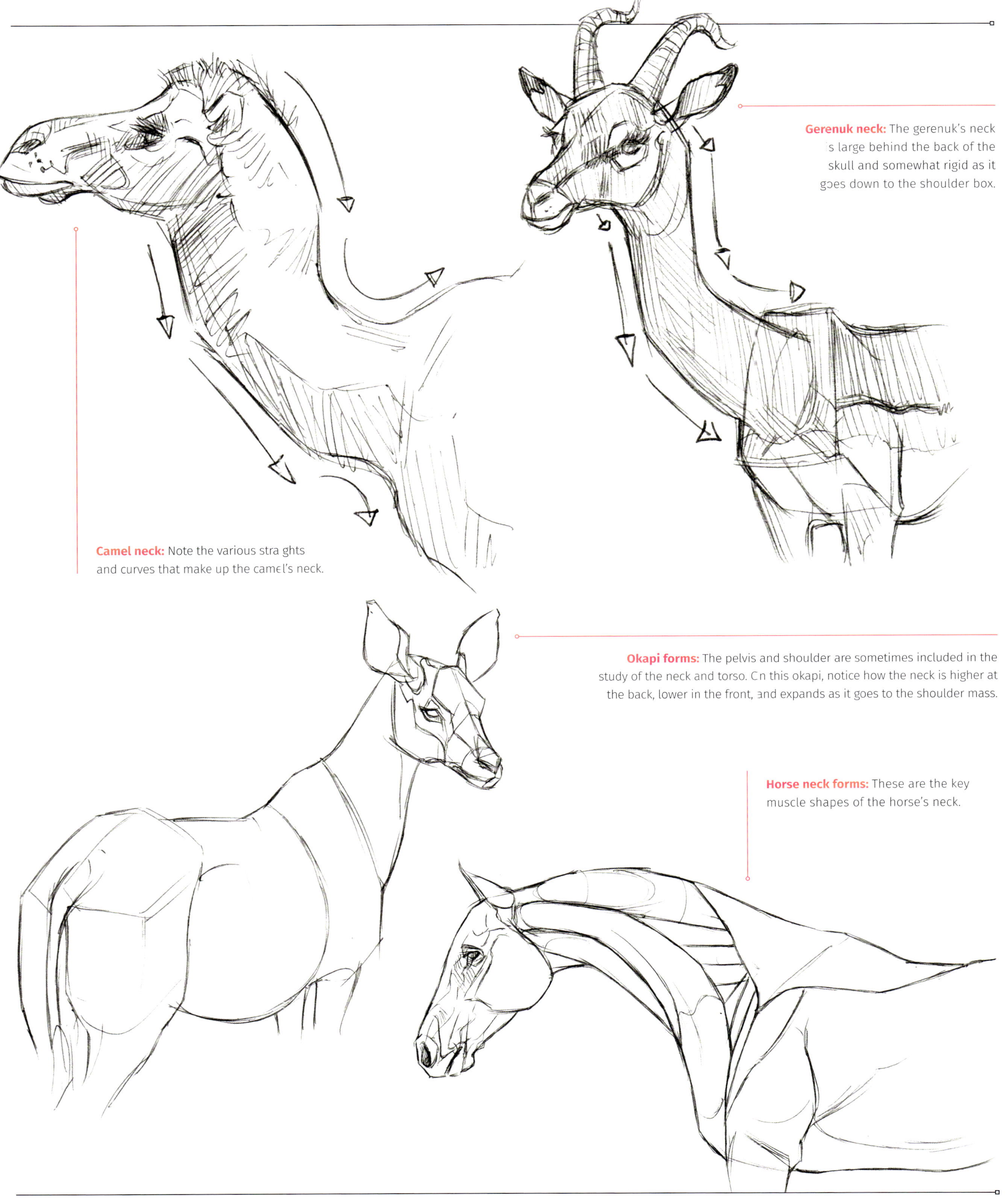

Gerenuk neck: The gerenuk's neck is large behind the back of the skull and somewhat rigid as it goes down to the shoulder box.

Camel neck: Note the various straights and curves that make up the camel's neck.

Okapi forms: The pelvis and shoulder are sometimes included in the study of the neck and torso. On this okapi, notice how the neck is higher at the back, lower in the front, and expands as it goes to the shoulder mass.

Horse neck forms: These are the key muscle shapes of the horse's neck.

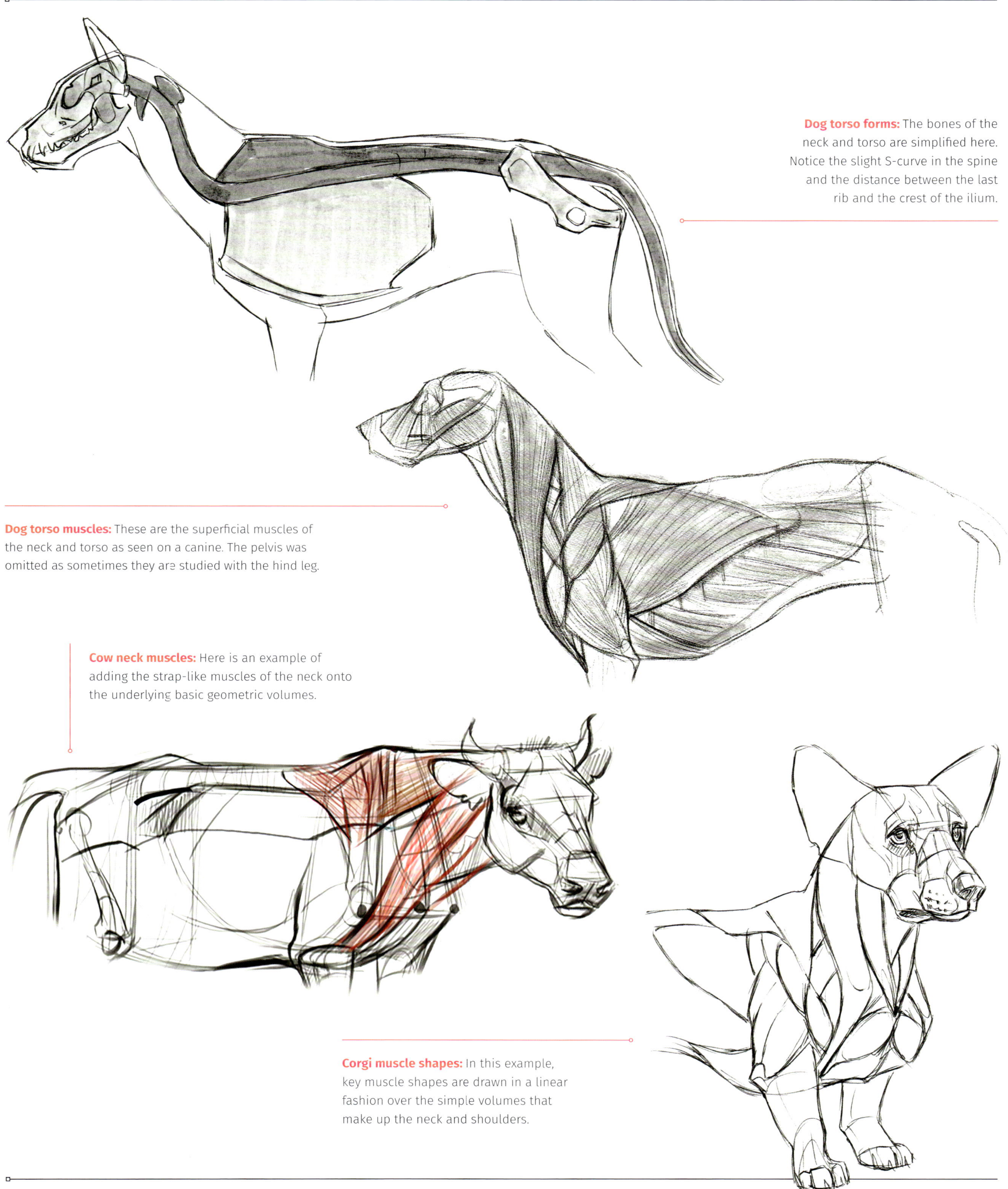

Dog torso forms: The bones of the neck and torso are simplified here. Notice the slight S-curve in the spine and the distance between the last rib and the crest of the ilium.

Dog torso muscles: These are the superficial muscles of the neck and torso as seen on a canine. The pelvis was omitted as sometimes they are studied with the hind leg.

Cow neck muscles: Here is an example of adding the strap-like muscles of the neck onto the underlying basic geometric volumes.

Corgi muscle shapes: In this example, key muscle shapes are drawn in a linear fashion over the simple volumes that make up the neck and shoulders.

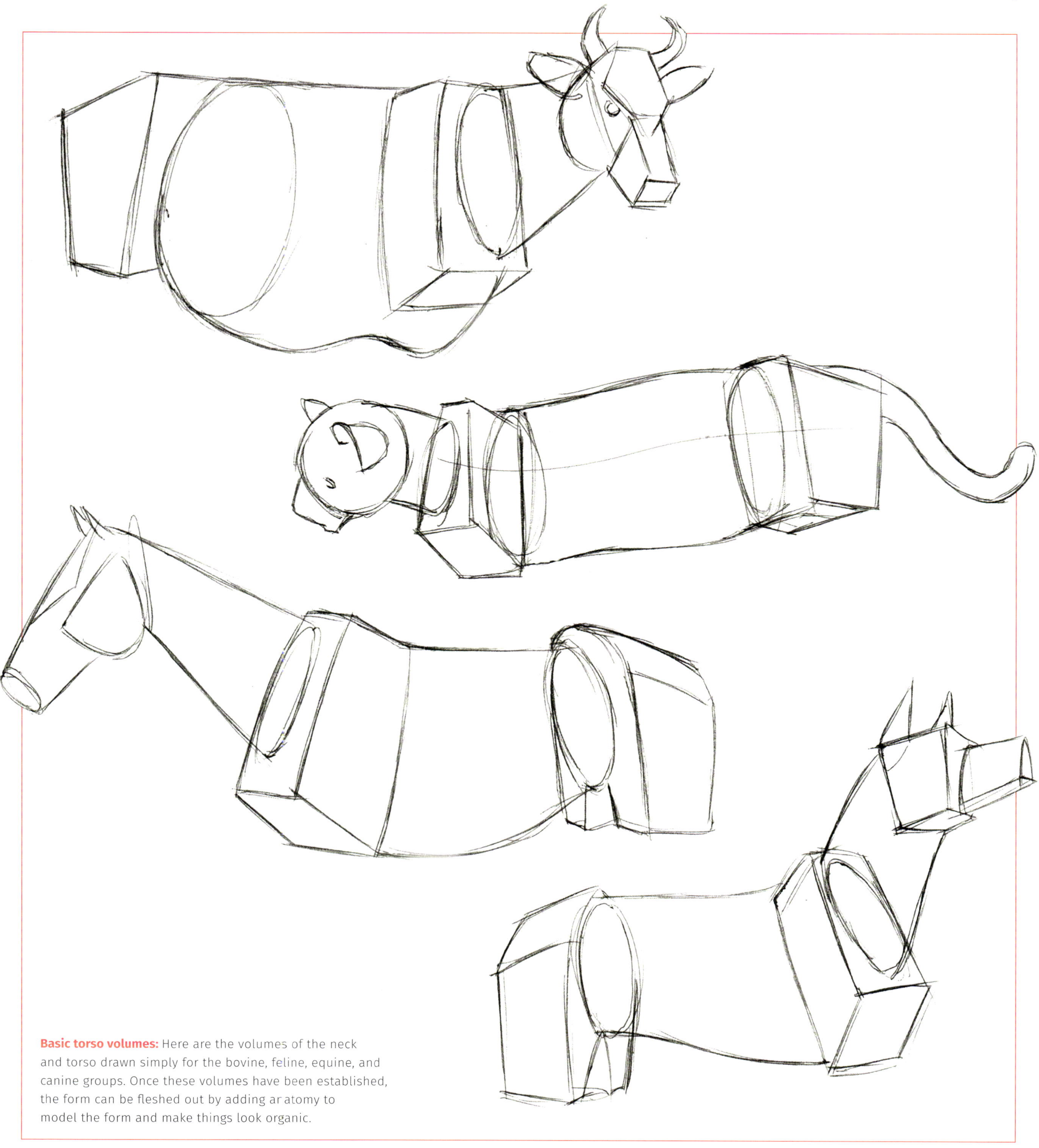

Basic torso volumes: Here are the volumes of the neck and torso drawn simply for the bovine, feline, equine, and canine groups. Once these volumes have been established, the form can be fleshed out by adding anatomy to model the form and make things look organic.

The simplified foreleg

The means of propulsion for most animals are two forelegs and two hind legs. When animals run, typically the forelegs take the weight when they land, while the hind legs push off (providing power). The shoulder is usually included in the study of the foreleg, so the scapula is where the bone arrangement begins. The shoulder blade, or scapula, is a free-floating bone held in by ligaments and plays an essential role in the motion of the foreleg. The spine of the scapula is always seen from the surface, as is the upper border. Watching big cats walk is a great way to see the scapula in motion as it rises above the thoracic vertebrae during a walk or gallop. These mobile bones dislodge from their usual location when big cats and canines reach out for their prey. ▸▸

Horse foreleg: In this series of horse foreleg drawings, the gesture is drawn first to establish the arrangement of bones in a loose, simplified fashion. Next is drawing the actual bones in the same arrangement, using simple form and cross contour. The muscles are then laid in. In this case, they are simplified, drawing the muscles of the shoulder blade, biceps, and triceps, and then the two masses of forearm muscles at the front and back of the arm. Finally, a construction drawing is included to show which simplified forms make up the profile view.

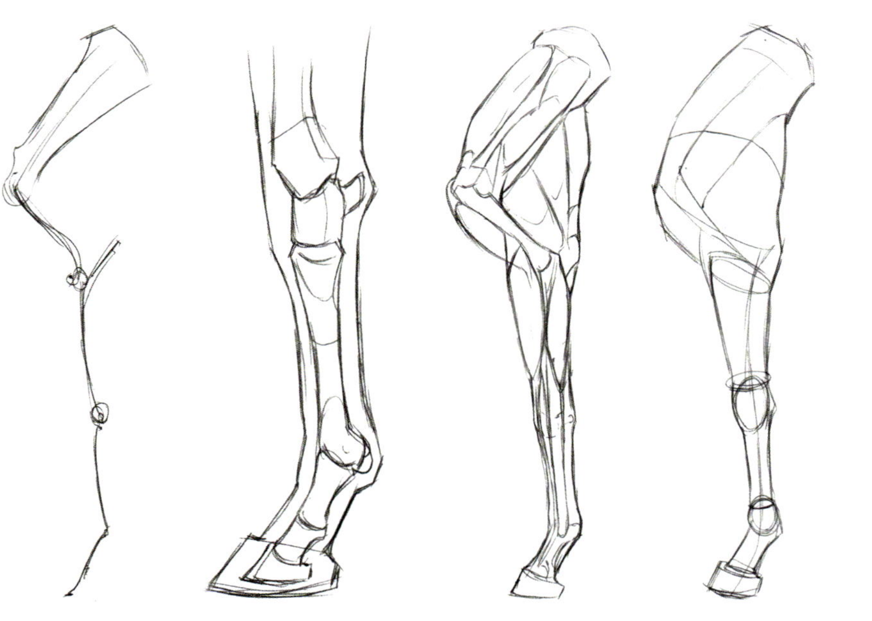

Lion foreleg: These two drawings show the simplified bones and muscles of a large carnivore (lion). Notice how the forearm has two bones and large claws, as opposed to the horse, who has two fused forearm bones that act as one, and only one toe inside the hoof with no claw.

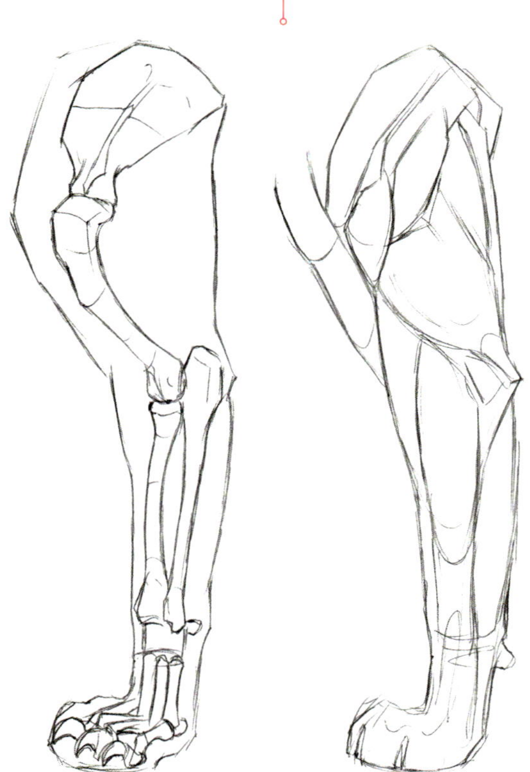

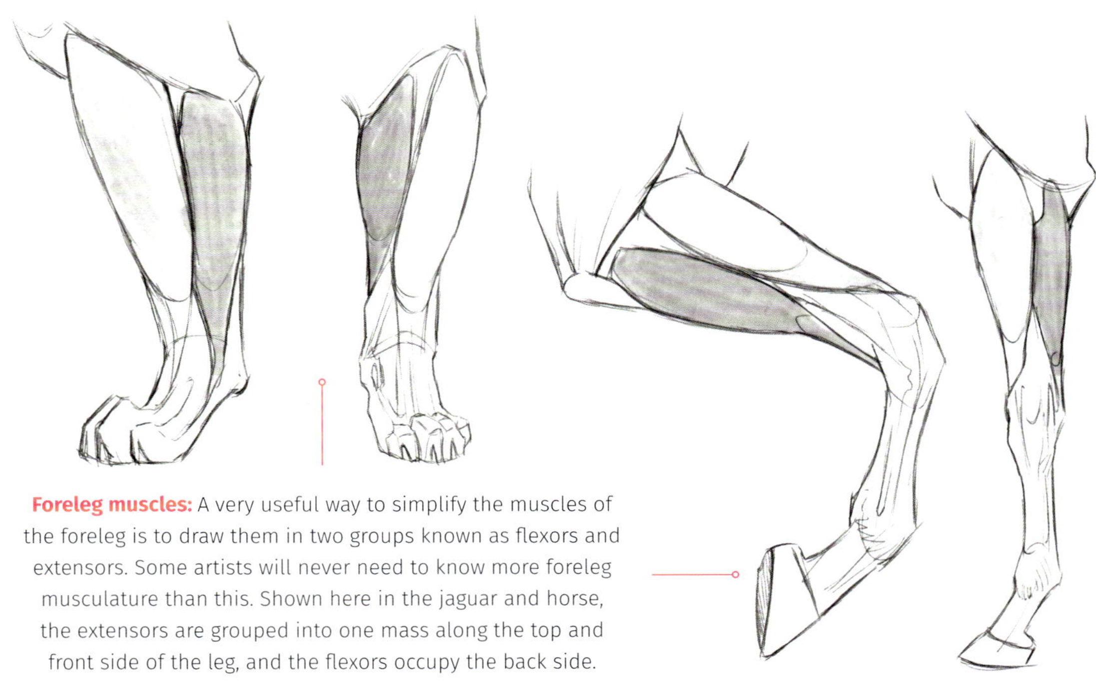

Foreleg muscles: A very useful way to simplify the muscles of the foreleg is to draw them in two groups known as flexors and extensors. Some artists will never need to know more foreleg musculature than this. Shown here in the jaguar and horse, the extensors are grouped into one mass along the top and front side of the leg, and the flexors occupy the back side.

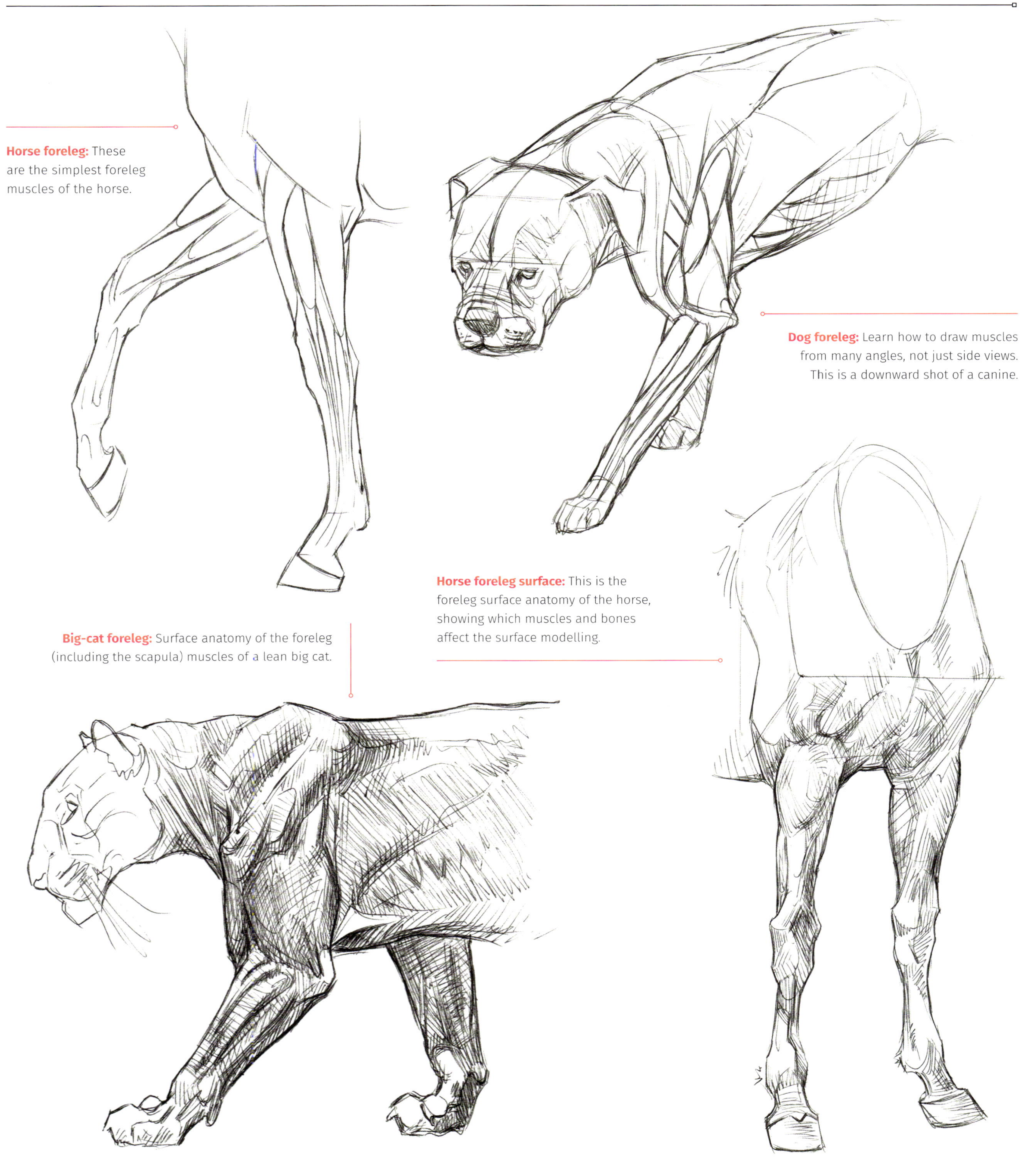

Horse foreleg: These are the simplest foreleg muscles of the horse.

Dog foreleg: Learn how to draw muscles from many angles, not just side views. This is a downward shot of a canine.

Horse foreleg surface: This is the foreleg surface anatomy of the horse, showing which muscles and bones affect the surface modelling.

Big-cat foreleg: Surface anatomy of the foreleg (including the scapula) muscles of a lean big cat.

The upper foreleg, or humerus, is the equivalent of a human upper arm, but in quadrupeds it is buried inside the trunk. What leaves the trunk or is exposed is the forearm, which has two bones, the radius and ulna. These bones are separate and capable of rotating in cats, less mobile in dogs, and fused in ungulates such as horses and cows.

Next up is the wrist, or carpal mass, which is a series of small bones transitioning to the forepaw or hoof. The paws are complex and require much study, especially in felines with a complex set of toes with nails that retract between the knuckles. Hooves are much simpler to draw, with the horse having one toe buried inside the hoof material and the cow having two, also known as a cloven foot. ◇

Toe-walkers: Most animals walk on the tips of their toes. In this comparison between two carnivores and two herbivores, note how they are all on their toes. Some animals, such as bears and raccoons, walk on their toes and on the plantar surfaces of their feet, but they are the minority. Notice also how the cow has two toes as opposed to the horse having just one. Bovines are all cloven-footed or 'split-hoofed'. The radius and ulna of the forearm is further apart in the lion than in the dog to allow for more movement with the wrist and forepaw.

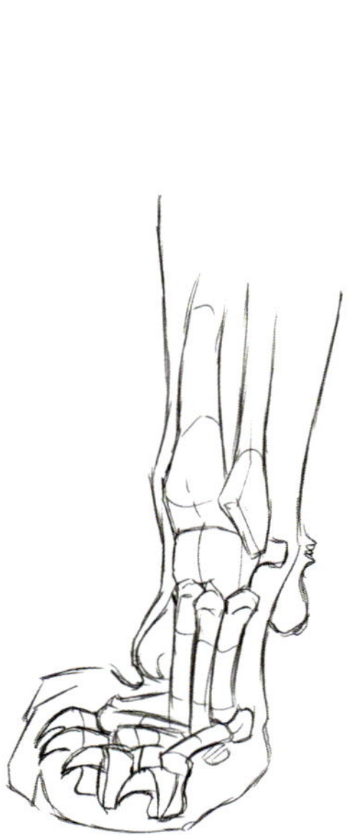

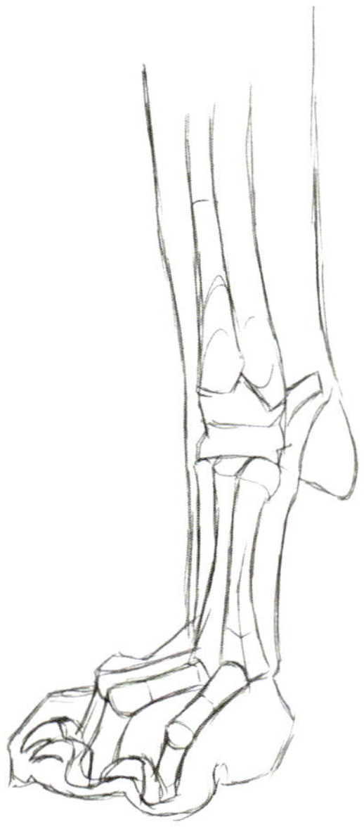

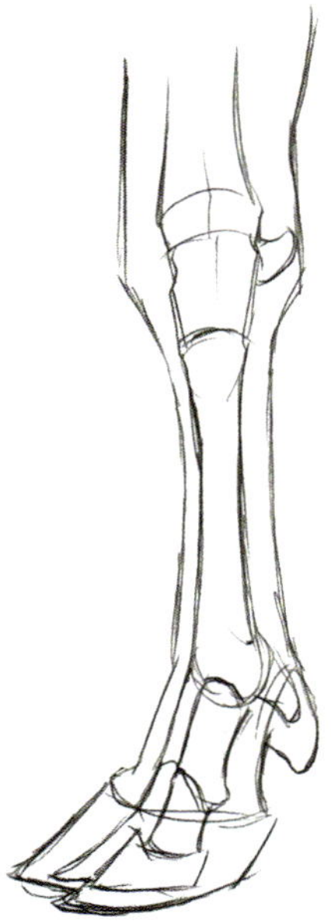

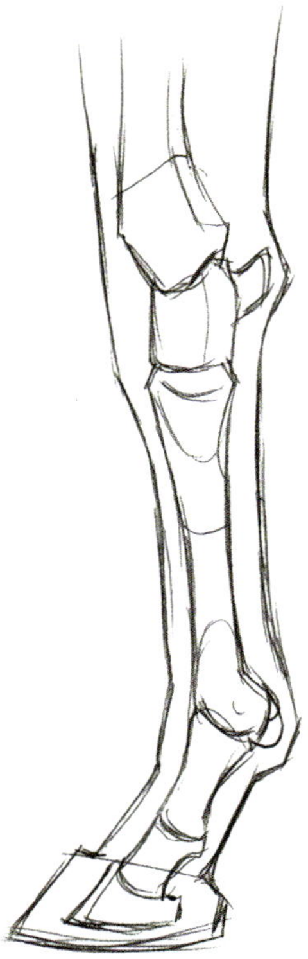

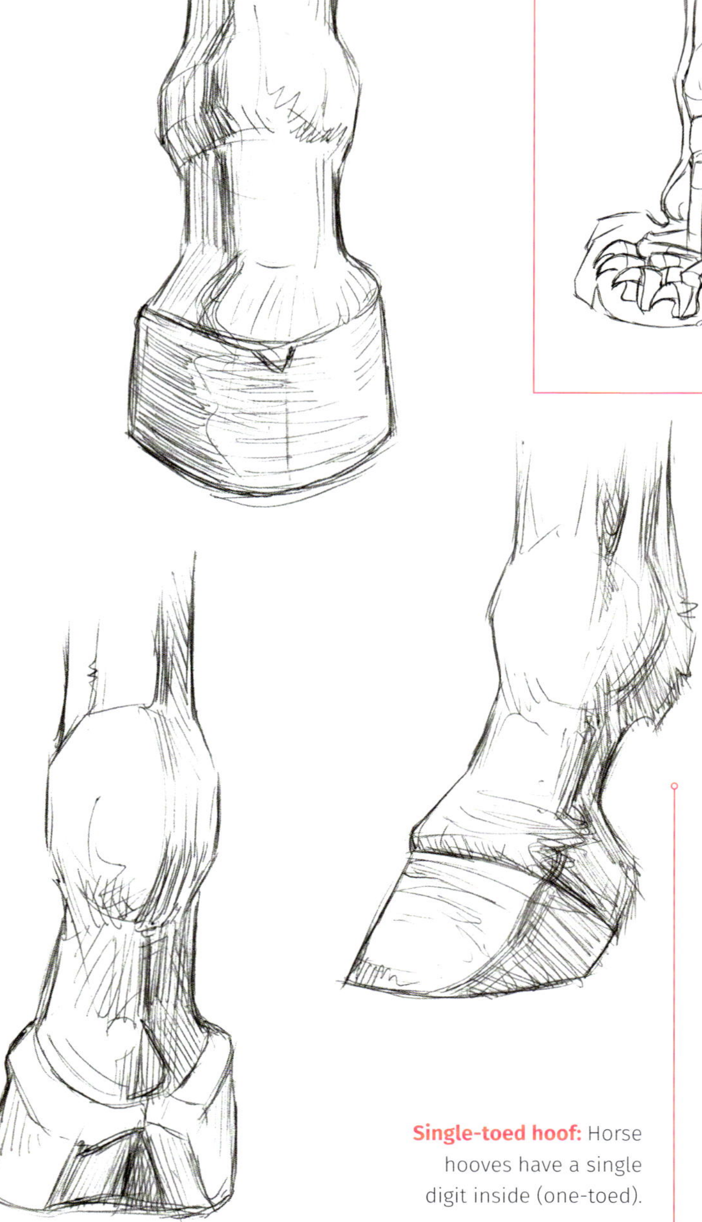

Single-toed hoof: Horse hooves have a single digit inside (one-toed).

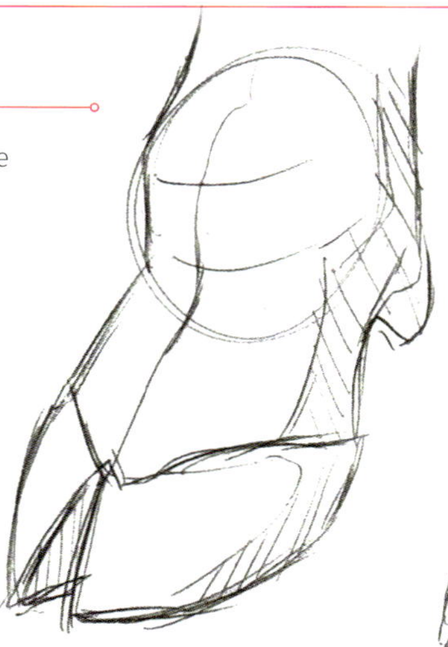

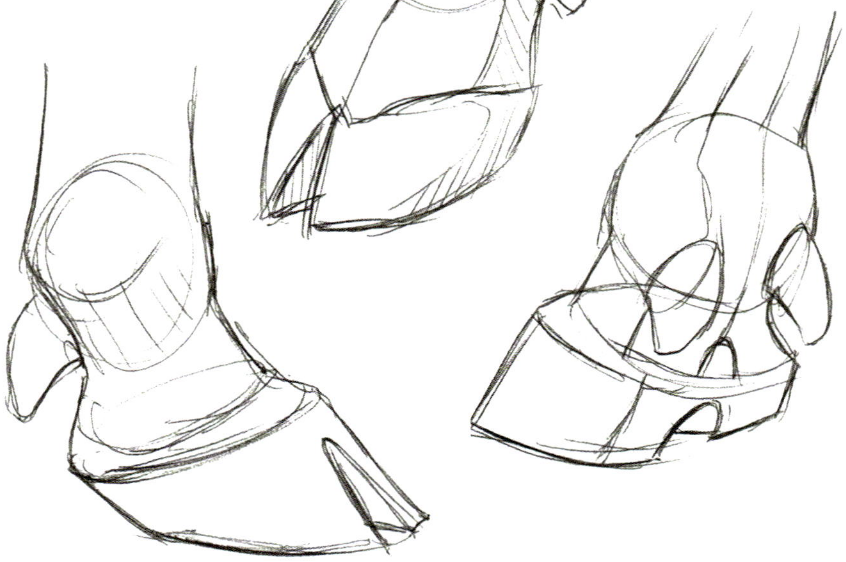

Cloven hooves: All cows are cloven-footed (two-toed).

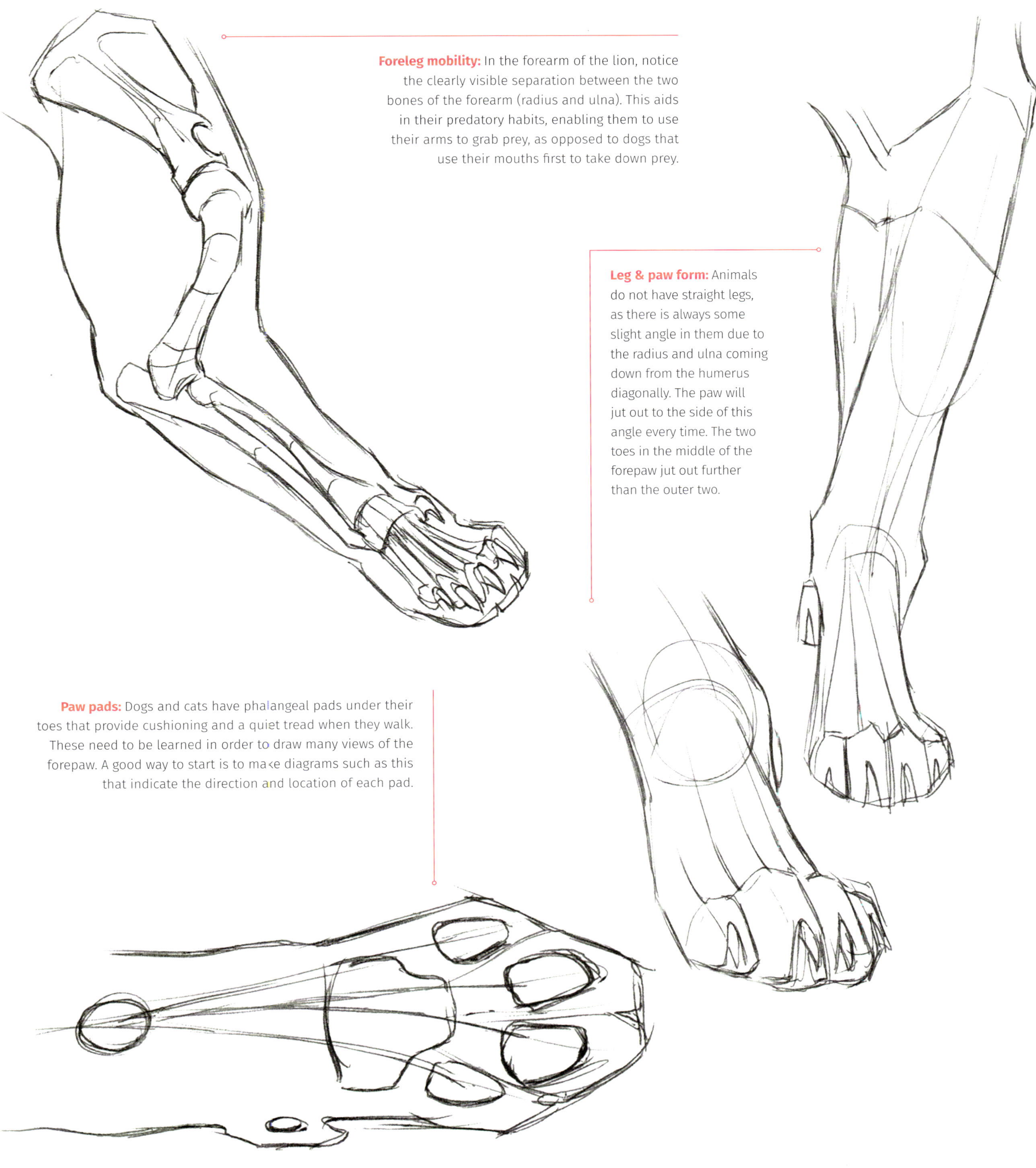

Foreleg mobility: In the forearm of the lion, notice the clearly visible separation between the two bones of the forearm (radius and ulna). This aids in their predatory habits, enabling them to use their arms to grab prey, as opposed to dogs that use their mouths first to take down prey.

Leg & paw form: Animals do not have straight legs, as there is always some slight angle in them due to the radius and ulna coming down from the humerus diagonally. The paw will jut out to the side of this angle every time. The two toes in the middle of the forepaw jut out further than the outer two.

Paw pads: Dogs and cats have phalangeal pads under their toes that provide cushioning and a quiet tread when they walk. These need to be learned in order to draw many views of the forepaw. A good way to start is to make diagrams such as this that indicate the direction and location of each pad.

The simplified hind leg

Drawing animals' hind legs takes specialized study, just as their forelegs do. The approach is the same. First, learn to simplify the arrangement of bones in a general way by finding the rhythm of the bones and how they connect in a gestural way. Next, practice drawing the basic forms of the pelvis, upper leg, lower leg, and hind foot. Finally, slowly start to draw the bones and muscles of the hind legs in a simplified yet accurate way.

The pelvis can be learned while drawing the torso, but it also makes sense to include it as the beginning bone to which the rest of the leg bones connect. The thigh bone, or femur, is buried inside the torso of many animals, but its ball-and-socket movement is where the action of the leg starts. Two essential landmarks that follow are the knee cap (or patella), which sits on the edge of the femur, and the crest of the tibia, which juts out very prominently below it. The knee cap is held in by a ligament and is therefore very mobile.

The calf or lower leg bones are below the femur and are called the tibia and fibula. These two bones are fused in ungulates but are slightly separated in carnivores. Finally, there is the ankle mass, foot, and toe(s). The hind foot or paw looks very similar to the forefoot and forepaw. ◇

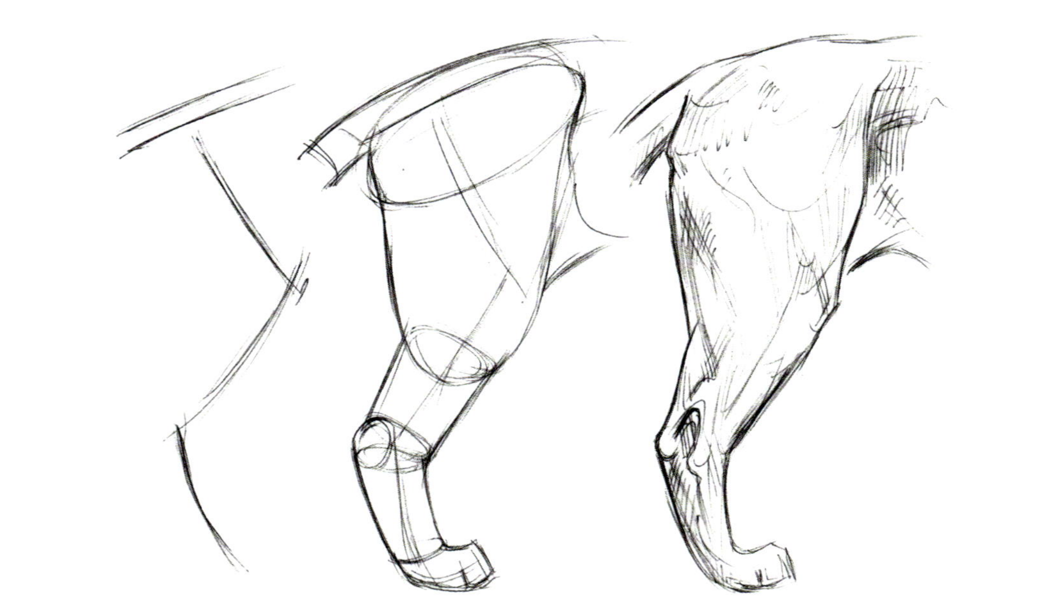

Drawing process: A great way to build a drawing is to start with 2D axis lines to establish the pose of the hind leg and lay down the direction of the bones. Next, basic forms are drawn on top of the 2D axis to establish a 3D form. Finally, the modelling of the form brings the drawing to completion.

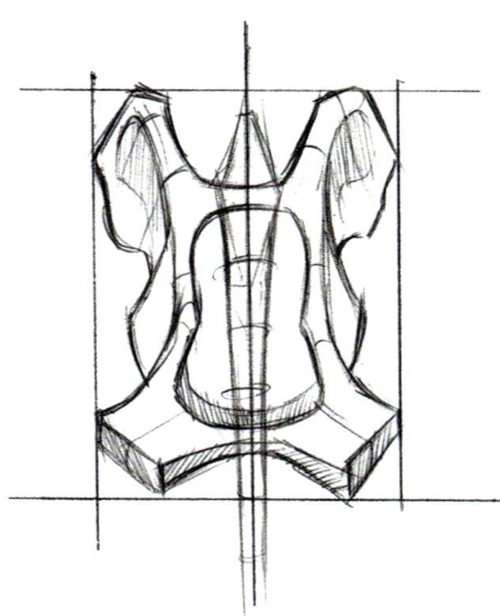

Lion pelvis: The pelvis of any animal needs particular study, but all pelvis bones have similar qualities. Here is the pelvis of a lion drawn from the top. Notice how narrow it is (which aids in running and motion) compared to the much broader horse or cow pelvis.

Feline pelvis: In cats, the hindquarters are tilted downwards to house the narrow pelvis. A box or rectangle is an ideal form to use for this, and it can be modified to look organic with the muscles of the hind leg. Cylindrical forms are used for the narrow calves and hind paws.

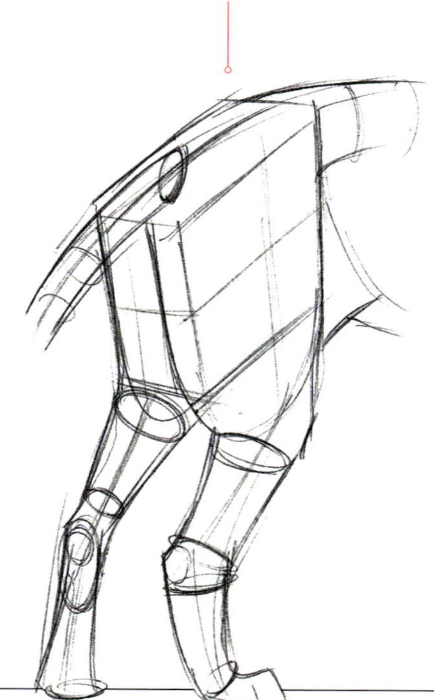

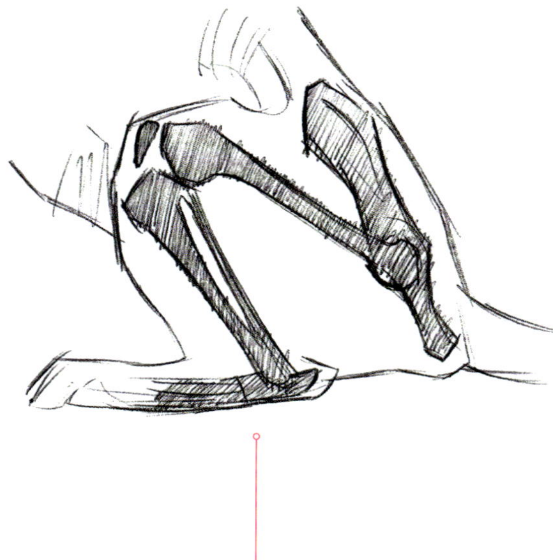

Seated hind leg: When animals are seated or in repose, their hind legs seem to swallow up the bones, making it confusing for the beginner to understand how to draw the leg. The way to always know how to draw a leg like this (foreshortened or otherwise) is to see how the bones fit inside and how they compress in an accordion-like fashion.

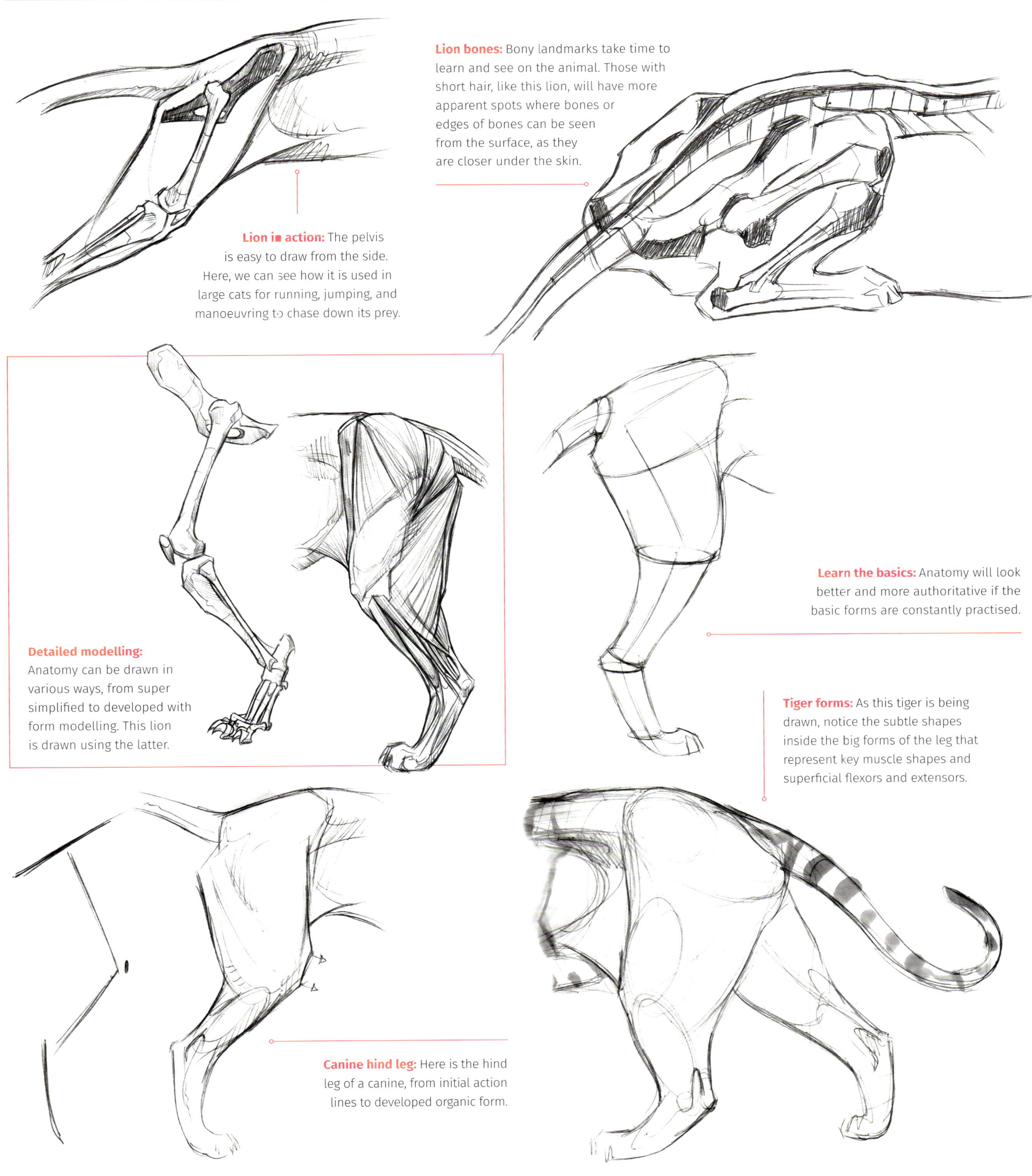

Lion bones: Bony landmarks take time to learn and see on the animal. Those with short hair, like this lion, will have more apparent spots where bones or edges of bones can be seen from the surface, as they are closer under the skin.

Lion in action: The pelvis is easy to draw from the side. Here, we can see how it is used in large cats for running, jumping, and manoeuvring to chase down its prey.

Detailed modelling: Anatomy can be drawn in various ways, from super simplified to developed with form modelling. This lion is drawn using the latter.

Learn the basics: Anatomy will look better and more authoritative if the basic forms are constantly practised.

Tiger forms: As this tiger is being drawn, notice the subtle shapes inside the big forms of the leg that represent key muscle shapes and superficial flexors and extensors.

Canine hind leg: Here is the hind leg of a canine, from initial action lines to developed organic form.

Horse muscles: Here are the horse hind-leg muscles with the fascia over the thighs removed to show which muscle masses comprise the quadriceps area. All the muscles are drawn as masses over the underlying skeletal framework.

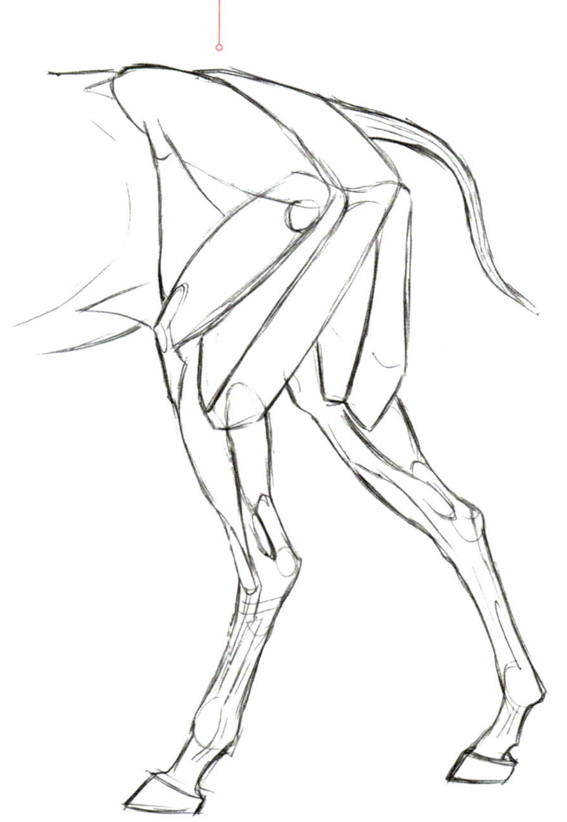

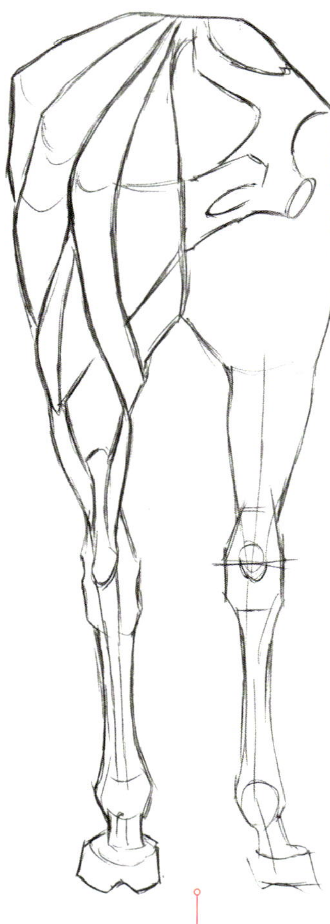

Horse muscles: Horse hindquarter muscles in the posterior view.

Horse bones: Shown here are the simple hind-leg bones of an equine. Note that some are close to the surface and others are deeper inside.

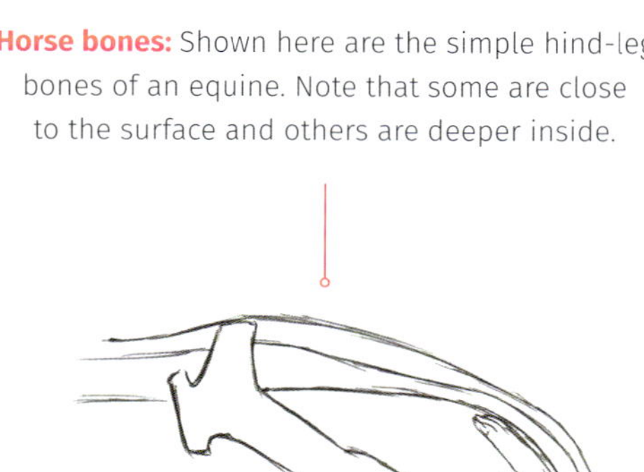

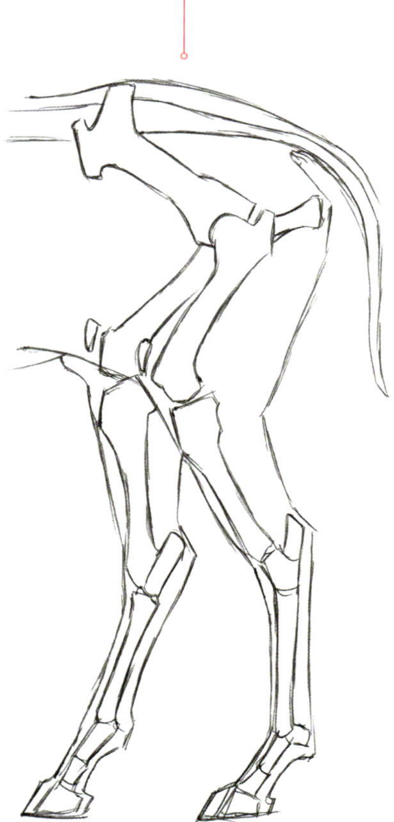

Dog muscles: Learning to draw muscles from a front or back three-quarter perspective is often a combination of drawing from a side view, using reference, and then drawing from imagination to foreshorten the muscle shapes.

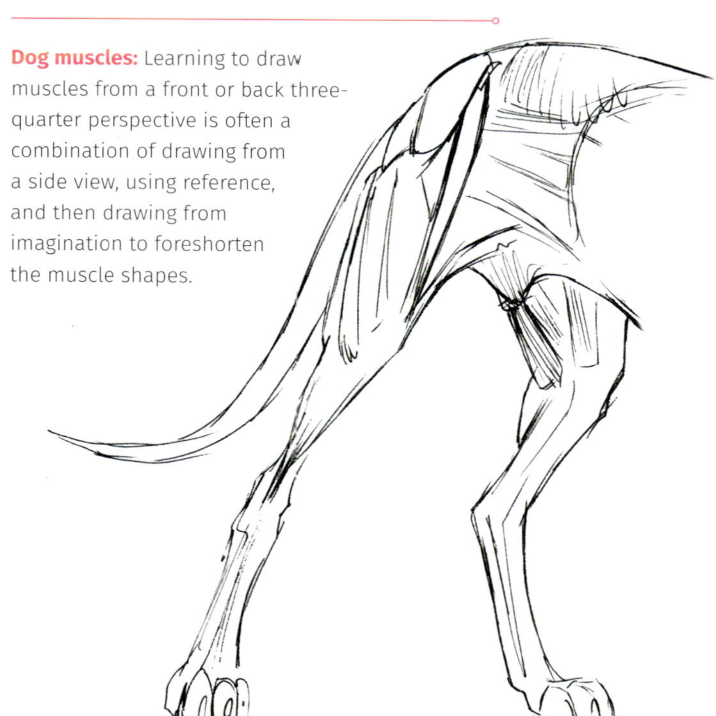

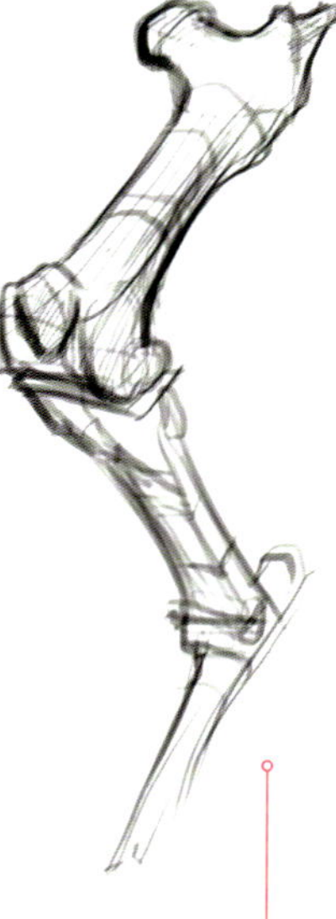

Horse bones:
Box-like forms are used to develop the hind-leg bones (like the femur and tibia), revealing the placement for the corners of the forms.

Horse construction:
This constructed drawing of the horse's hindquarters uses a box for the pelvis area. Notice how the strong Achilles tendons are very obvious in almost all animals and become an essential feature to include every time the calf and lower leg are drawn. Also, notice how legs are not straight in the back but rather come in towards each other (knock-heeled).

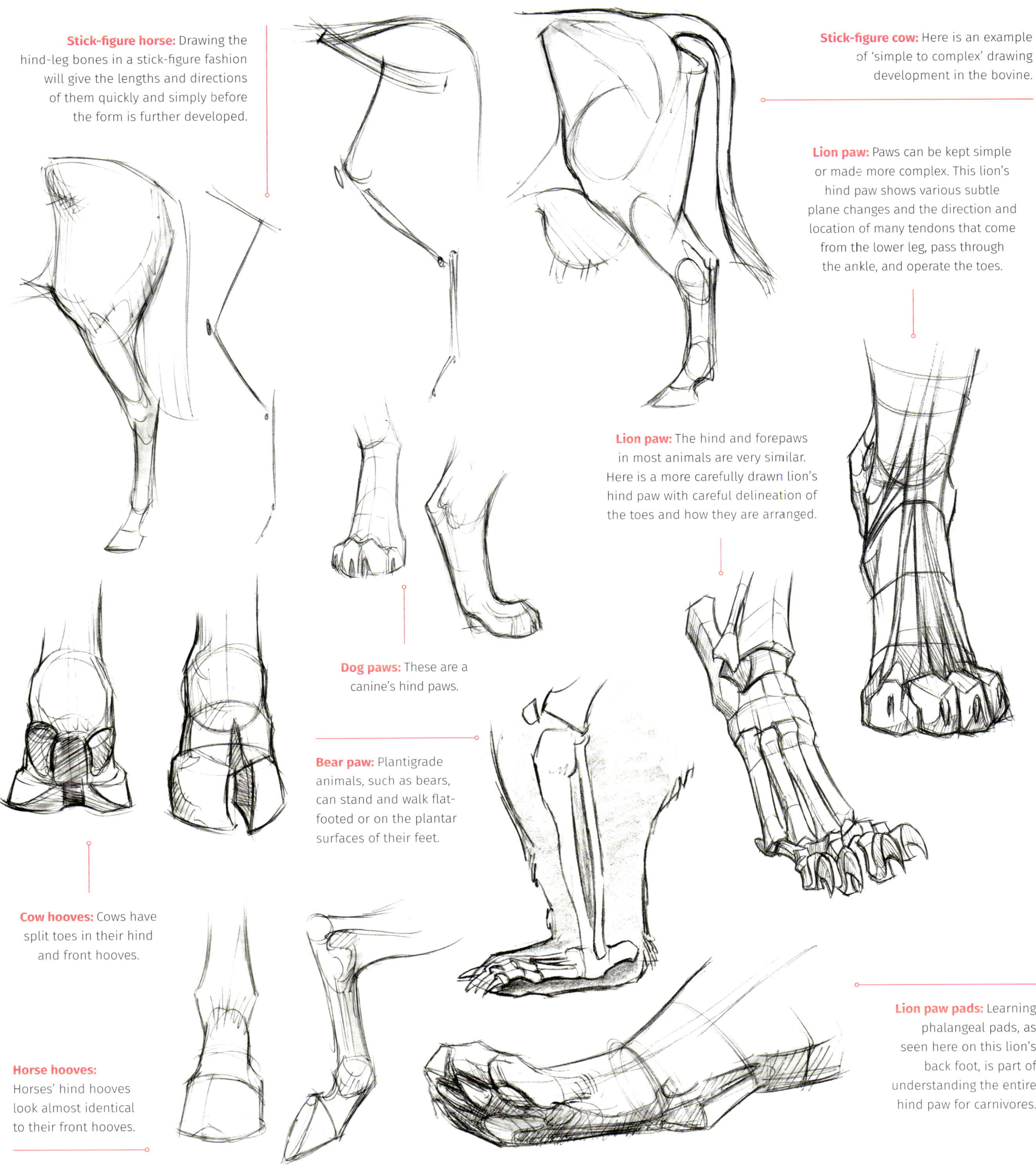
Stick-figure horse: Drawing the hind-leg bones in a stick-figure fashion will give the lengths and directions of them quickly and simply before the form is further developed.

Stick-figure cow: Here is an example of 'simple to complex' drawing development in the bovine.

Lion paw: Paws can be kept simple or made more complex. This lion's hind paw shows various subtle plane changes and the direction and location of many tendons that come from the lower leg, pass through the ankle, and operate the toes.

Lion paw: The hind and forepaws in most animals are very similar. Here is a more carefully drawn lion's hind paw with careful delineation of the toes and how they are arranged.

Dog paws: These are a canine's hind paws.

Bear paw: Plantigrade animals, such as bears, can stand and walk flat-footed or on the plantar surfaces of their feet.

Cow hooves: Cows have split toes in their hind and front hooves.

Horse hooves: Horses' hind hooves look almost identical to their front hooves.

Lion paw pads: Learning phalangeal pads, as seen here on this lion's back foot, is part of understanding the entire hind paw for carnivores.

Comparative anatomy

The study of comparative anatomy is of great importance when learning to draw animals. Here is a brief introduction to the topic, but there is much more to know about this fascinating subject. At first glance, the human's outward appearance seems vastly different from another mammal's, but we can see how much they have in common when they are carefully compared. Most animals stand on all four legs and the tips of their toes, but they share the same bones (such as a skull, backbone, ribcage, pelvis, and legs) with humans. The muscles also resemble those of a human, although they are placed somewhat differently, and some muscles have different but similar shapes.

While studying comparative anatomy, you will discover on an animal where things such as the true wrist, elbow, knee, and ankle are located, and how they correspond to those found in humans. Apes and a few other animals are built more like humans, but most of the animals dealt with in this chapter are constructed similarly to each other and stand on their toes. If we put a human in a crouched position (similar to how a runner begins a race) on the tips of their fingers and toes, that is how an animal is all the time, except the human would tire out quickly and not be able to hold that position. The animals shown here are always like this, and do not get tired because they have particular tendons and brace ligaments to keep their bodies effortlessly held in this position. What you already know about human figure-drawing will help with your animal drawing, and vice versa. ◇

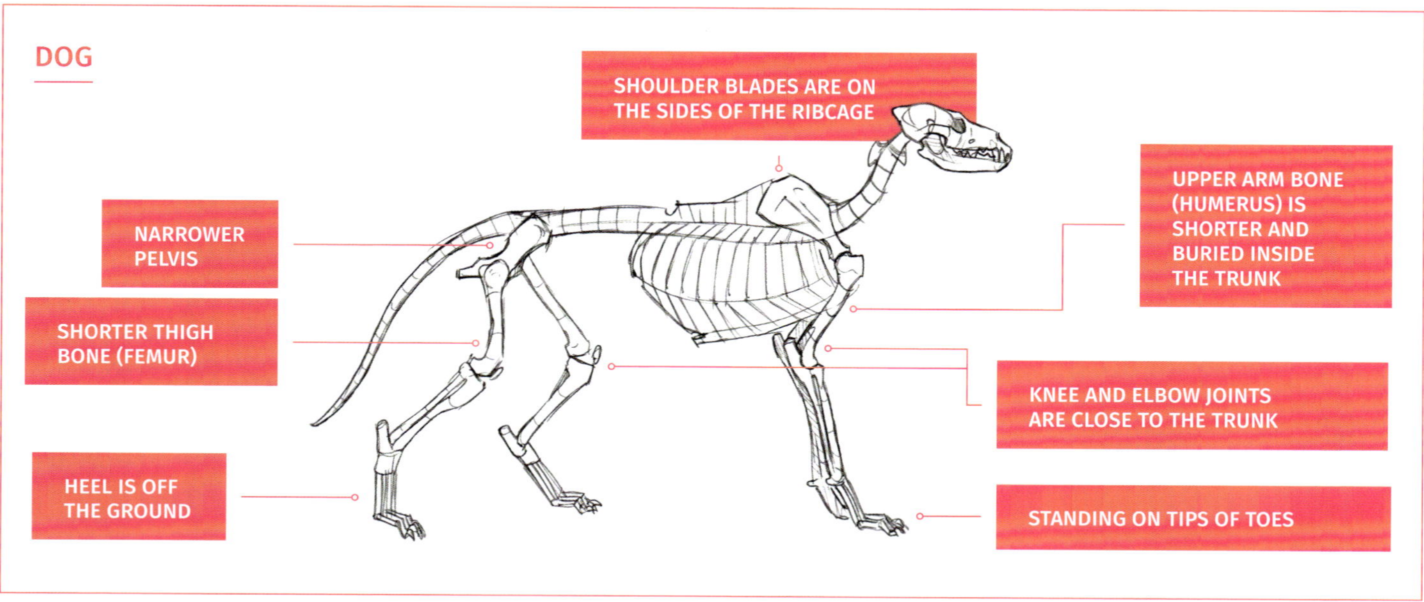

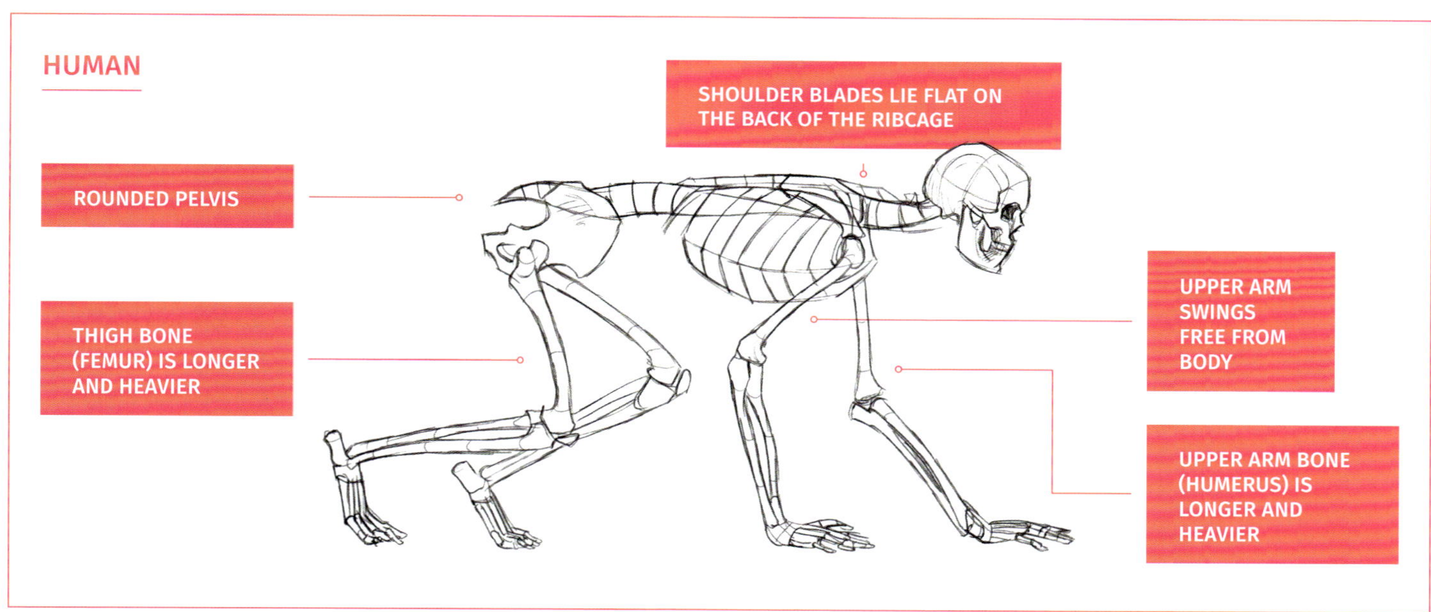

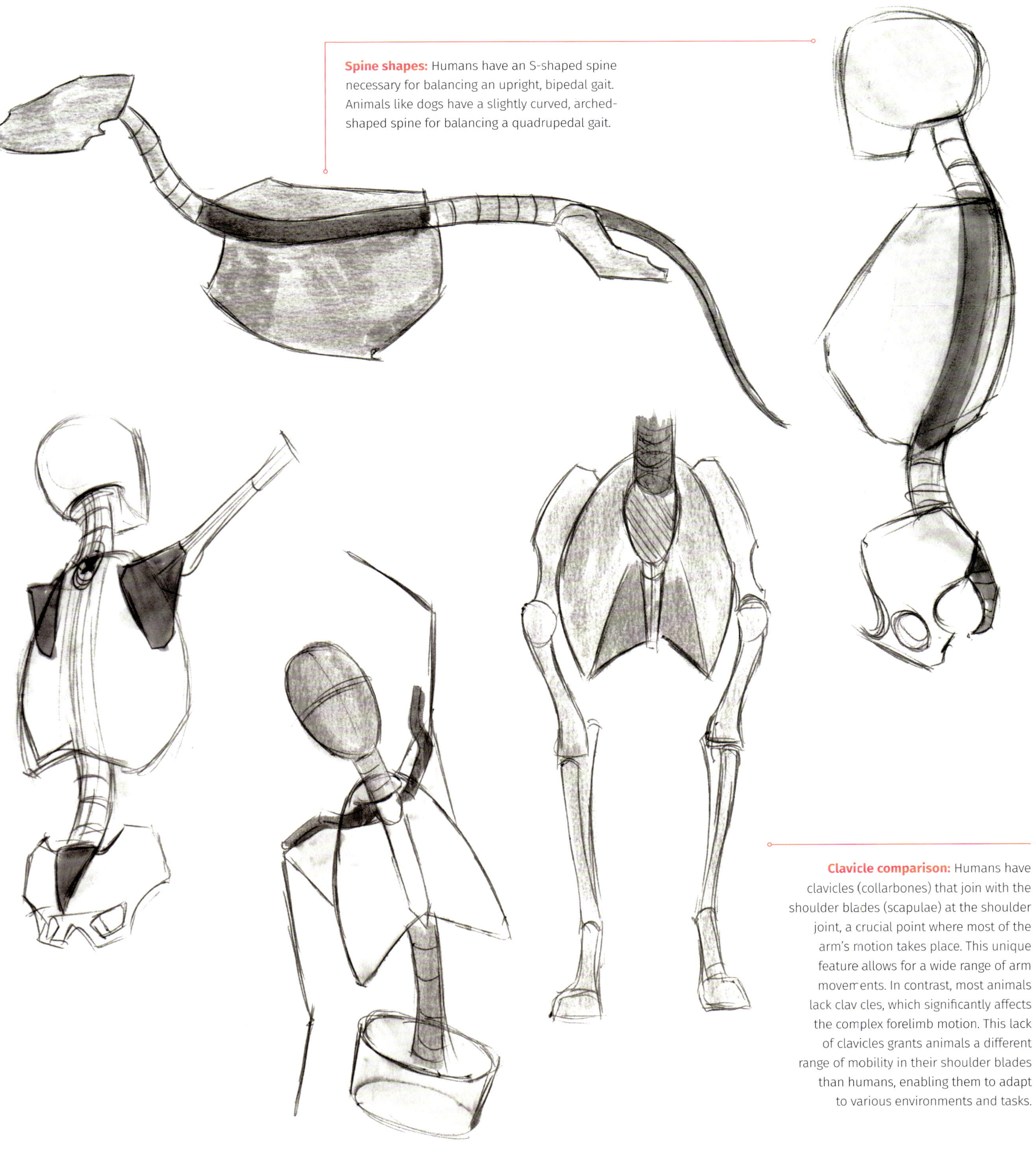

Spine shapes: Humans have an S-shaped spine necessary for balancing an upright, bipedal gait. Animals like dogs have a slightly curved, arched-shaped spine for balancing a quadrupedal gait.

Clavicle comparison: Humans have clavicles (collarbones) that join with the shoulder blades (scapulae) at the shoulder joint, a crucial point where most of the arm's motion takes place. This unique feature allows for a wide range of arm movements. In contrast, most animals lack clavicles, which significantly affects the complex forelimb motion. This lack of clavicles grants animals a different range of mobility in their shoulder blades than humans, enabling them to adapt to various environments and tasks.

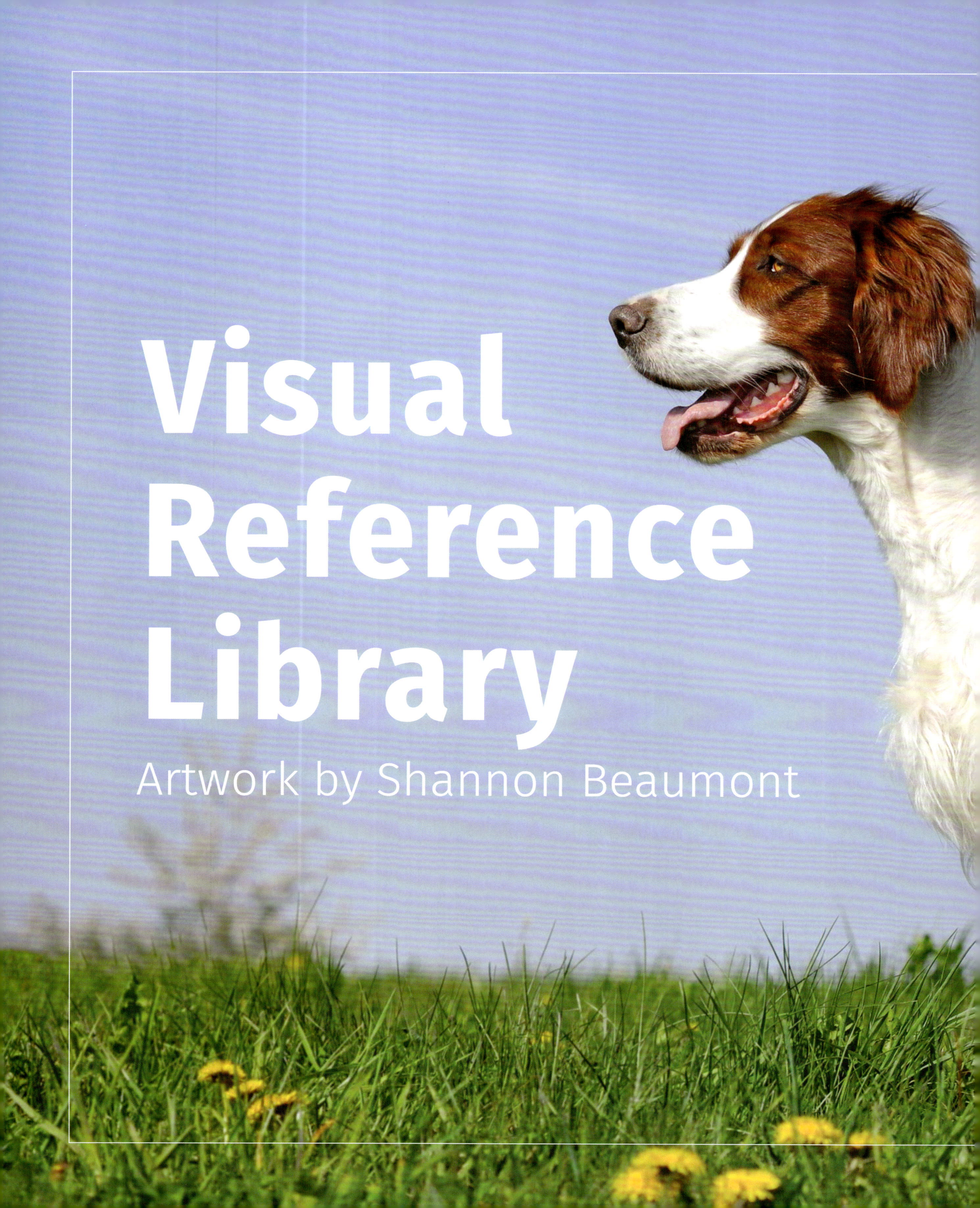
Visual
Reference
Library
Artwork by Shannon Beaumont

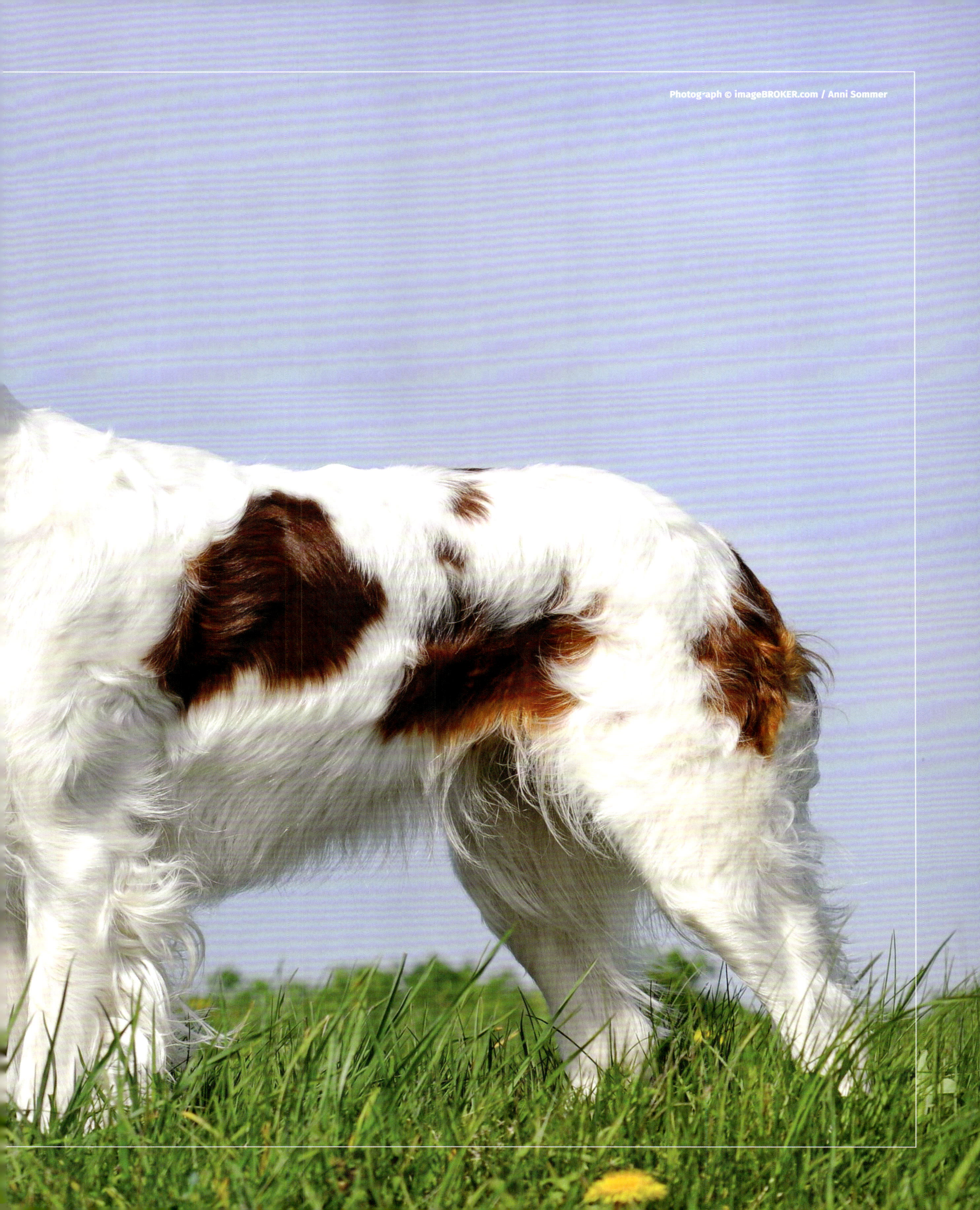

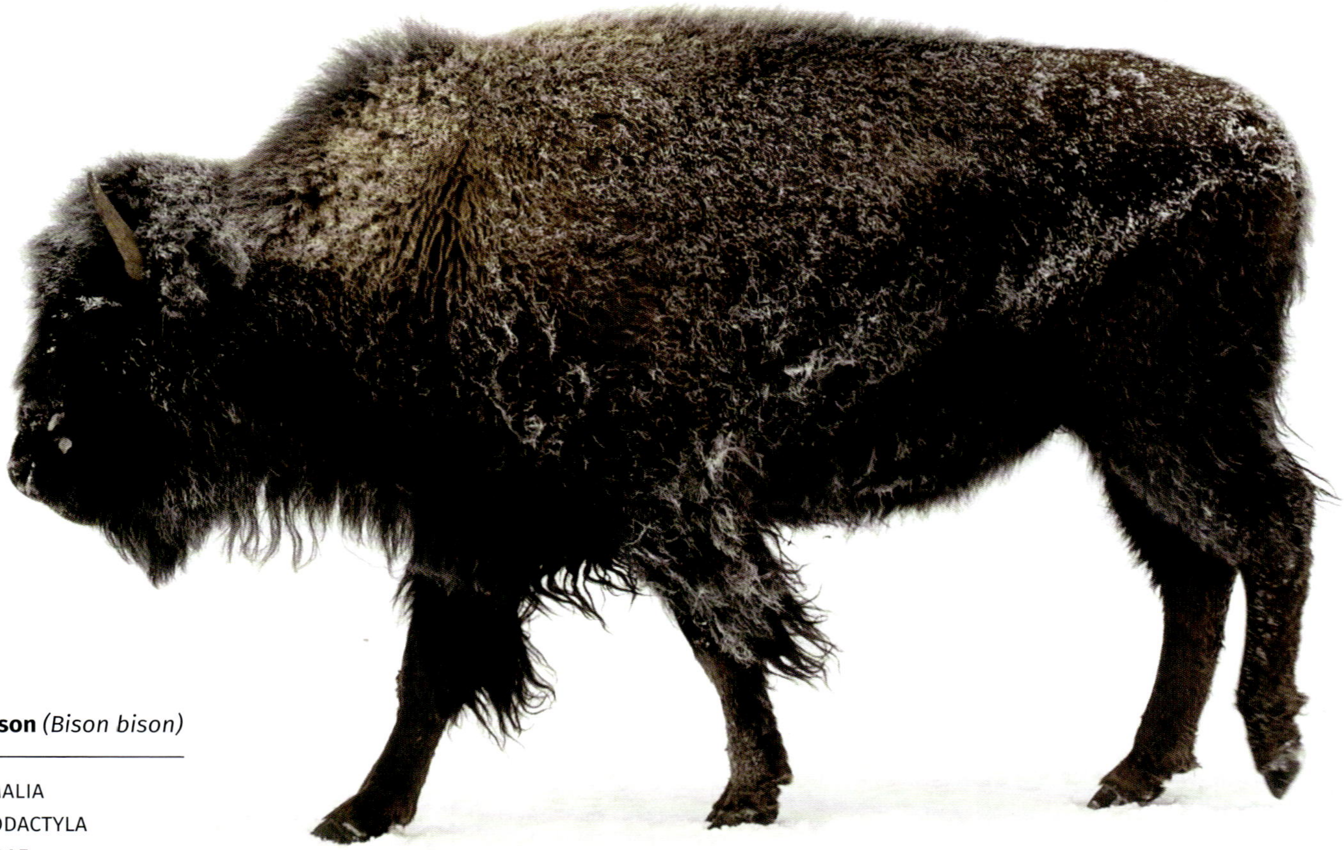

Bison

American bison *(Bison bison)*

CLASS: MAMMALIA
ORDER: ARTIODACTYLA
FAMILY: BOVIDAE

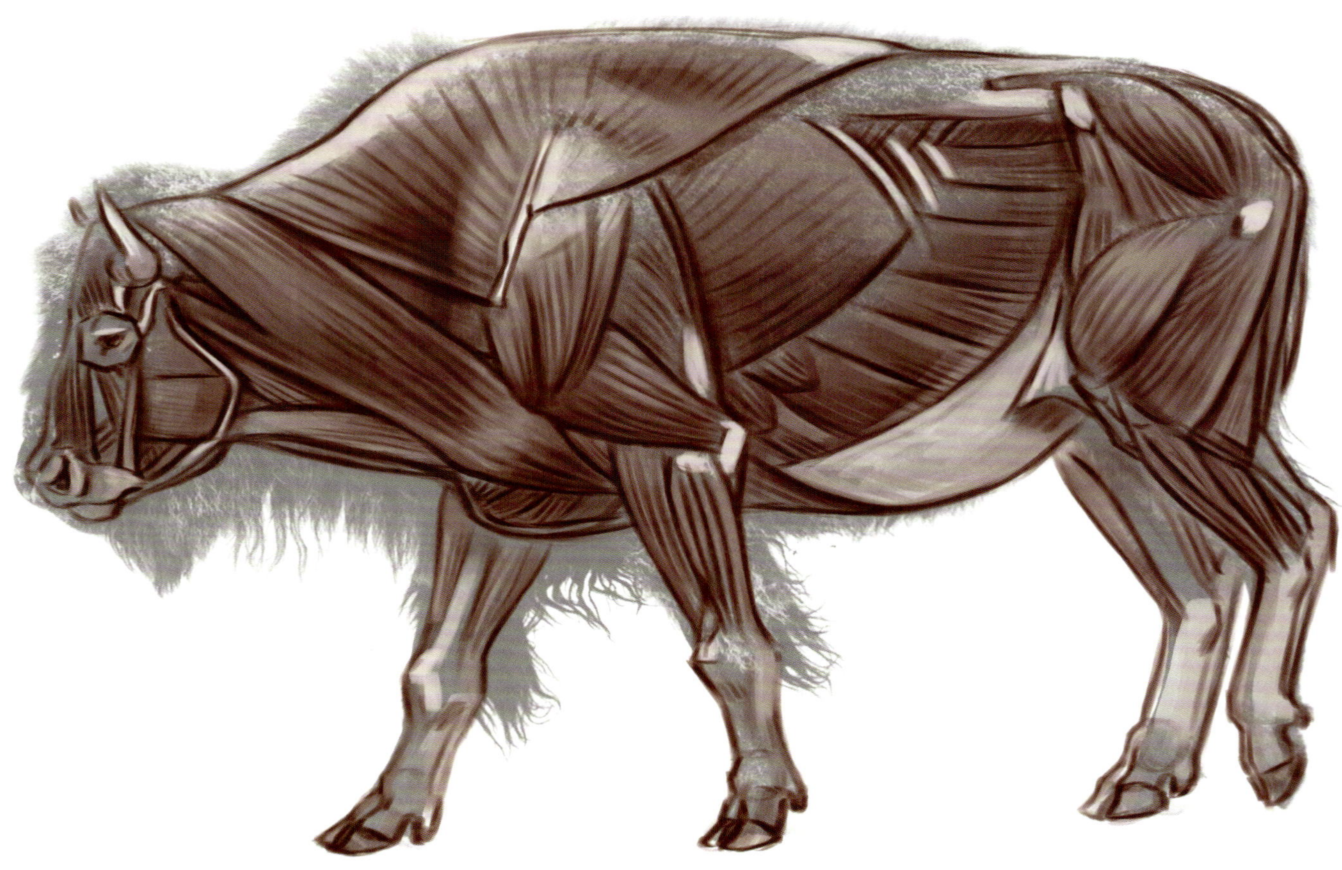

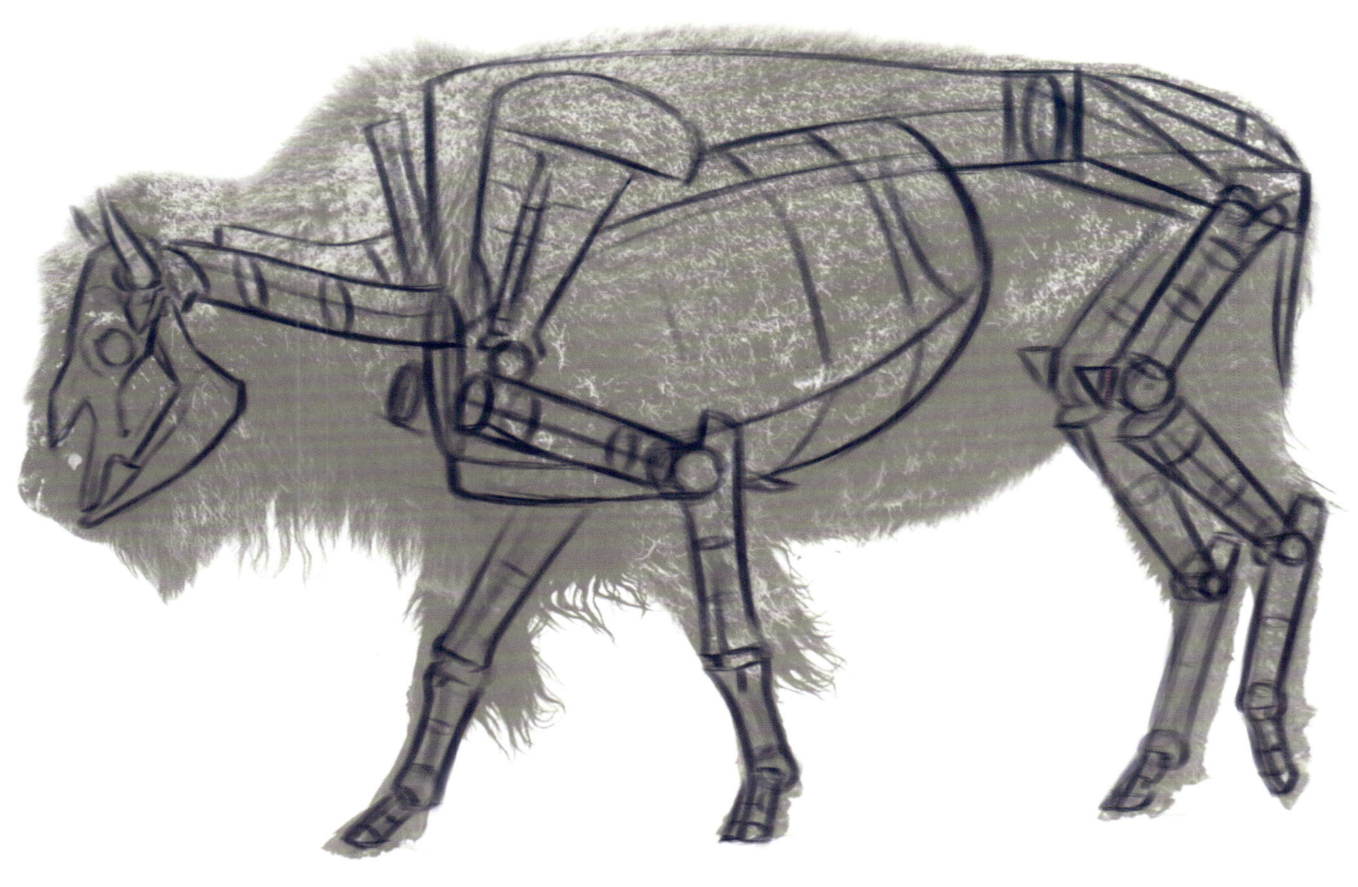

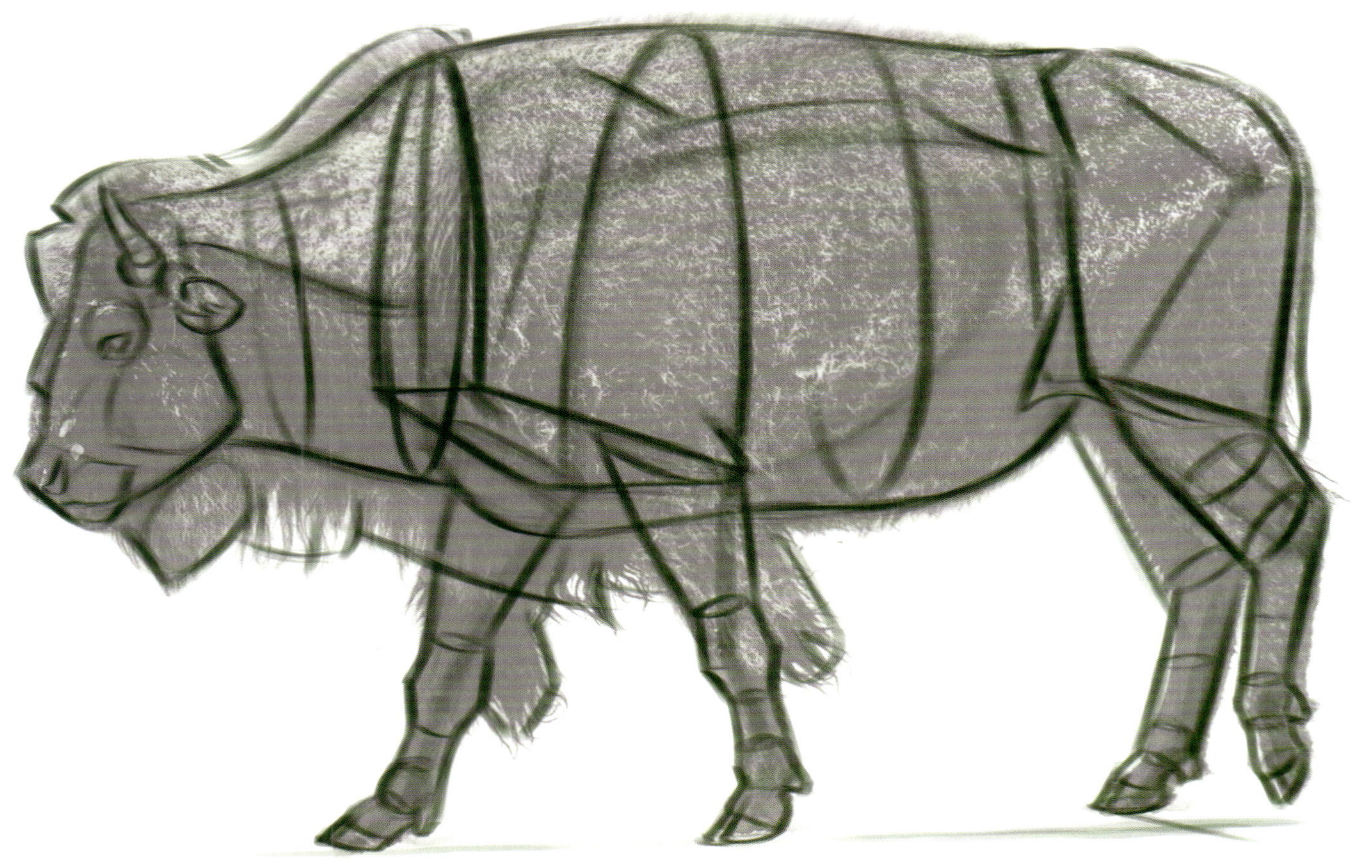

Photograph © Caroline Piek / Agami.nl

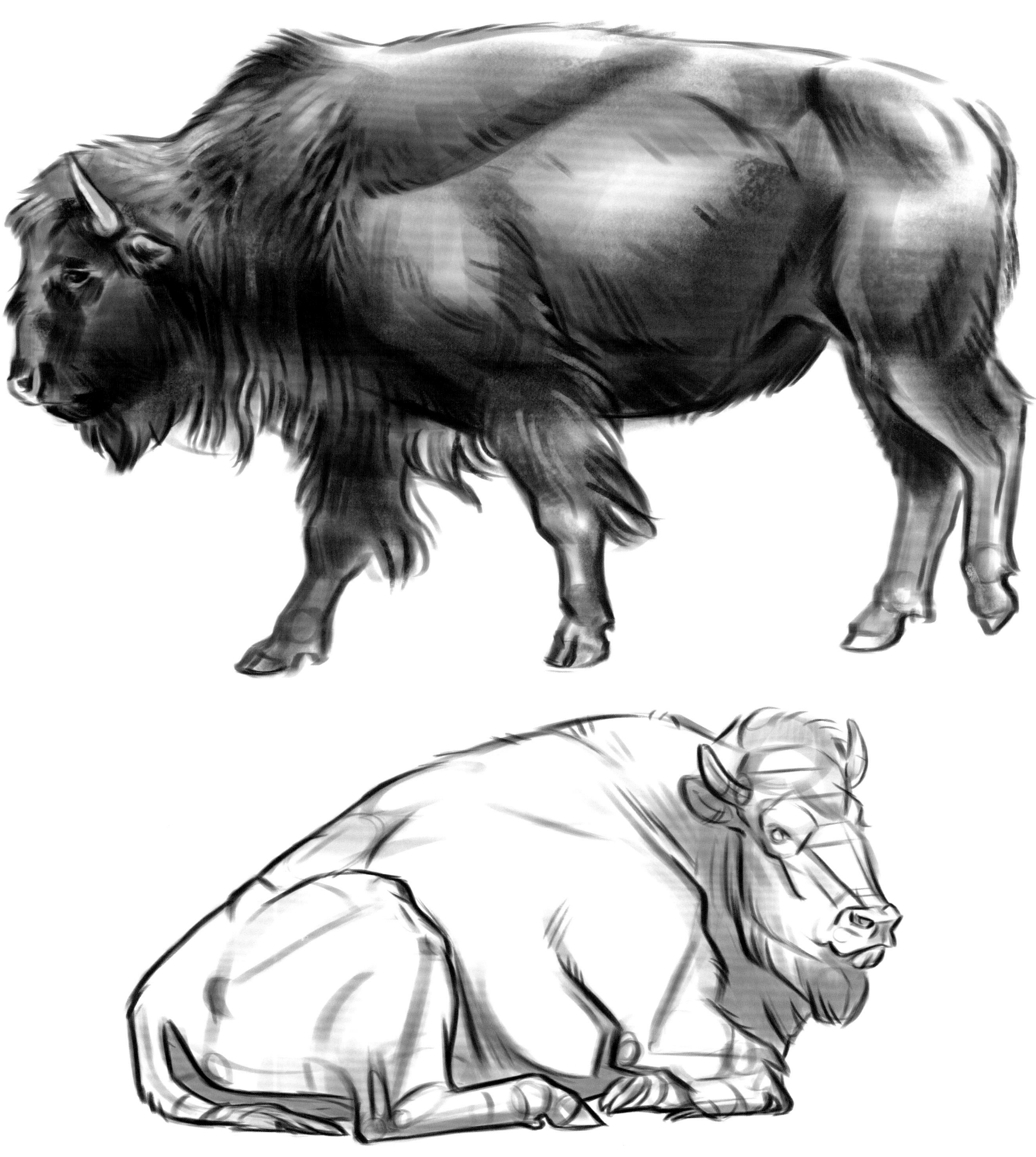

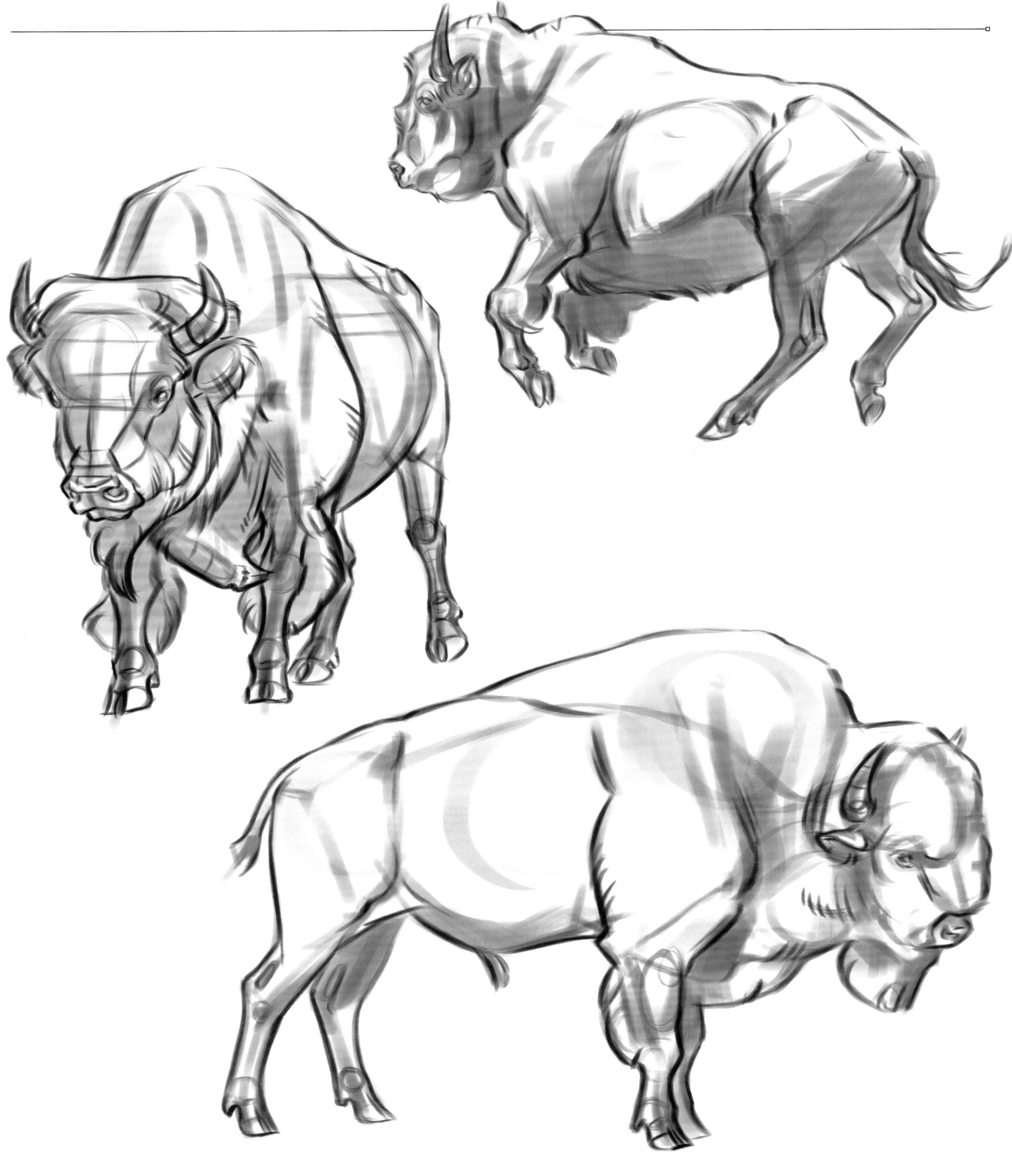

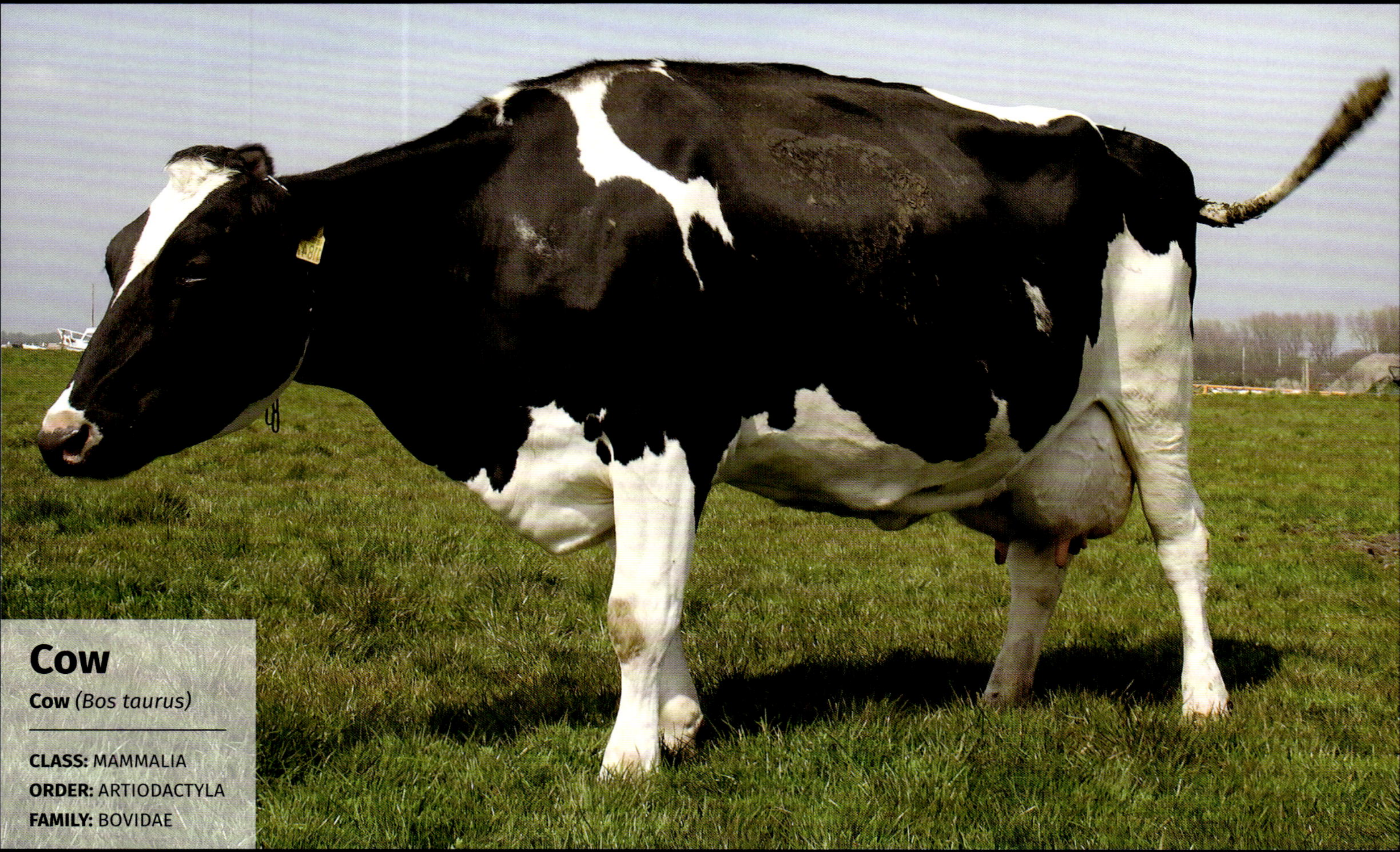

Cow

Cow *(Bos taurus)*

CLASS: MAMMALIA
ORDER: ARTIODACTYLA
FAMILY: BOVIDAE

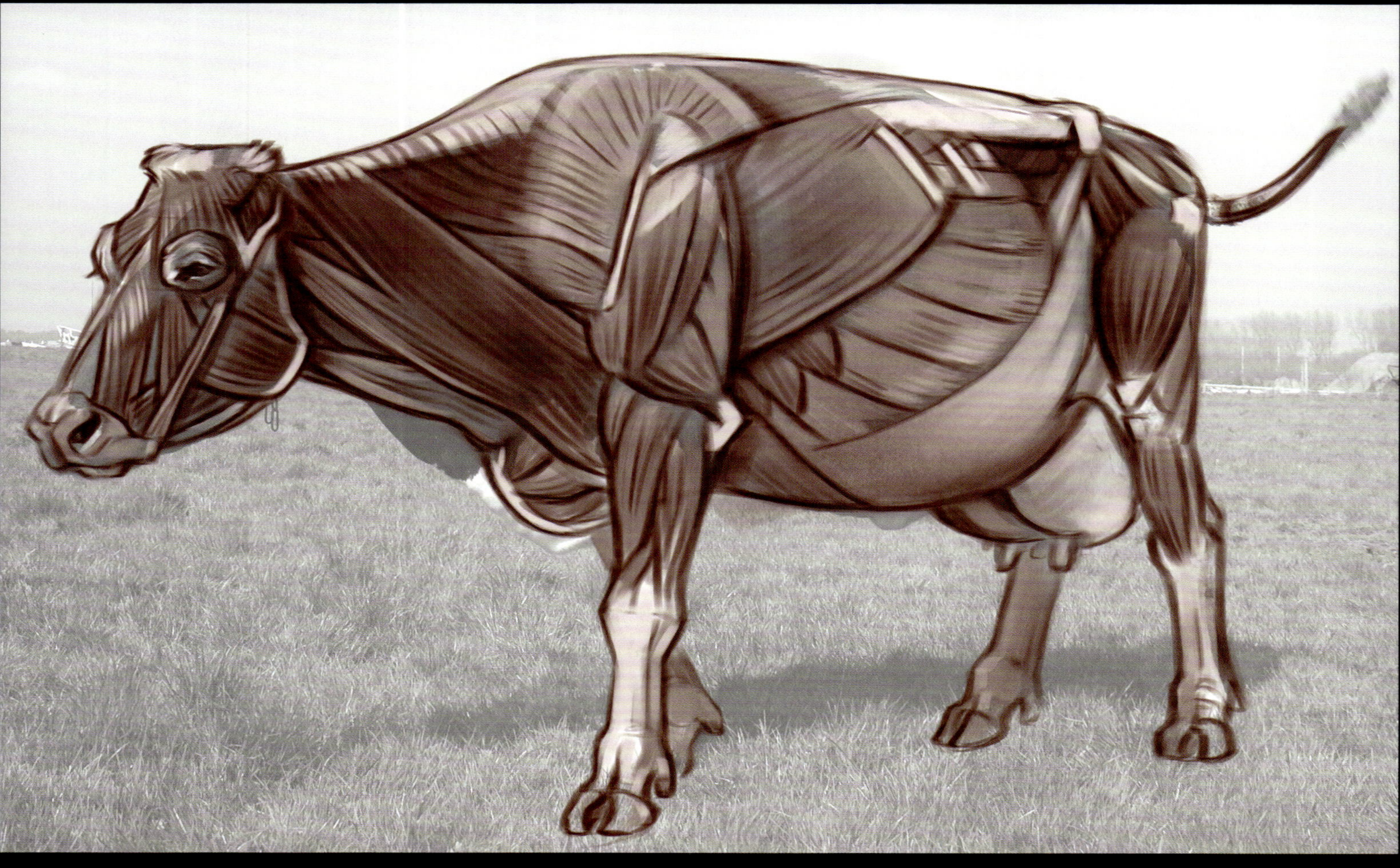

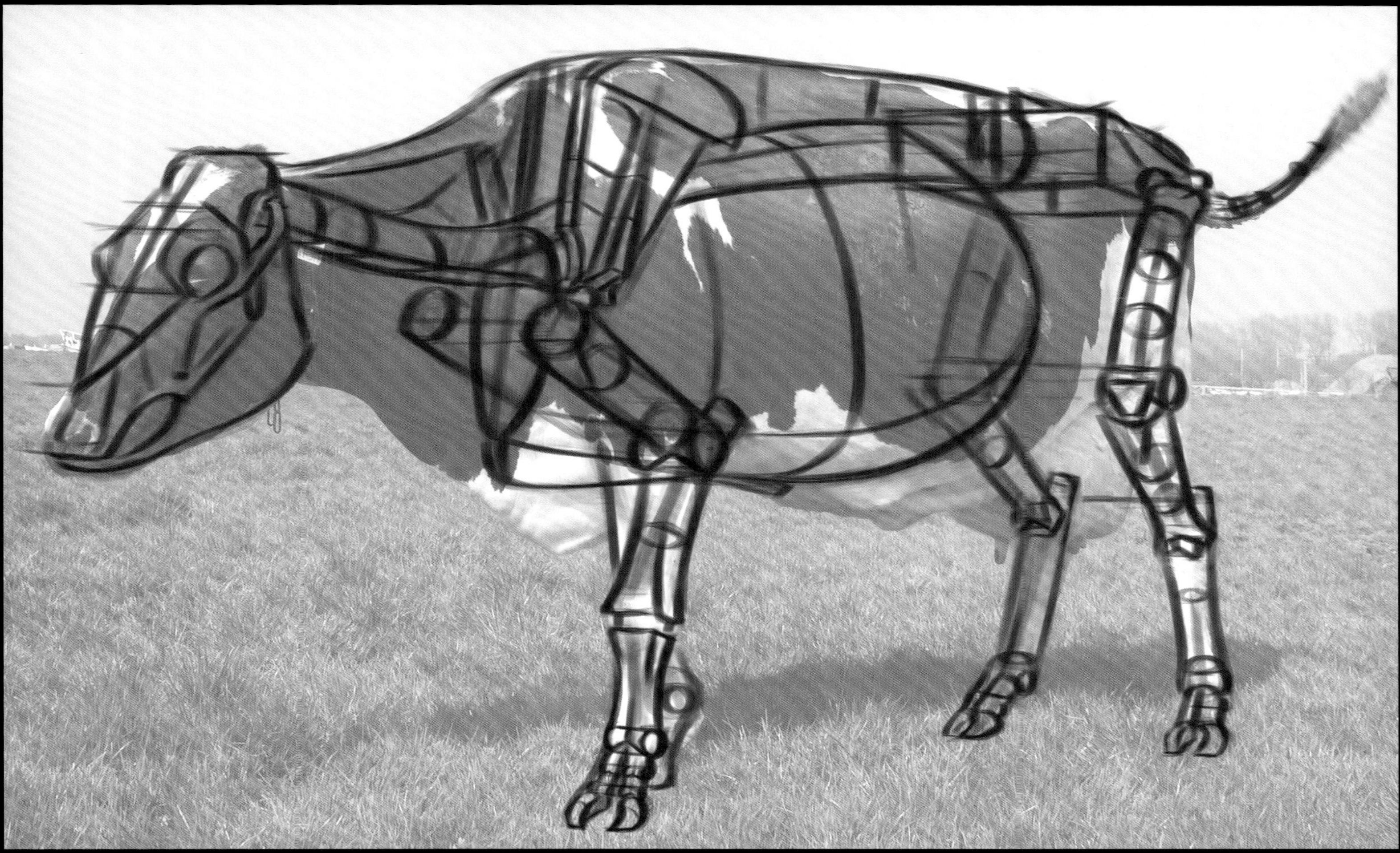

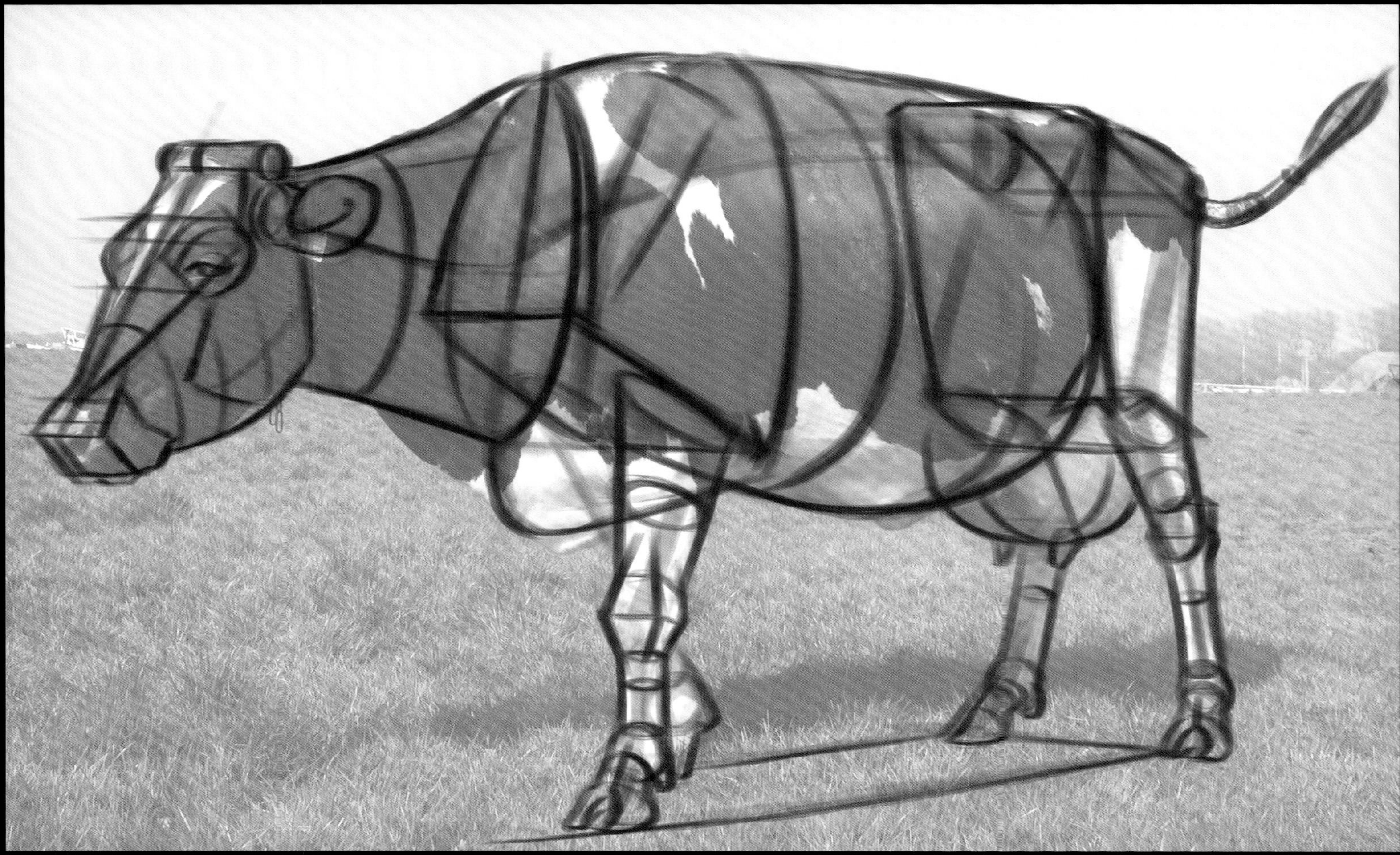

Photograph © Arnold Meijer / Agami.nl

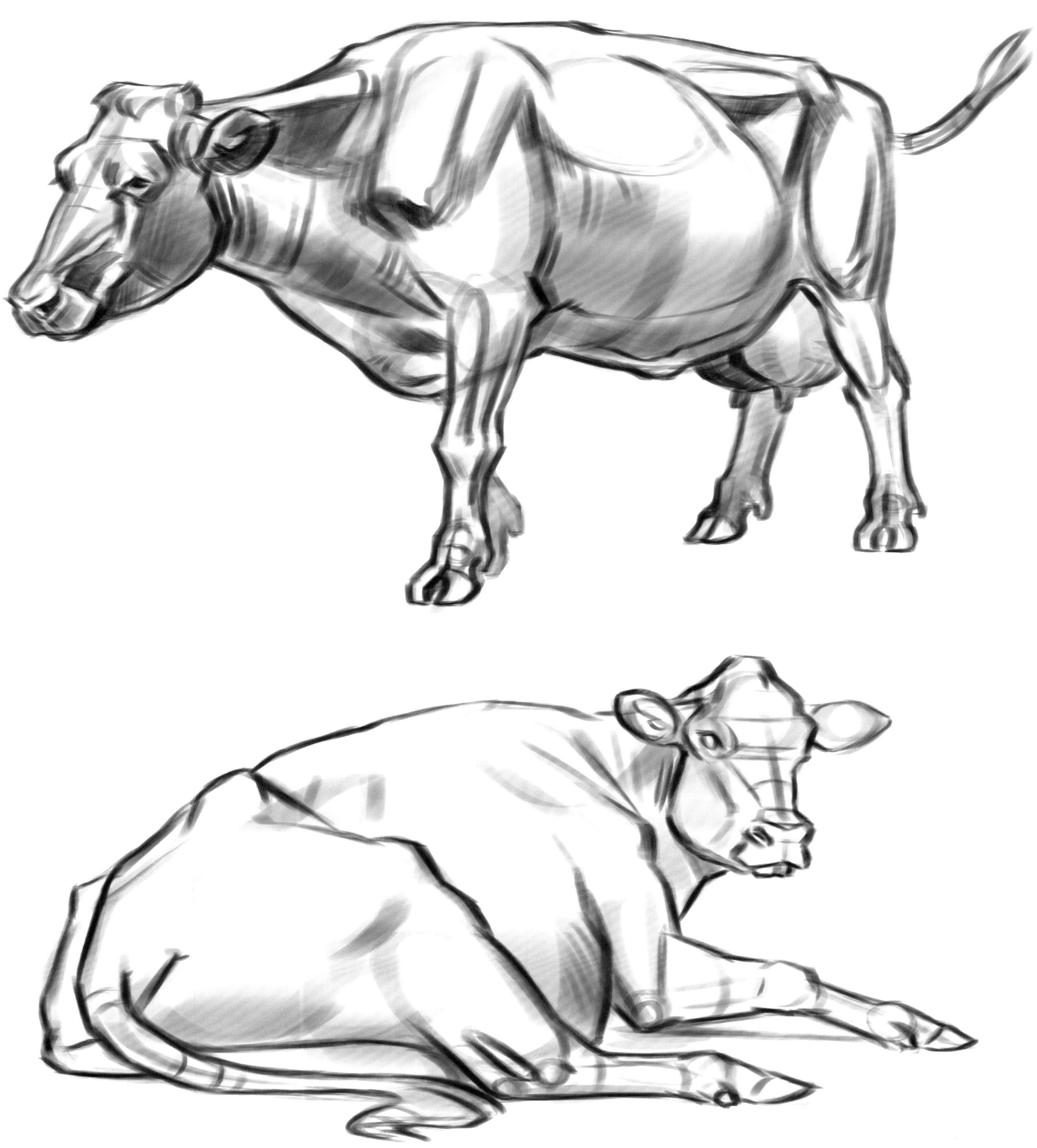

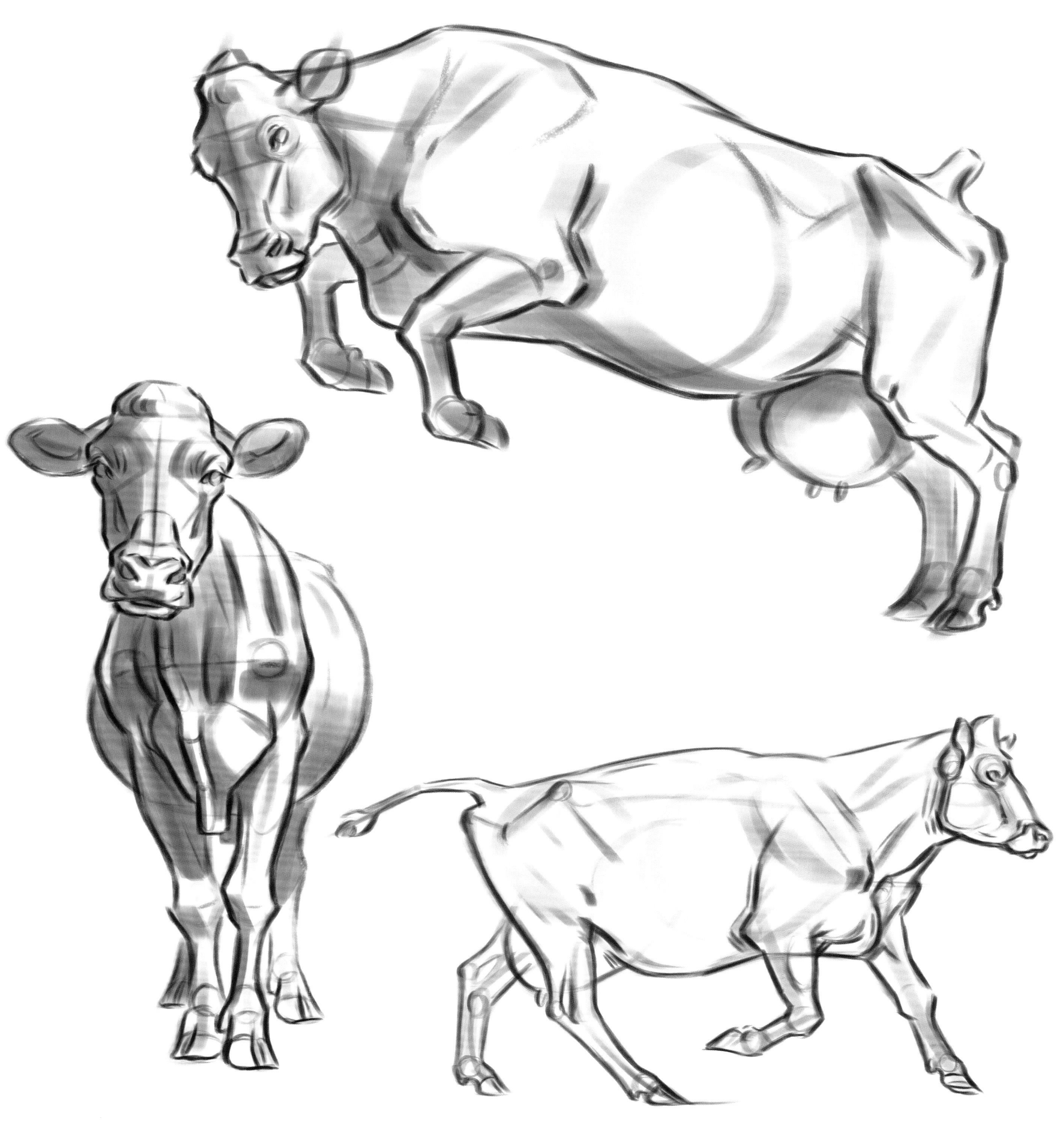

Goat

Domestic goat

(Capra aegagrus hircus)

CLASS: MAMMALIA
ORDER: ARTIODACTYLA
FAMILY: BOVIDAE

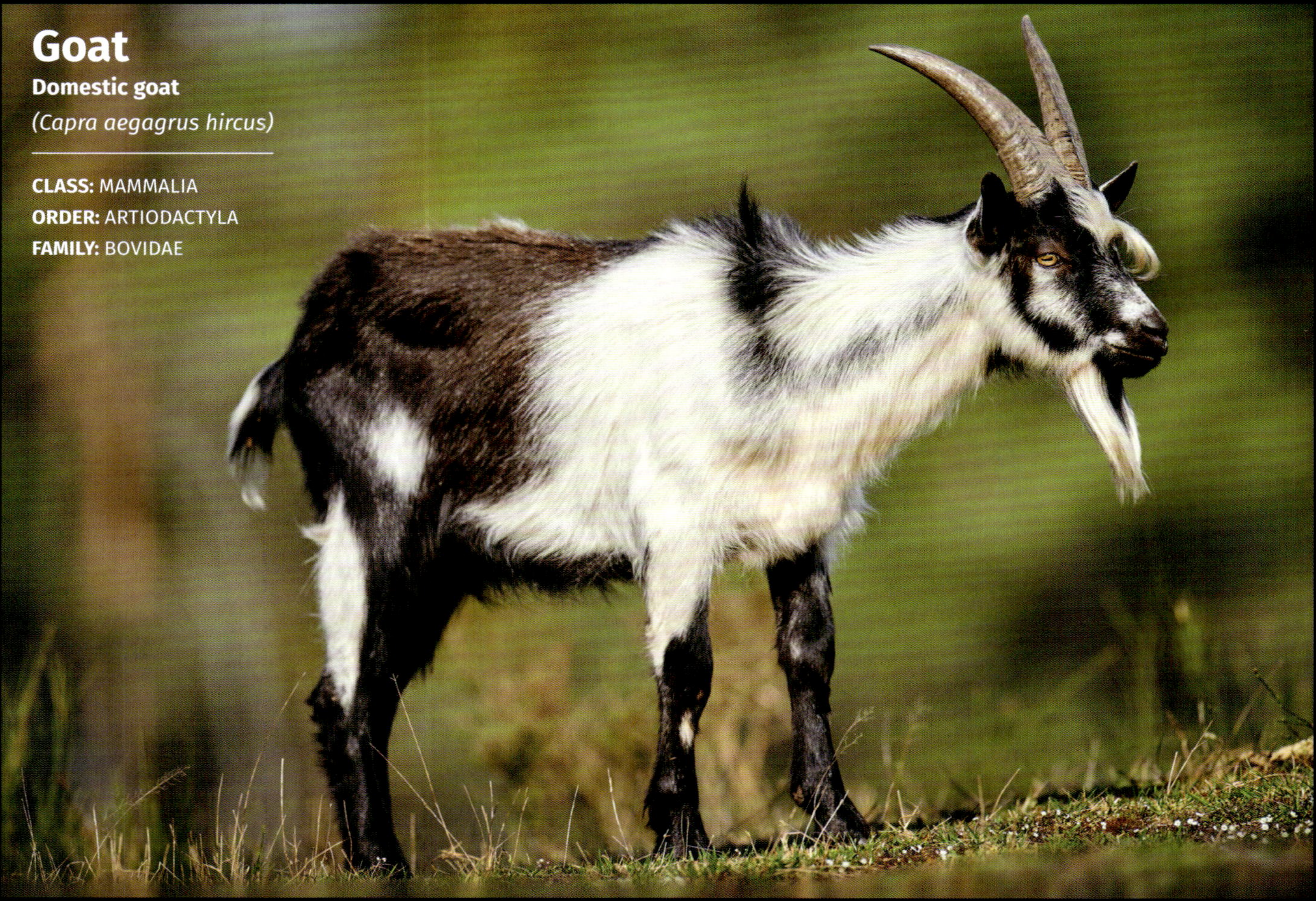

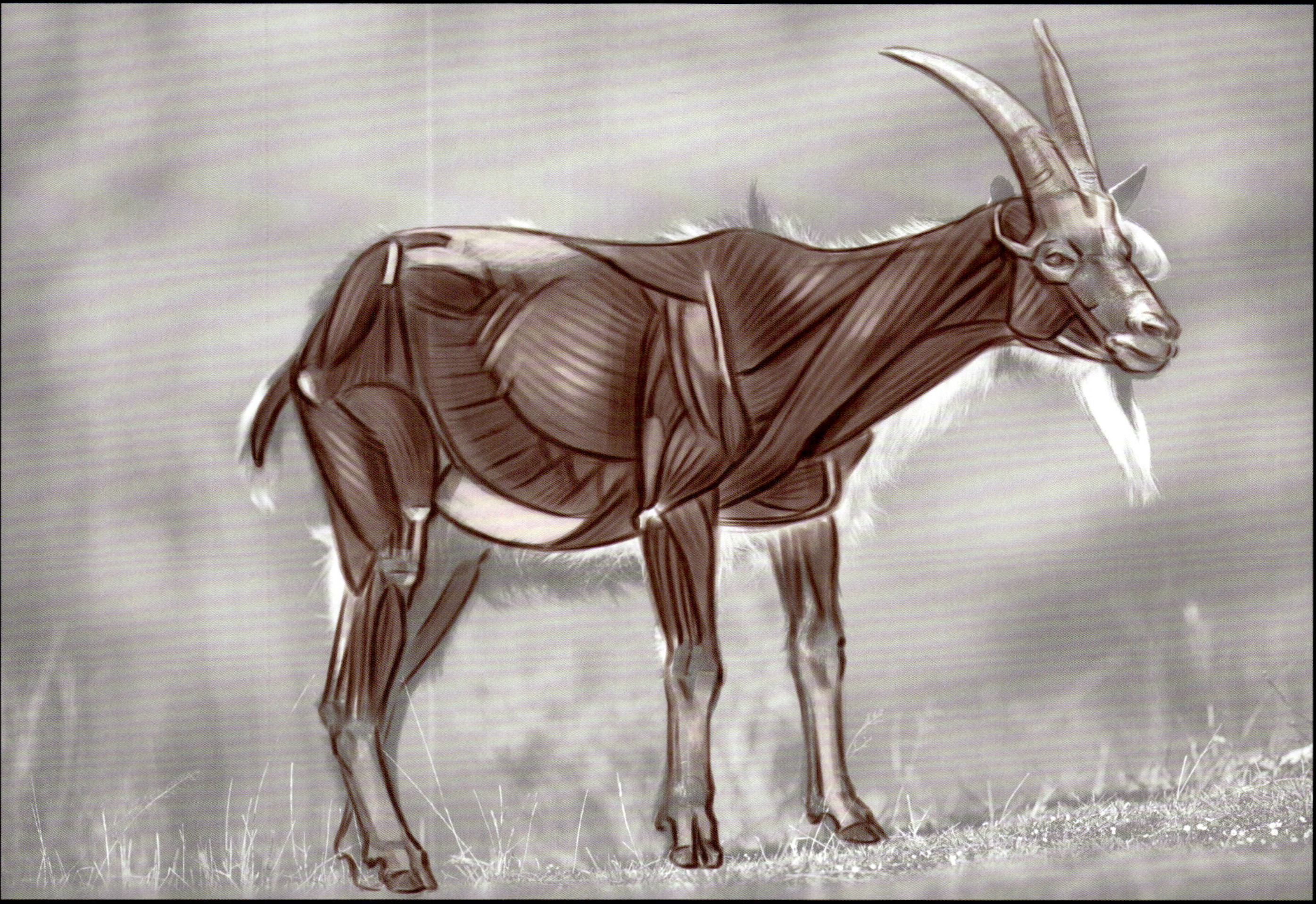

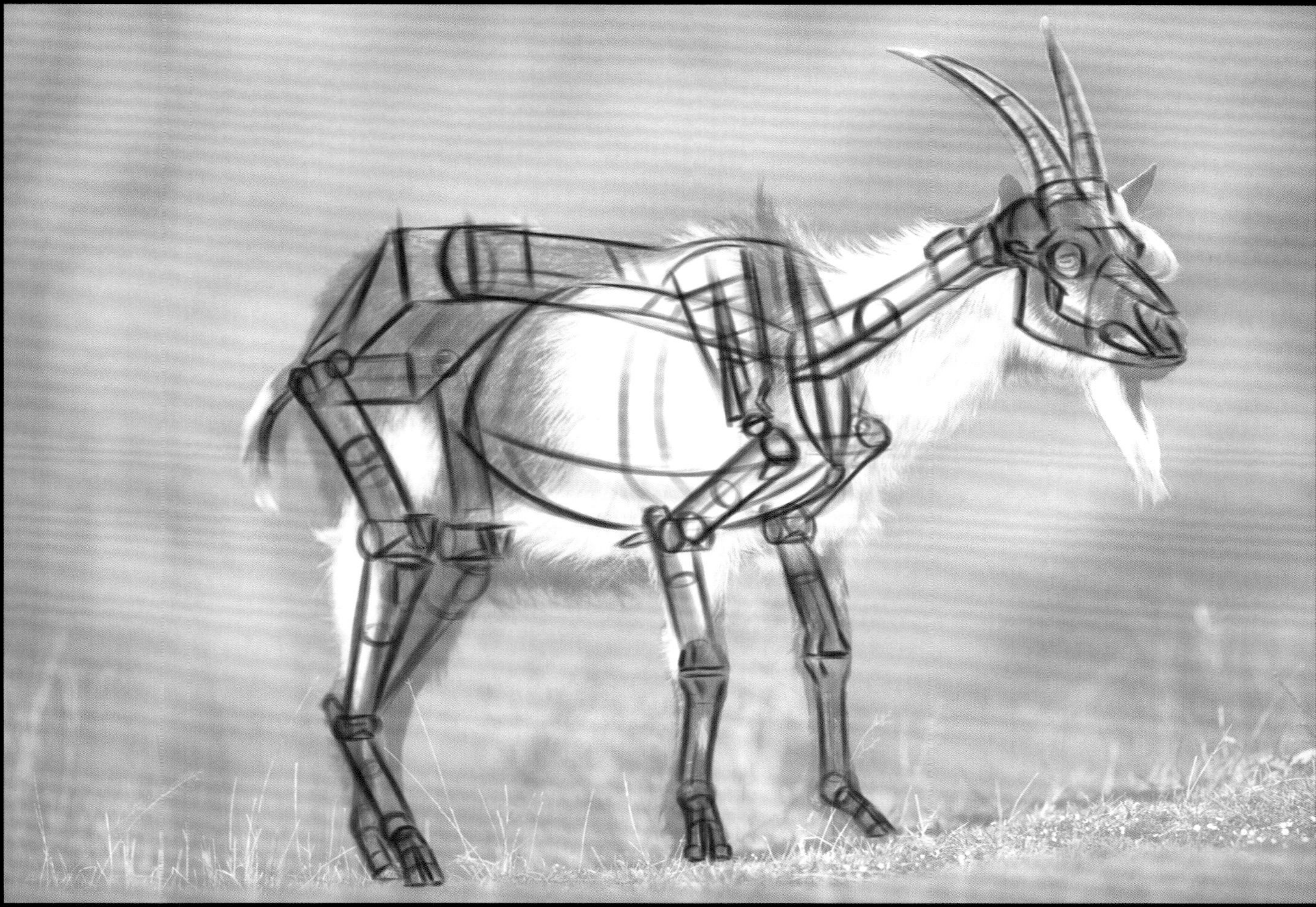

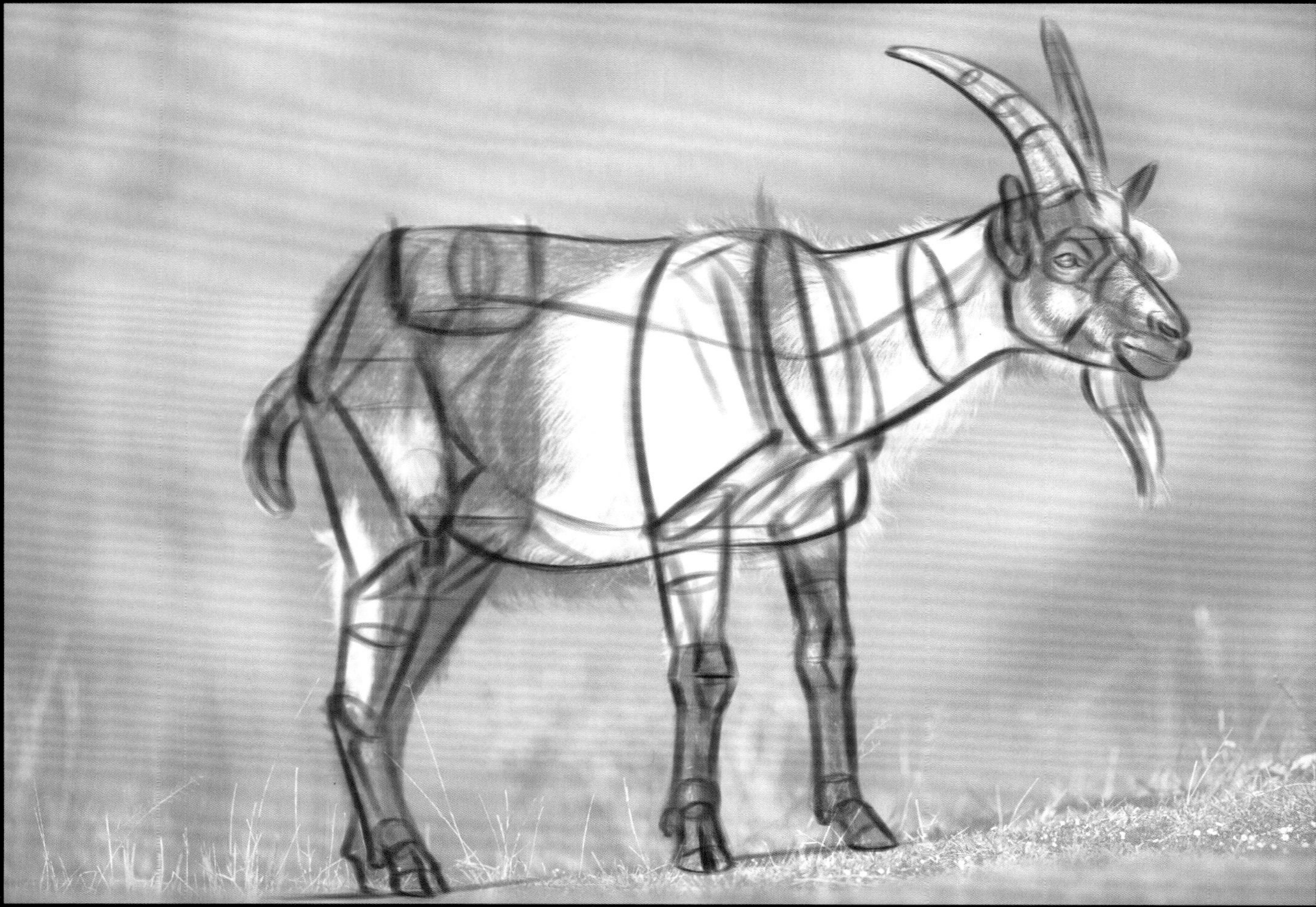

Photograph © imageBROKER.com / David & Micha Sheldon

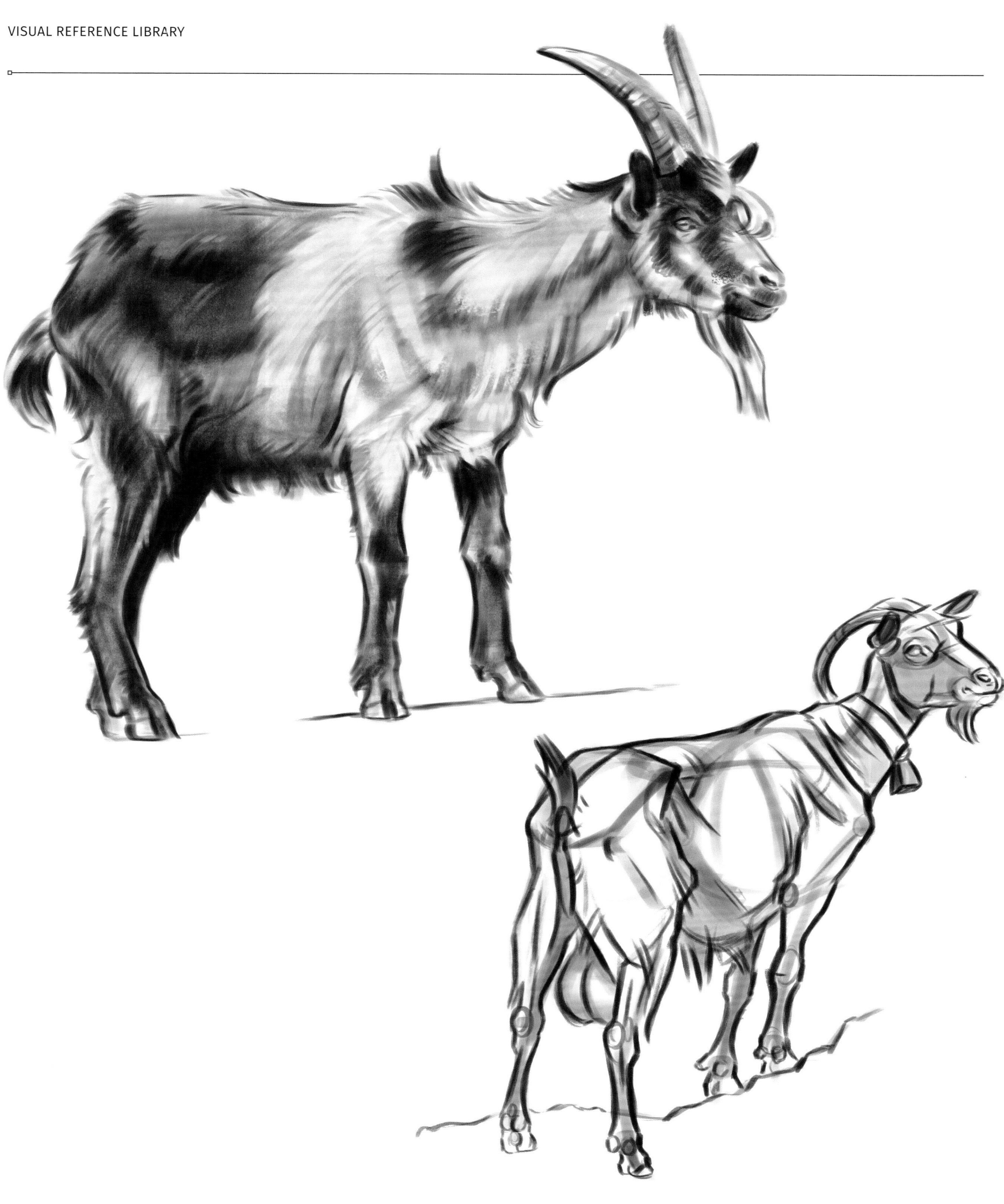

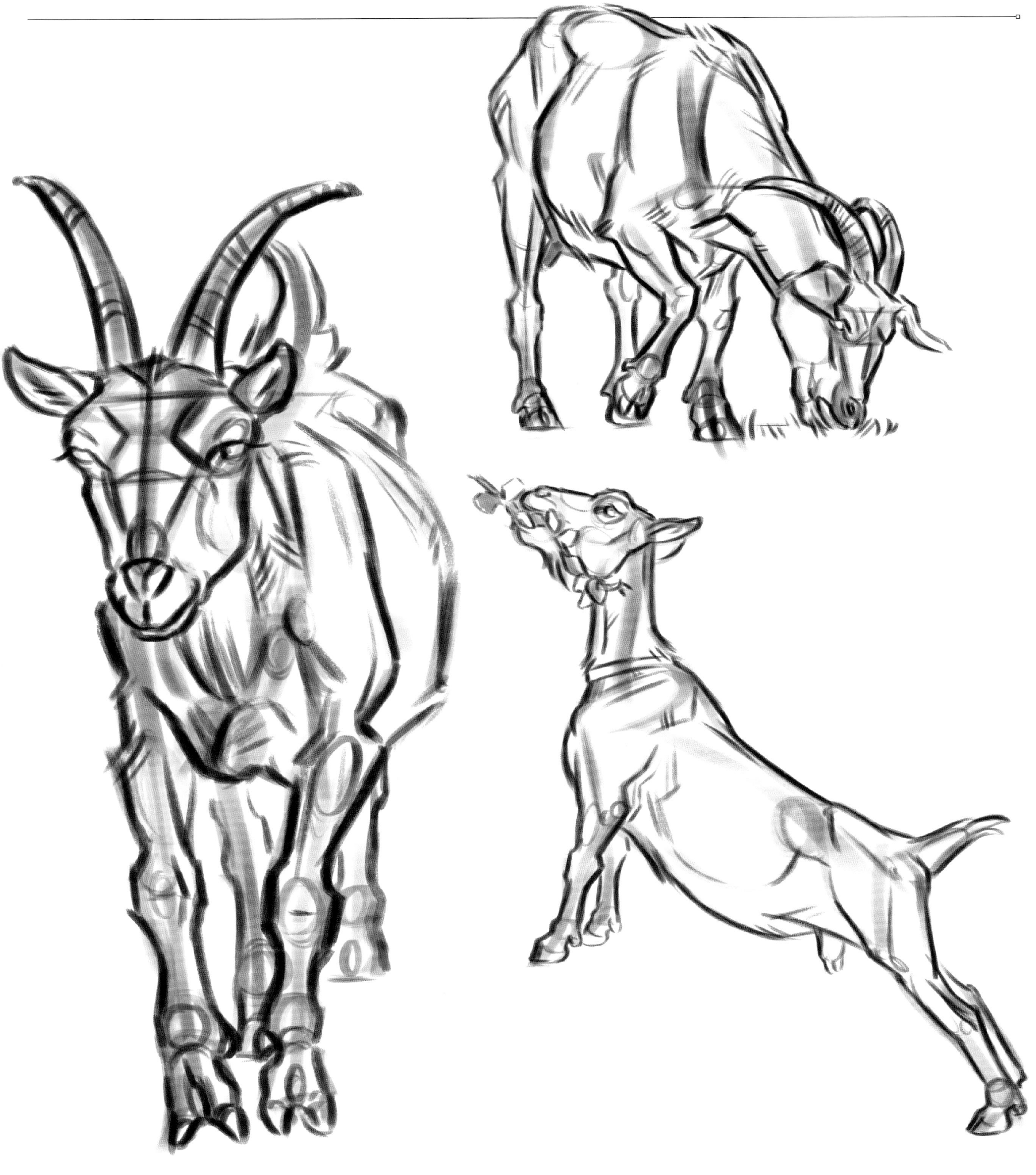

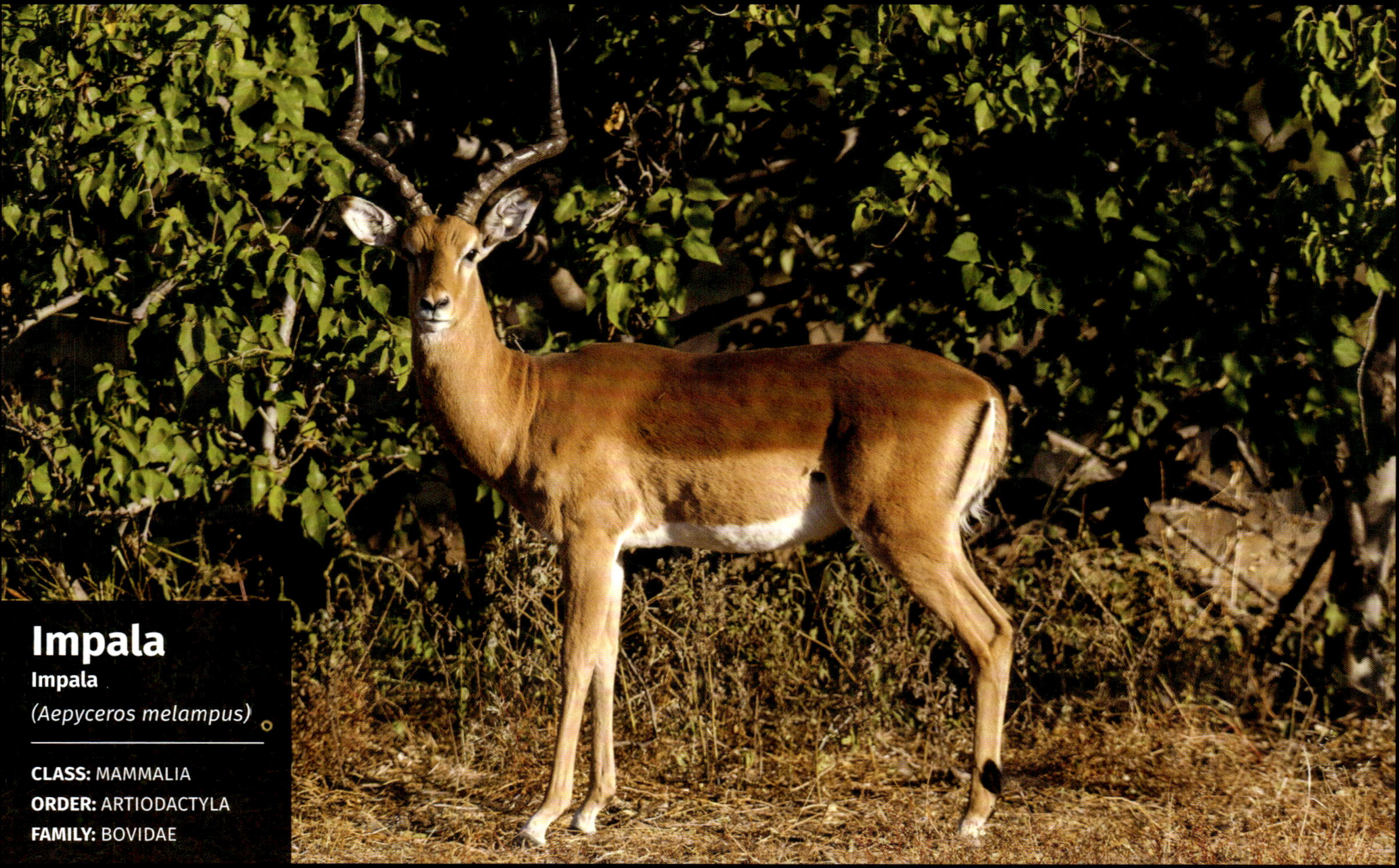

Impala

Impala

(Aepyceros melampus)

CLASS: MAMMALIA

ORDER: ARTIODACTYLA

FAMILY: BOVIDAE

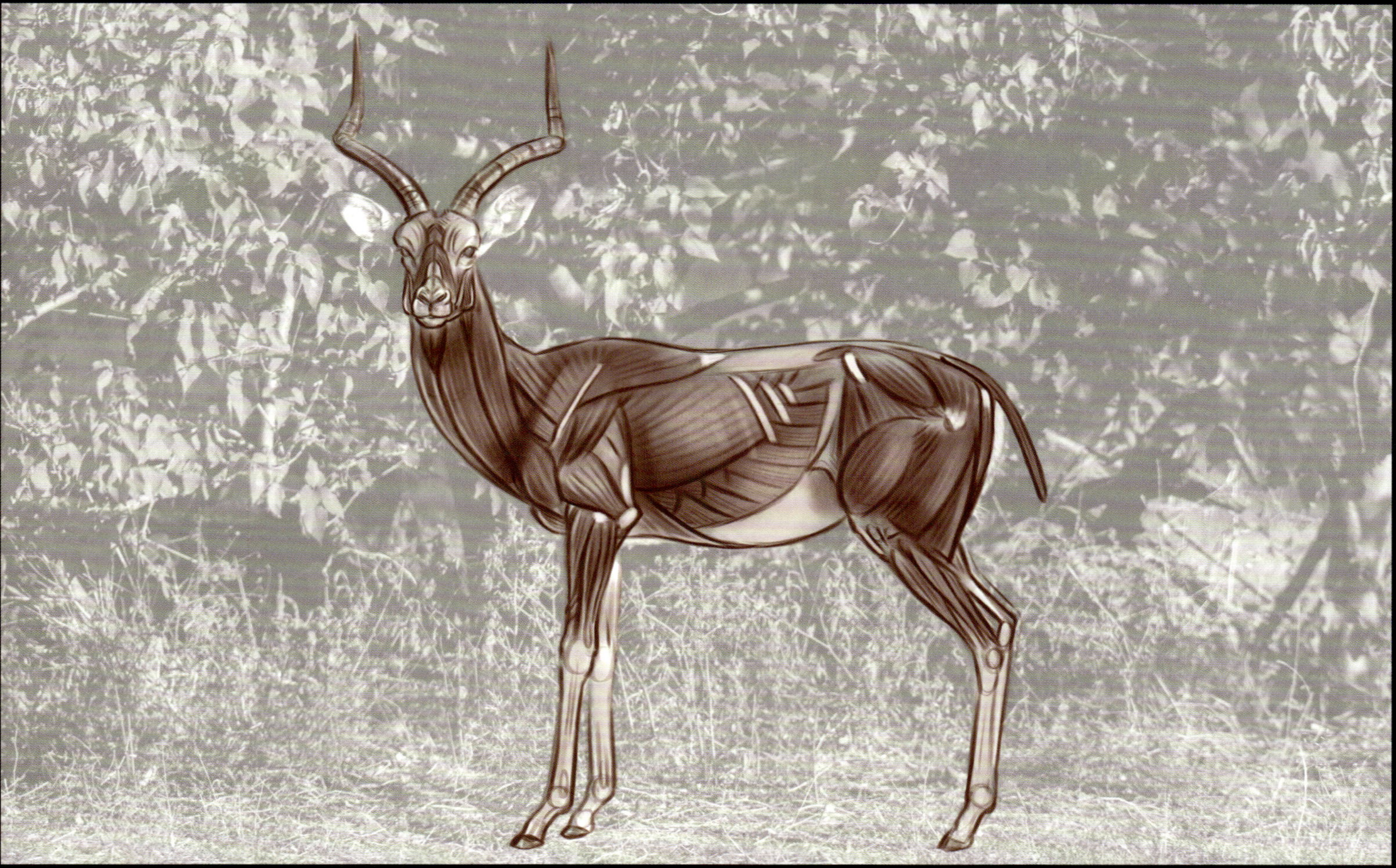

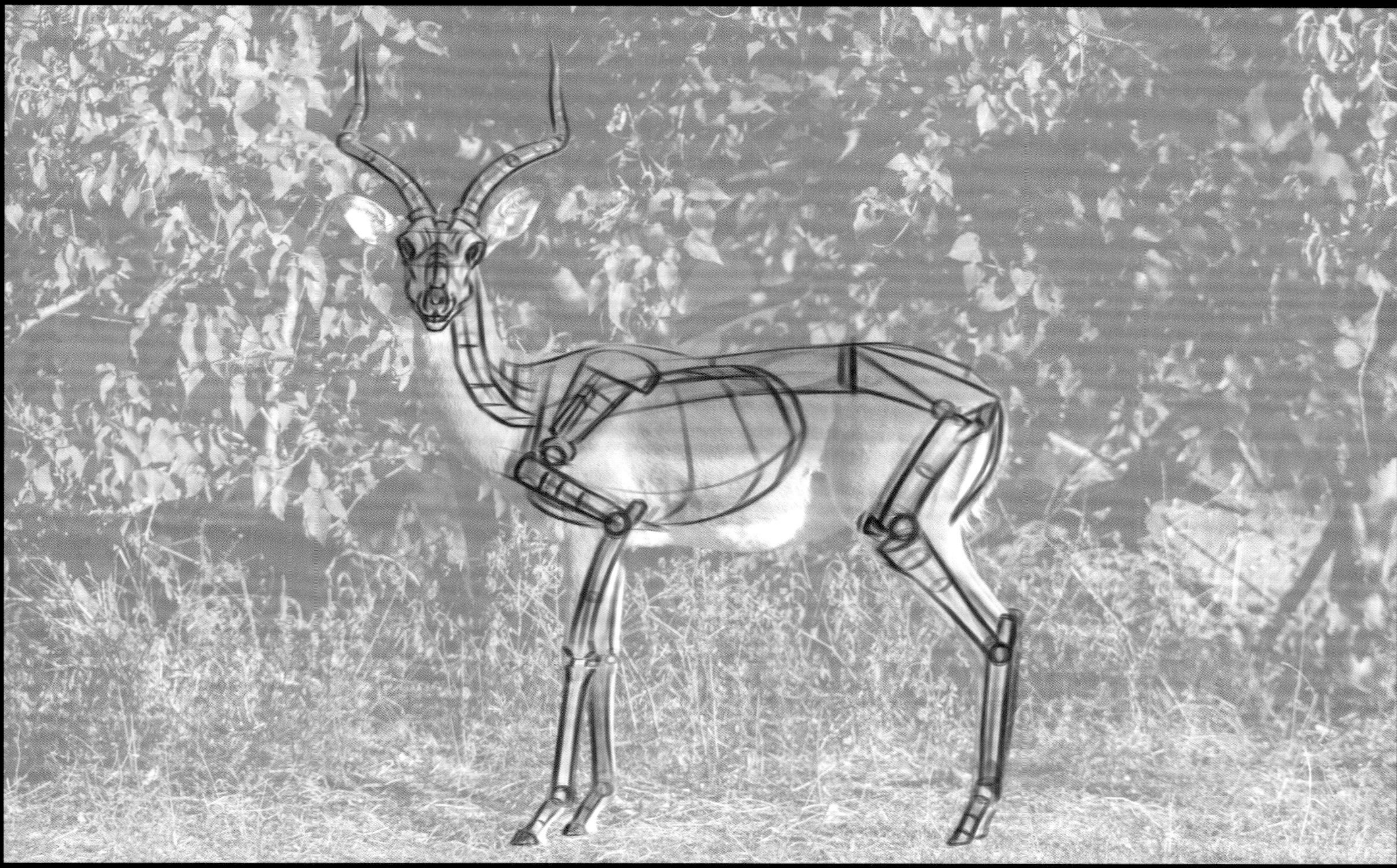

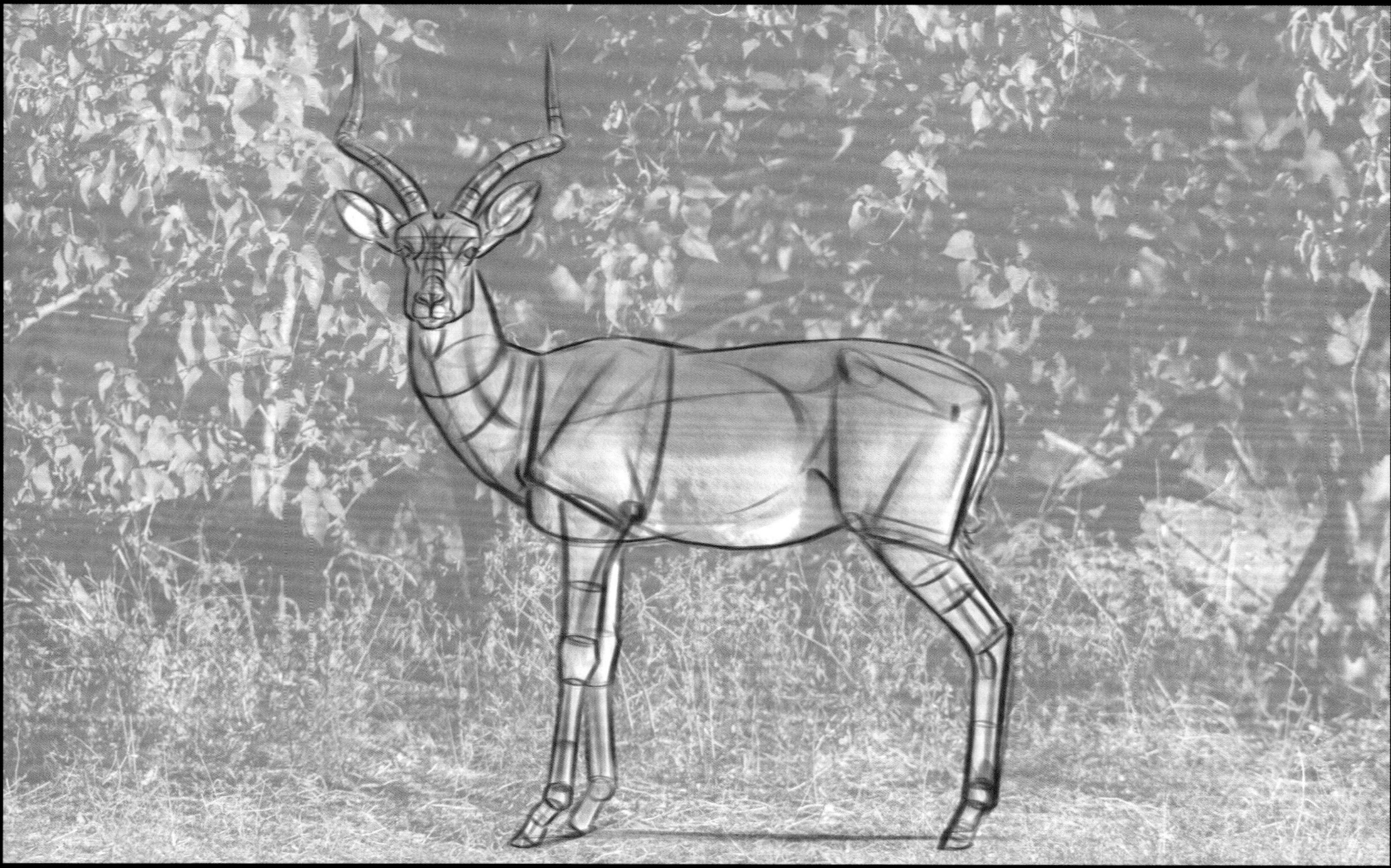

Photograph © Sergio Pitamitz/ Agami.nl

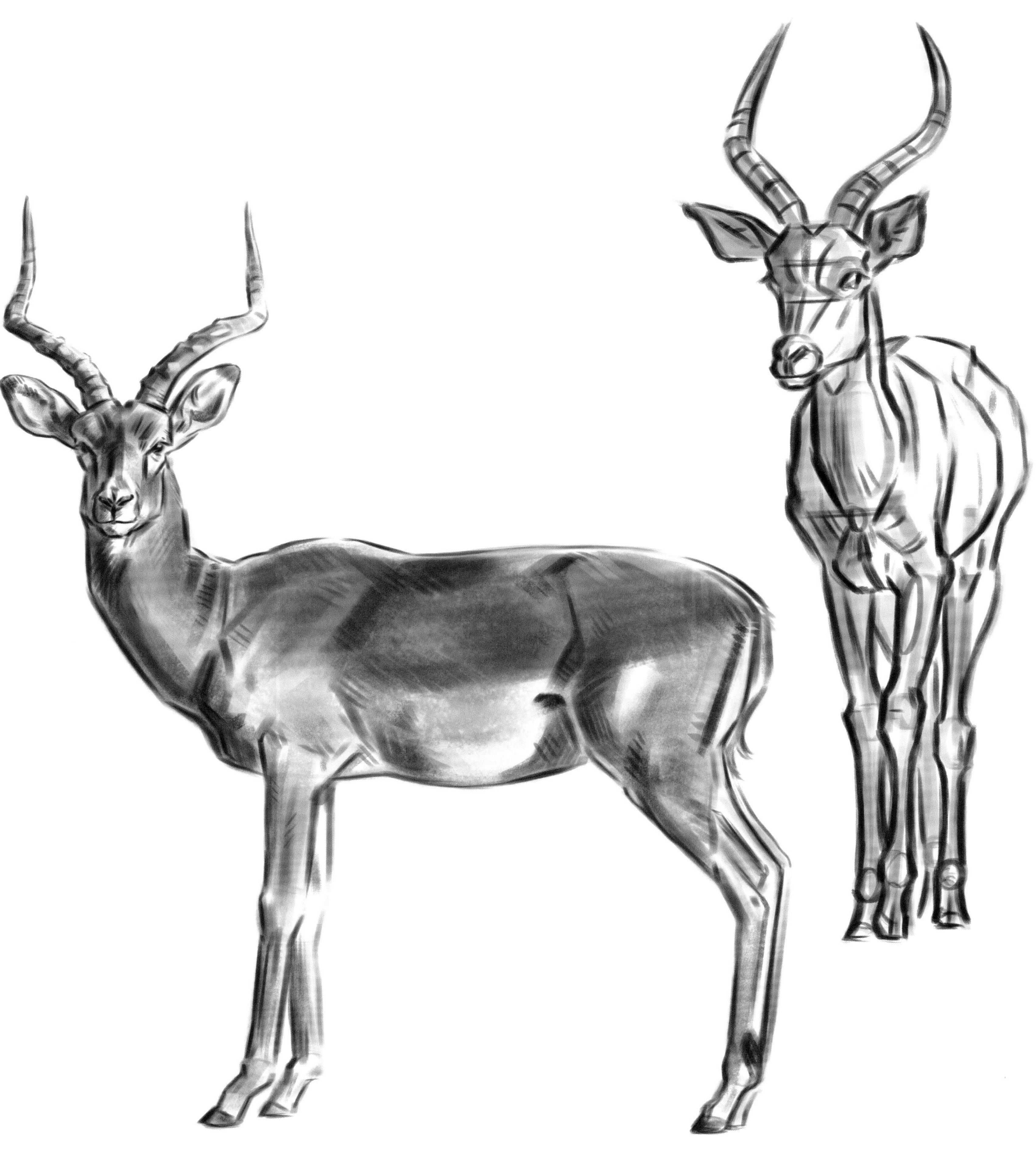

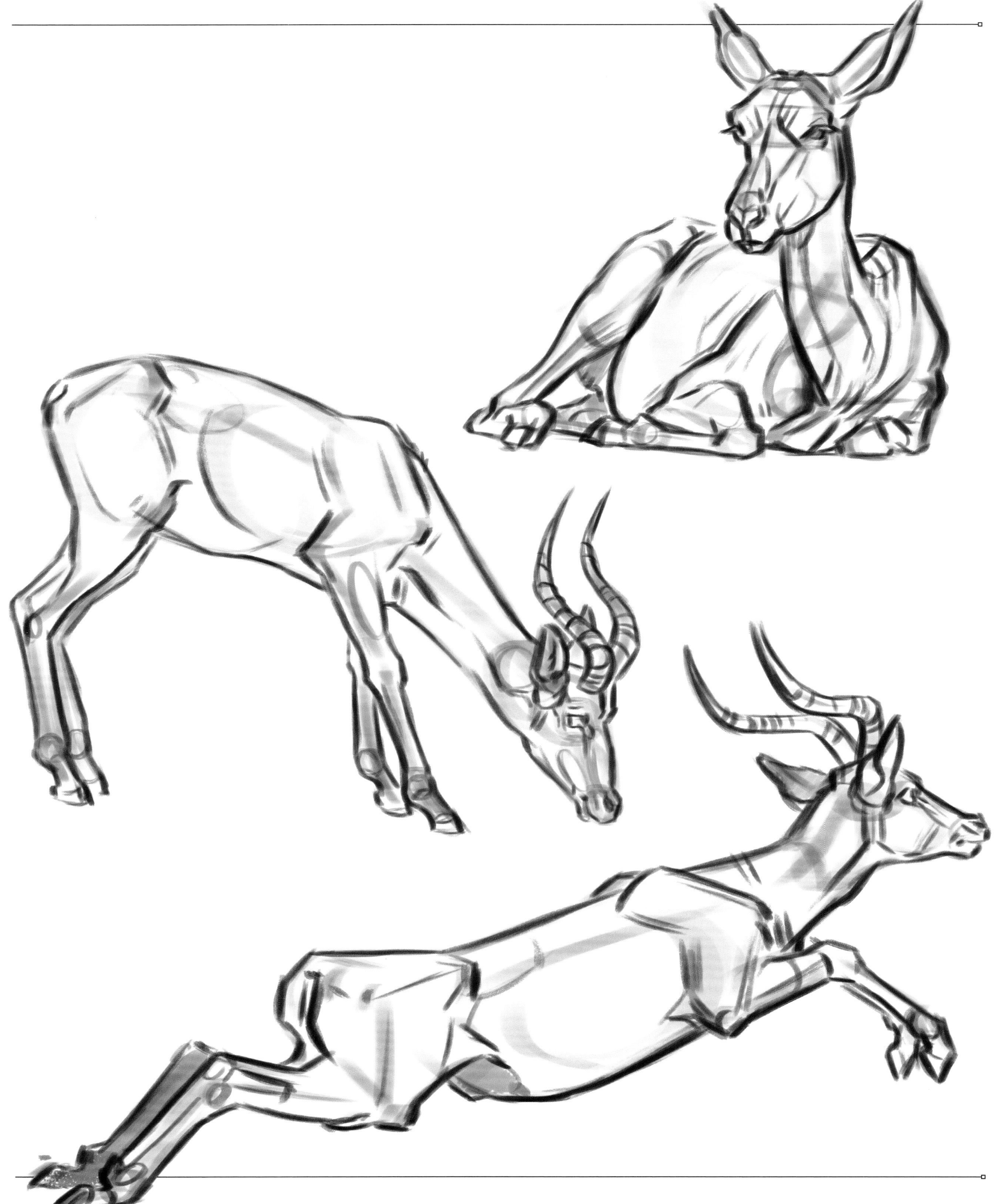

Sheep

Drents Friese sheep

(Ovis aries)

CLASS: MAMMALIA
ORDER: ARTIODACTYLA
FAMILY: BOVIDAE

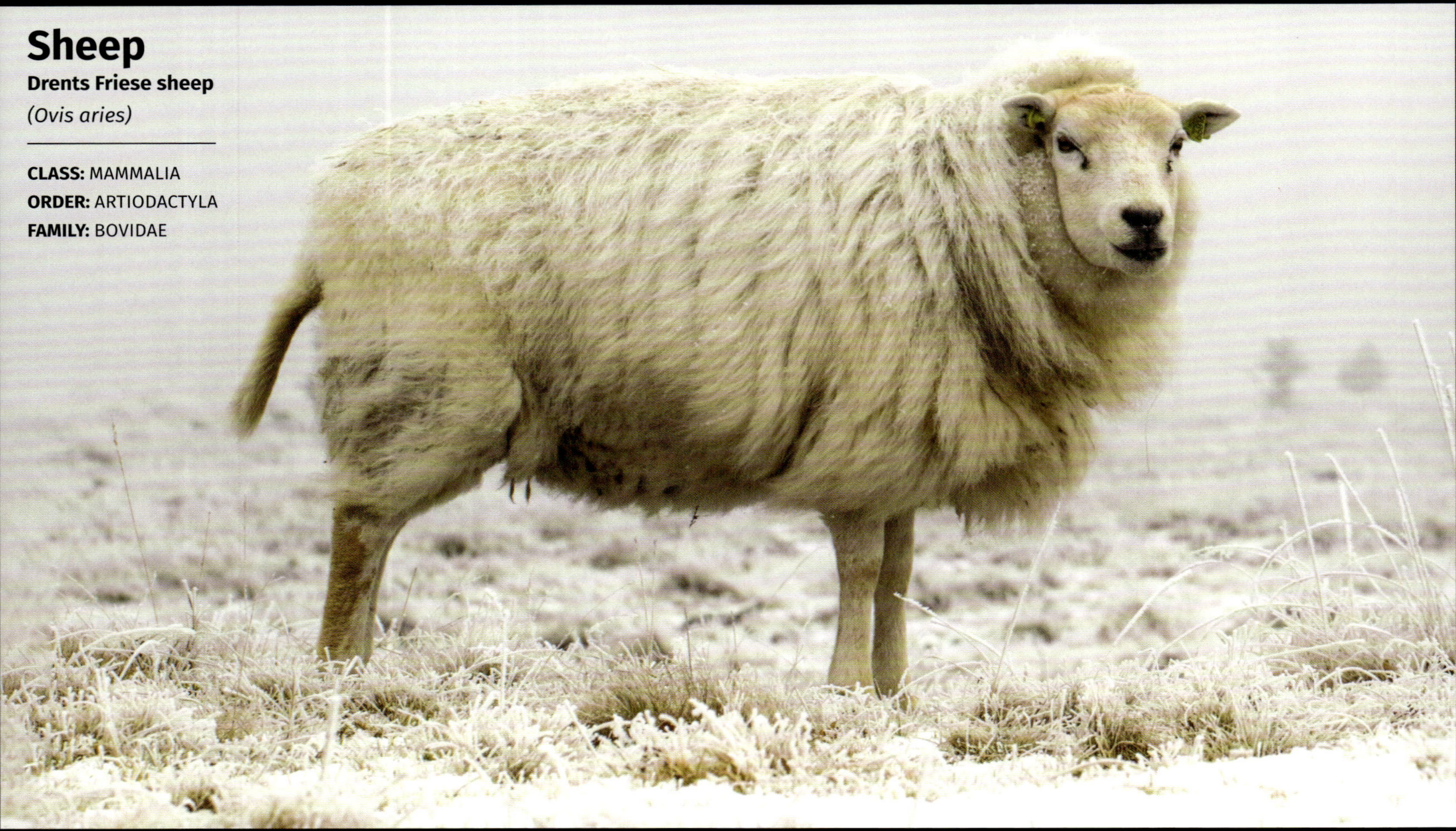

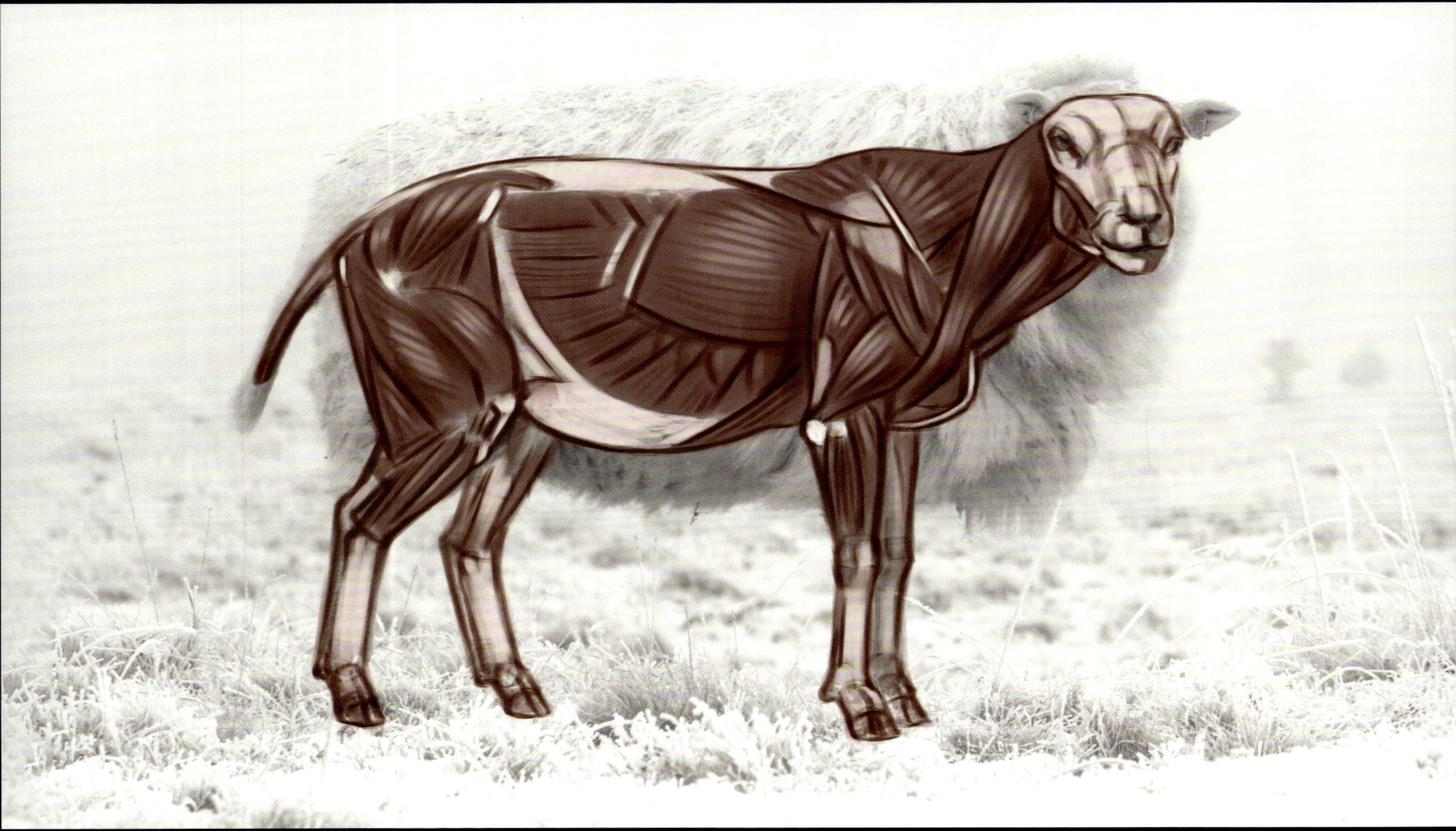

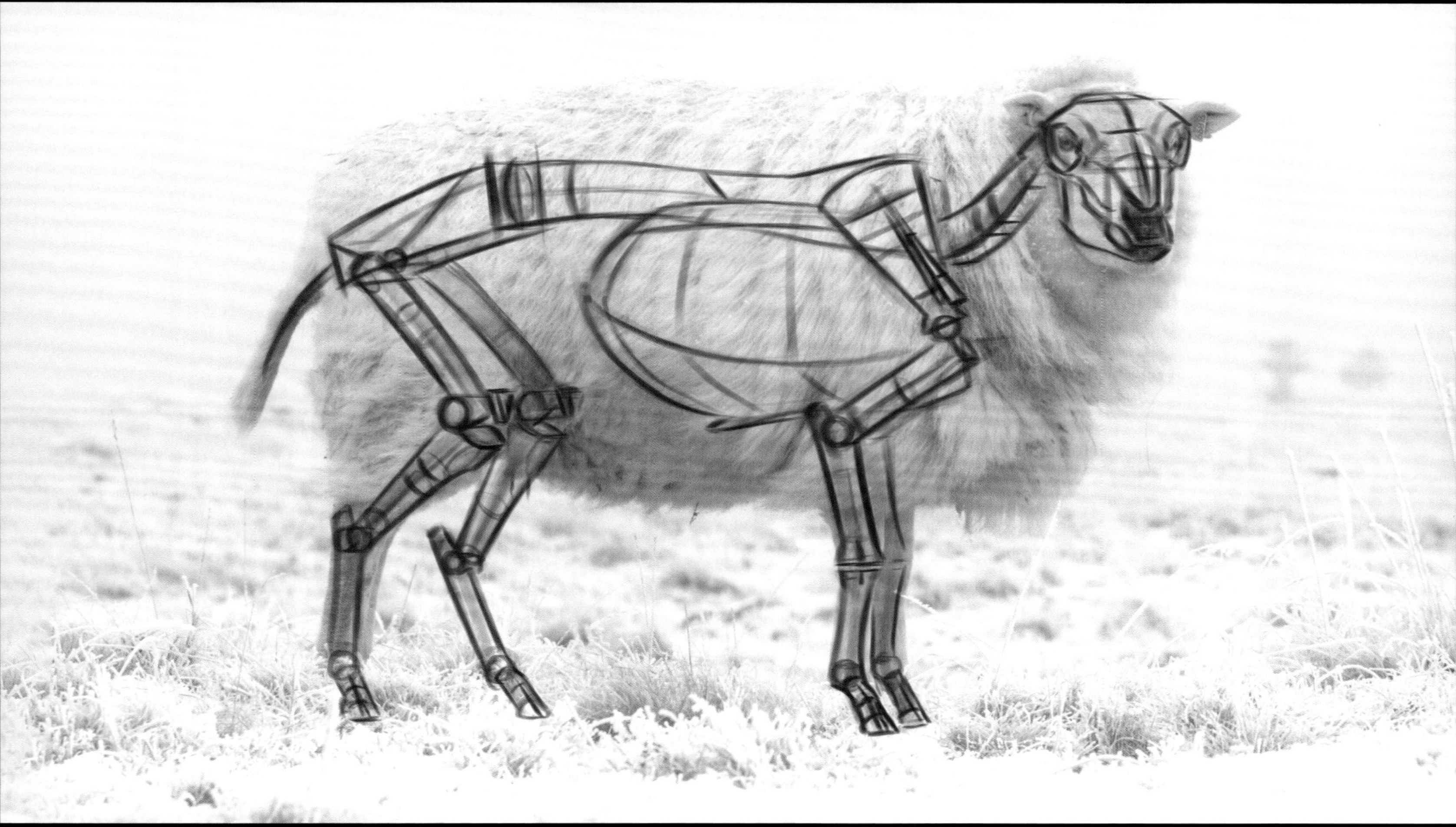

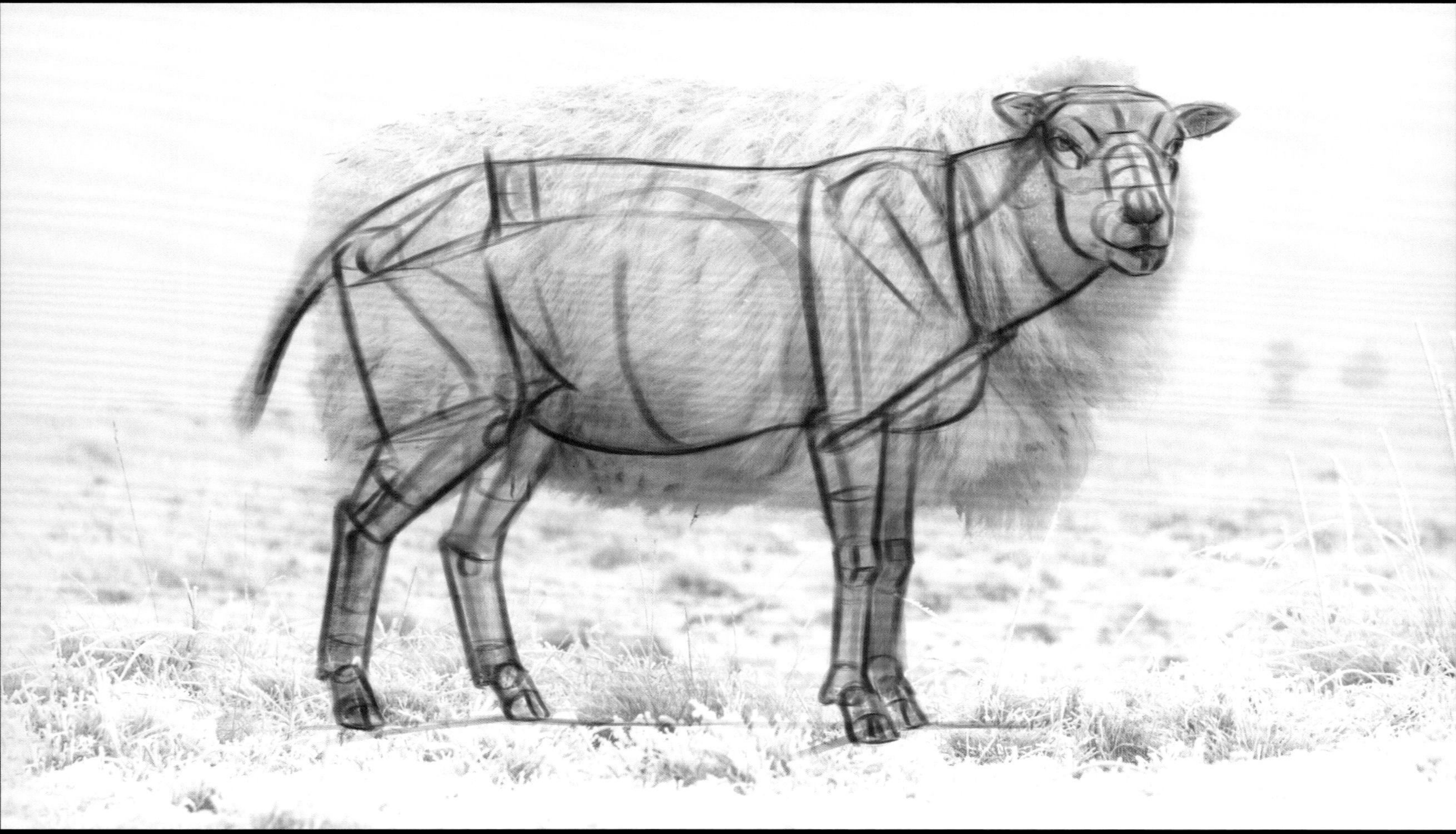

Photograph © Wil Leurs/ Agami.nl

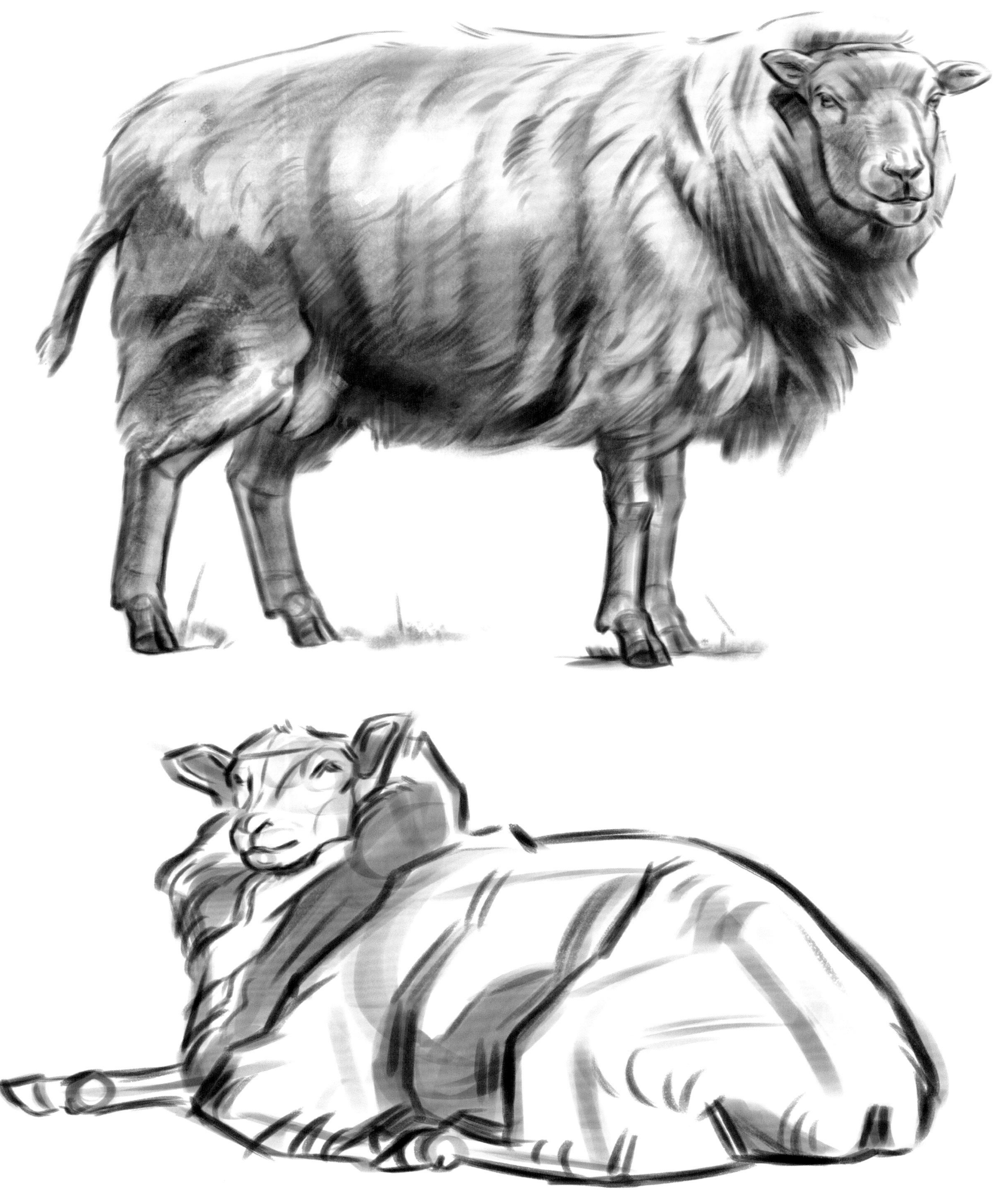

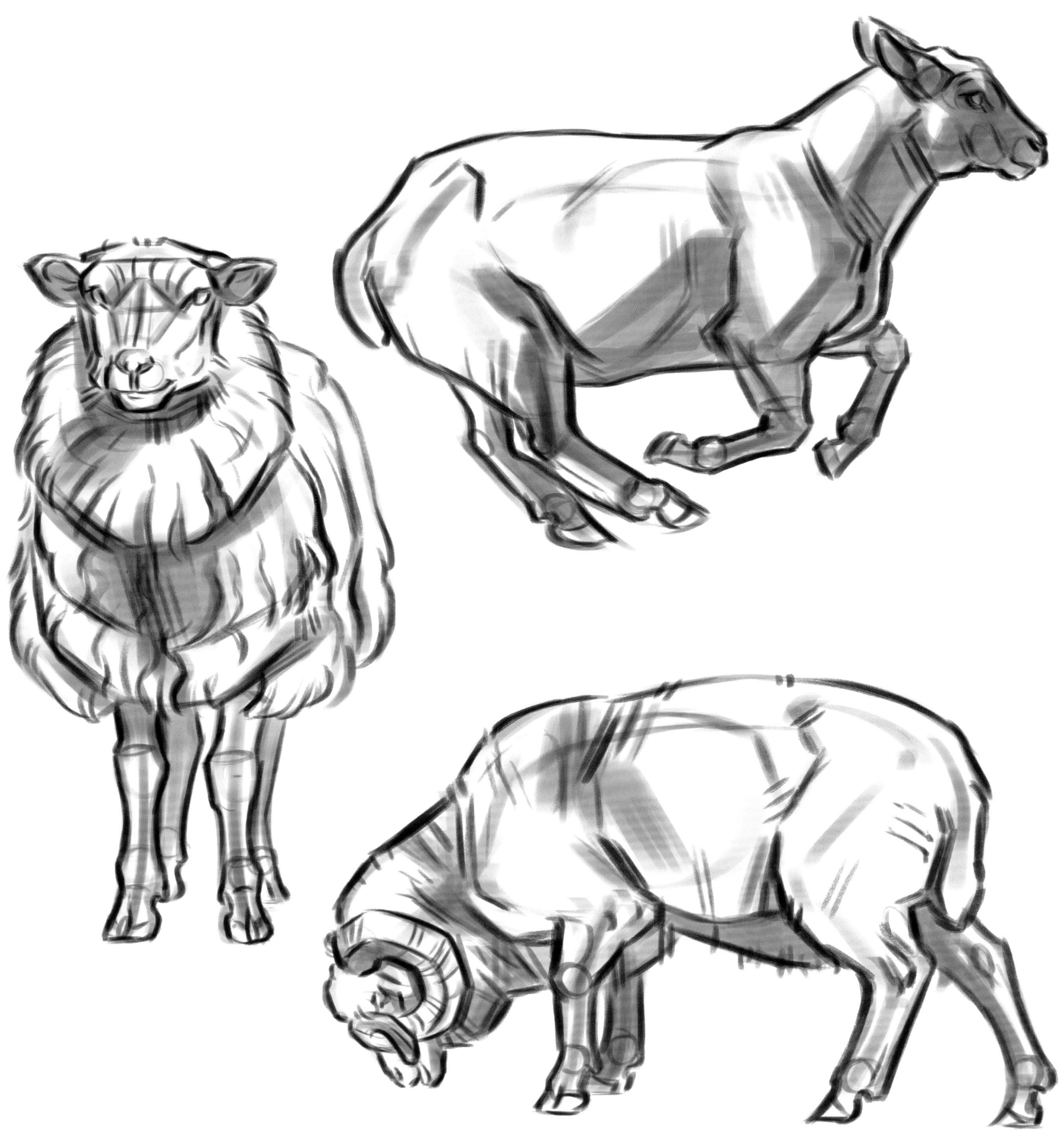

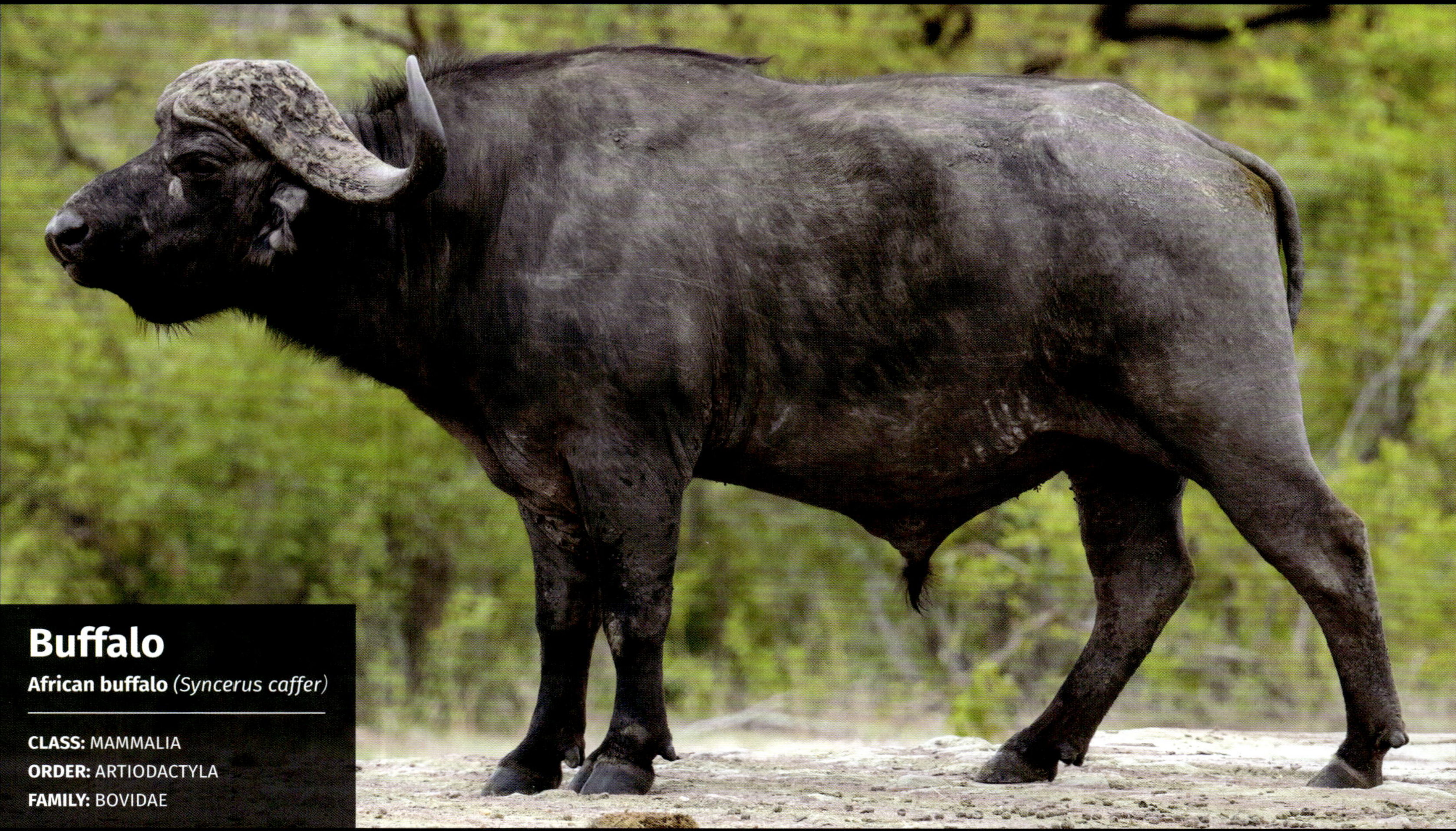

Buffalo

African buffalo *(Syncerus caffer)*

CLASS: MAMMALIA
ORDER: ARTIODACTYLA
FAMILY: BOVIDAE

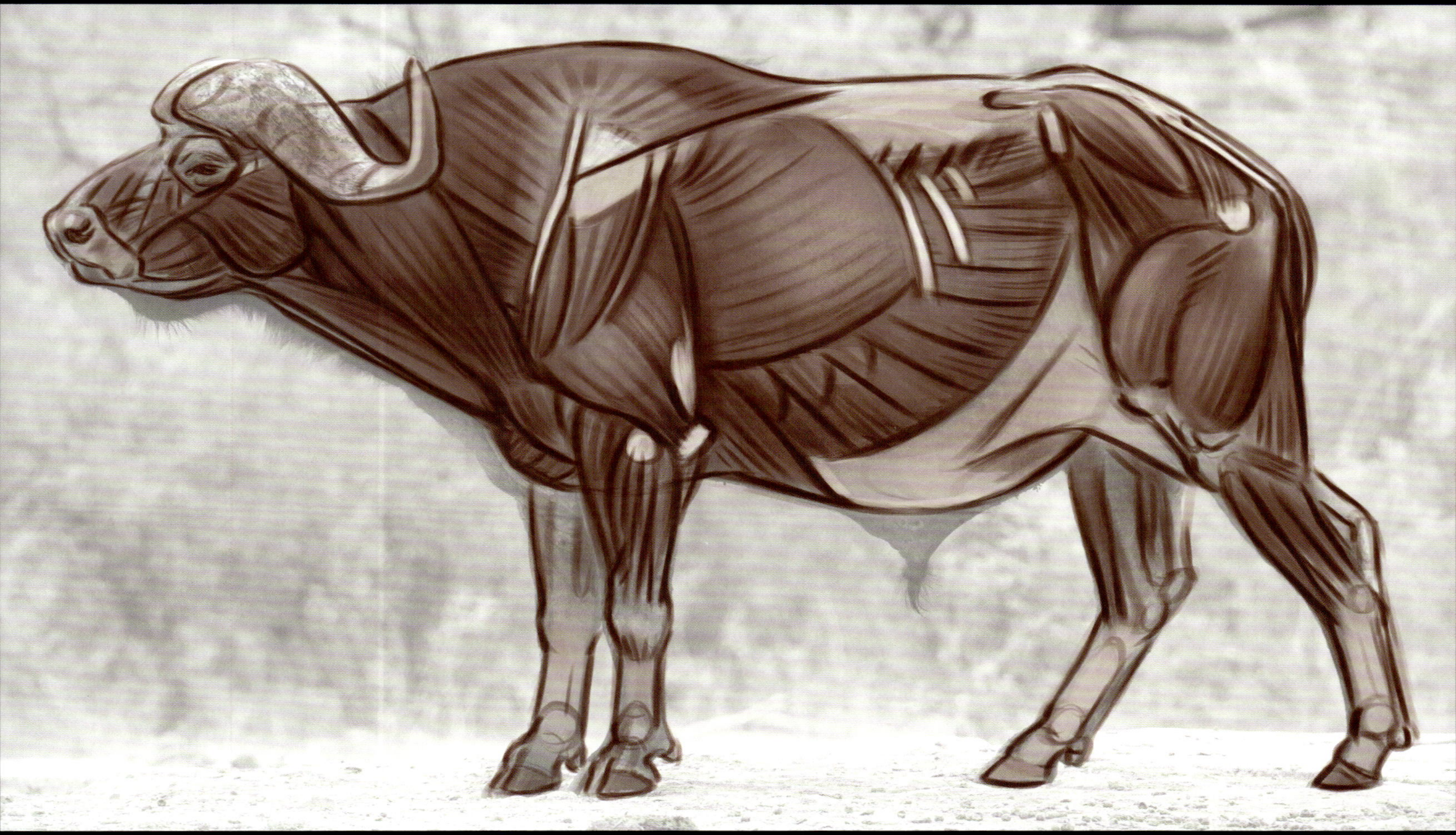

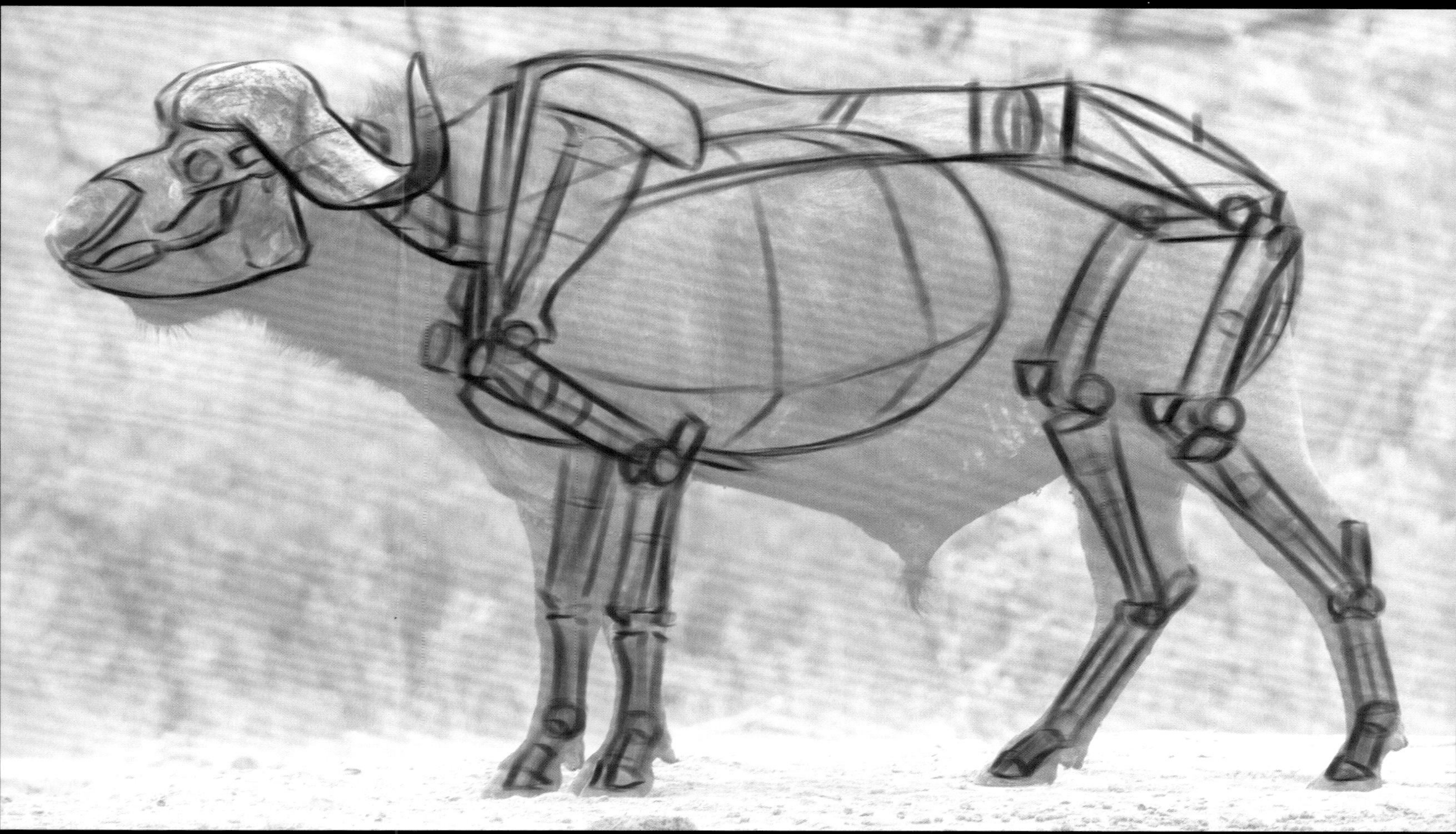

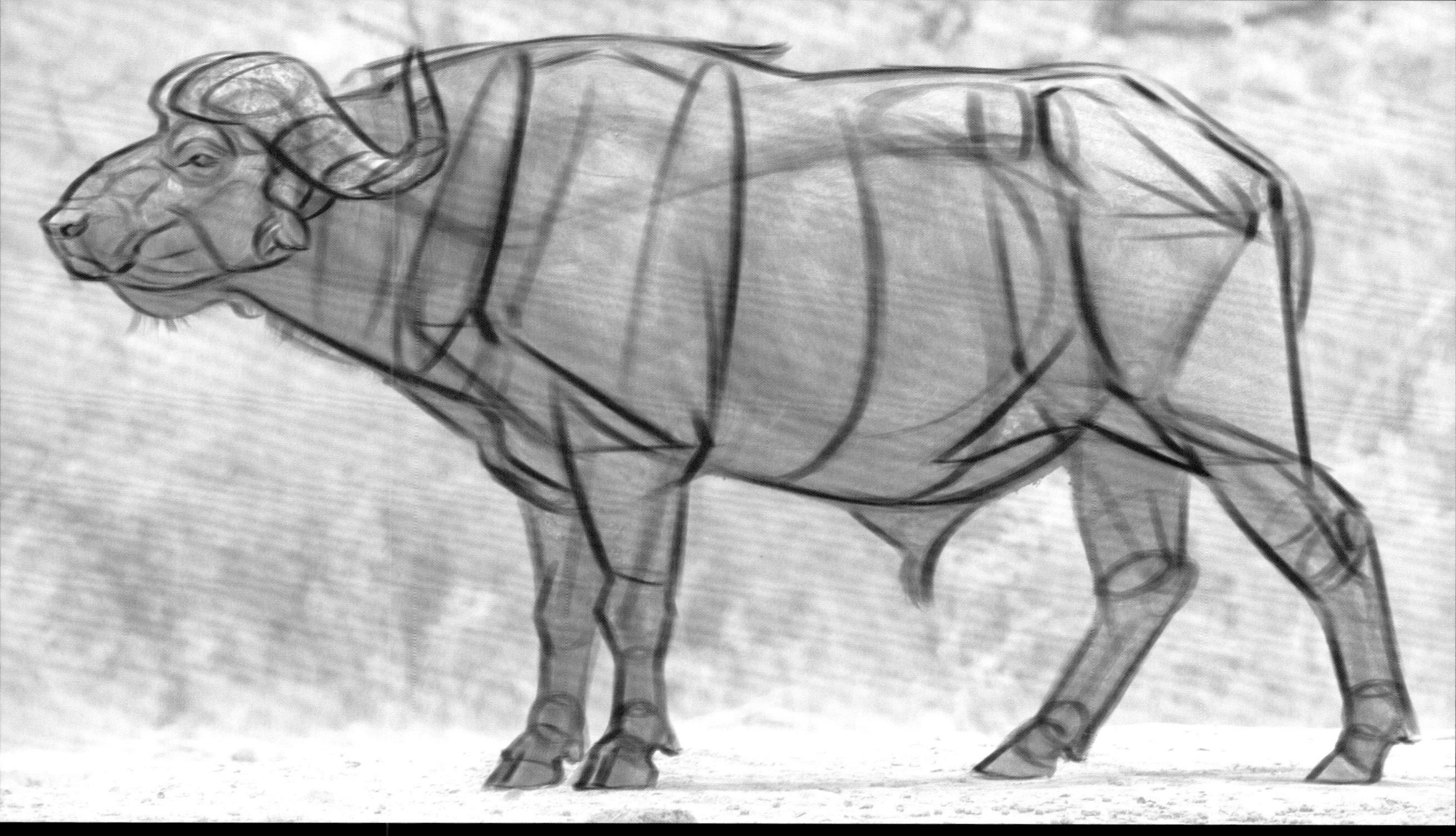

Photograph © Saverio Gatto / Agami.nl

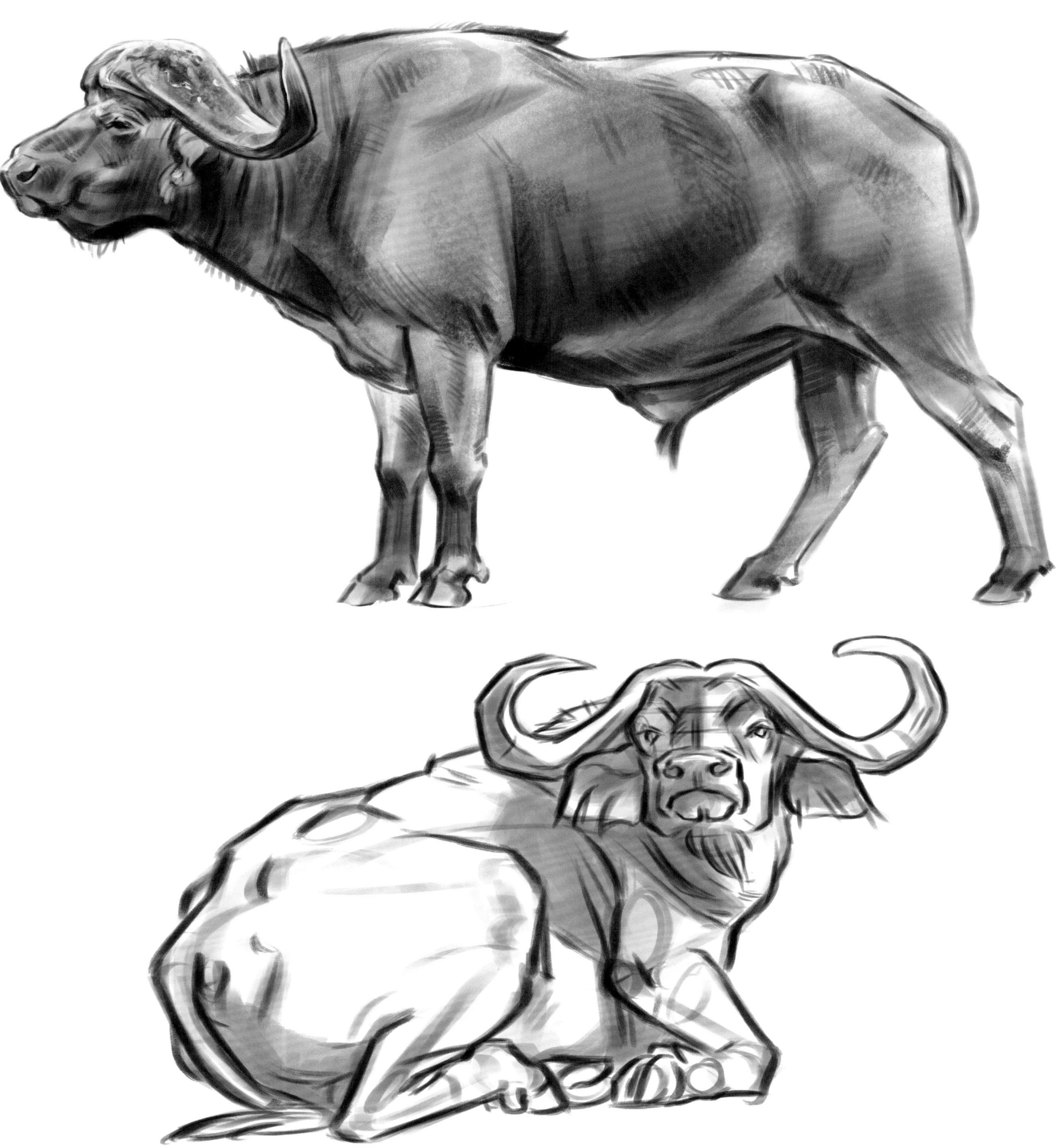

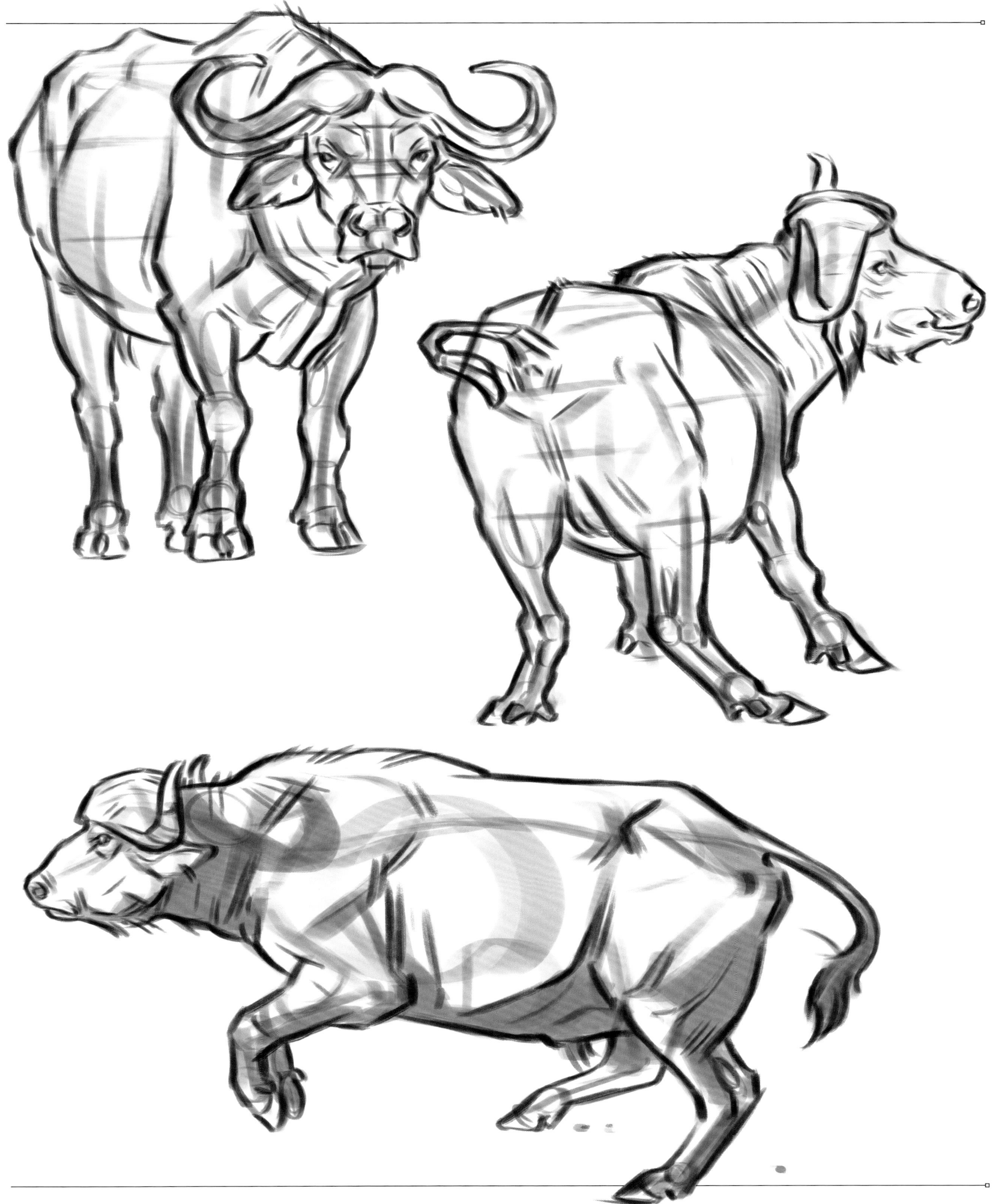

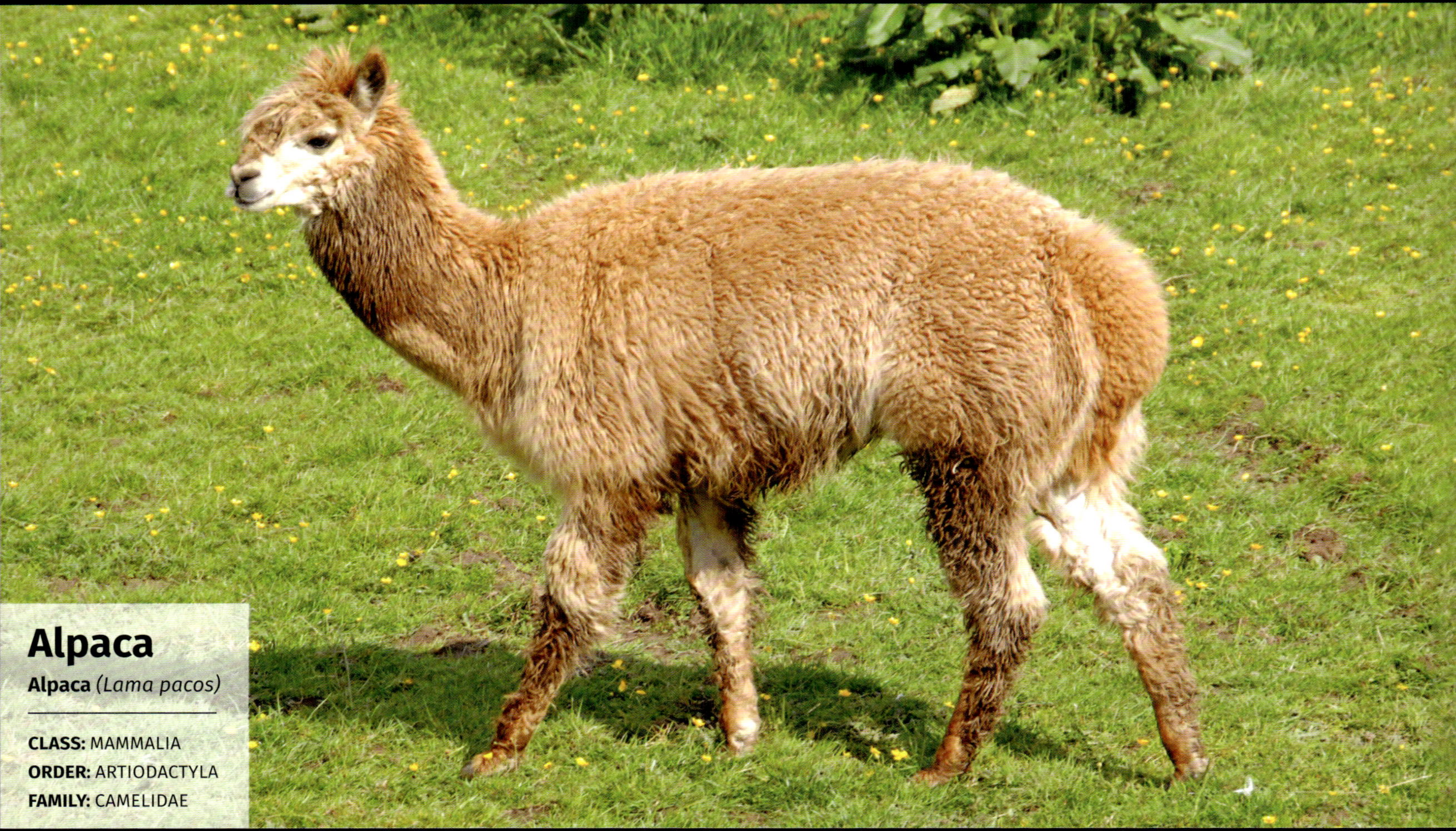

Alpaca

Alpaca *(Lama pacos)*

CLASS: MAMMALIA
ORDER: ARTIODACTYLA
FAMILY: CAMELIDAE

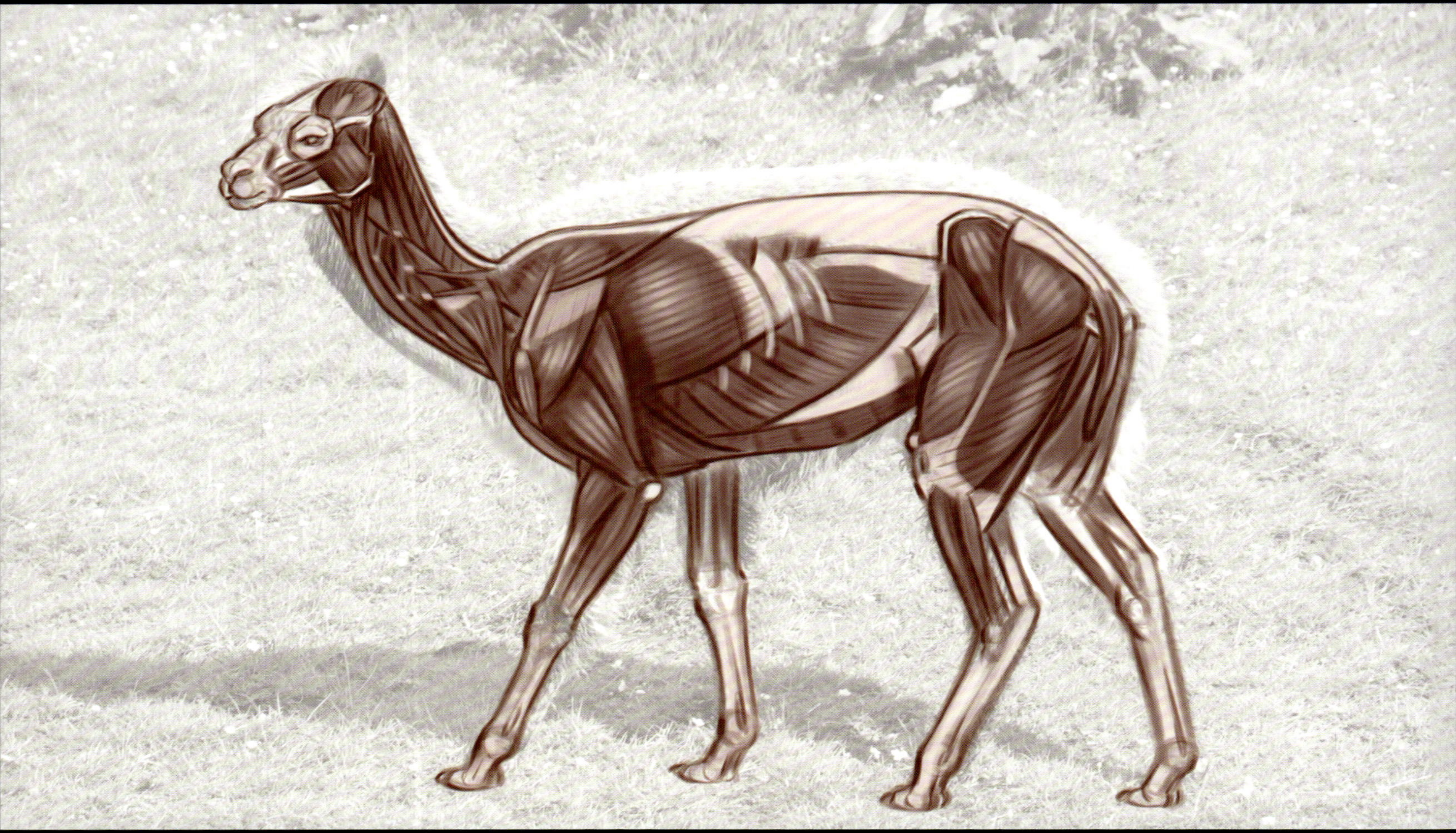

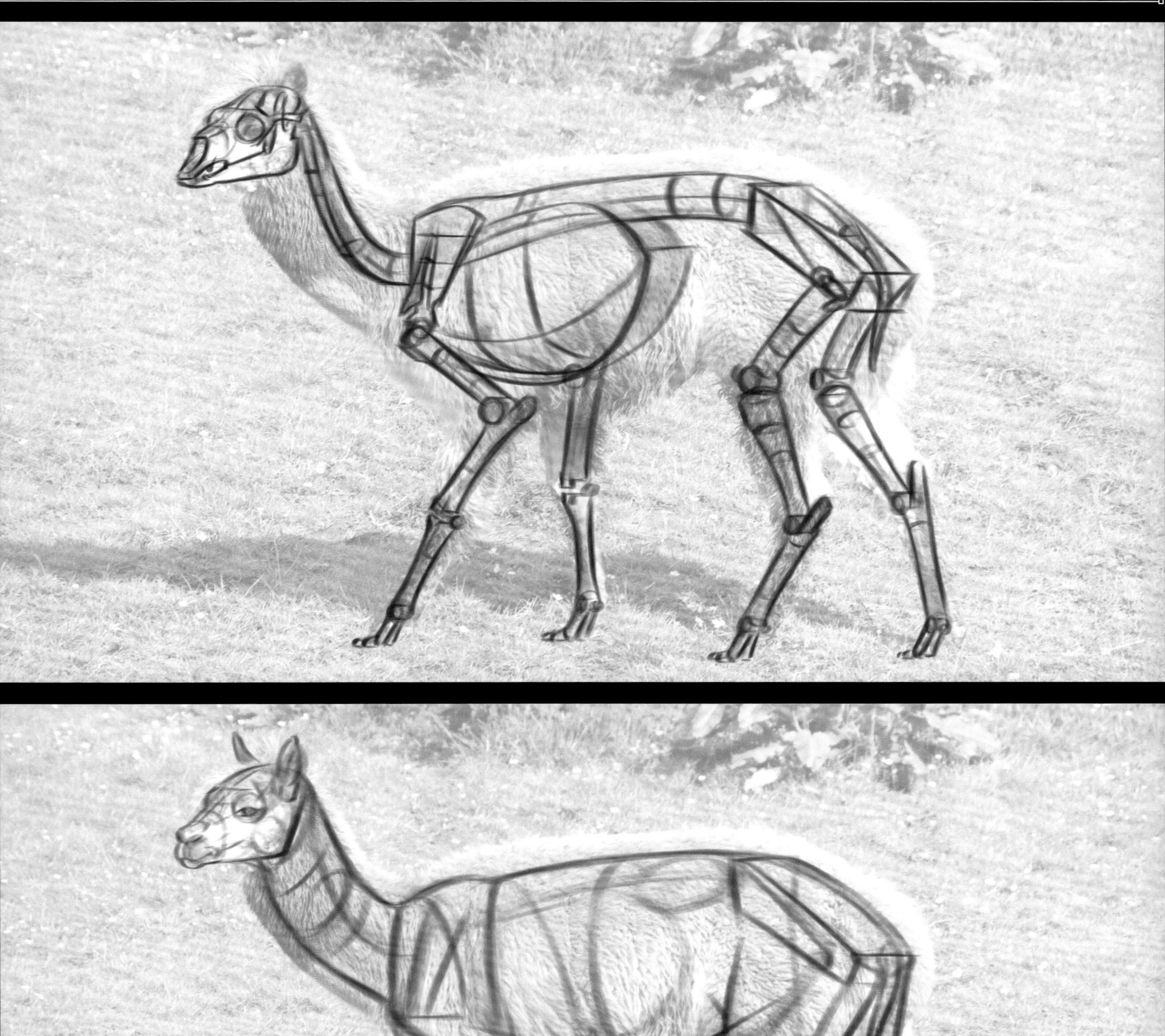

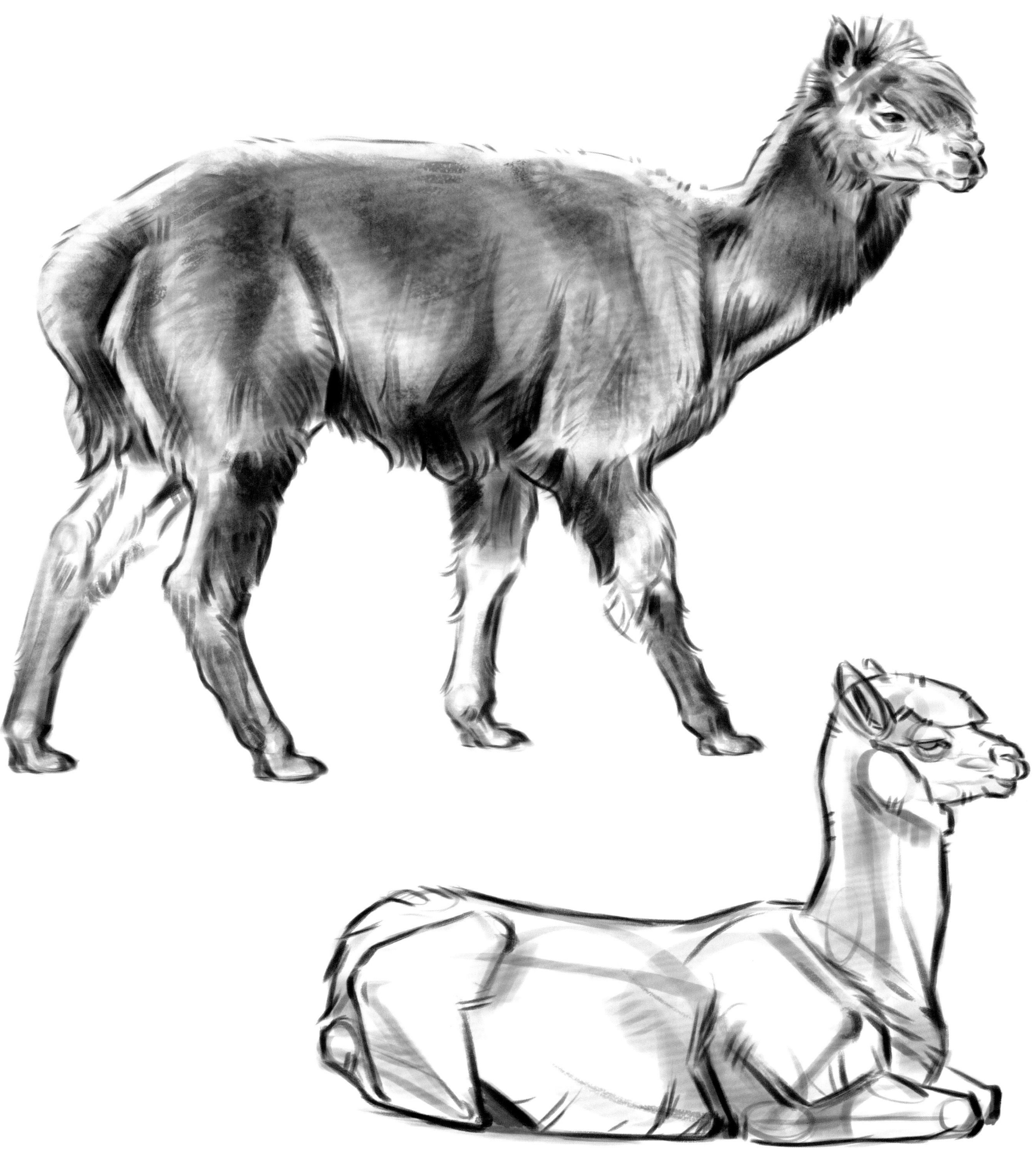

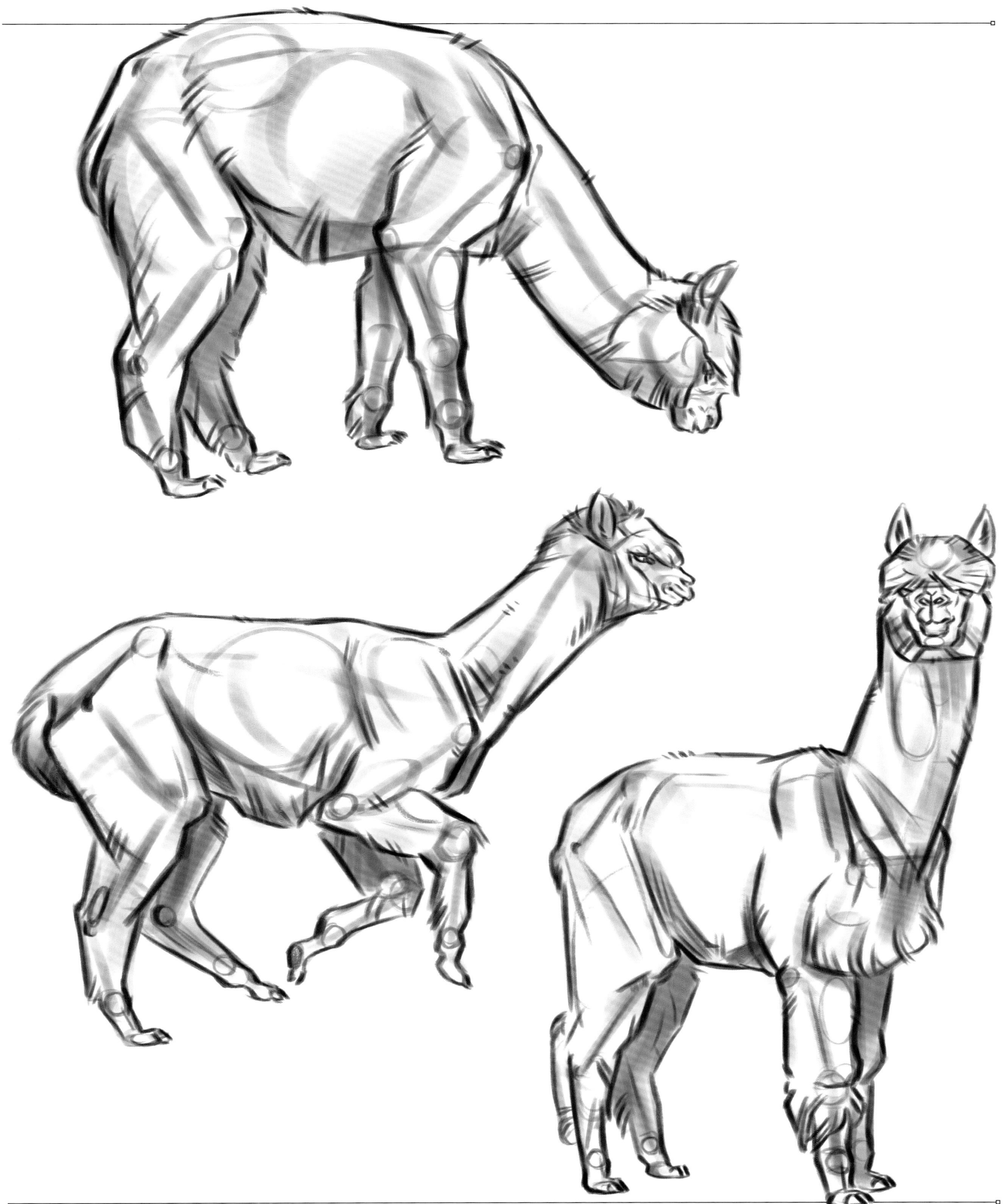

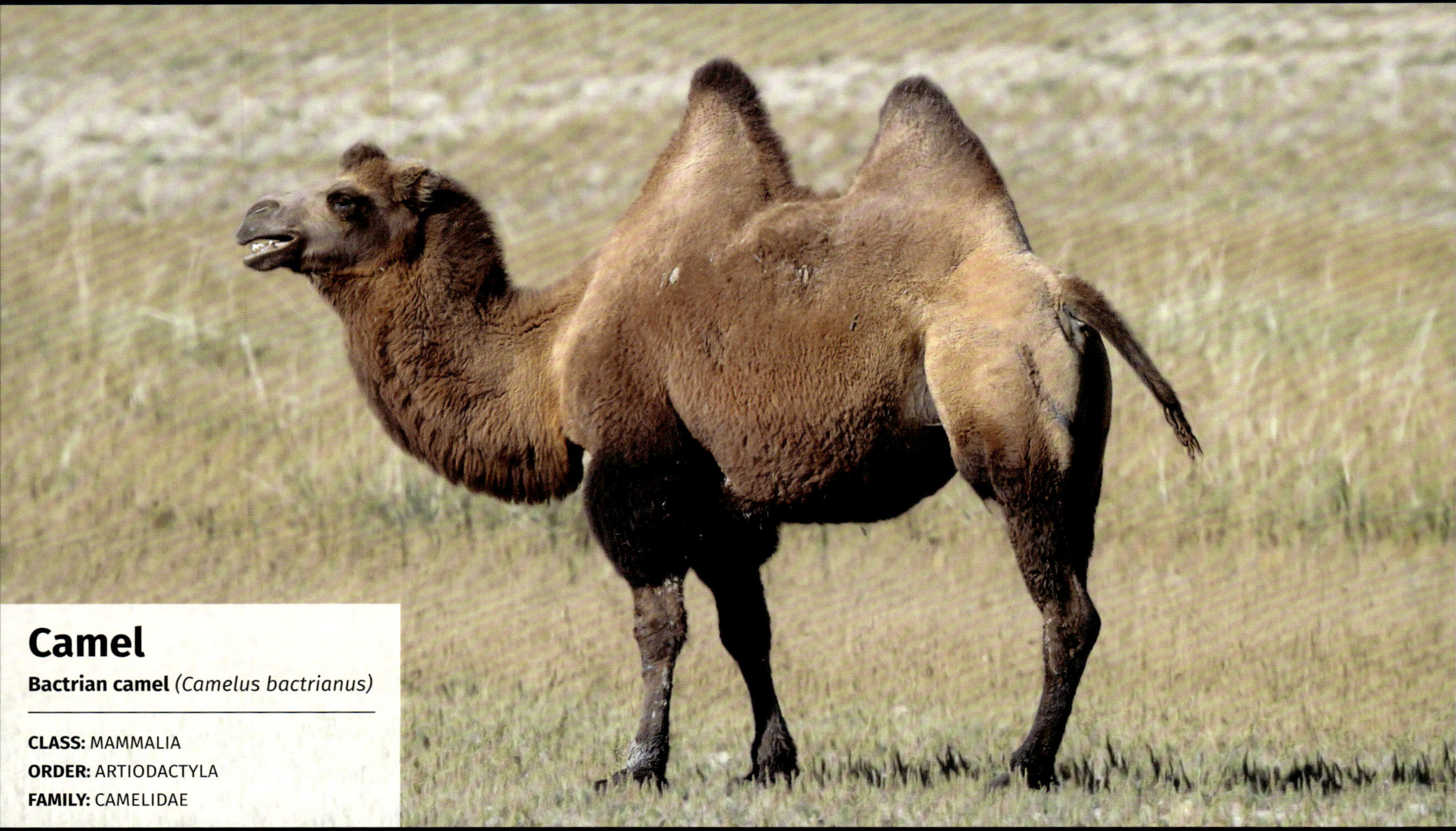

Camel

Bactrian camel *(Camelus bactrianus)*

CLASS: MAMMALIA
ORDER: ARTIODACTYLA
FAMILY: CAMELIDAE

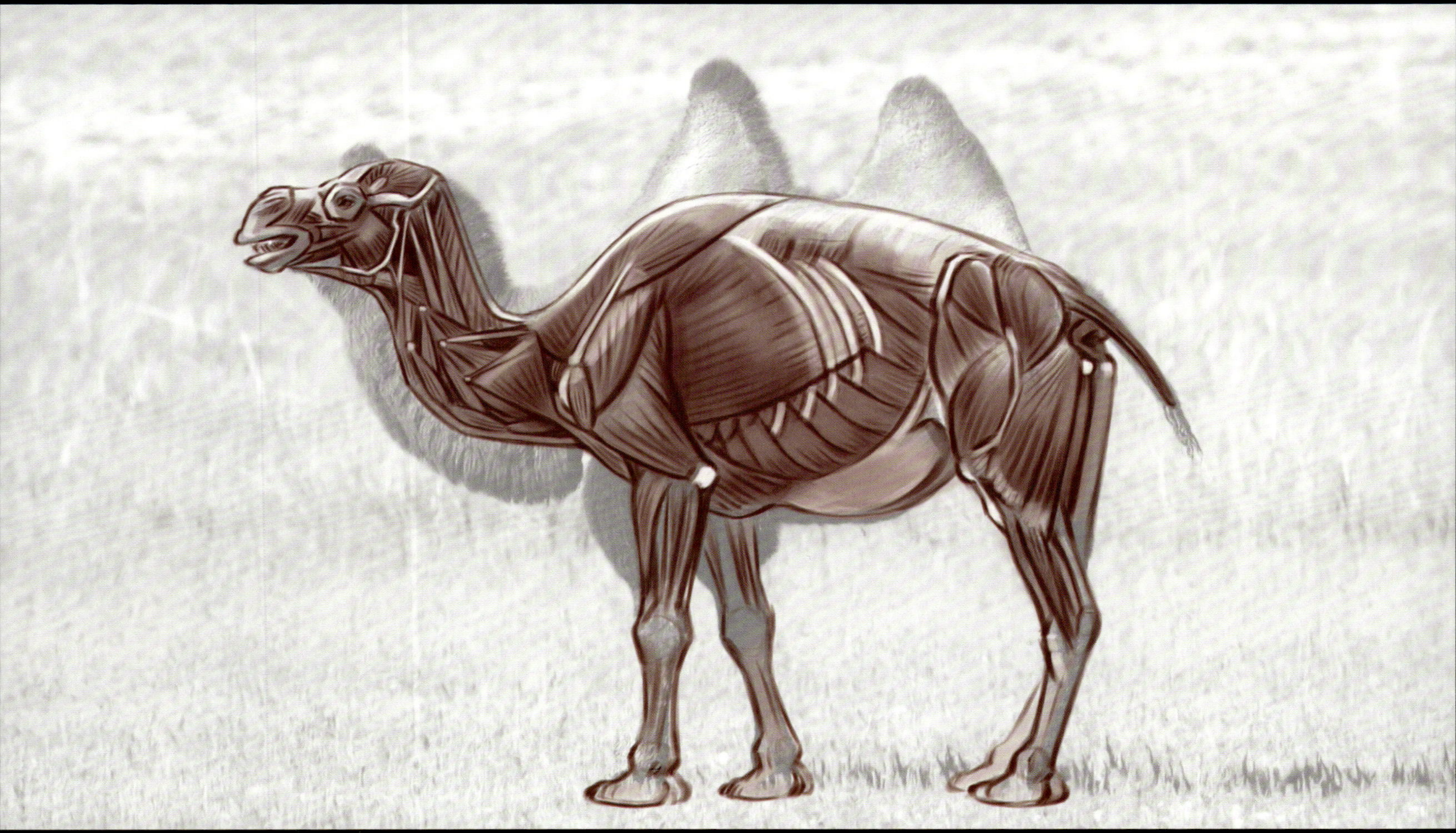

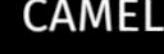

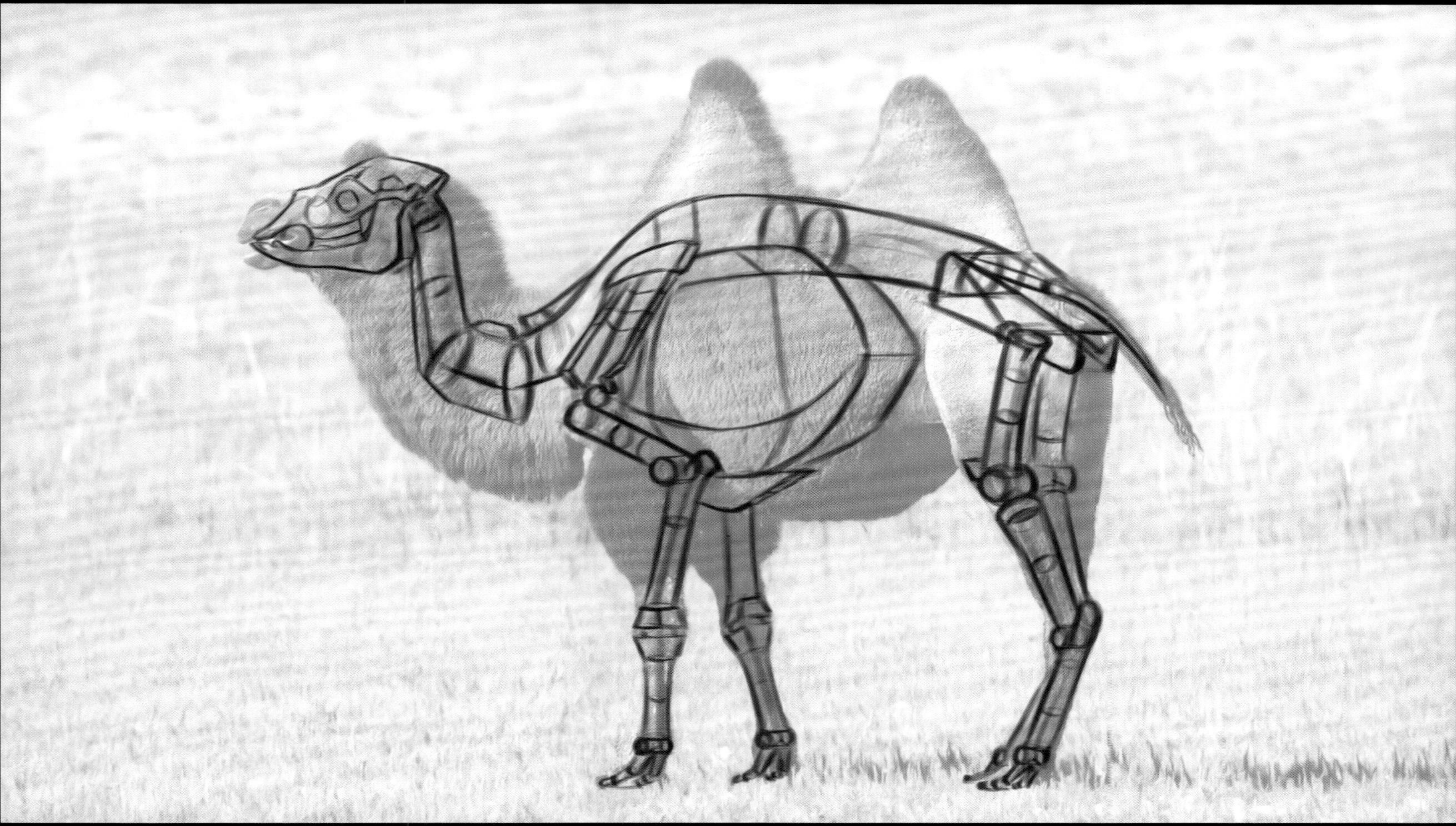

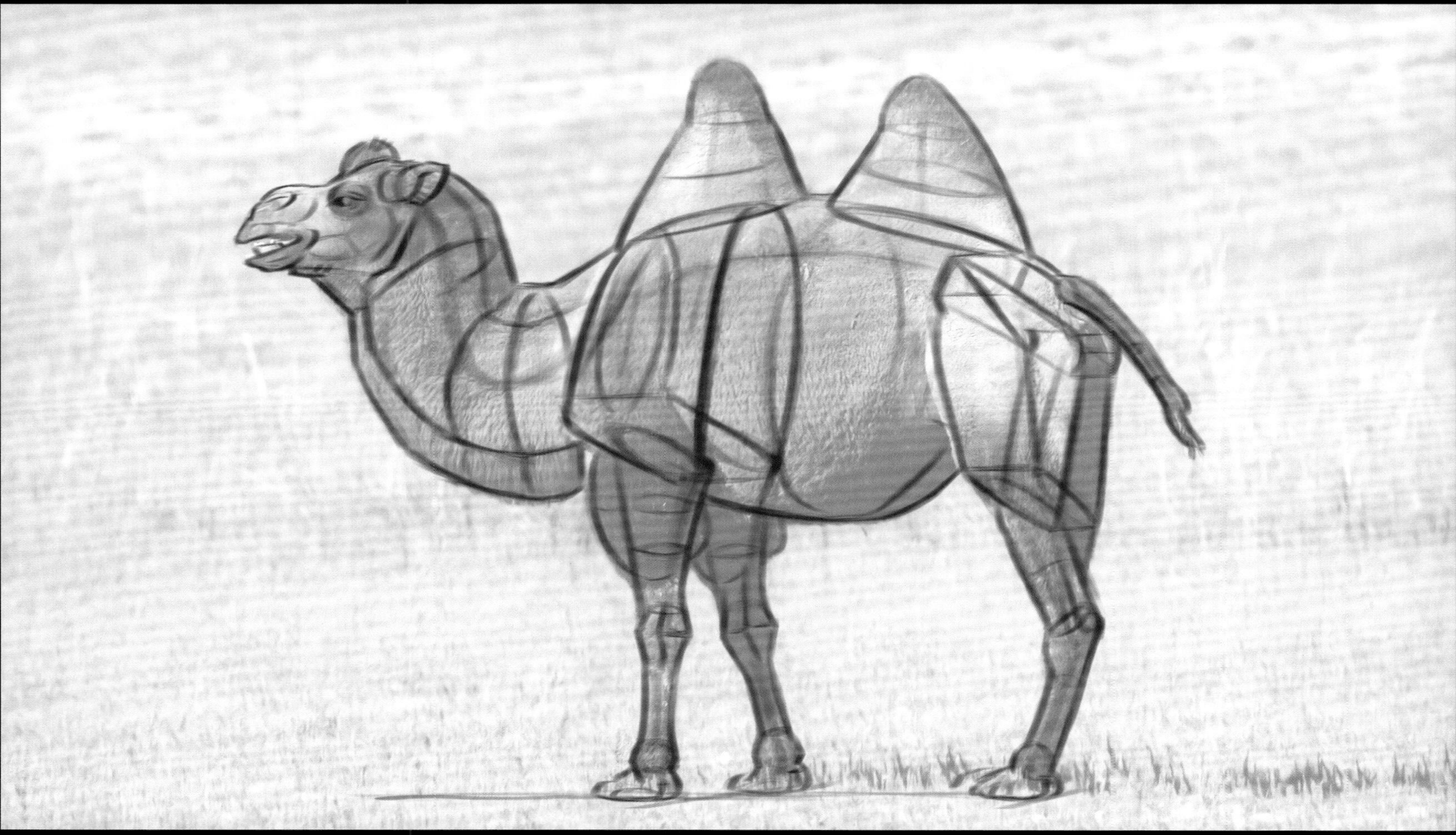

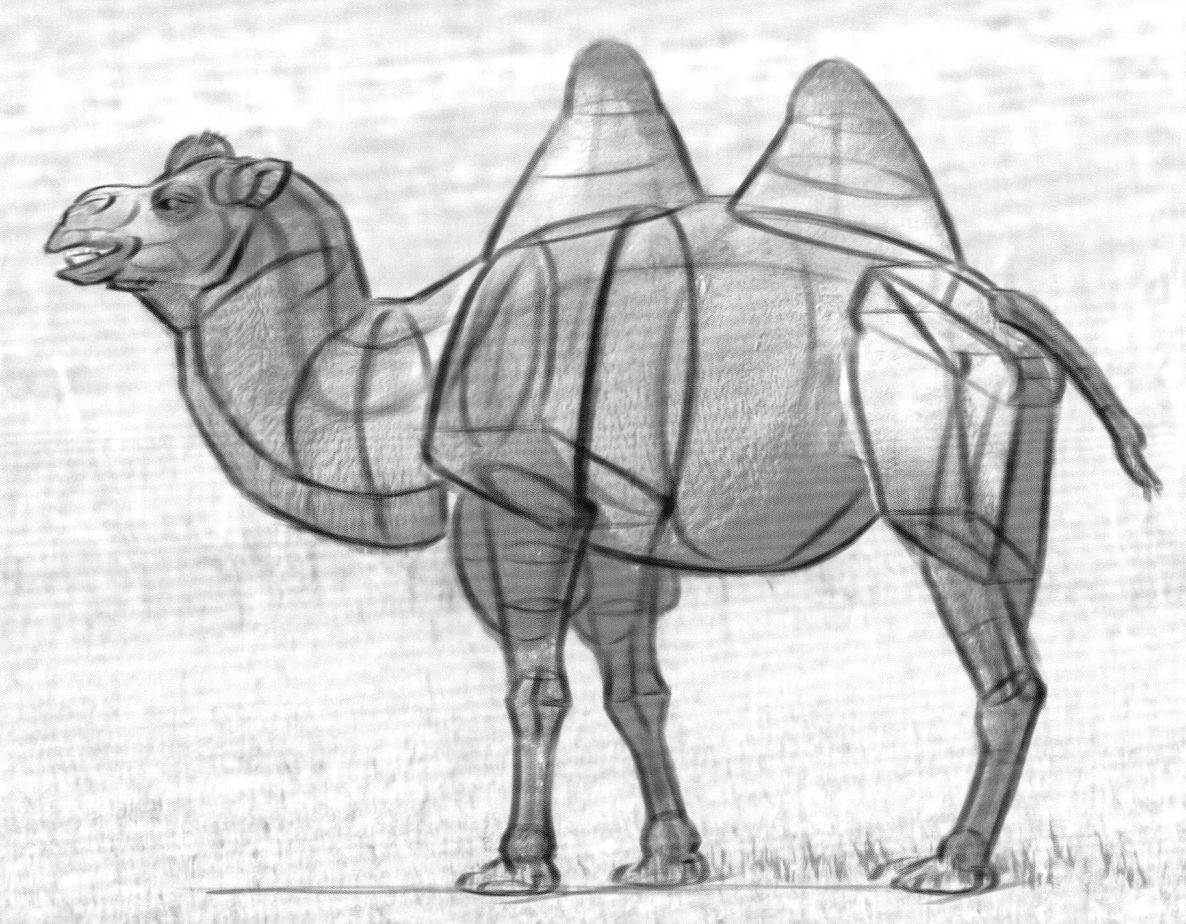

Photograph © Aurélien Audevard / Agami.nl

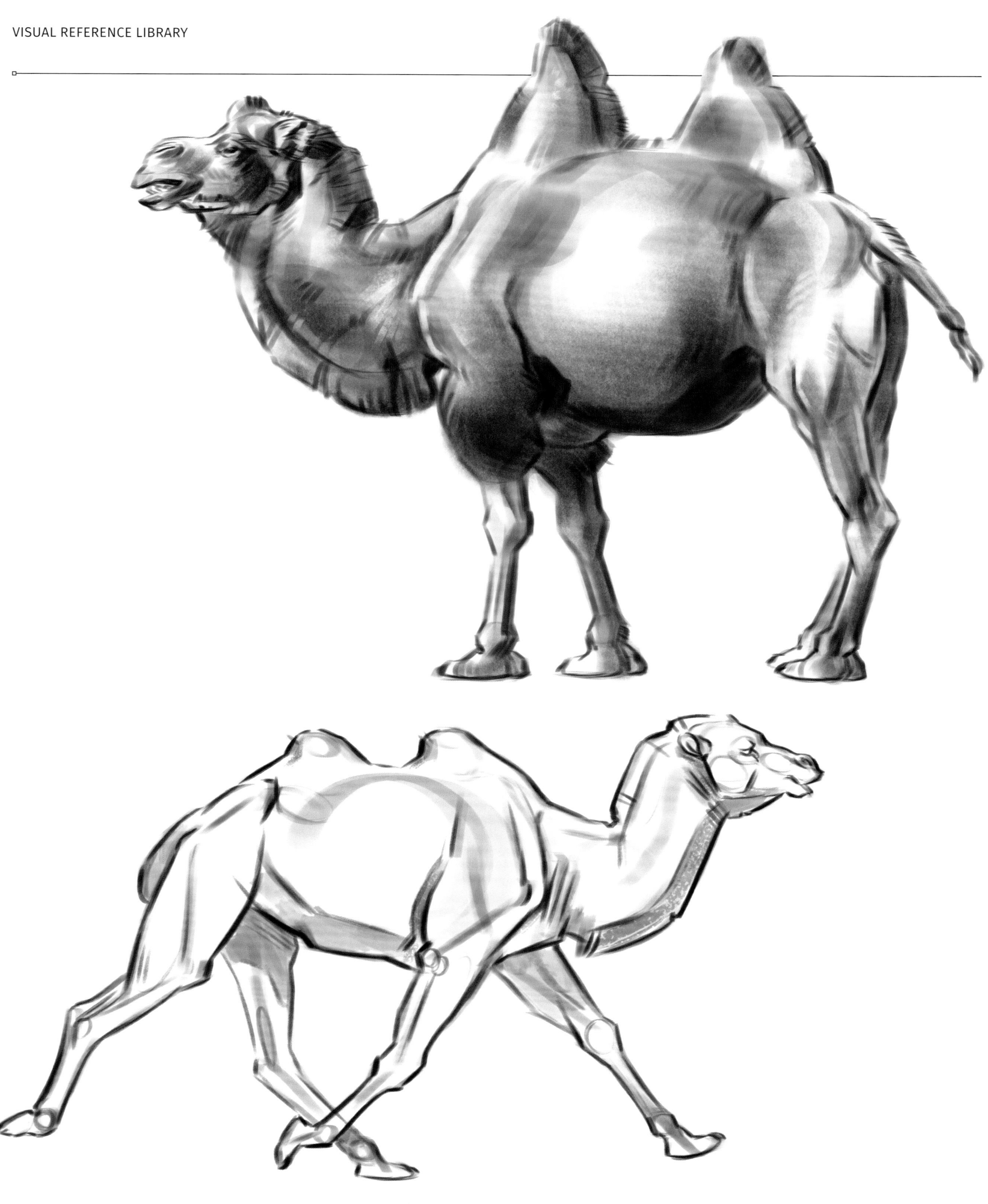

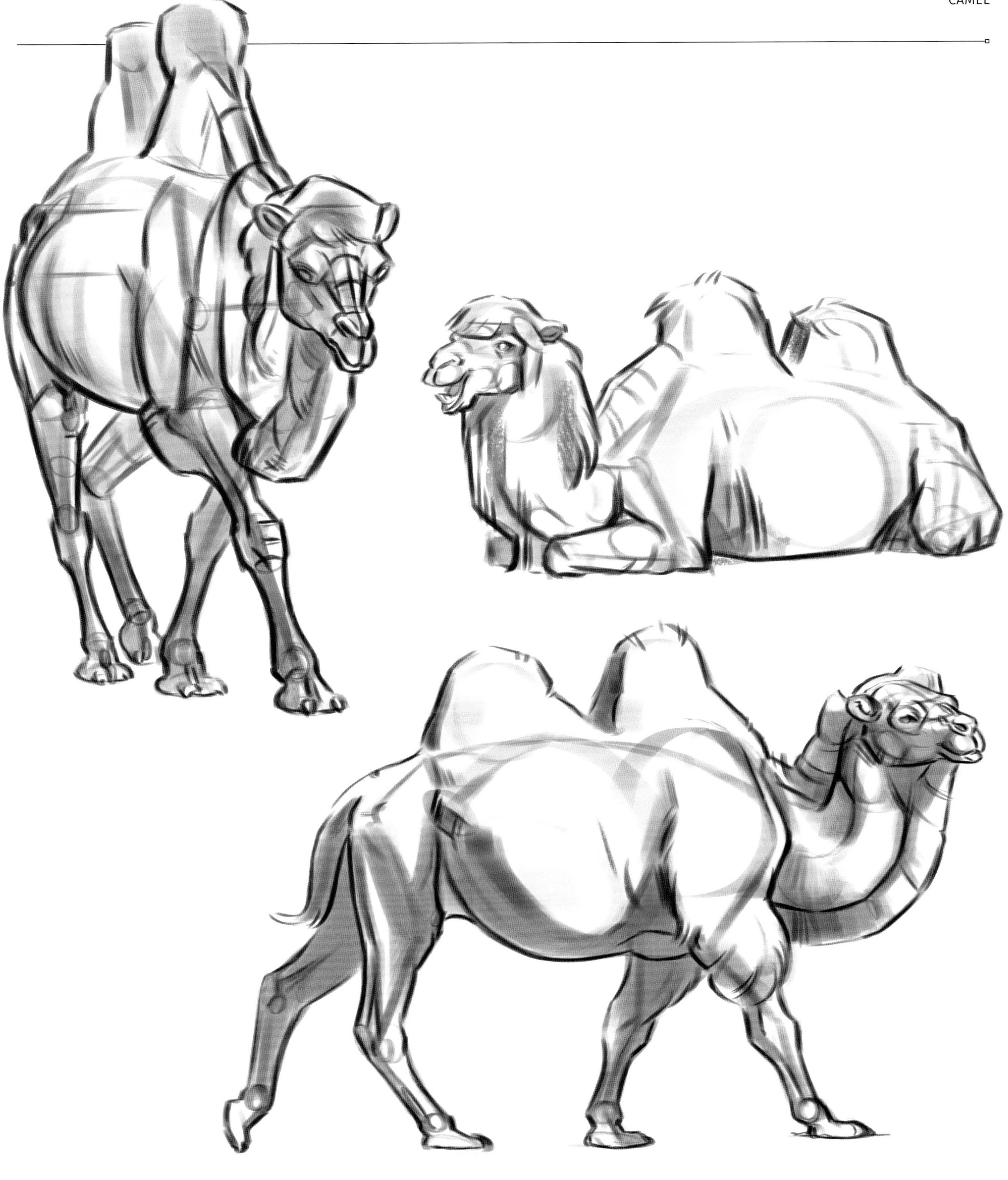

Deer

Red deer *(Cervus elaphus)*

CLASS: MAMMALIA
ORDER: ARTIODACTYLA
FAMILY: CERVIDAE

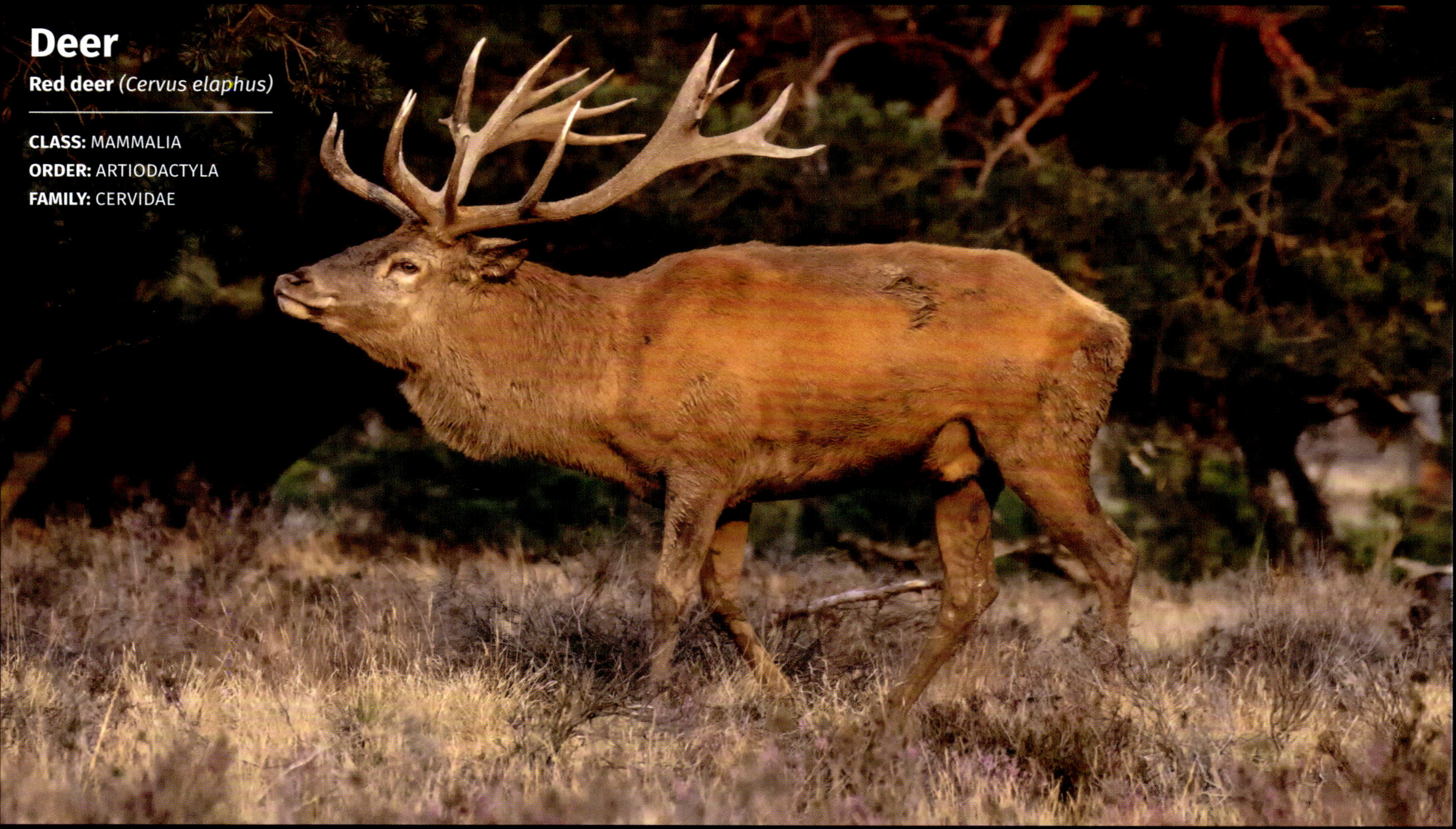

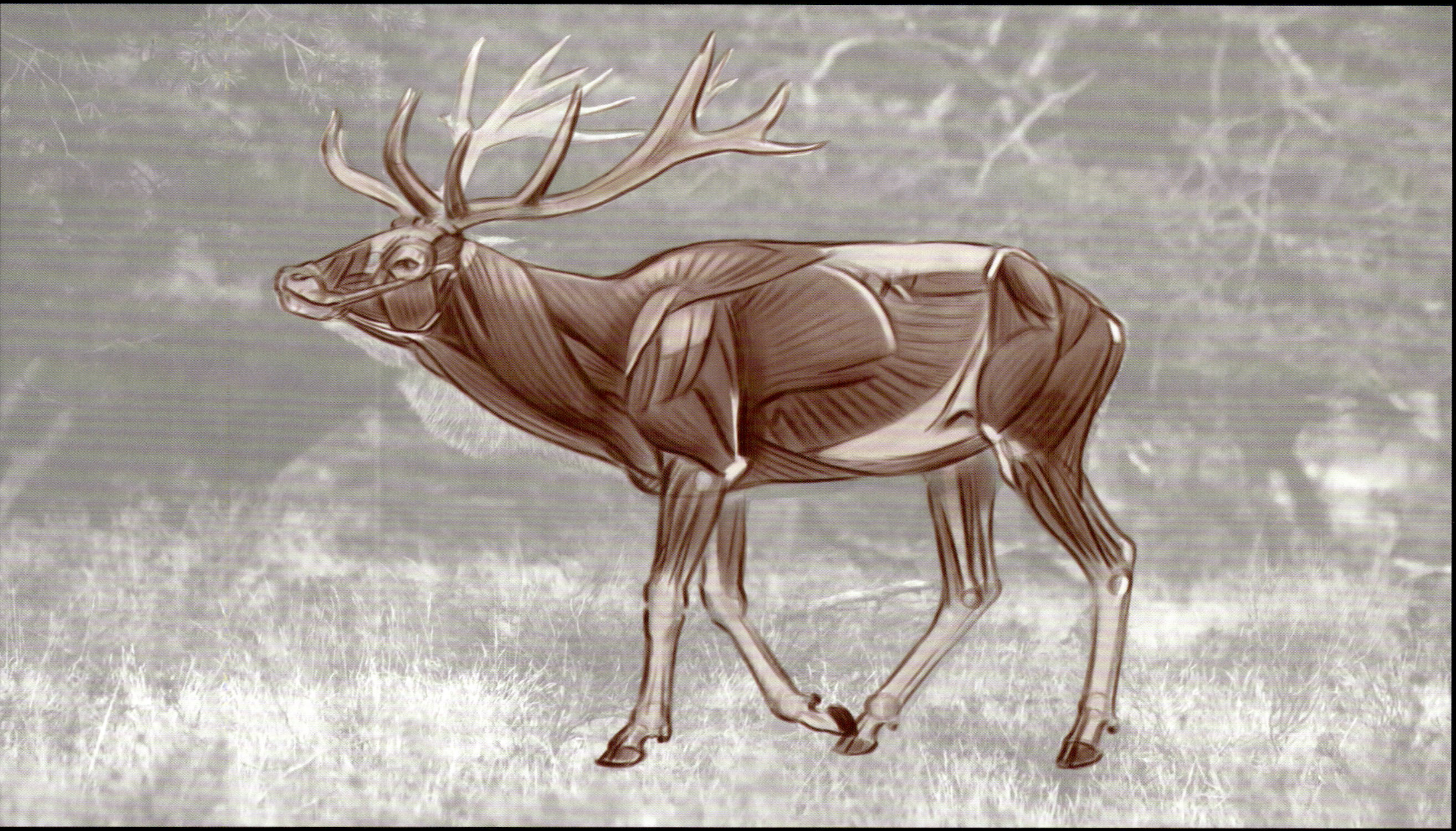

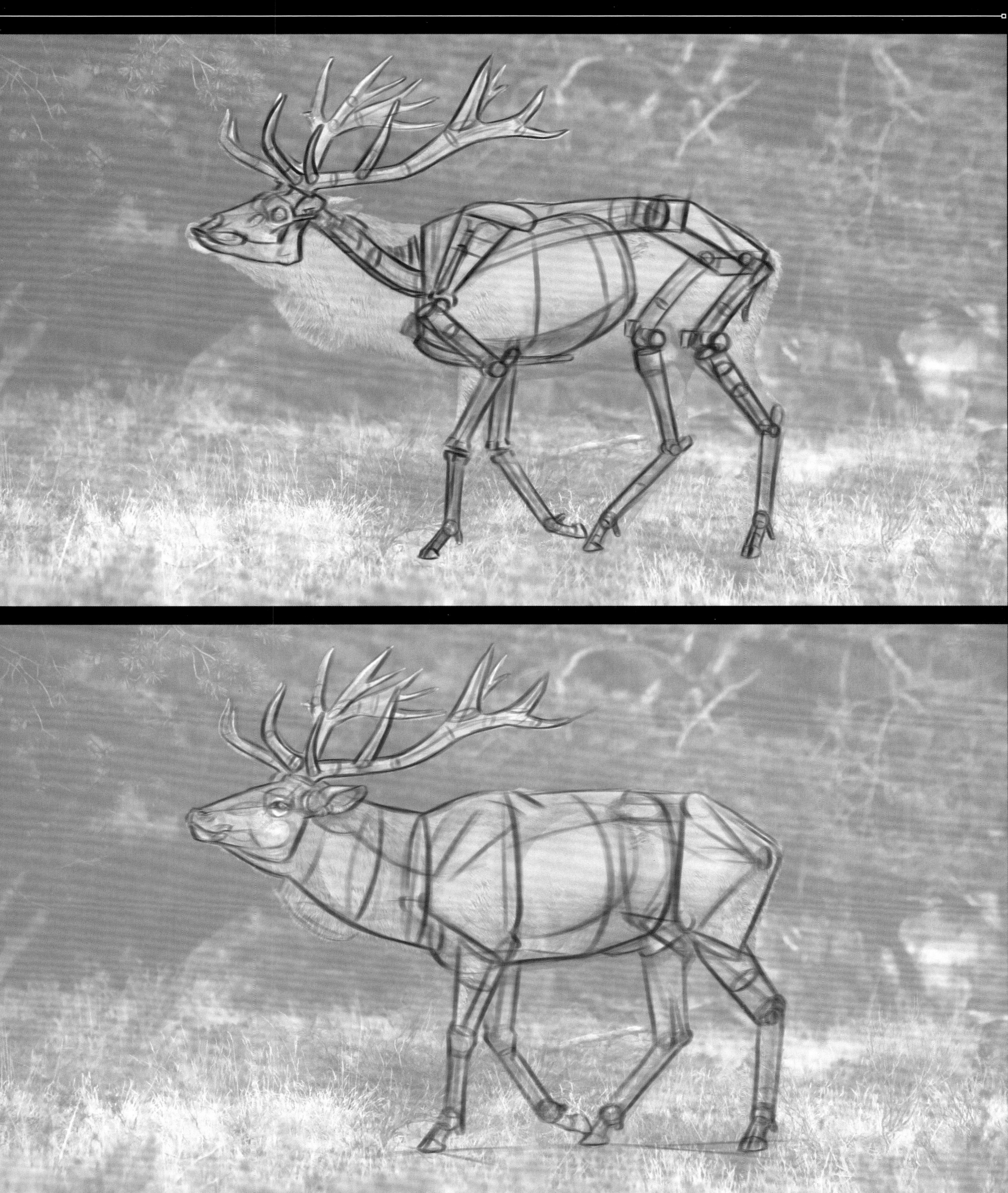

Photograph © Hans Germeraad / Agami.nl

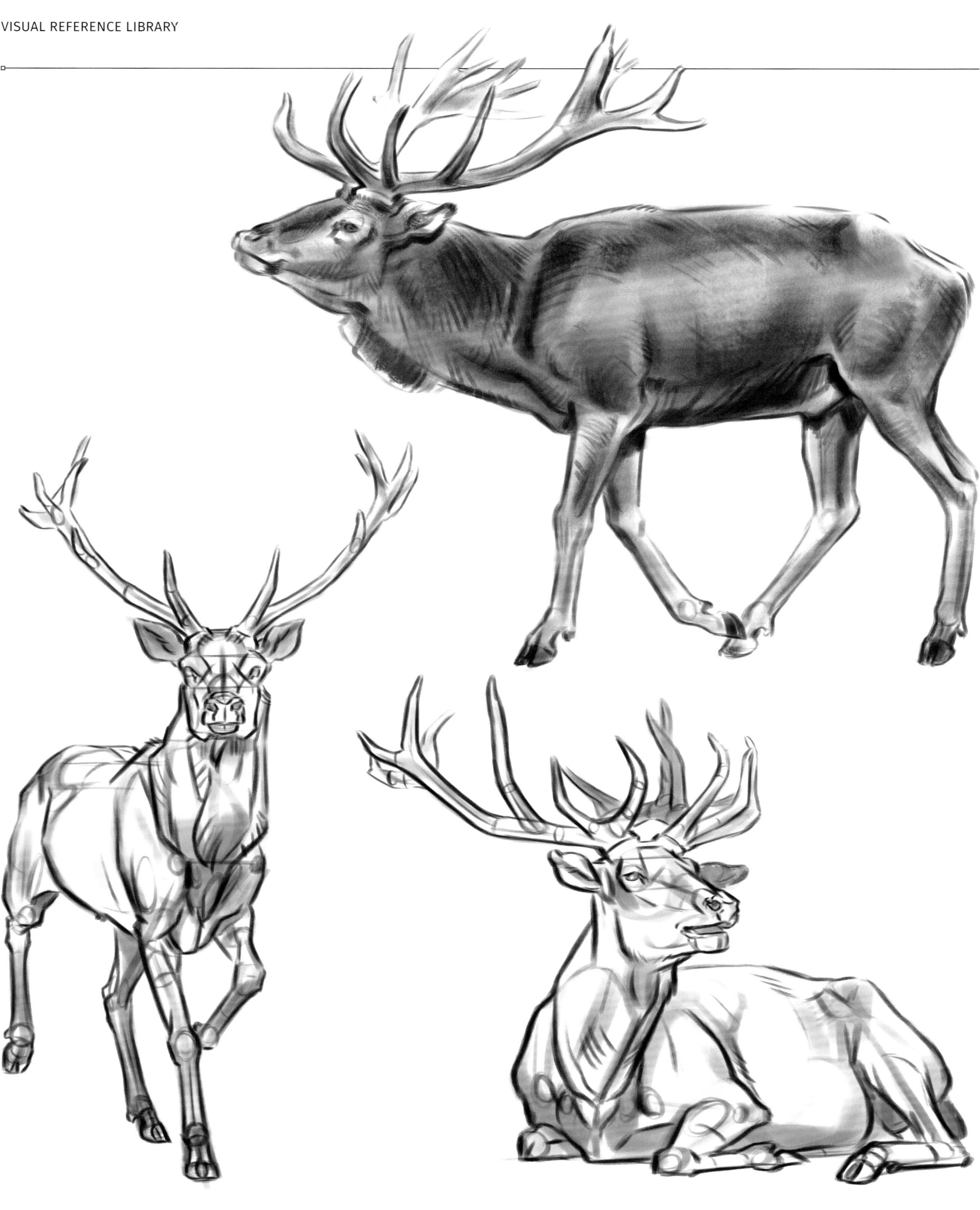

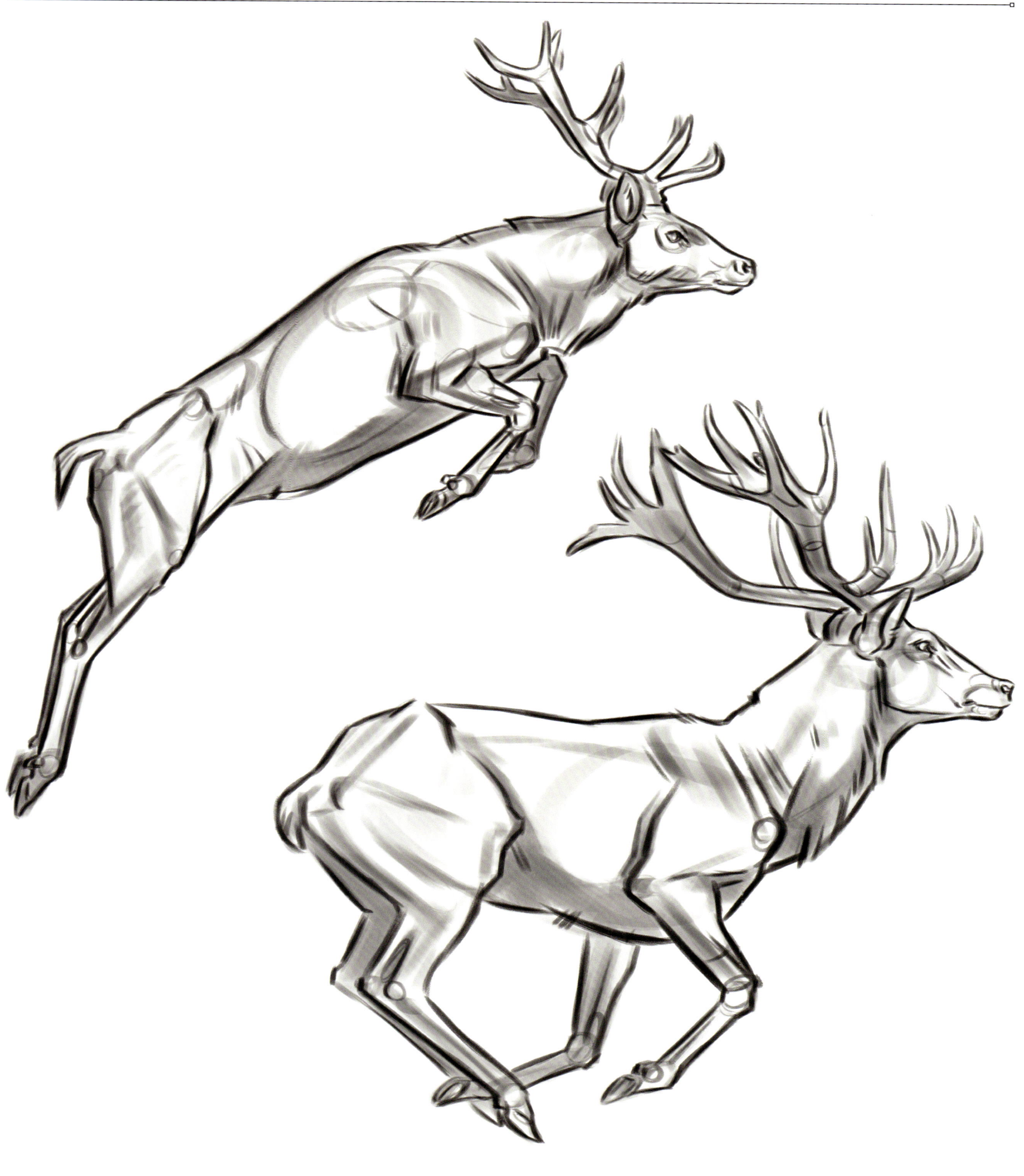

Moose

Moose *(Alces alces)*

CLASS: MAMMALIA
ORDER: ARTIODACTYLA
FAMILY: CERVIDAE

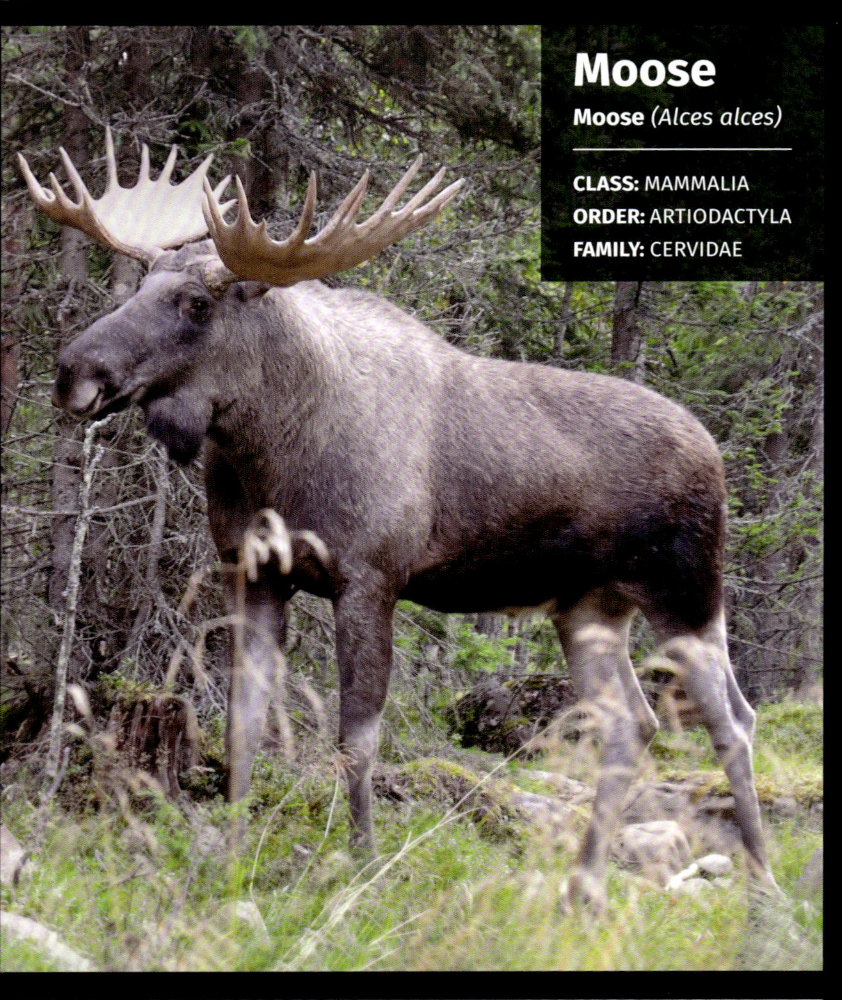

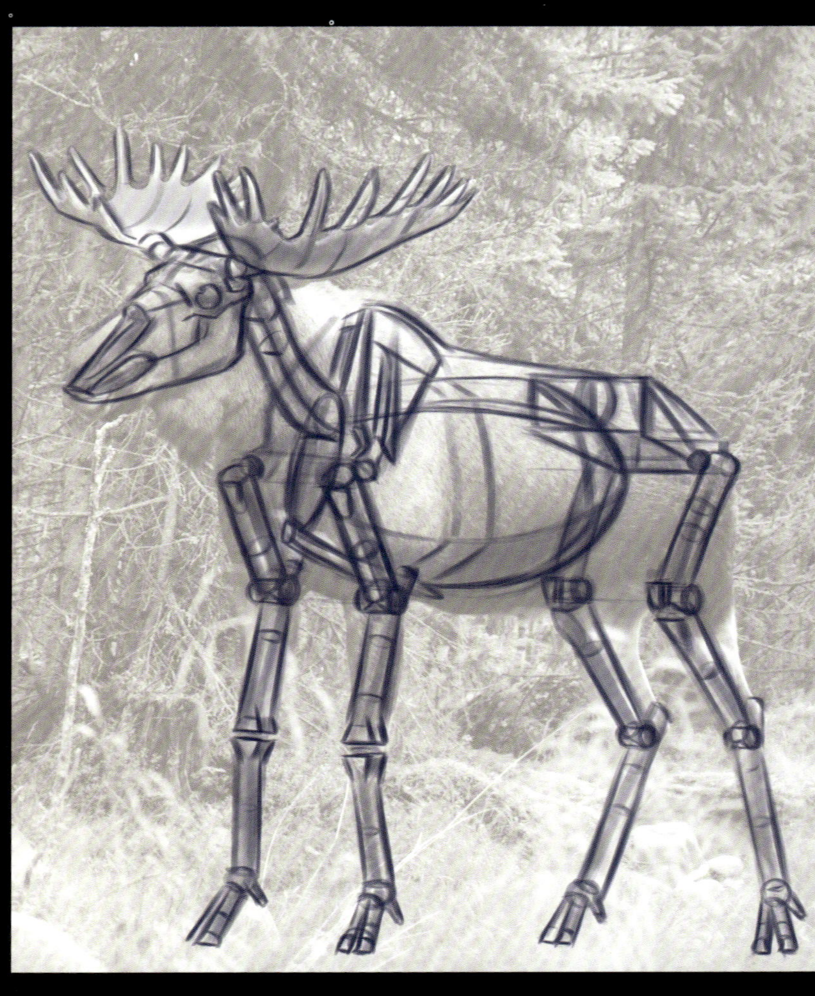

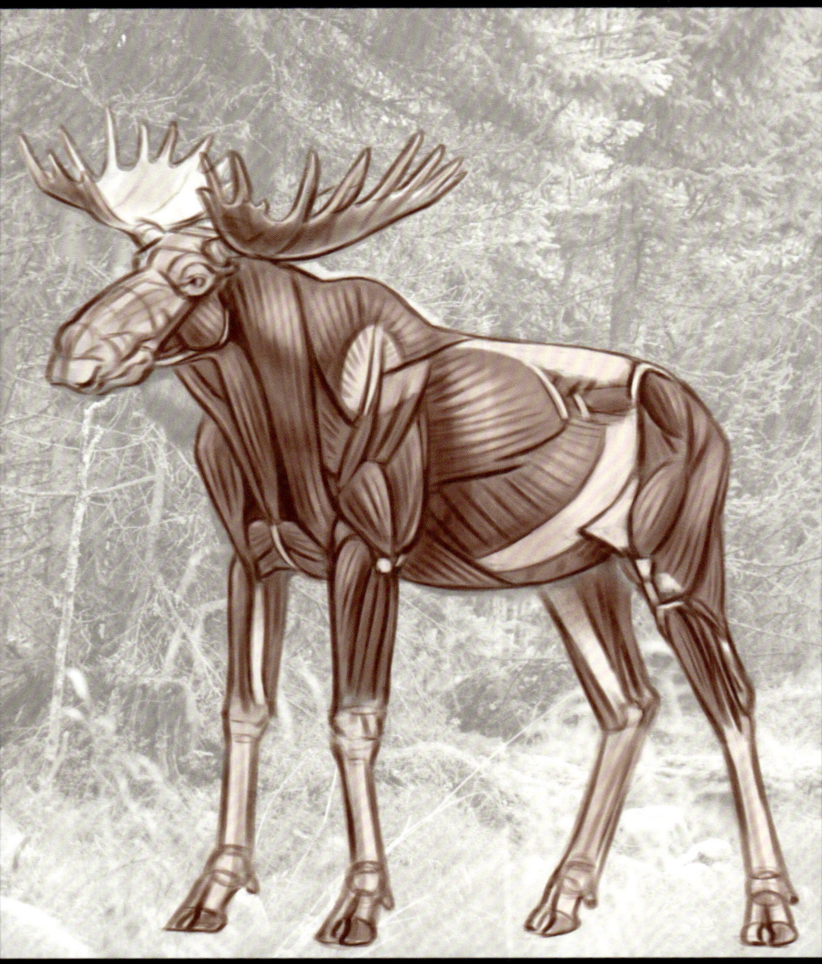

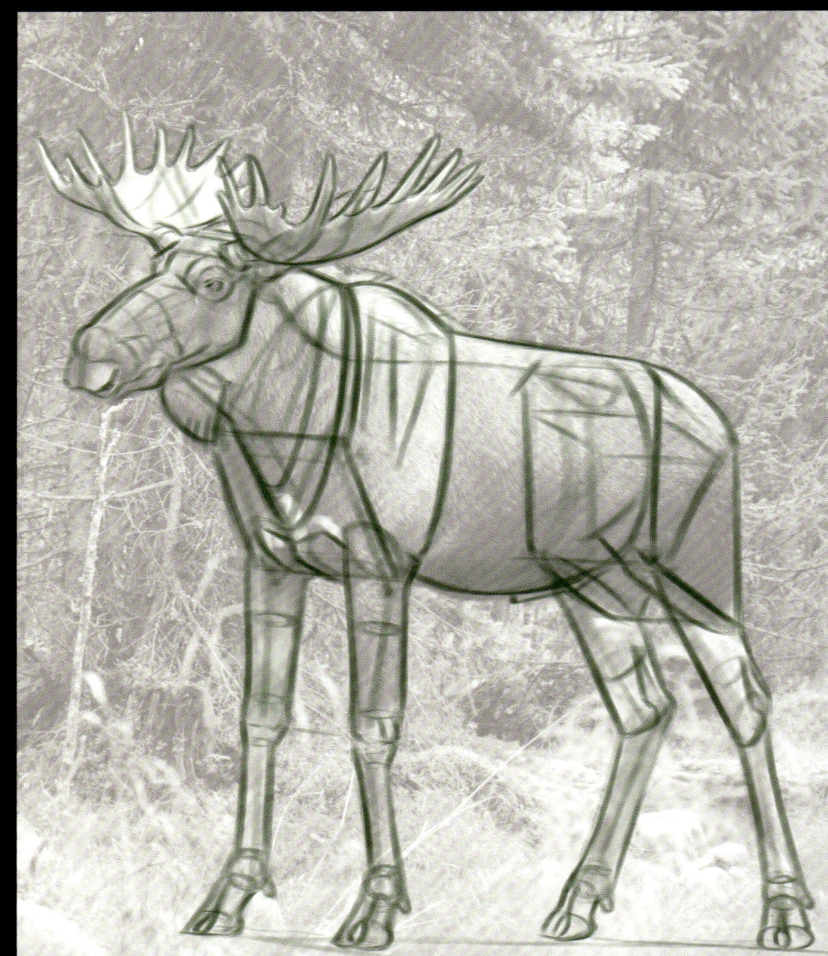

Photograph © Rob Riemer / Agami.nl

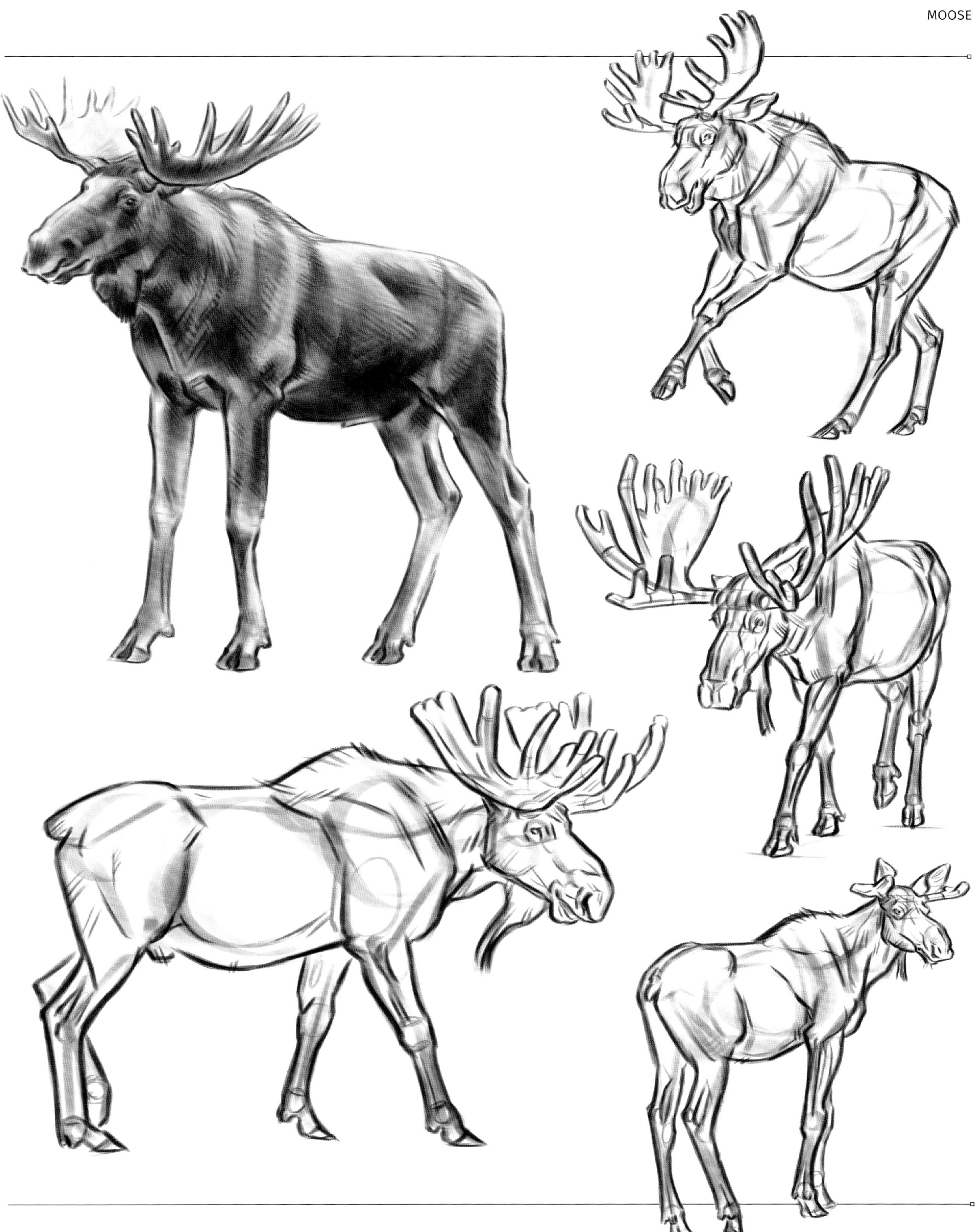

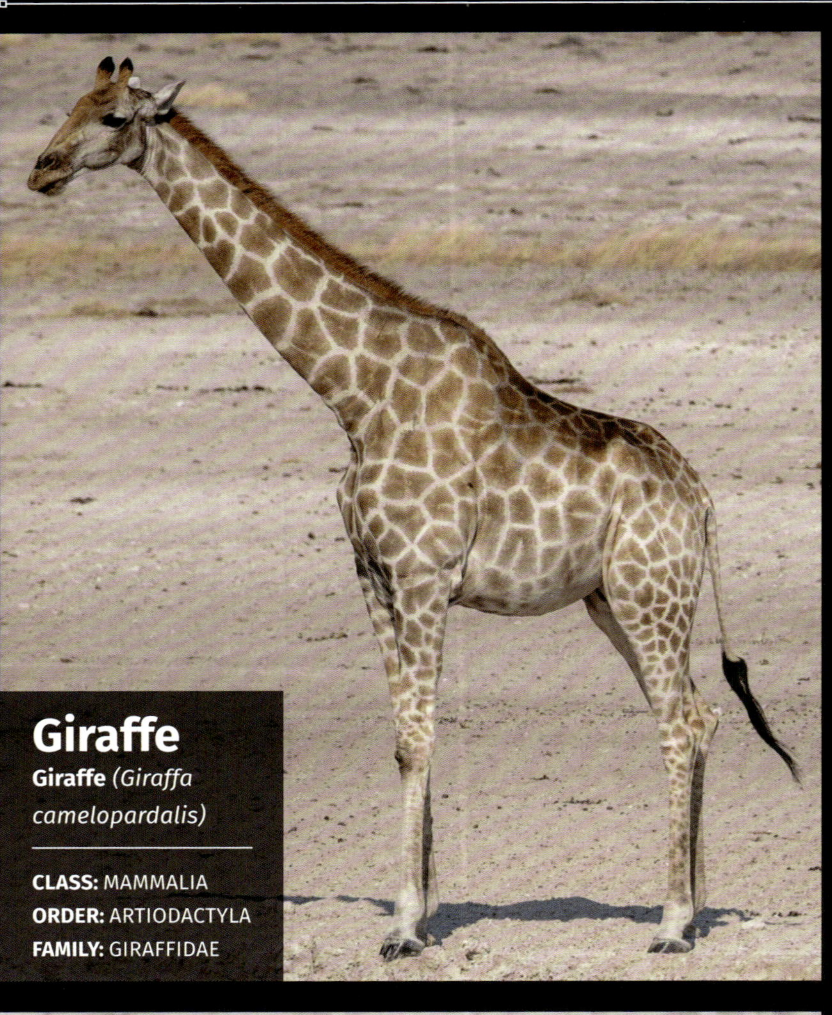

Giraffe

Giraffe *(Giraffa camelopardalis)*

CLASS: MAMMALIA
ORDER: ARTIODACTYLA
FAMILY: GIRAFFIDAE

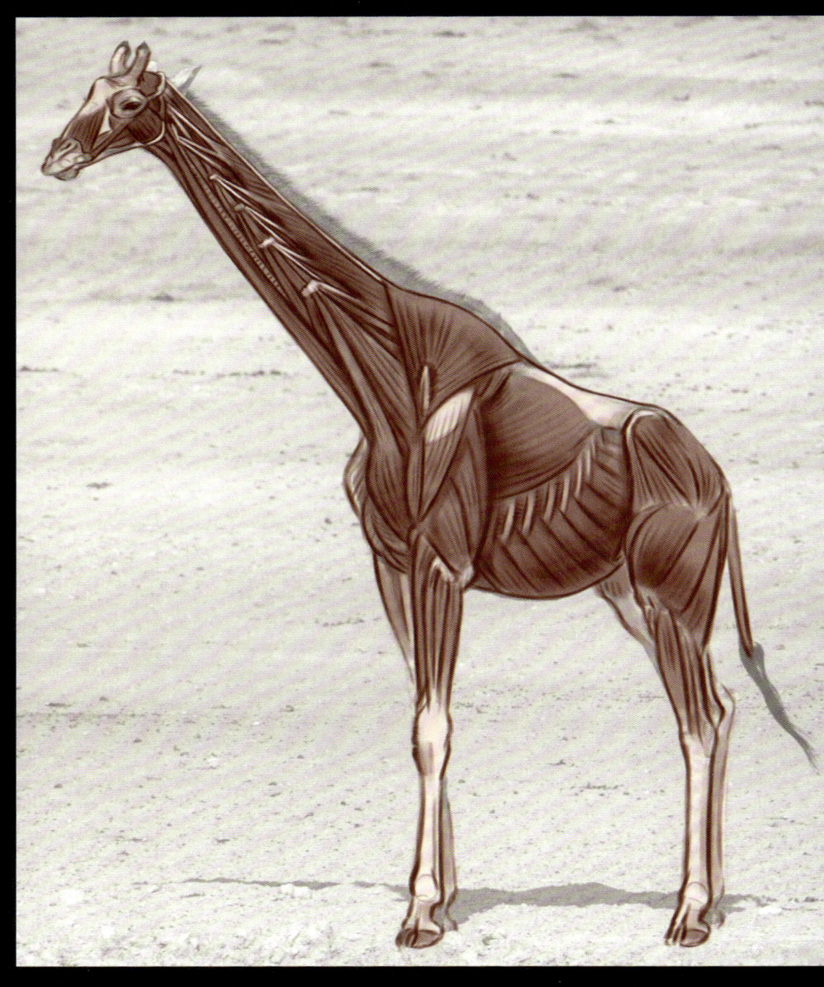

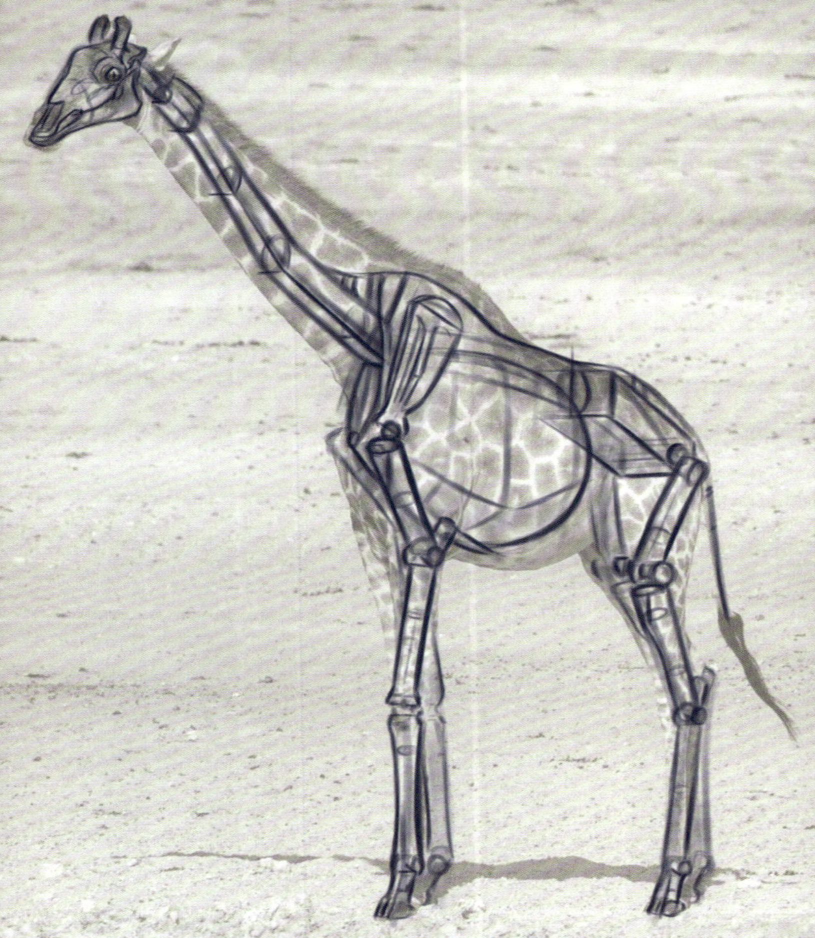

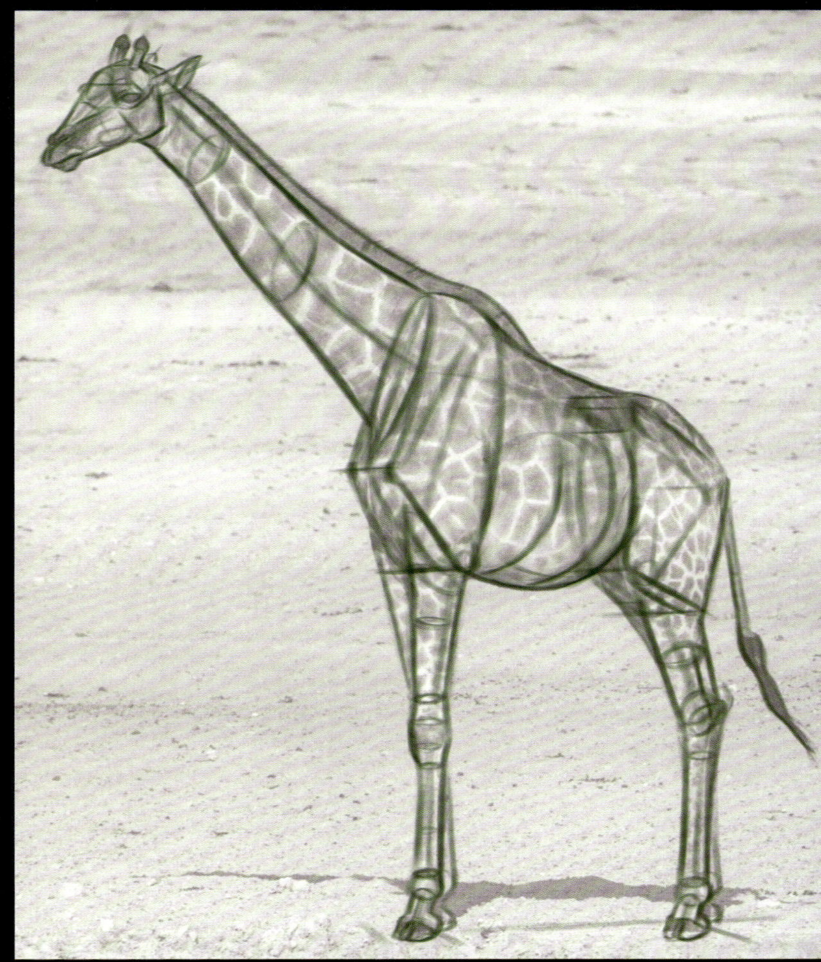

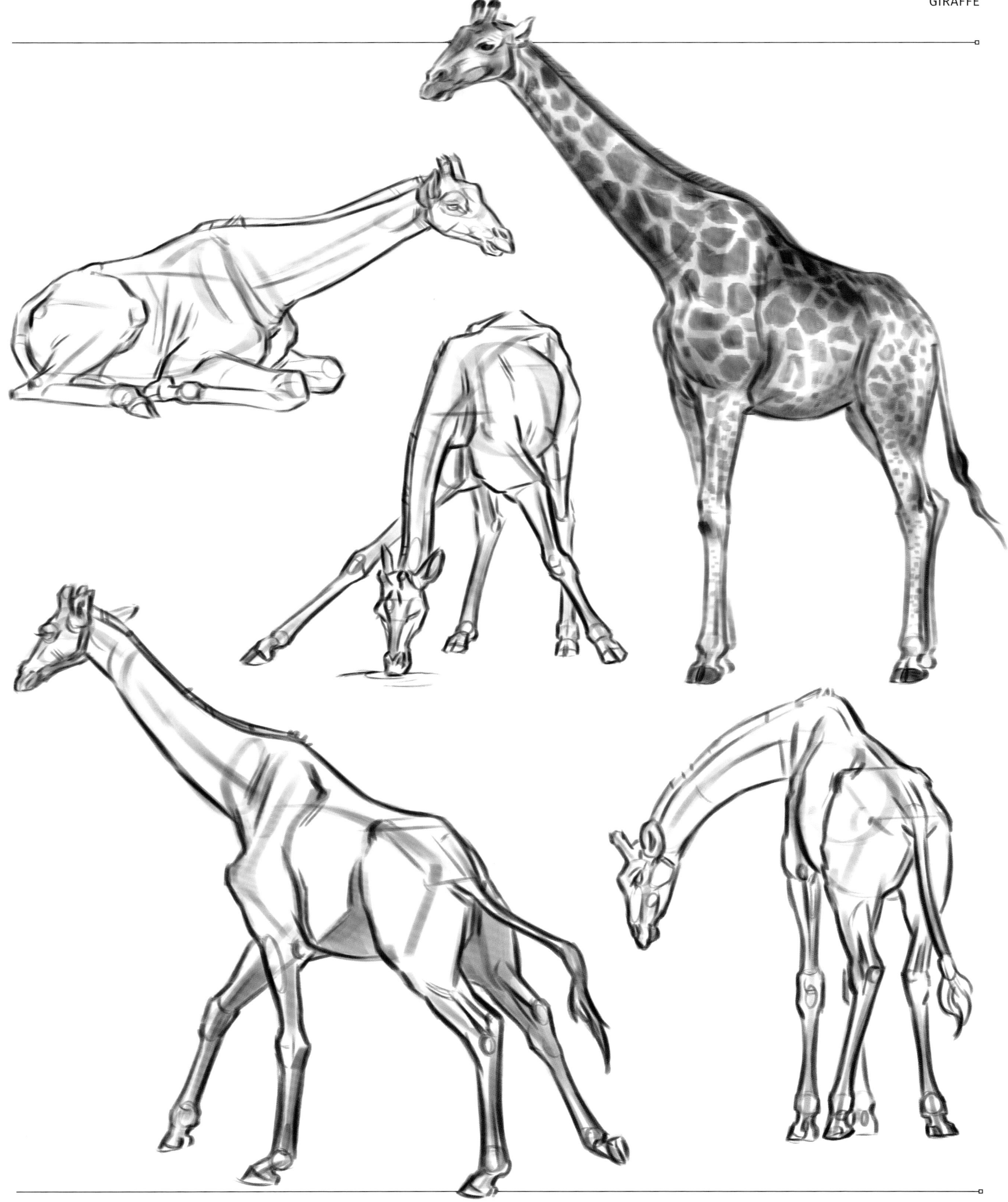

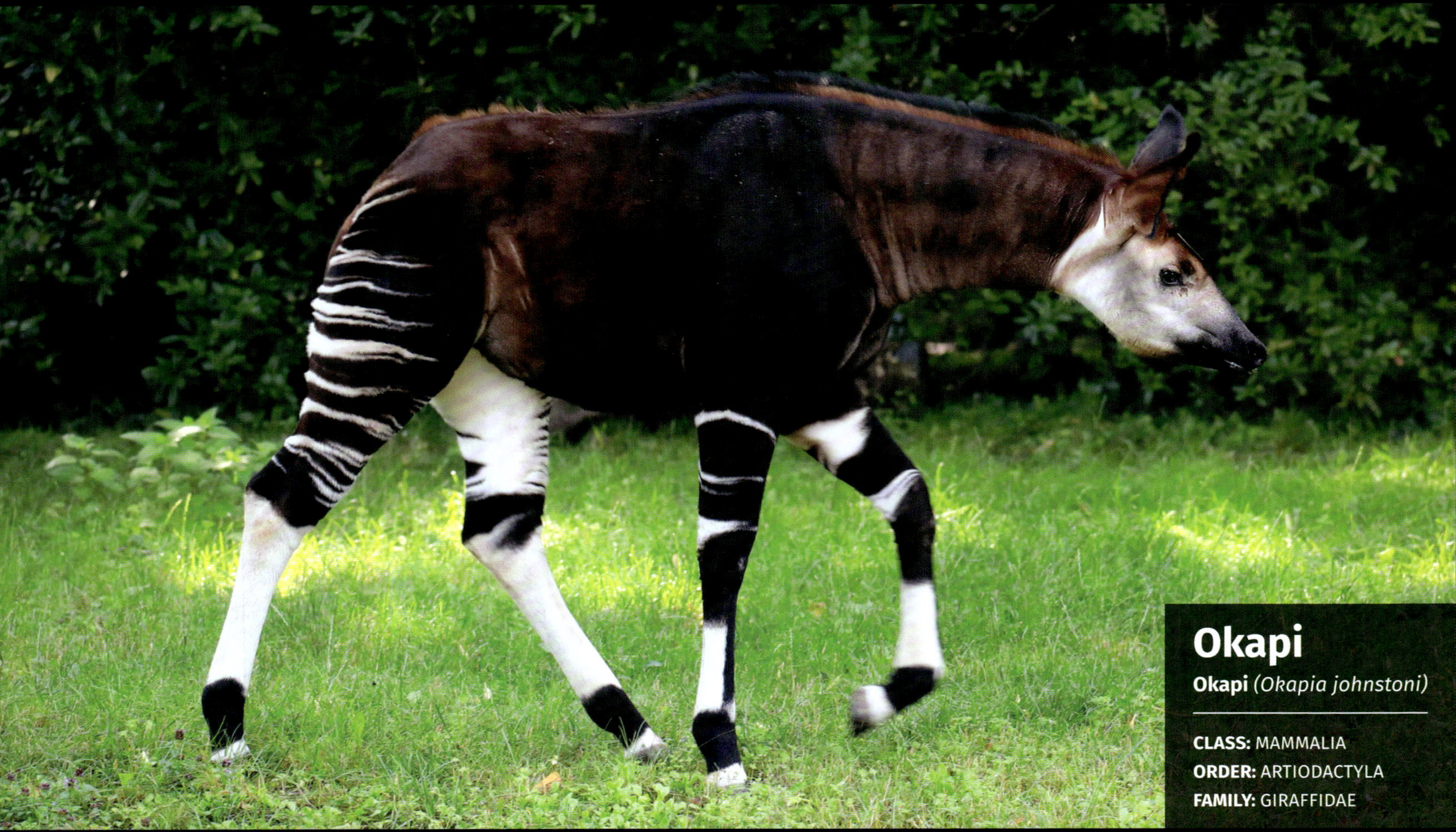

Okapi

Okapi *(Okapia johnstoni)*

CLASS: MAMMALIA
ORDER: ARTIODACTYLA
FAMILY: GIRAFFIDAE

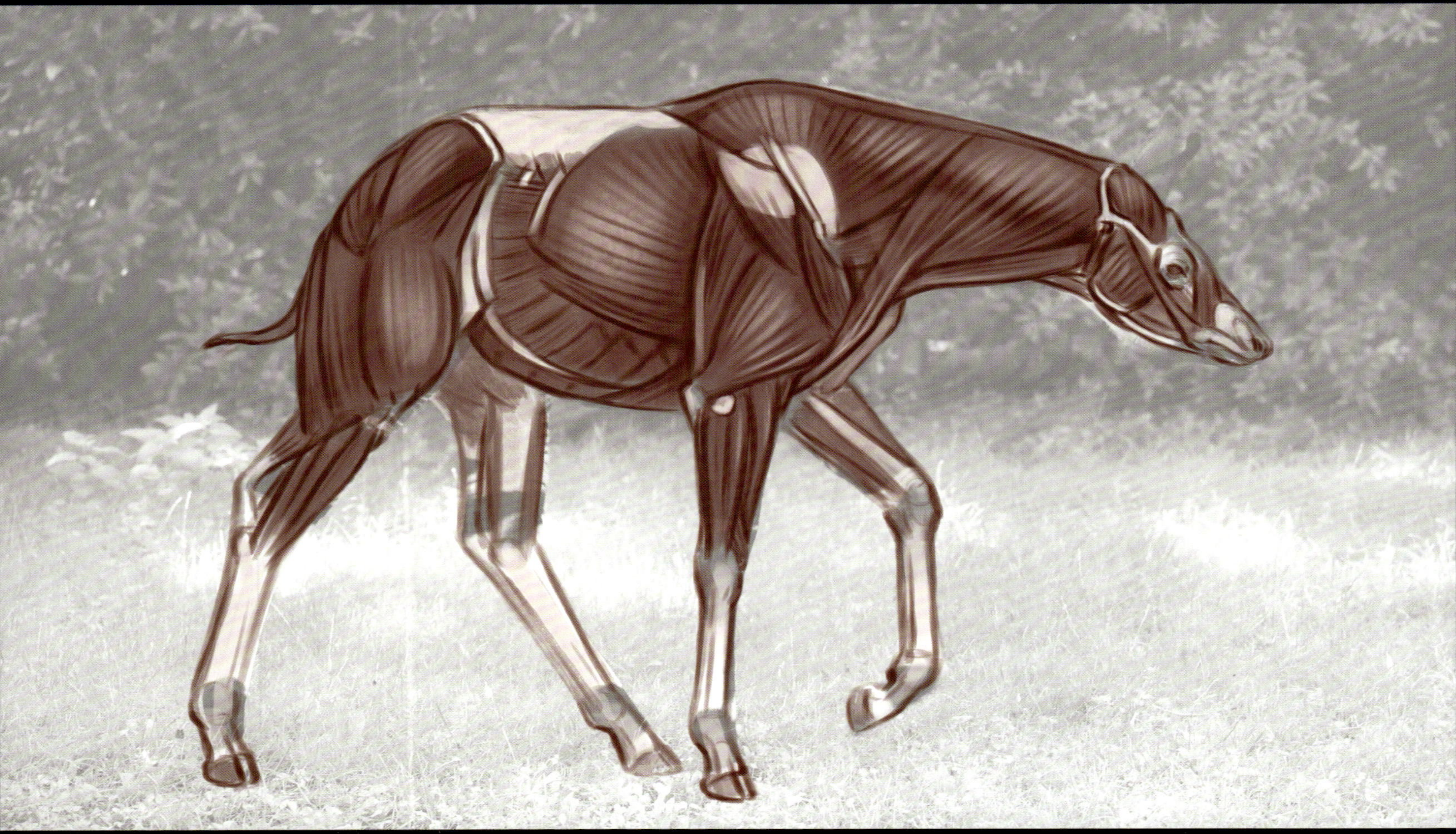

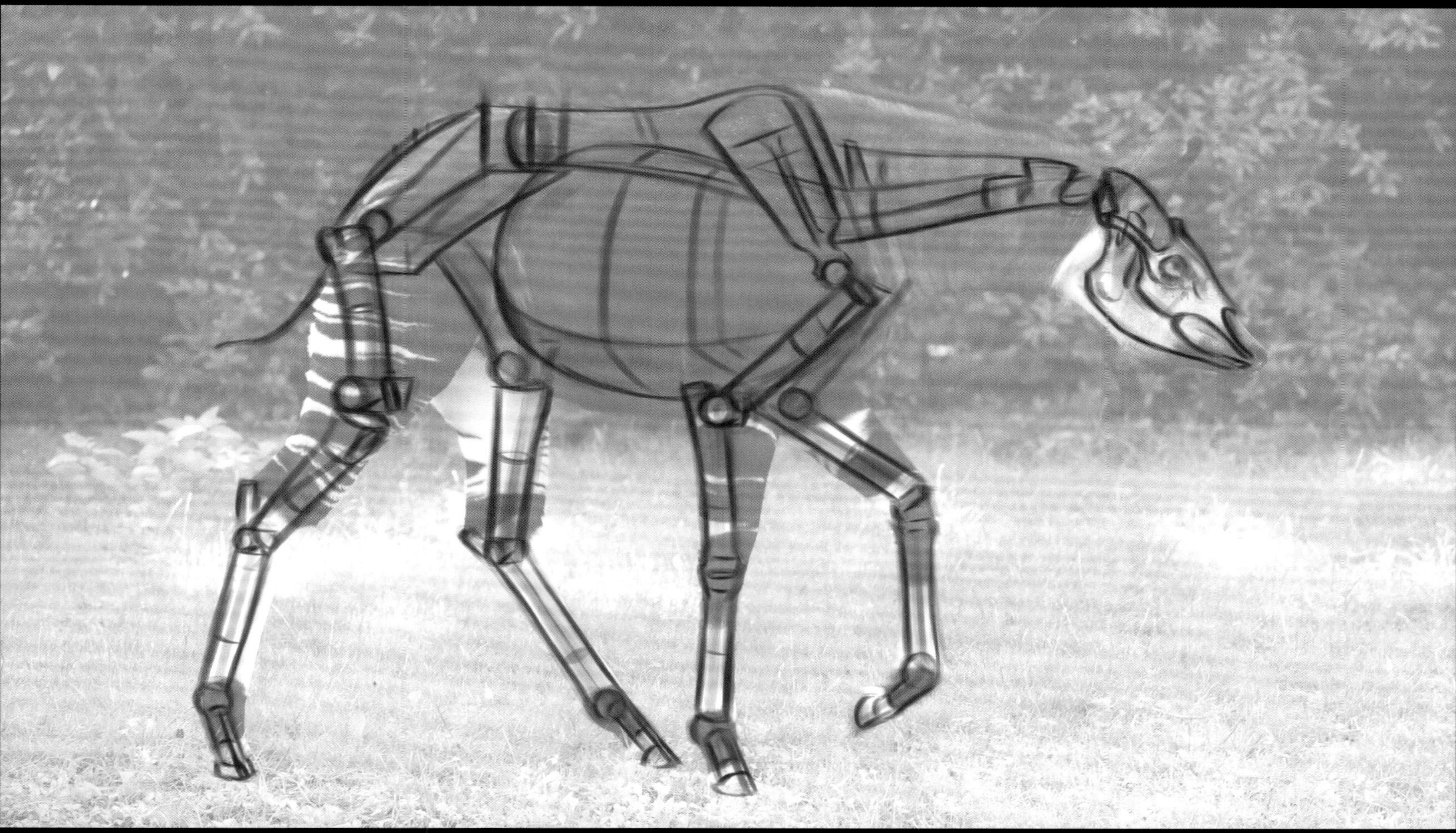

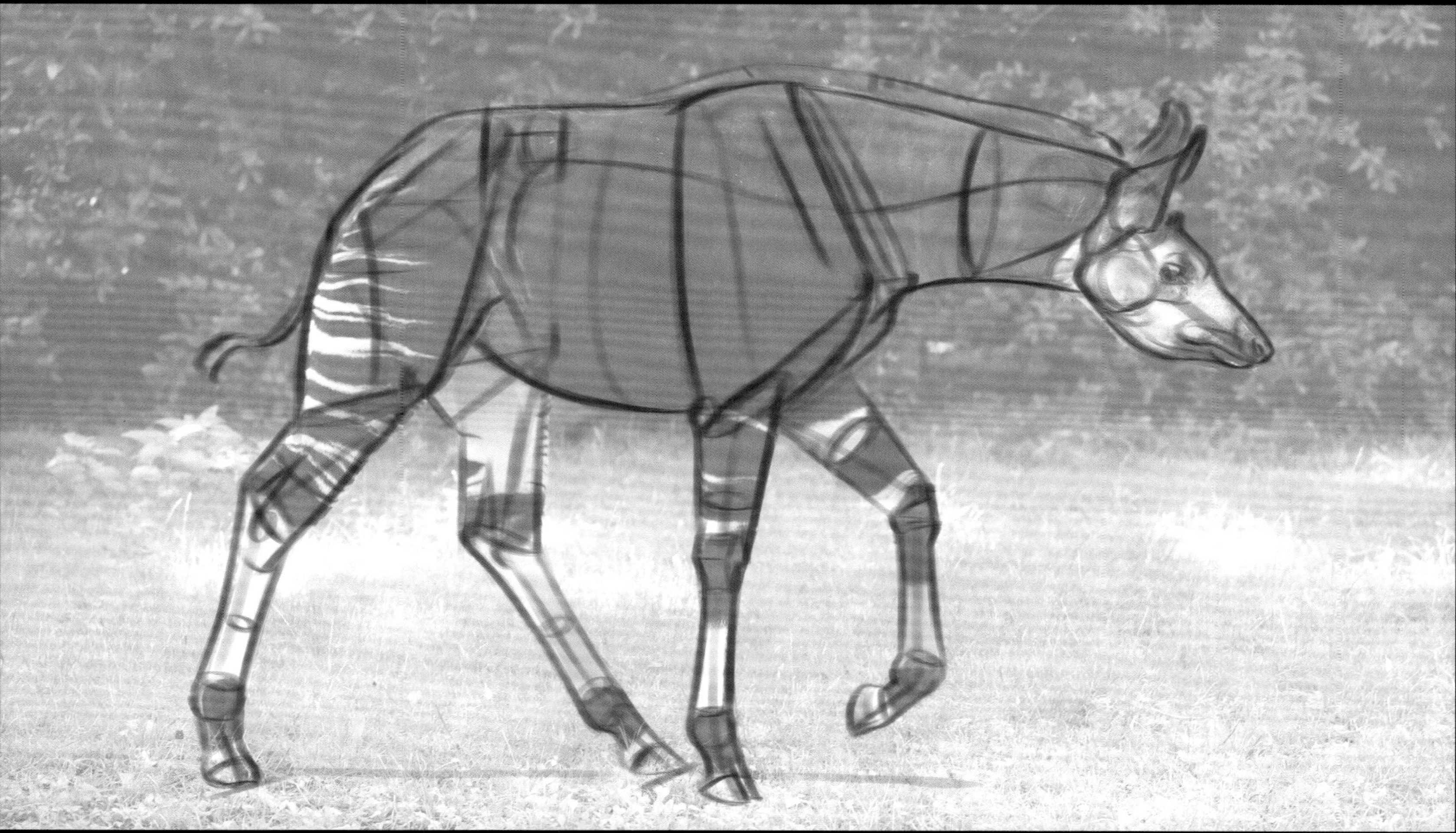

Photograph © imageBROKER.com / Jürgen & Christine Sohns

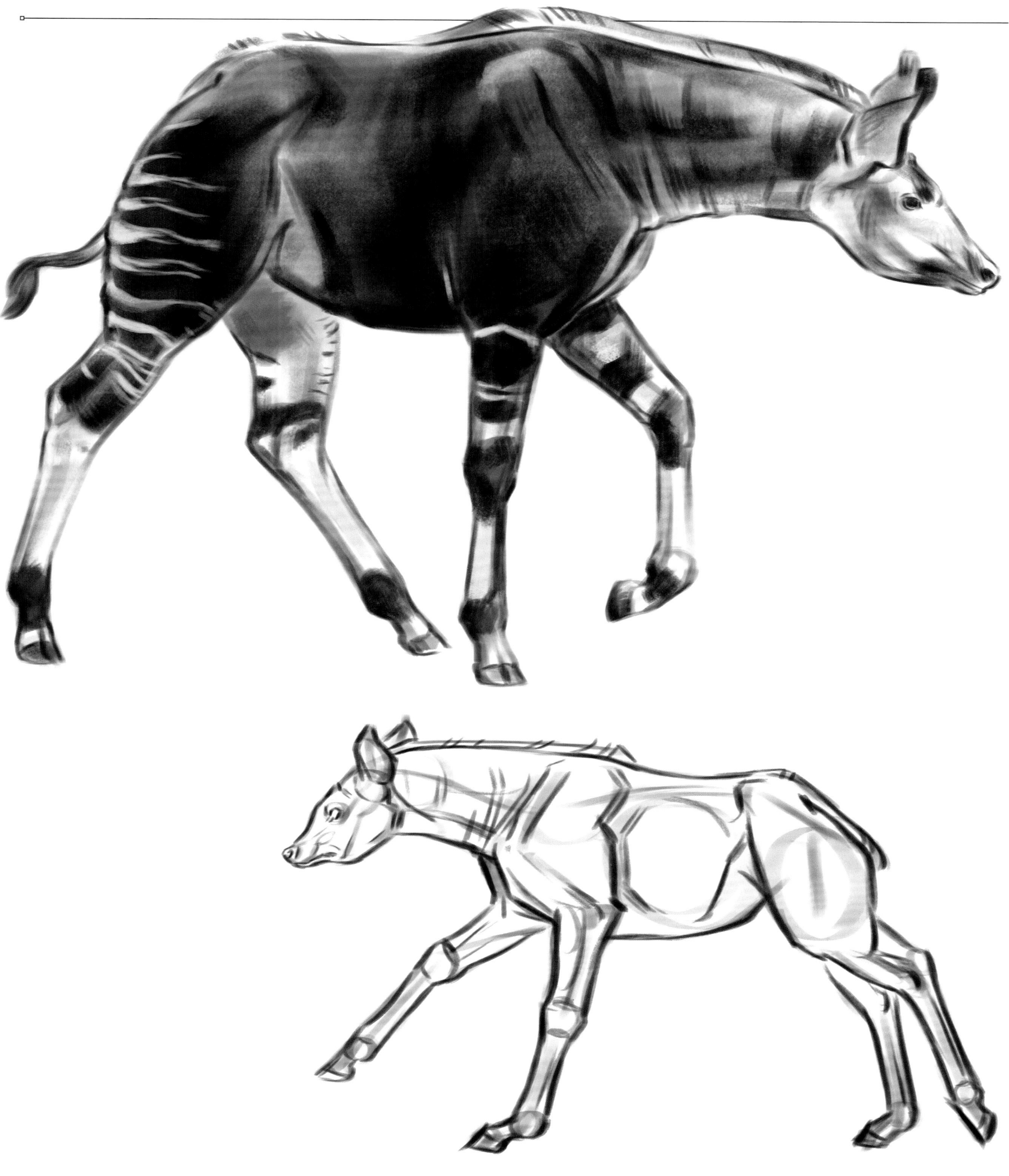

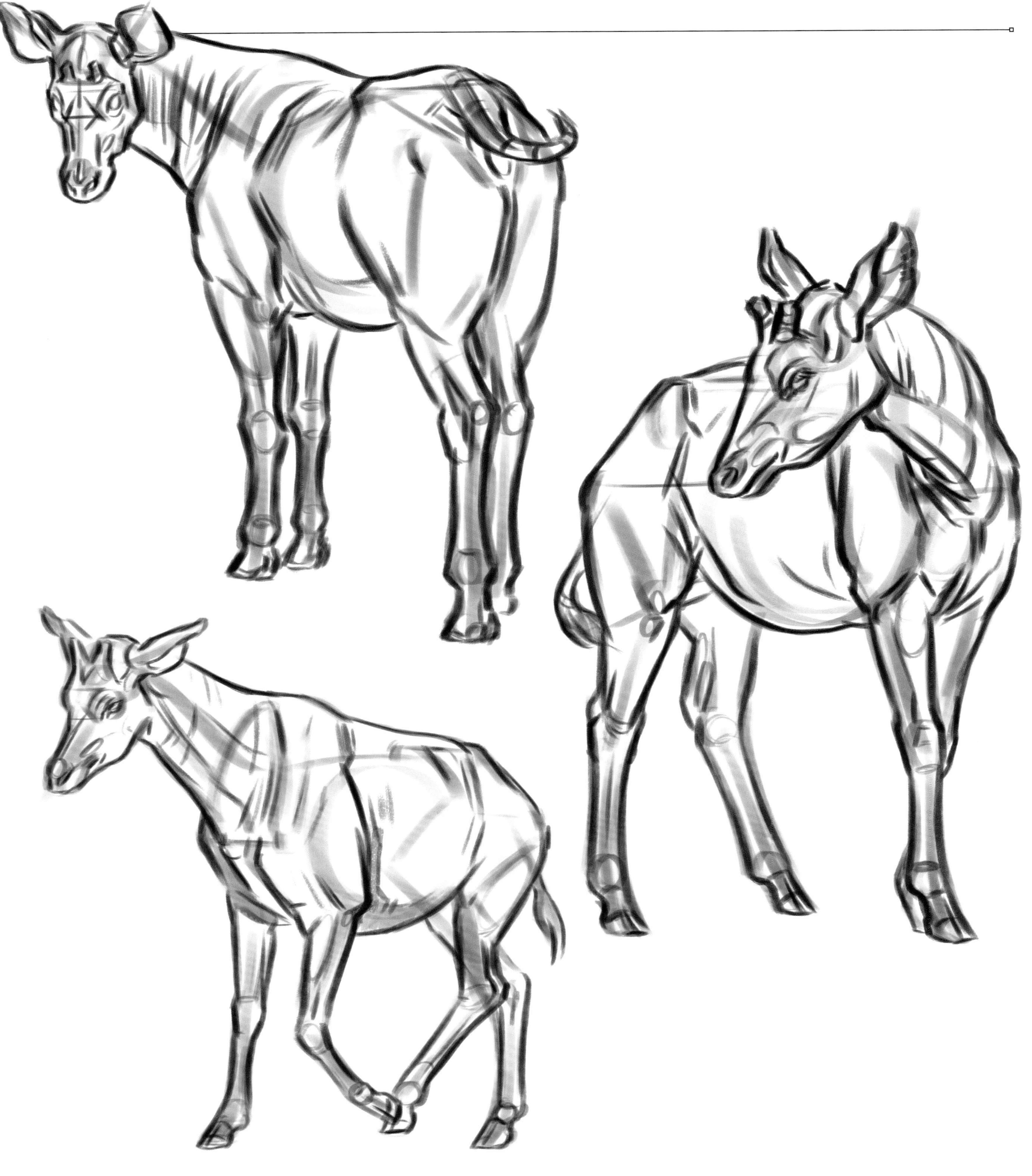

Hippopotamus

Hippopotamus

(Hippopotamus amphibius)

CLASS: MAMMALIA
ORDER: ARTIODACTYLA
FAMILY: HIPPOPOTAMIDAE

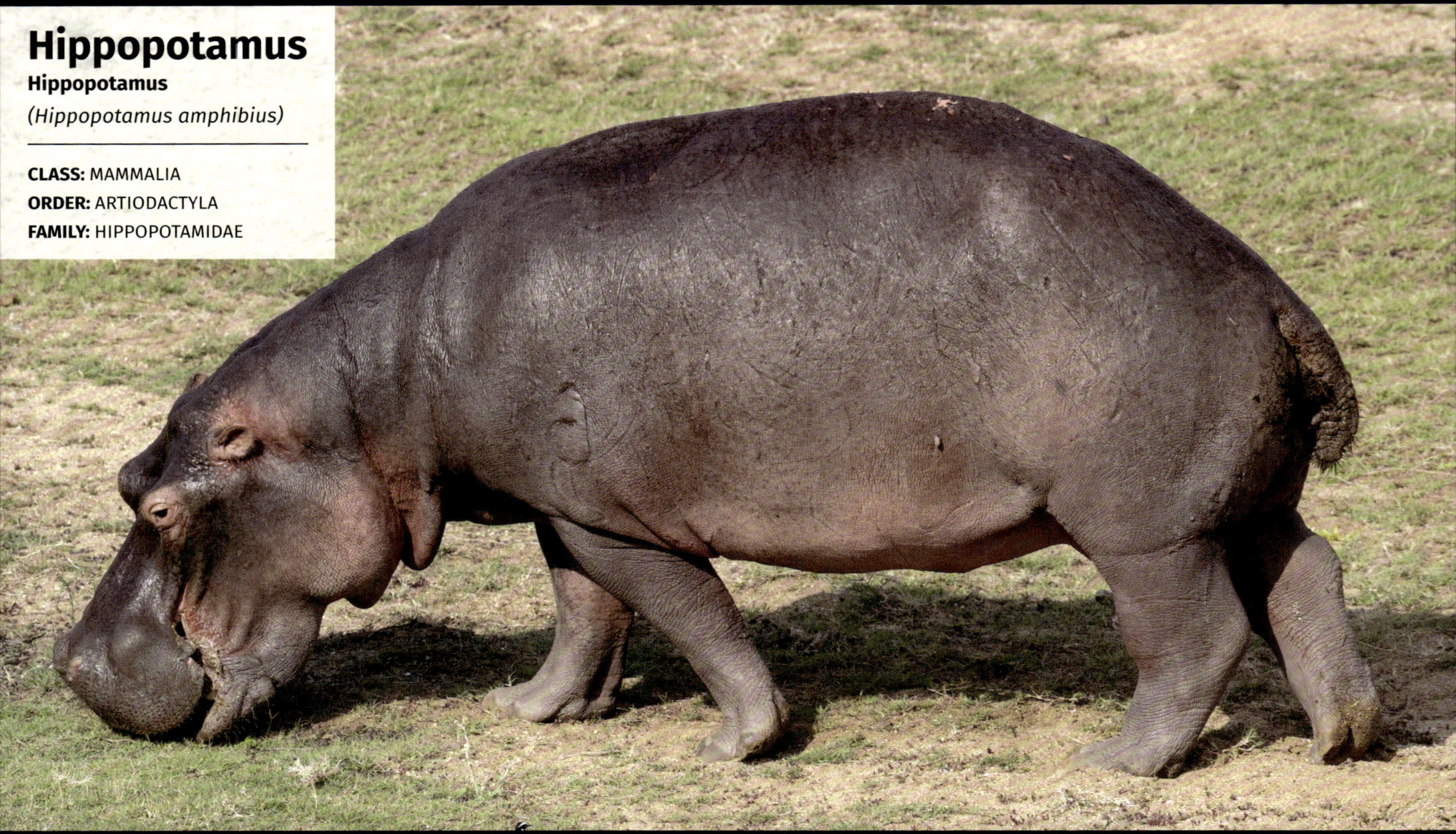

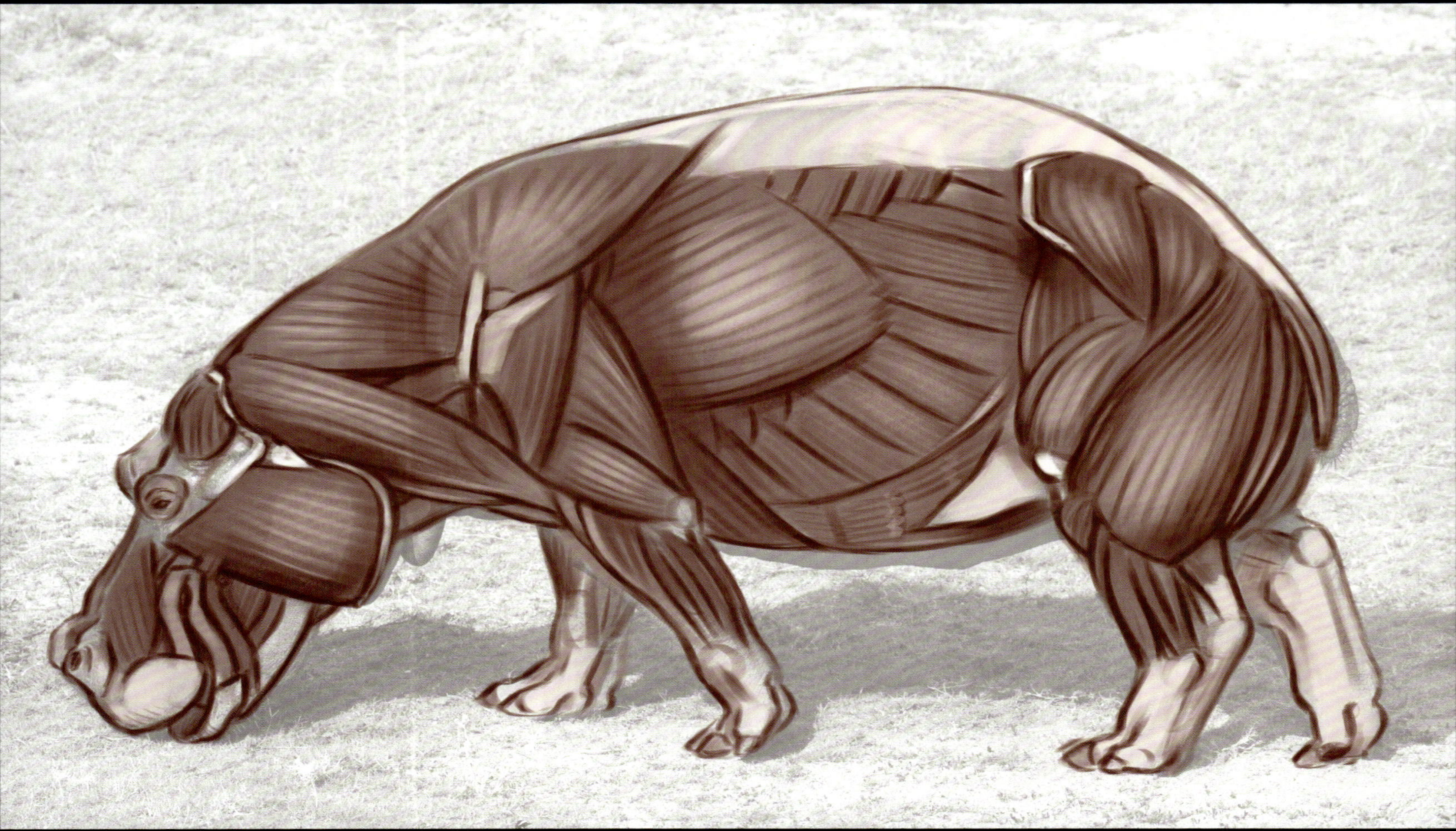

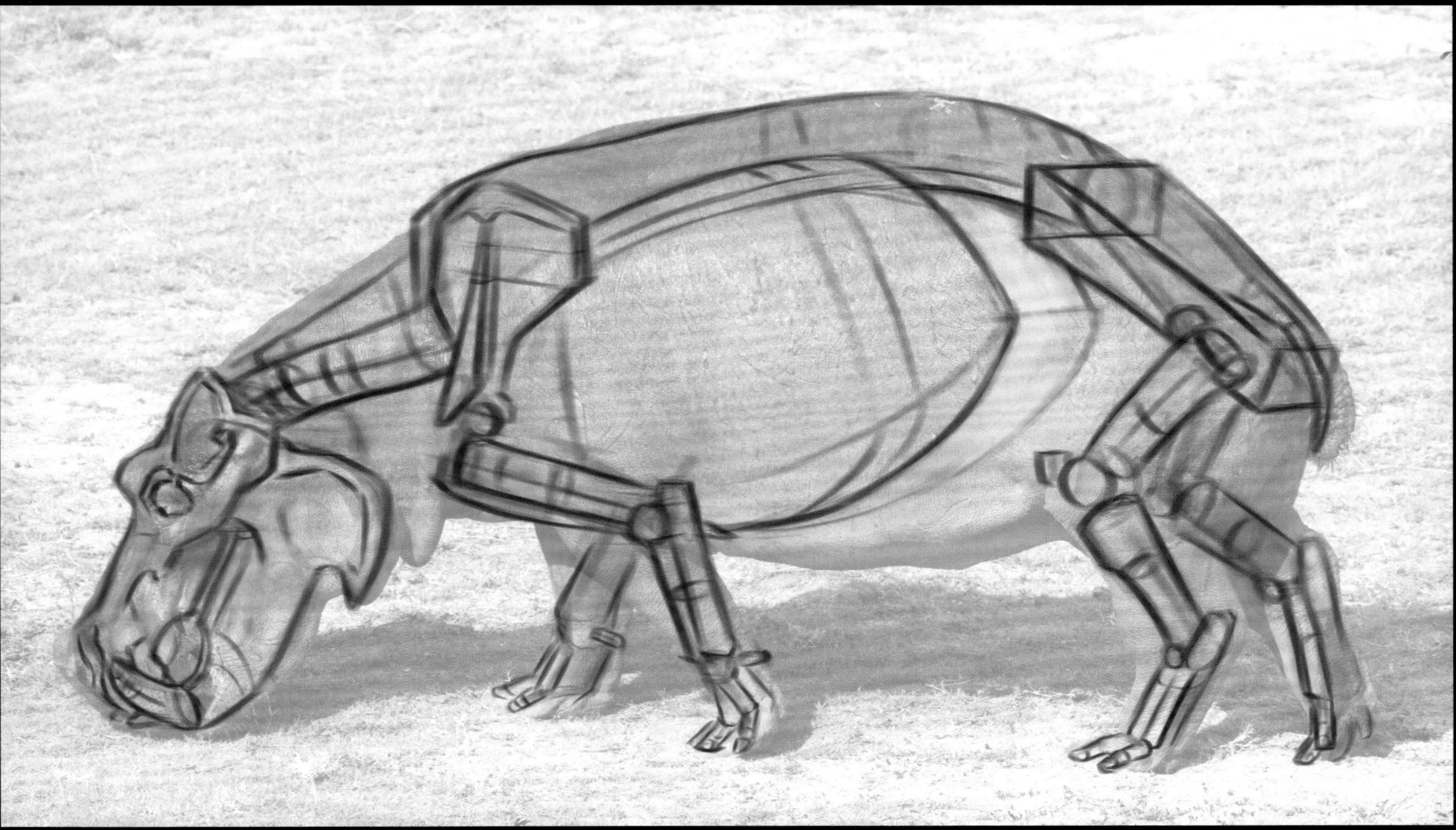

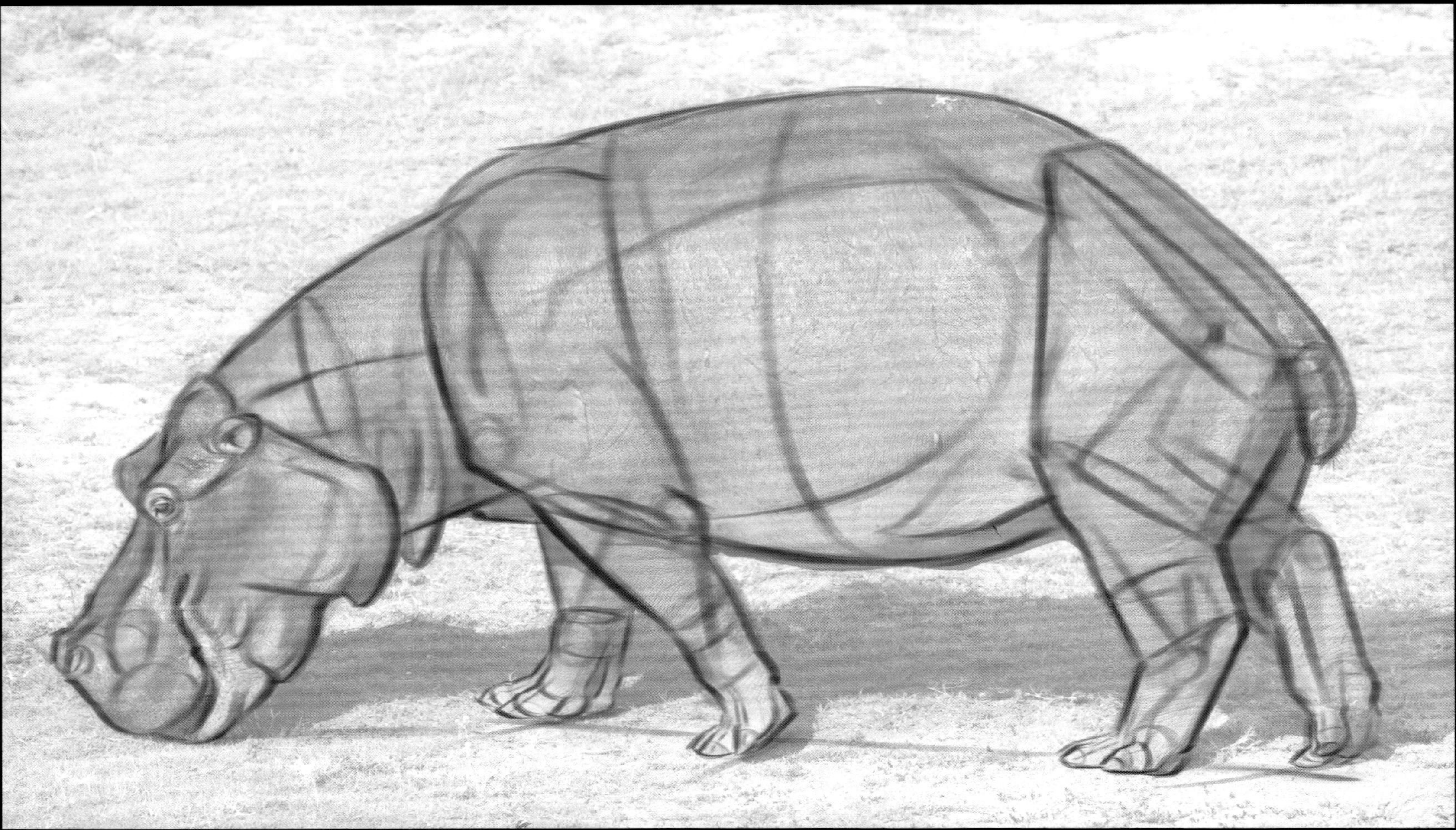

Photograph © Saverio Gatto / Agami.nl

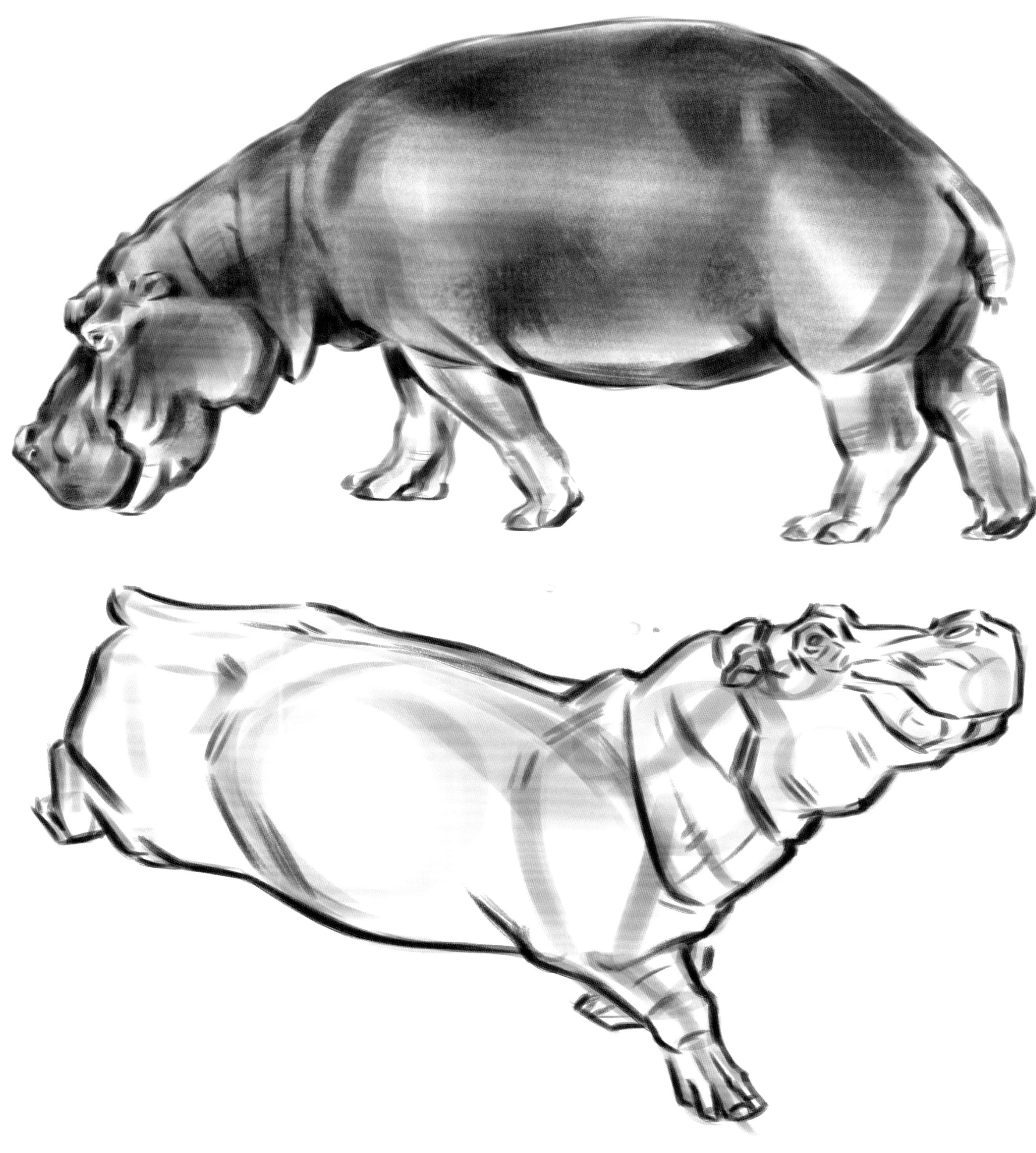

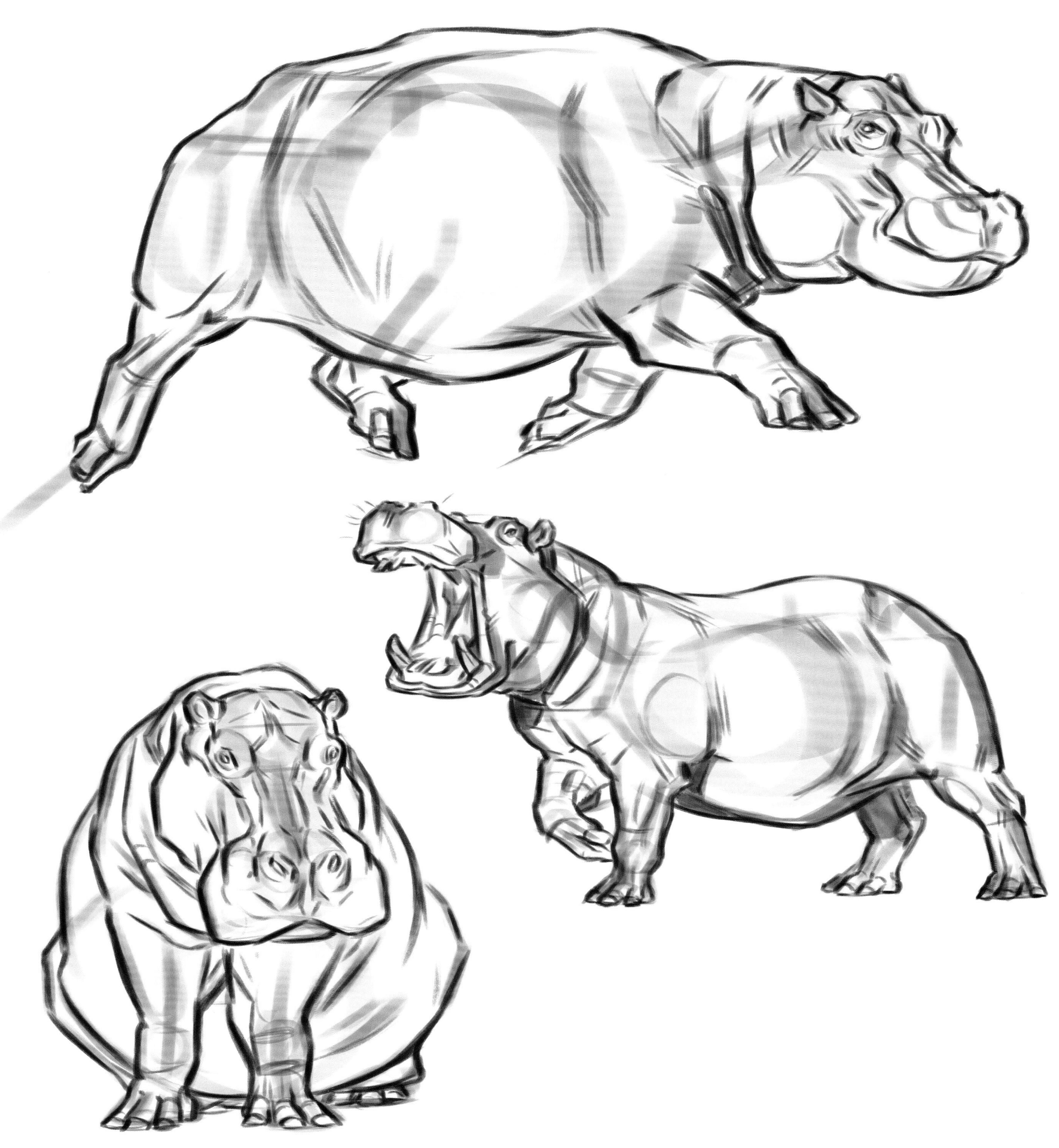

Dog

Irish red & white setter

(Canis lupus familiaris)

CLASS: MAMMALIA

ORDER: CARNIVORA

FAMILY: CANIDAE

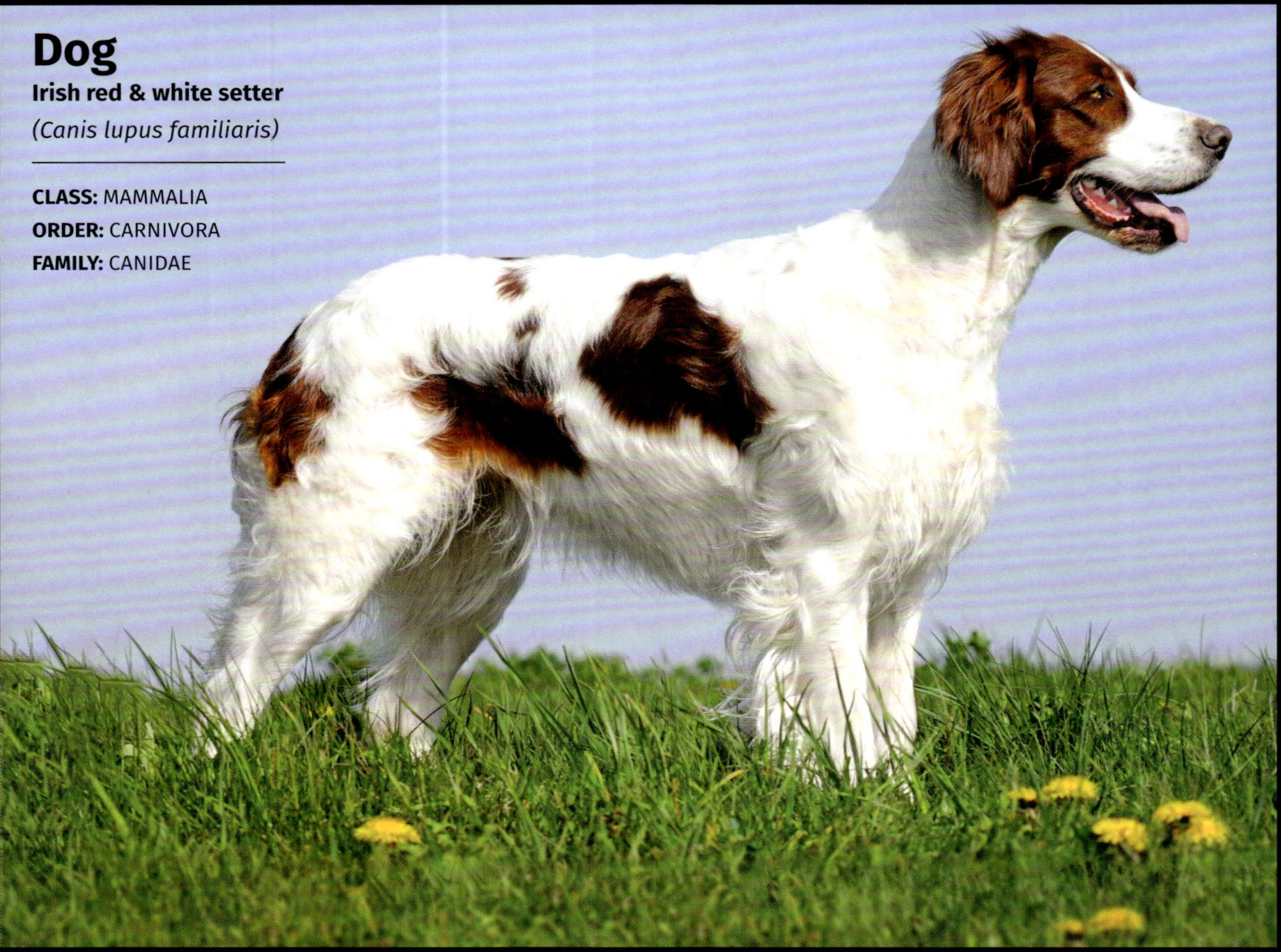

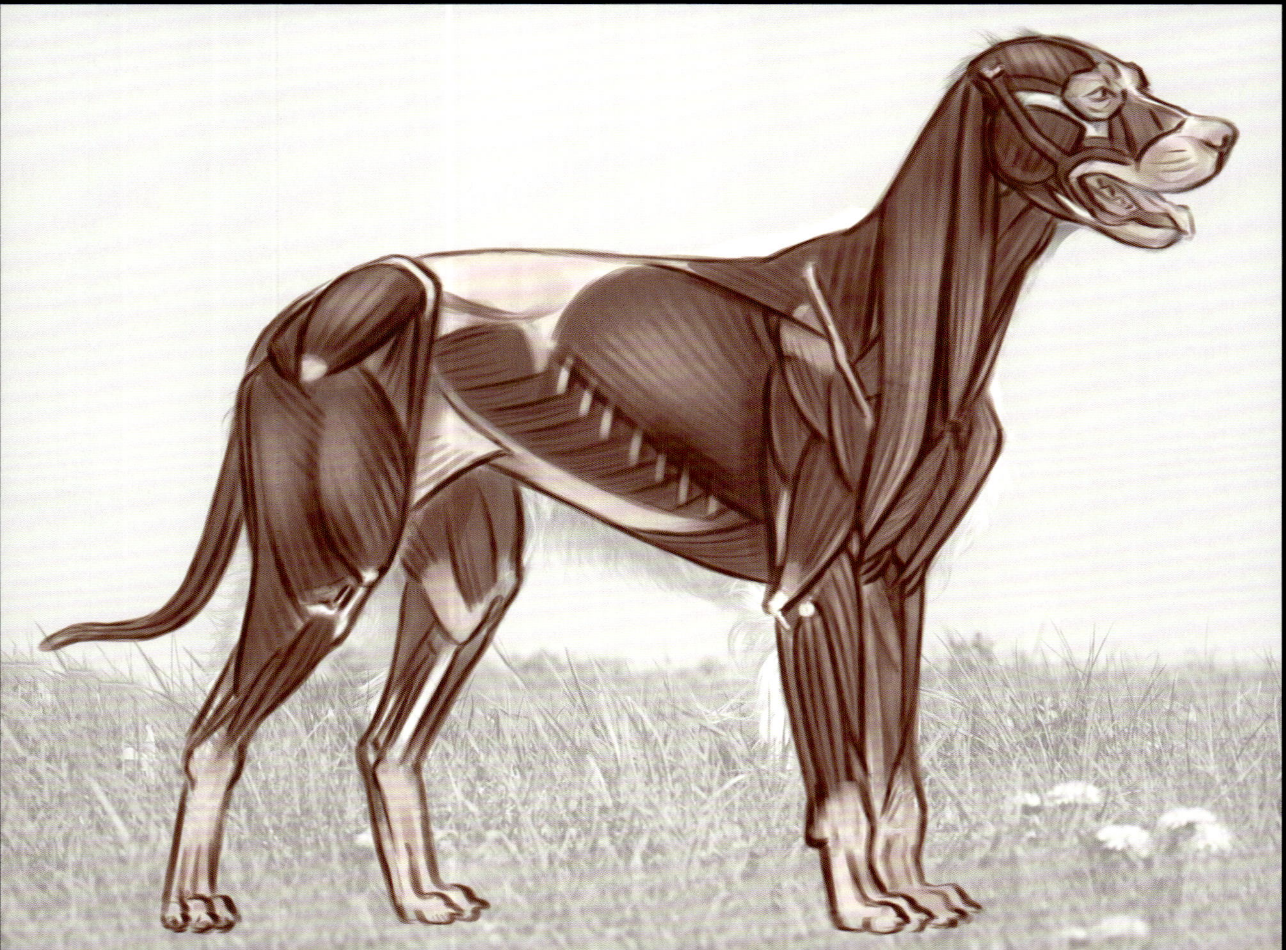

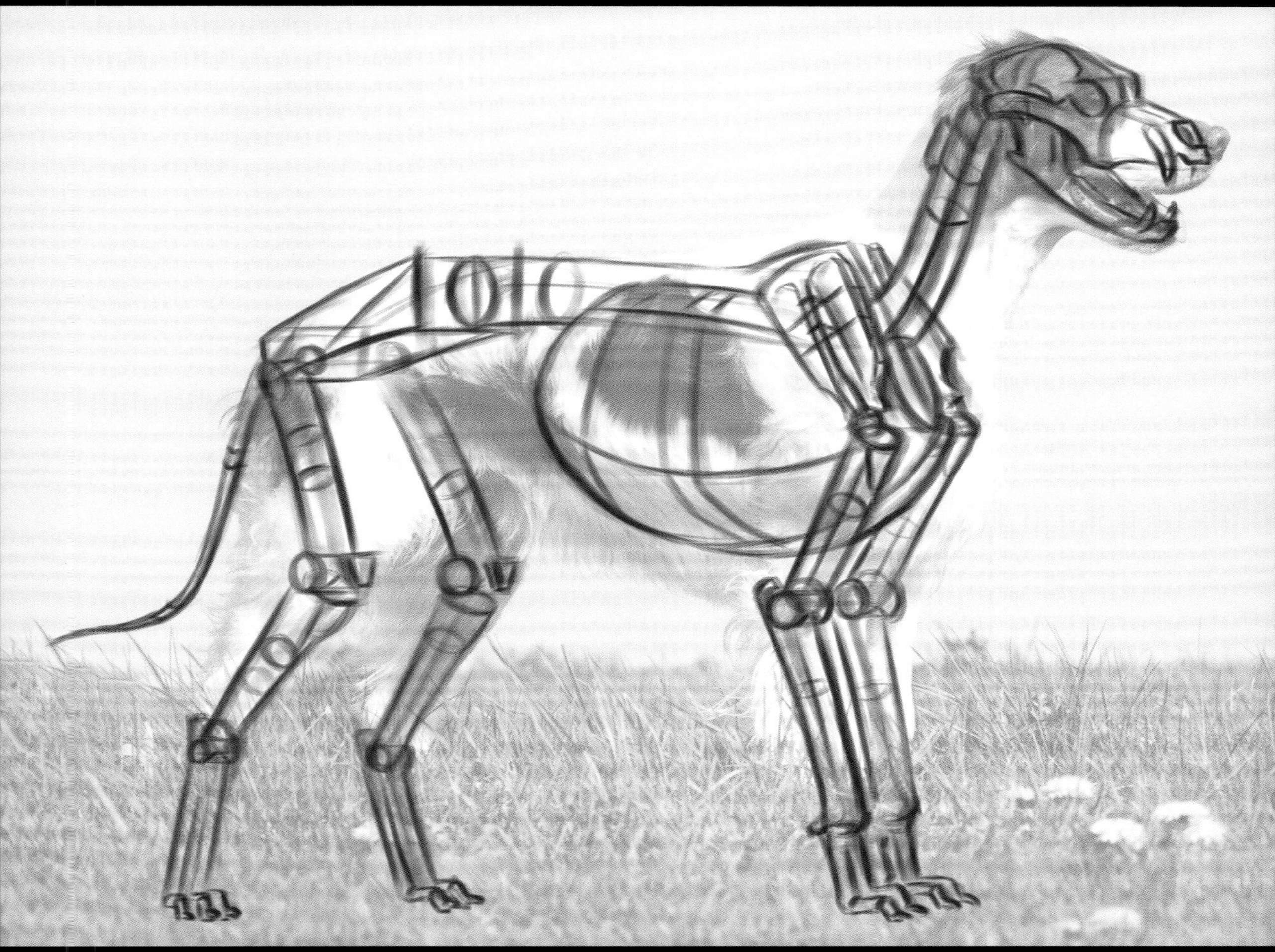

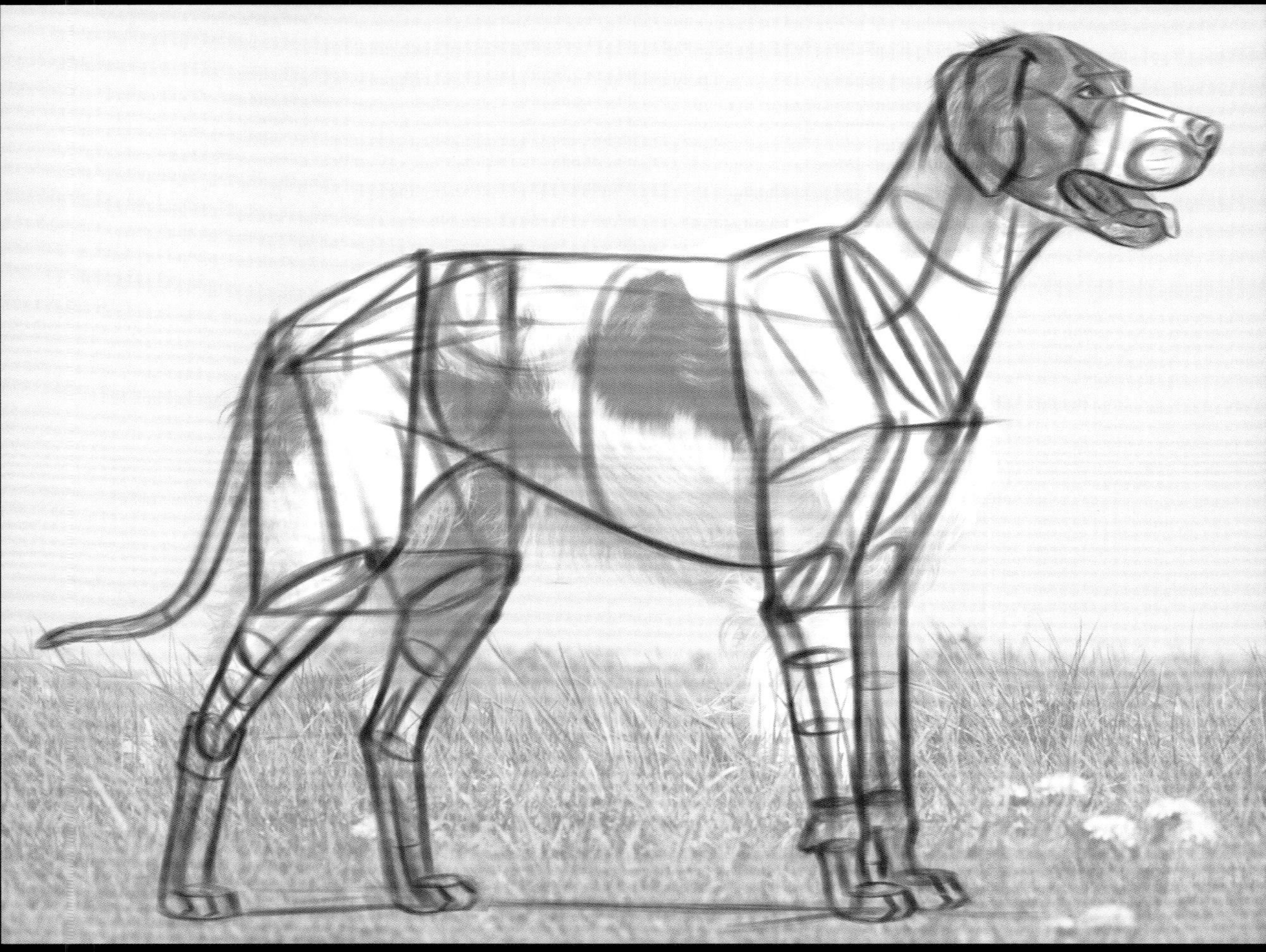

Photograph © imageBROKER.com / Anni Sommer

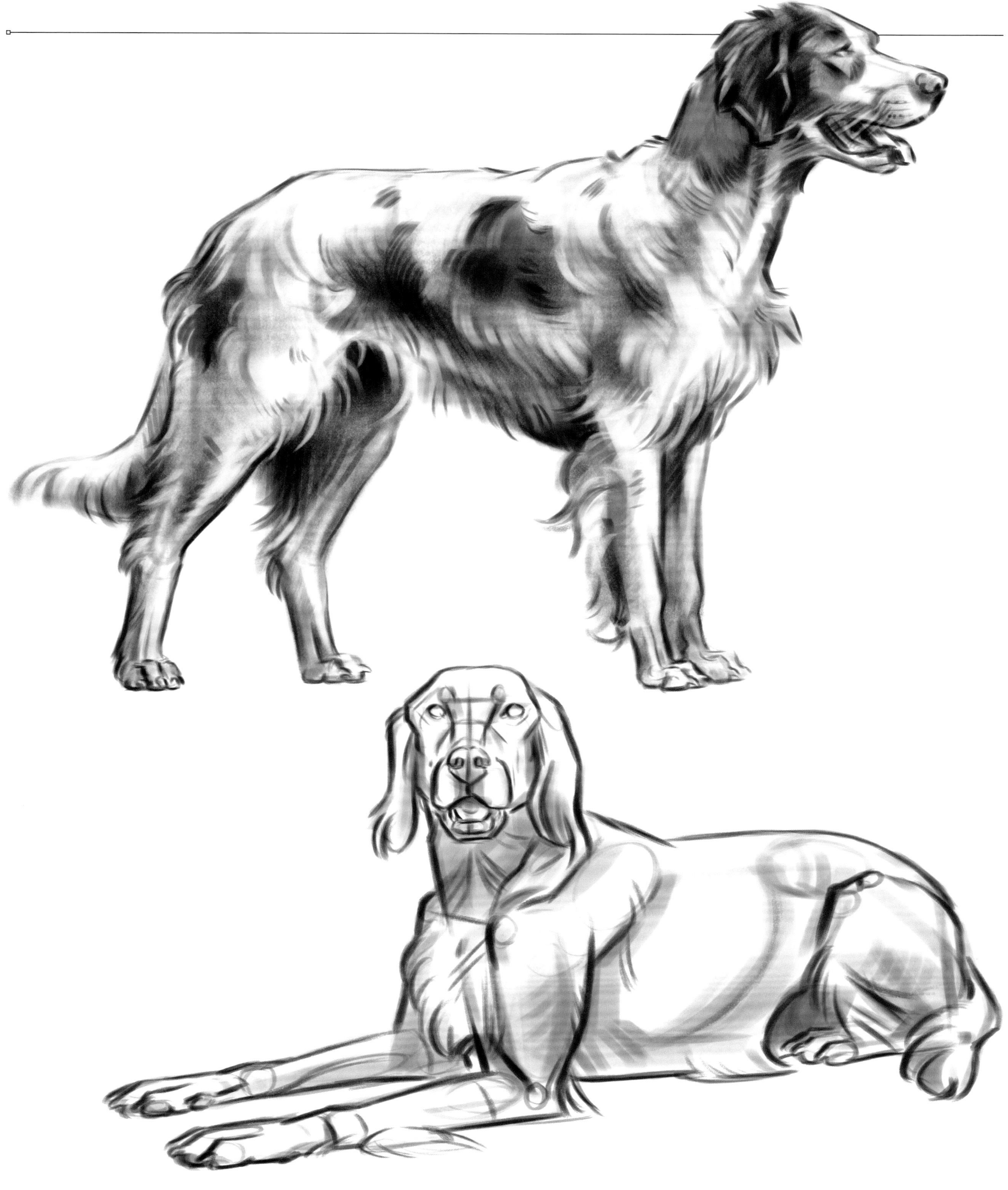

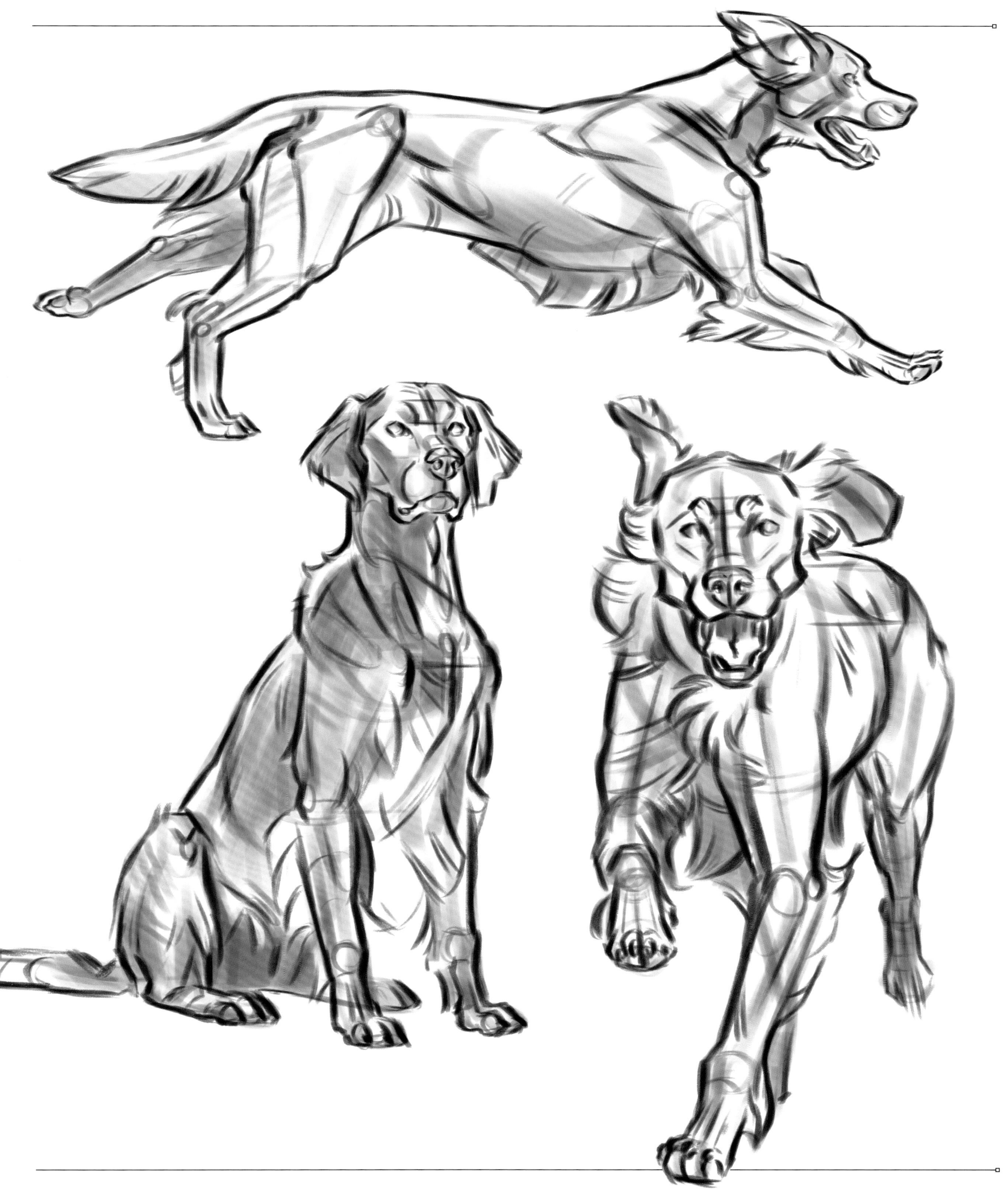

Fox

Red fox *(Vulpes vulpes)*

CLASS: MAMMALIA
ORDER: CARNIVORA
FAMILY: CANIDAE

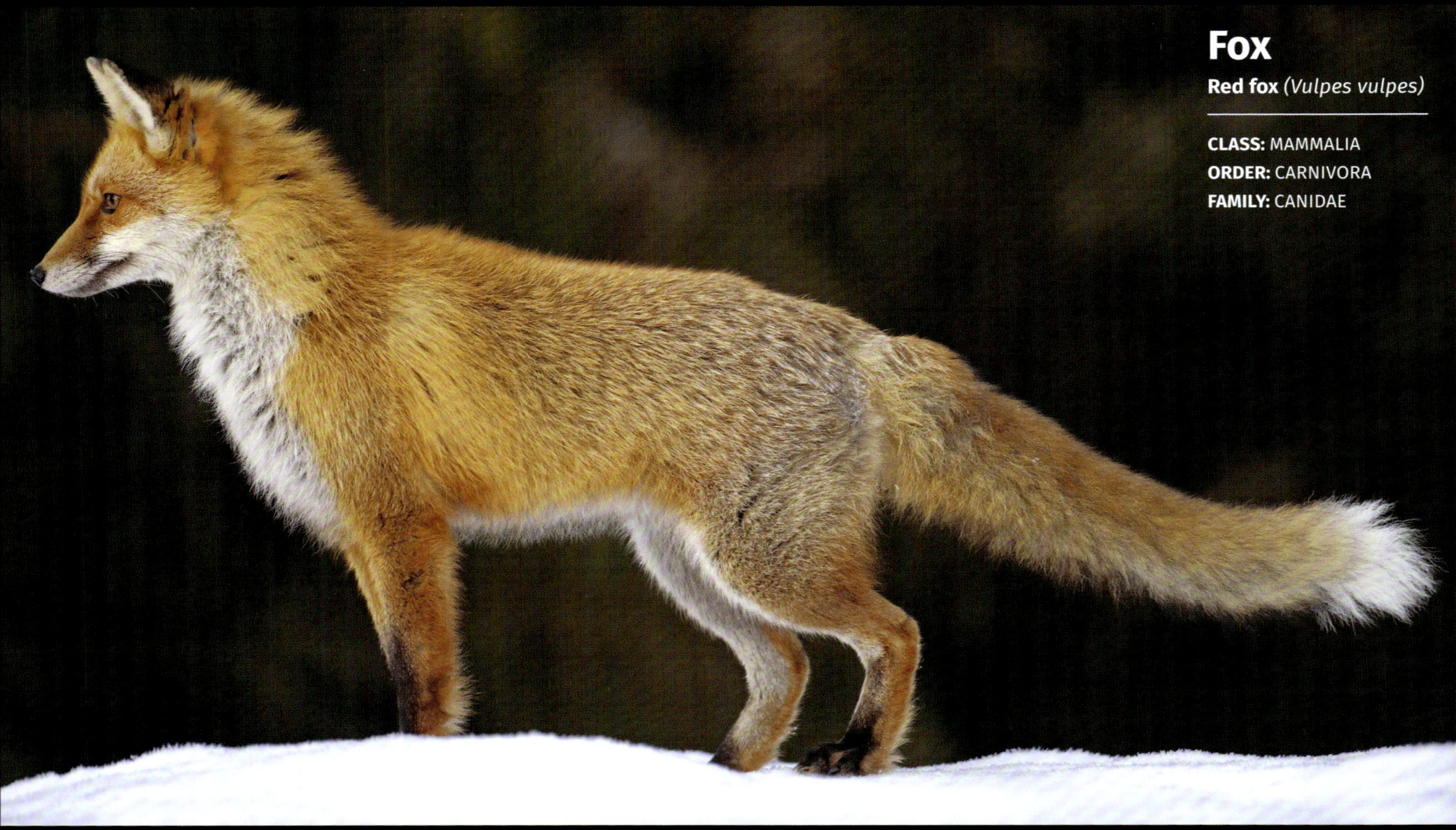

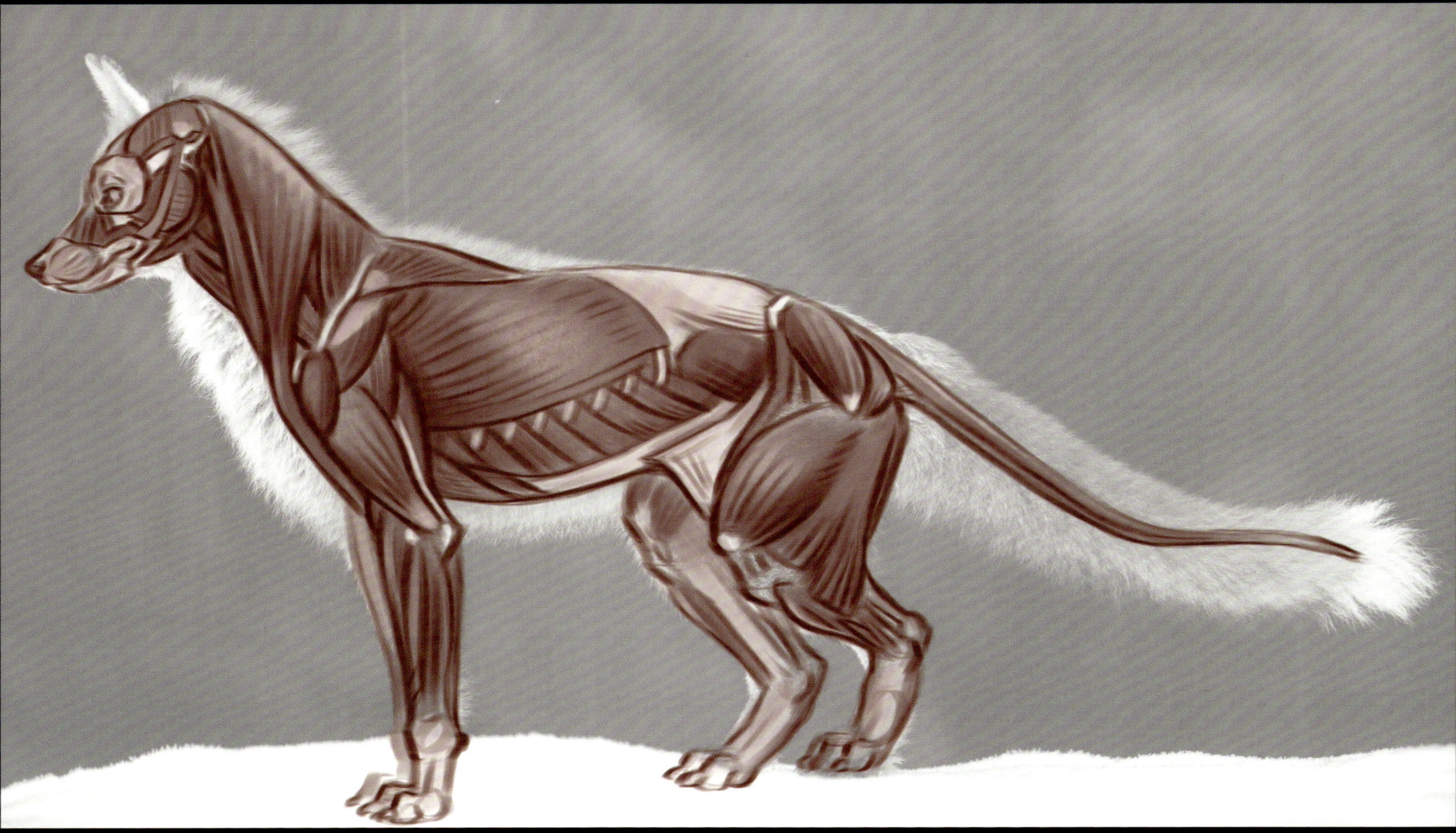

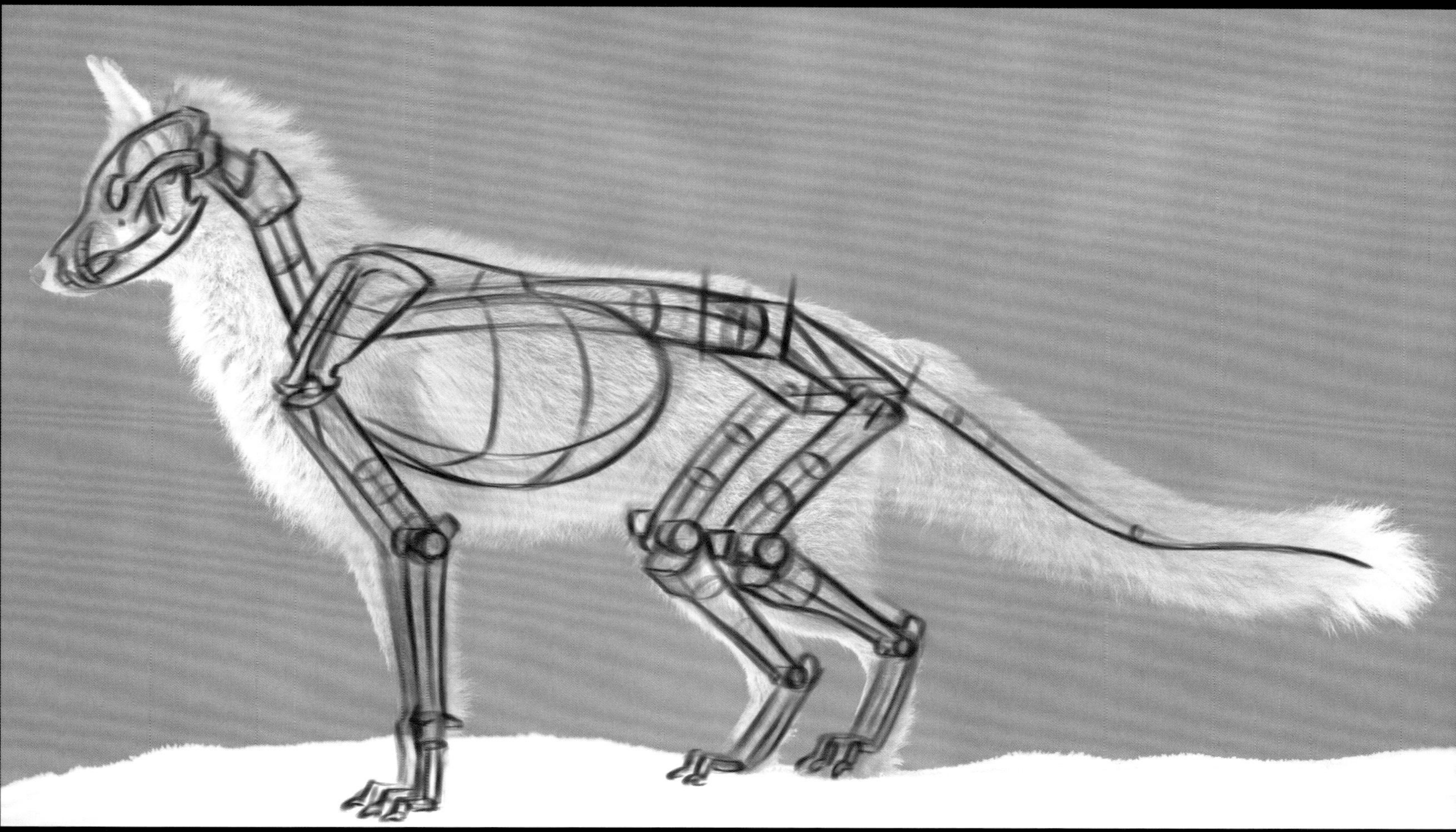

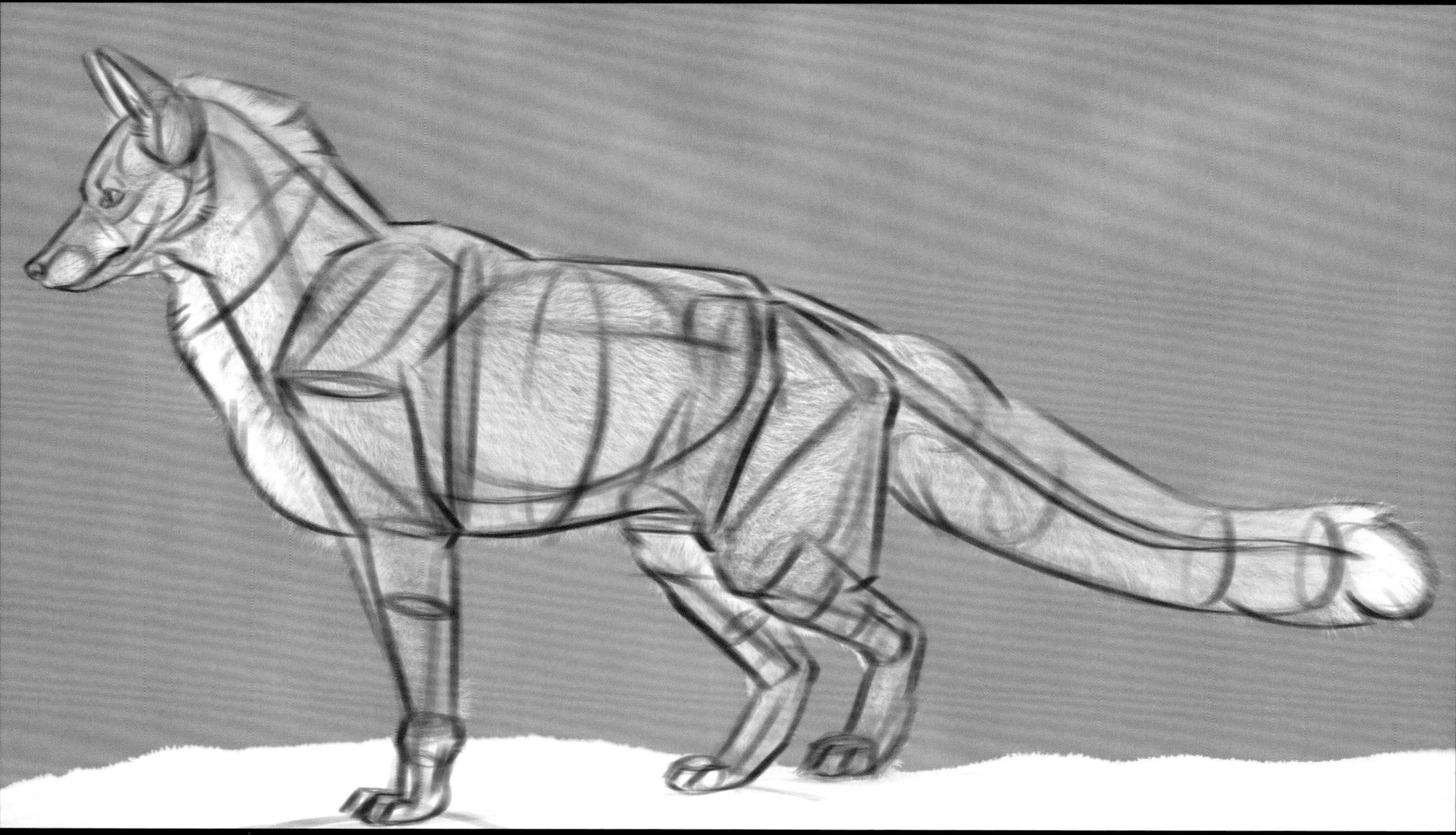

Photograph © Markus Varesvuo / Agami.nl

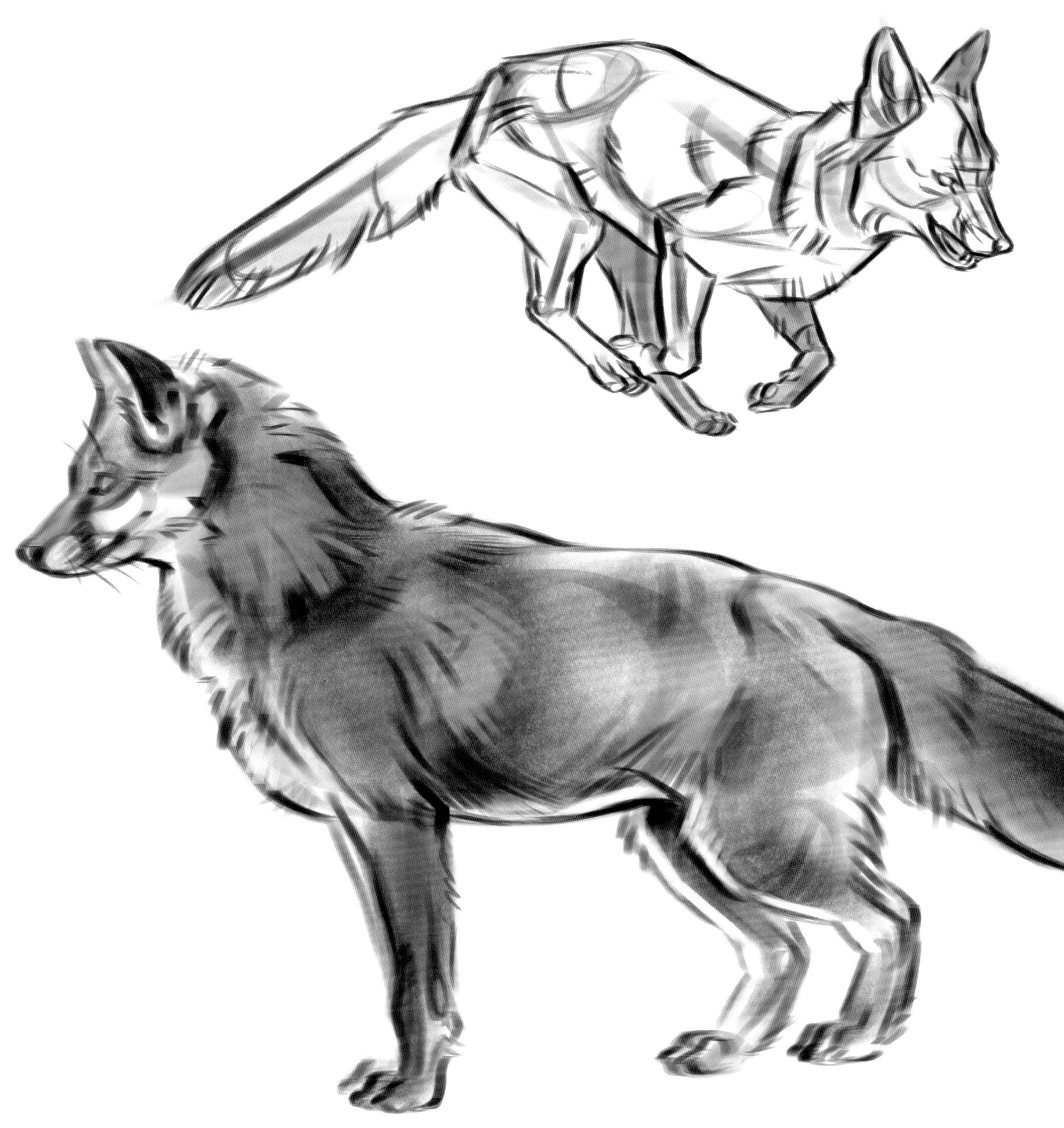

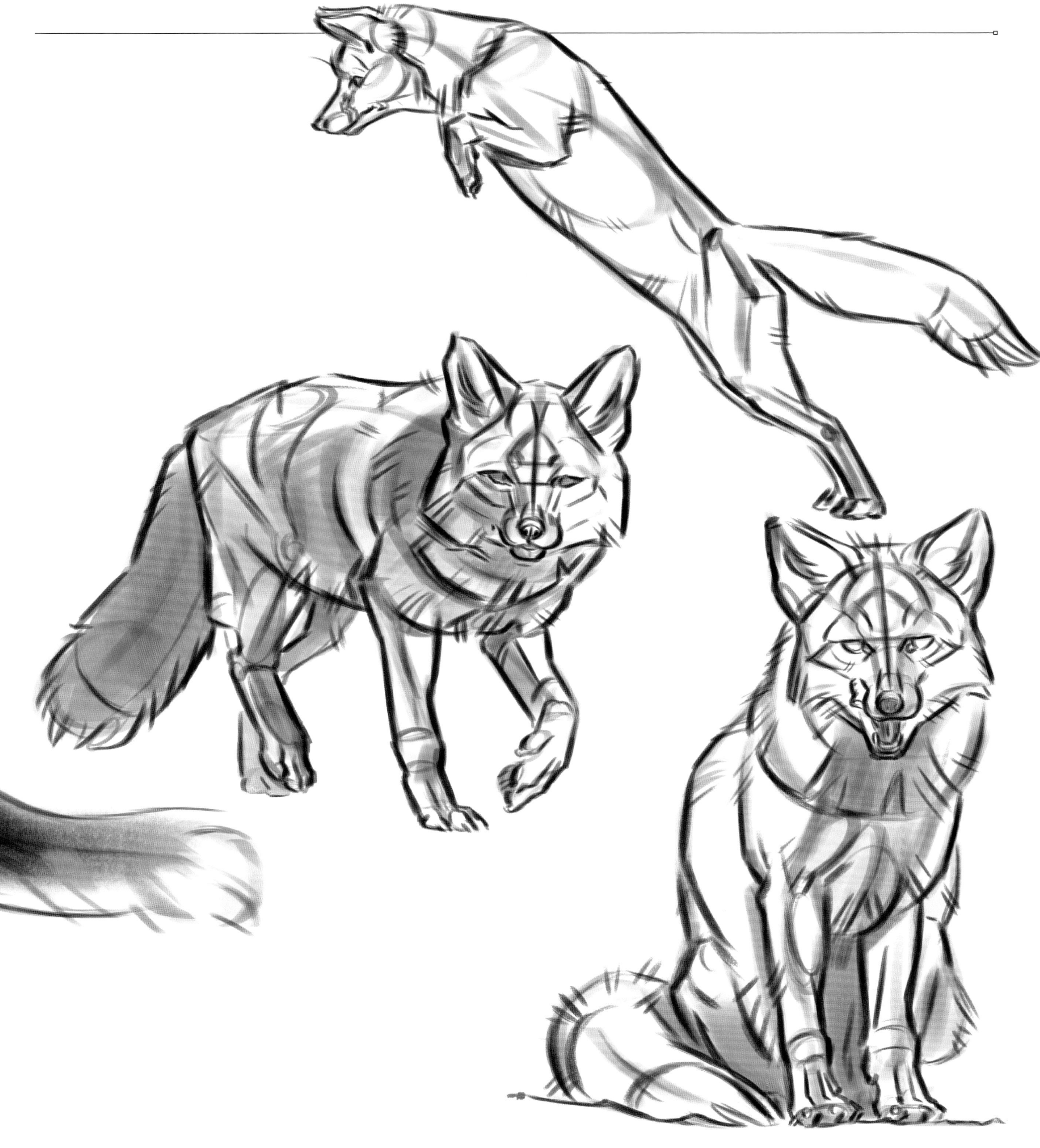

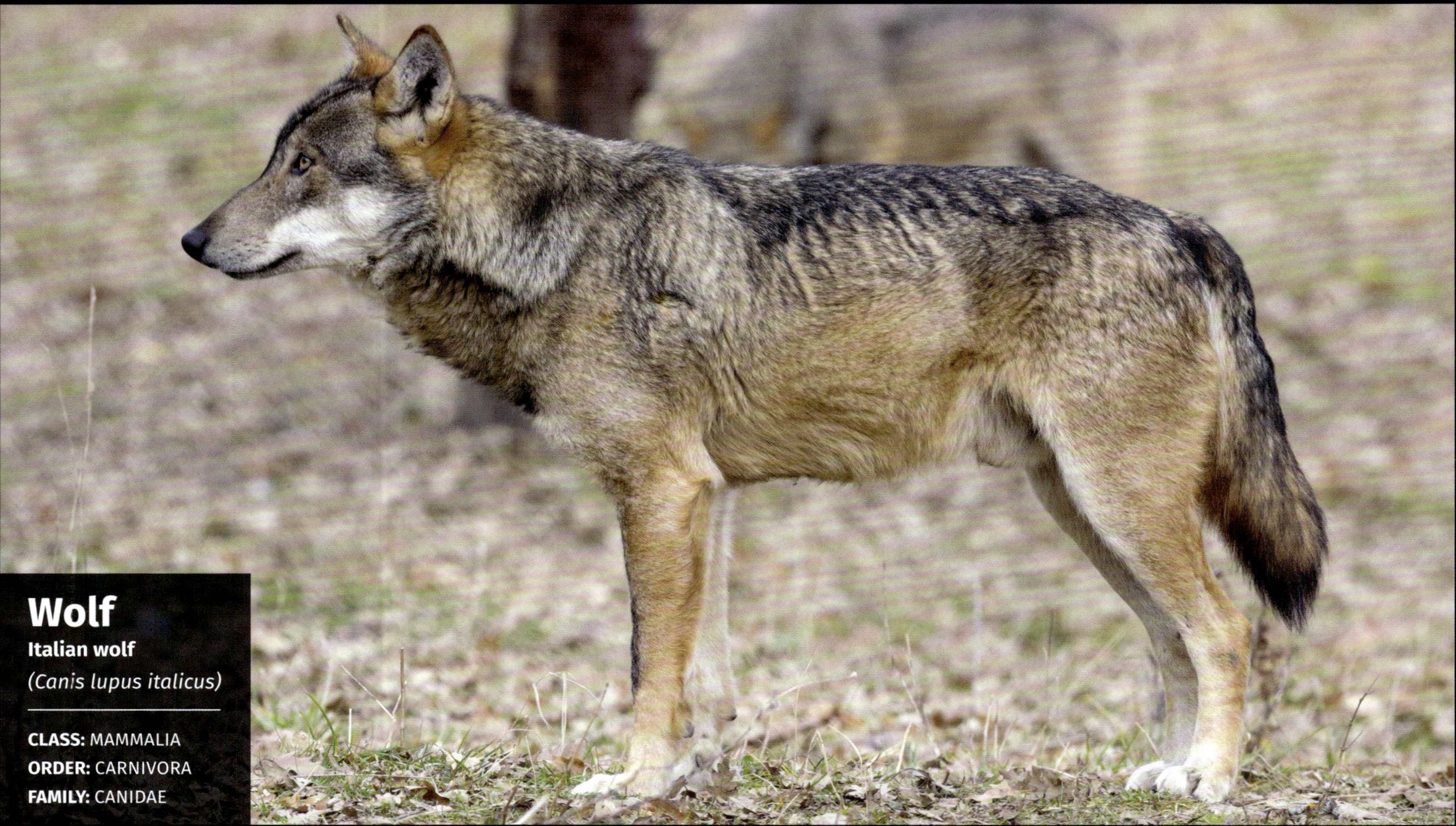

Wolf

Italian wolf

(Canis lupus italicus)

CLASS: MAMMALIA
ORDER: CARNIVORA
FAMILY: CANIDAE

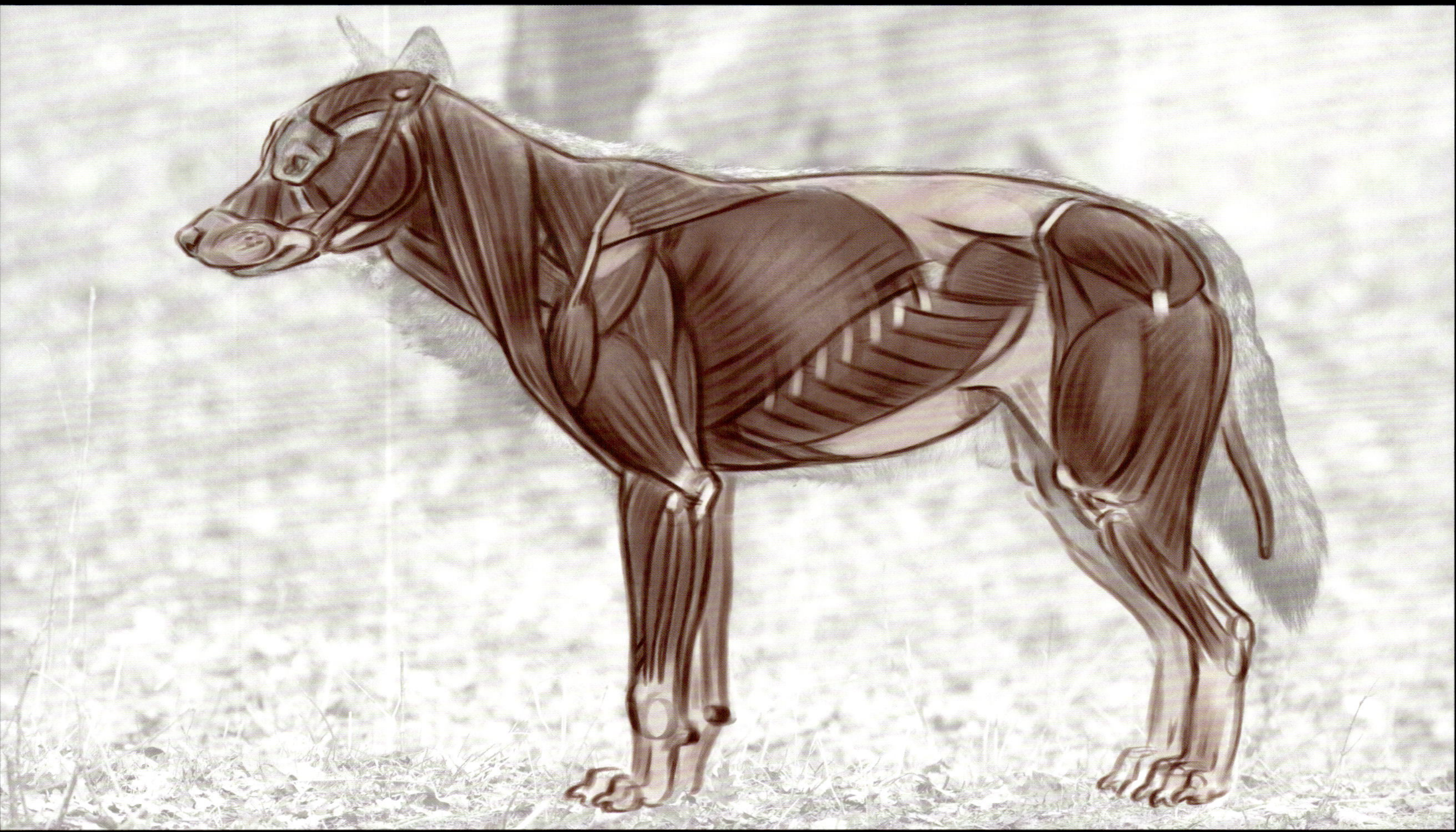

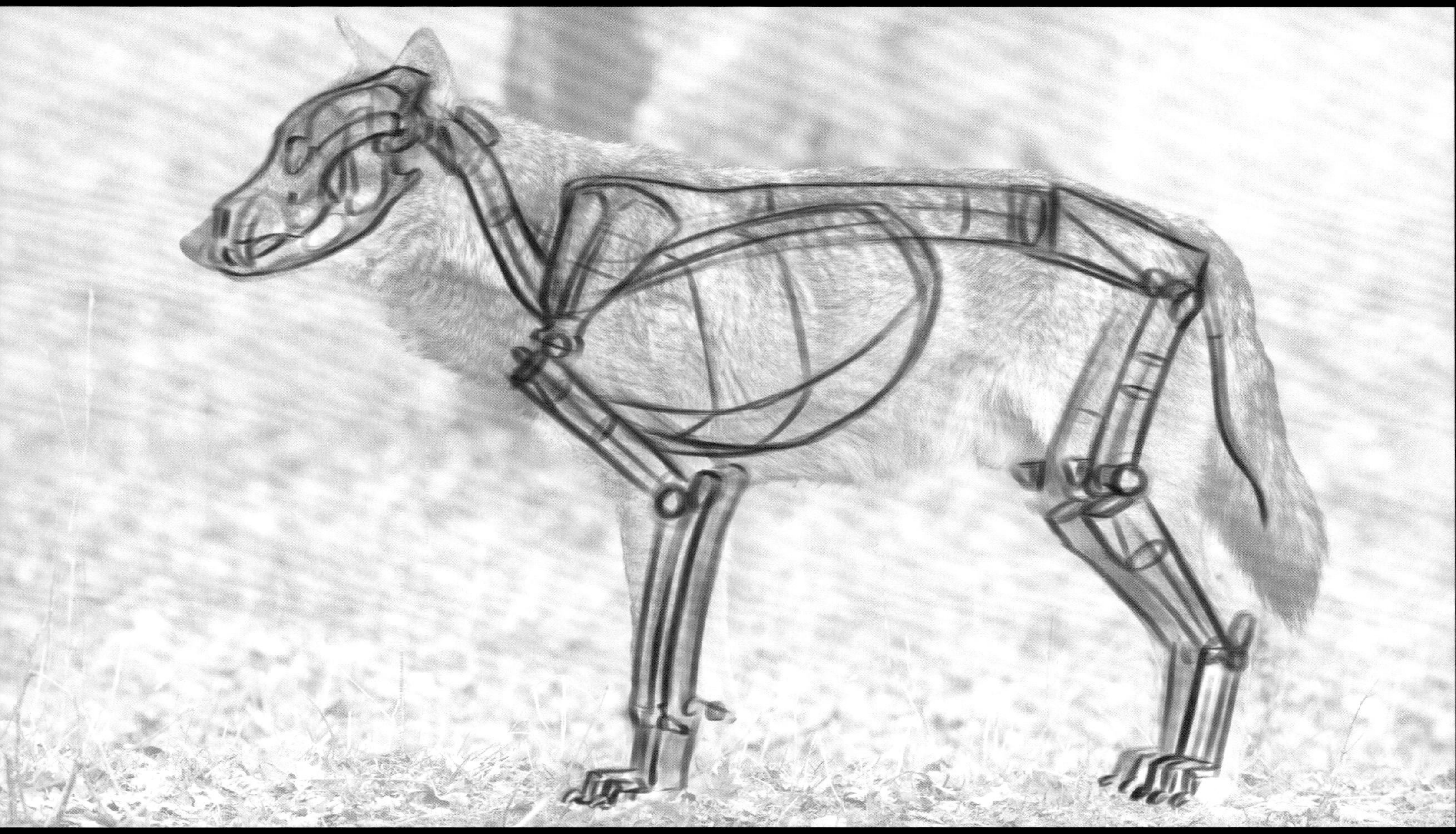

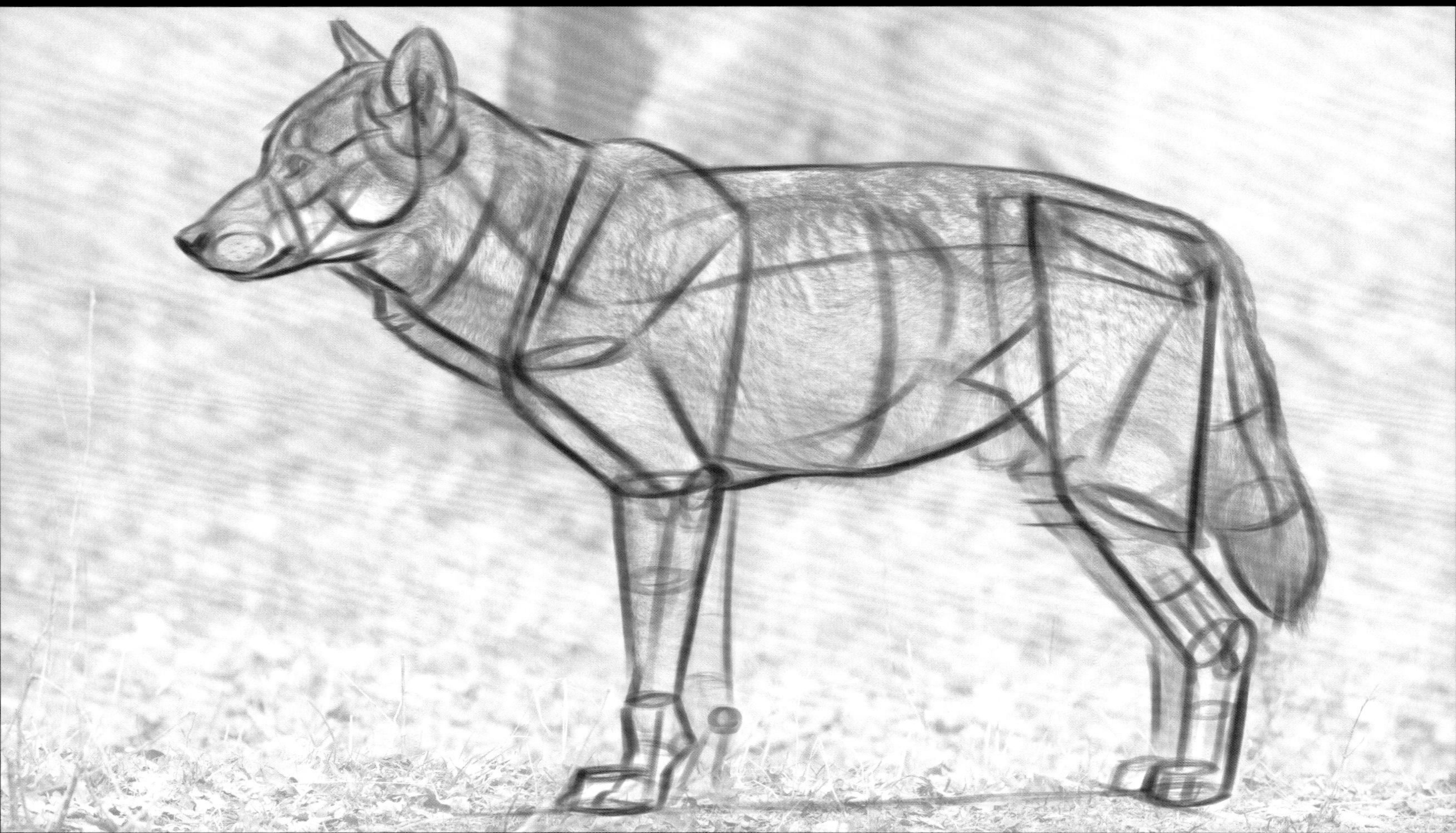

Photograph © Saverio Gatto / Agami.nl

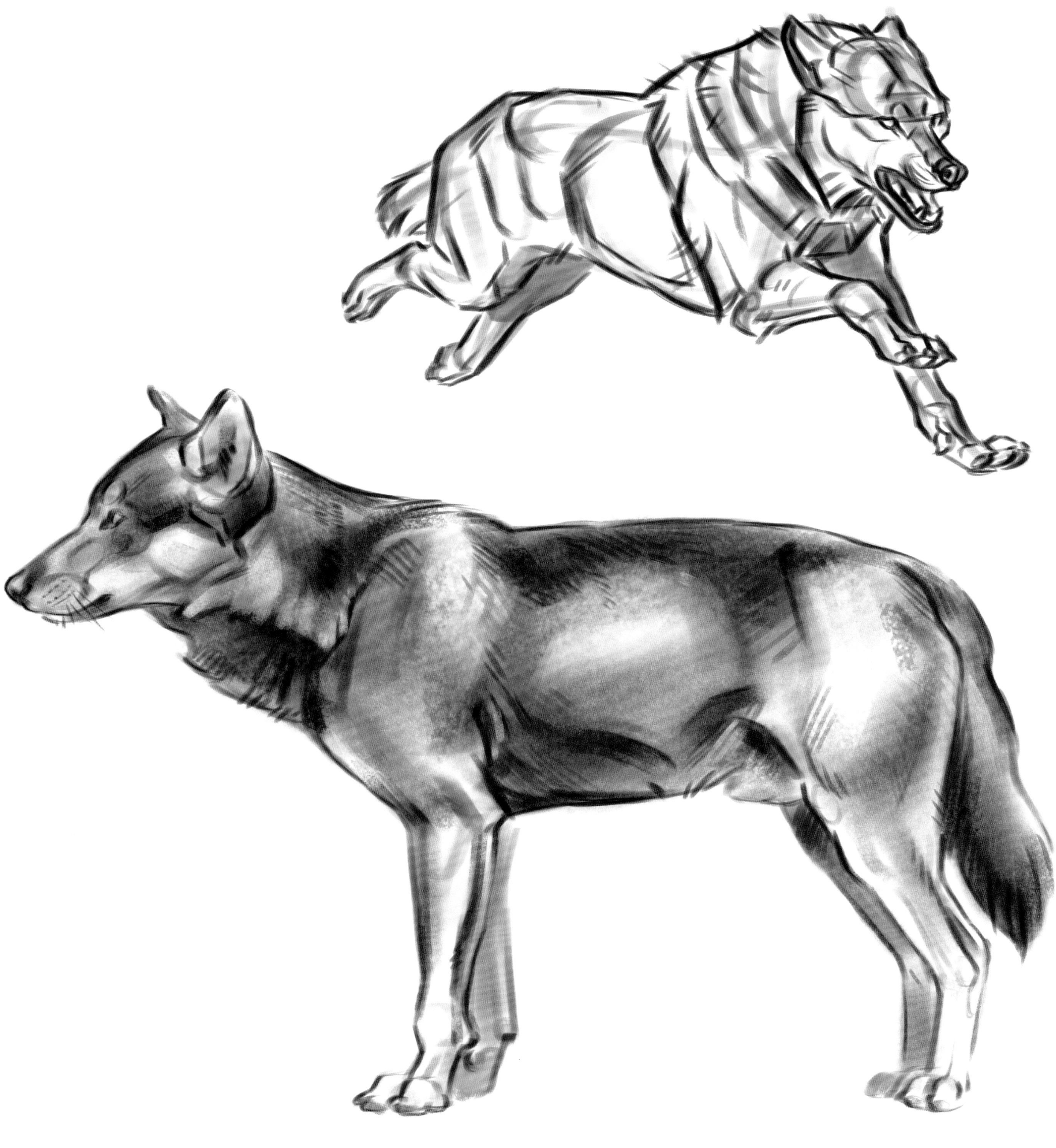

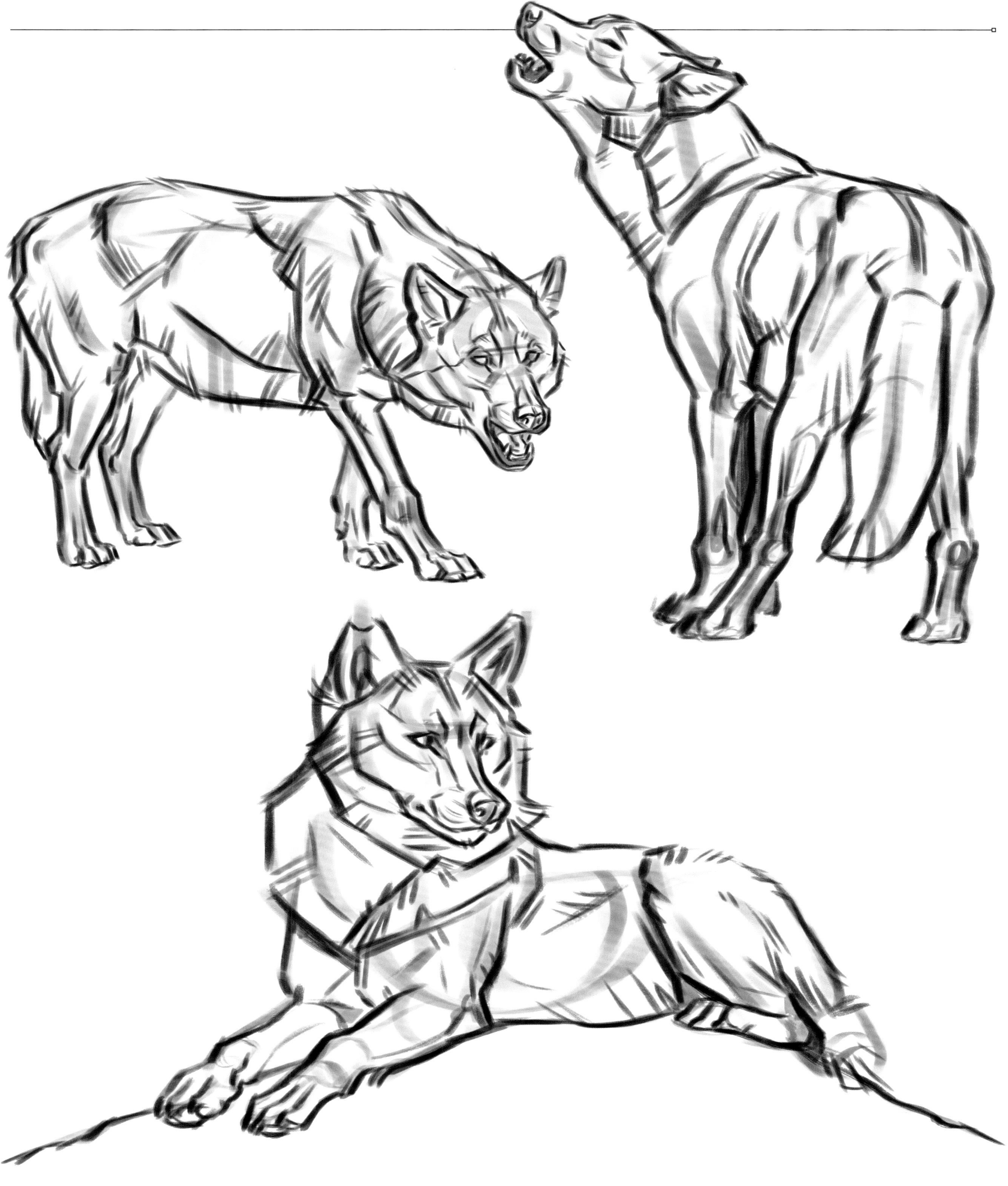

Cat

Bengal domestic cat

(Felis catus)

CLASS: MAMMALIA
ORDER: CARNIVORA
FAMILY: FELIDAE

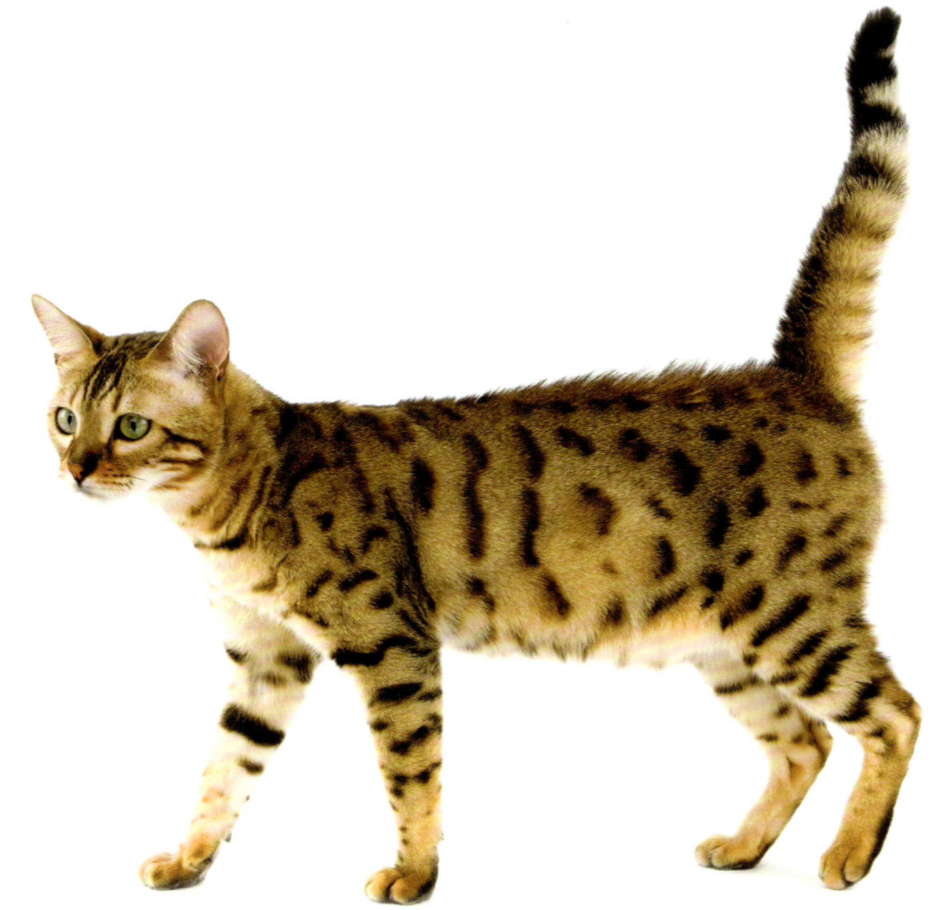

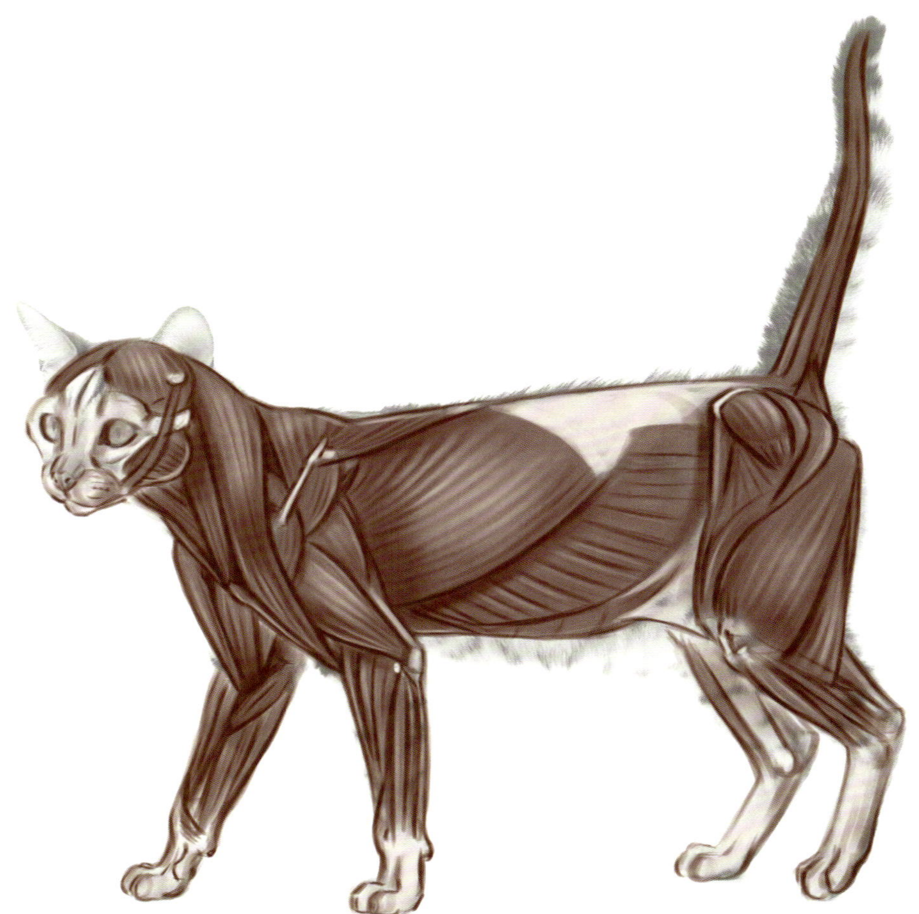

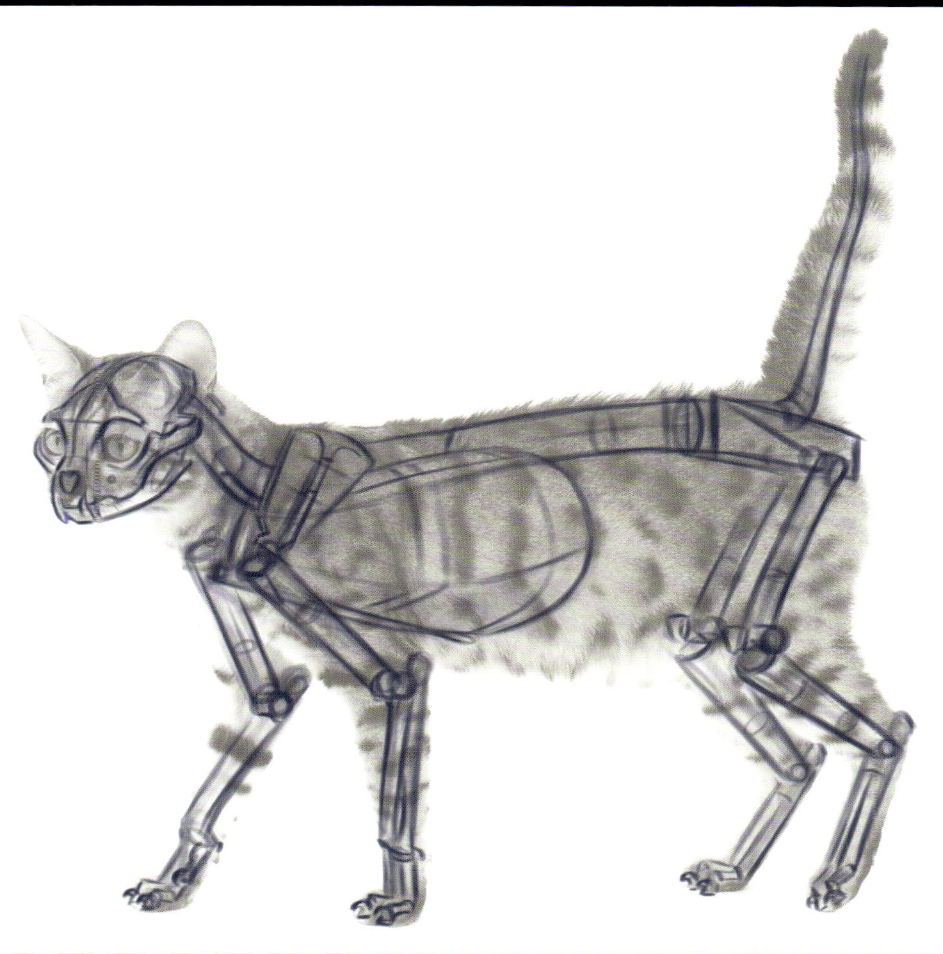

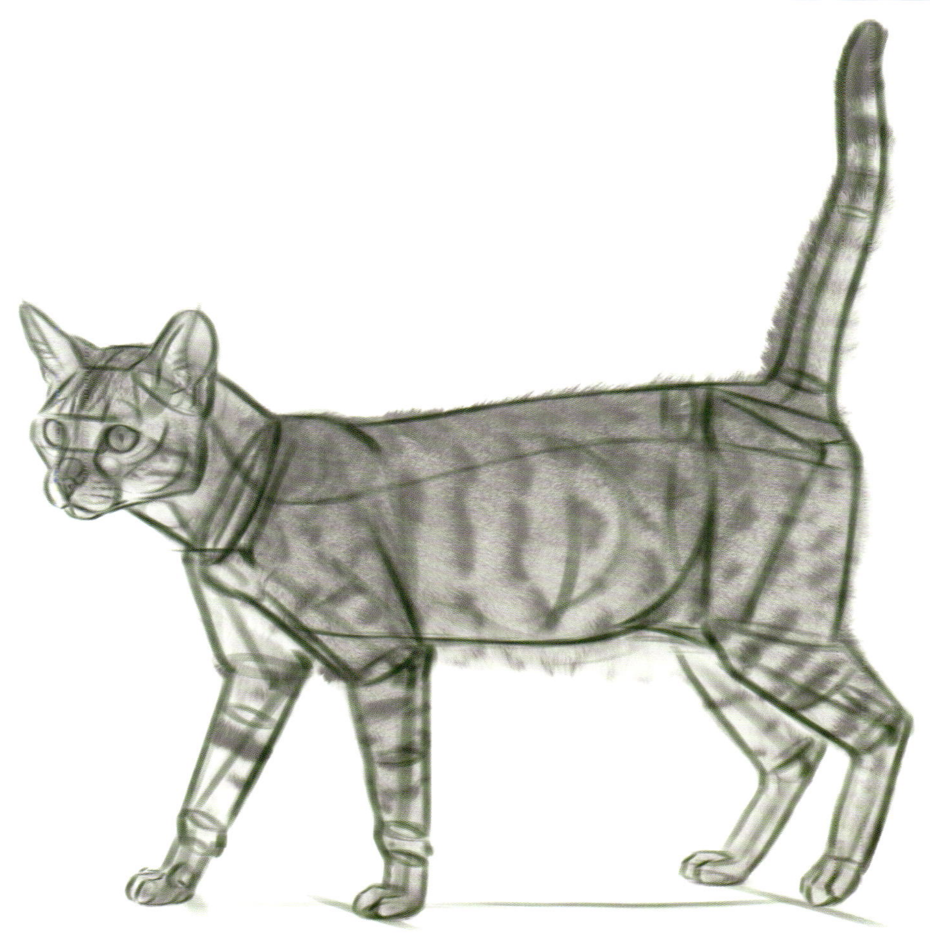

Photograph © imageBROKER.com / G. Lacz

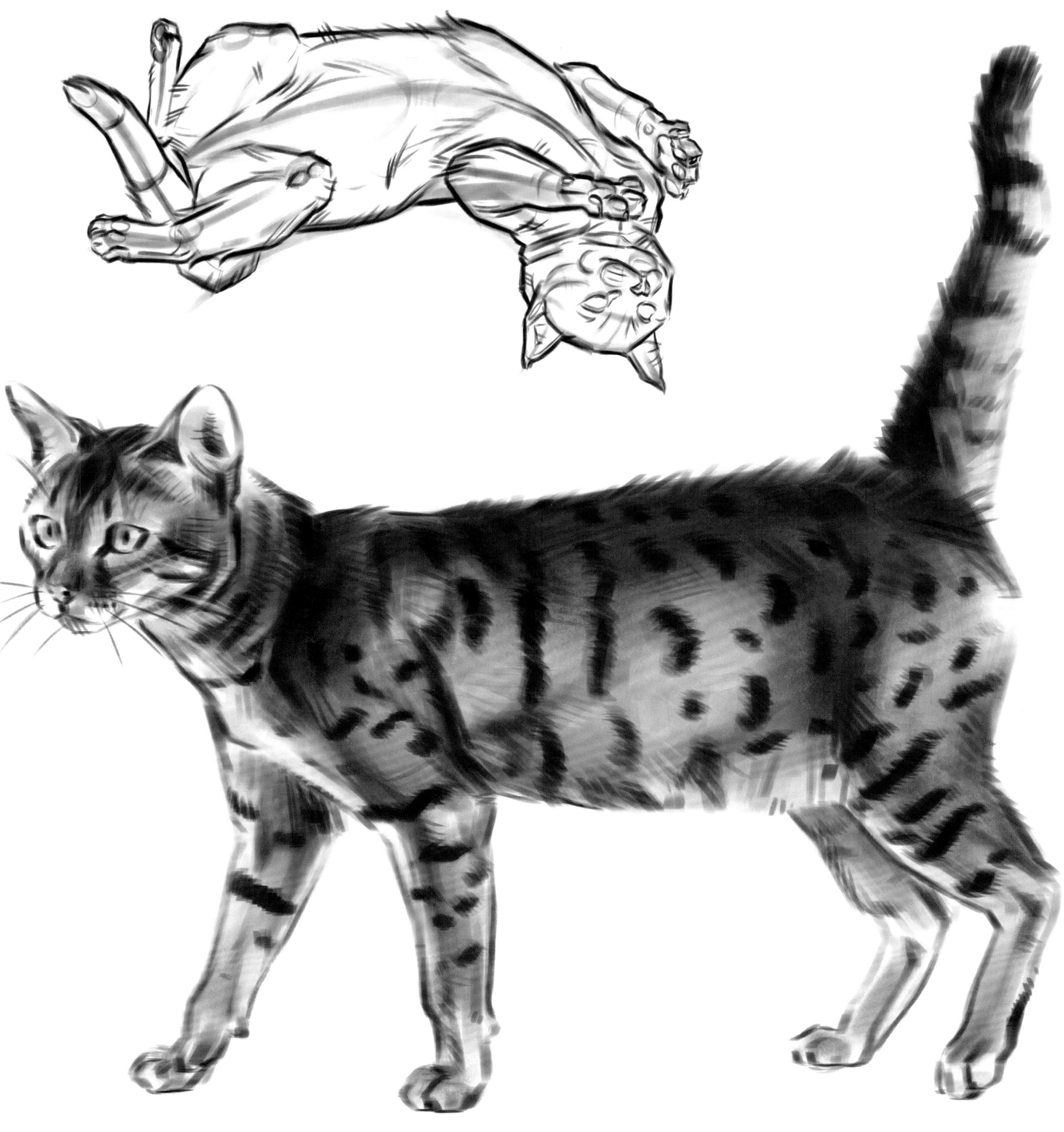

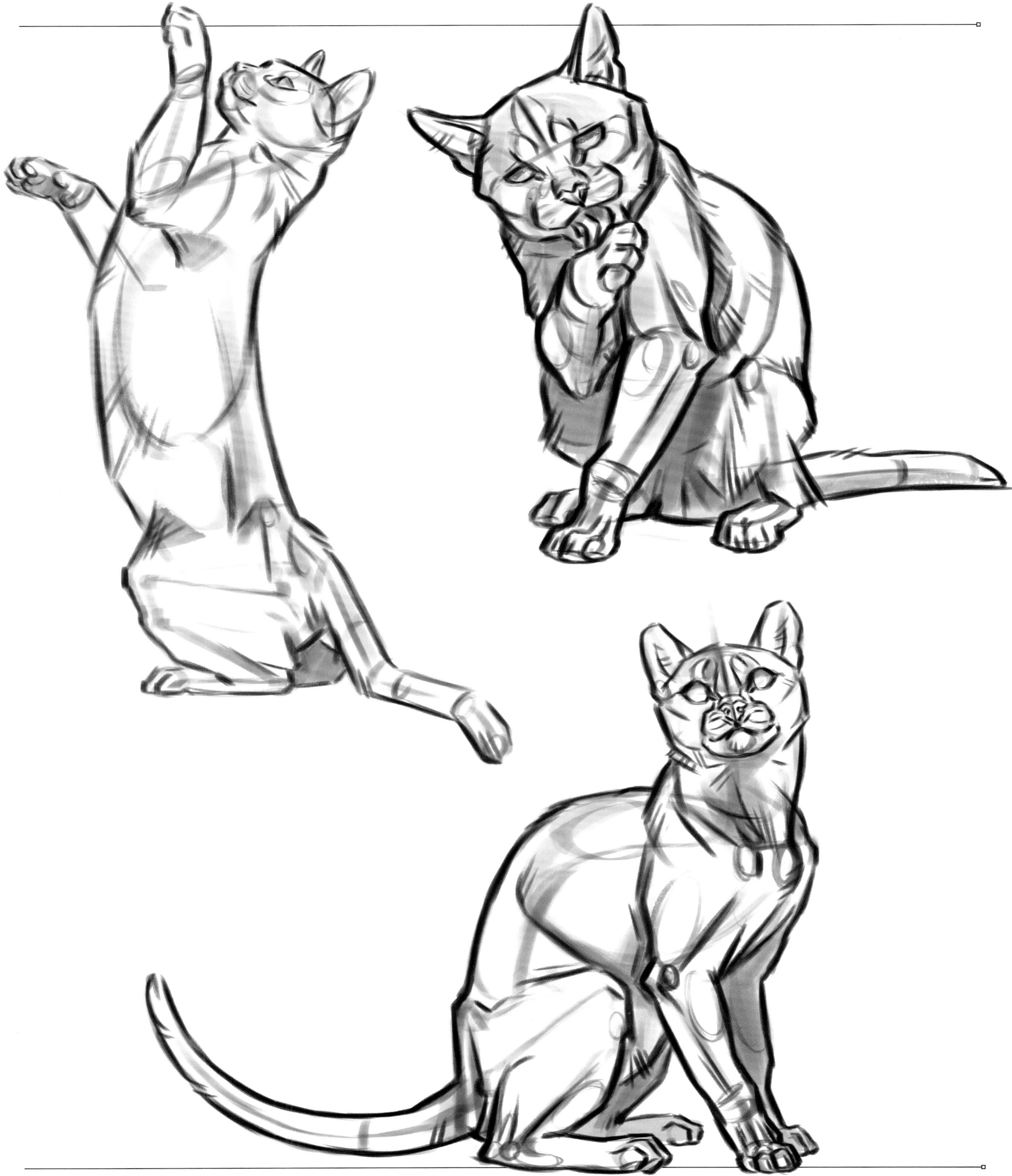

Cheetah

Cheetah

(Acinonyx jubatus)

CLASS: MAMMALIA
ORDER: CARNIVORA
FAMILY: FELIDAE

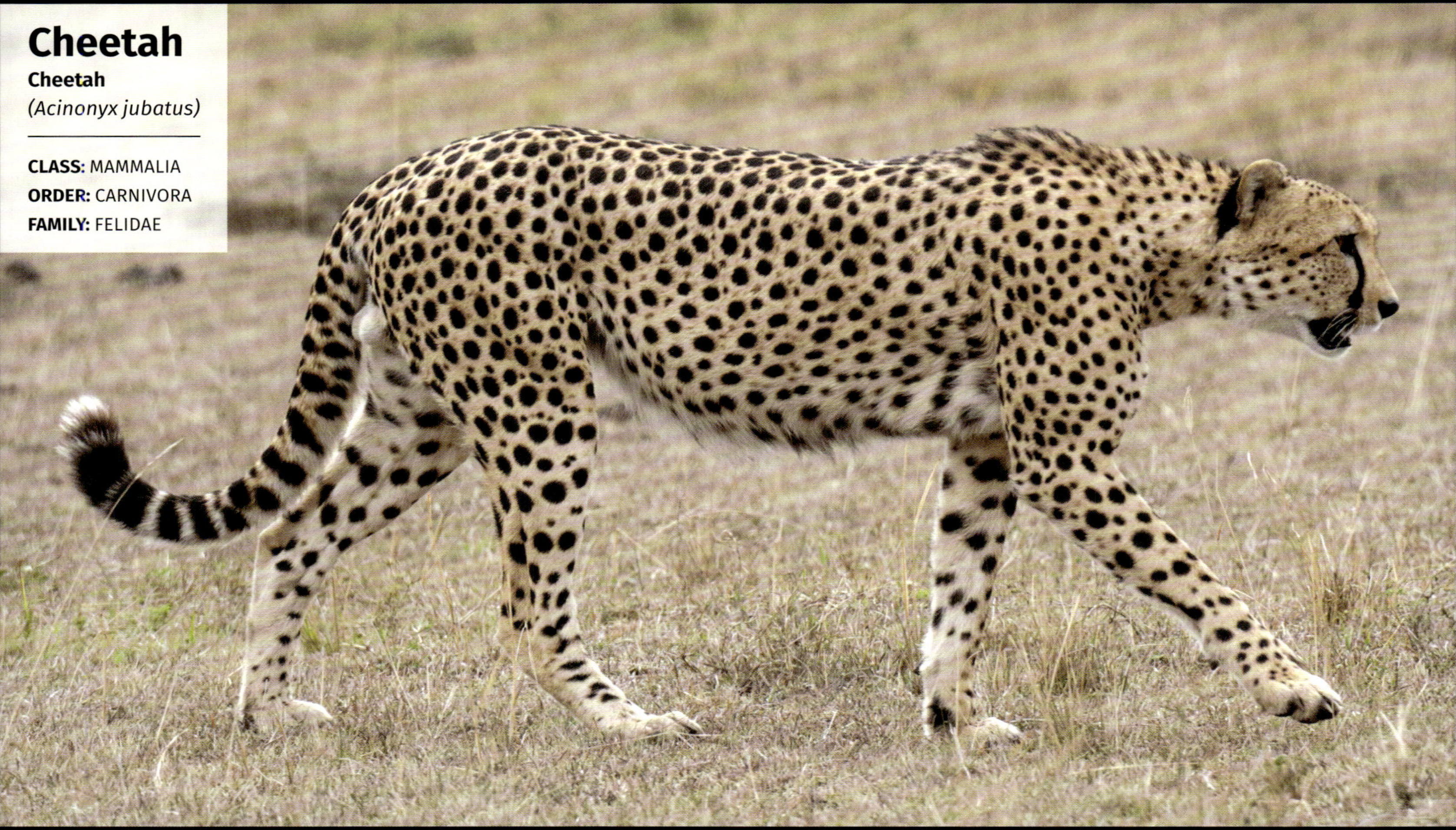

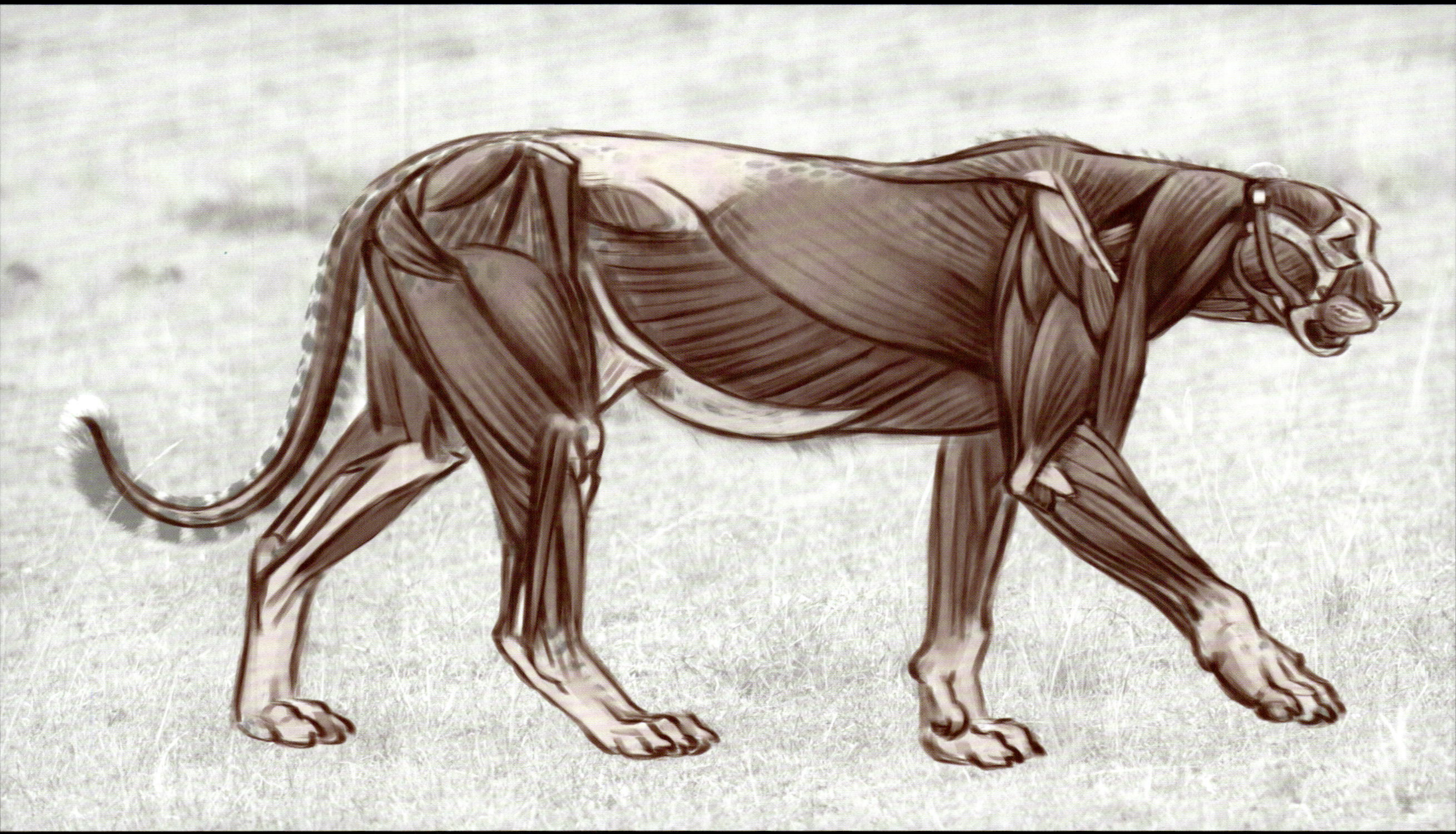

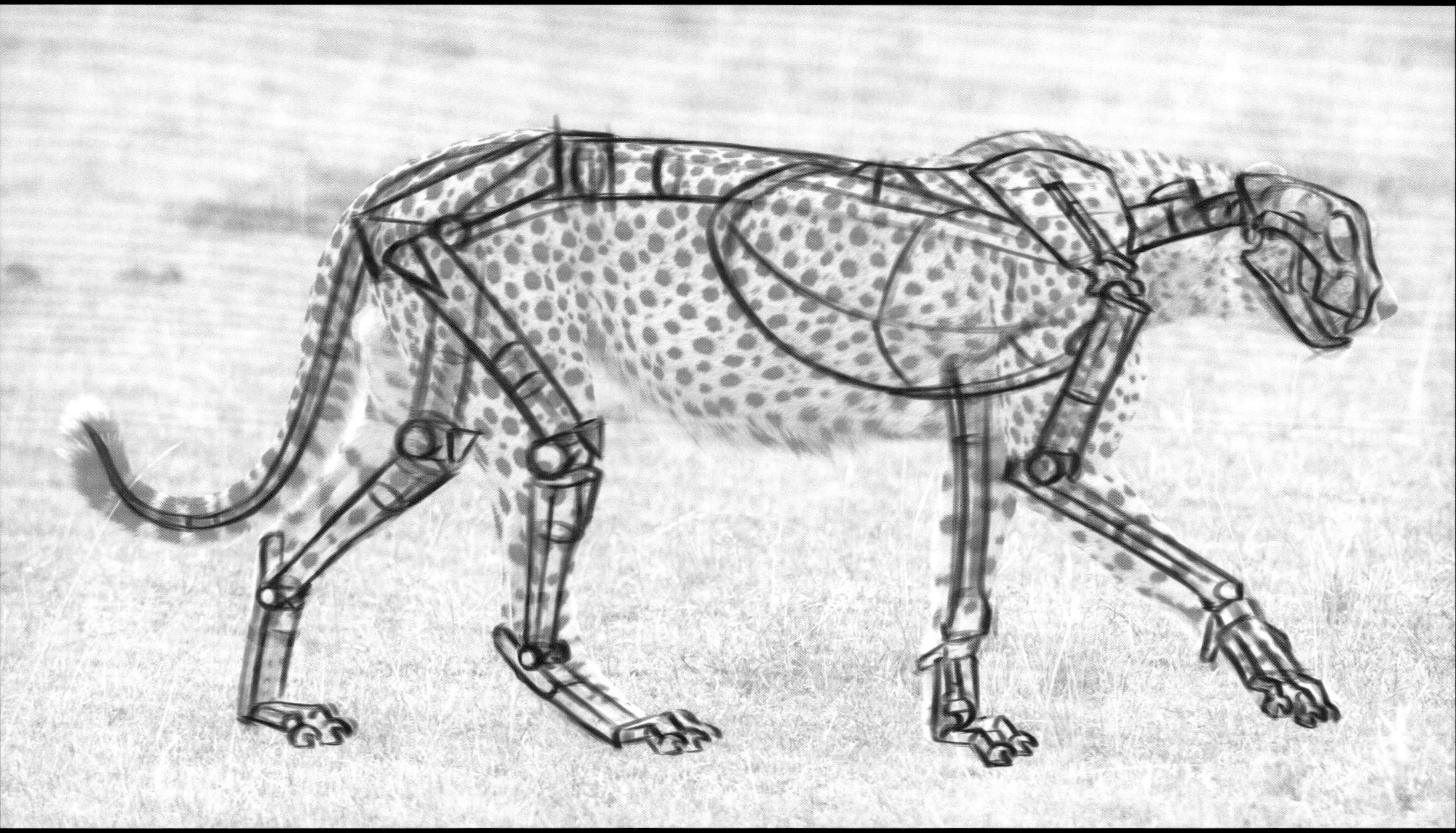

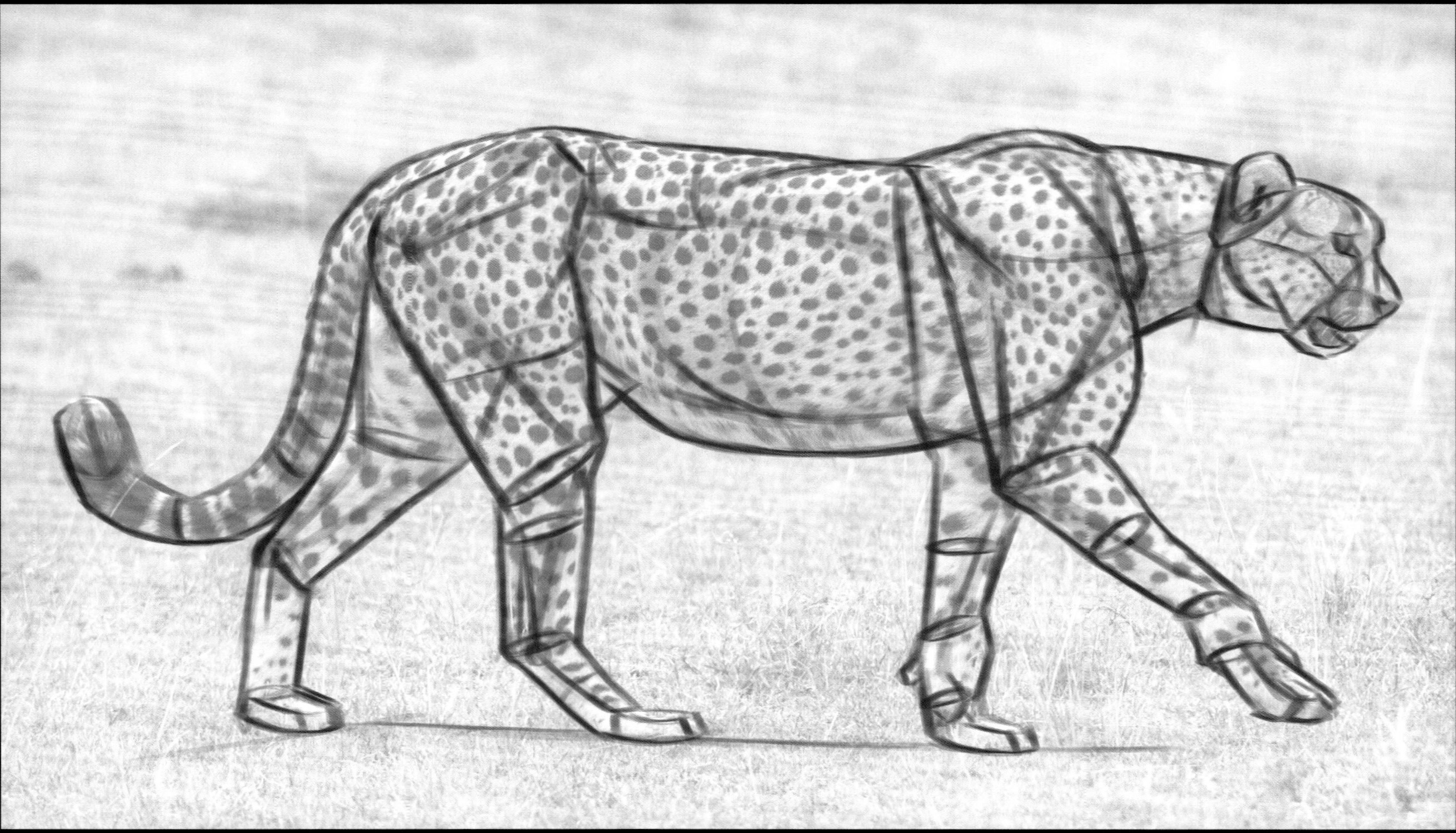

Photograph © Sergio Pitamitz / Agami.nl

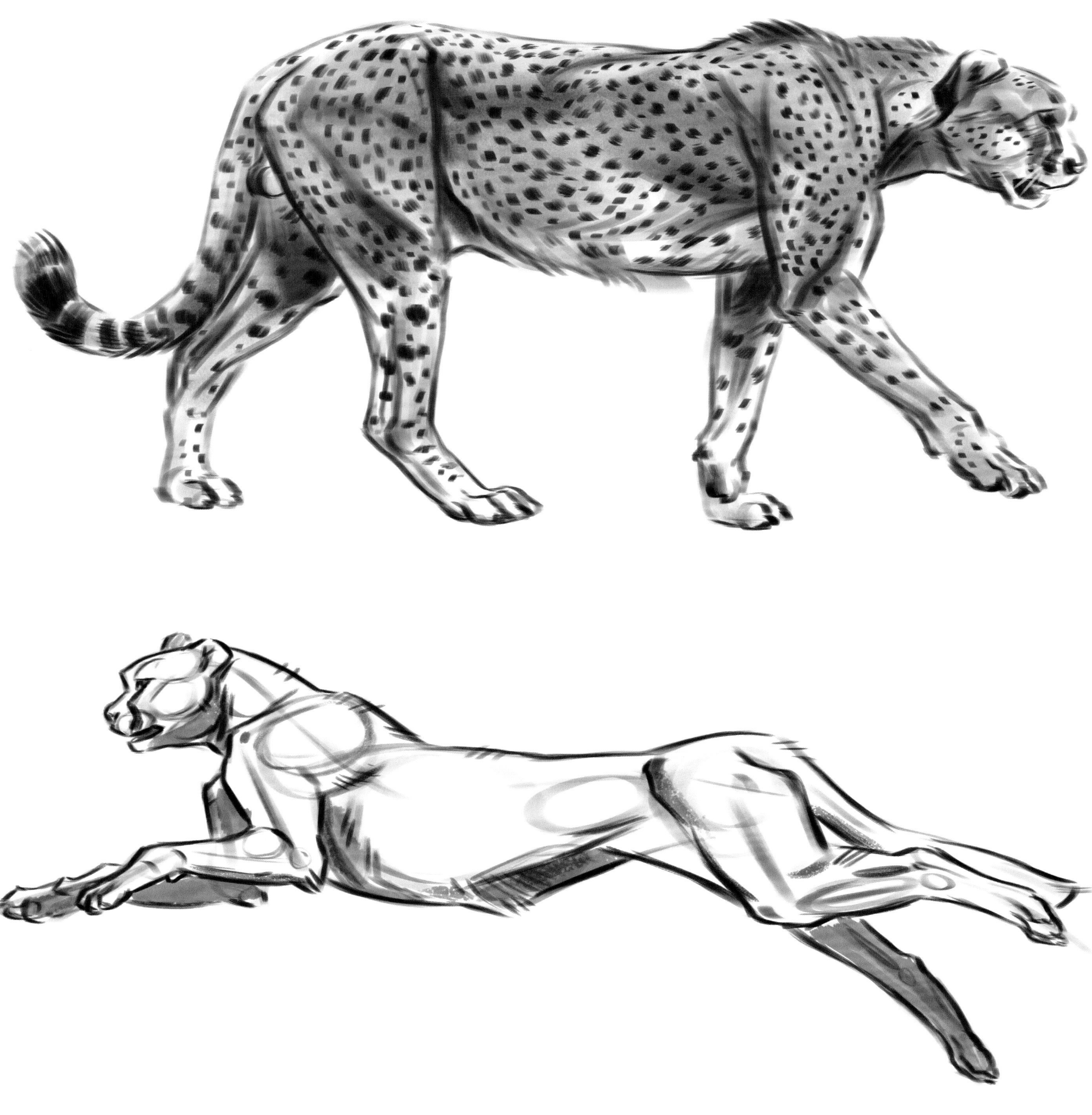

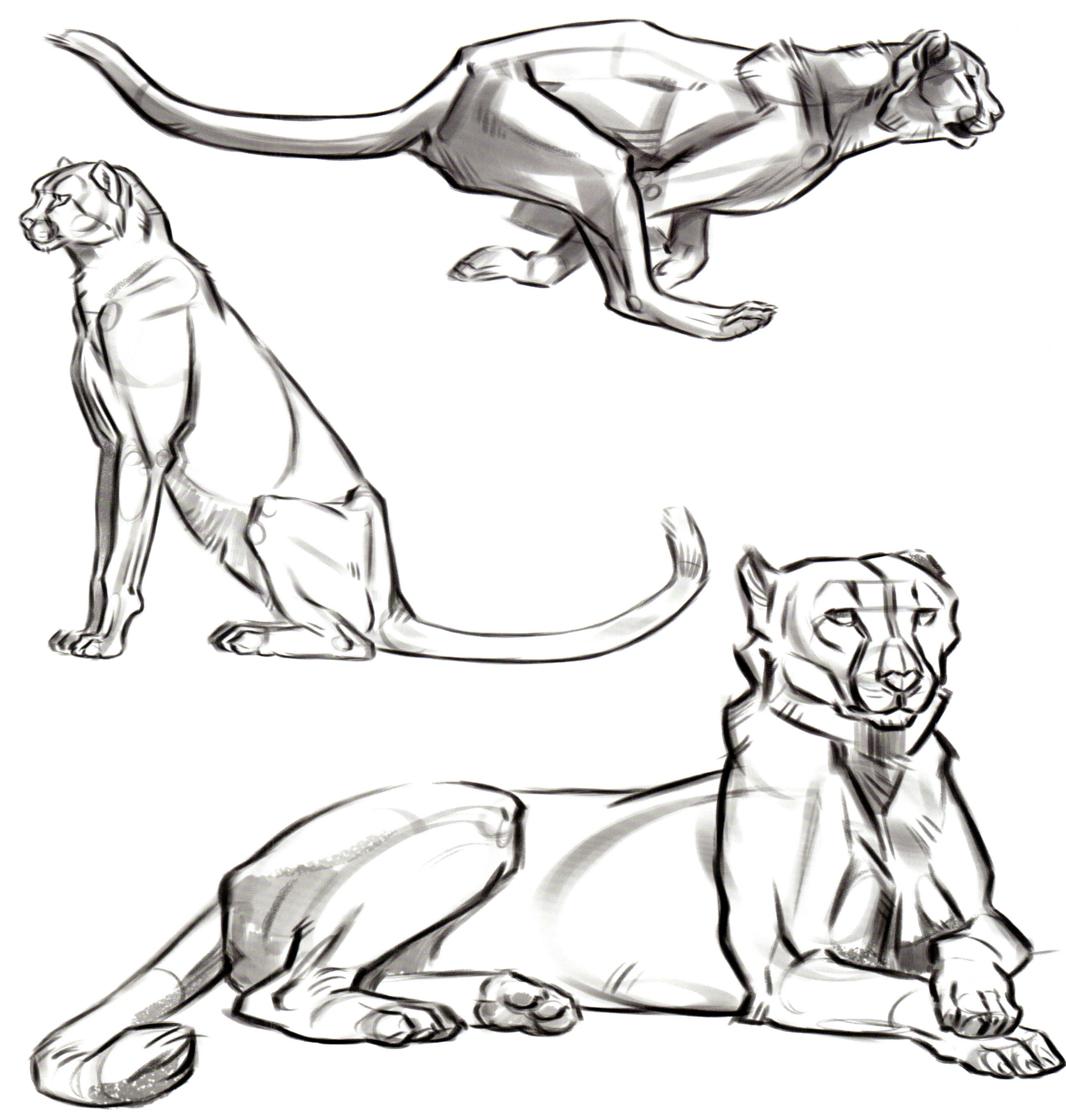

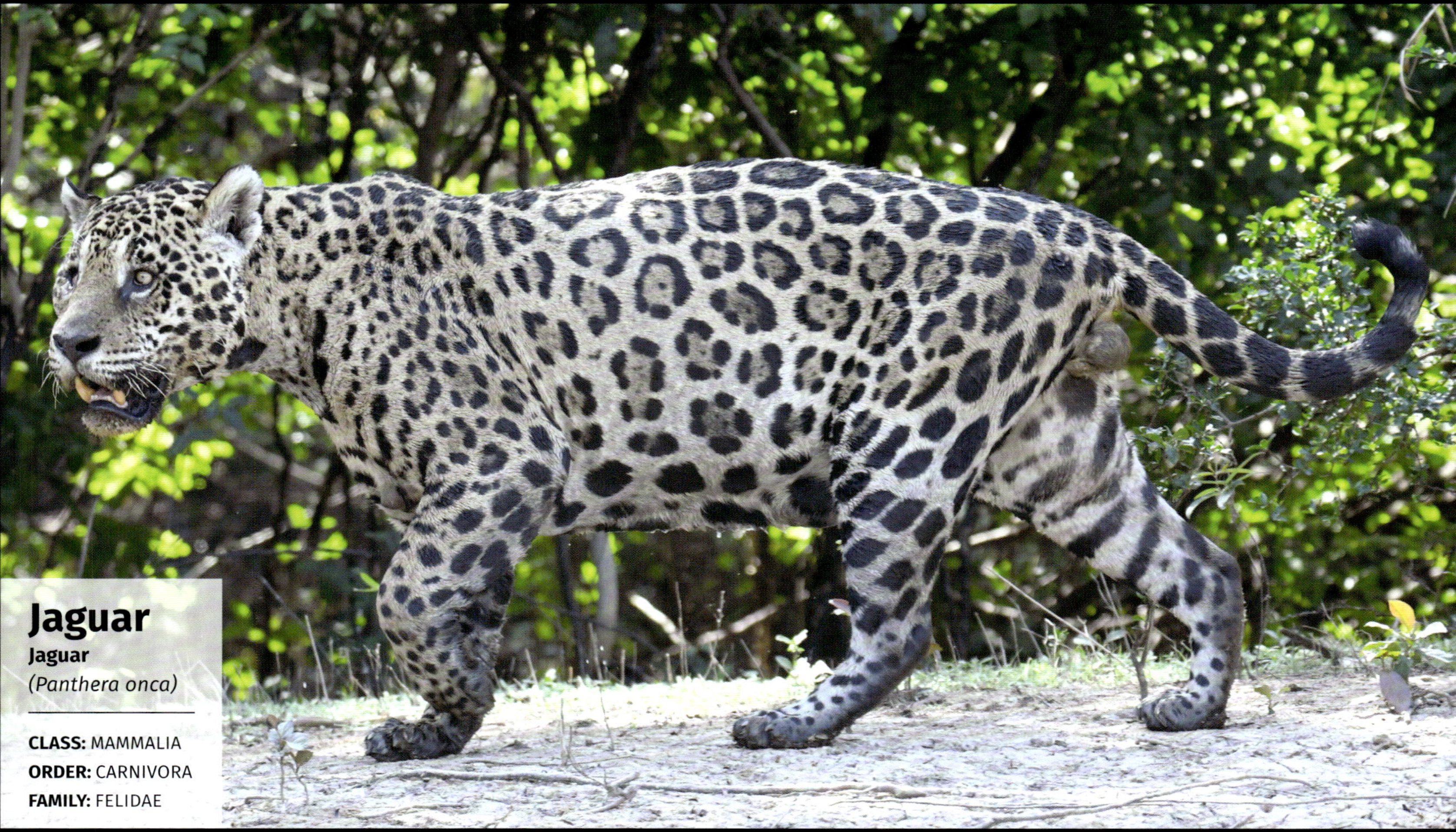

Jaguar

Jaguar
(Panthera onca)

CLASS: MAMMALIA
ORDER: CARNIVORA
FAMILY: FELIDAE

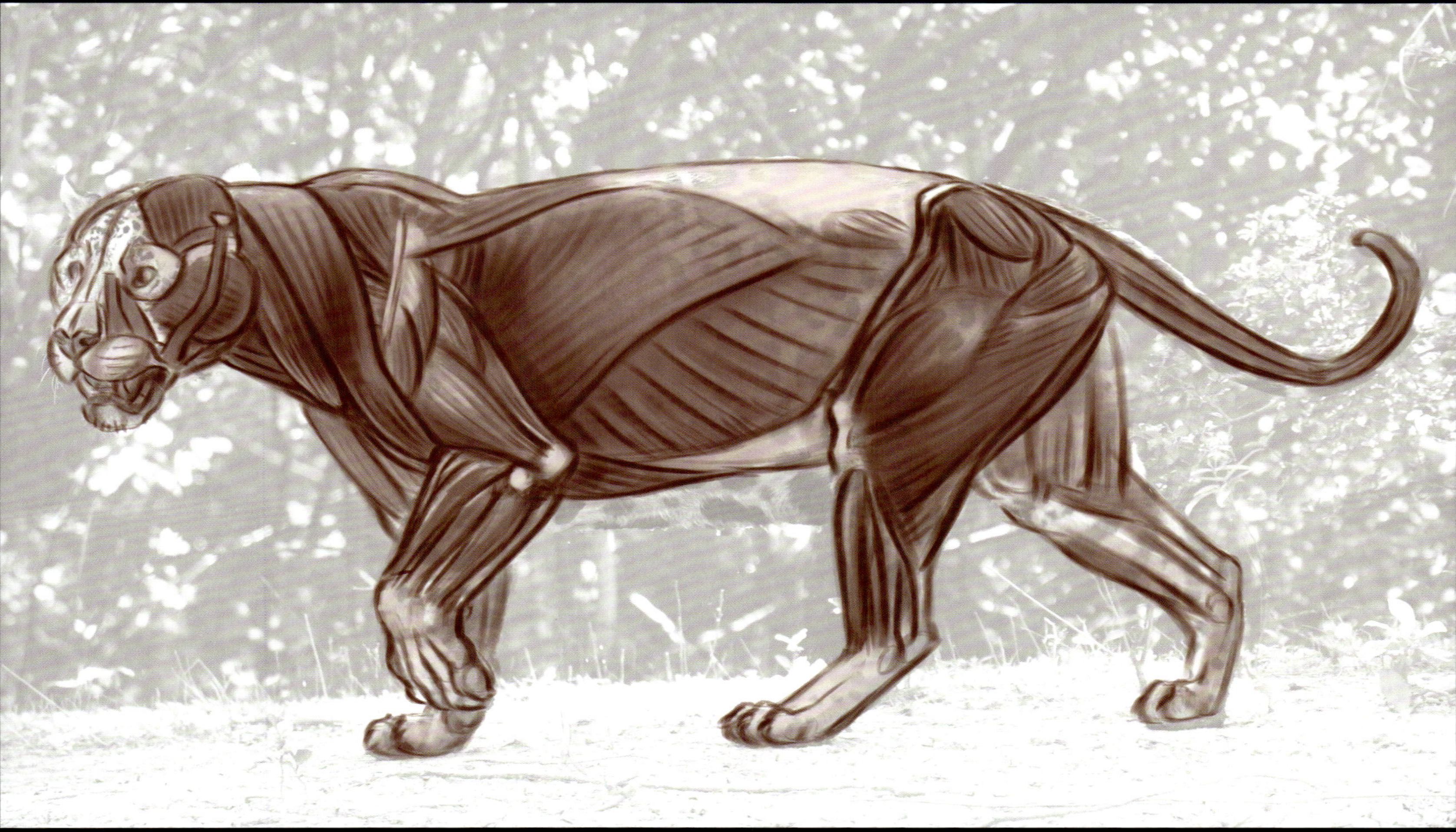

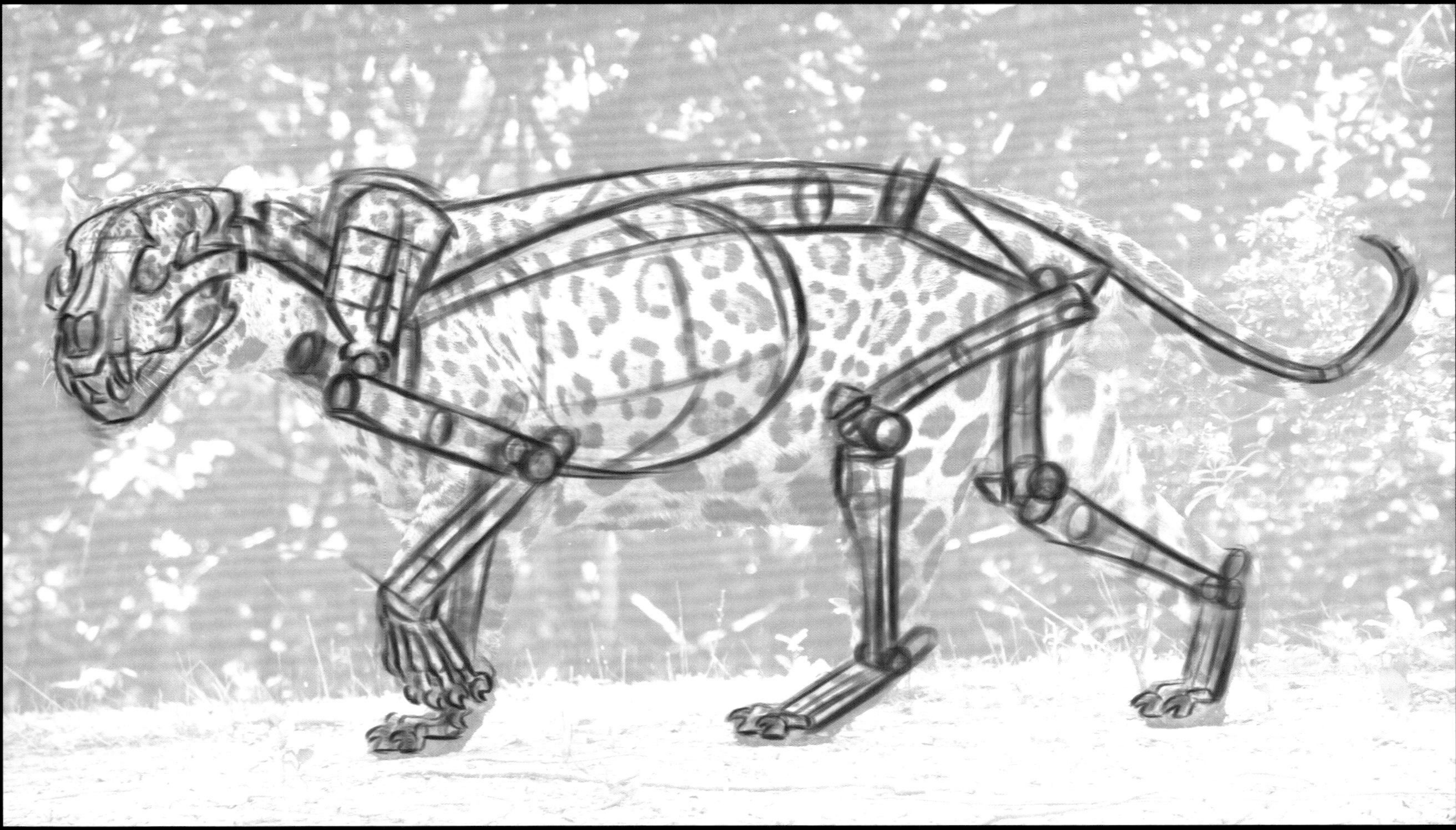

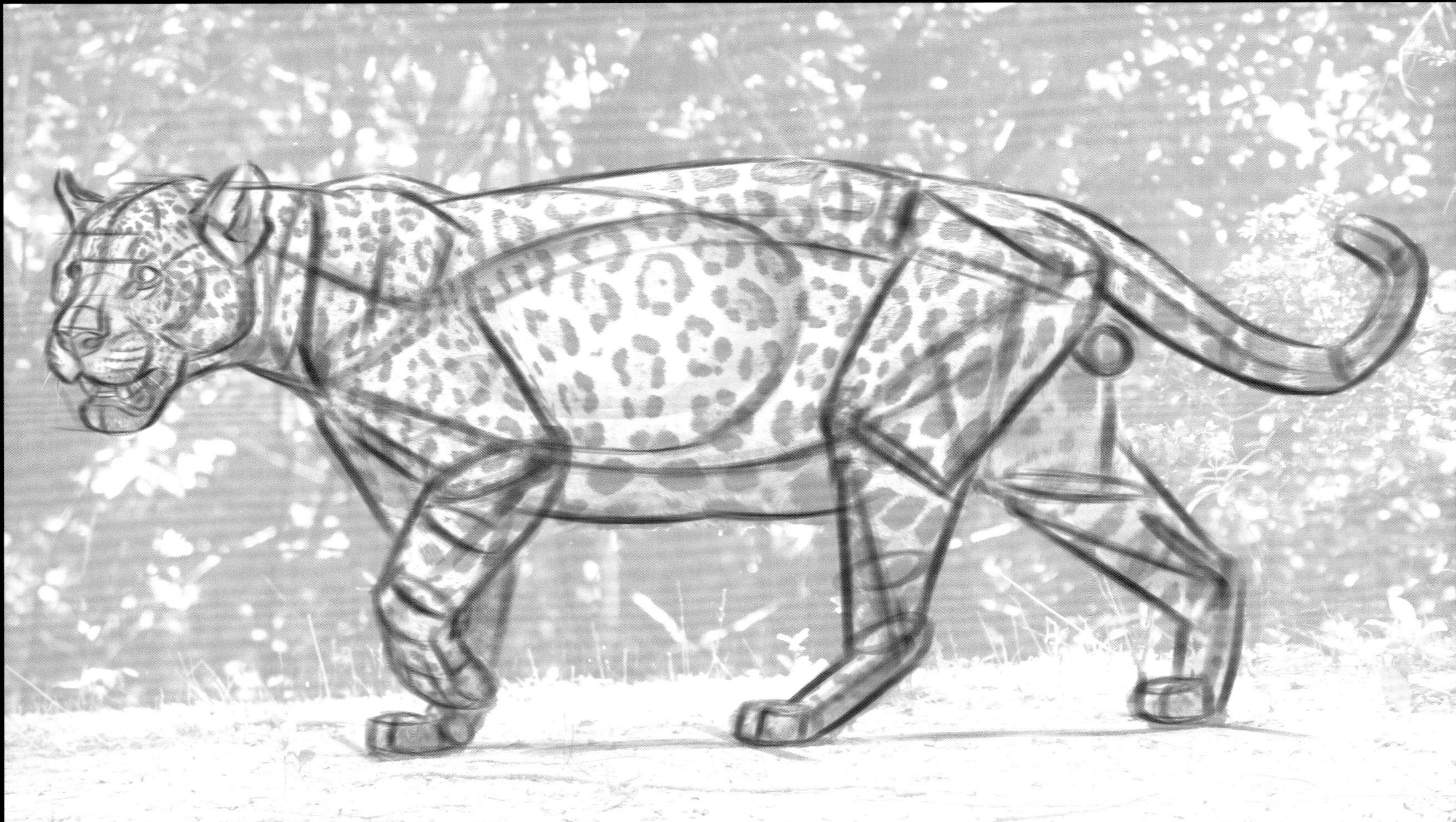

Photograph © Eduard Sangster / Agami.nl

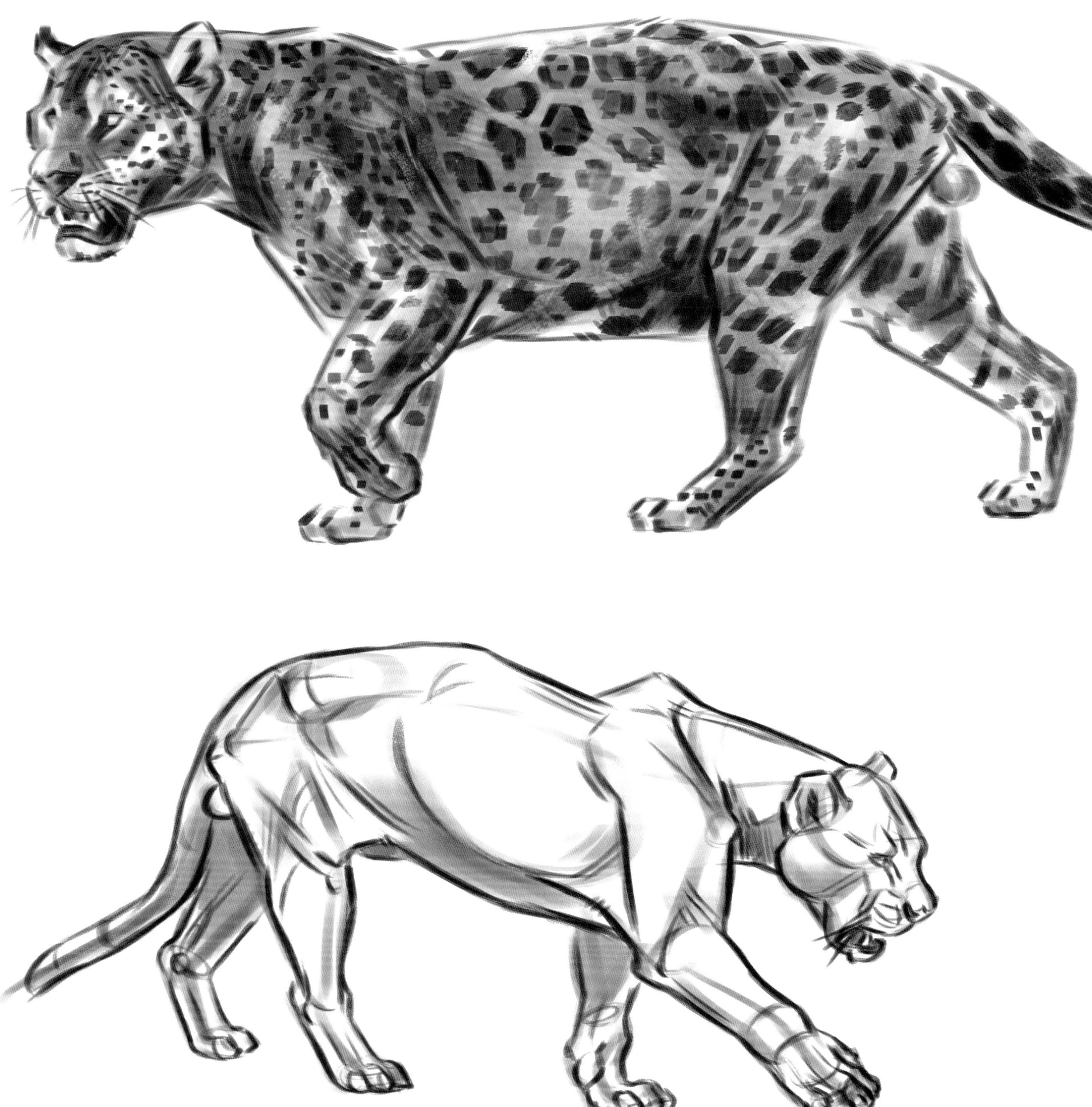

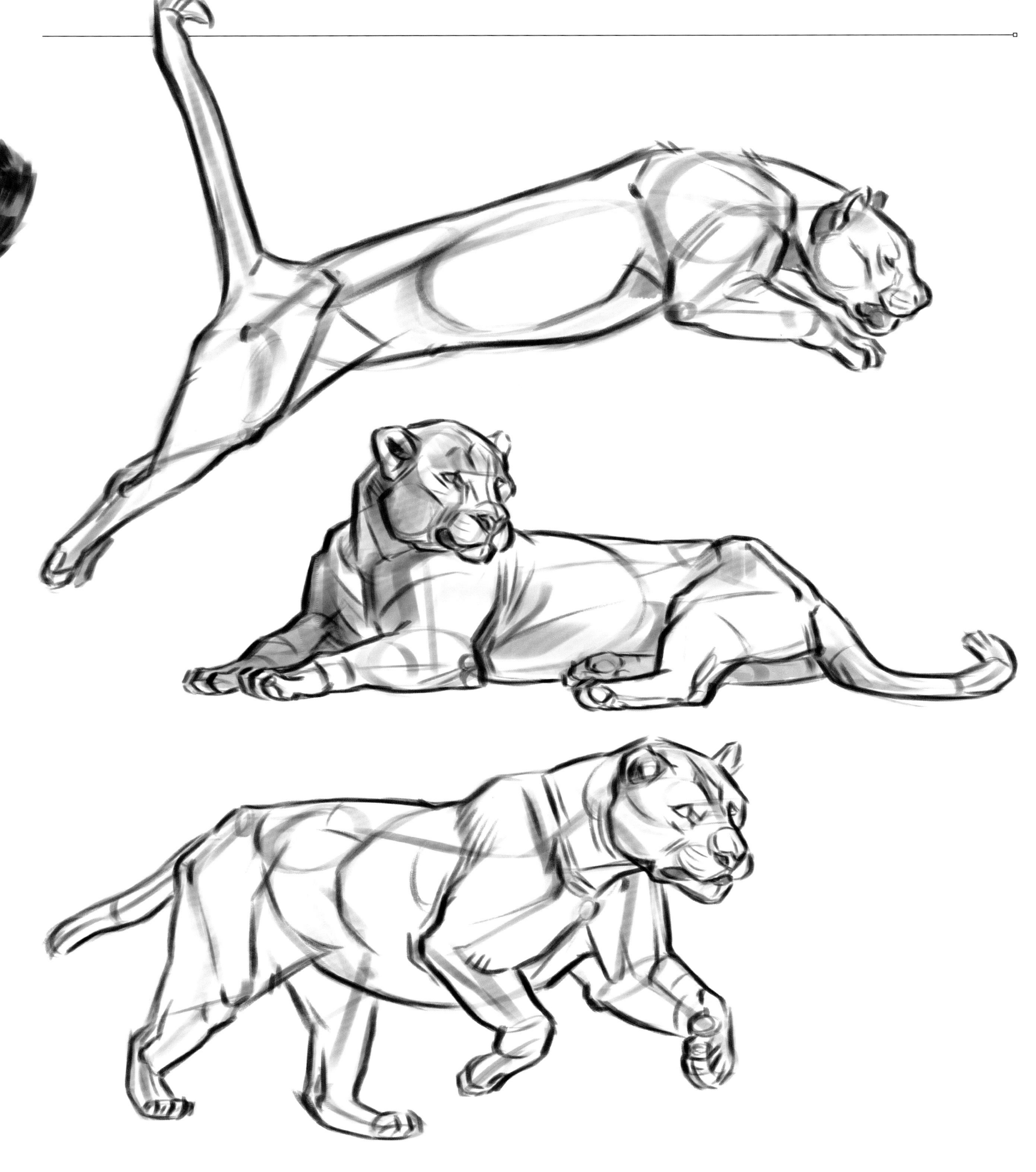

Lioness

Lioness *(Panthera leo)*

CLASS: MAMMALIA
ORDER: CARNIVORA
FAMILY: FELIDAE

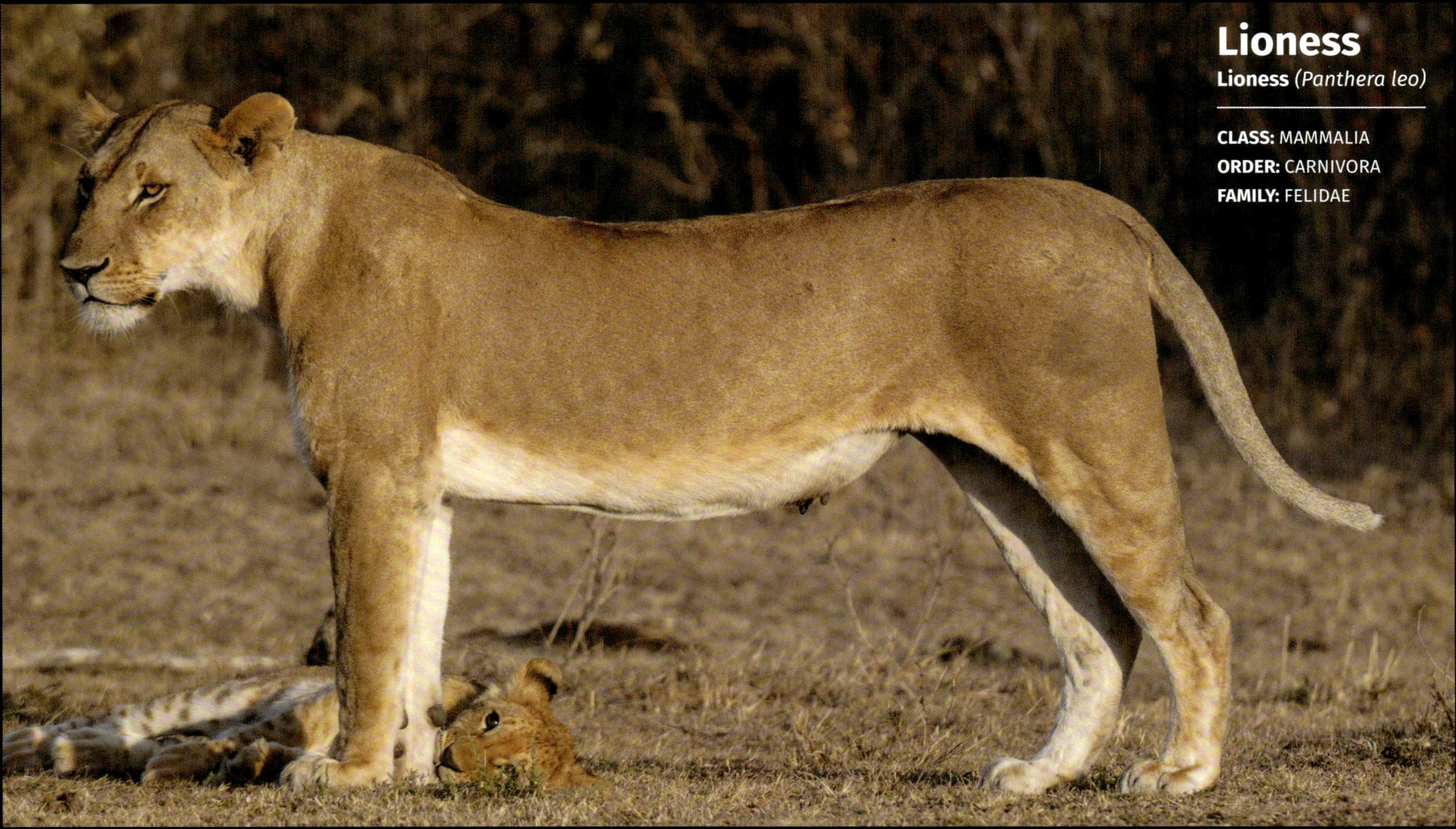

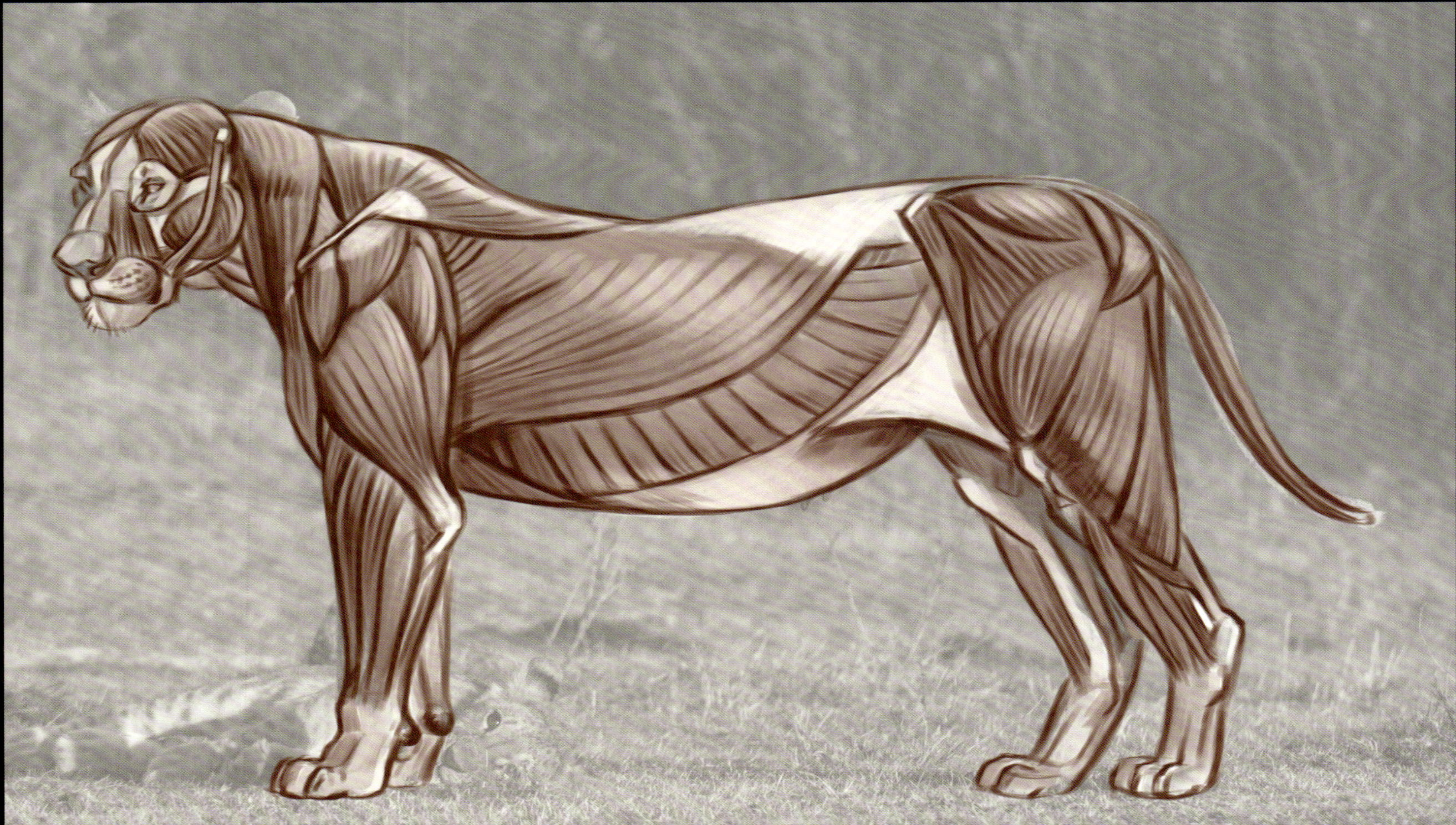

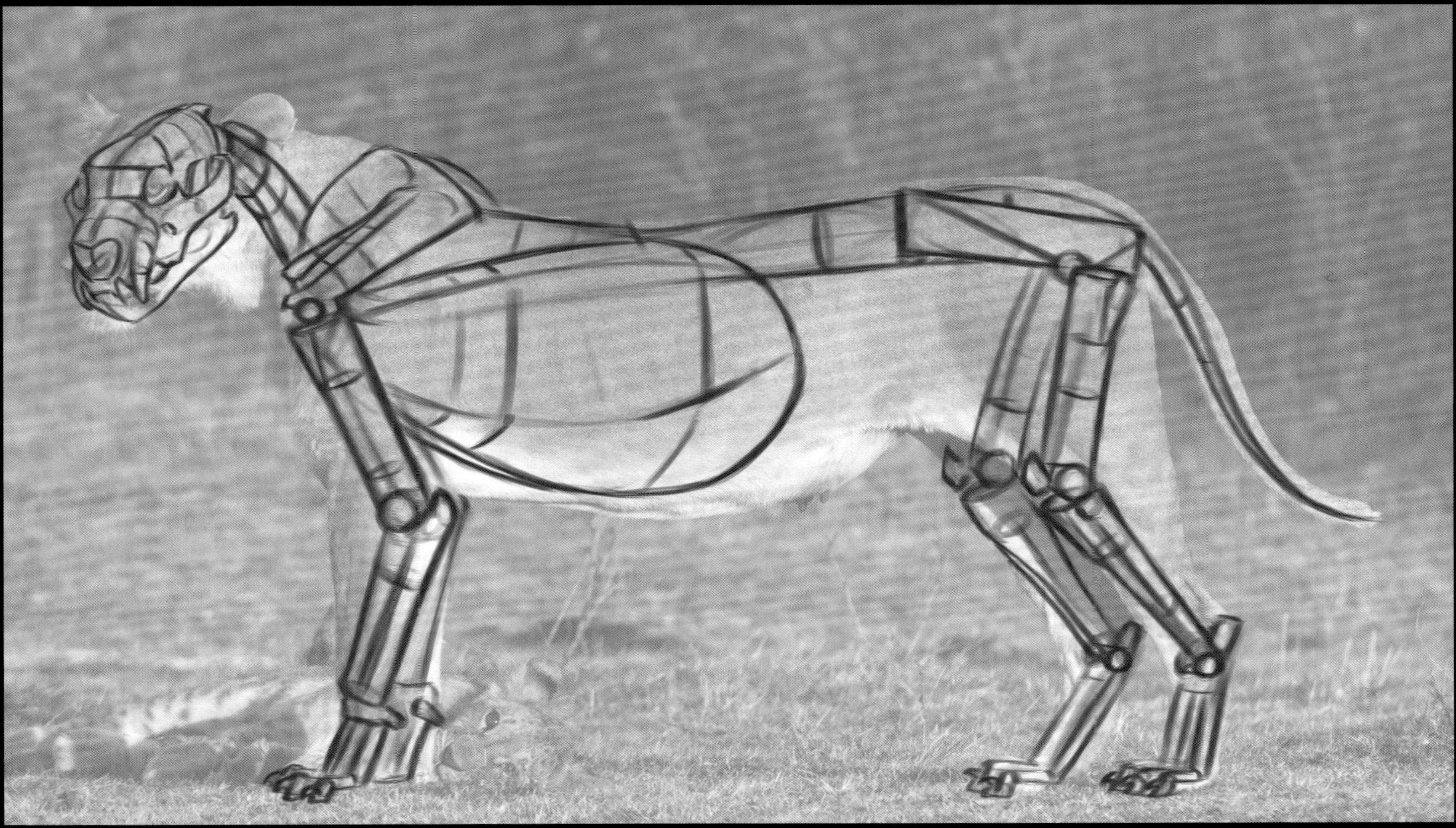

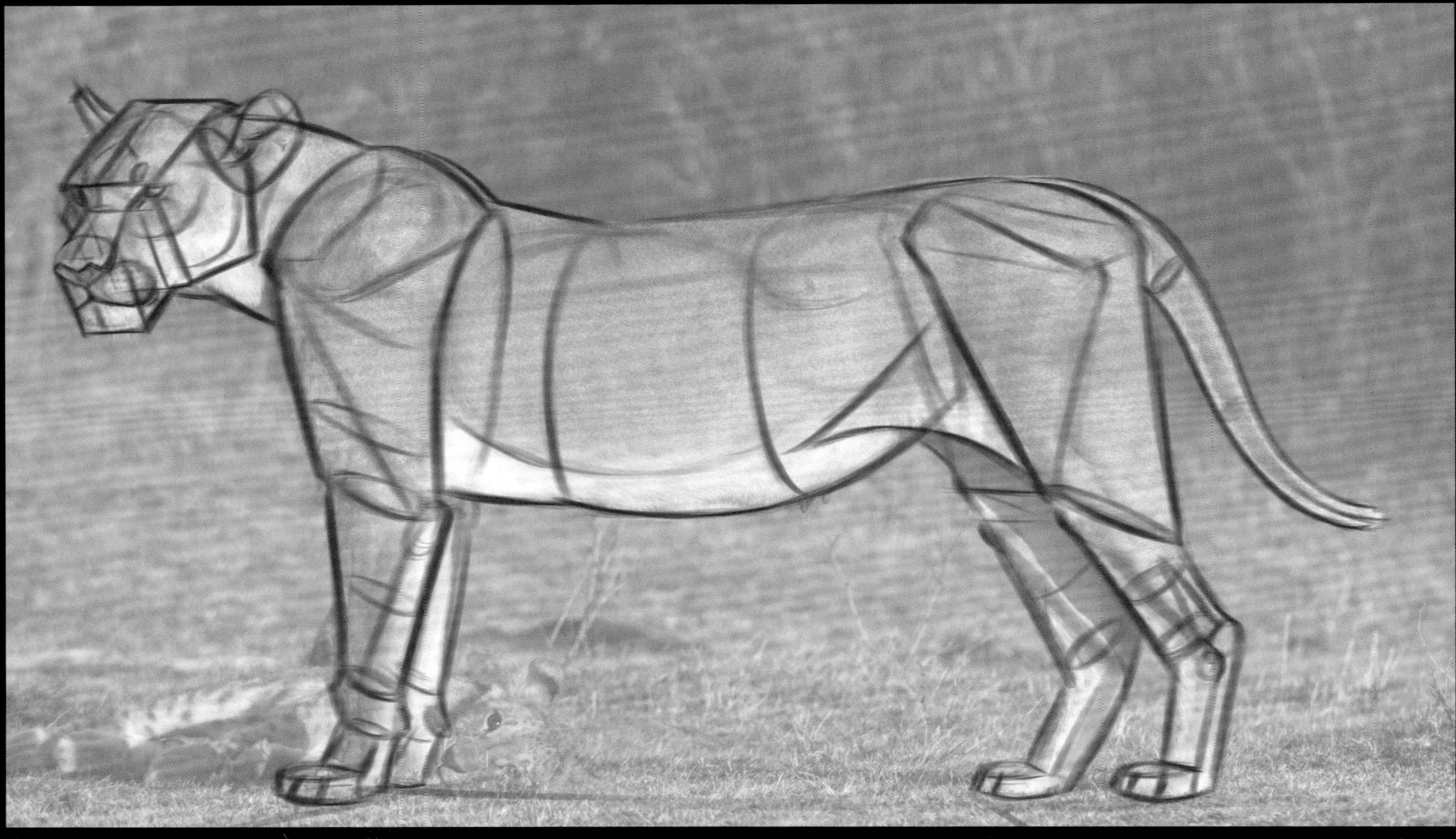

Photograph © Sergio Pitamitz / Agami.nl

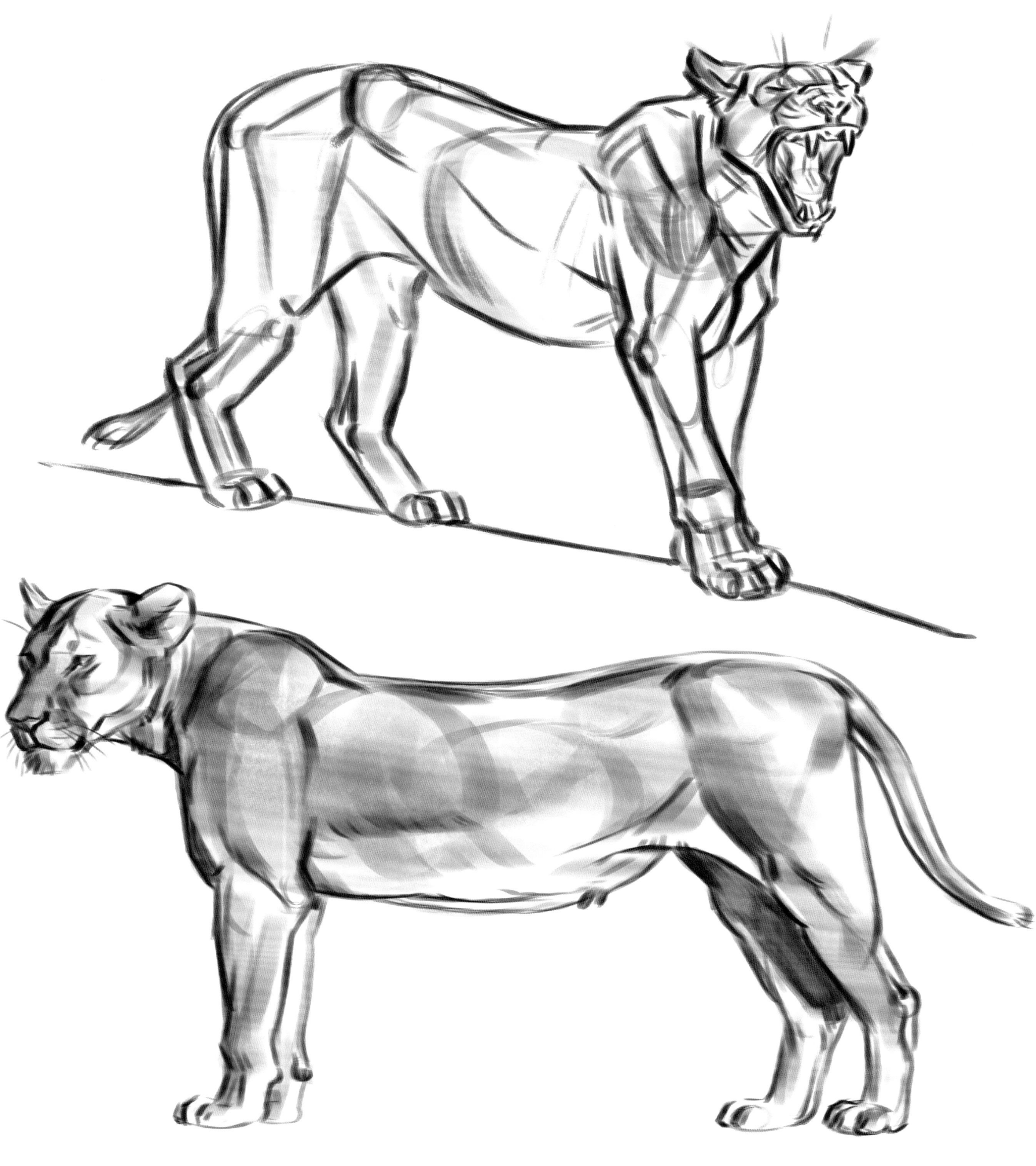

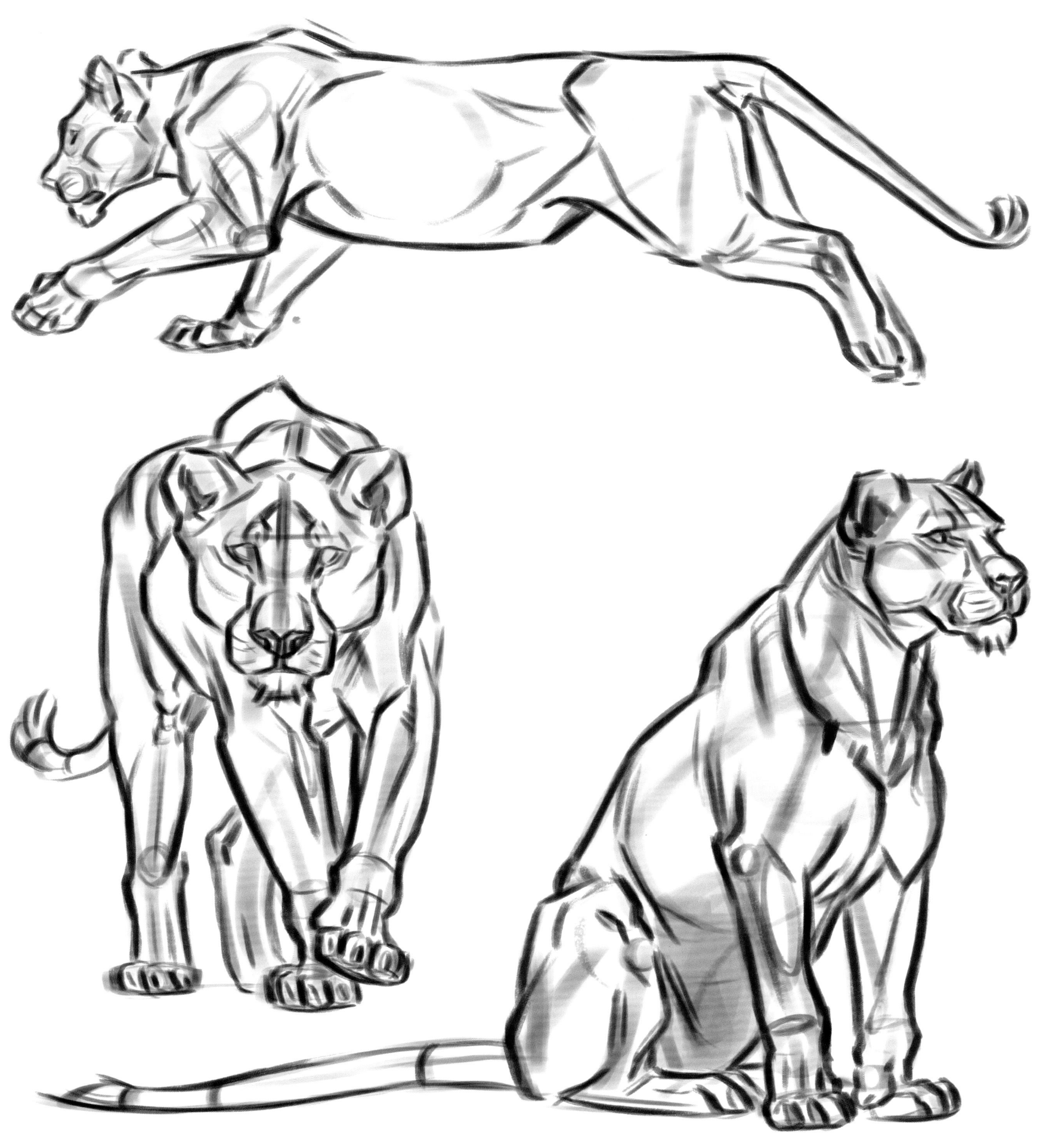

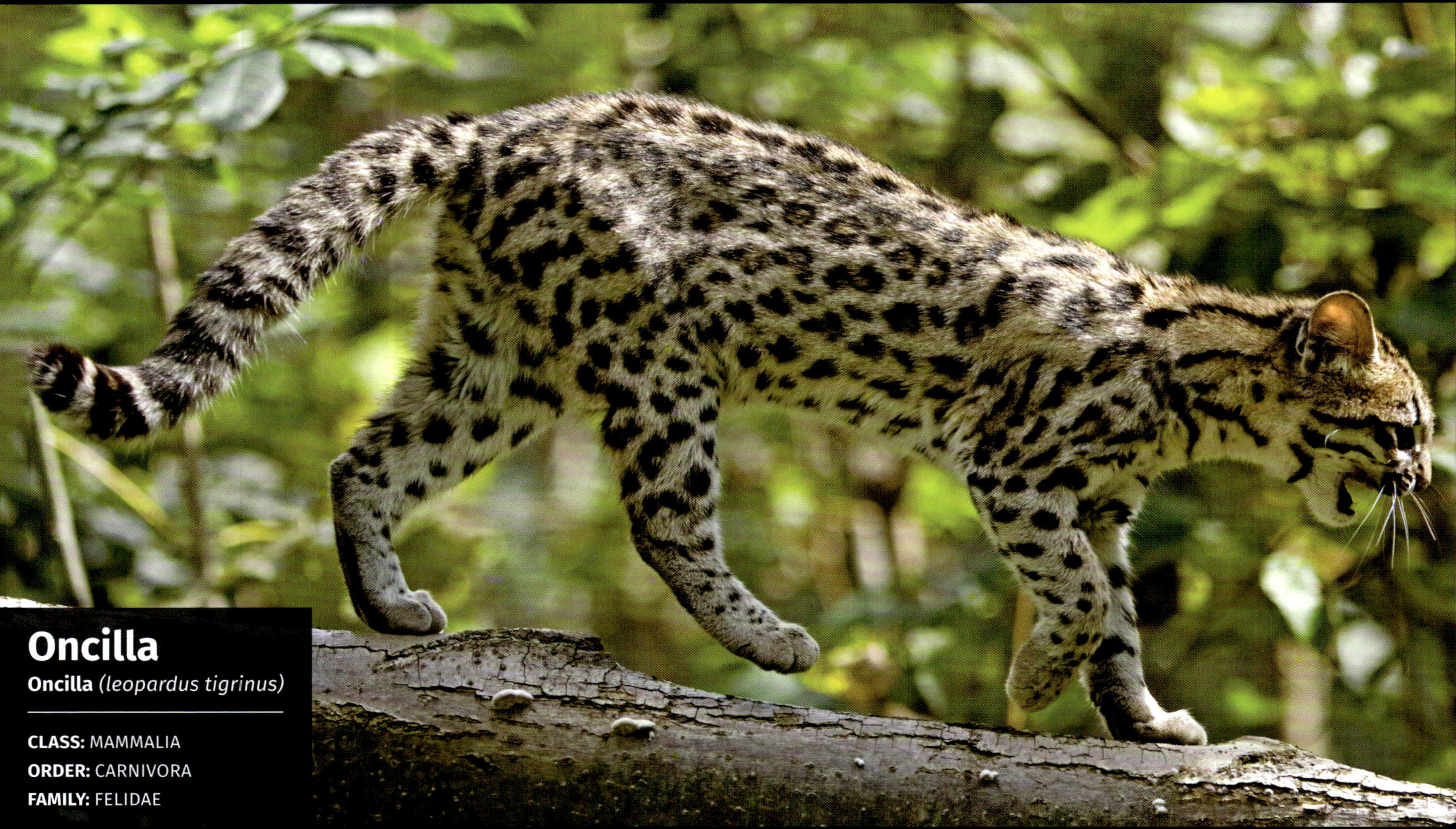

Oncilla

Oncilla *(leopardus tigrinus)*

CLASS: MAMMALIA
ORDER: CARNIVORA
FAMILY: FELIDAE

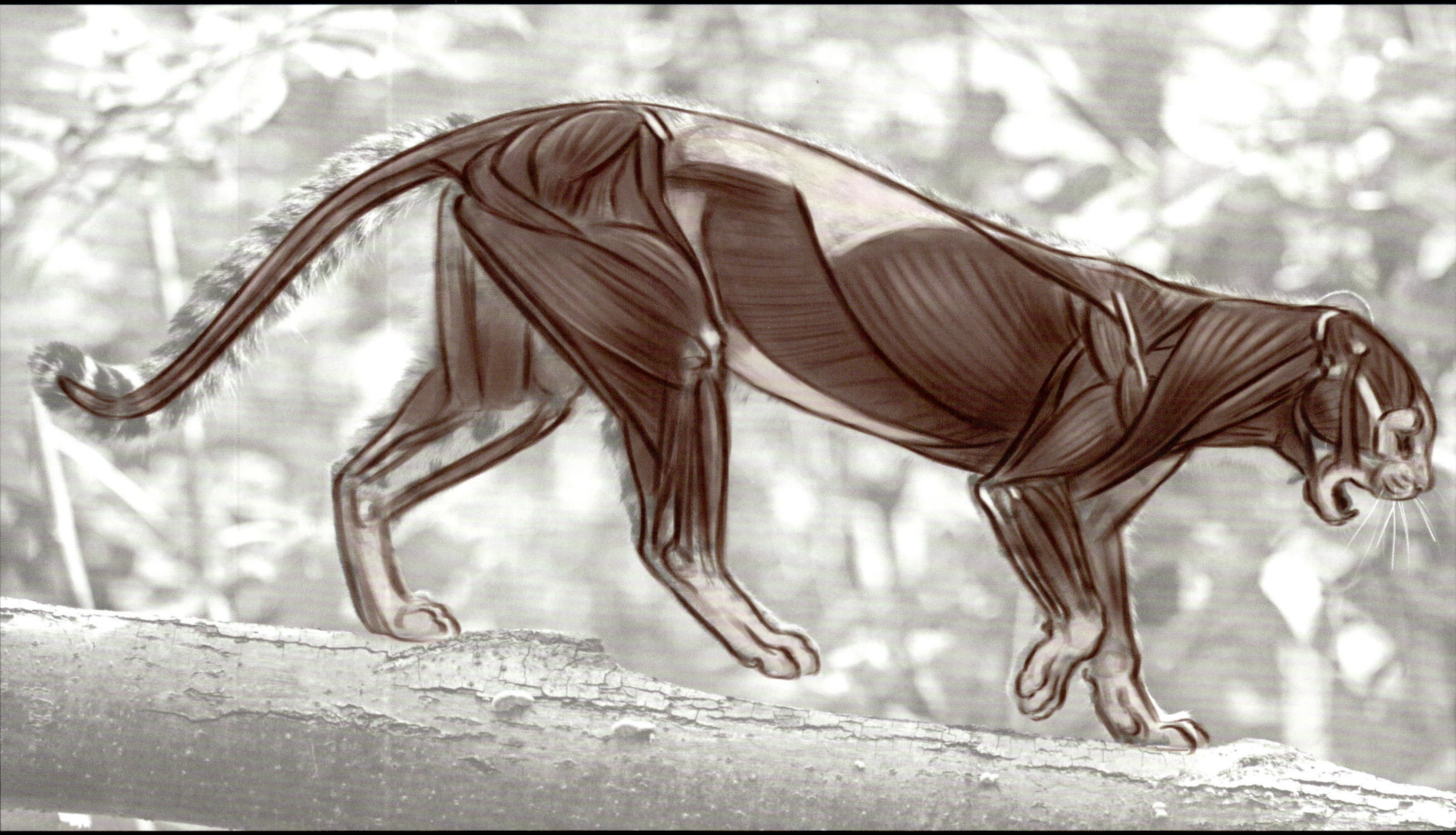

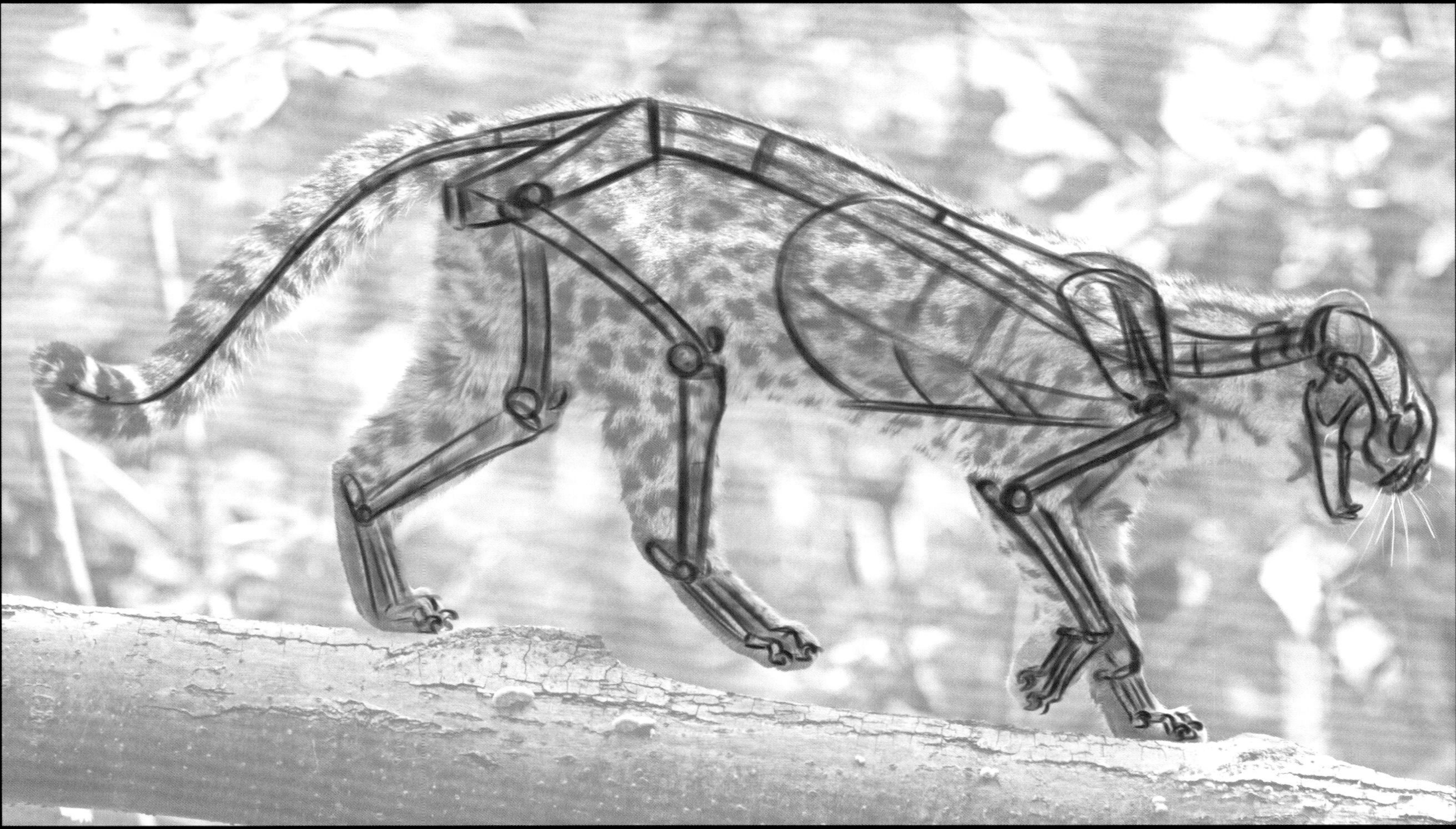

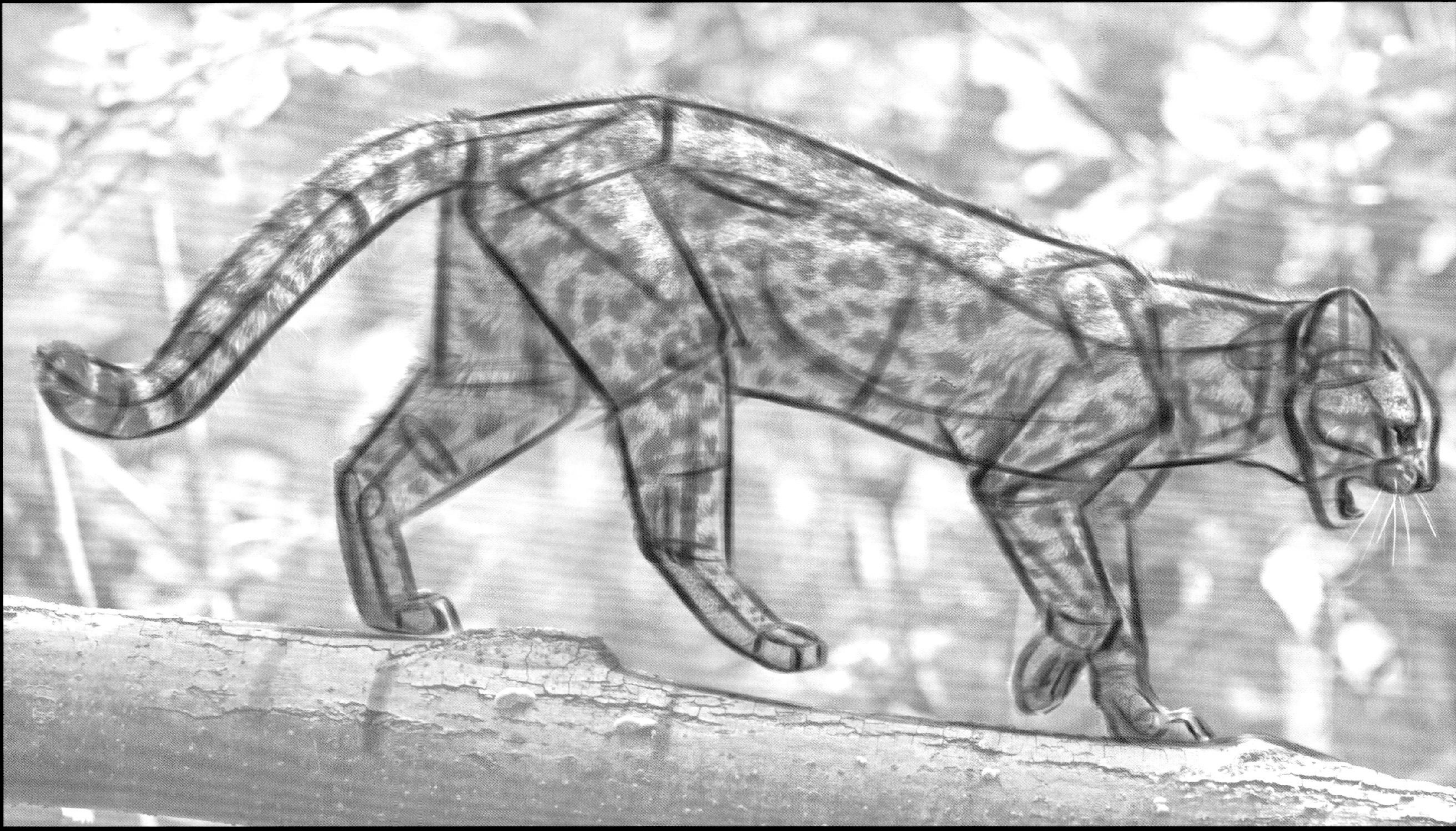

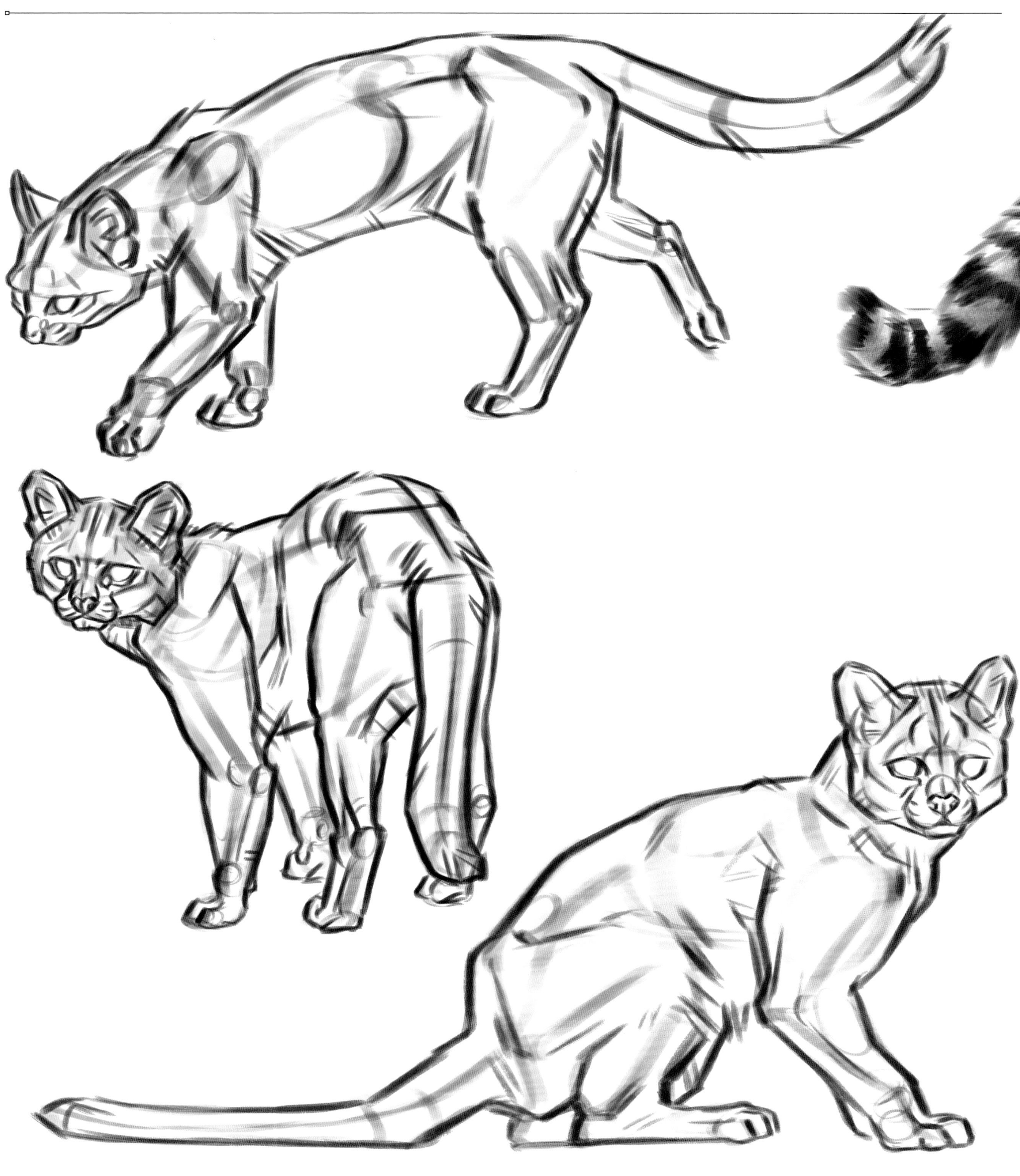

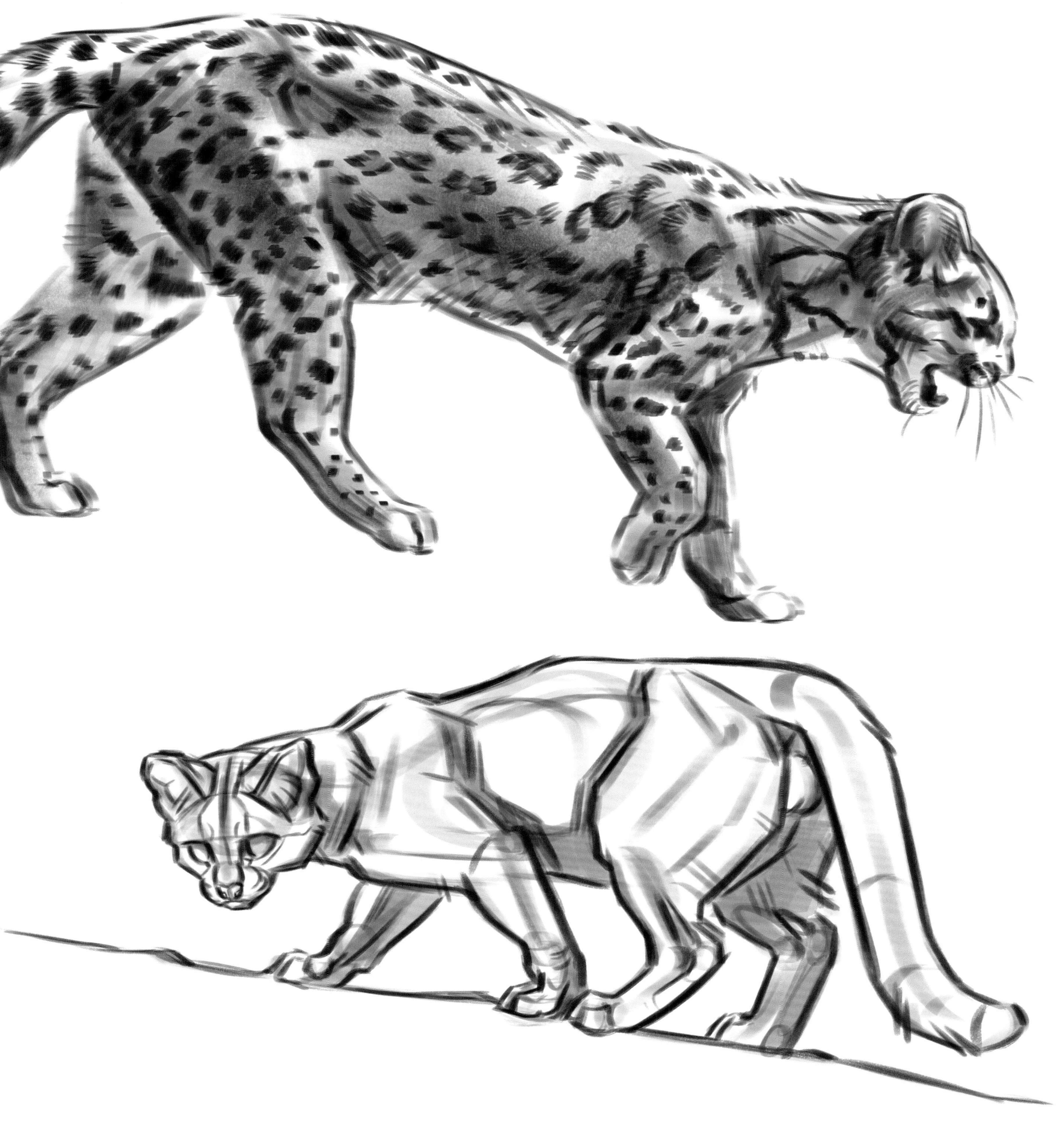

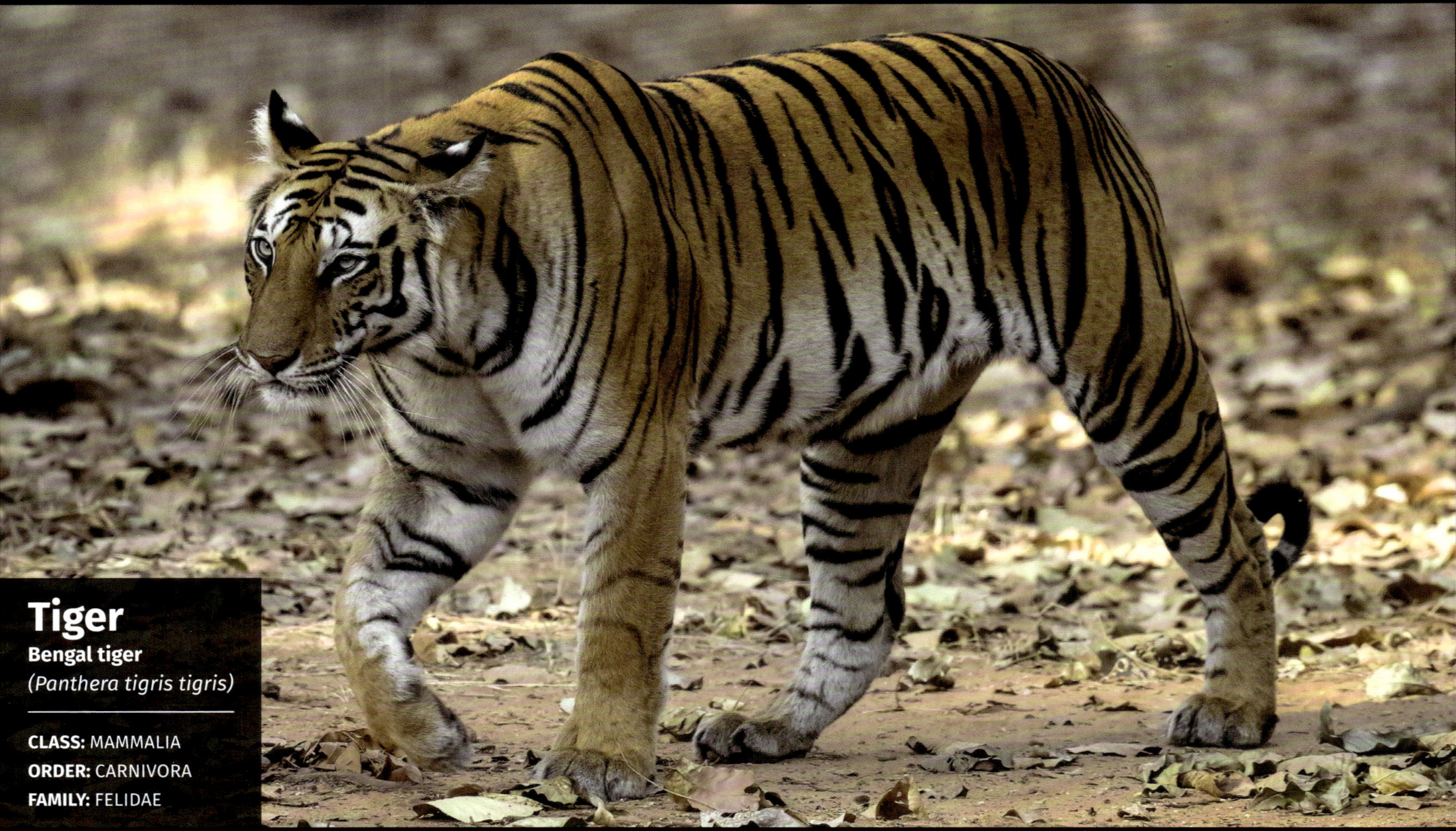

Tiger

Bengal tiger

(Panthera tigris tigris)

CLASS: MAMMALIA
ORDER: CARNIVORA
FAMILY: FELIDAE

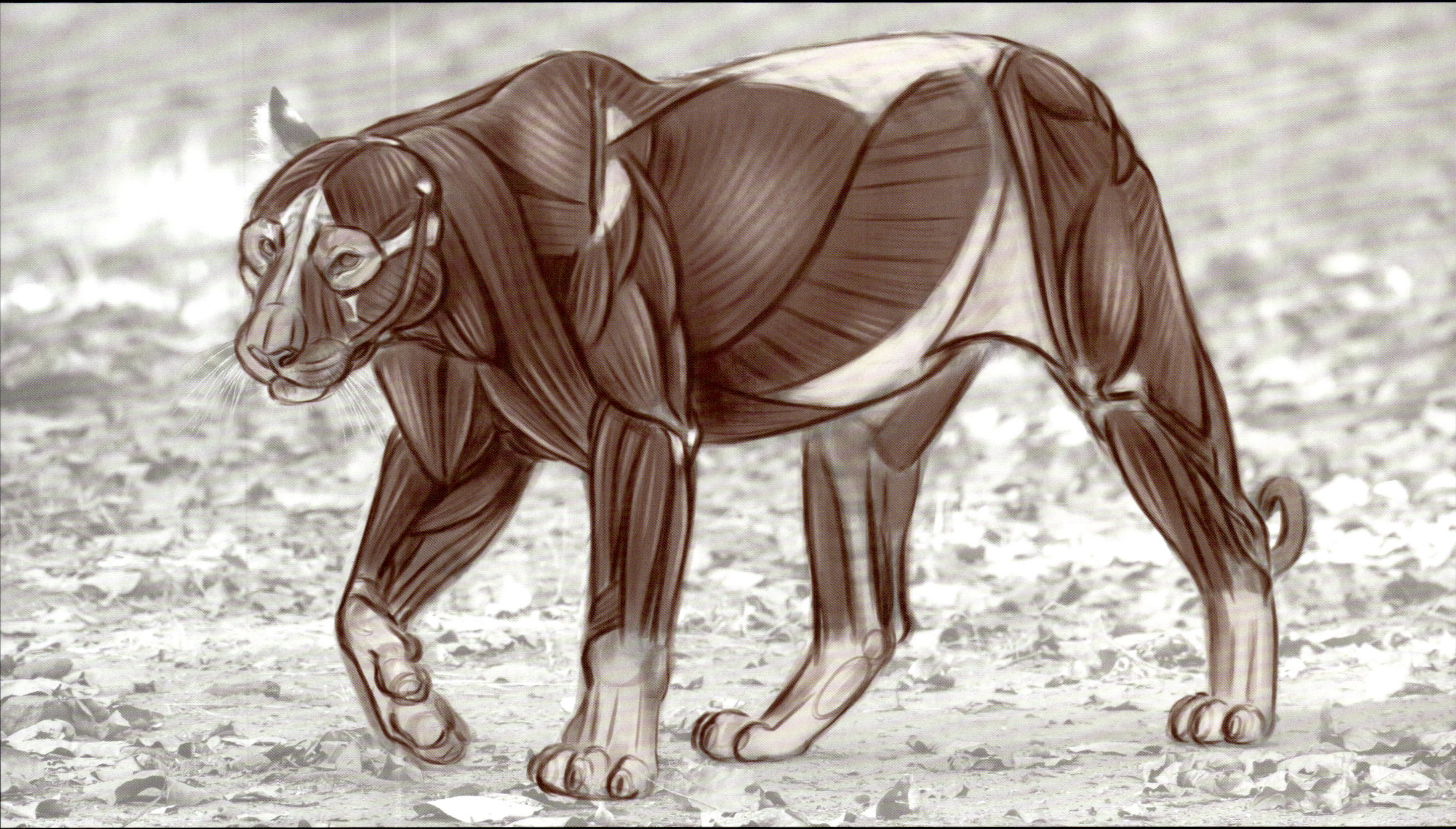

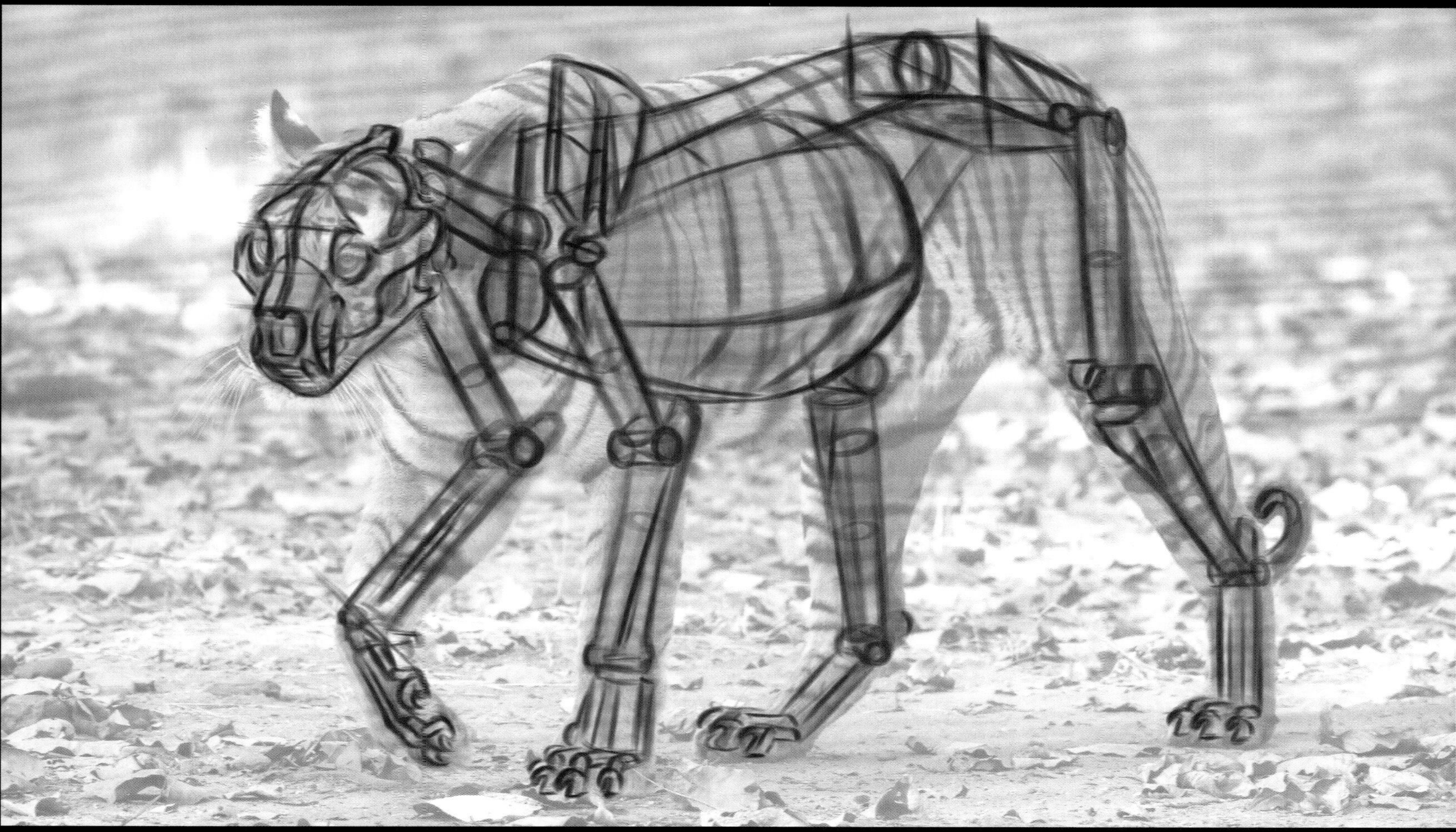

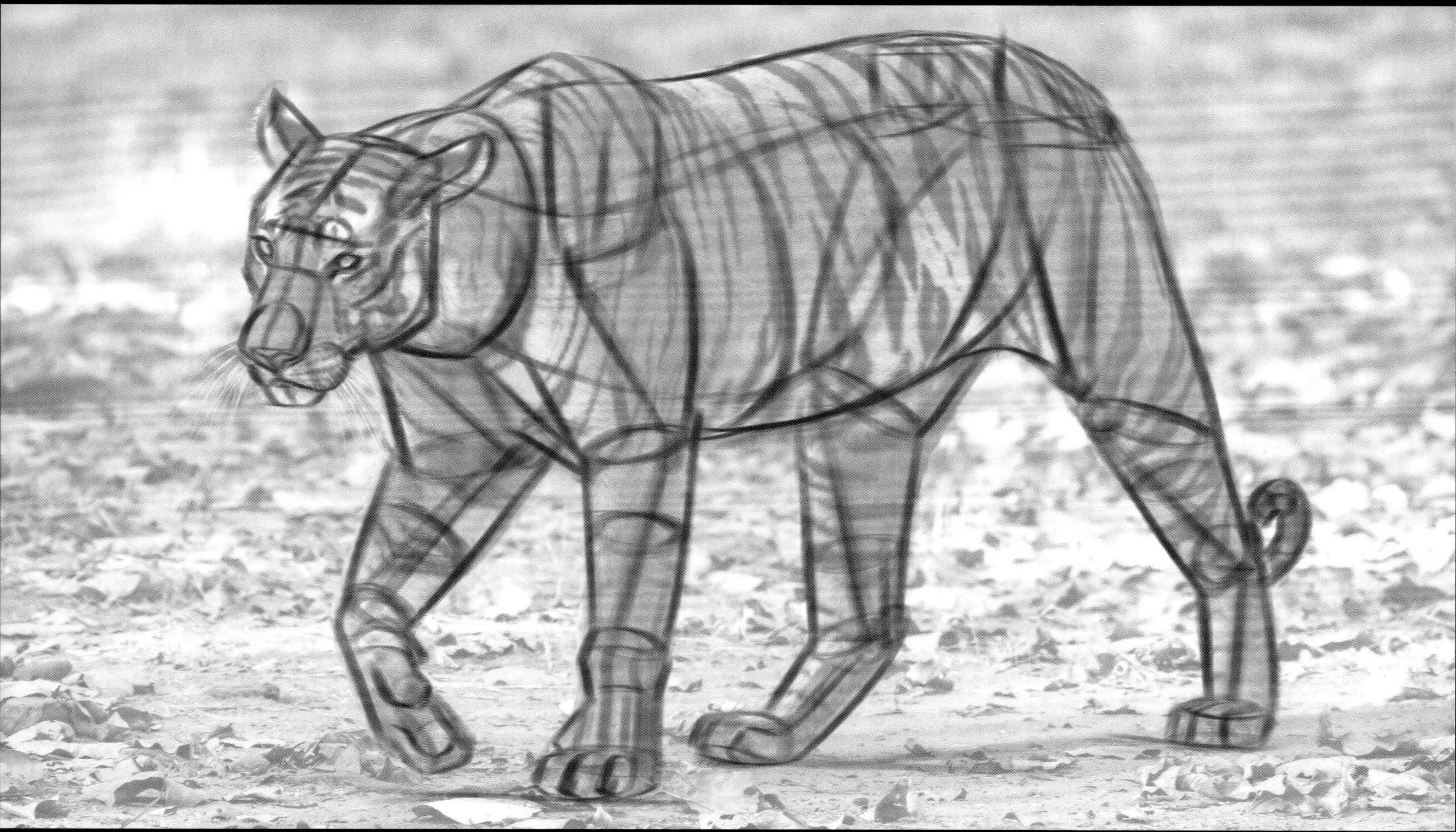

Photograph © Vincent Legrand / Agami.nl

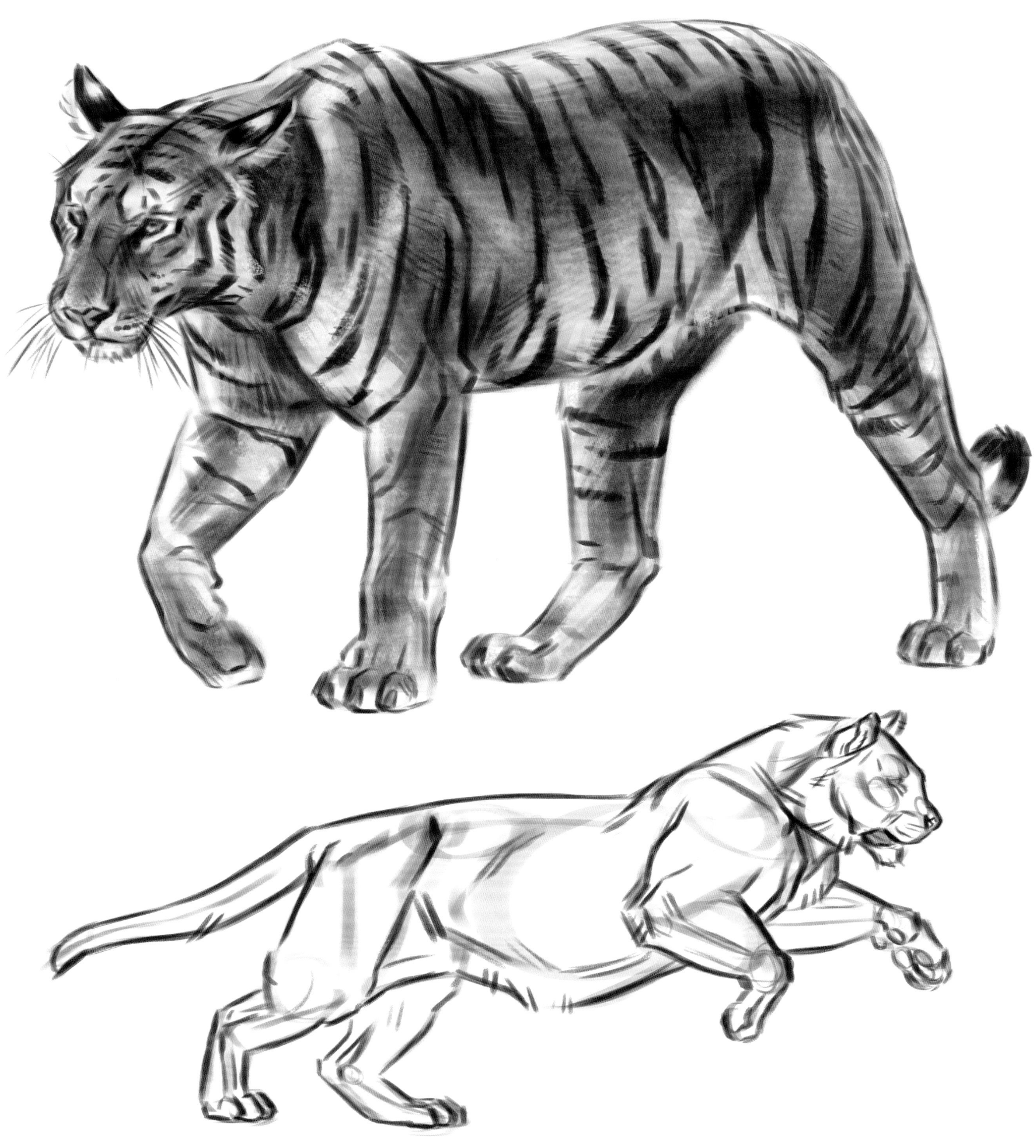

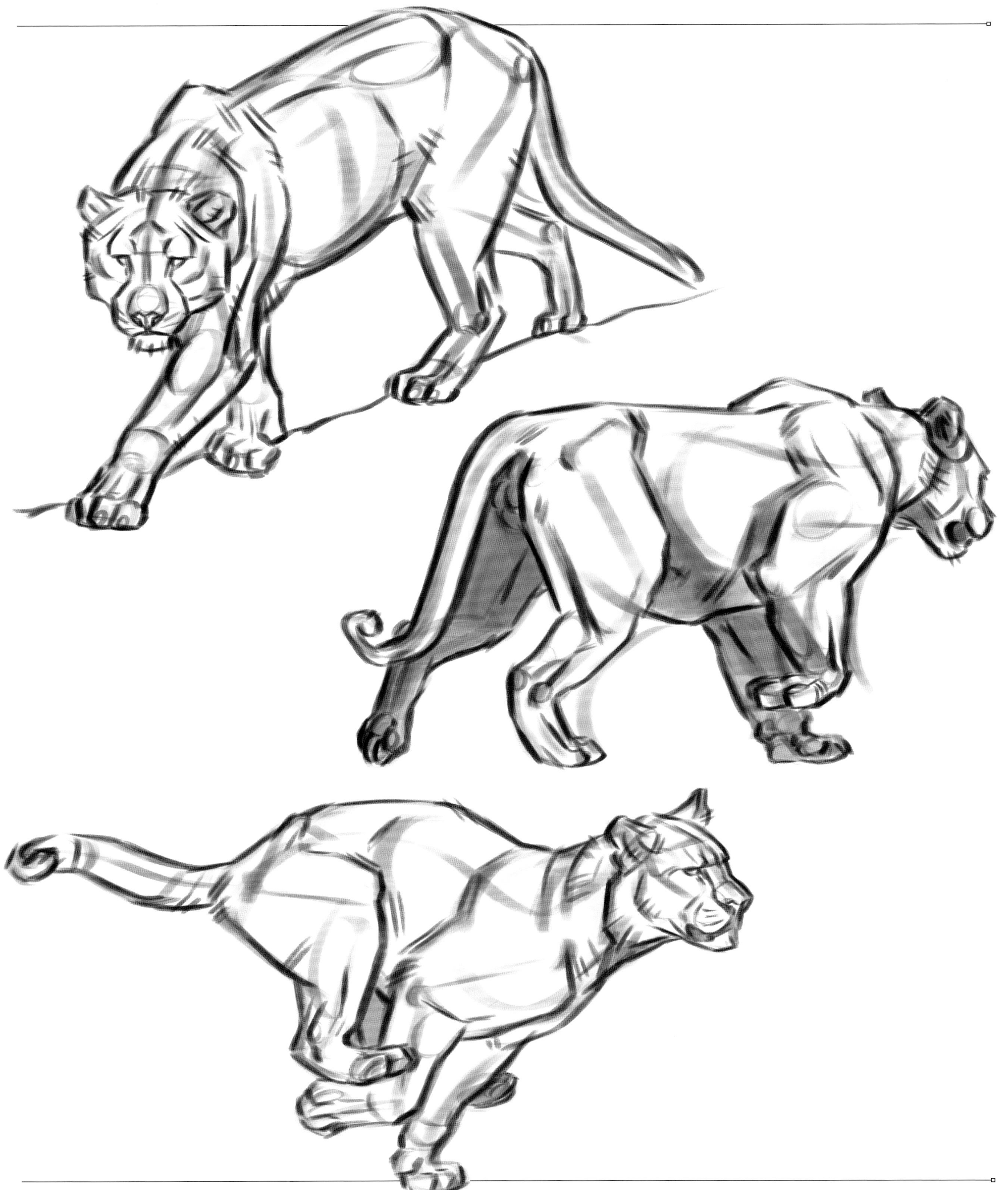

Meerkat

Meerkat
(Suricata suricatta)

CLASS: MAMMALIA
ORDER: CARNIVORA
FAMILY: HERPESTIDAE

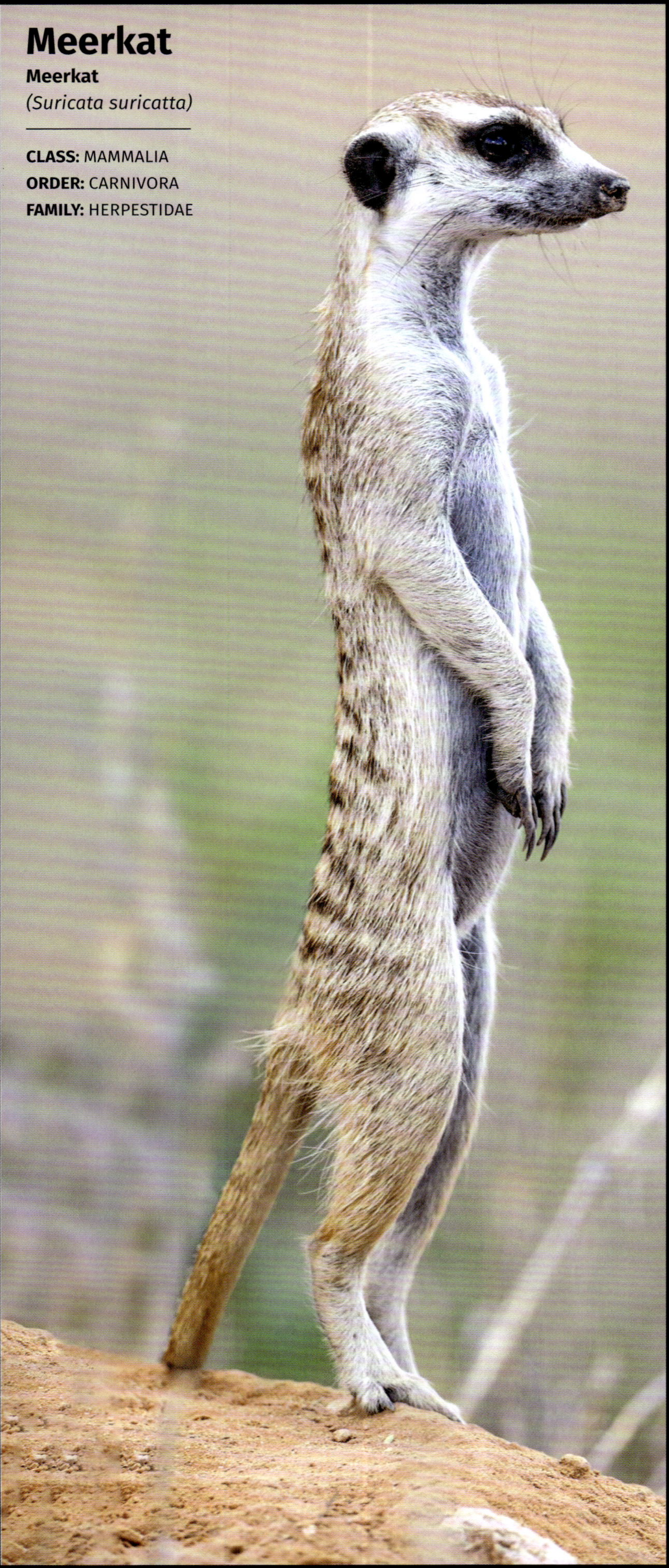

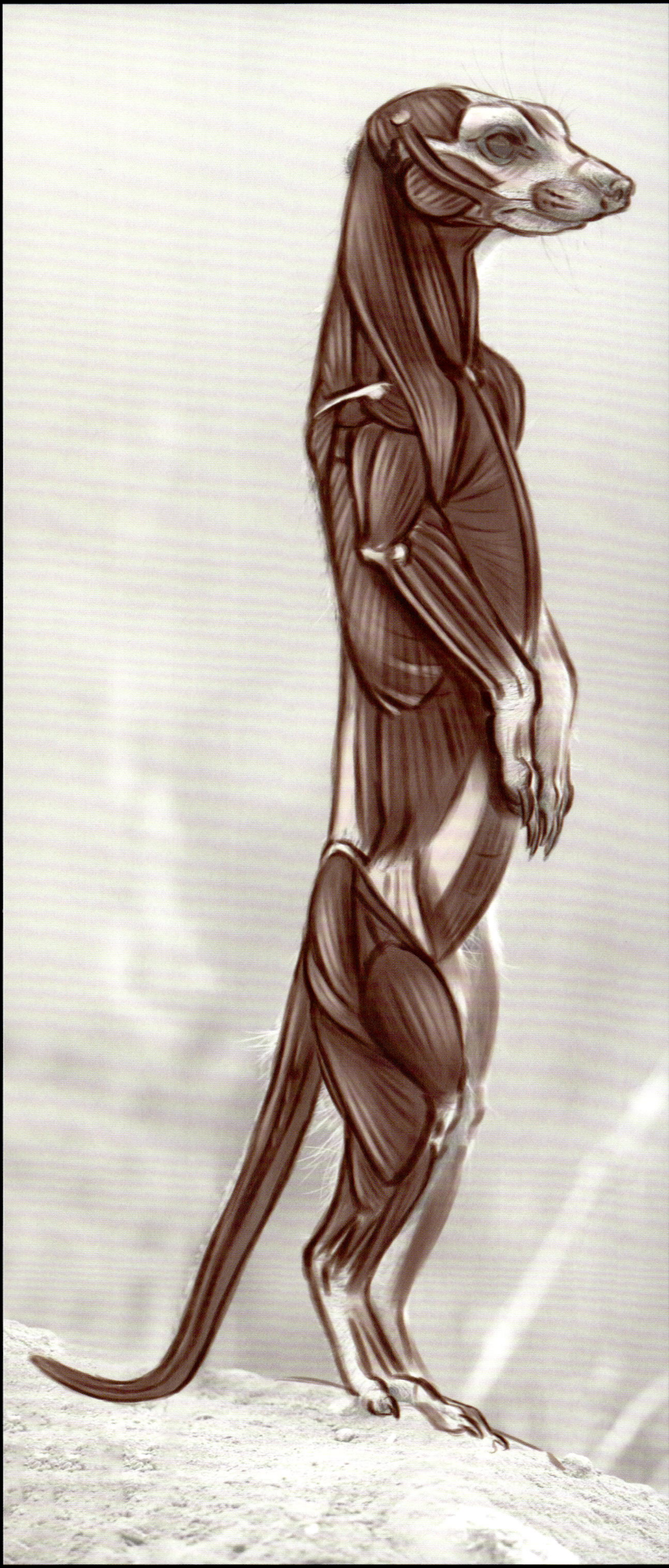

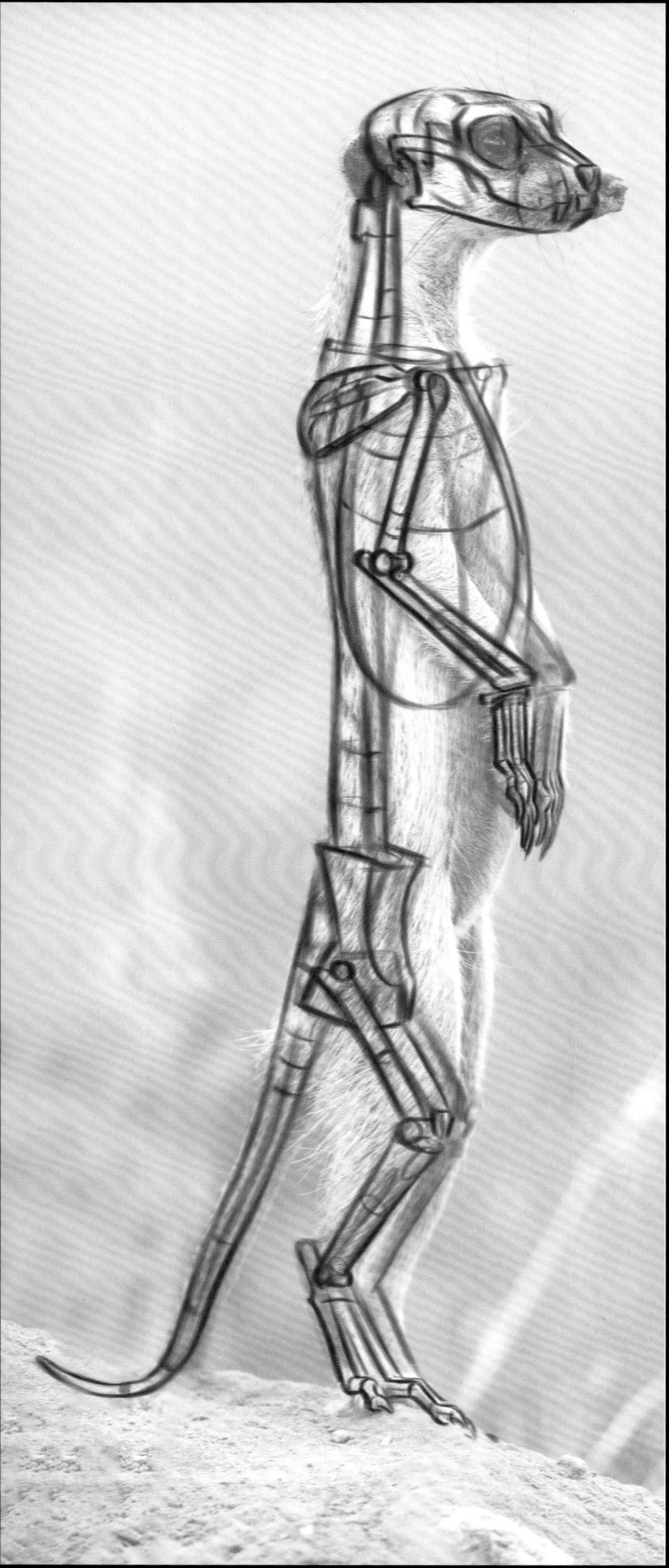

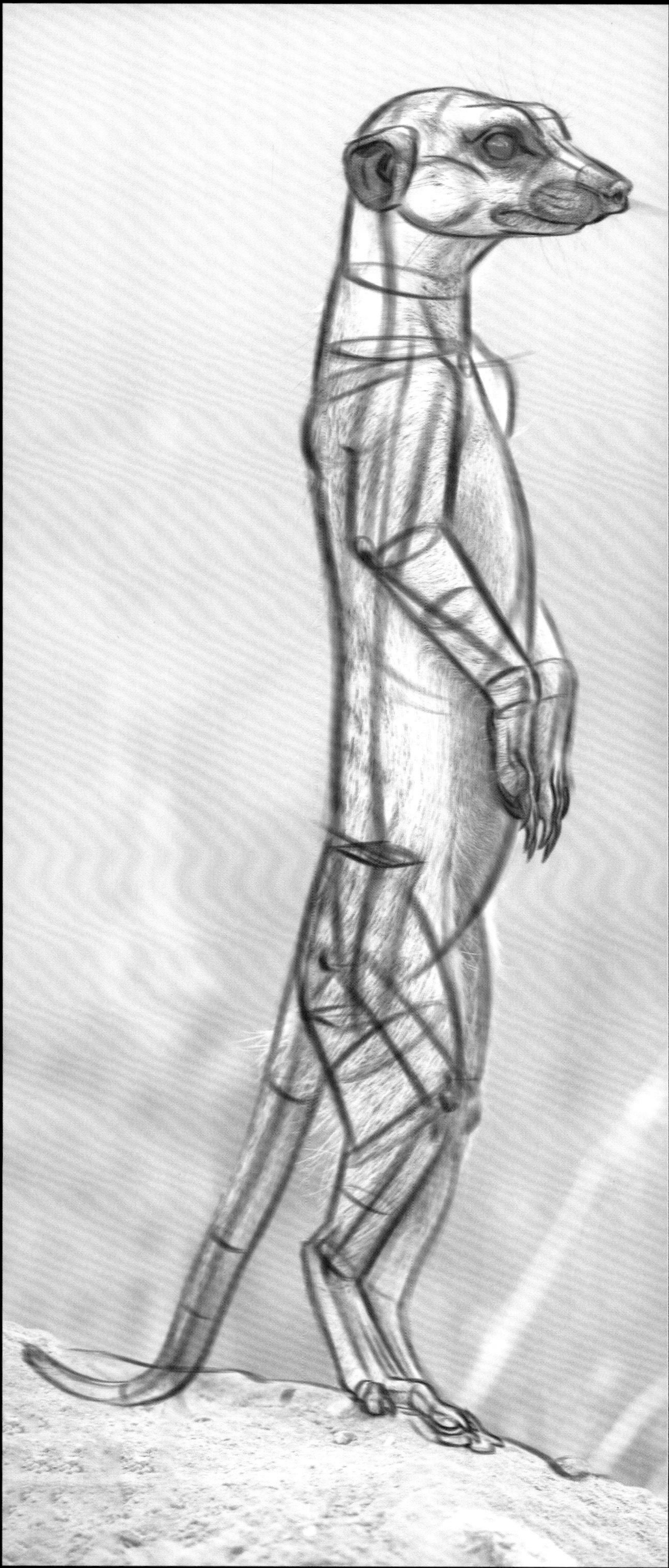

Photograph © imageBROKER.com / Thomas Dressler

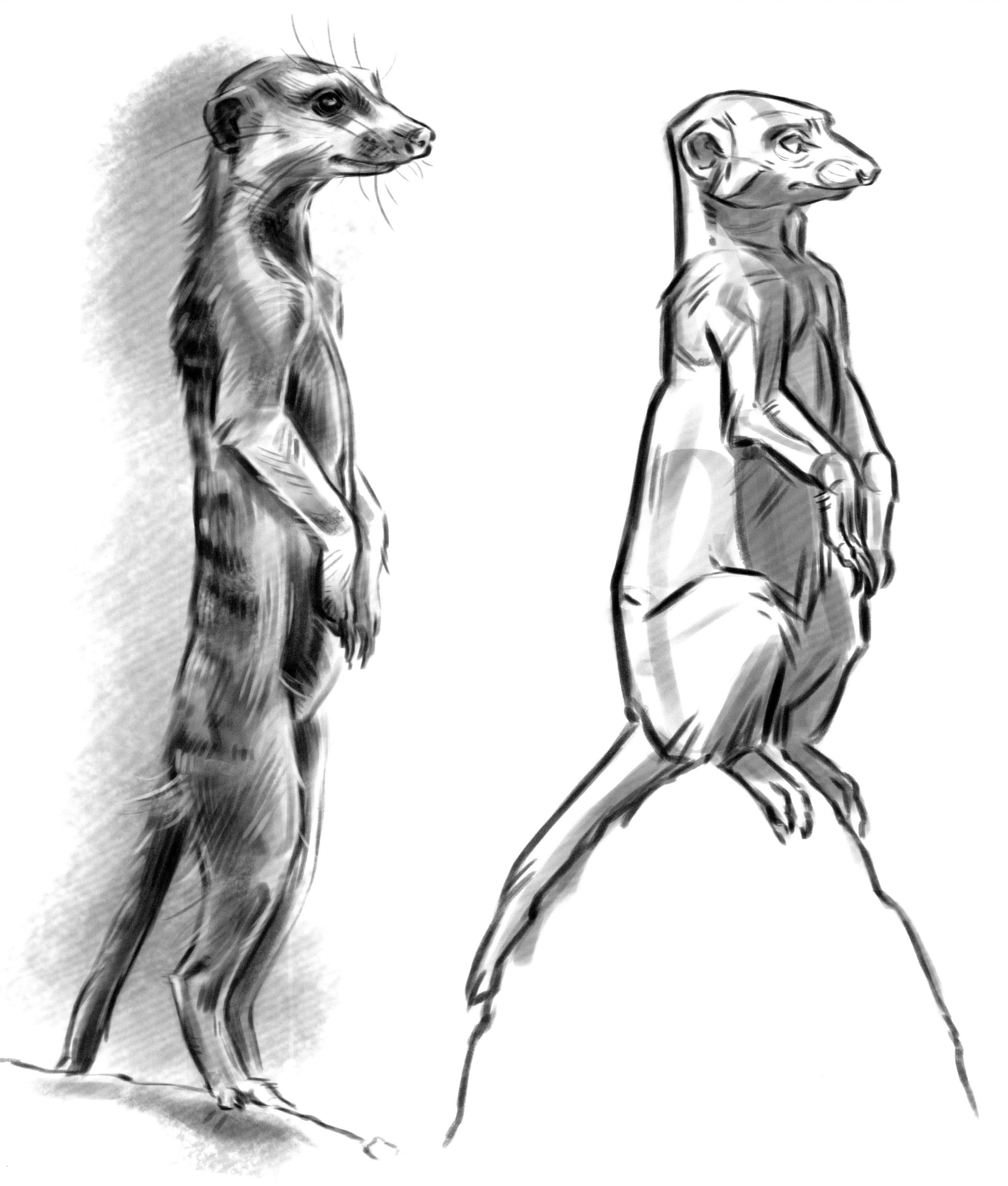

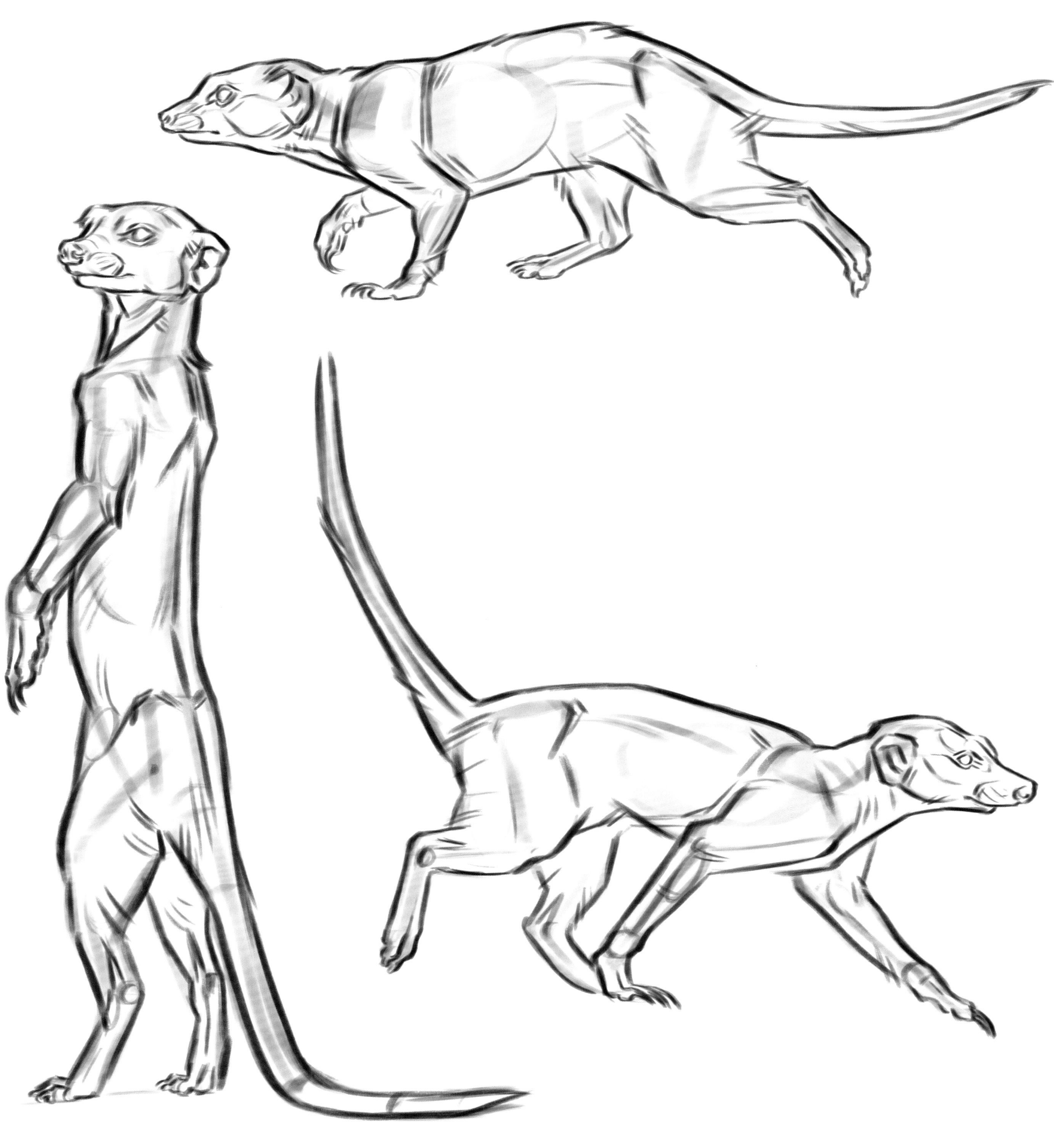

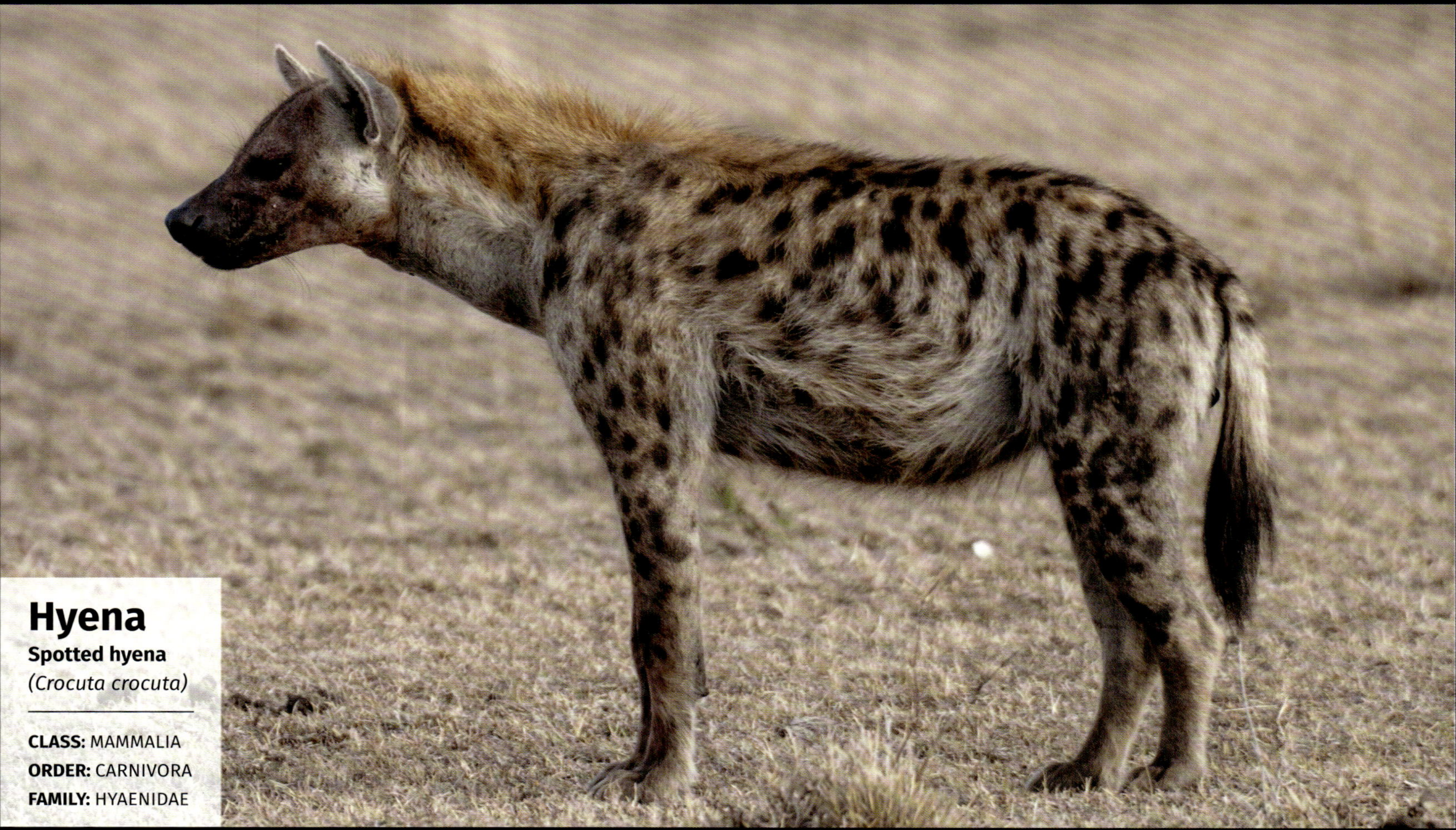

Hyena

Spotted hyena
(Crocuta crocuta)

CLASS: MAMMALIA
ORDER: CARNIVORA
FAMILY: HYAENIDAE

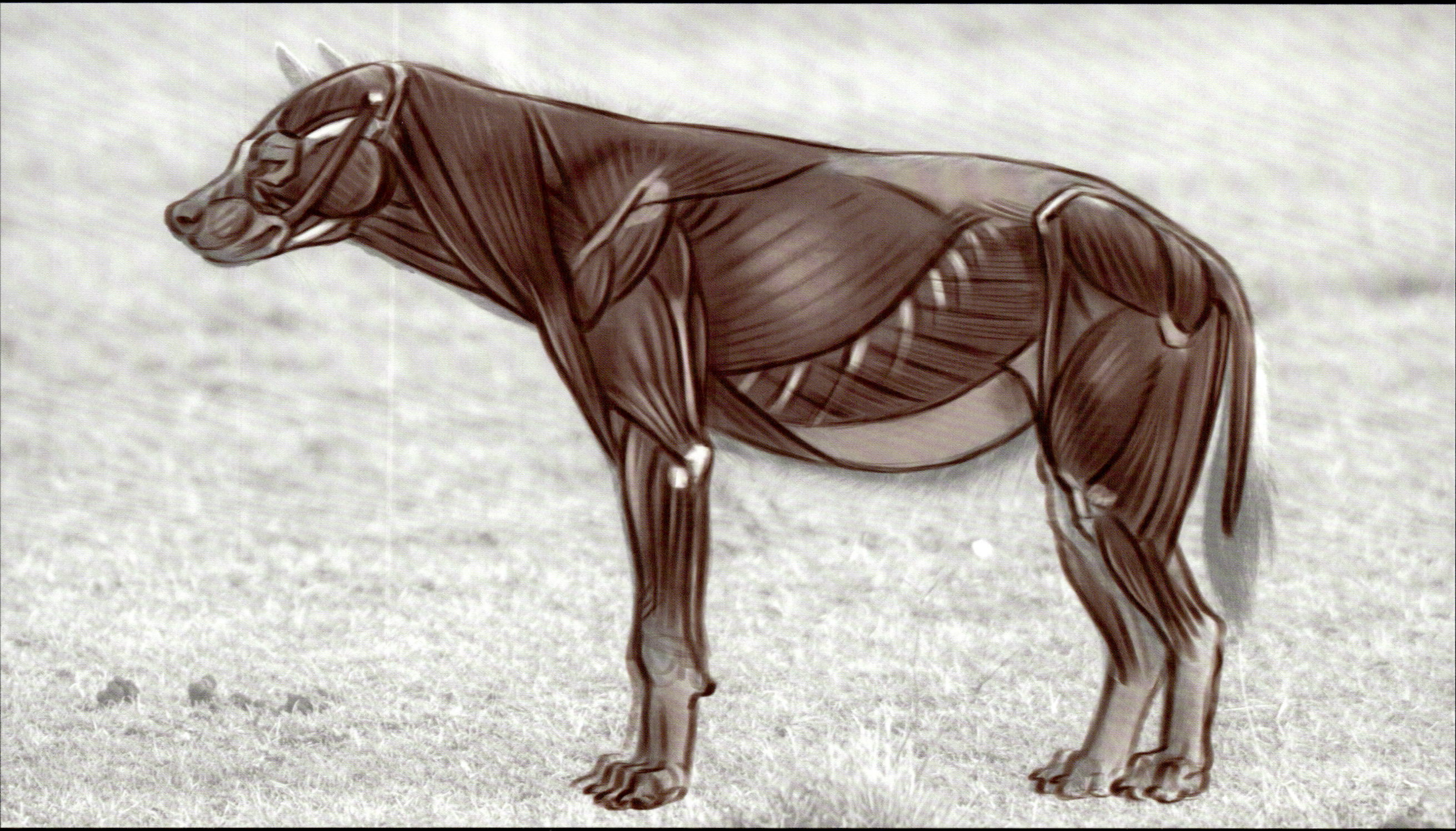

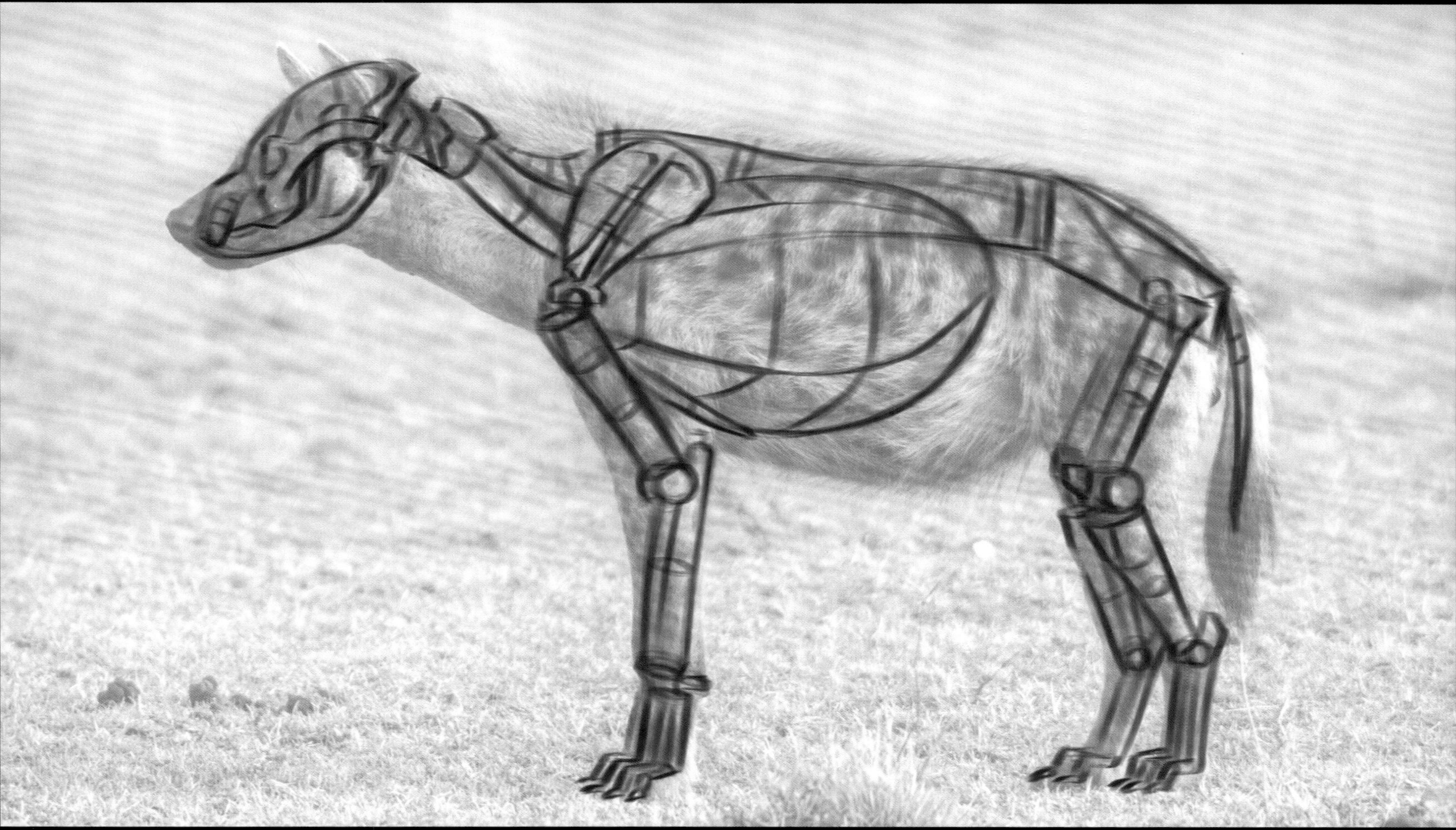

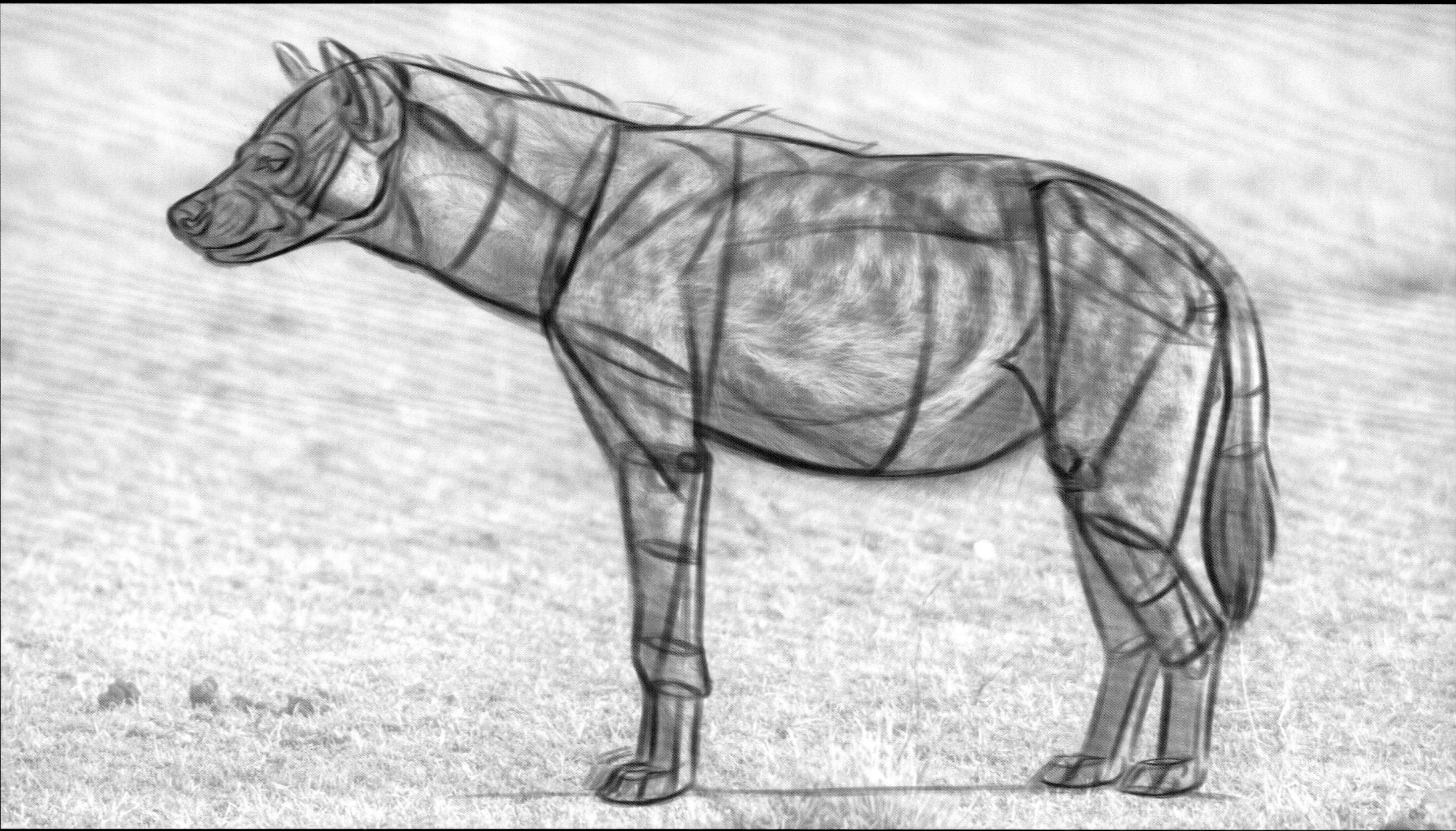

Photograph © Sergio Pitamitz / Agami.nl

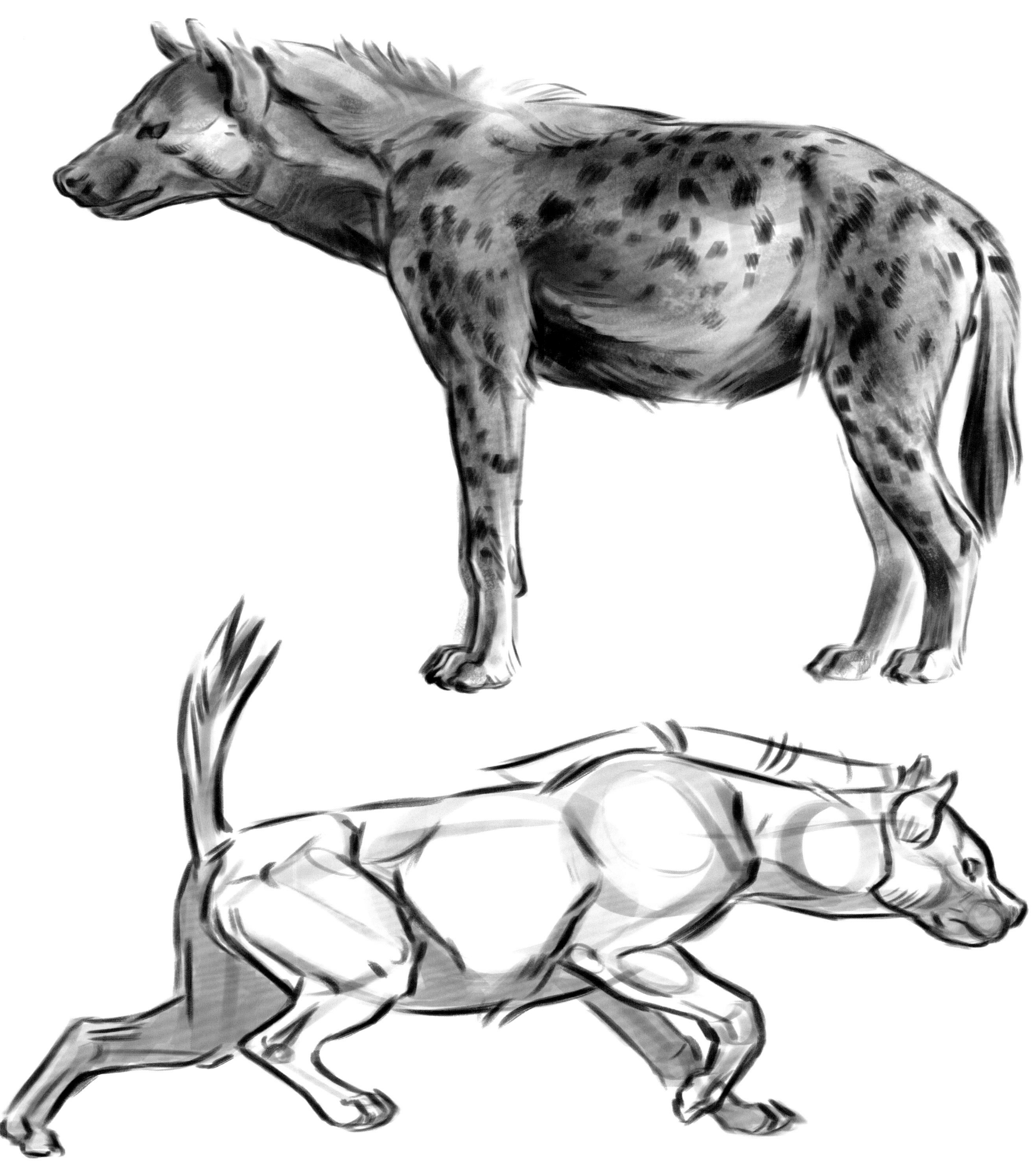

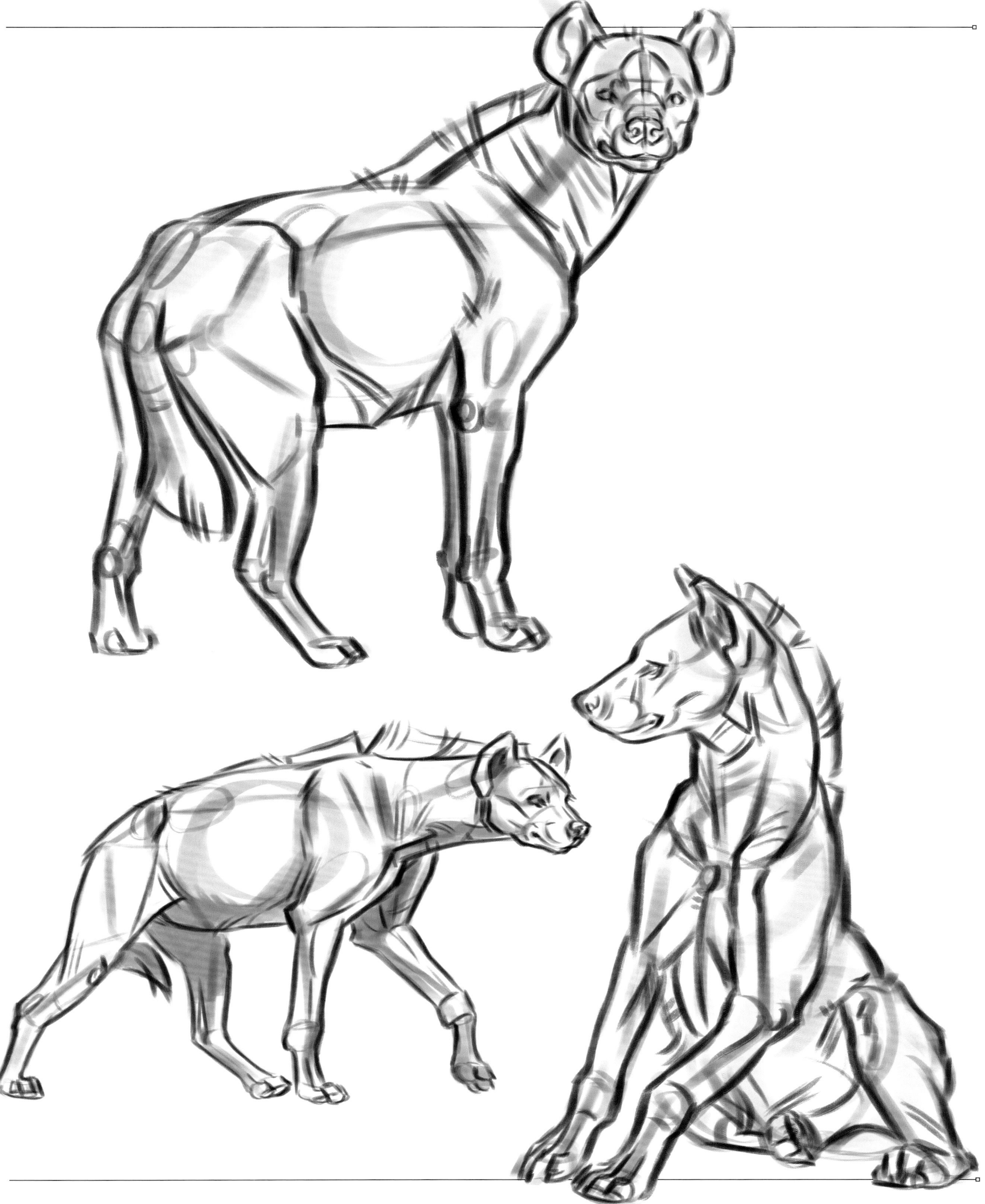

Badger

European badger

(Meles meles)

CLASS: MAMMALIA
ORDER: CARNIVORA
FAMILY: MUSTELIDAE

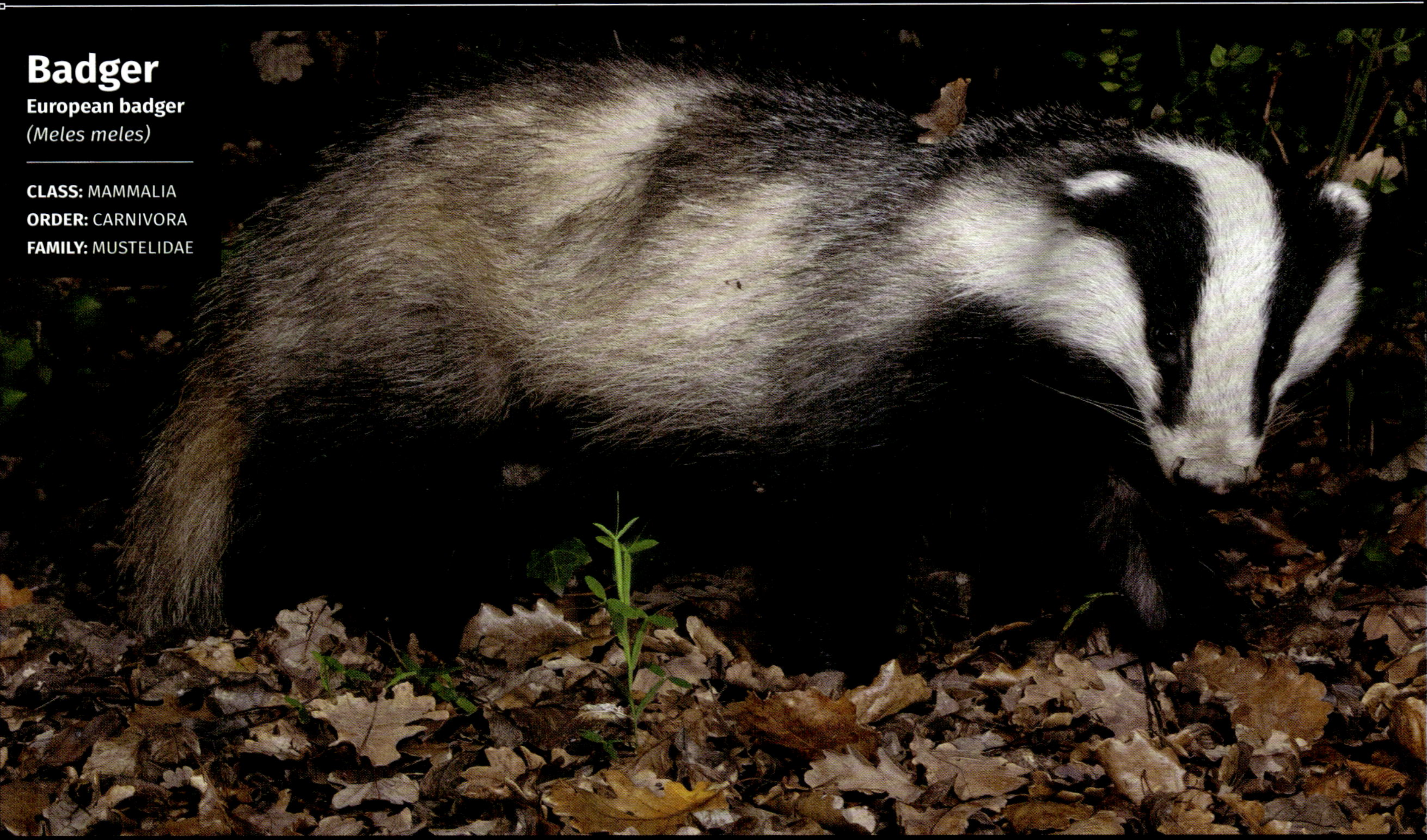

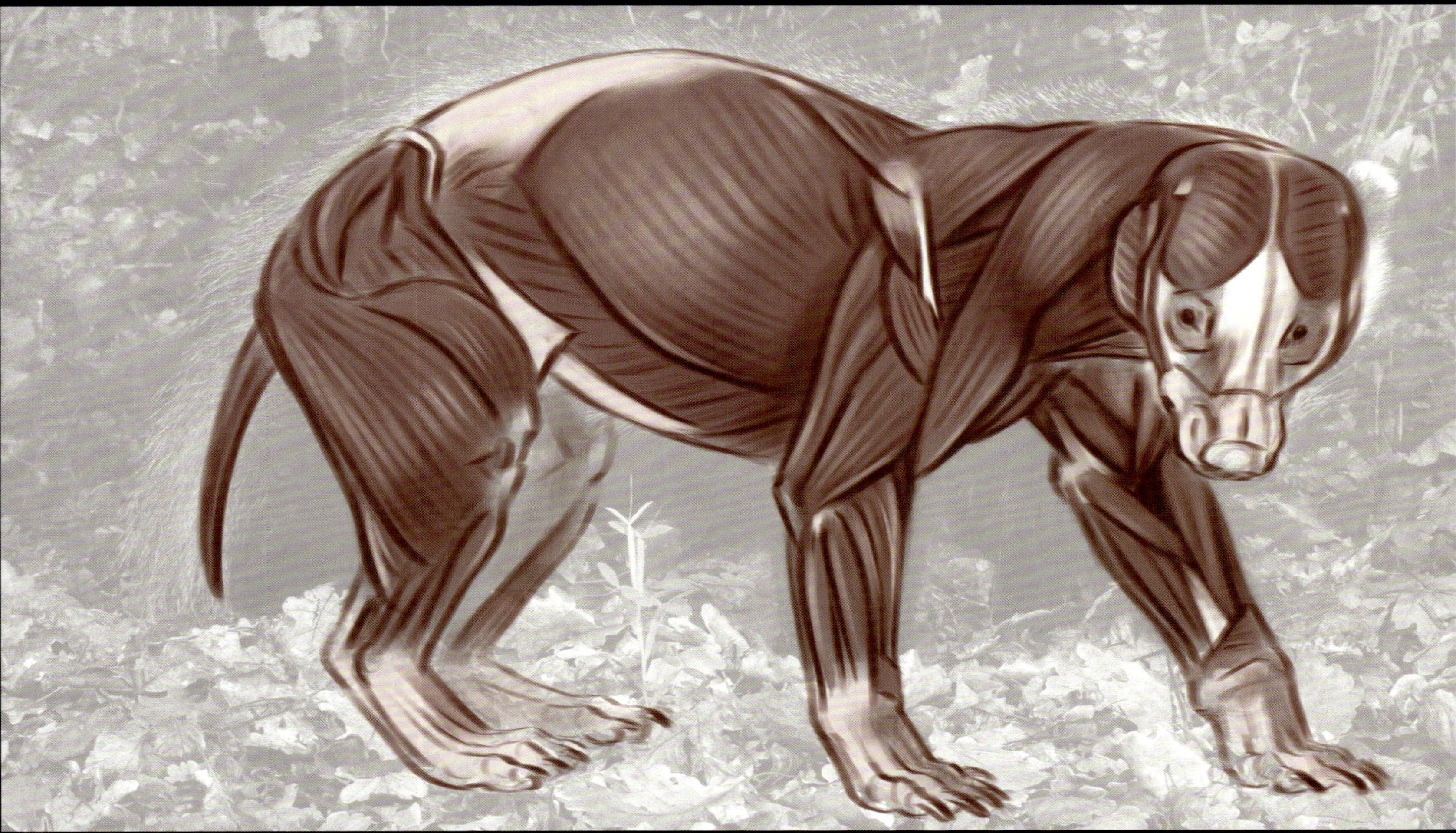

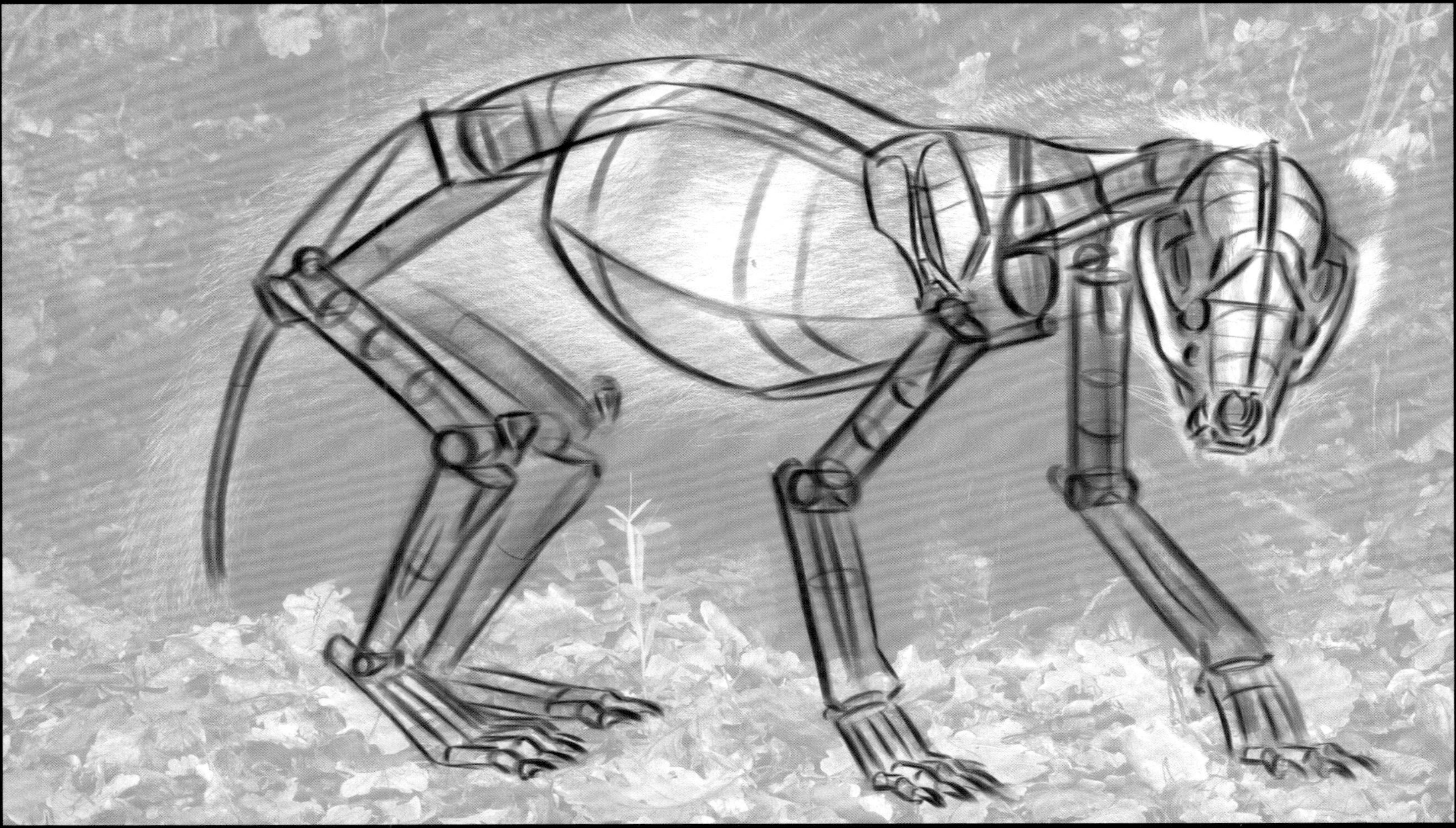

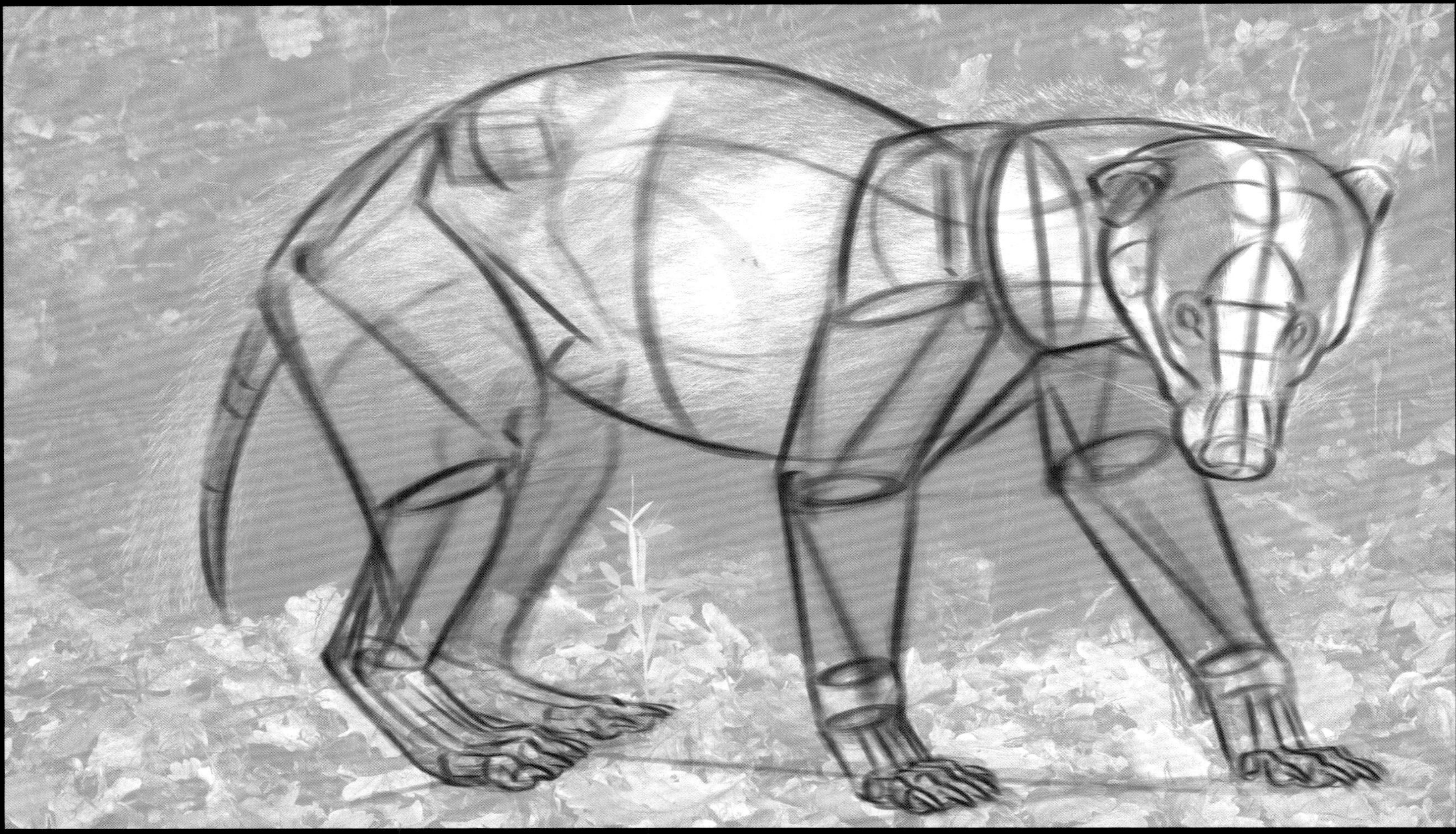

Photograph © Saverio Gatto / Agami.nl

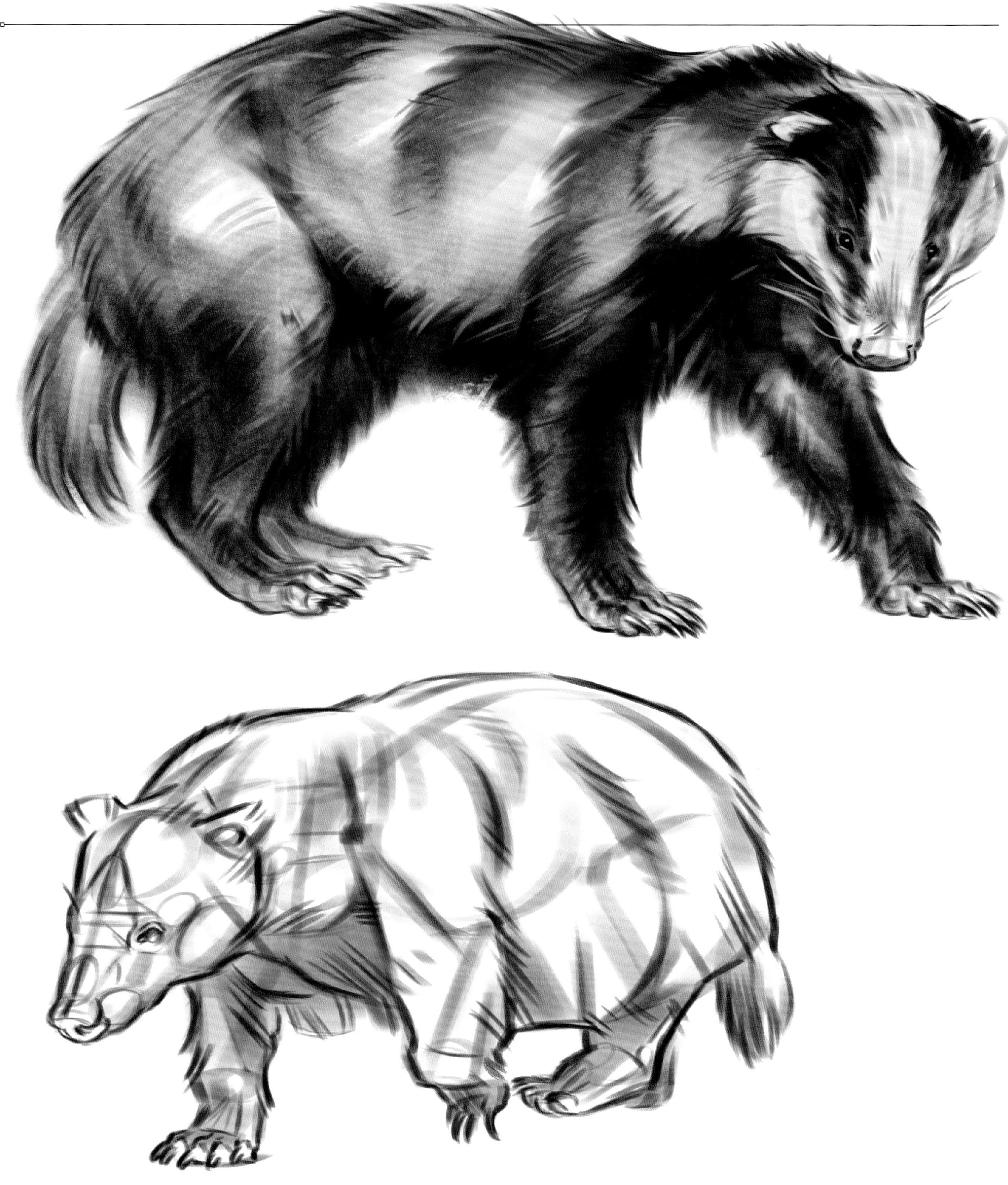

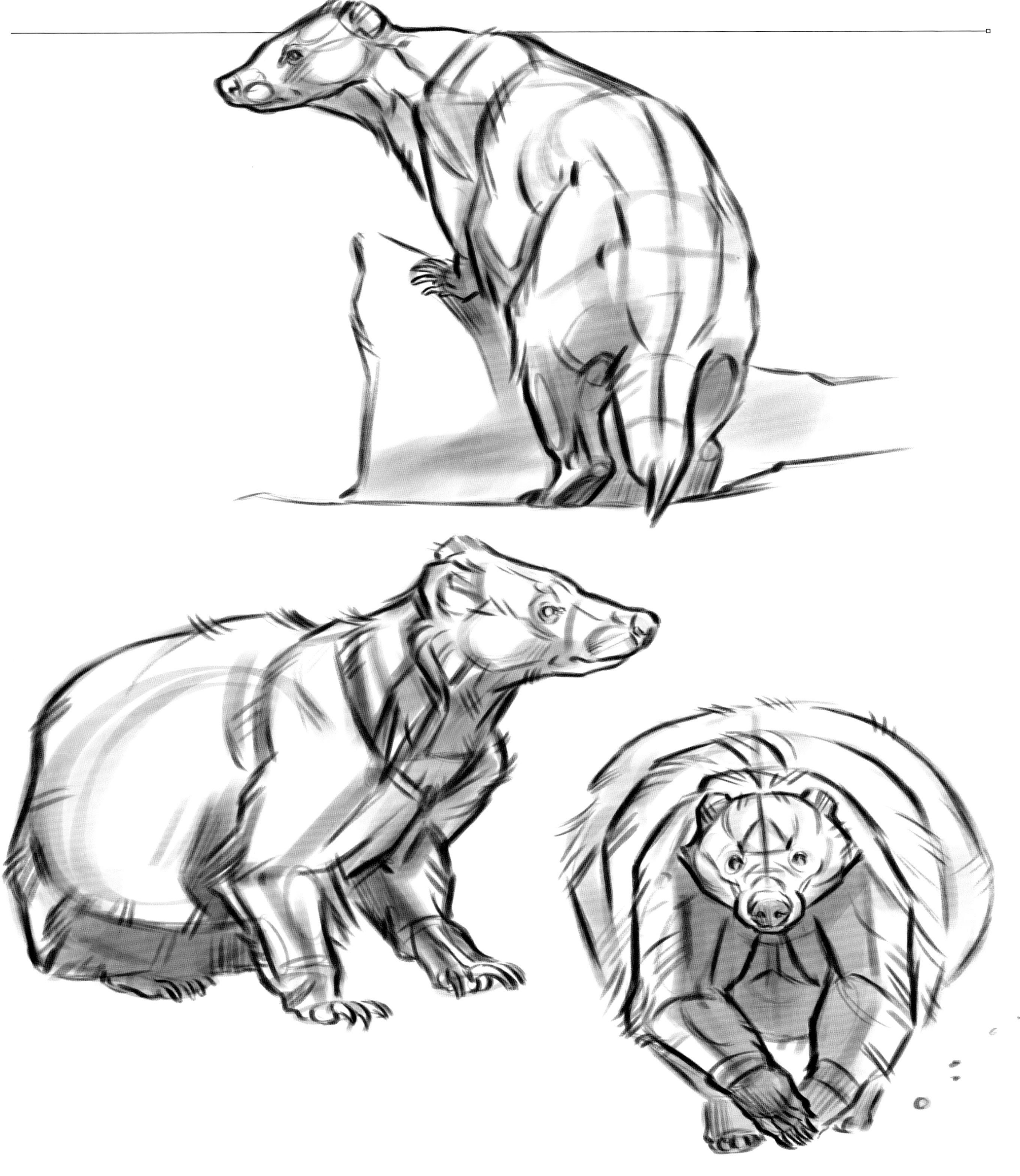

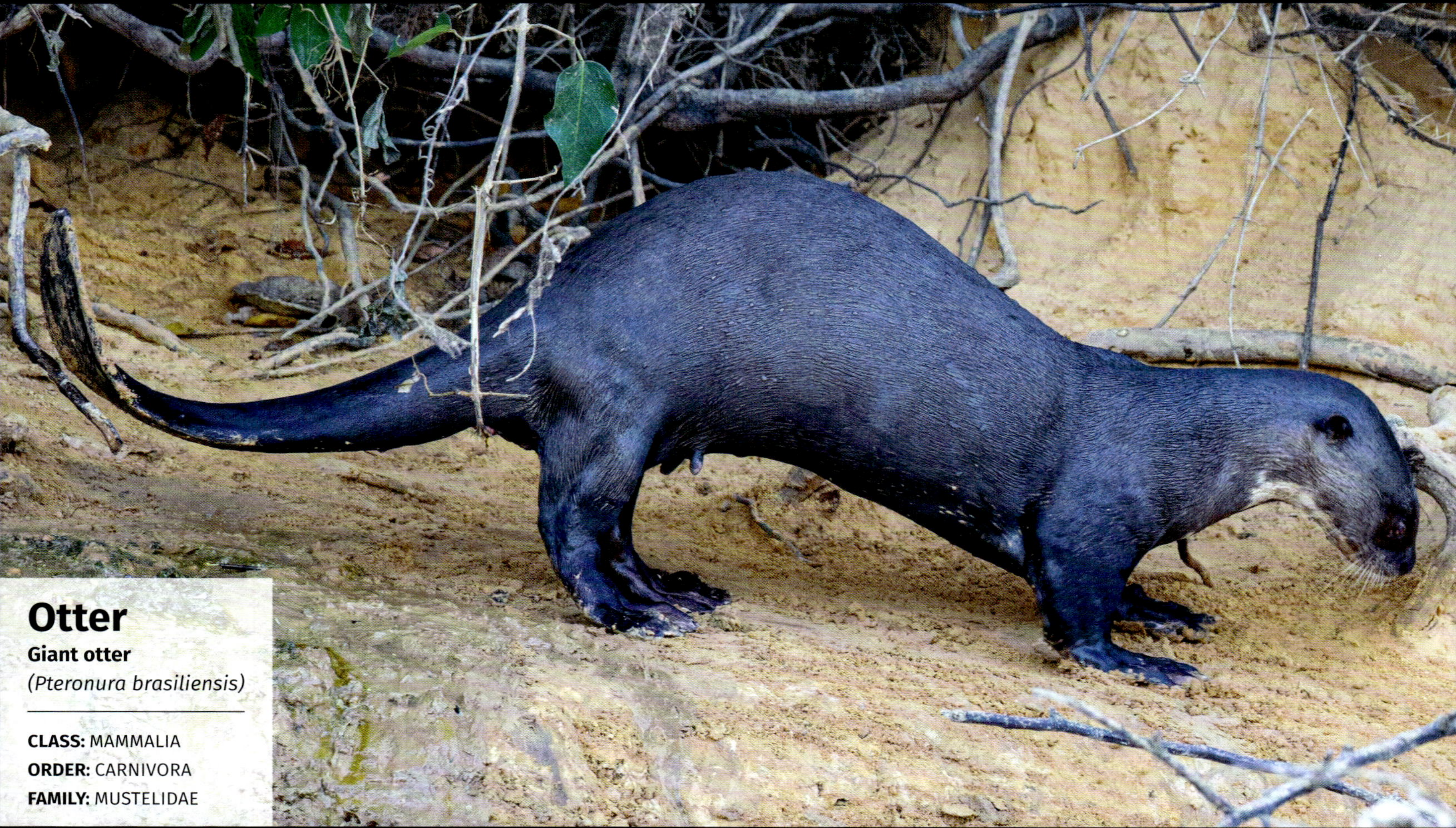

Otter

Giant otter

(Pteronura brasiliensis)

CLASS: MAMMALIA
ORDER: CARNIVORA
FAMILY: MUSTELIDAE

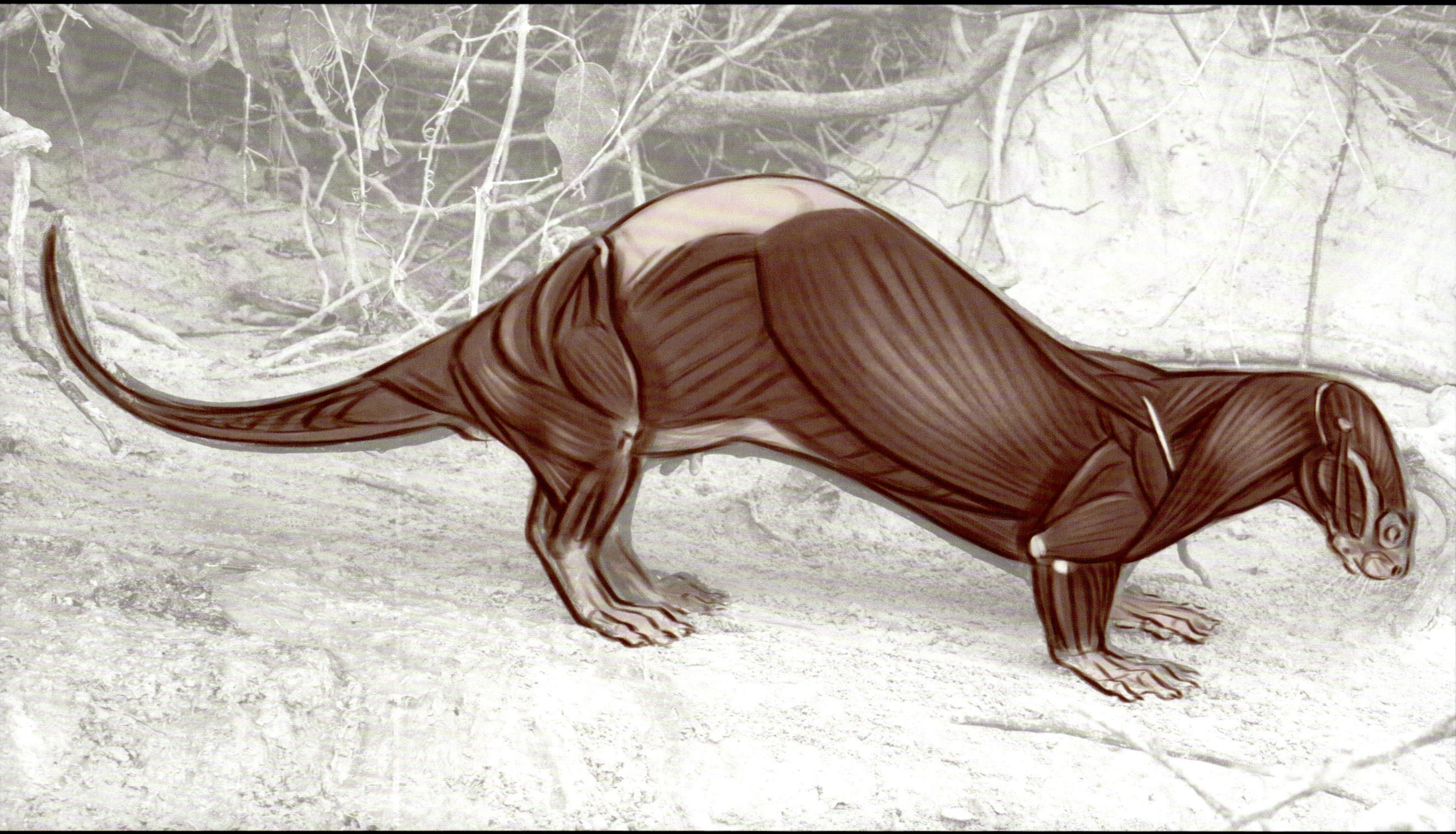

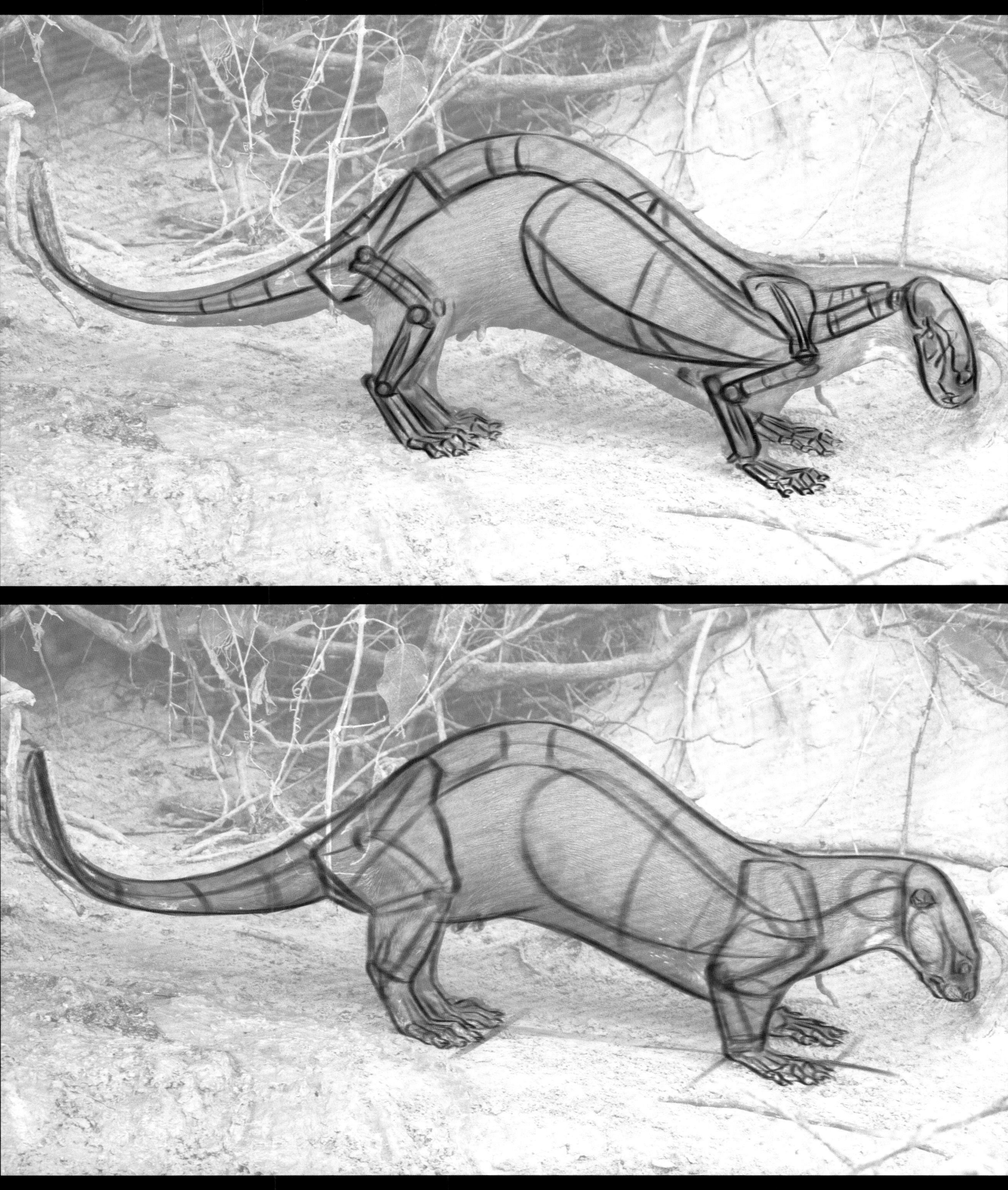

Photograph © imageBROKER.com / Hermann Brehm

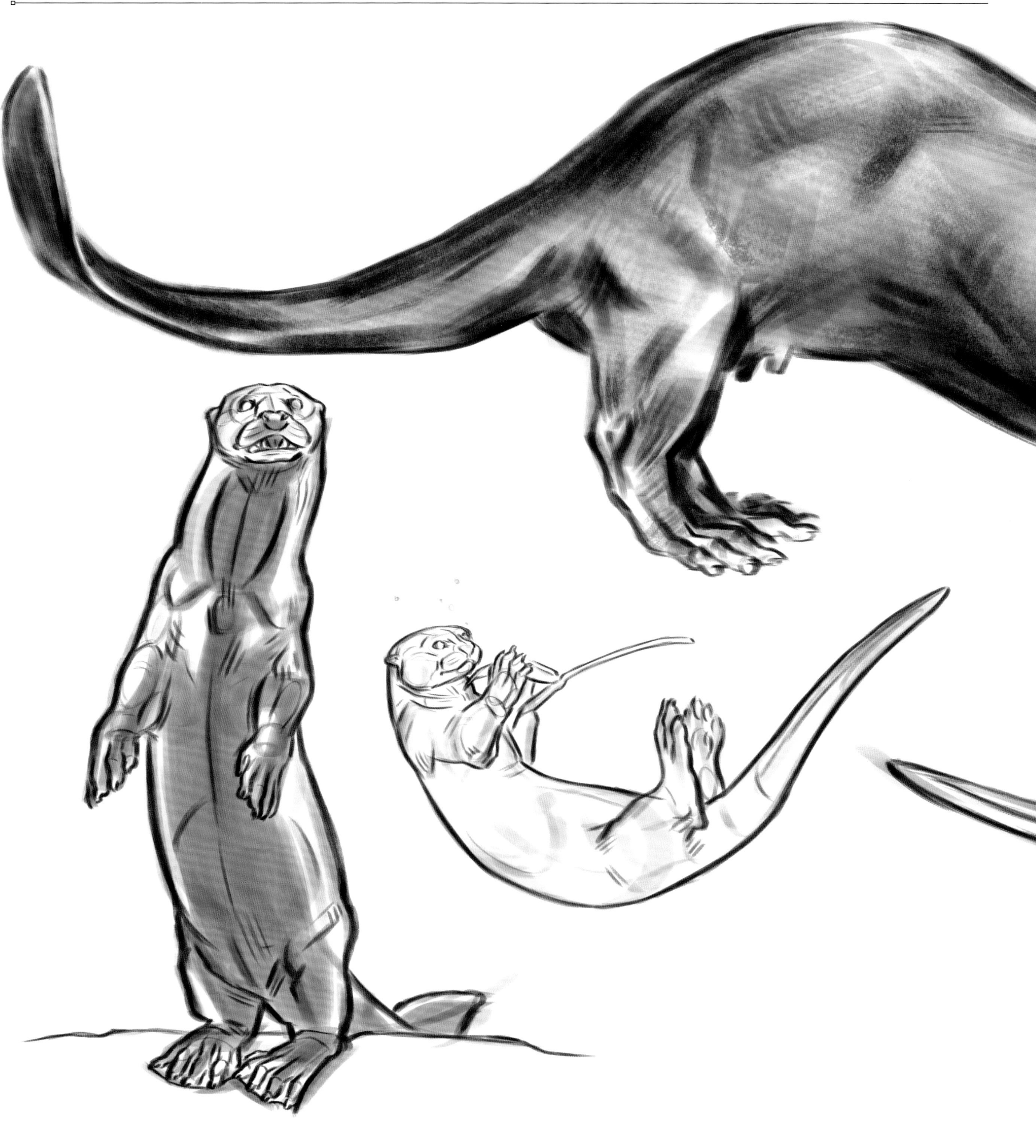

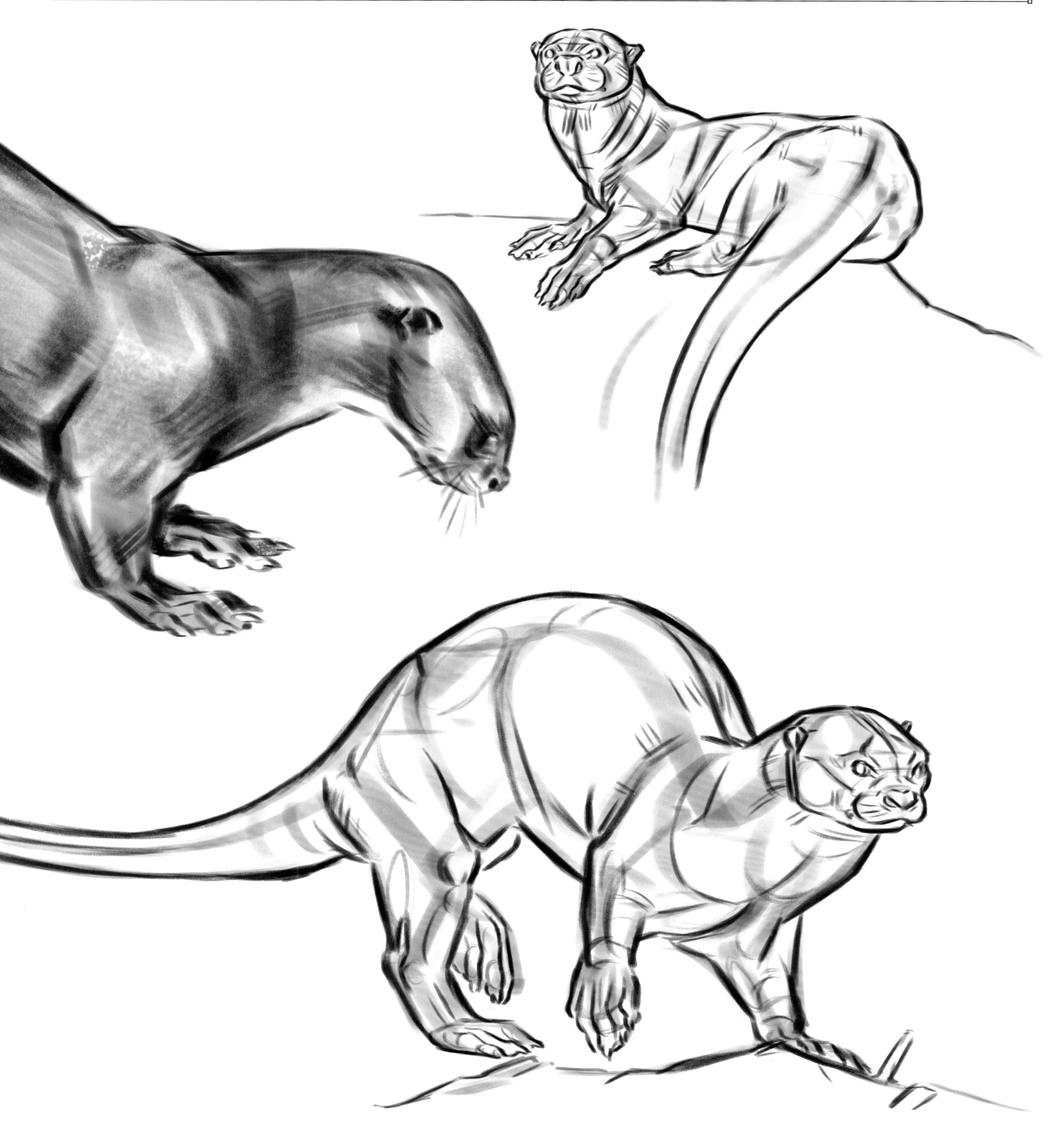

Weasel

Least weasel

(Mustela nivalis)

CLASS: MAMMALIA
ORDER: CARNIVORA
FAMILY: MUSTELIDAE

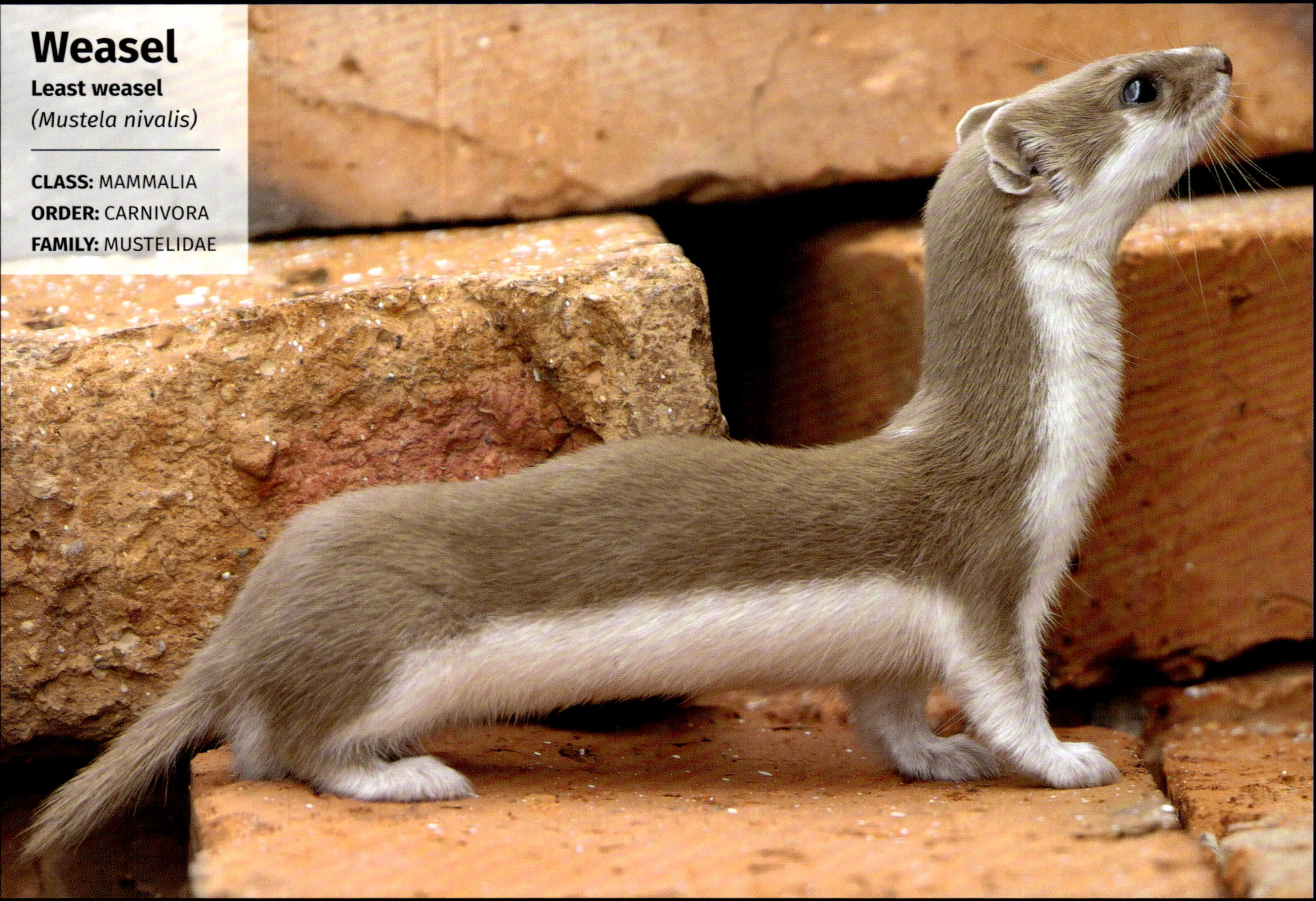

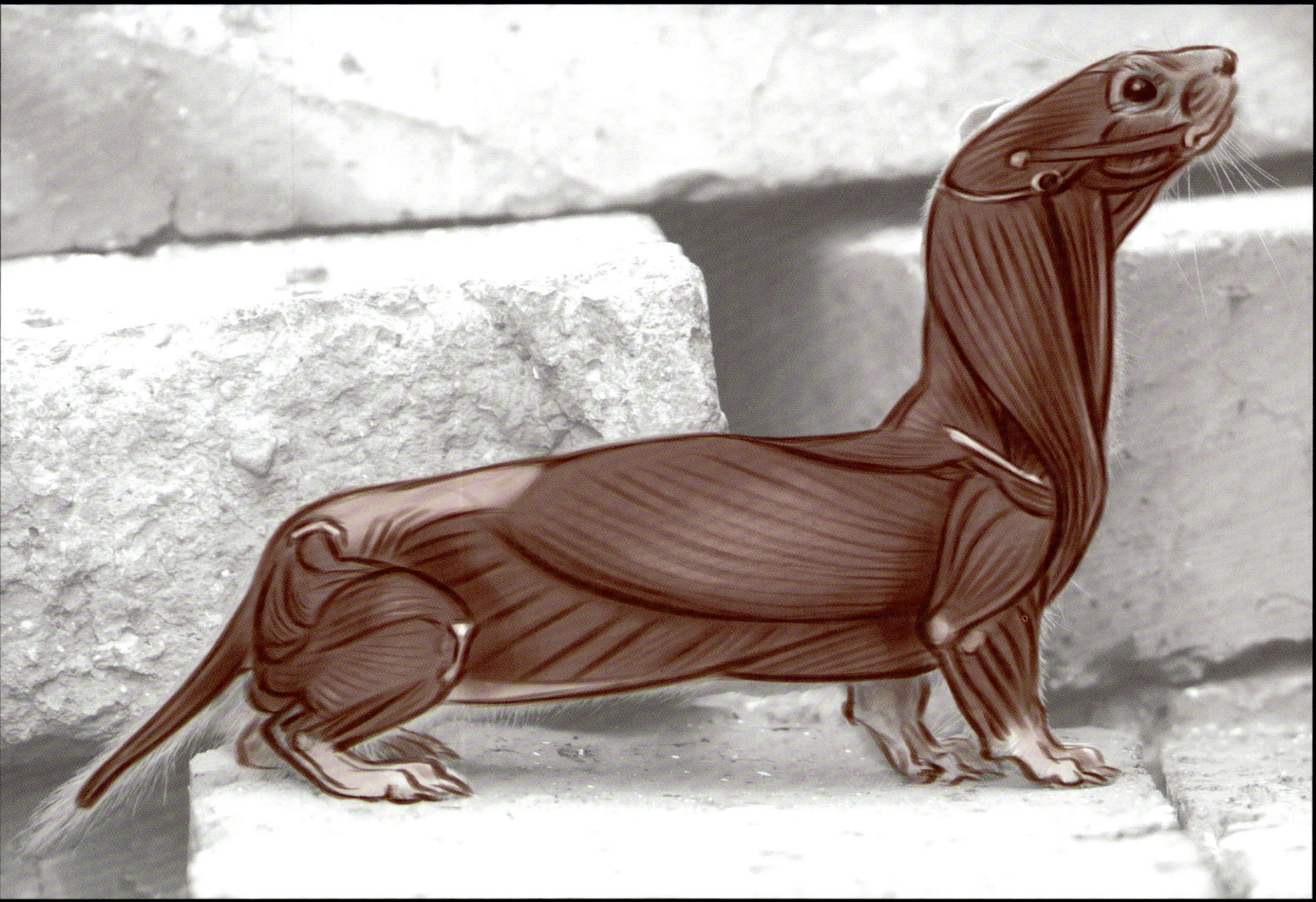

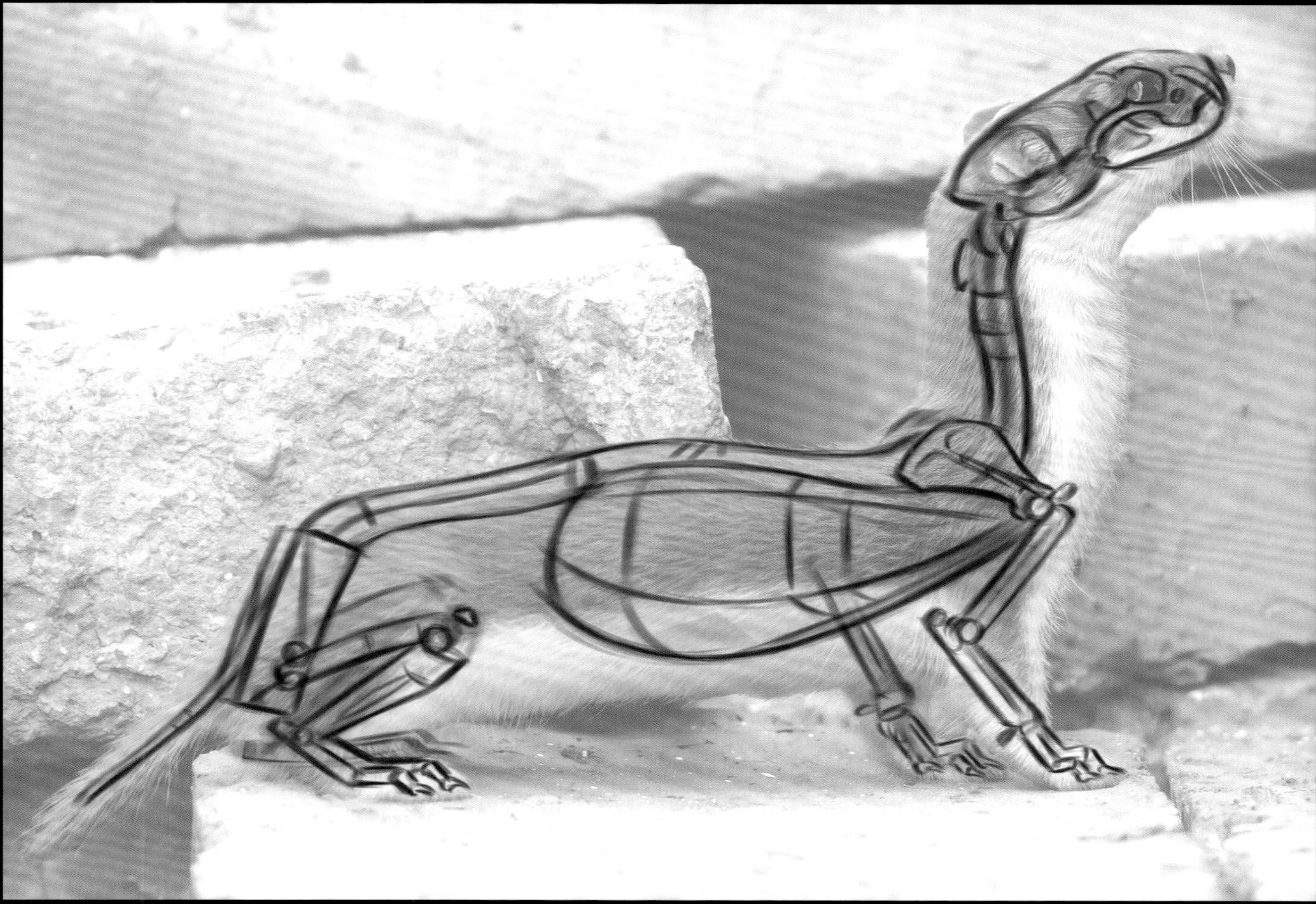

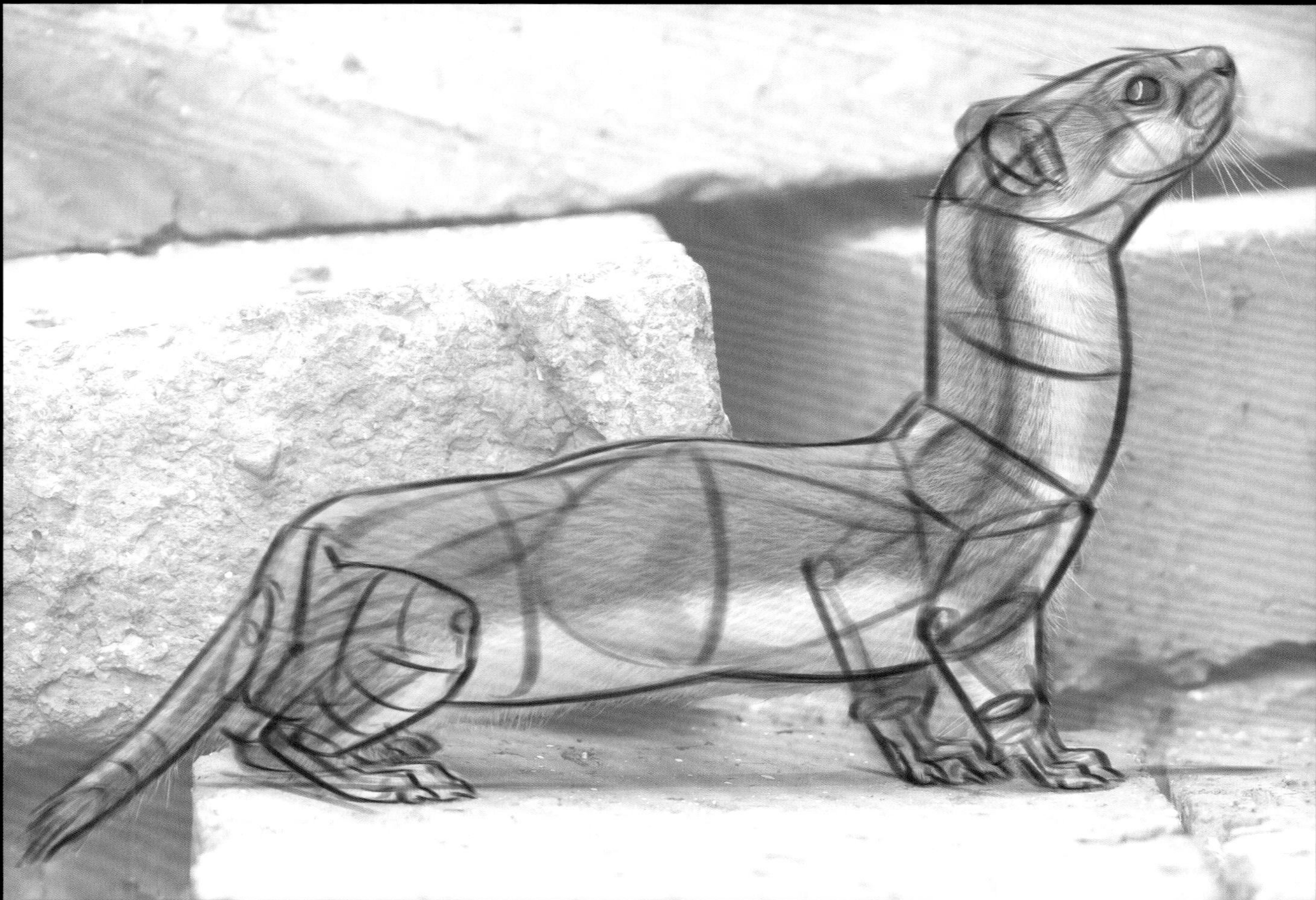

Photograph © Dani Lopez Velasco / Agami.nl

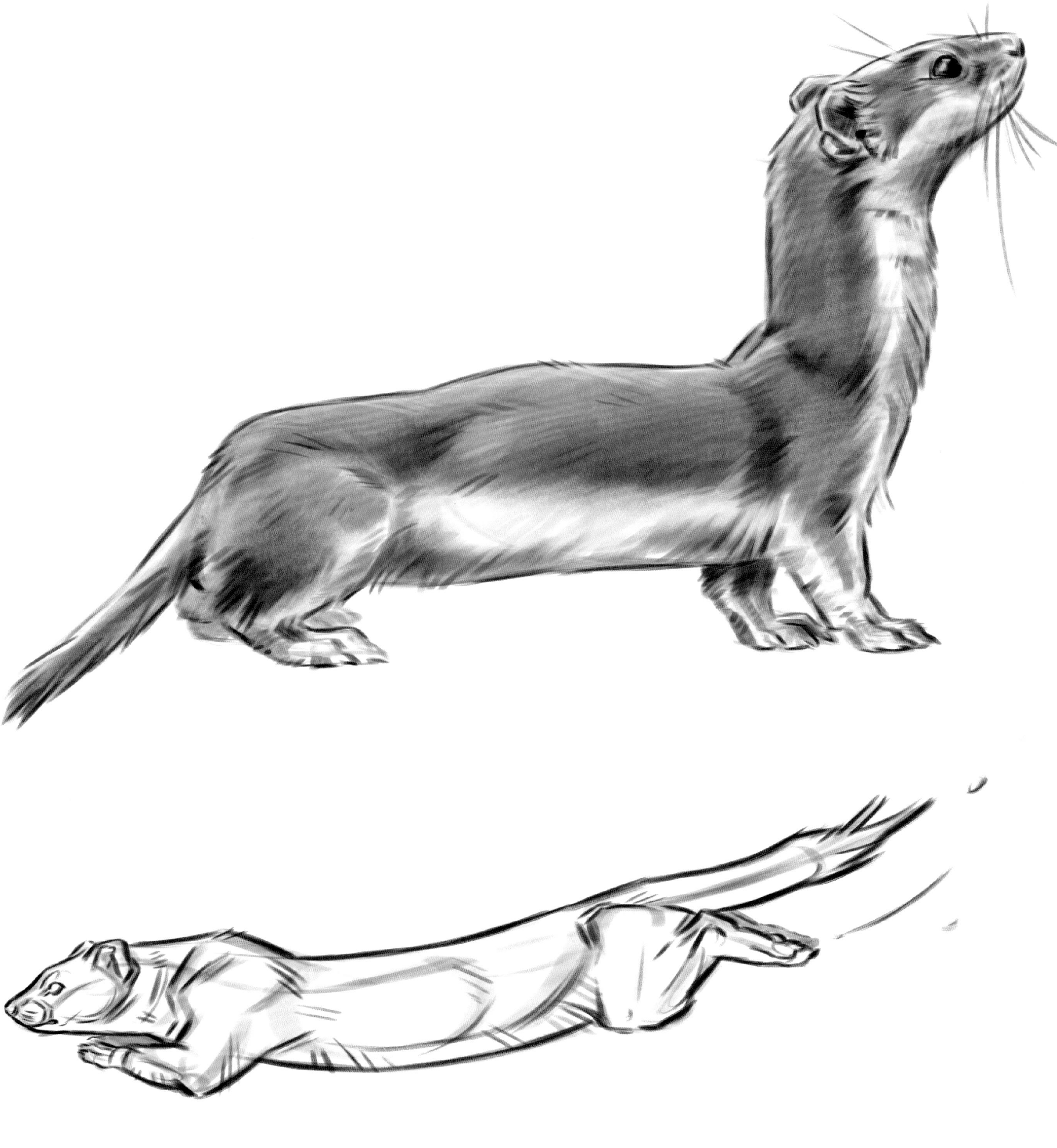

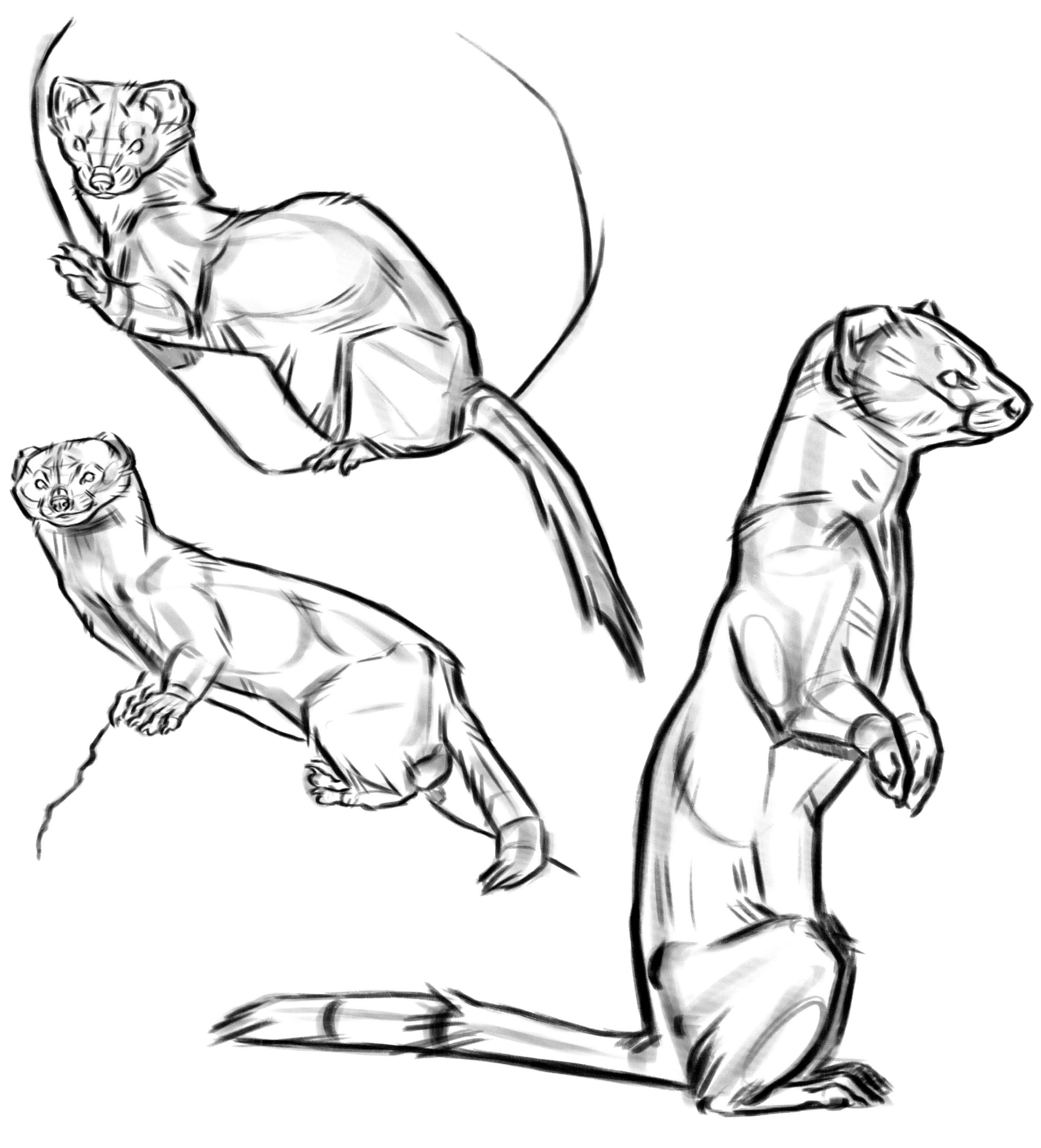

Wolverine

Wolverine *(Gulo gulo)*

CLASS: MAMMALIA
ORDER: CARNIVORA
FAMILY: MUSTELIDAE

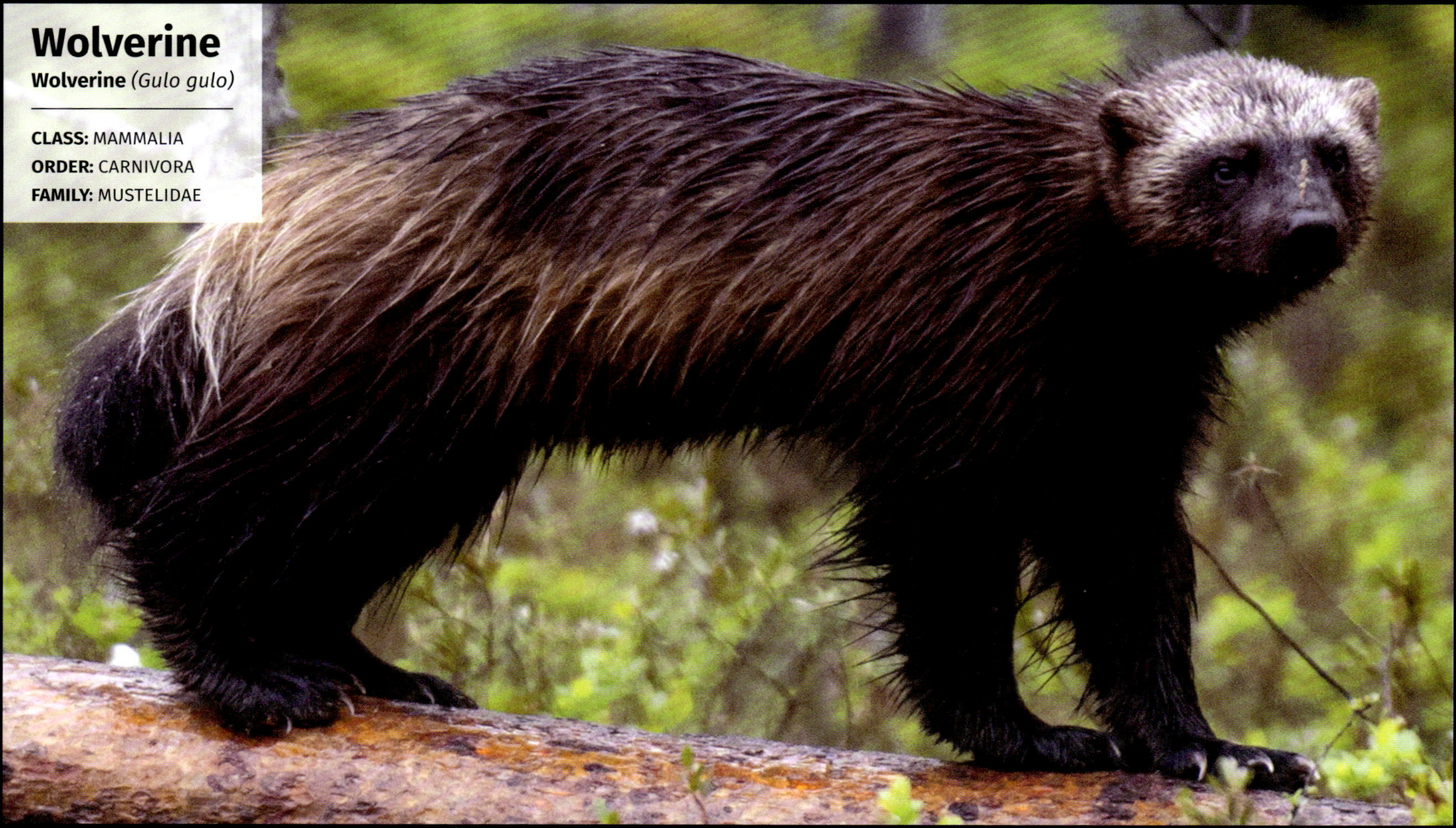

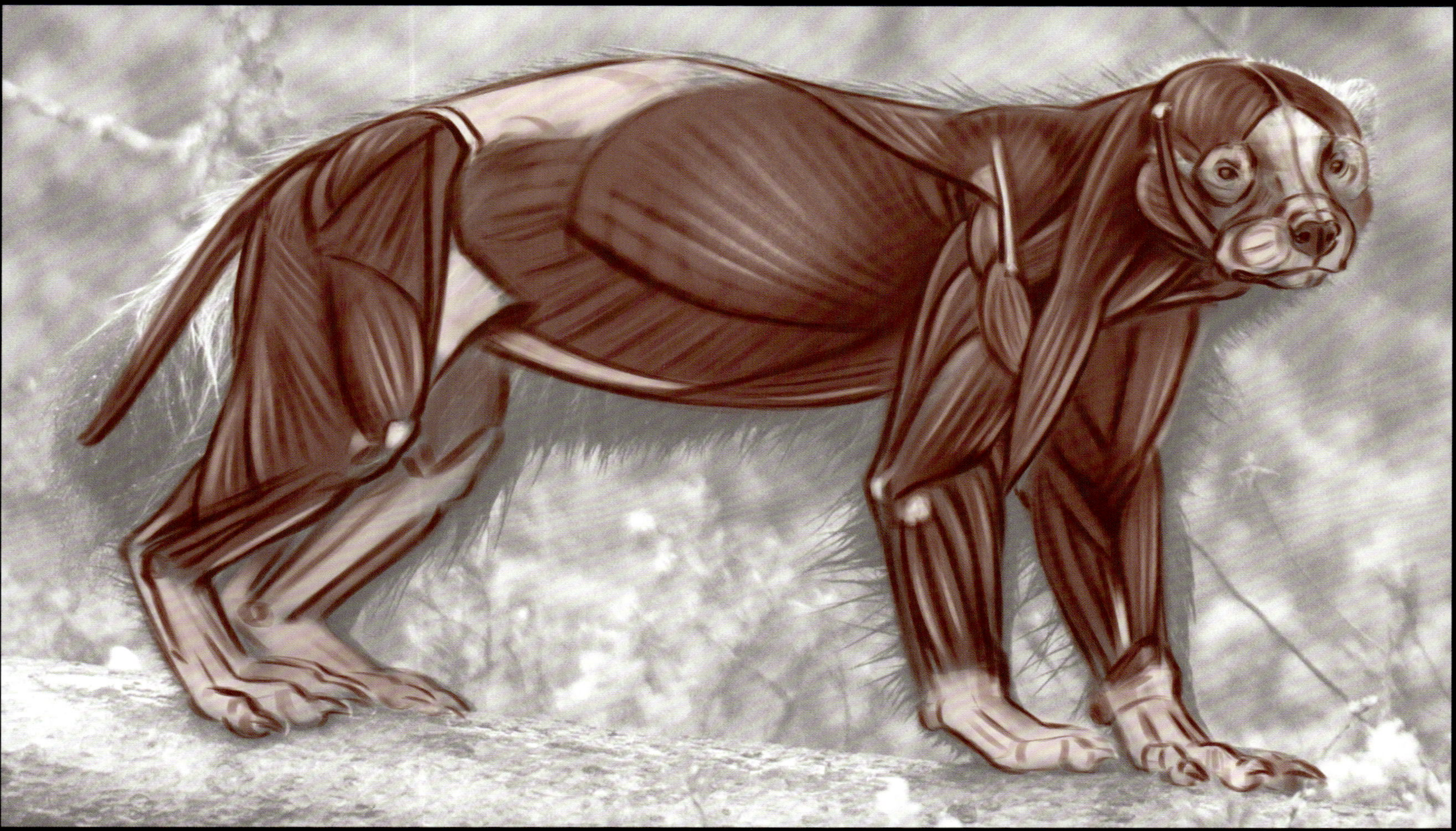

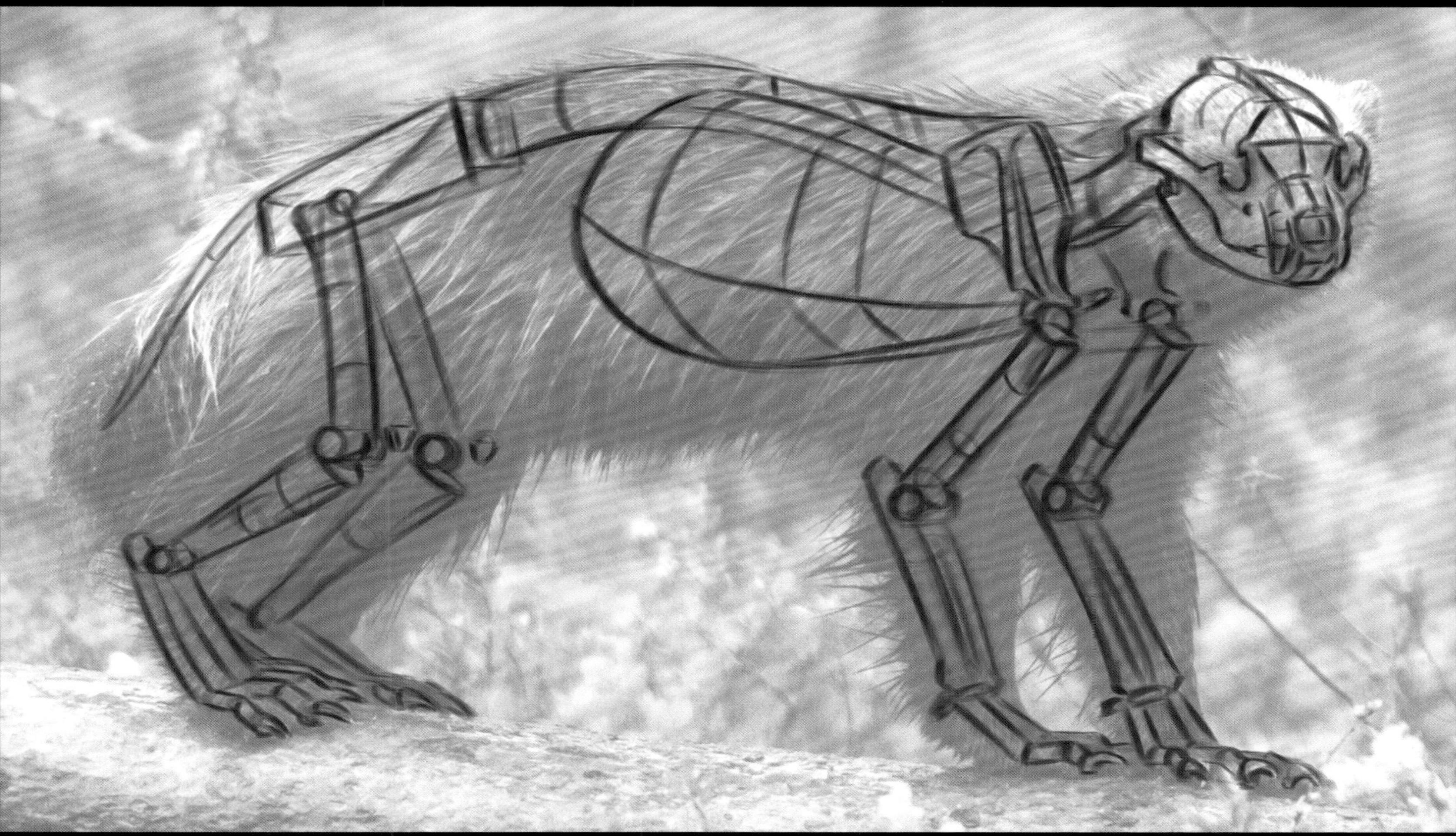

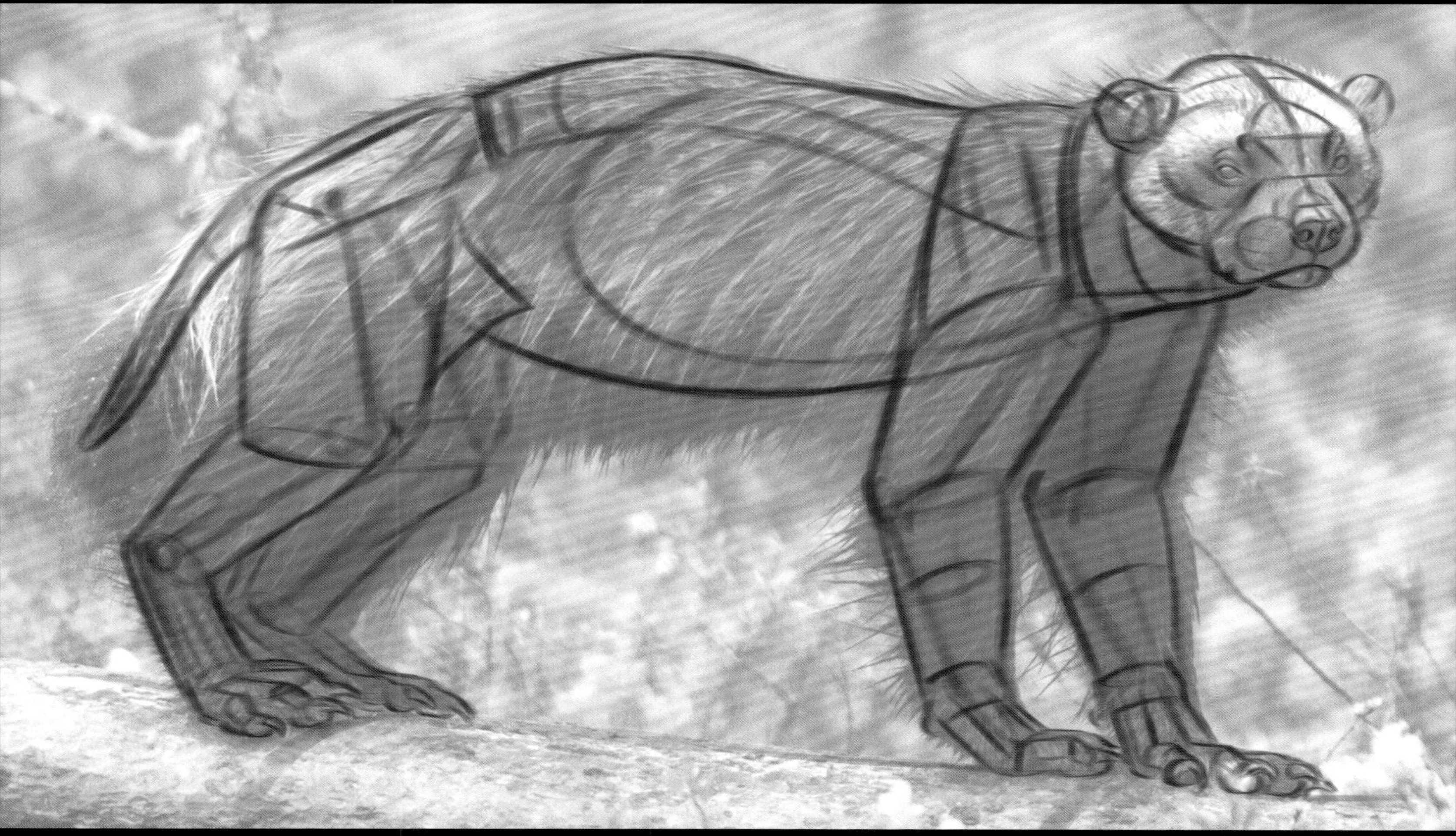

Photograph © Sergio Pitamitz / Agami.nl

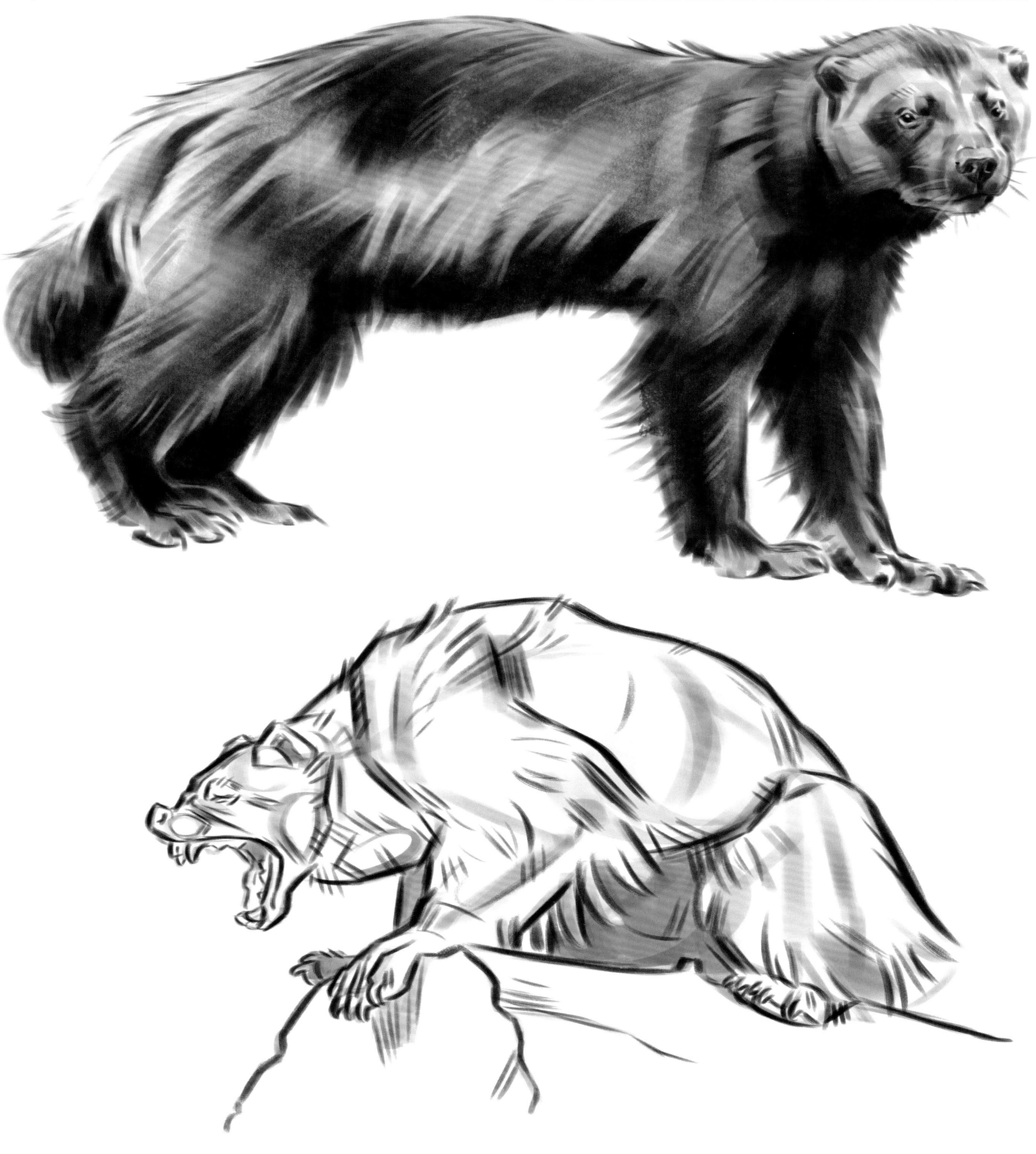

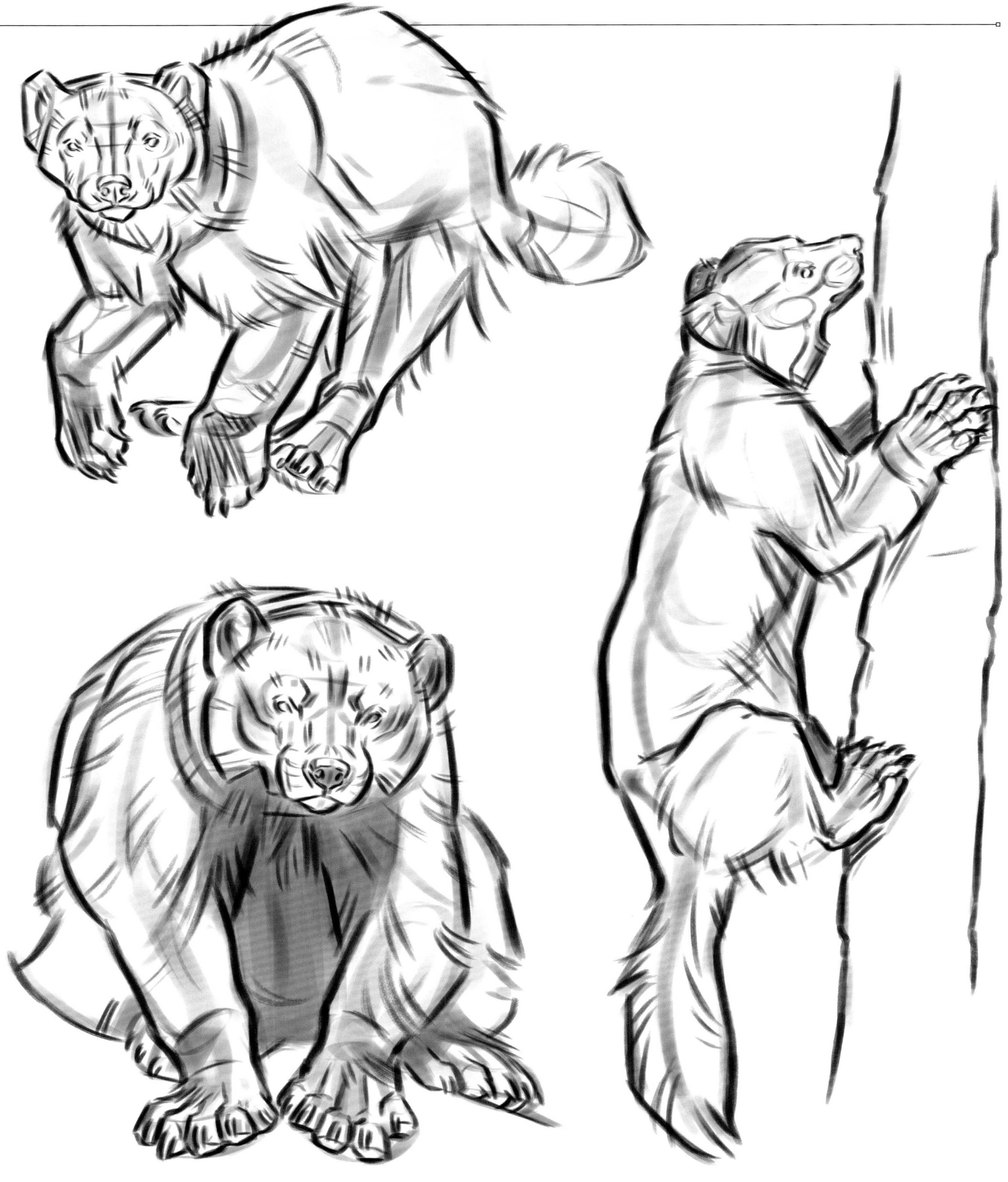

Sea lion

Galápagos sea lion
(Zalophus wollebaeki)

CLASS: MAMMALIA
ORDER: CARNIVORA
FAMILY: OTARIIDAE

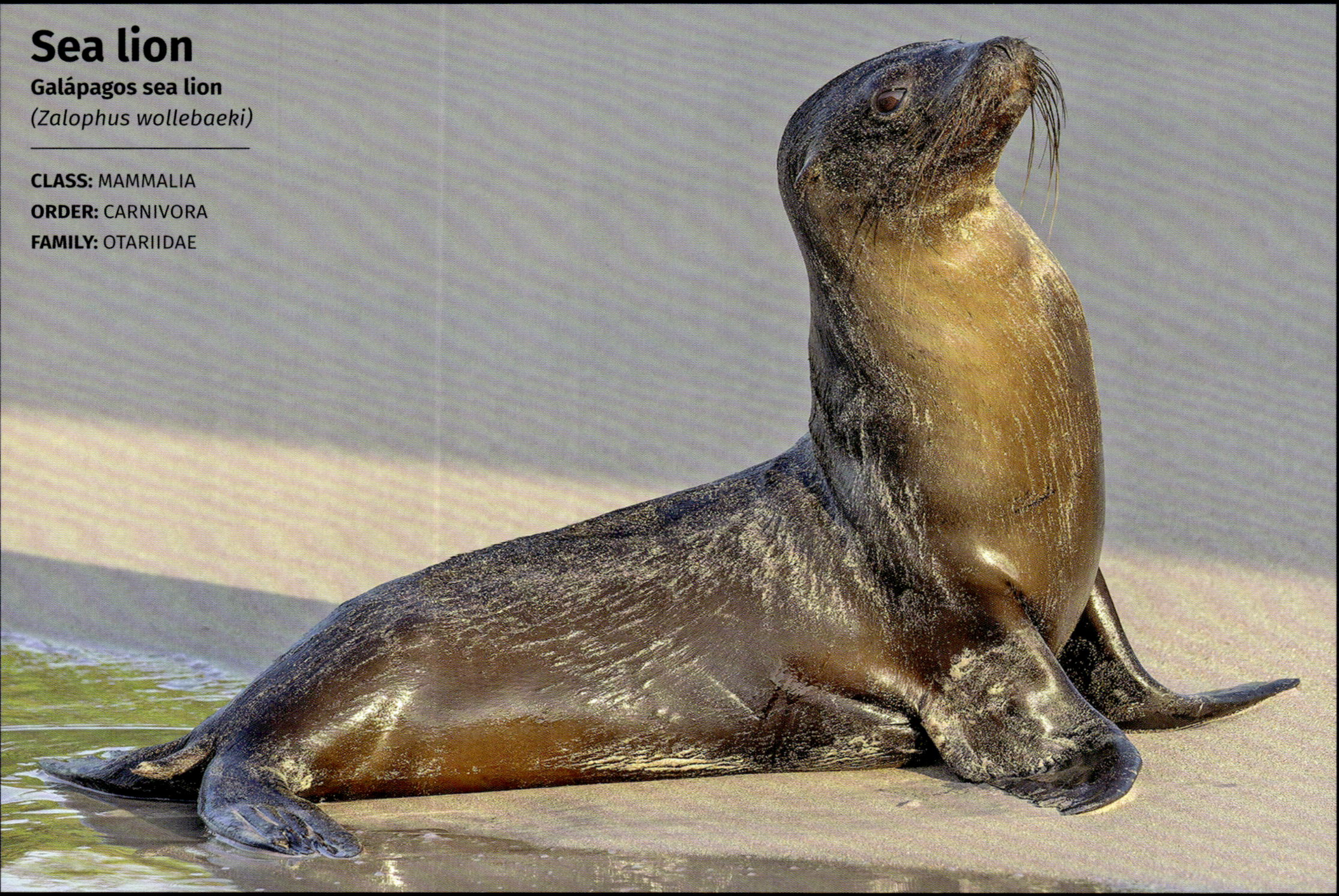

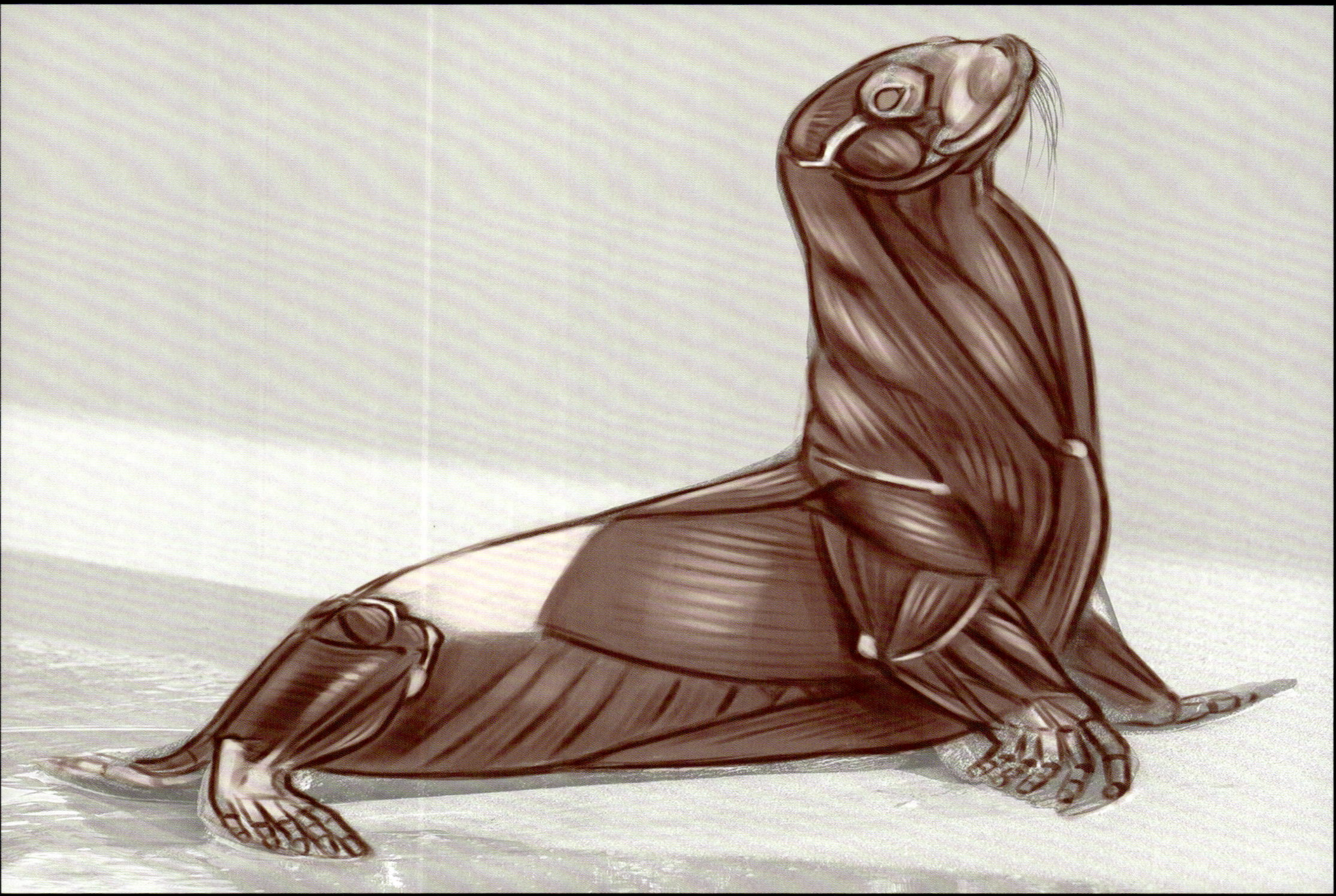

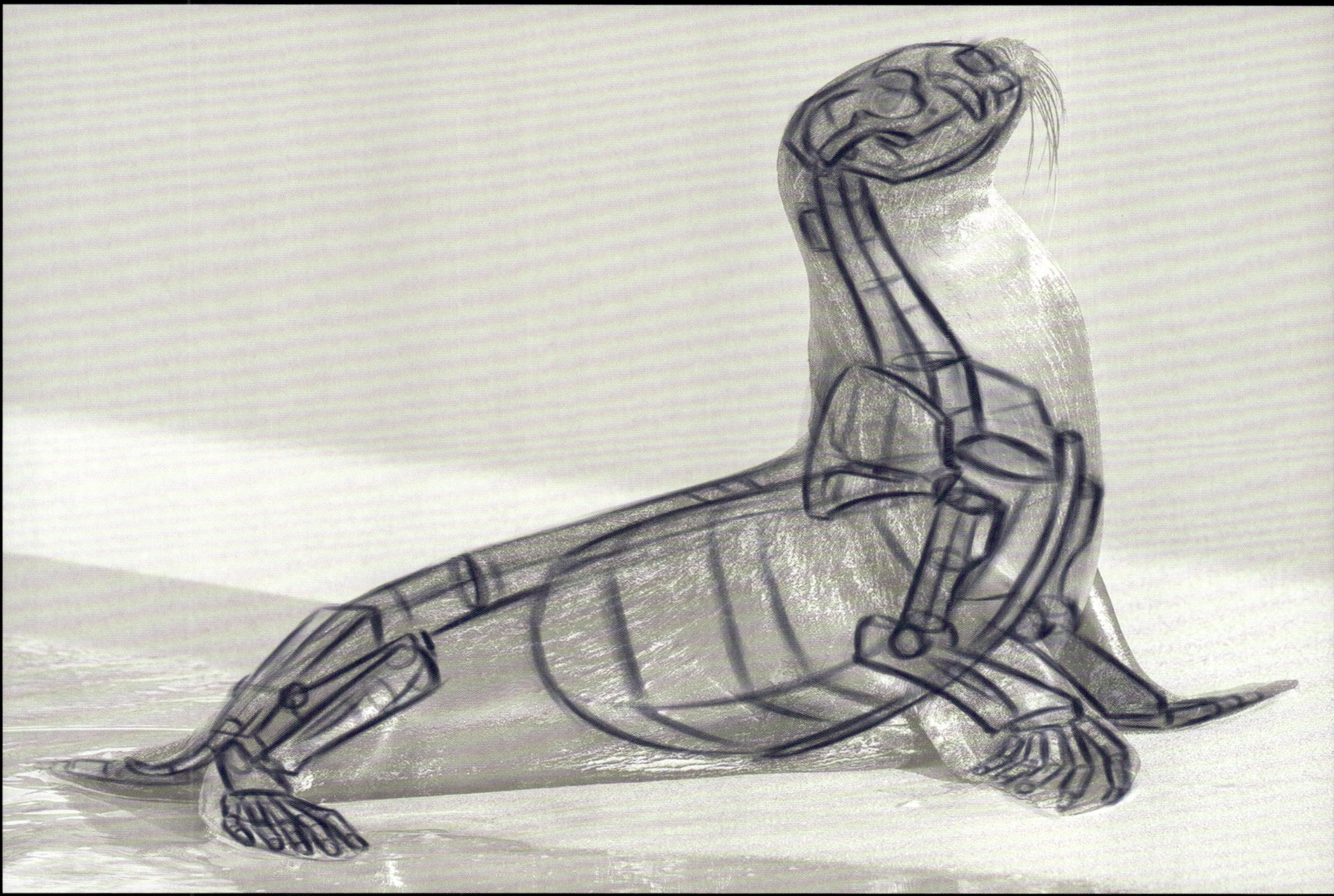

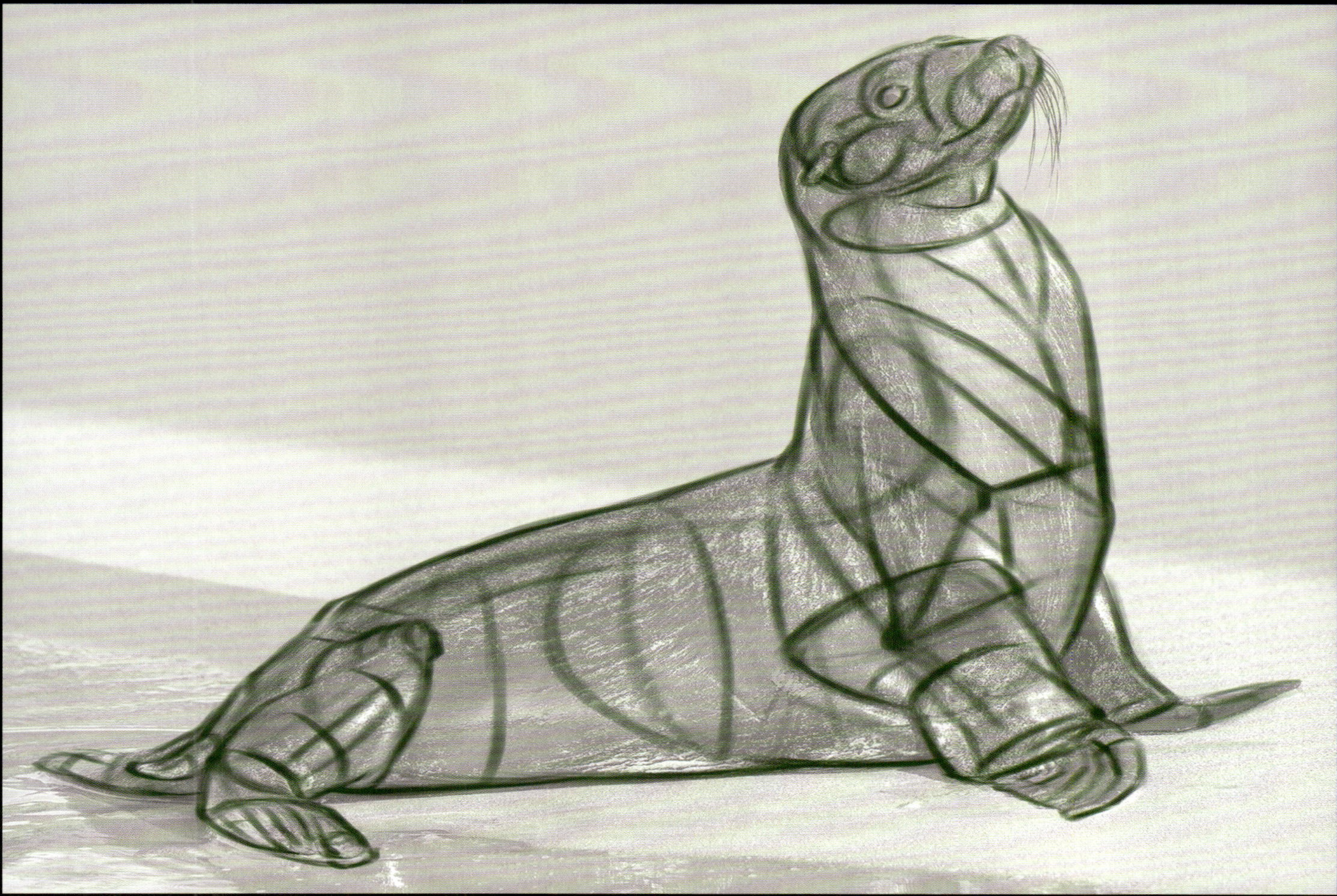

Photograph © Pete Morris / Agami.nl

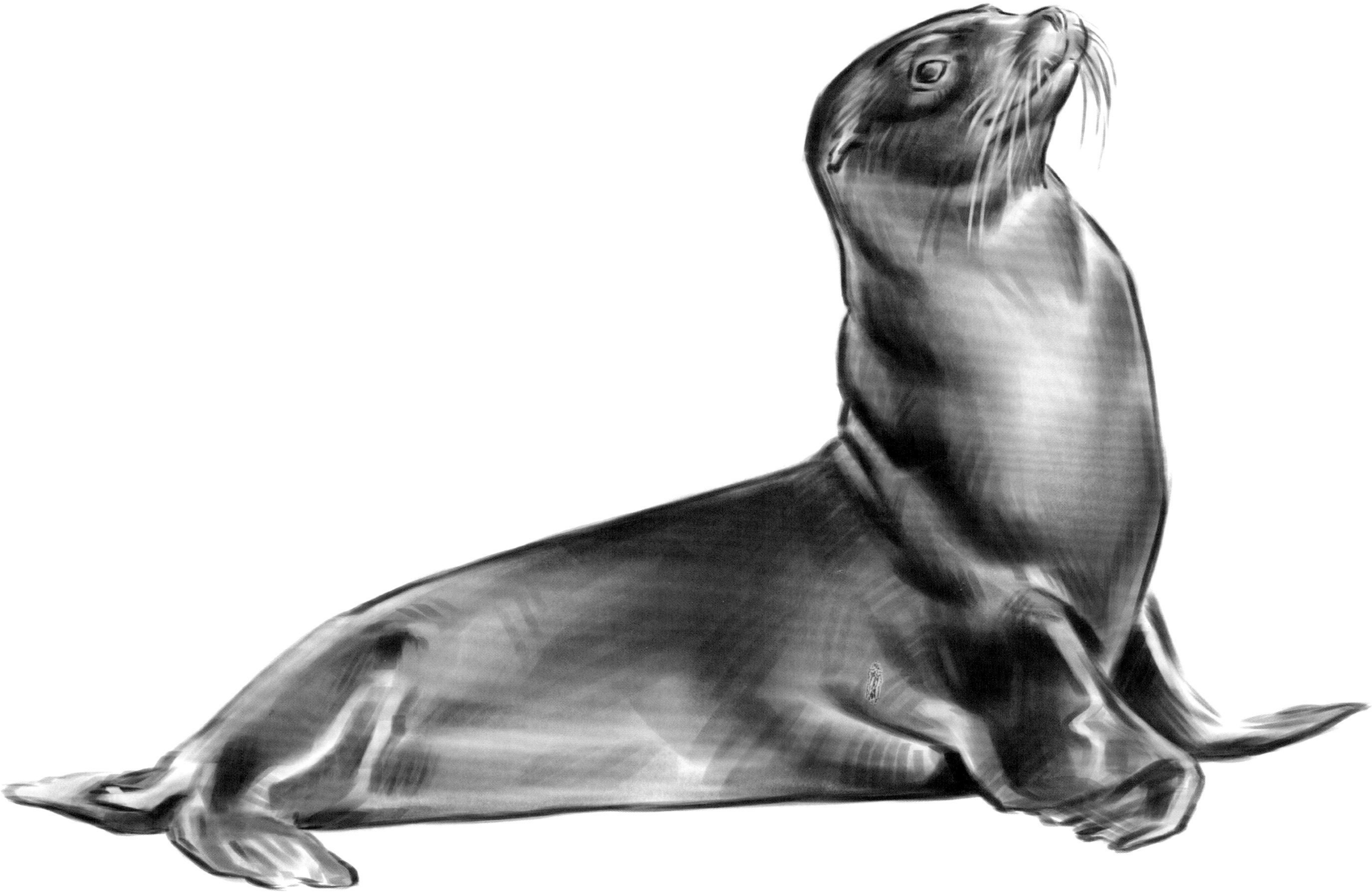

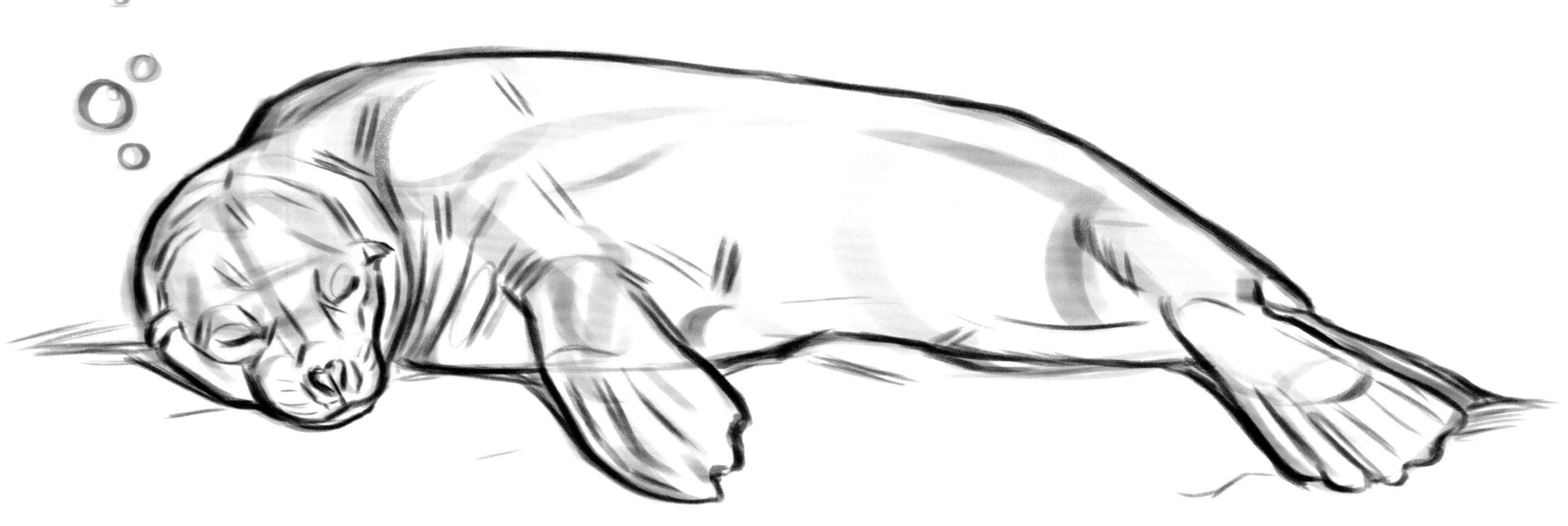

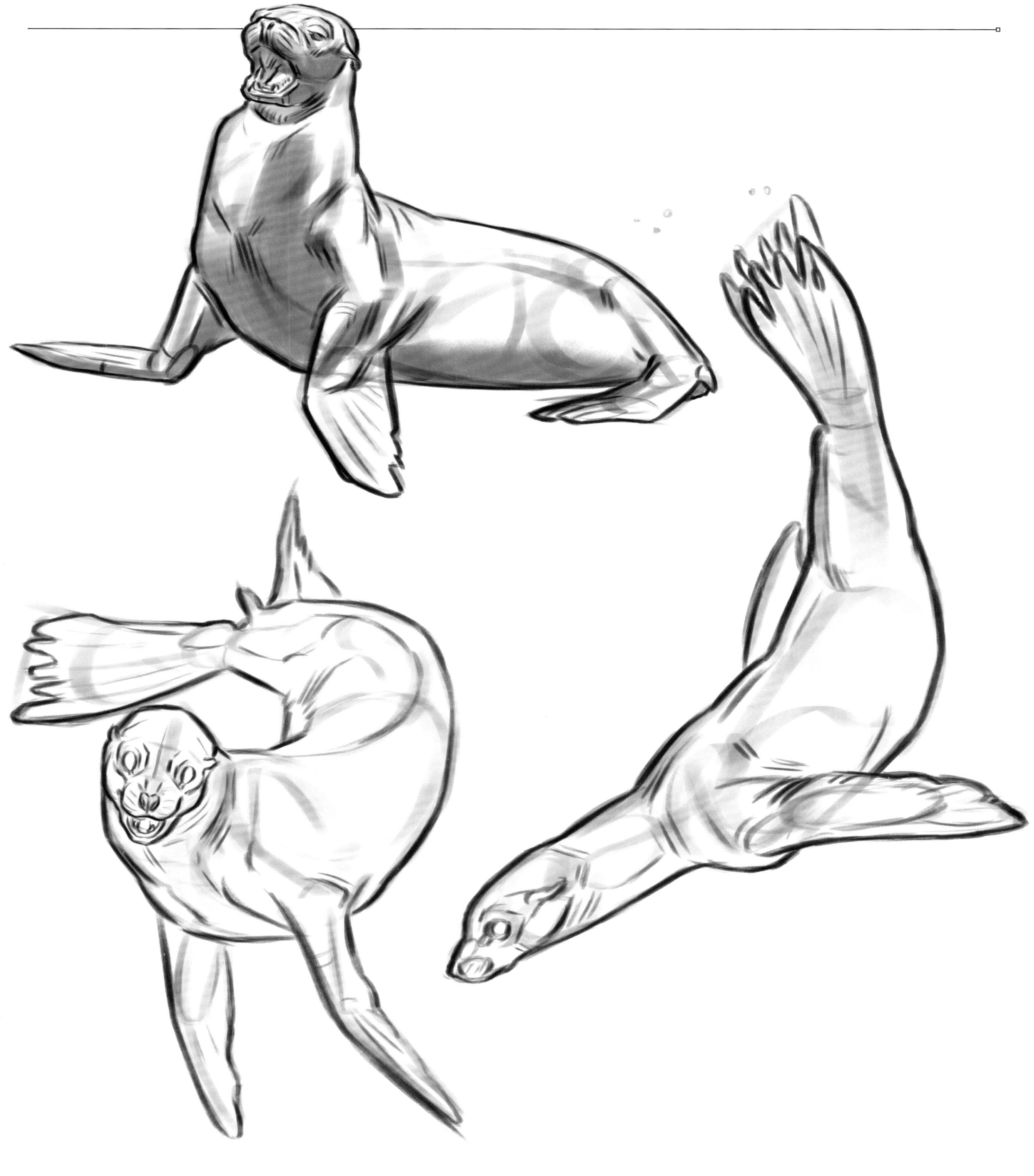

Racoon

Raccoon
(Procyon lotor)

CLASS: MAMMALIA
ORDER: CARNIVORA
FAMILY: PROCYONIDAE

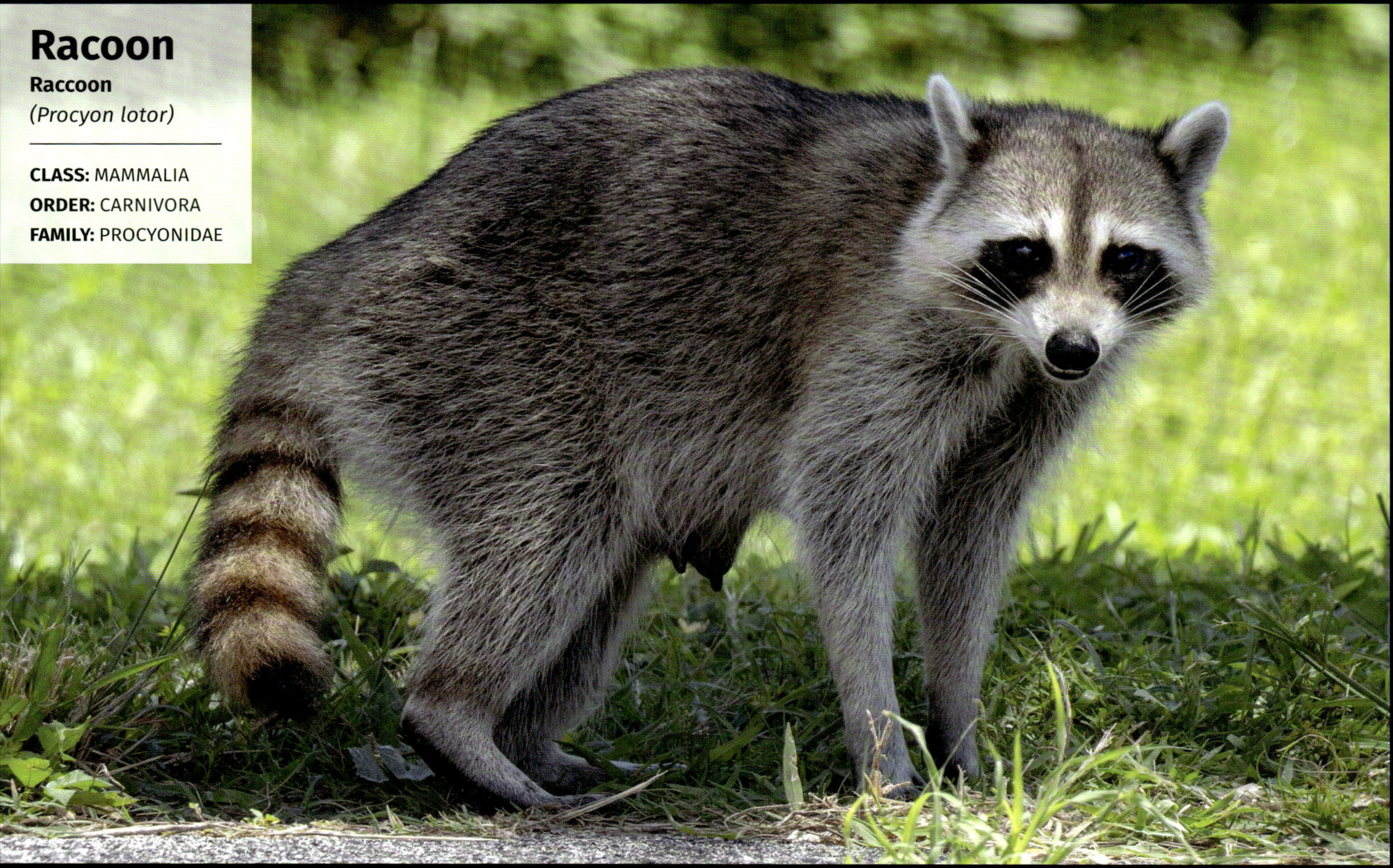

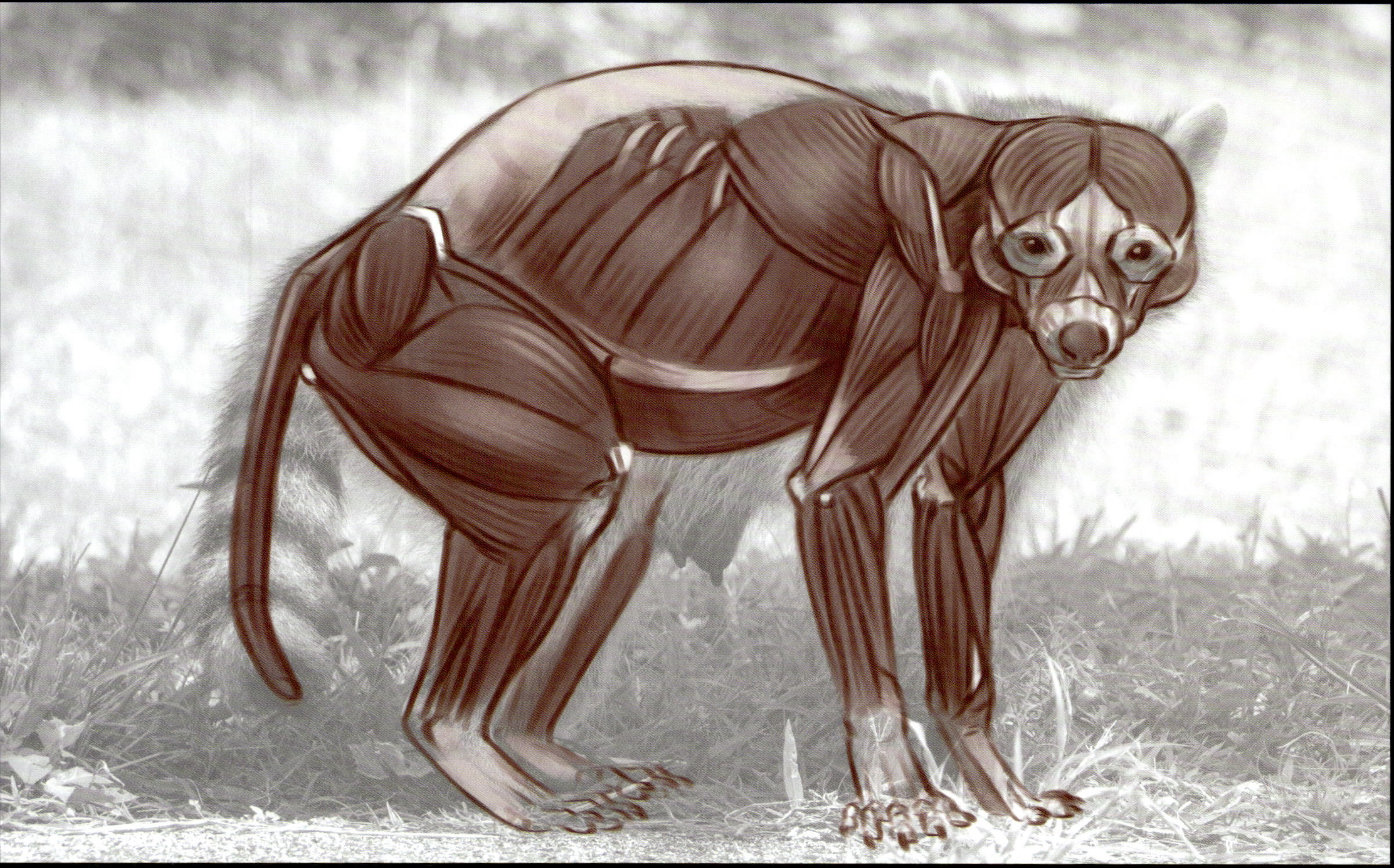

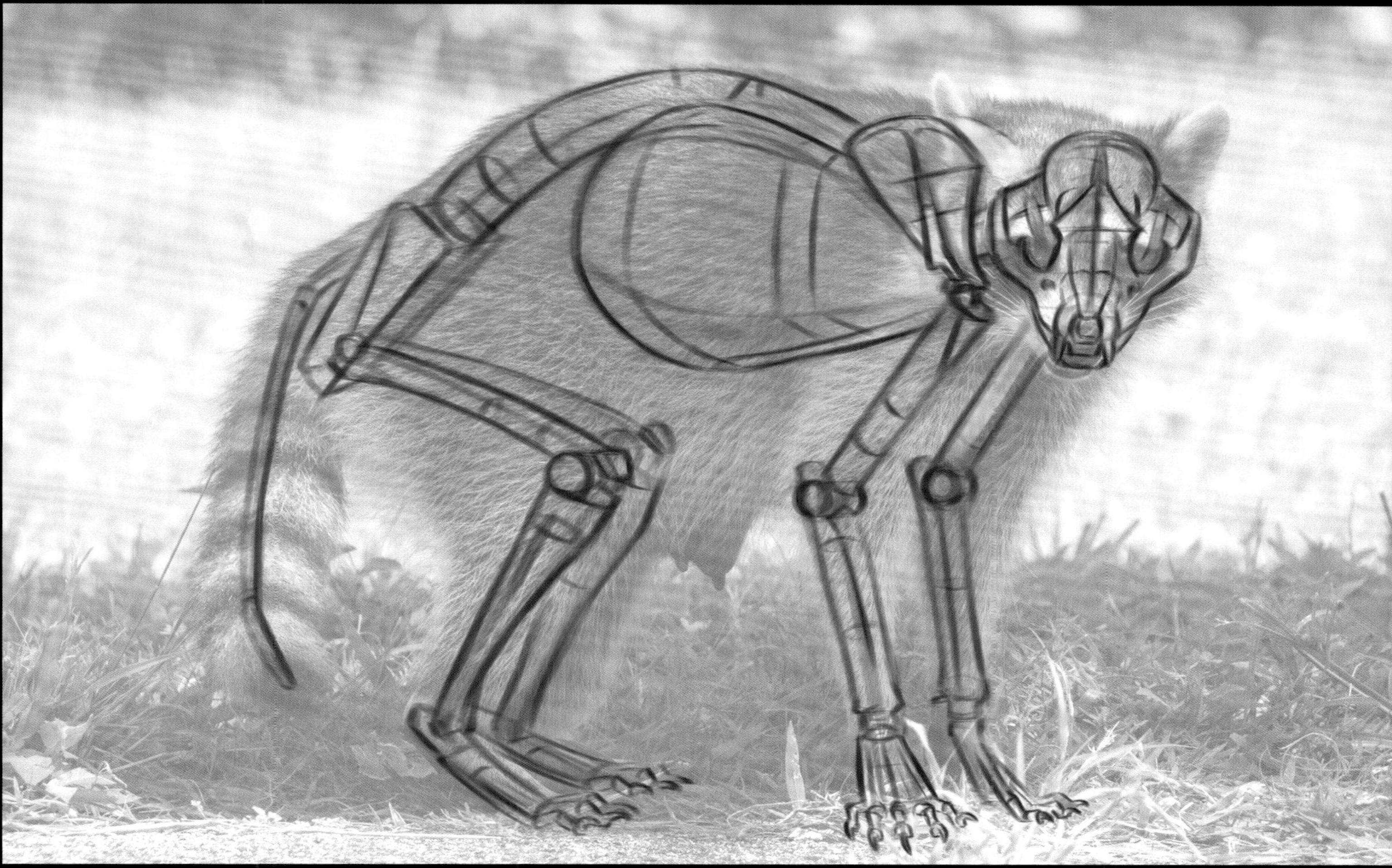

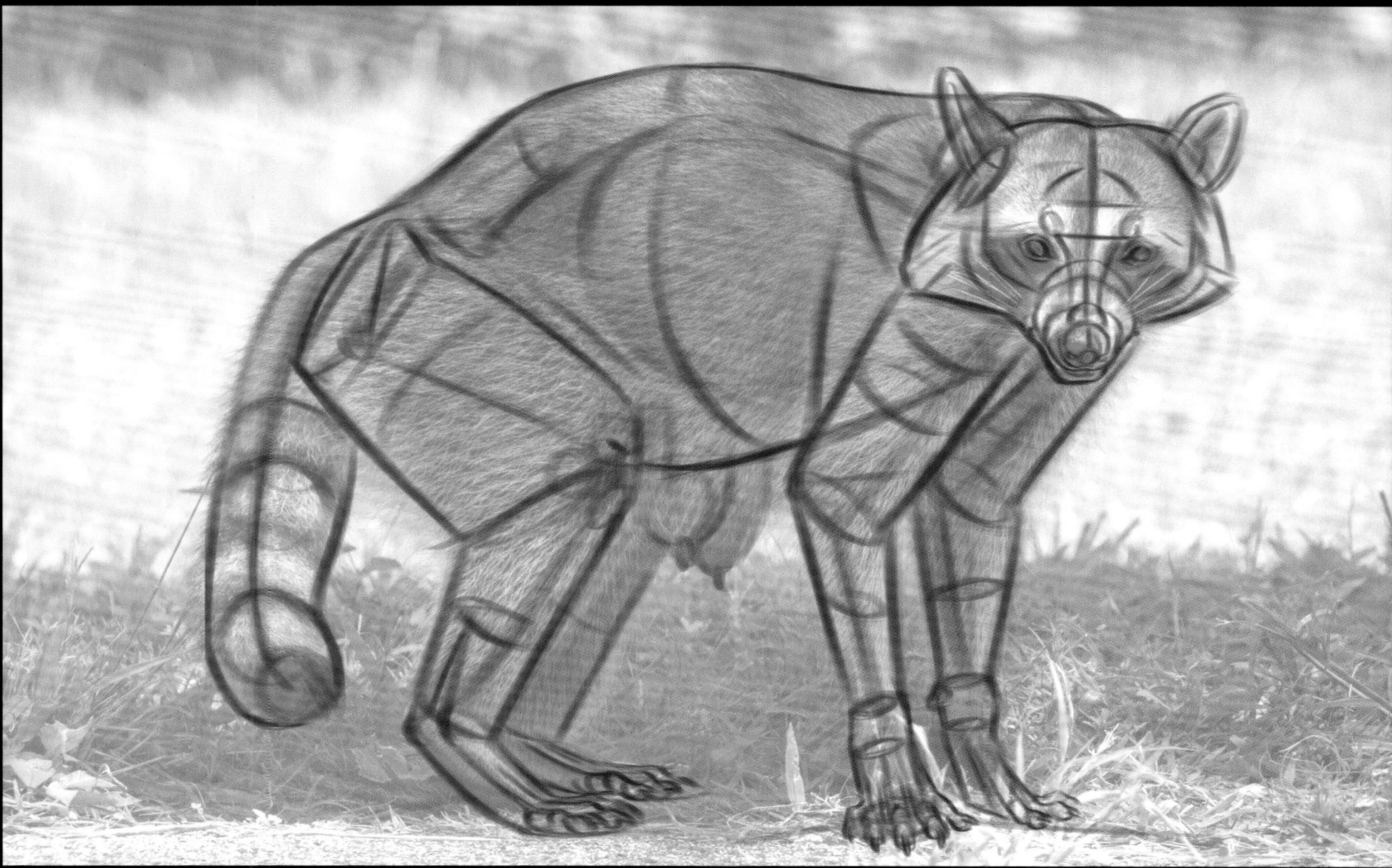

Photograph © Roy de Haas/ Agami.nl

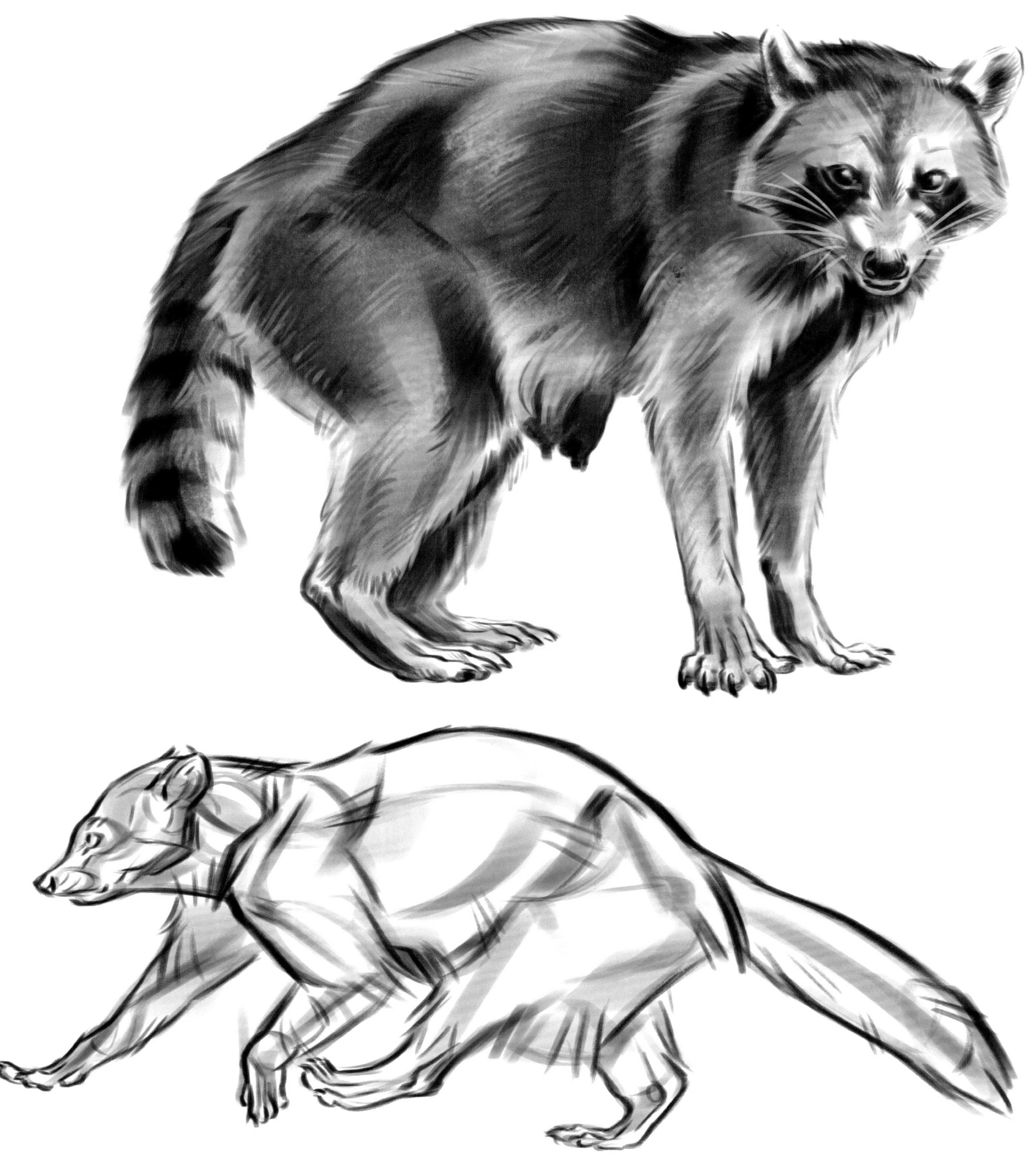

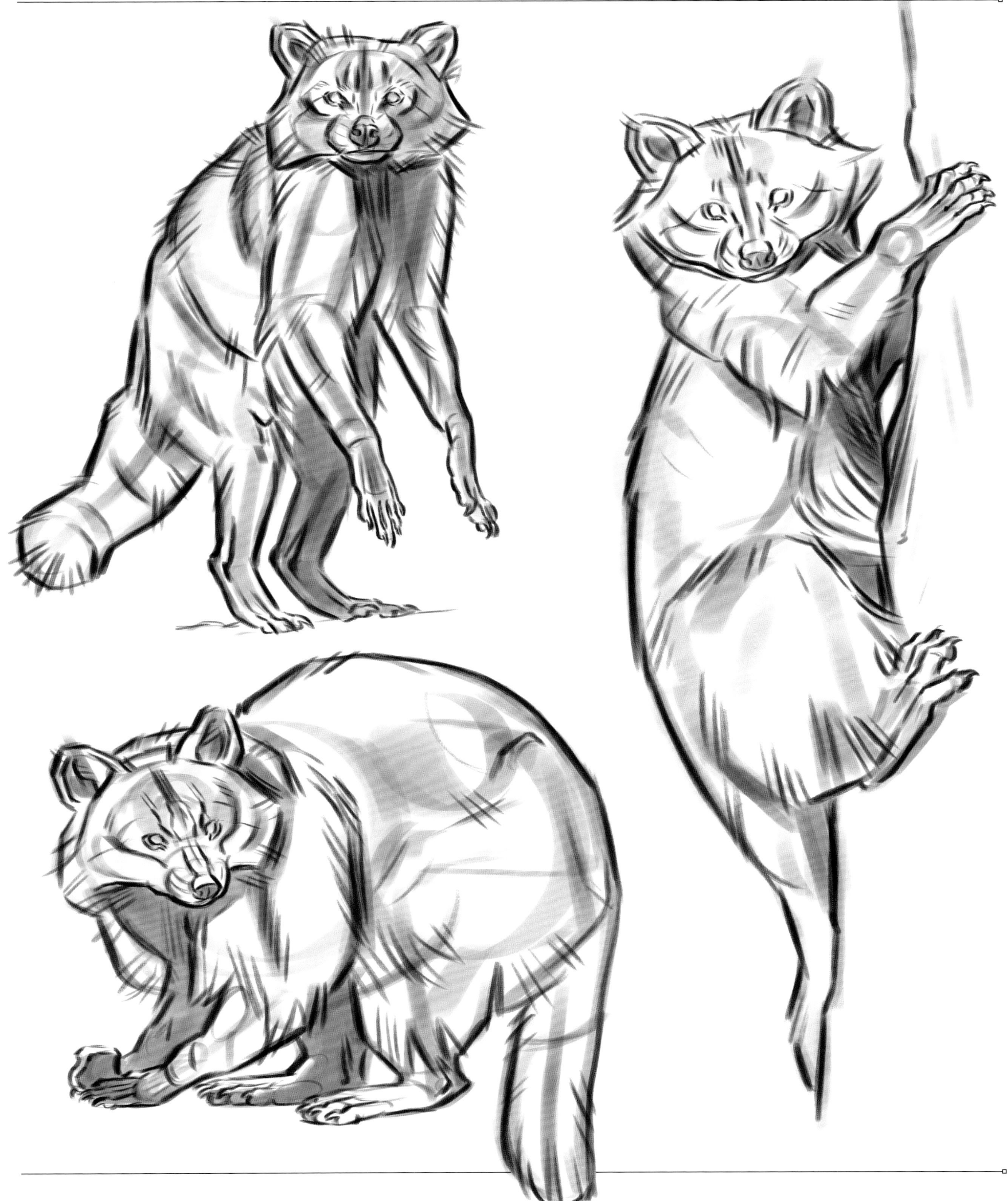

Grizzly Bear

Grizzly bear

(Ursus arctos horribilis)

CLASS: MAMMALIA
ORDER: CARNIVORA
FAMILY: URSIDAE

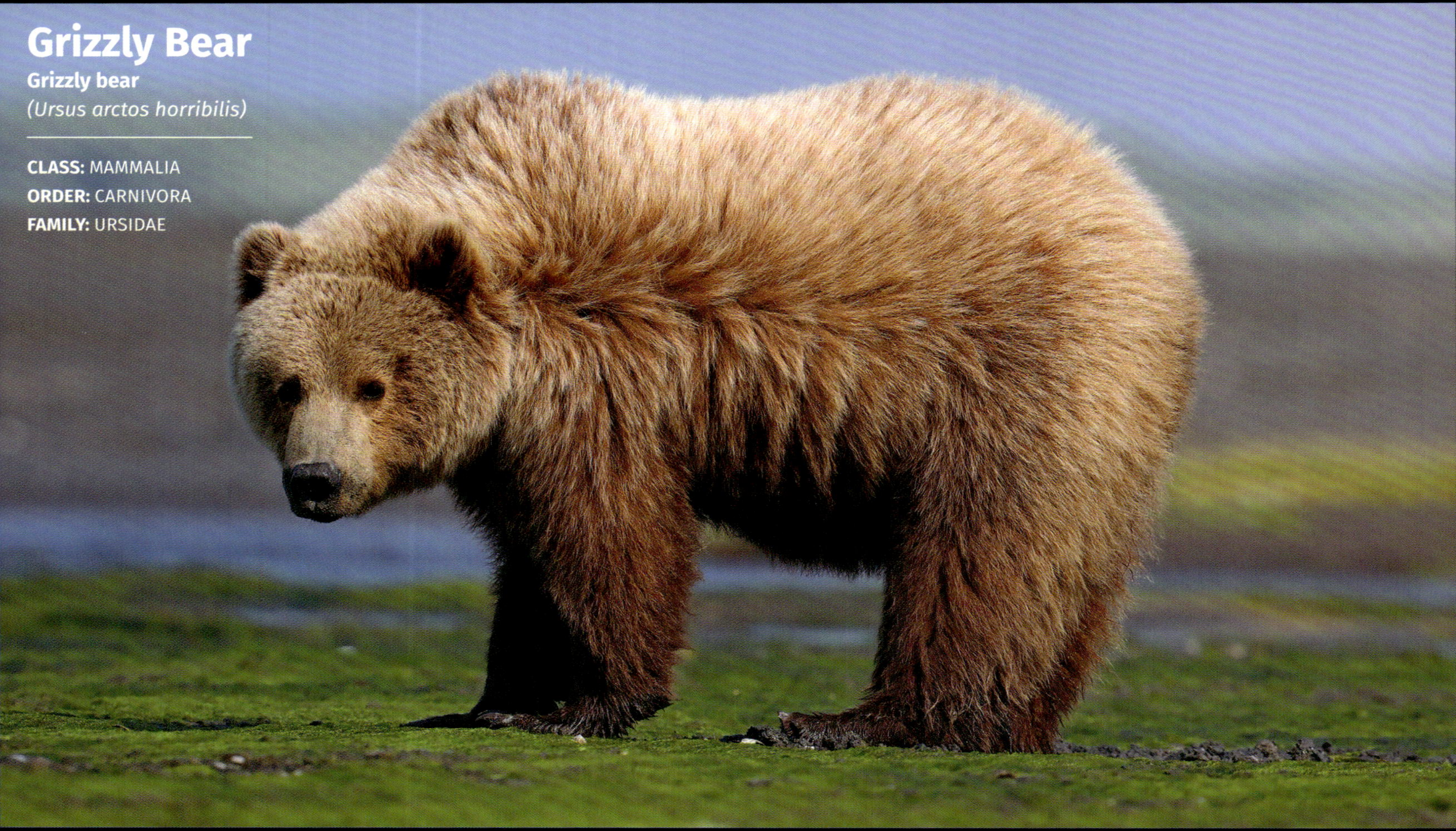

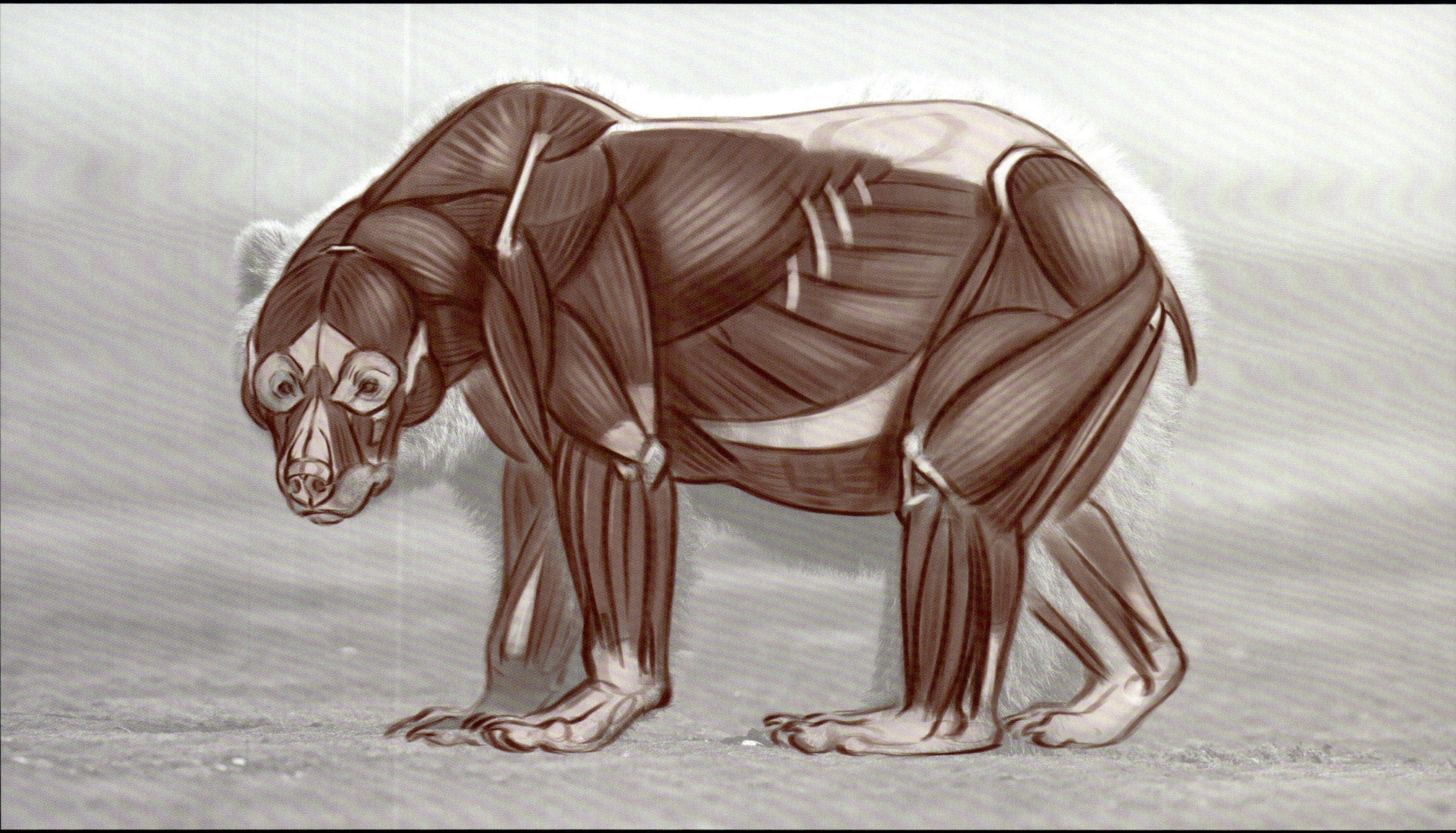

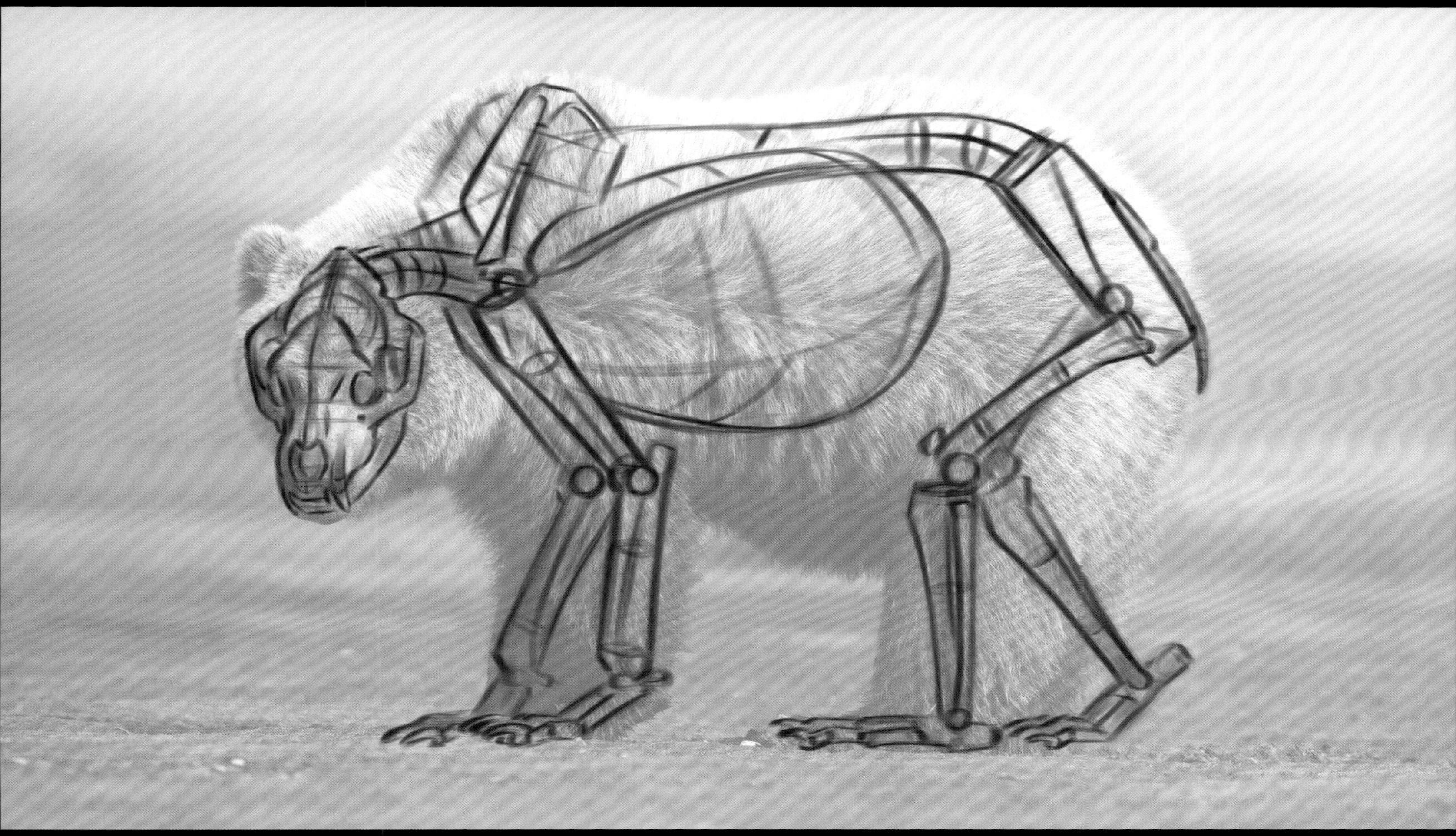

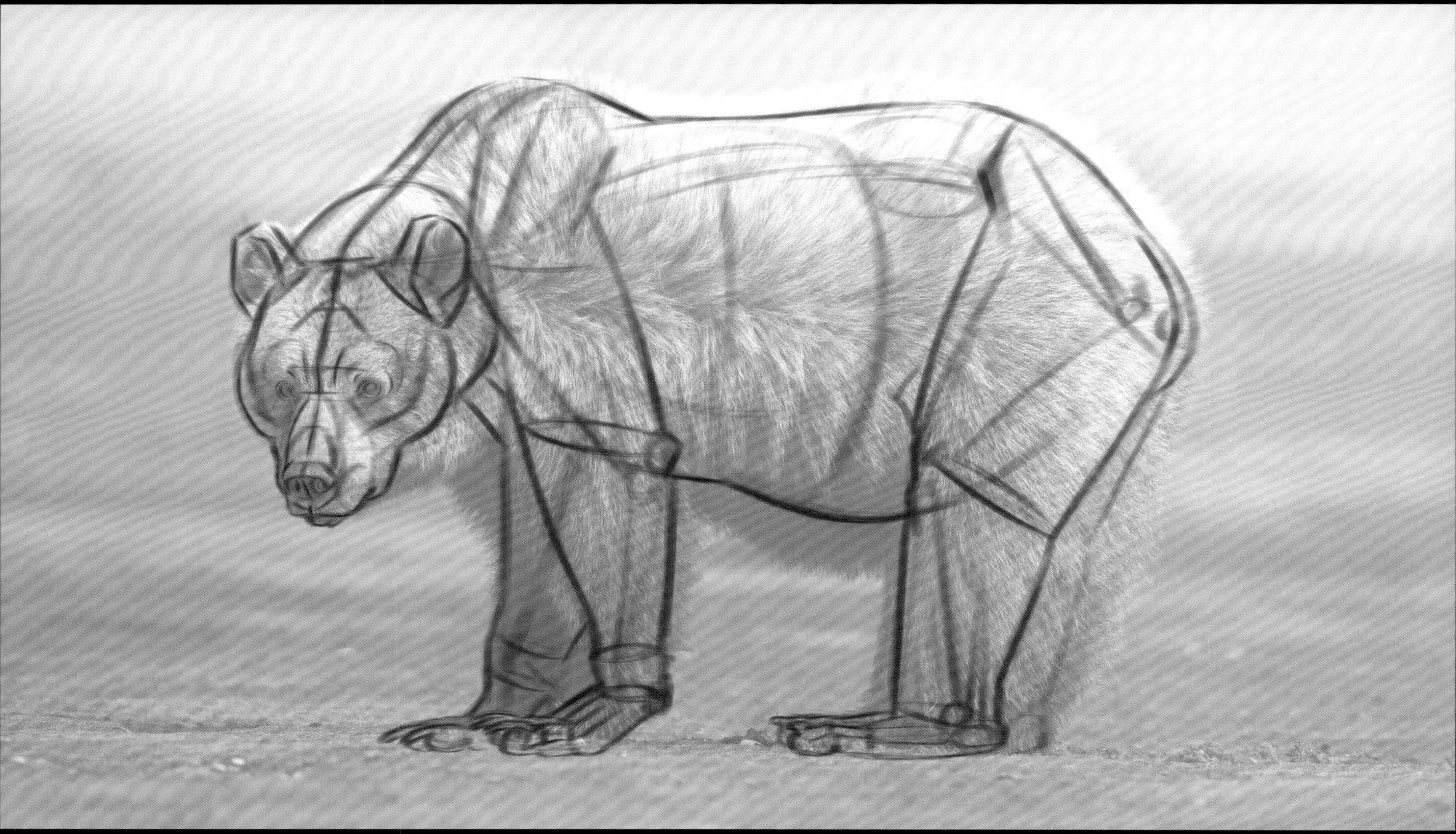

Photograph © Aurélien Audevard/ Agami.nl

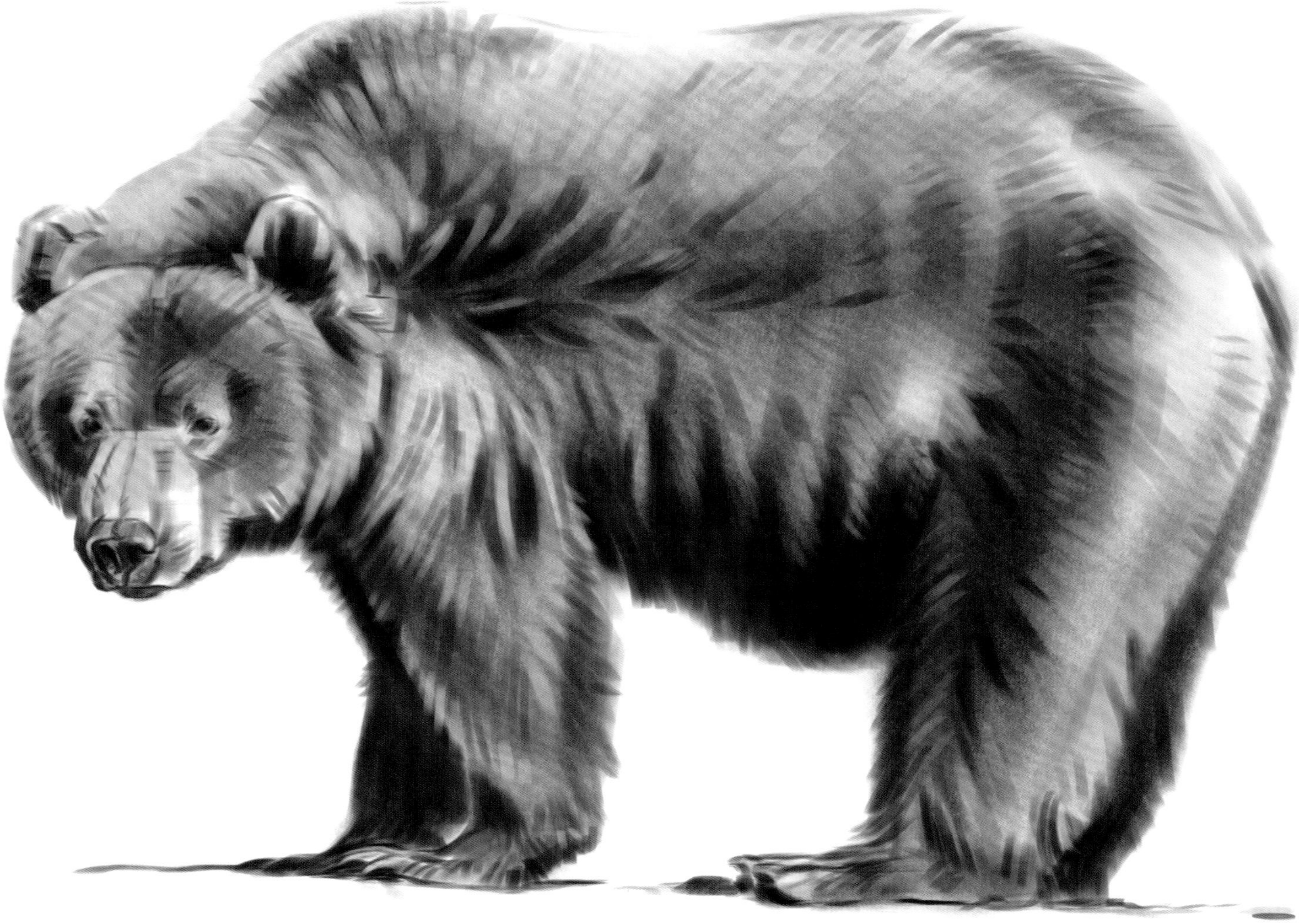

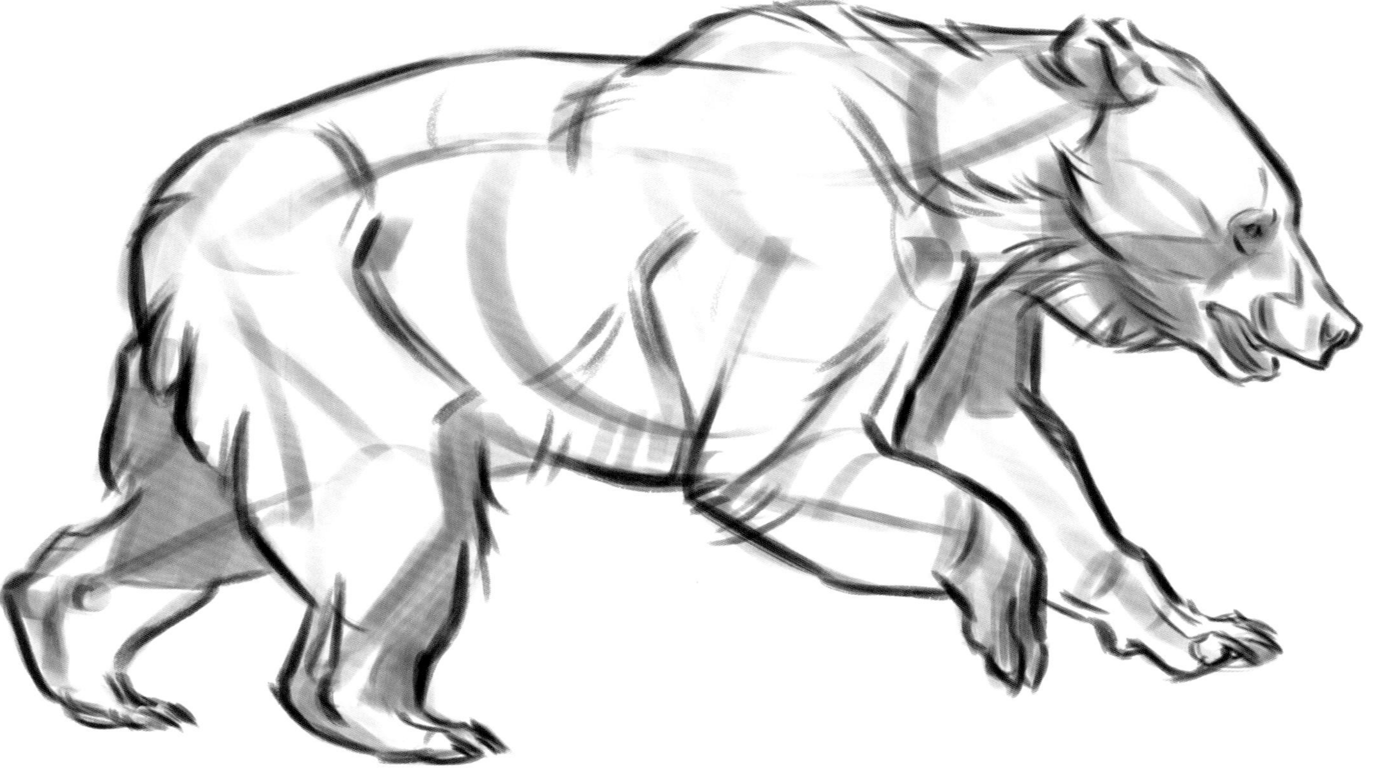

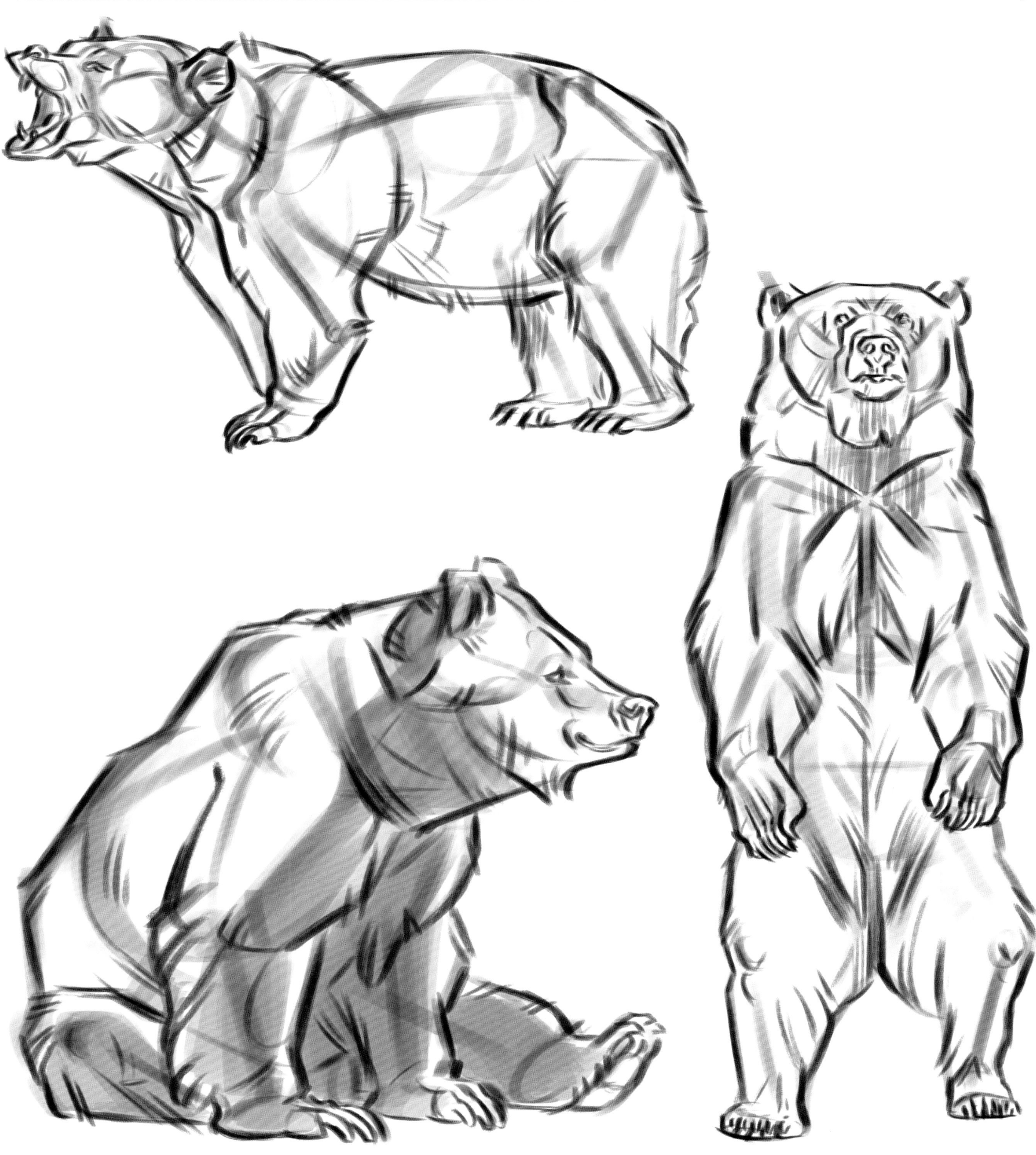

Polar bear

Polar bear
(Ursus maritimus)

CLASS: MAMMALIA
ORDER: CARNIVORA
FAMILY: URSIDAE

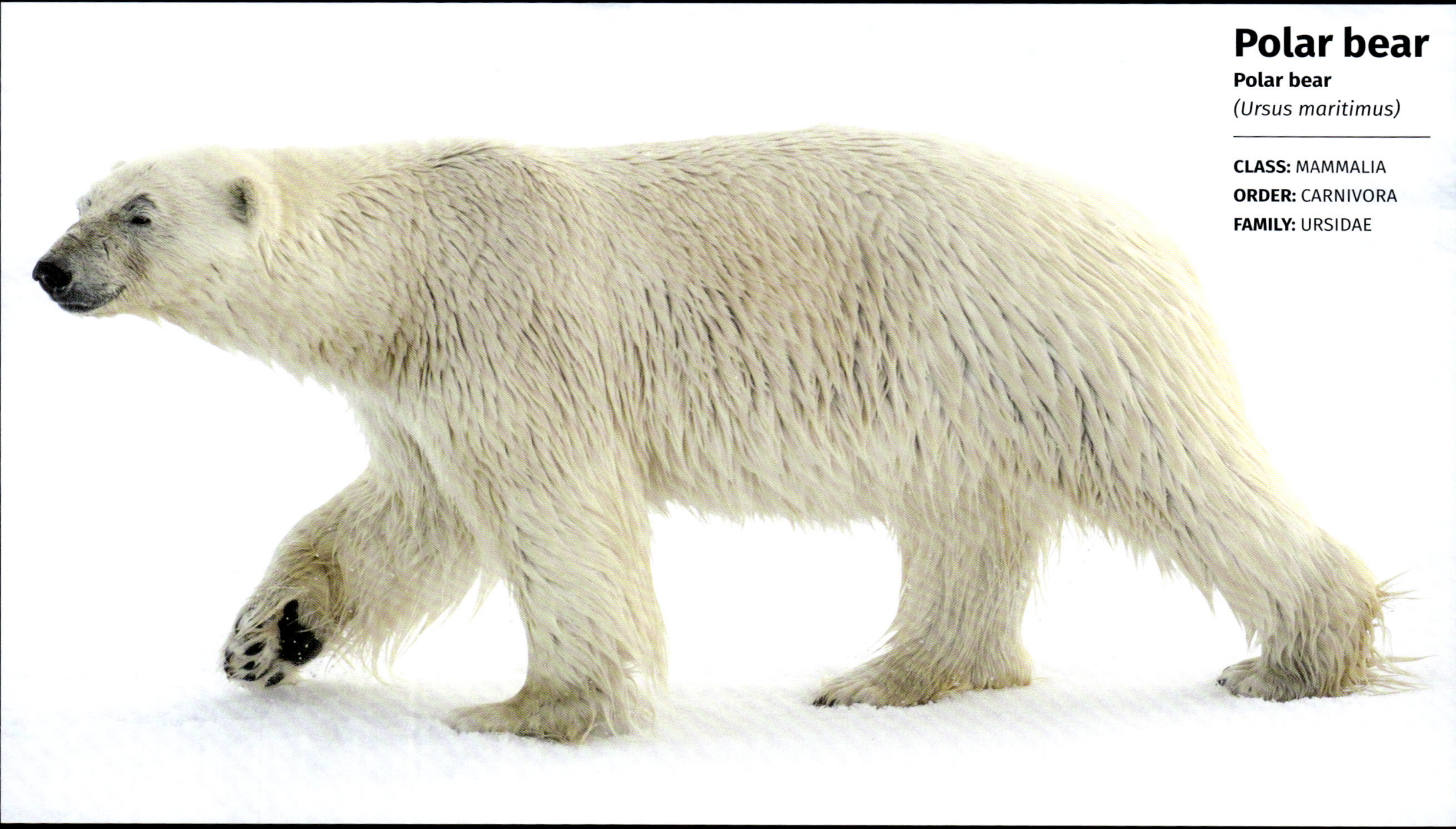

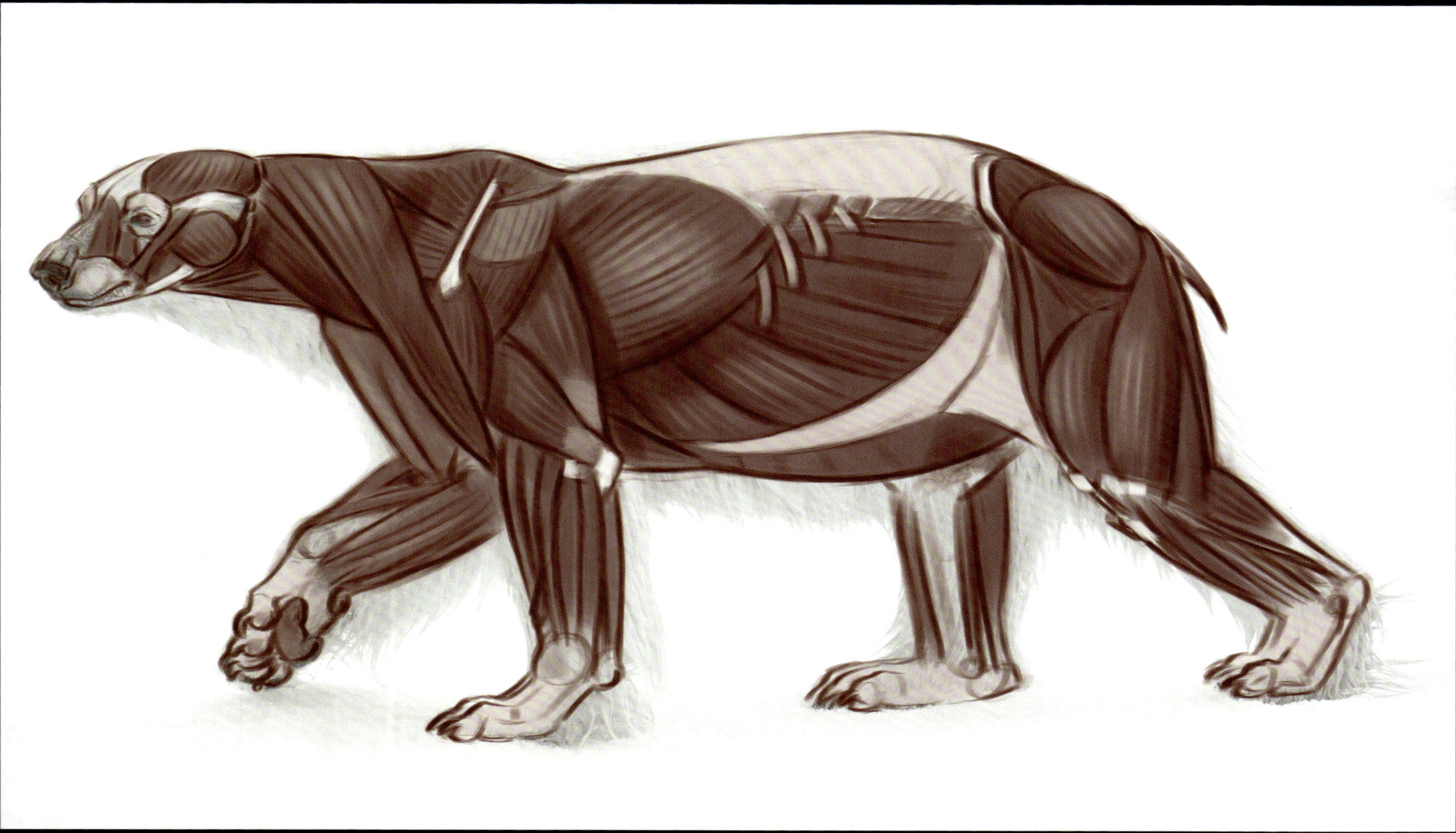

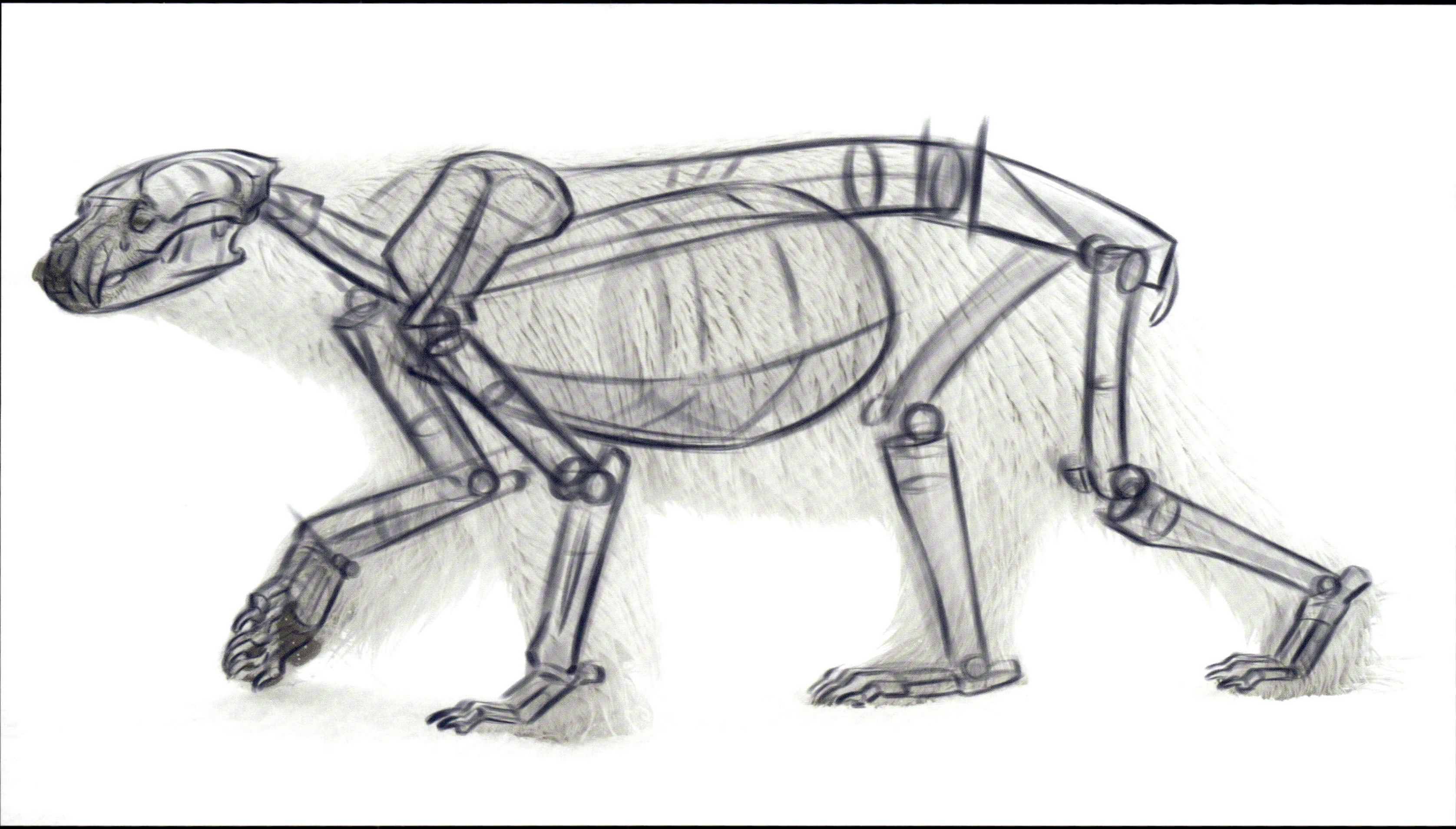

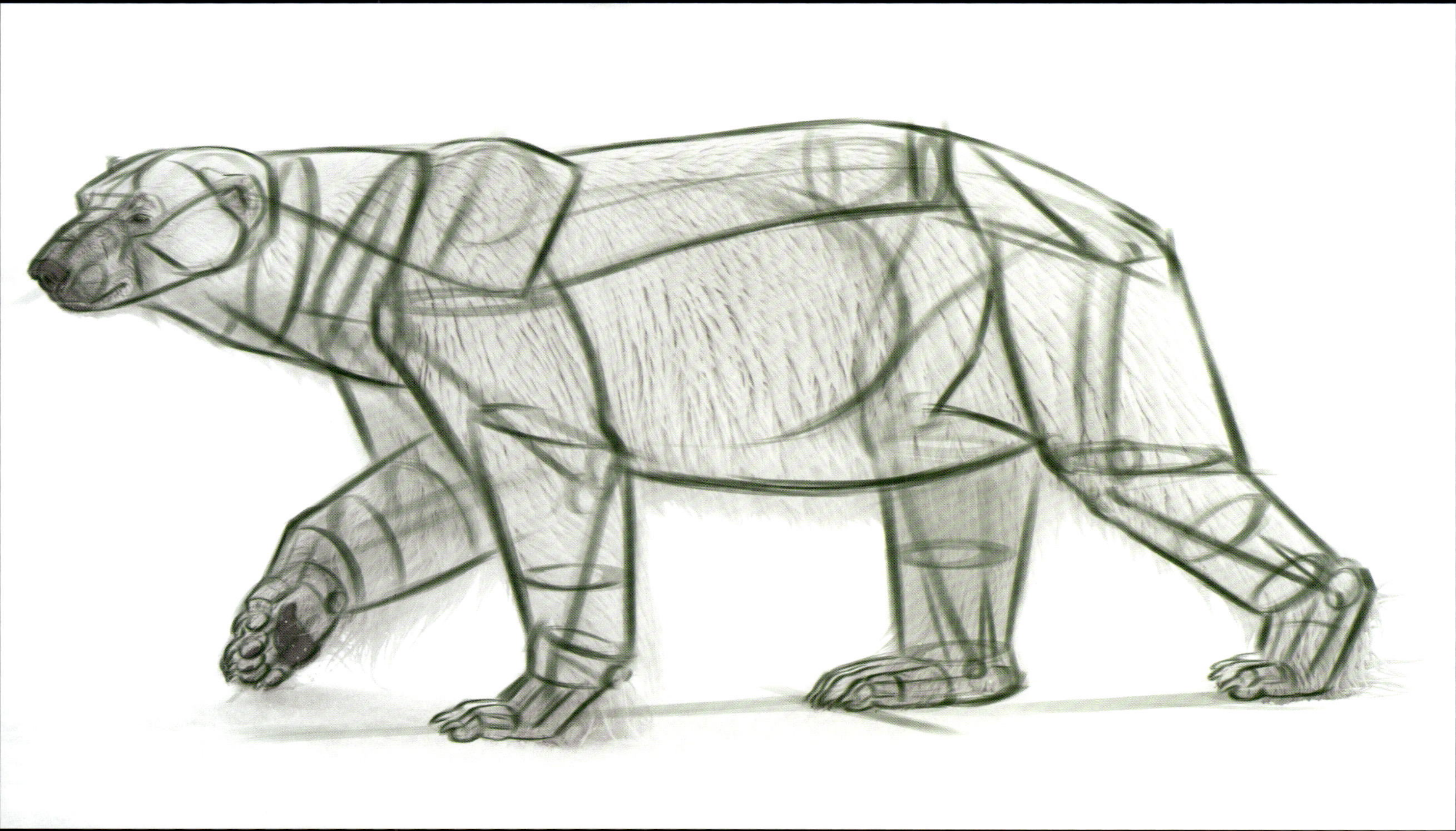

Photograph © Marc Guyt / Agami.nl

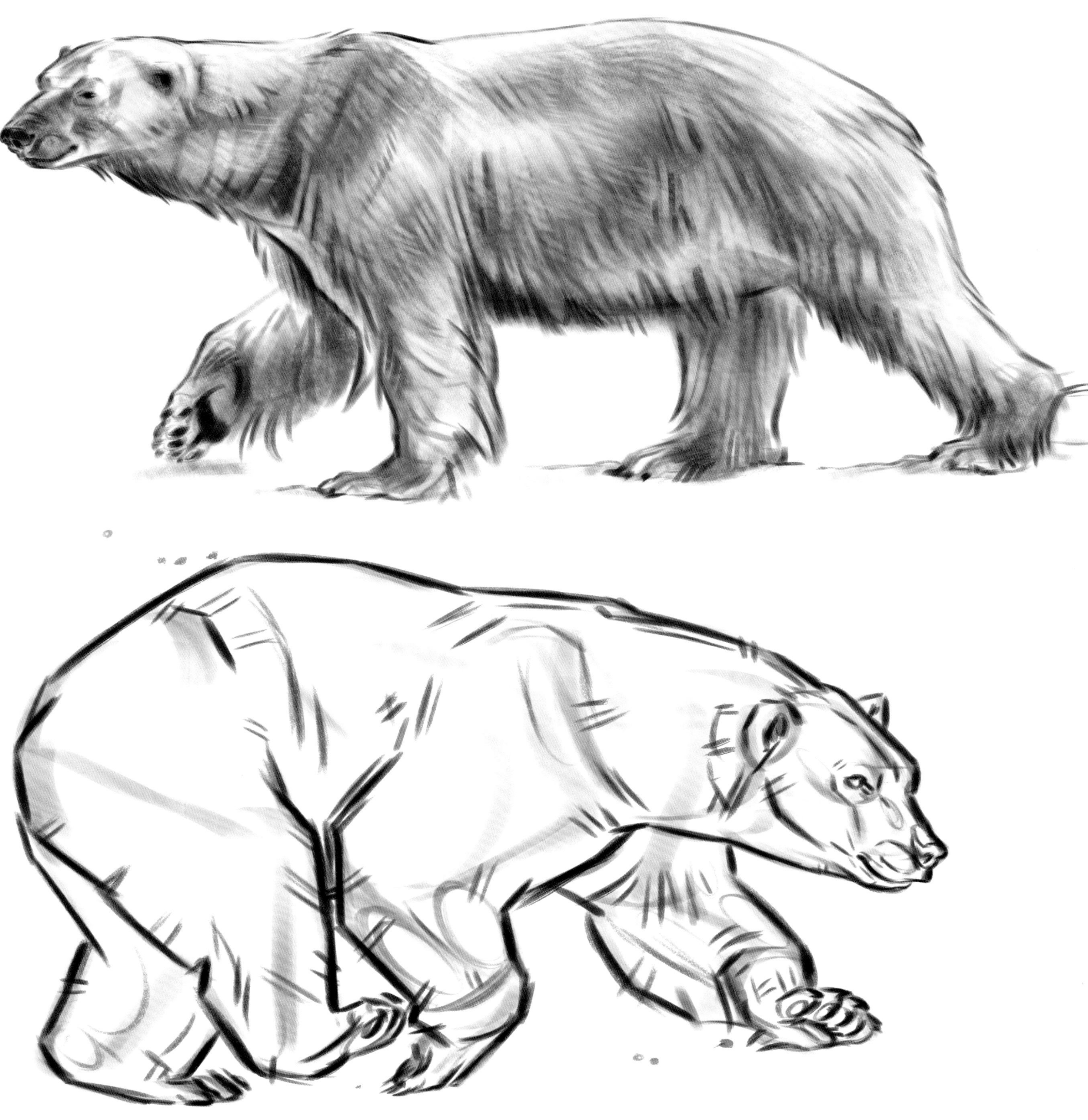

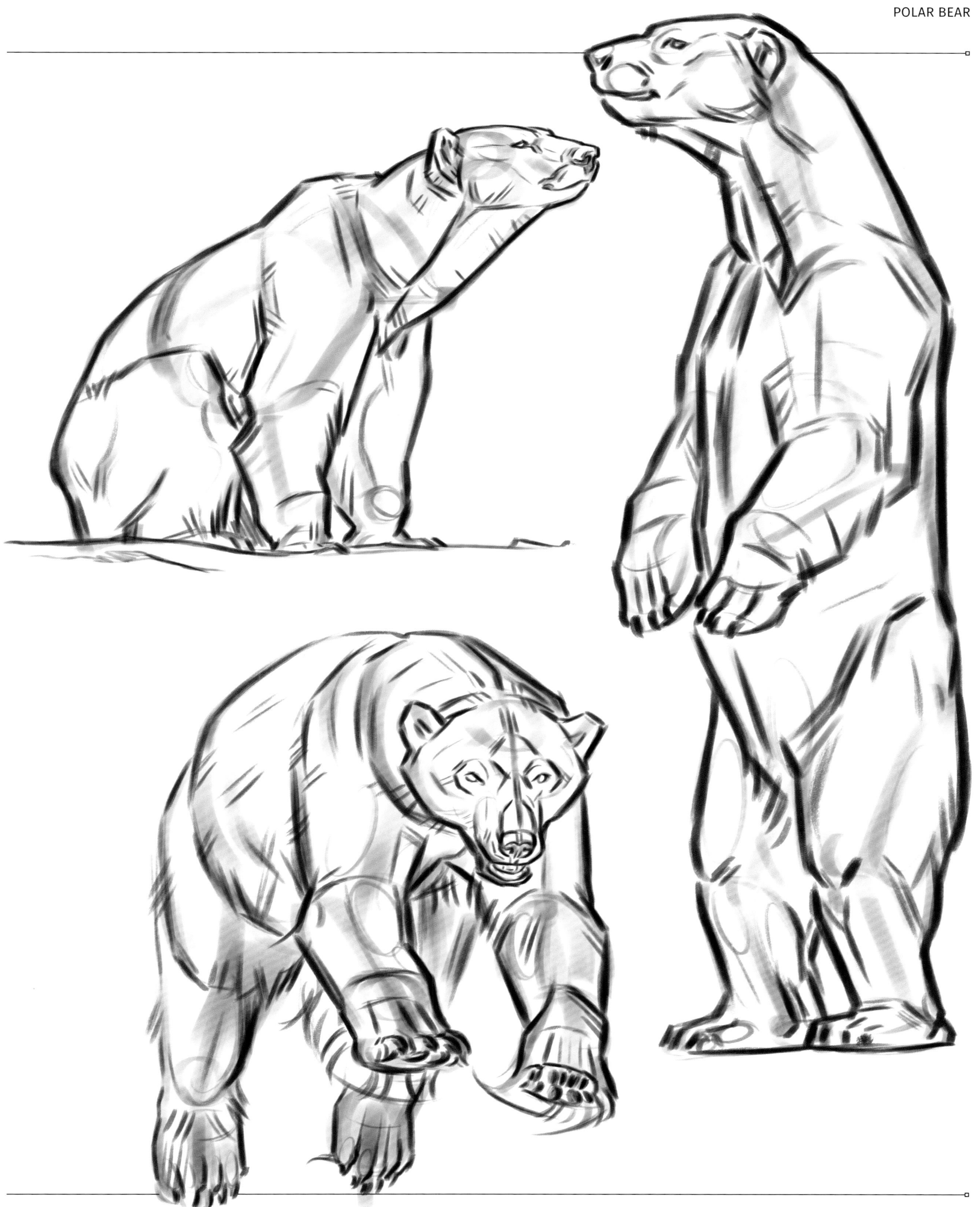

Bat

Escalera's bat

(Myotis escalerai)

CLASS: MAMMALIA

ORDER: CHIROPTERA

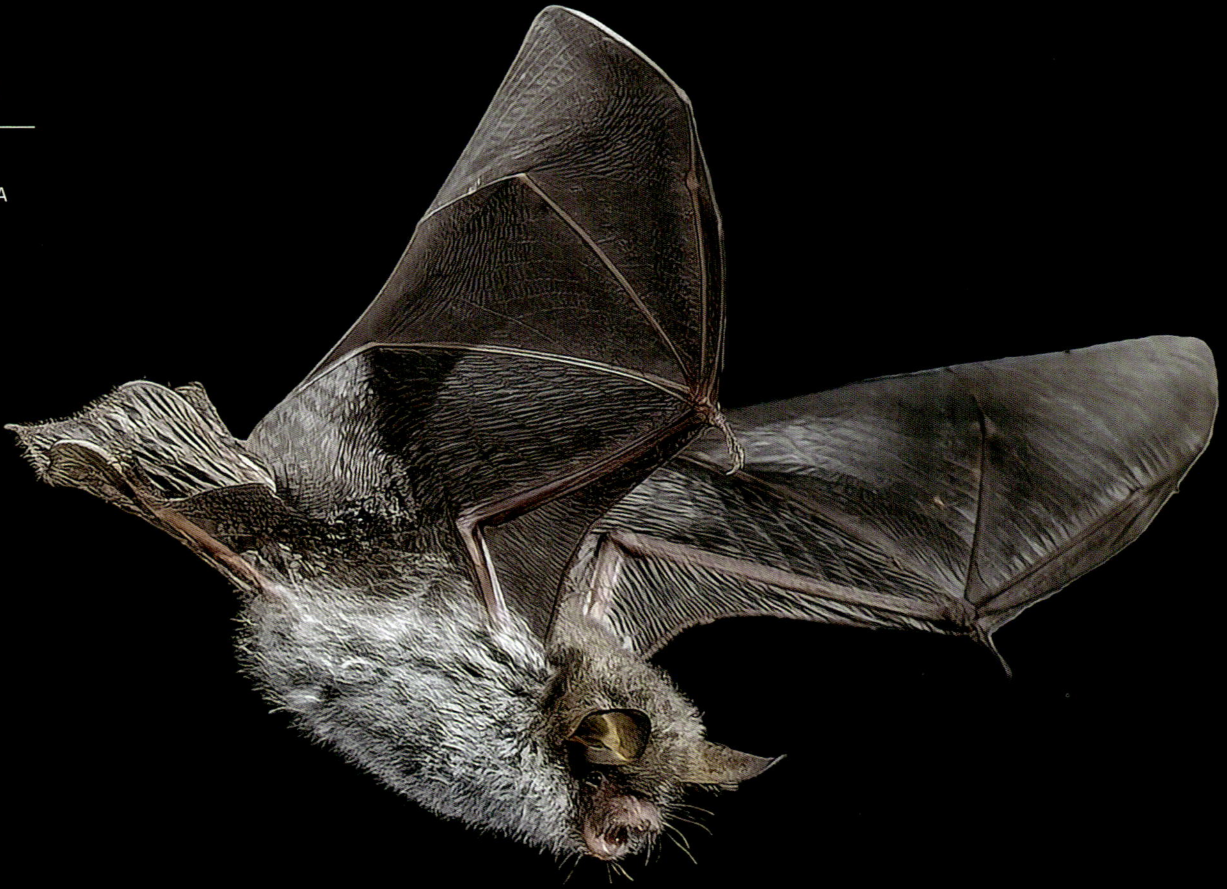

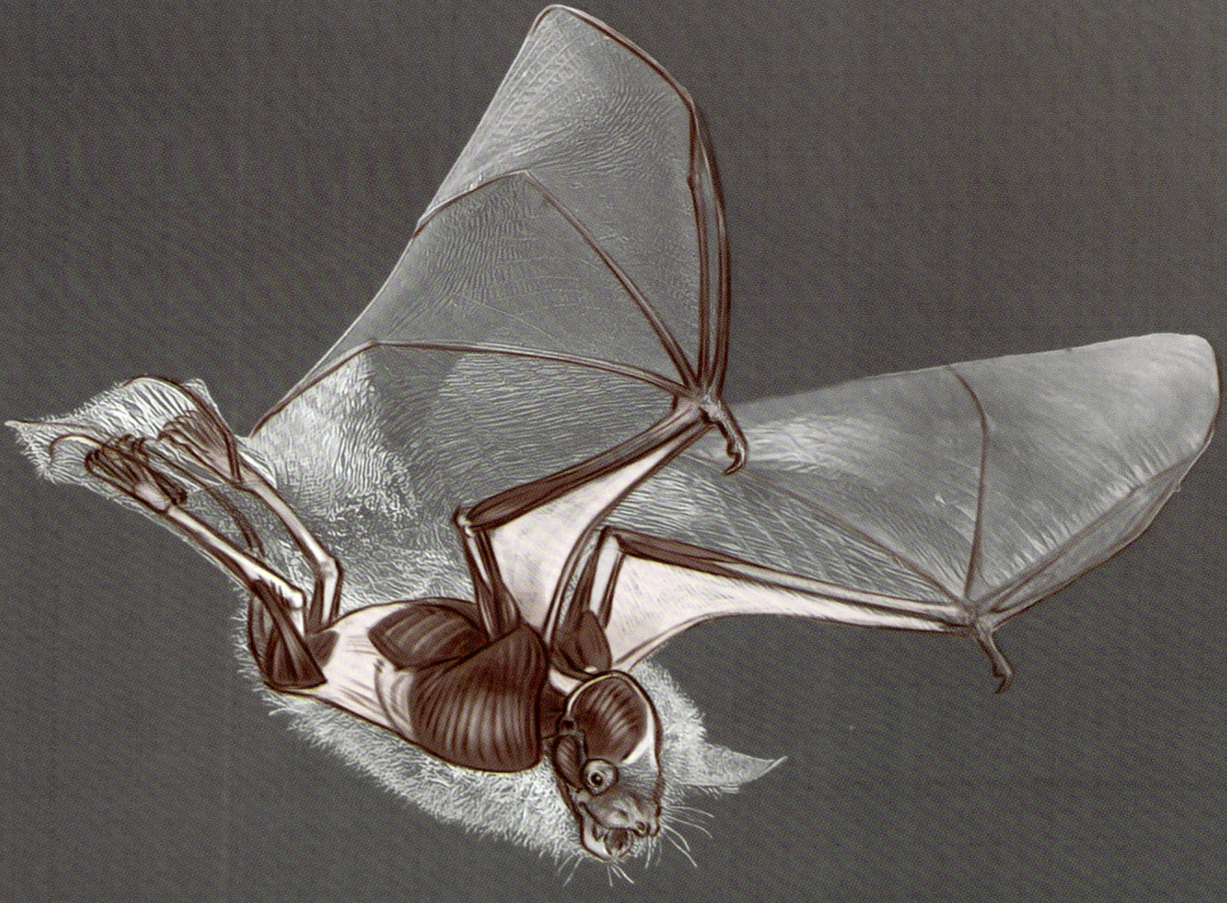

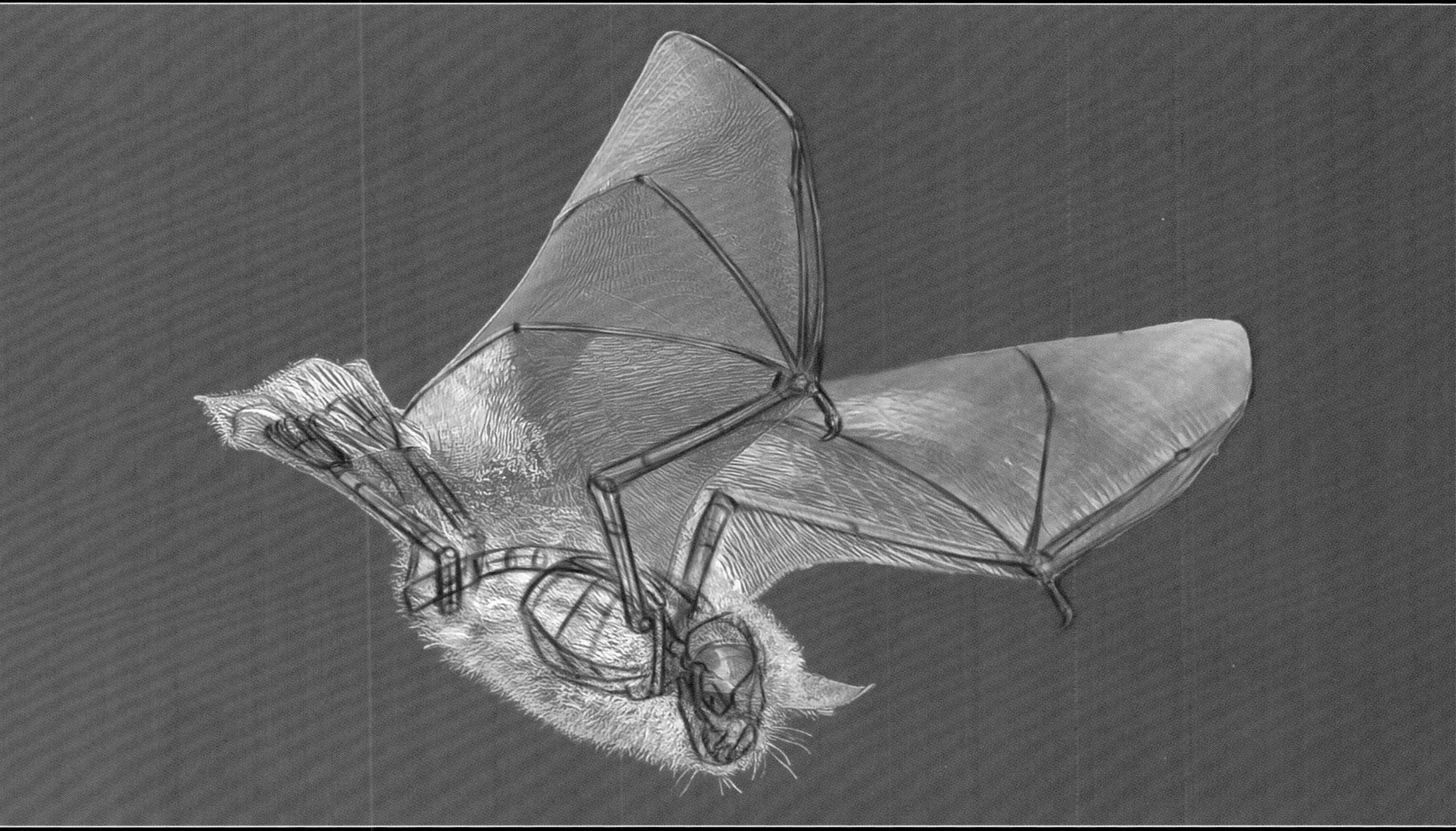

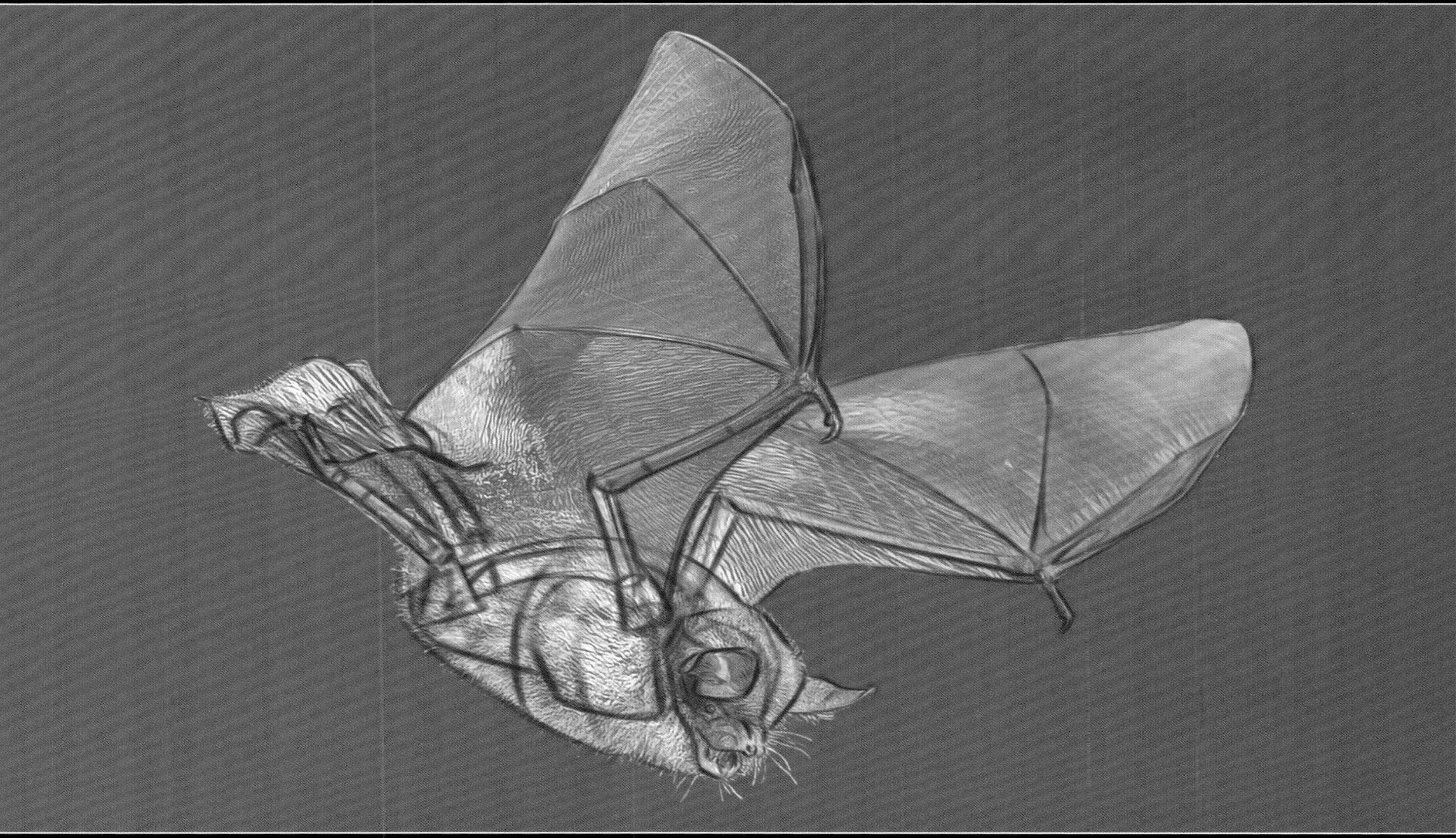

Photograph © Vincent Legrand / Agami.nl

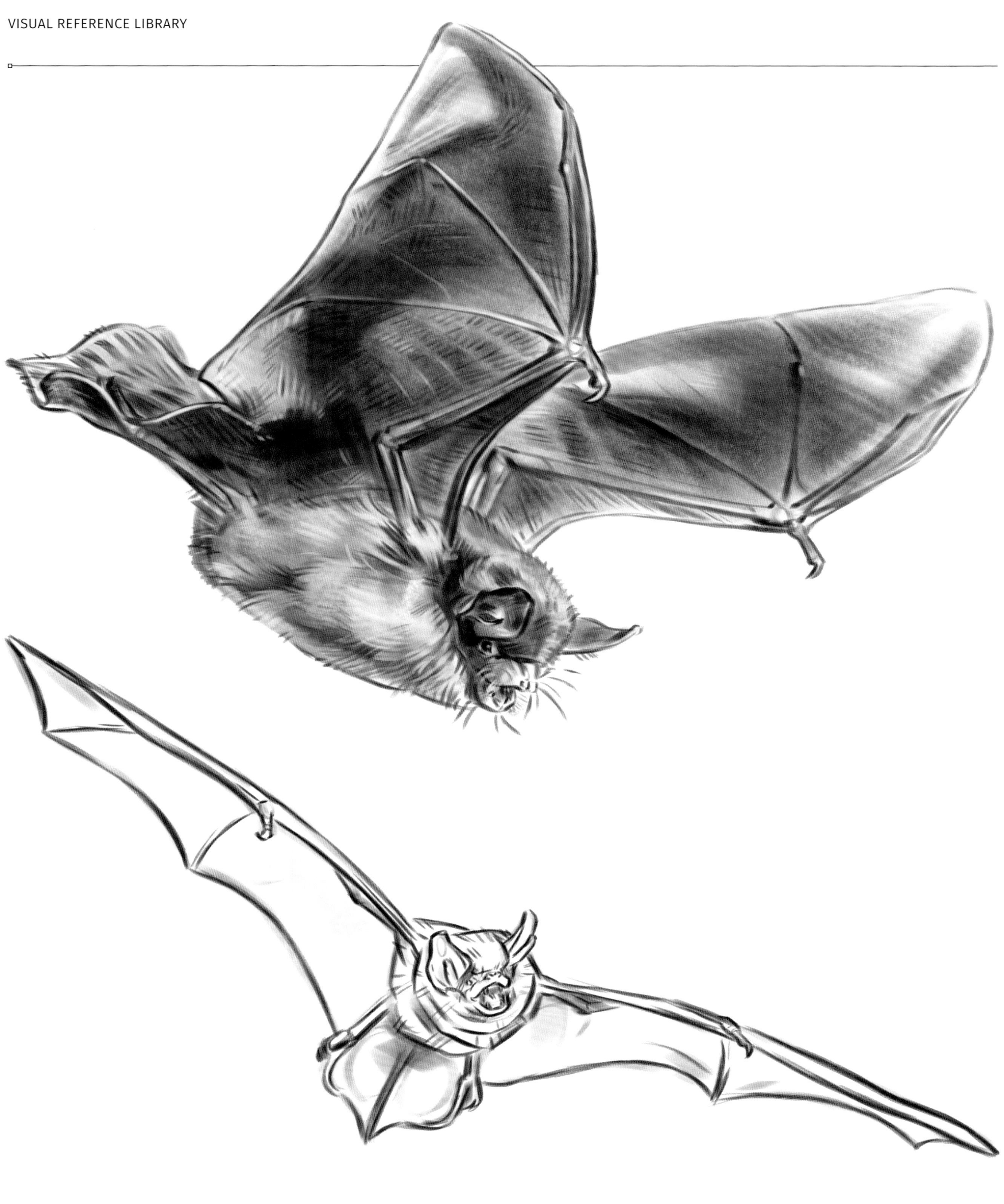

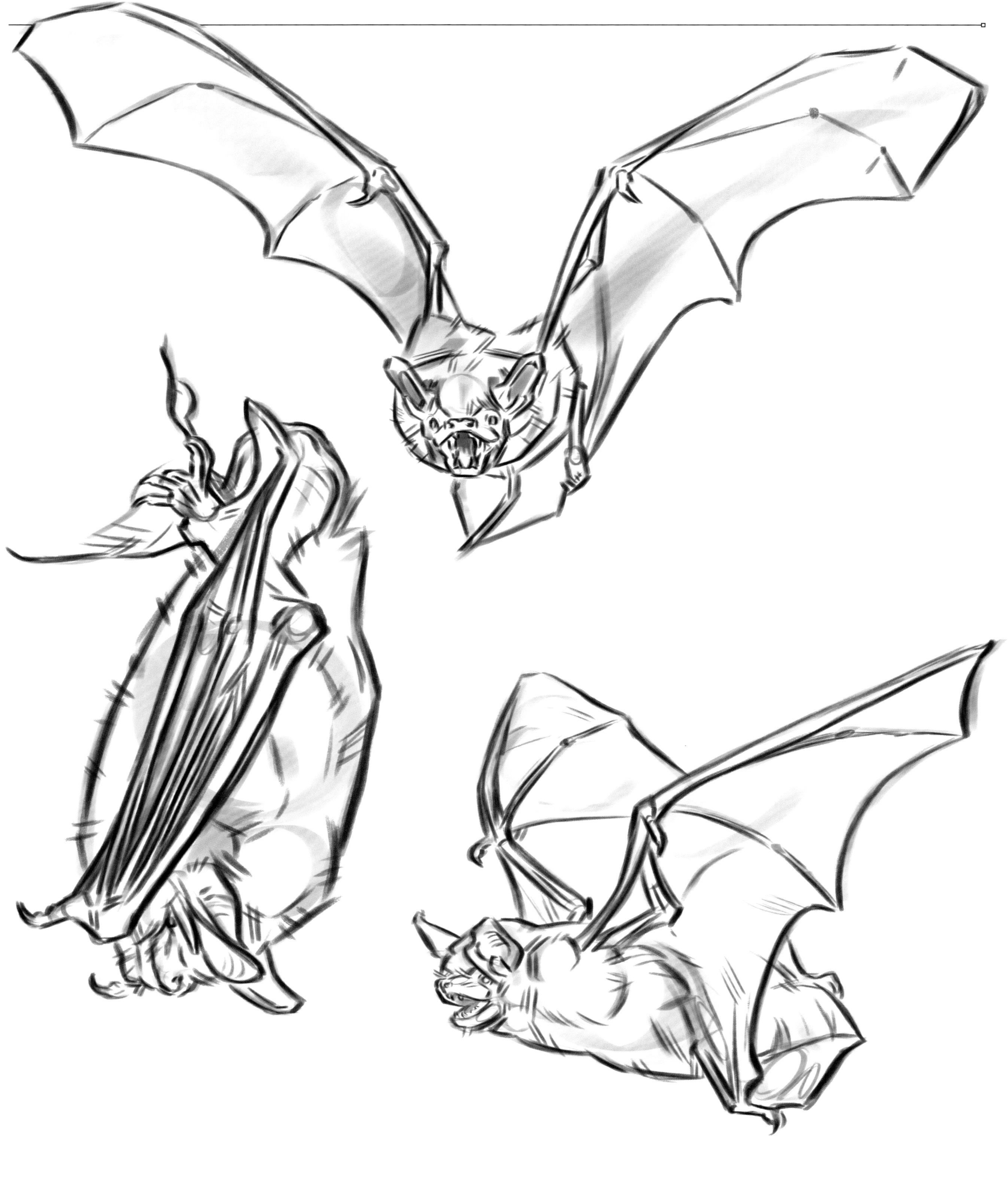

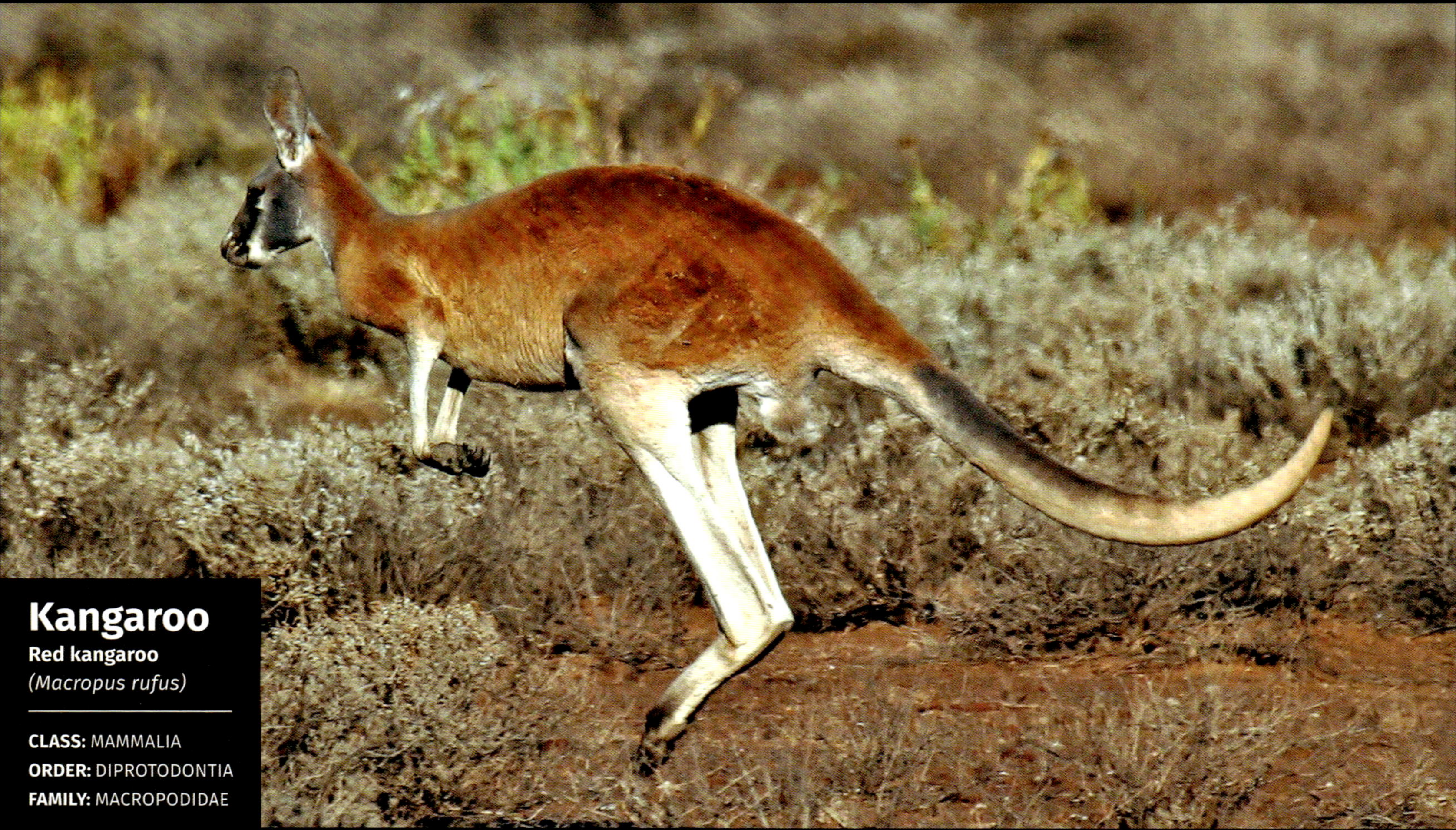

Kangaroo

Red kangaroo
(Macropus rufus)

CLASS: MAMMALIA
ORDER: DIPROTODONTIA
FAMILY: MACROPODIDAE

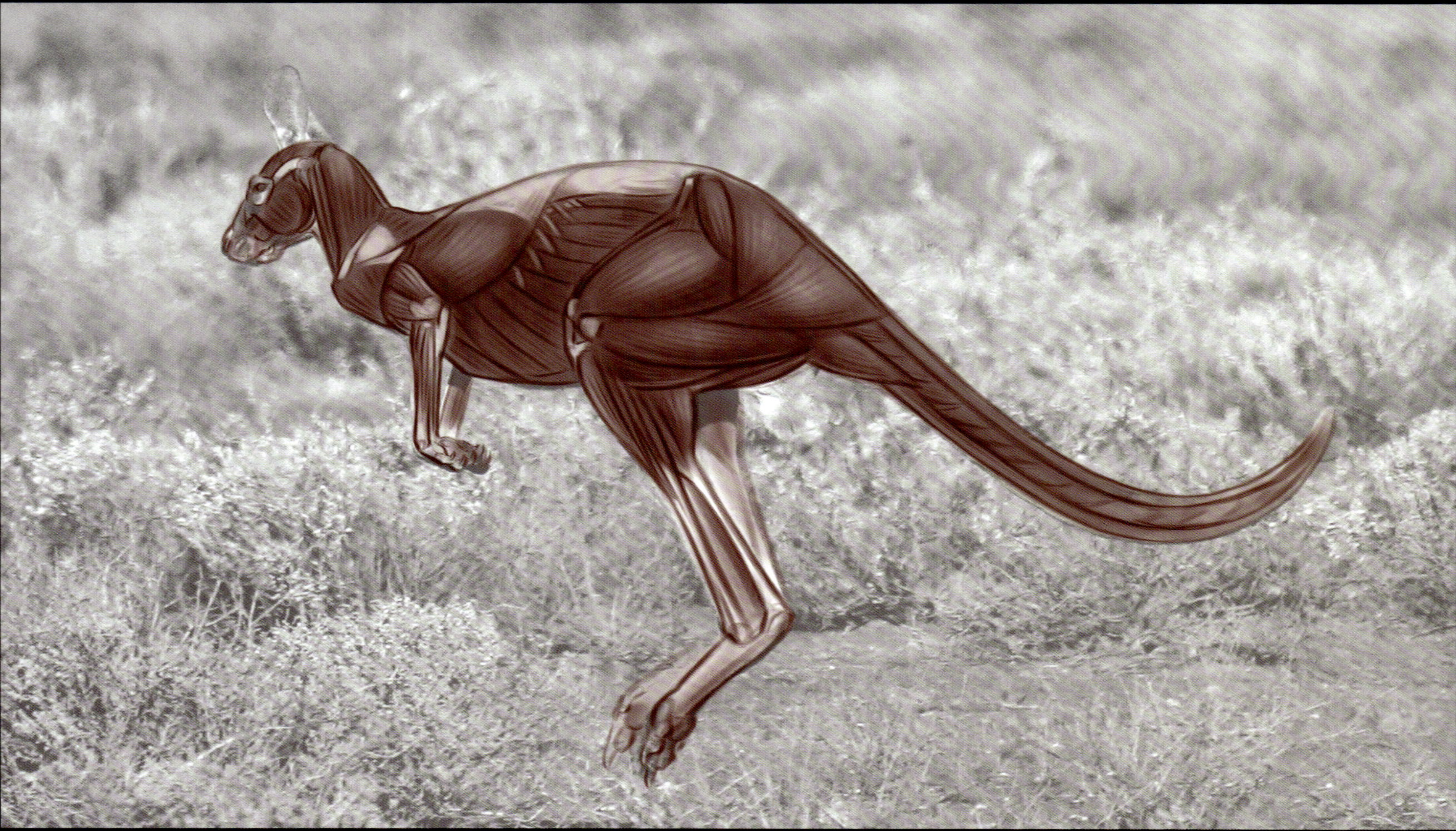

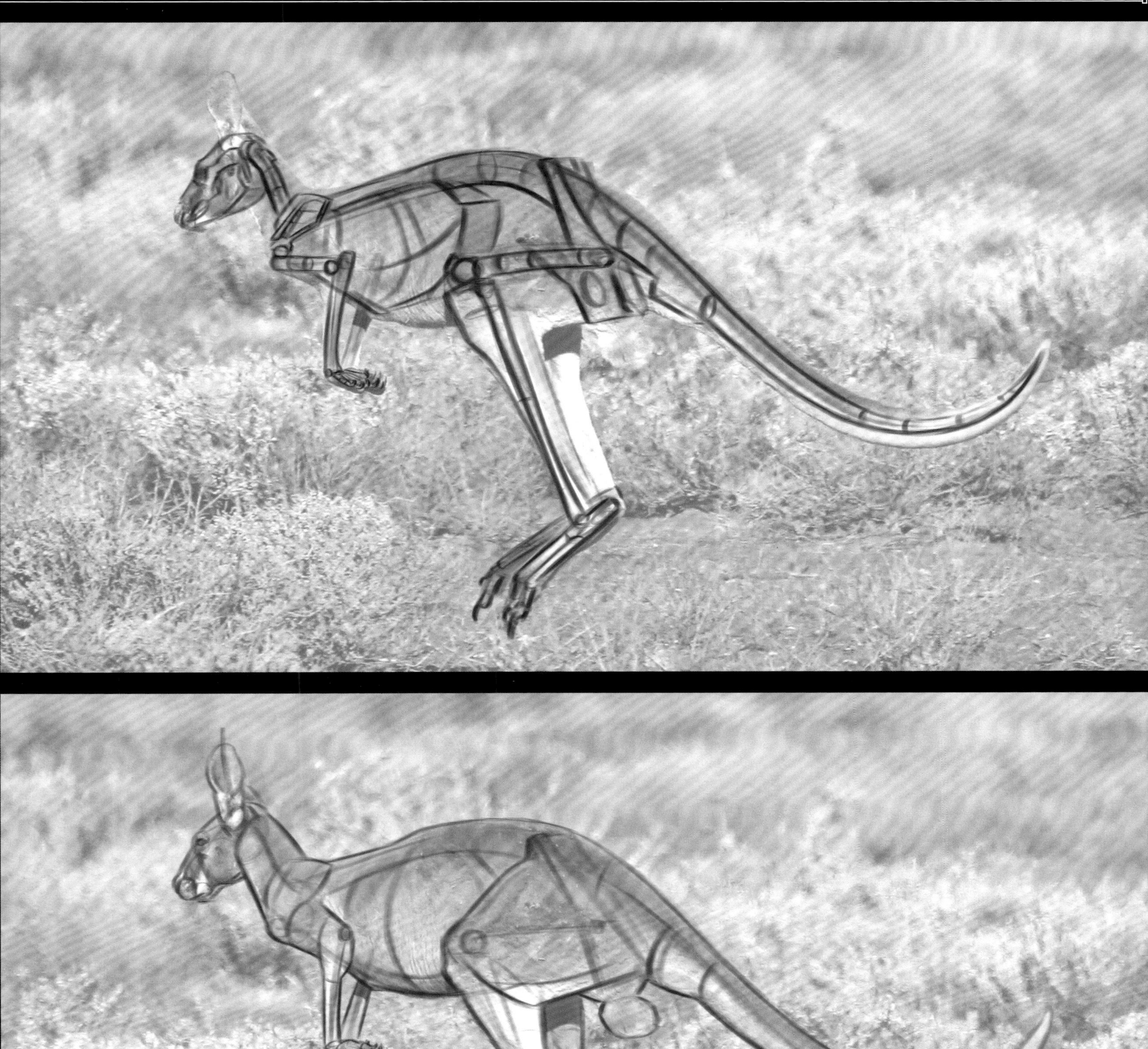

Photograph © Pete Morris / Agami.nl

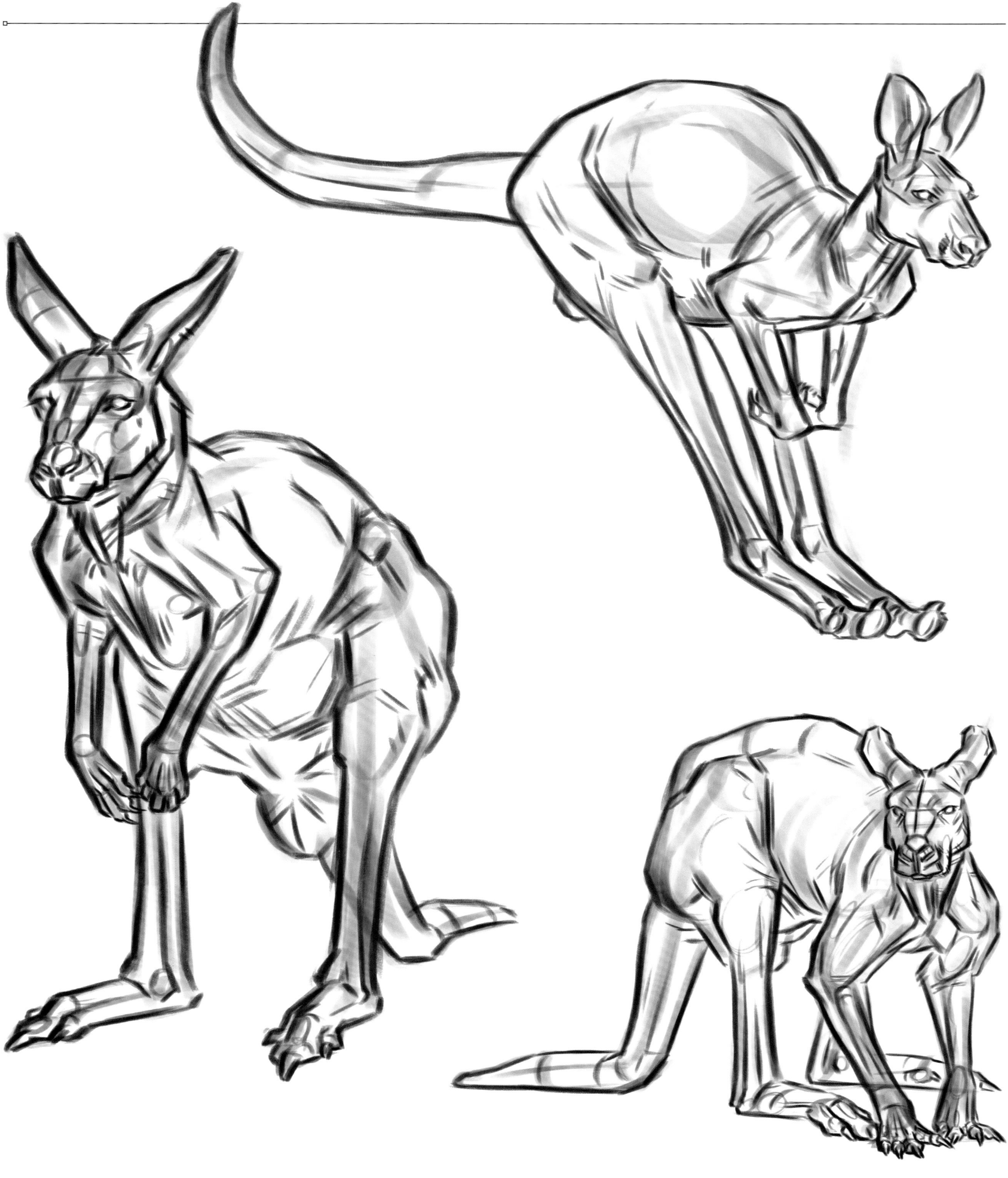

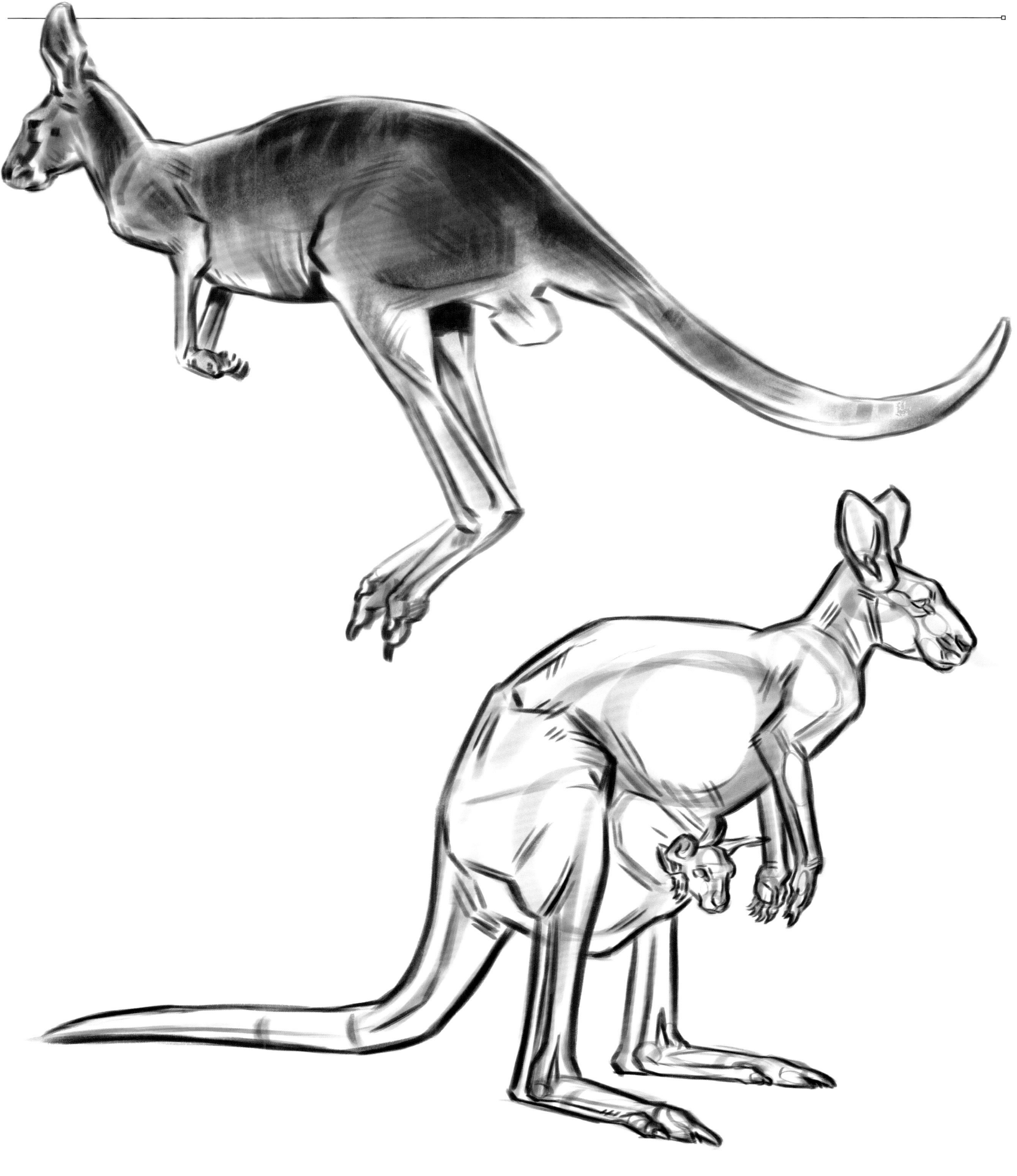

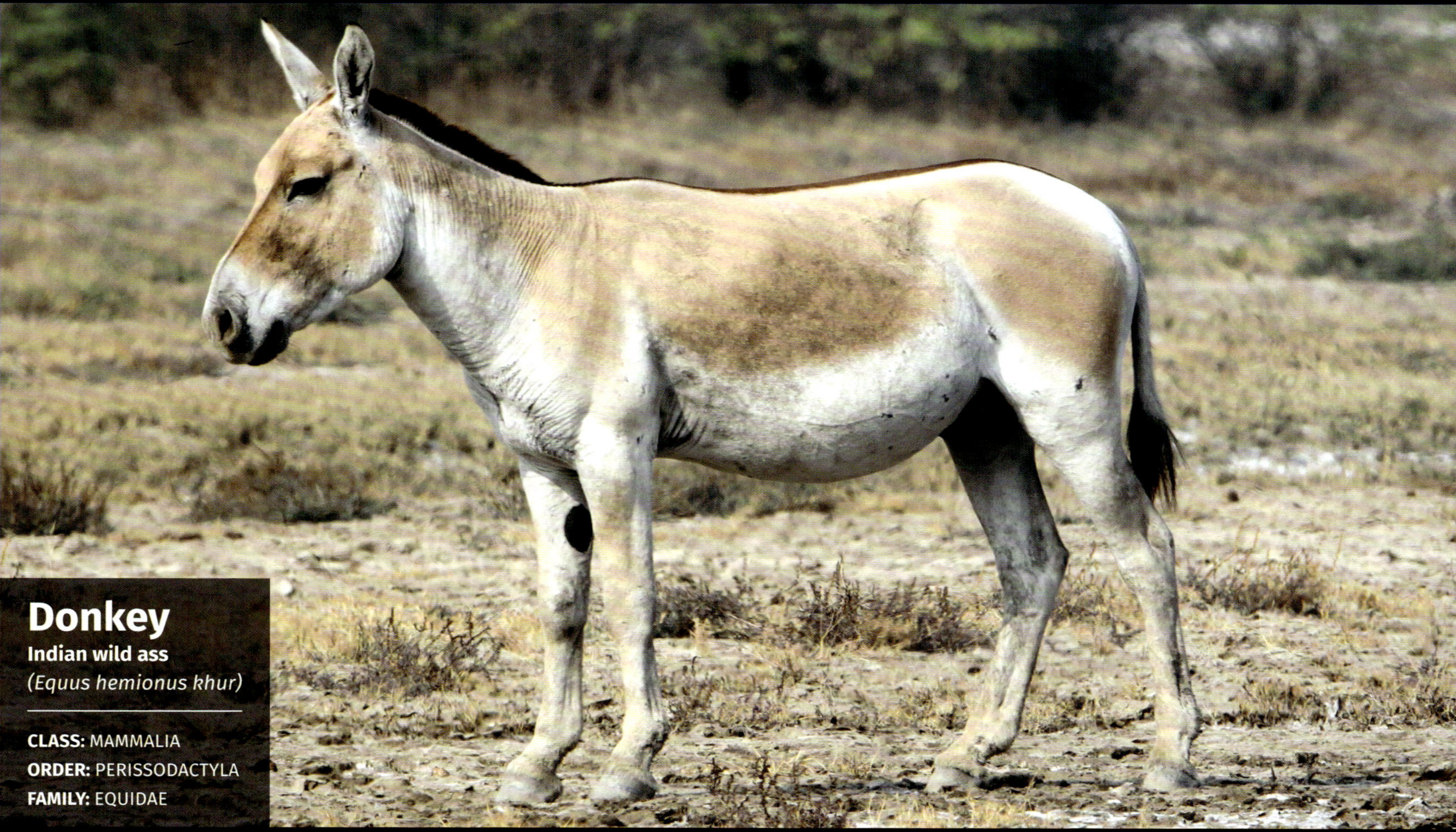

Donkey

Indian wild ass

(Equus hemionus khur)

CLASS: MAMMALIA
ORDER: PERISSODACTYLA
FAMILY: EQUIDAE

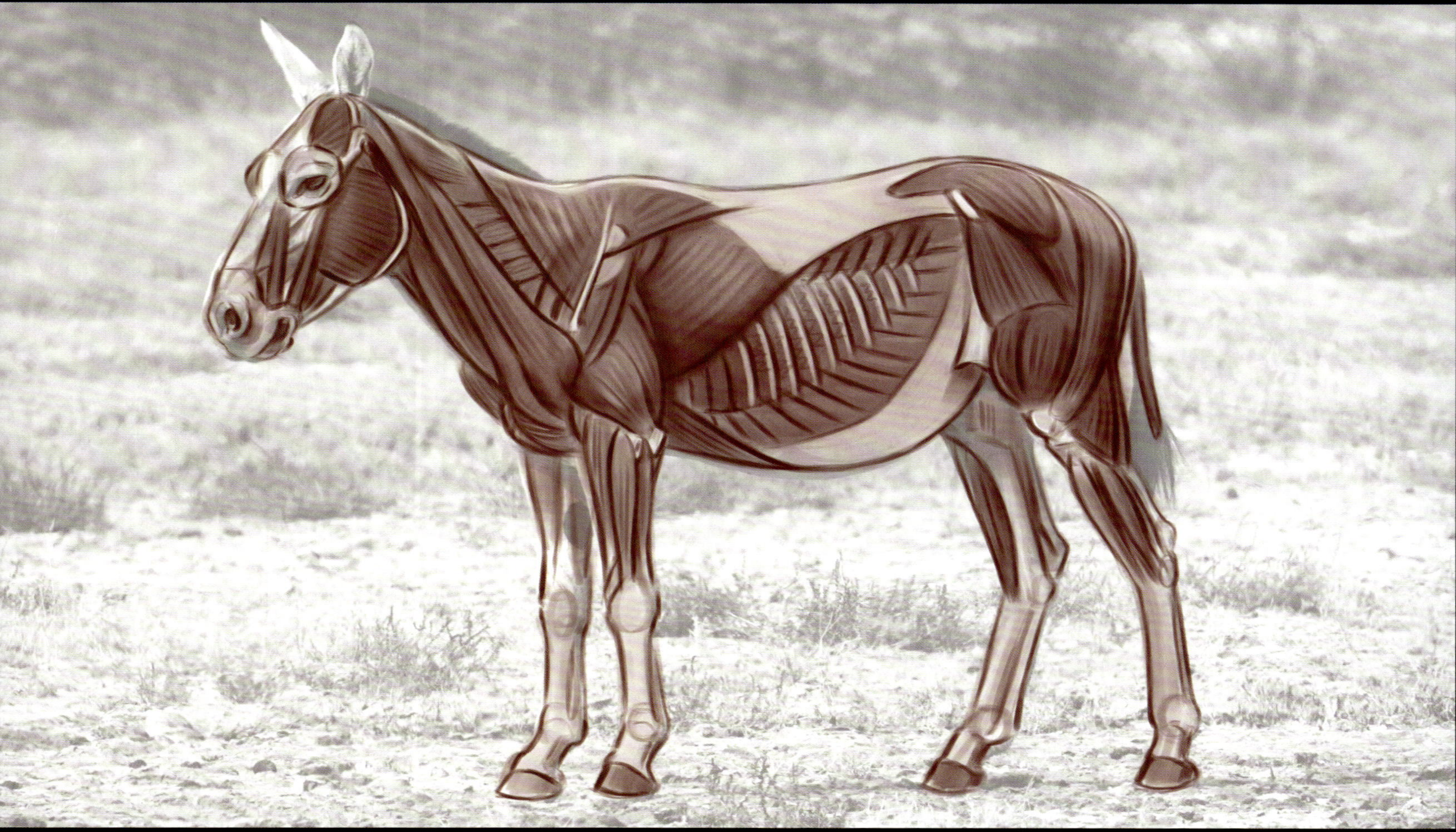

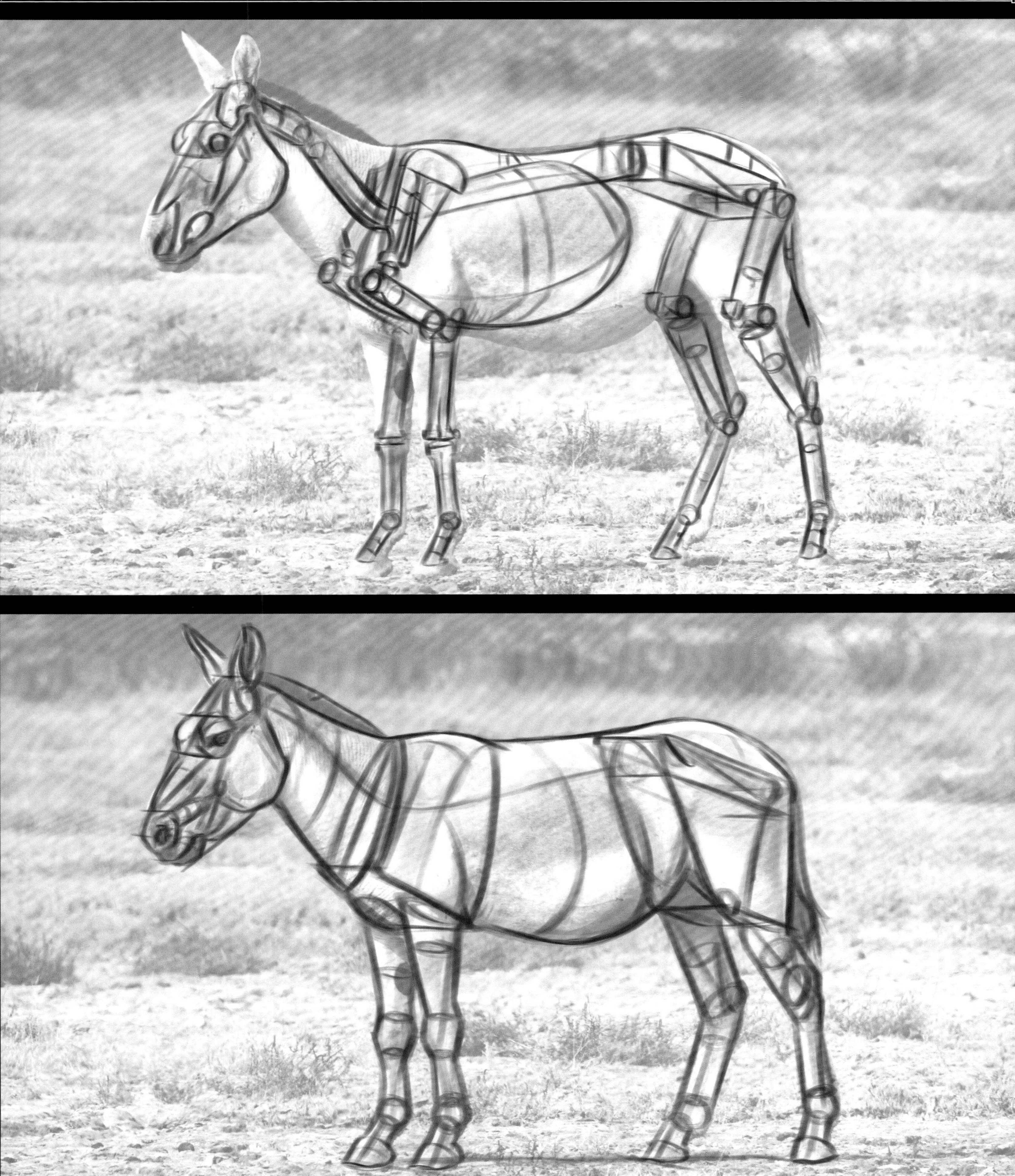

Photograph © James Eaton / Agami.nl

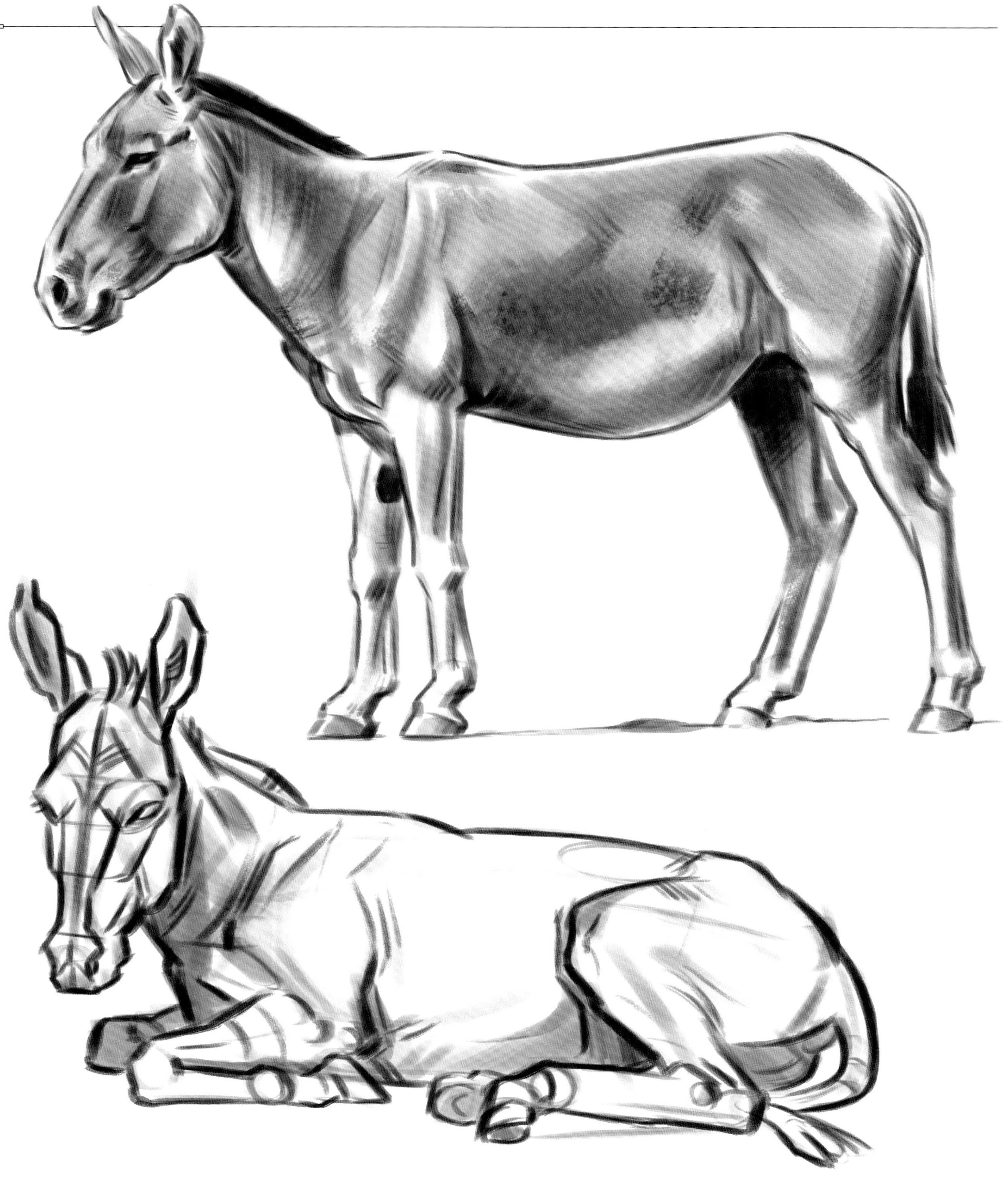

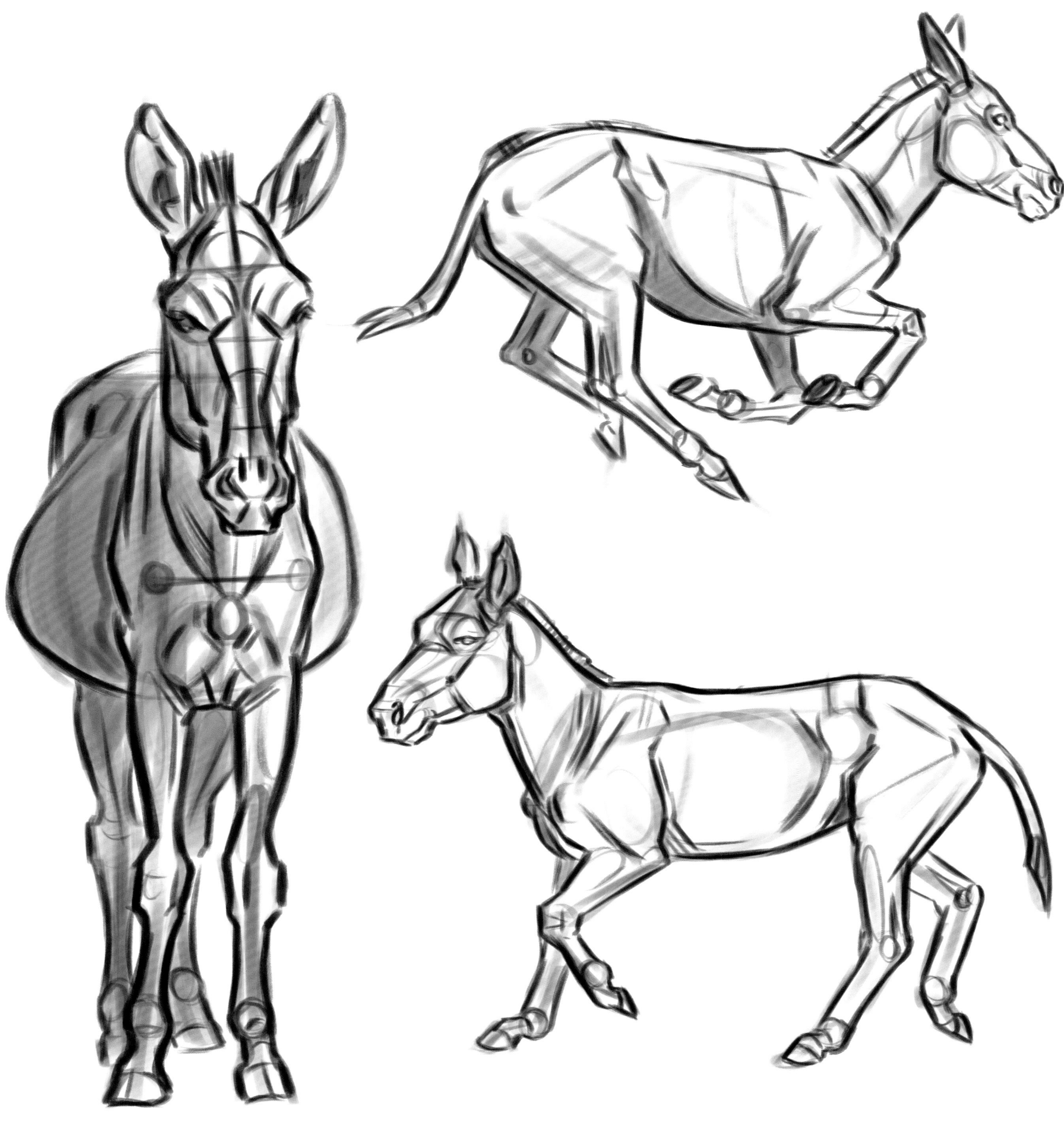

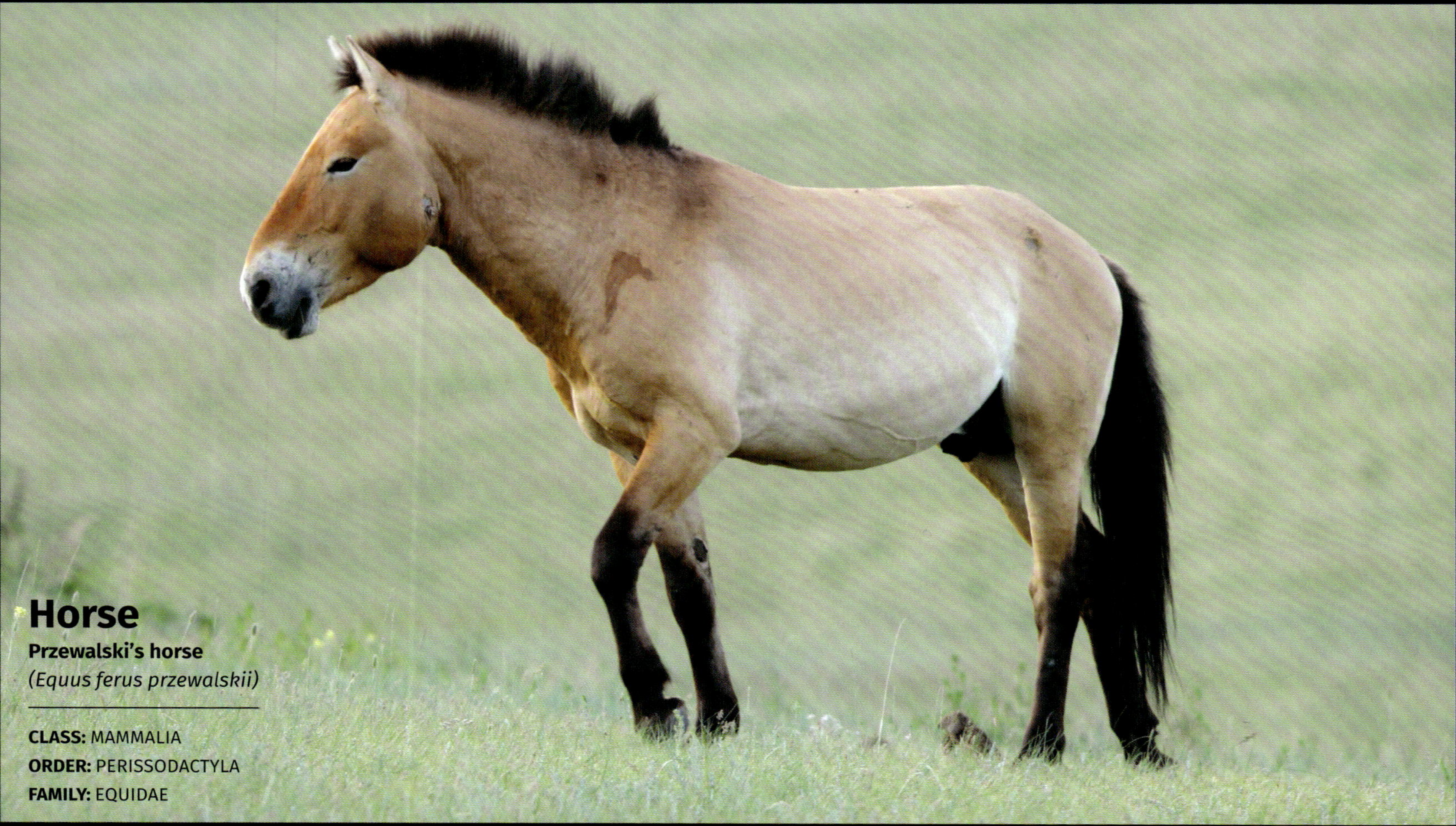

Horse

Przewalski's horse
(Equus ferus przewalskii)

CLASS: MAMMALIA
ORDER: PERISSODACTYLA
FAMILY: EQUIDAE

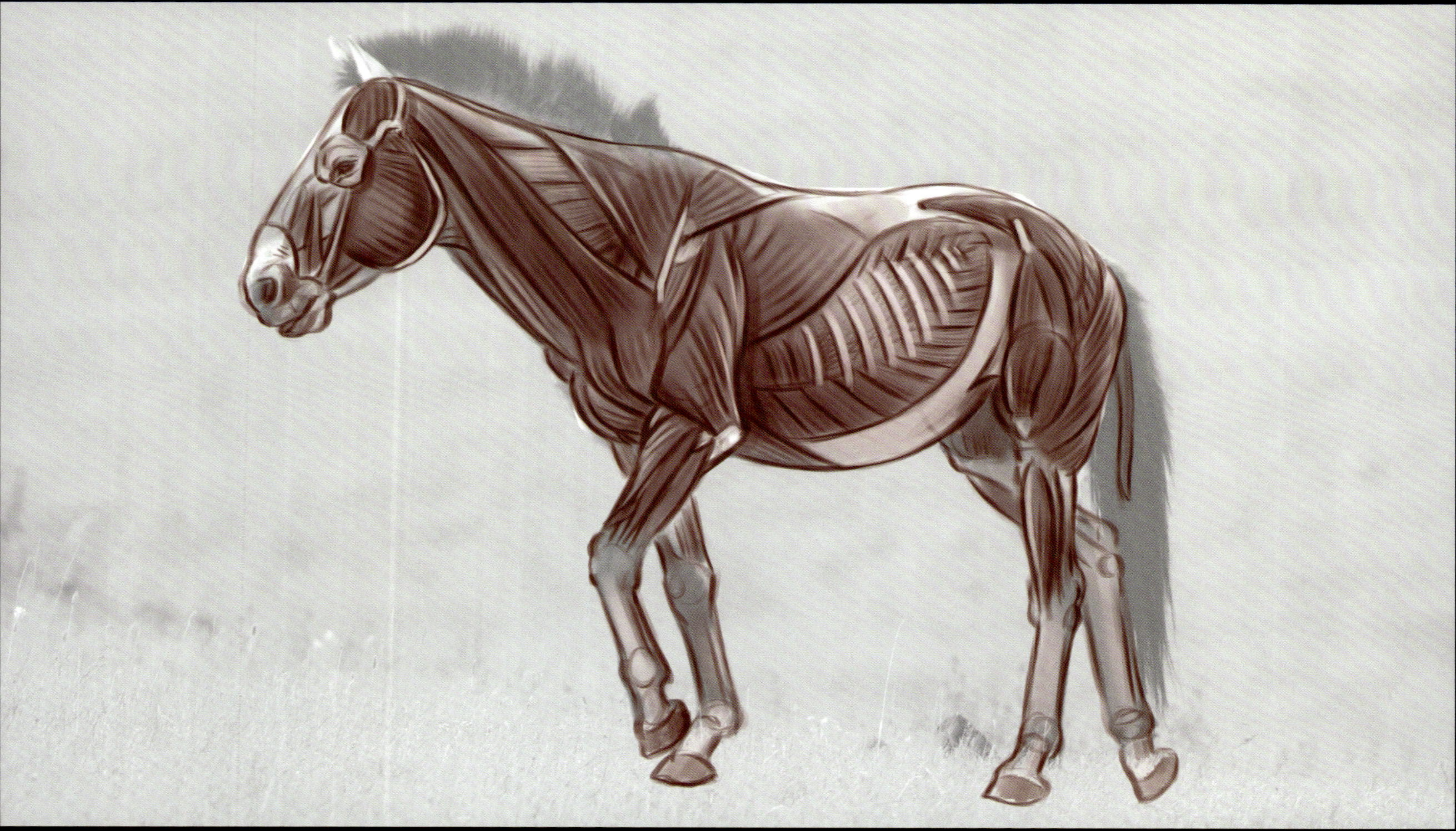

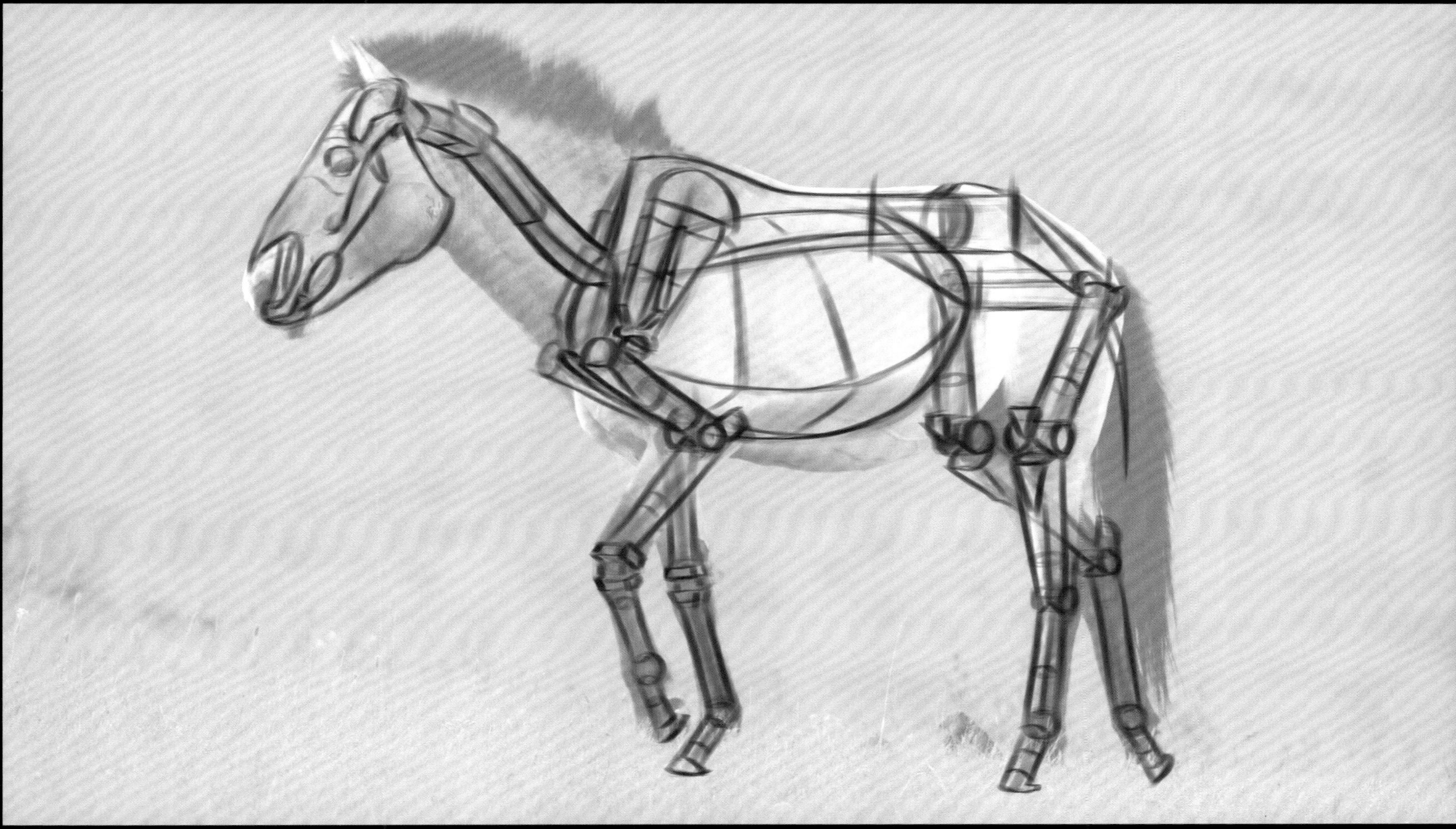

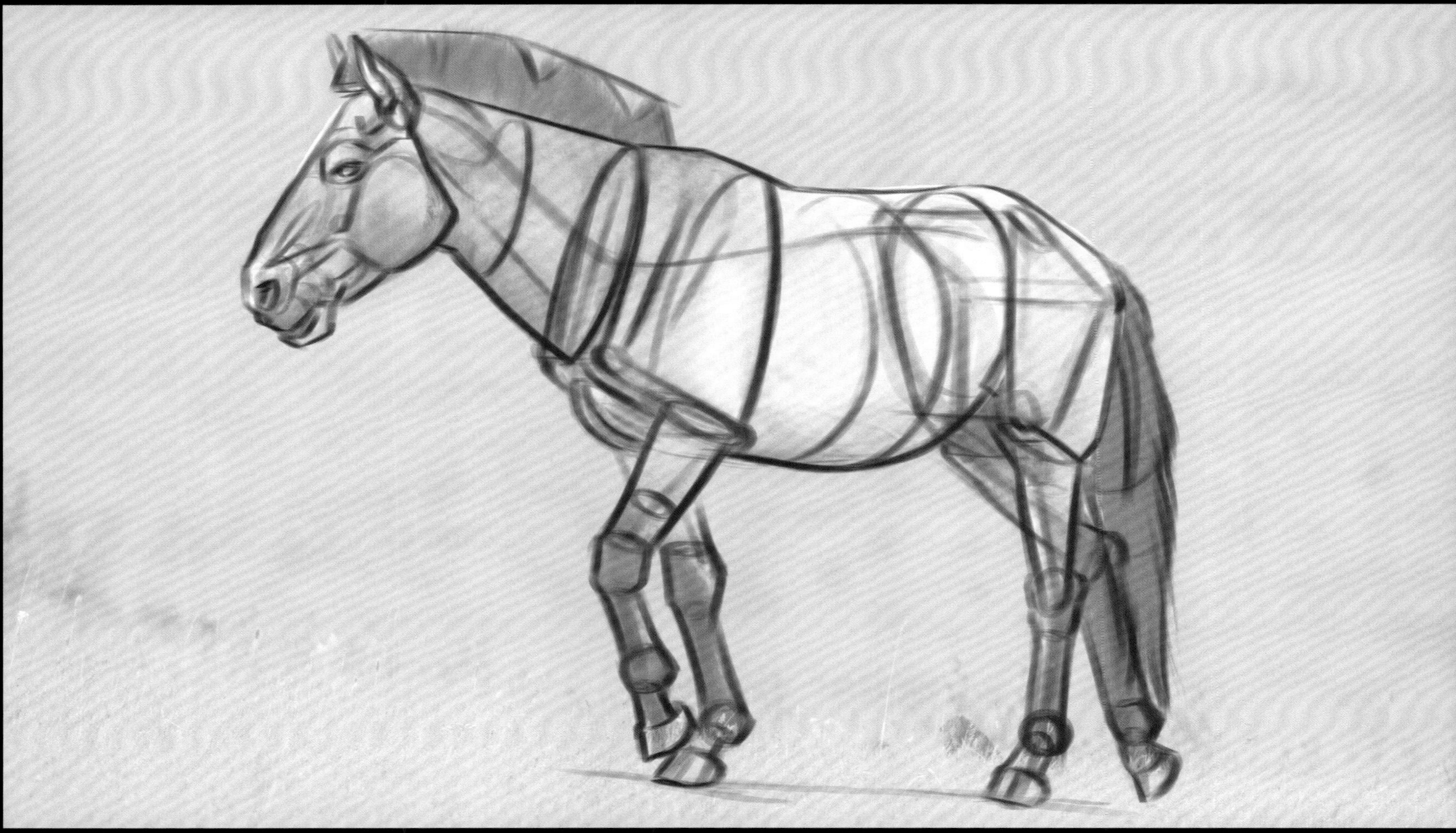

Photograph © James Eaton / Agami.nl

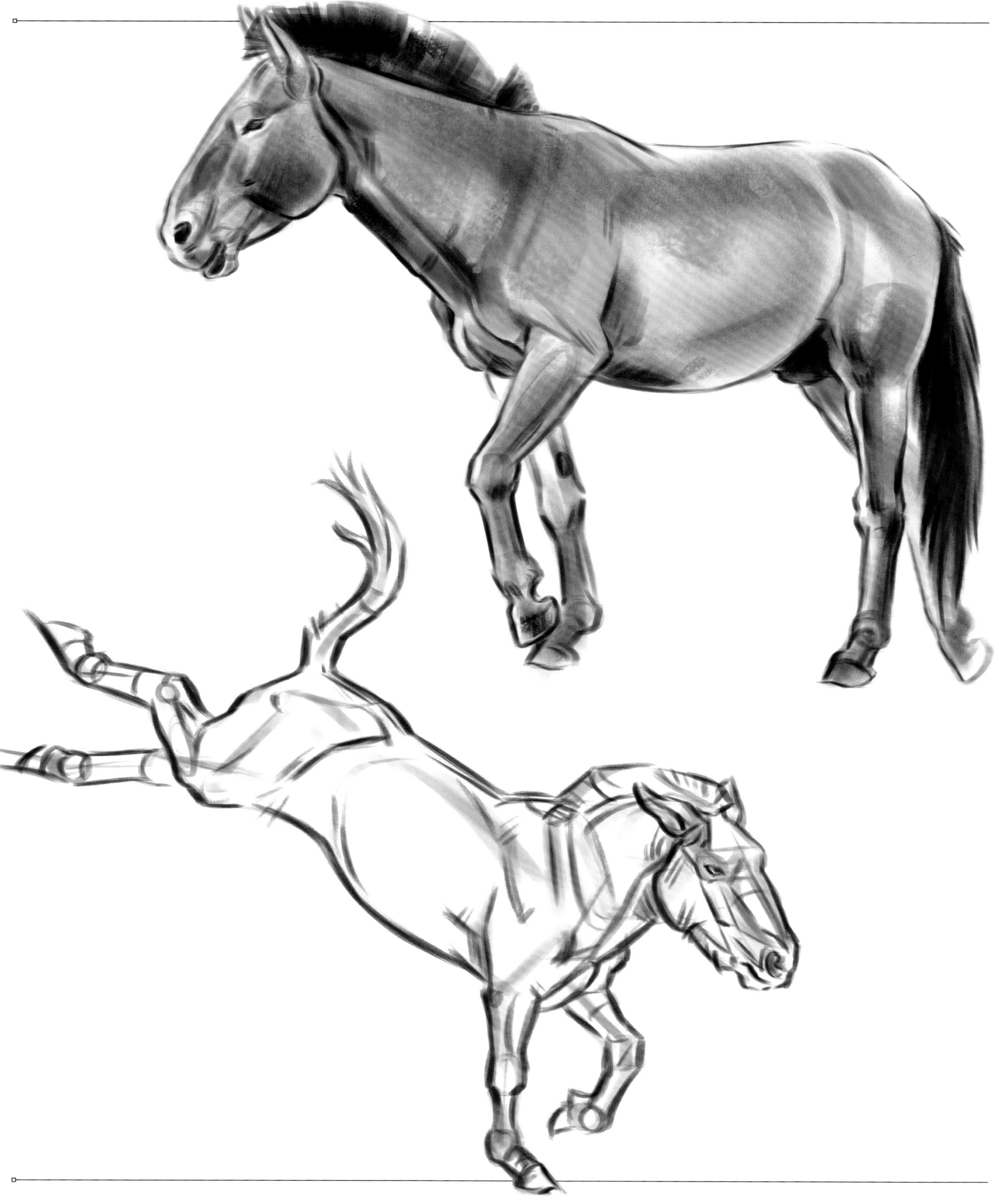

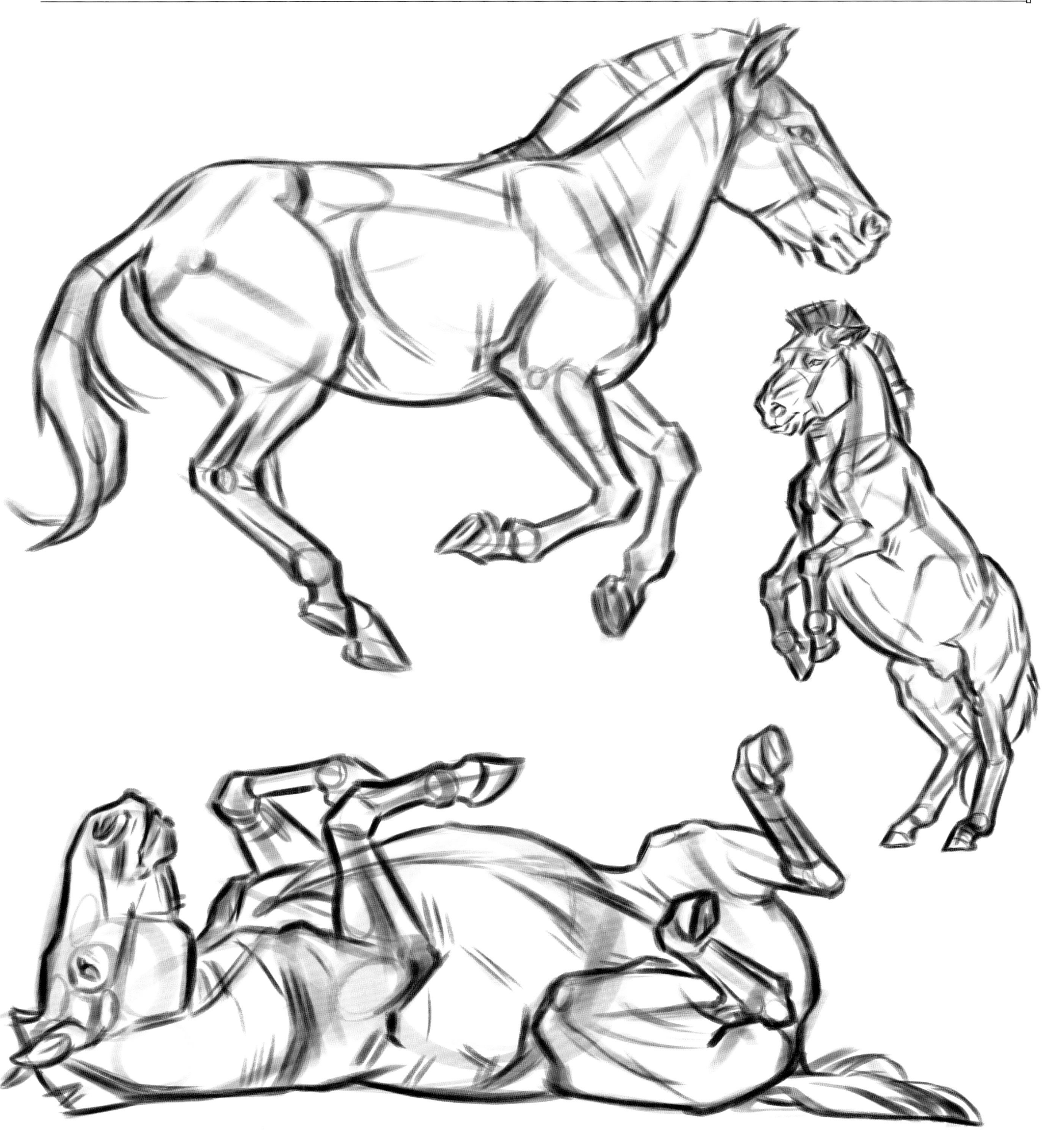

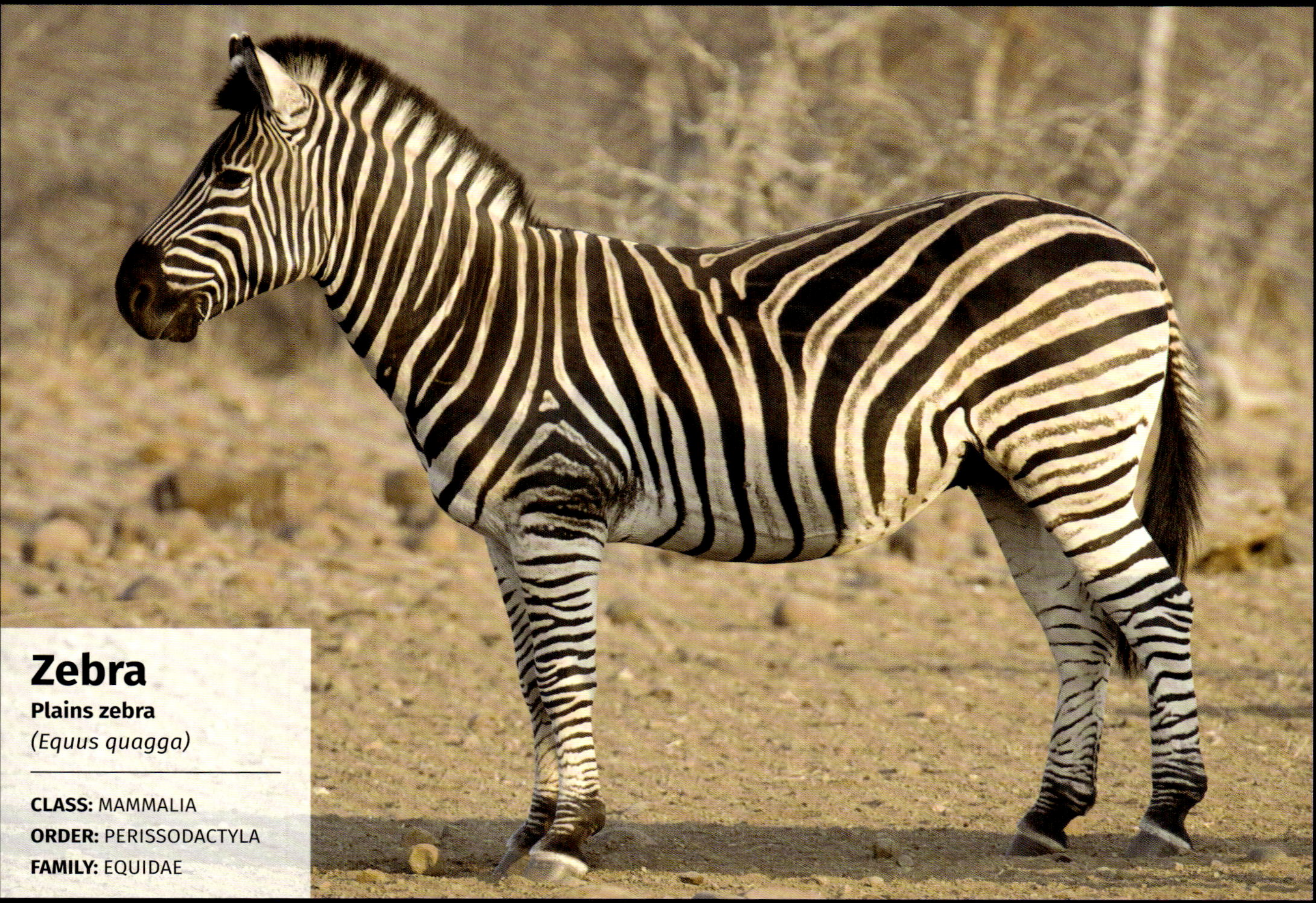

Zebra

Plains zebra

(Equus quagga)

CLASS: MAMMALIA
ORDER: PERISSODACTYLA
FAMILY: EQUIDAE

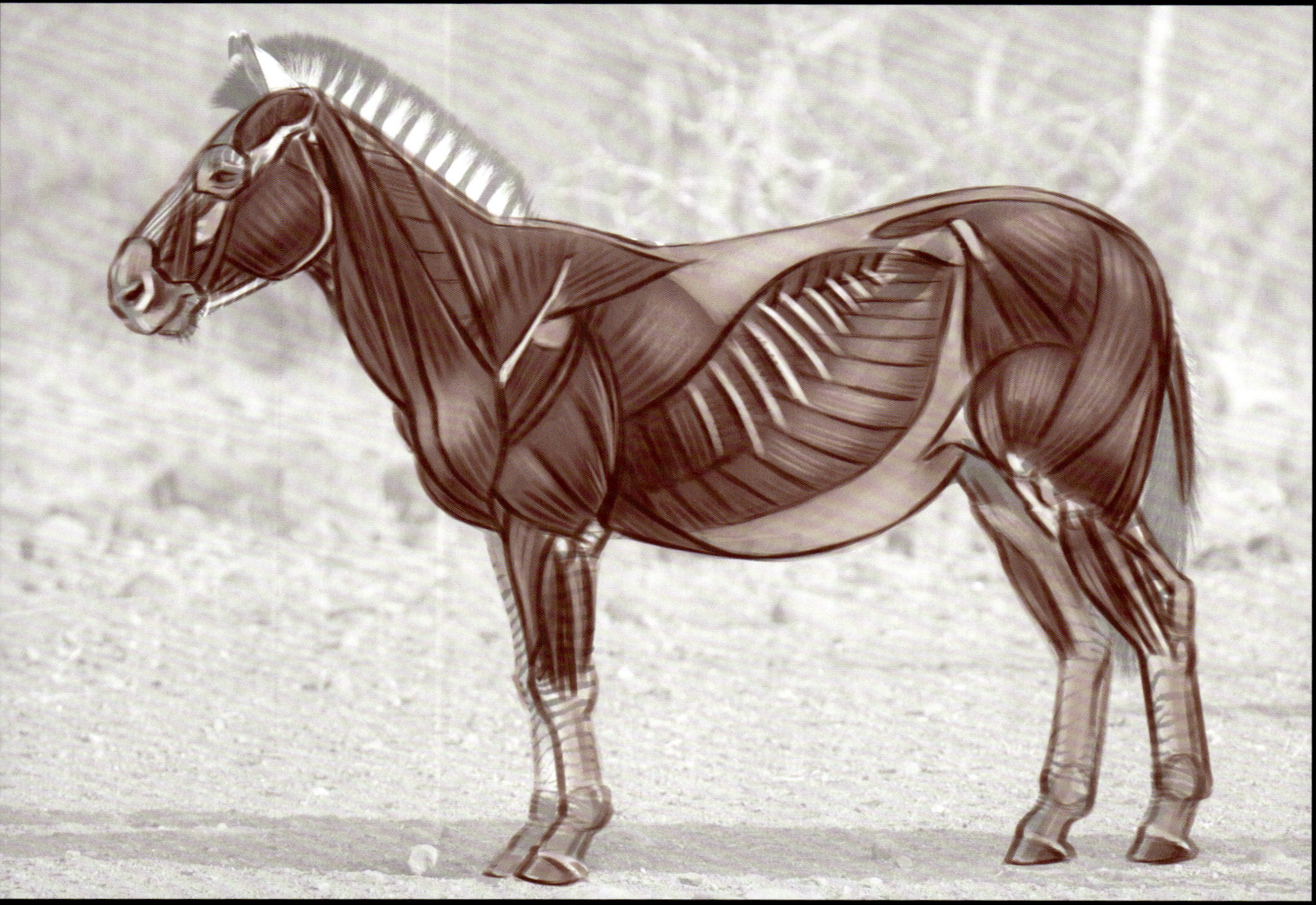

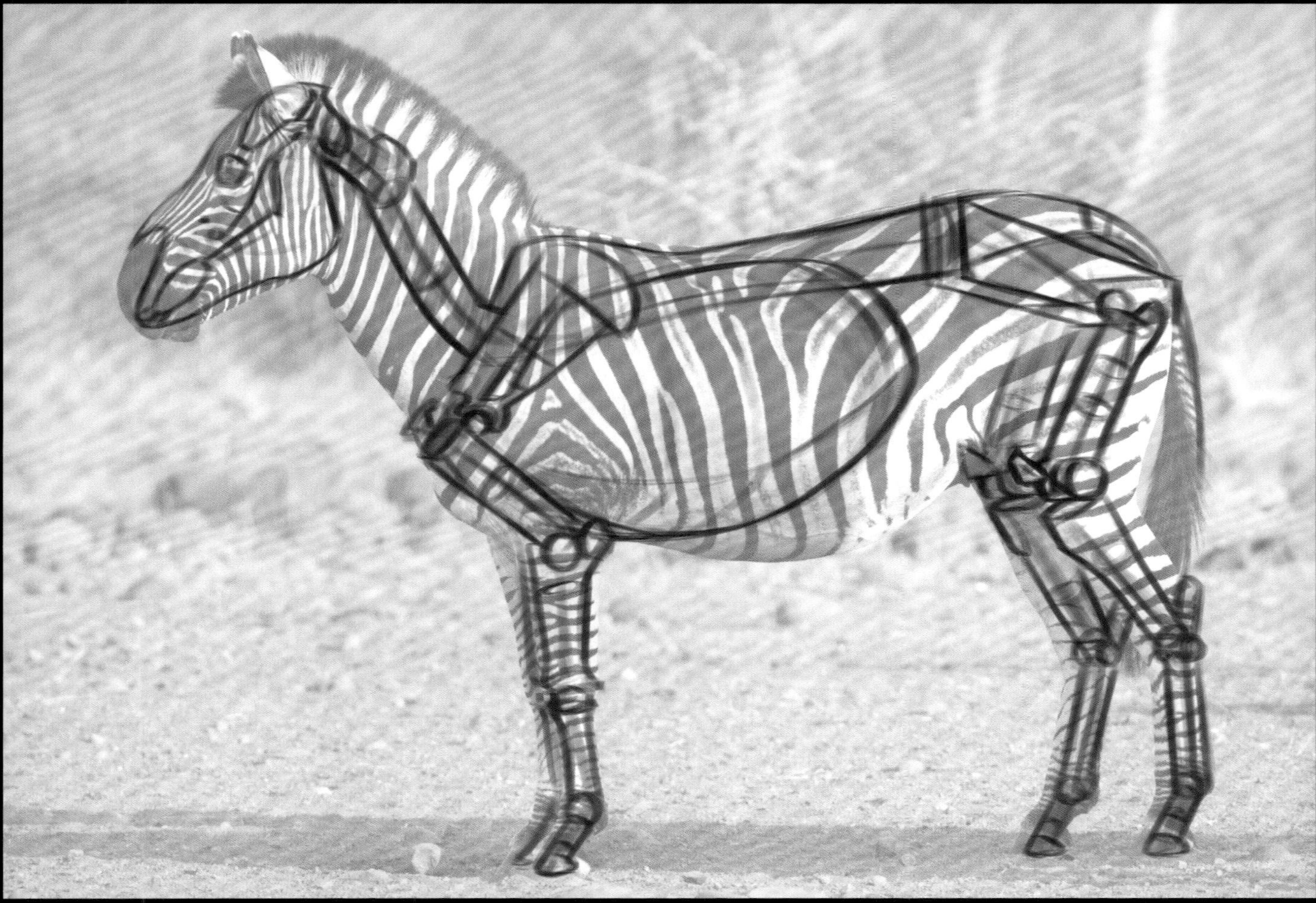

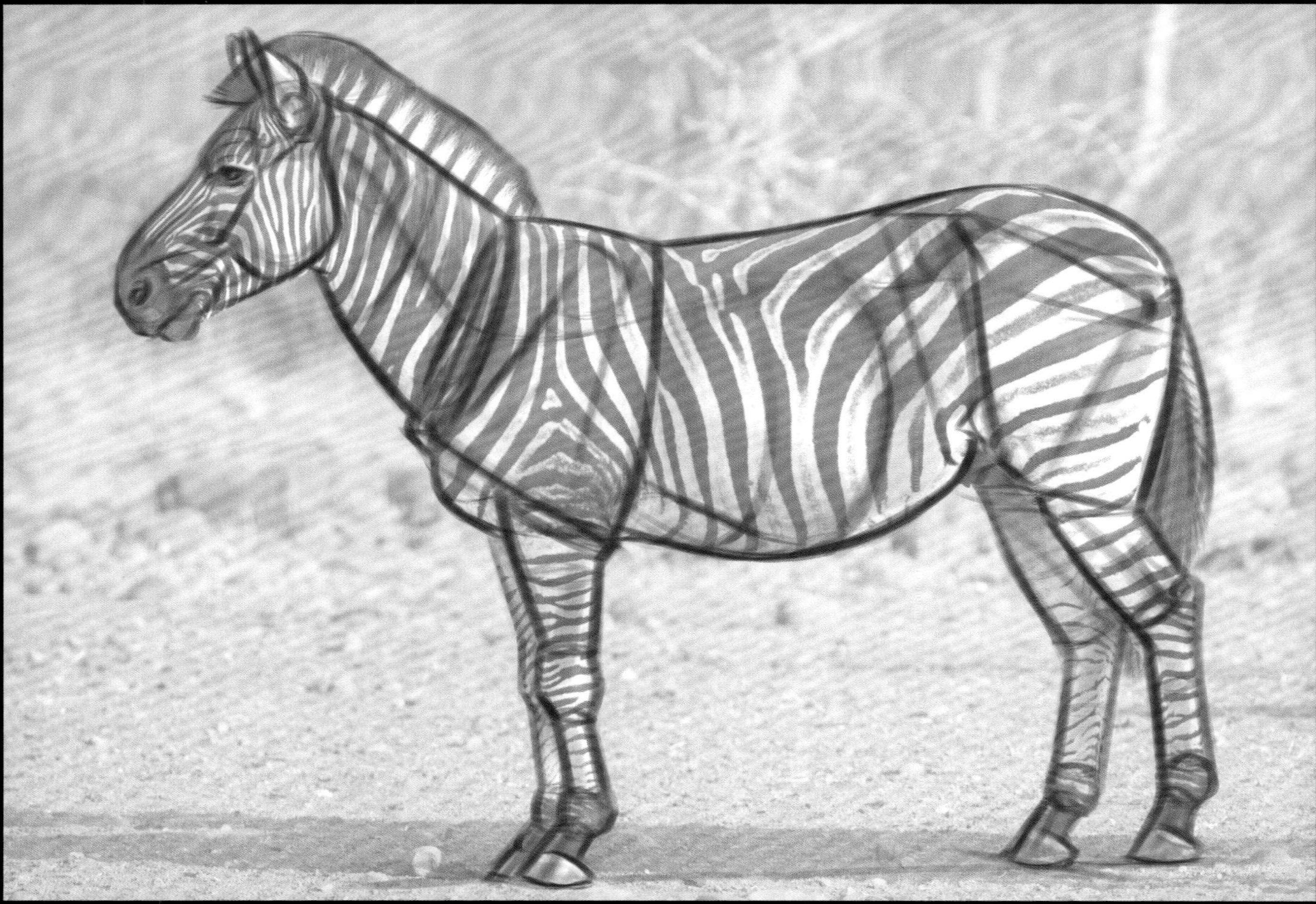

Photograph © Marc Guyt / Agami.nl

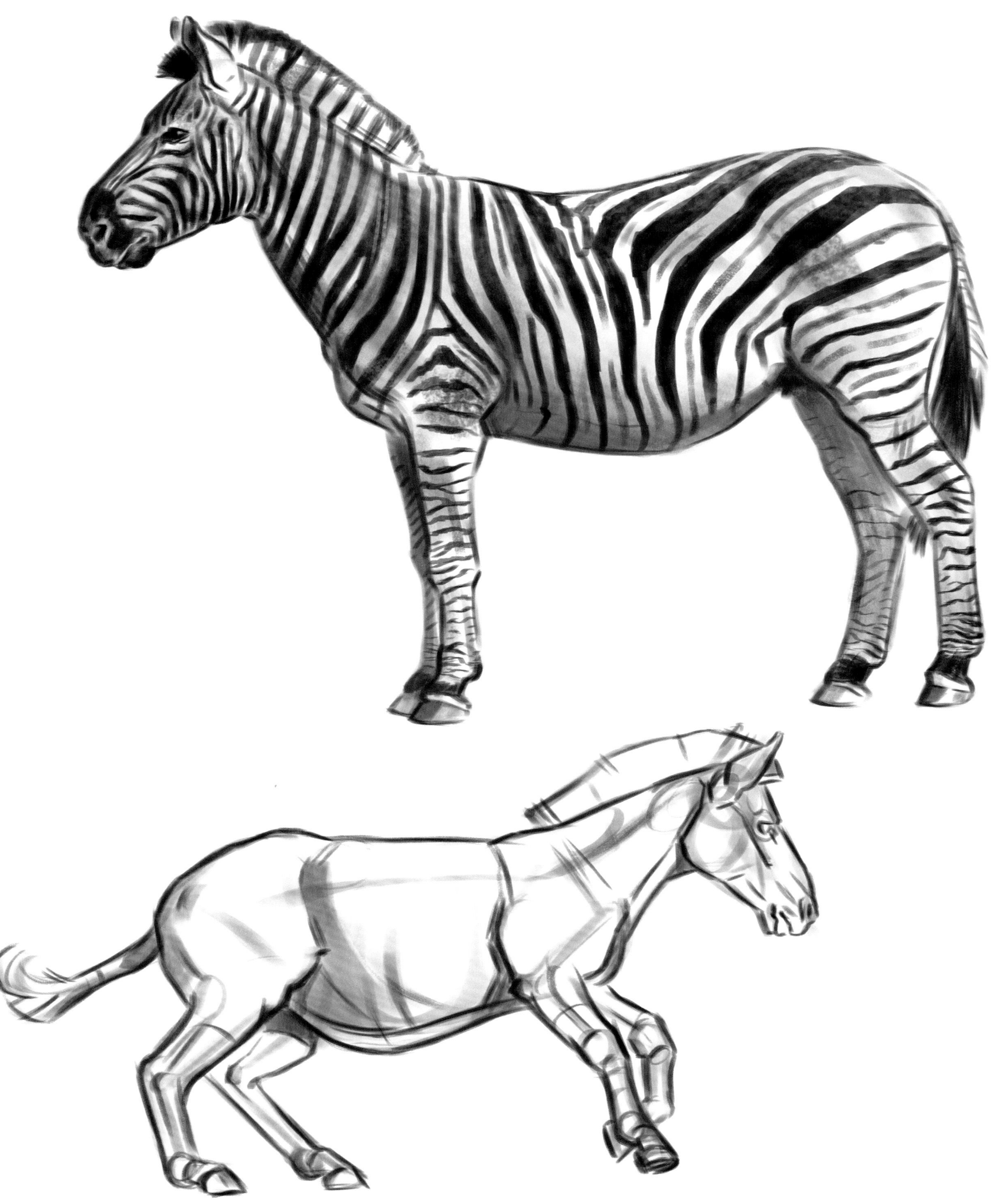

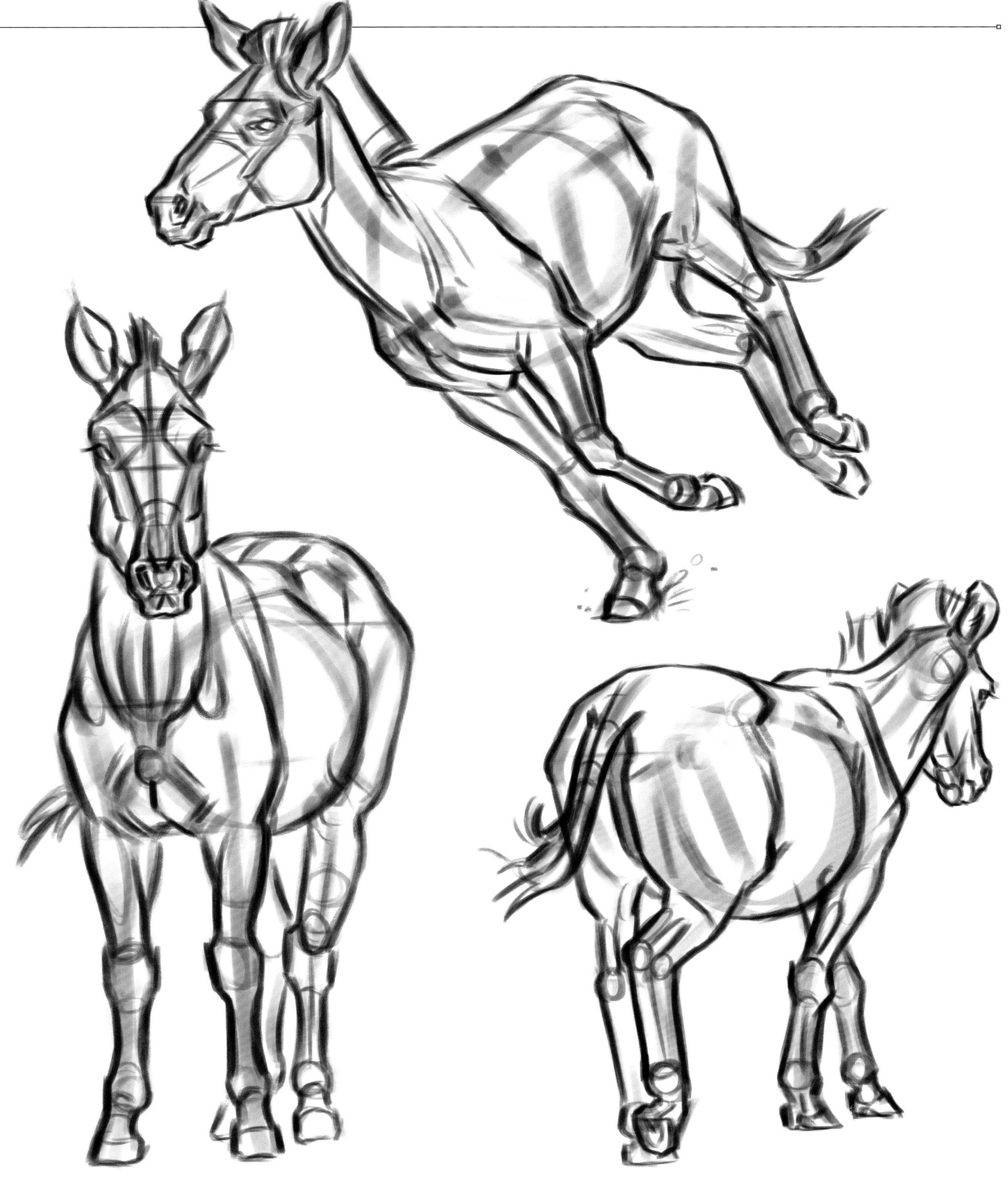

Rhinoceros

Southern white rhinoceros
(Ceratotherium simum)

CLASS: MAMMALIA
ORDER: PERISSODACTYLA
FAMILY: RHINOCEROTIDAE

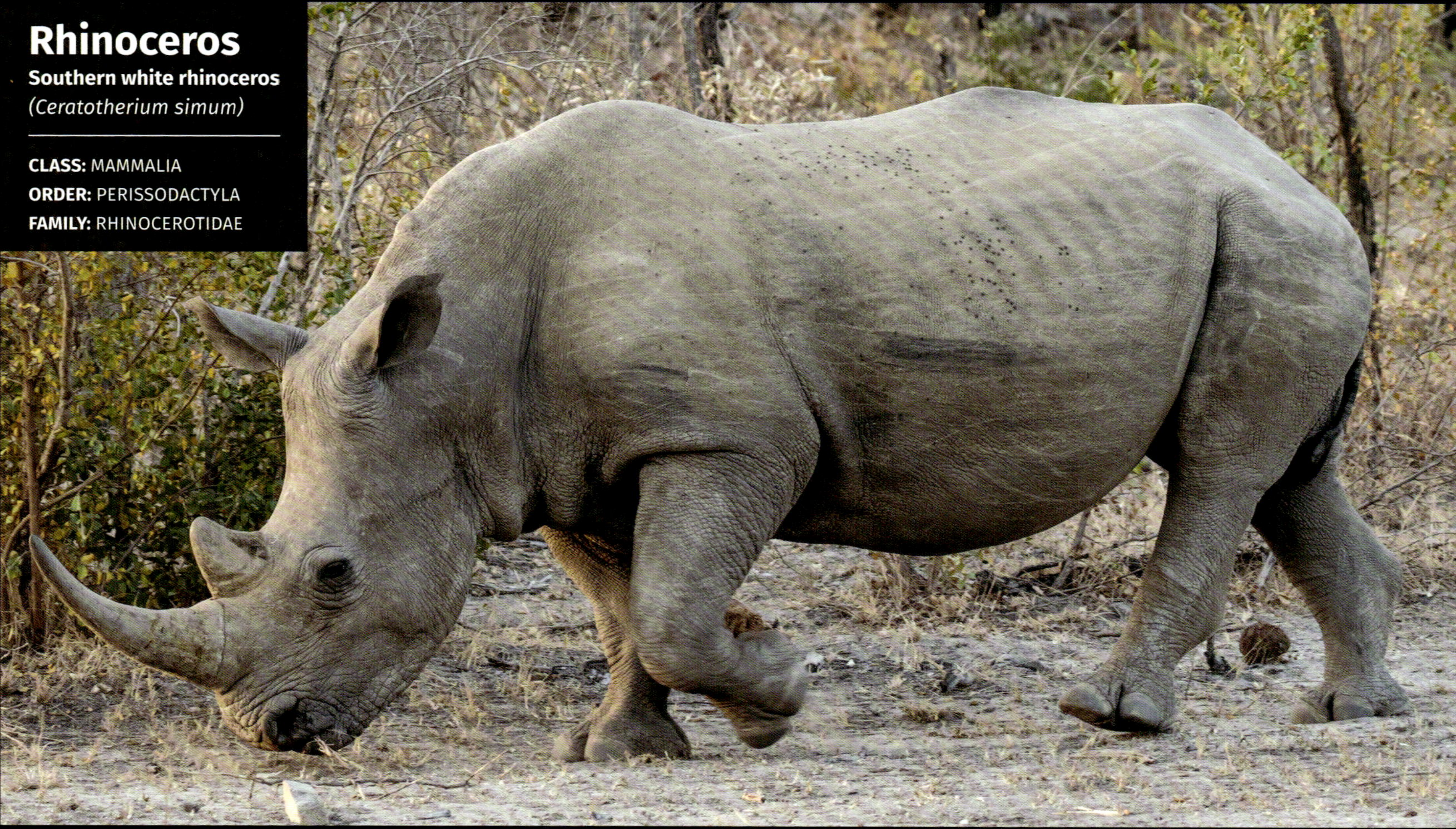

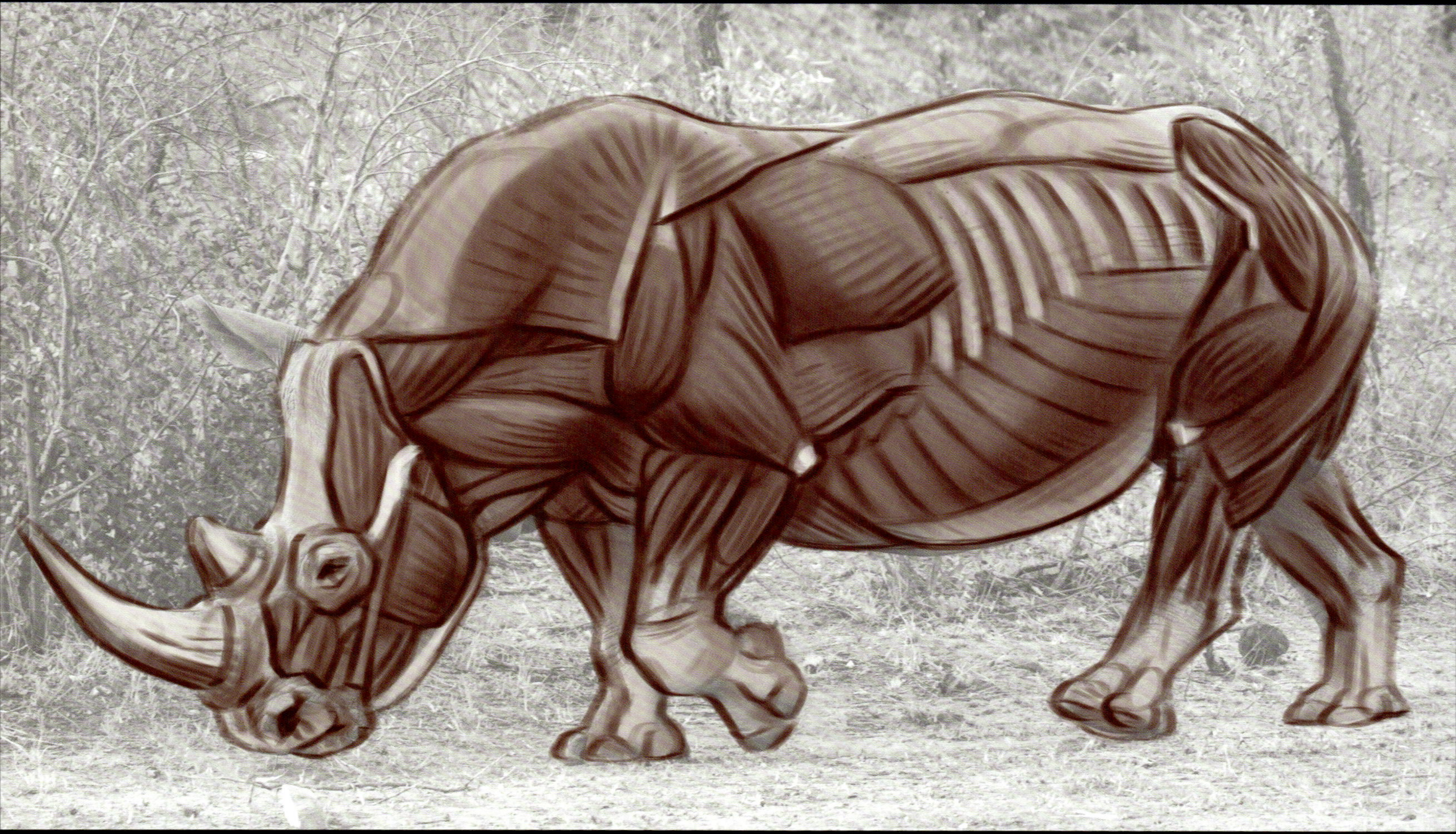

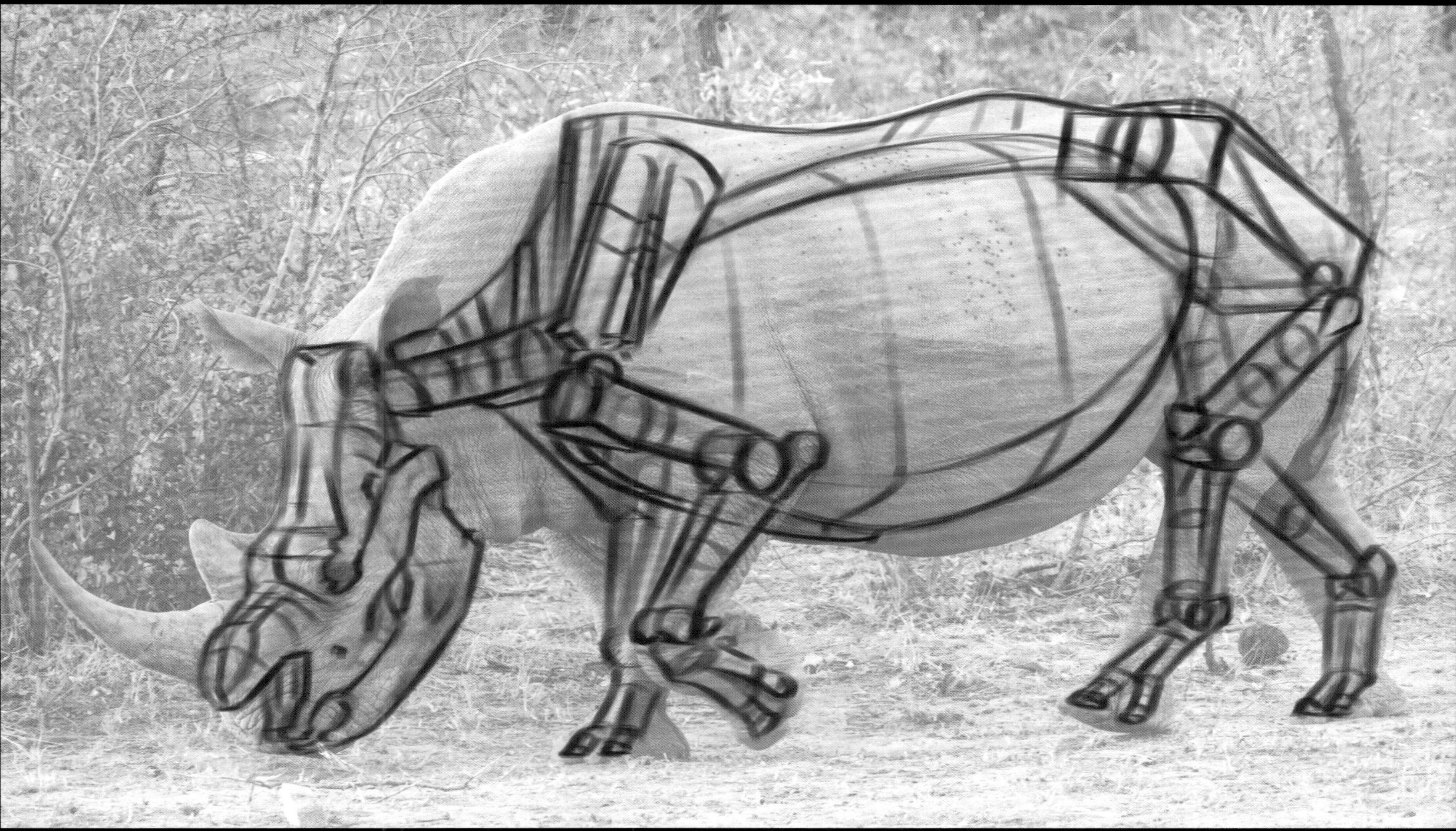

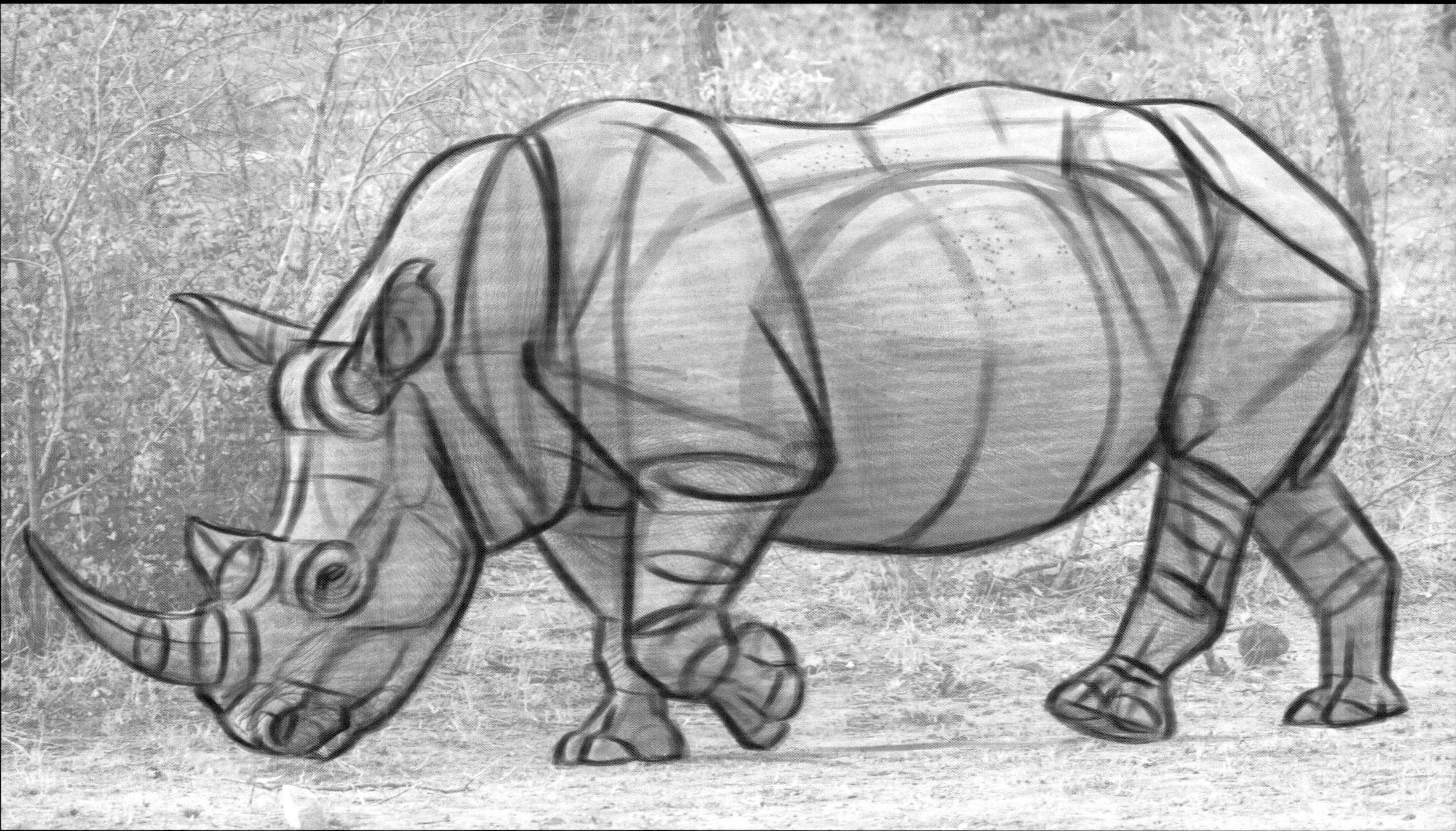

Photograph © Pete Morris / Agami.nl

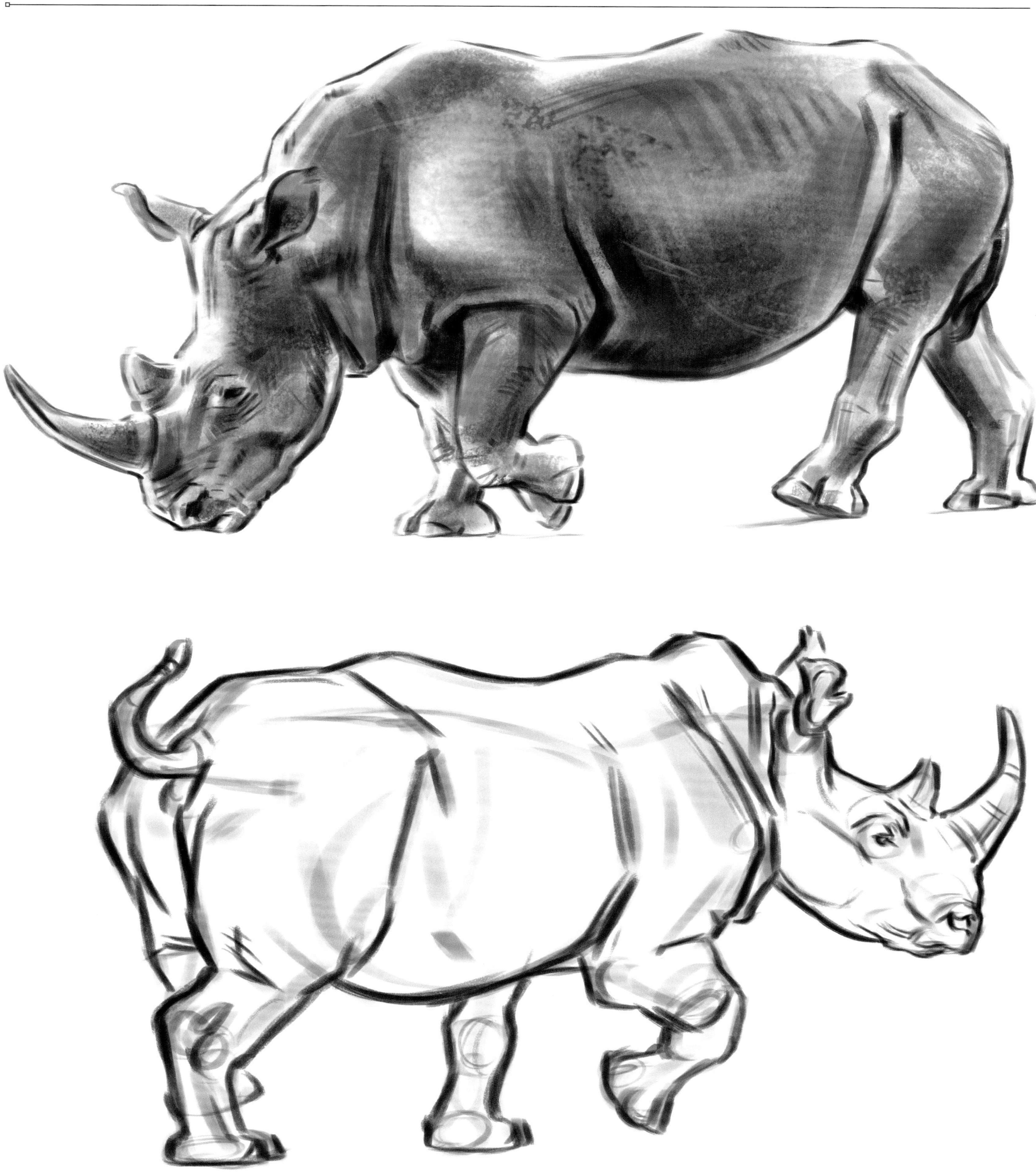

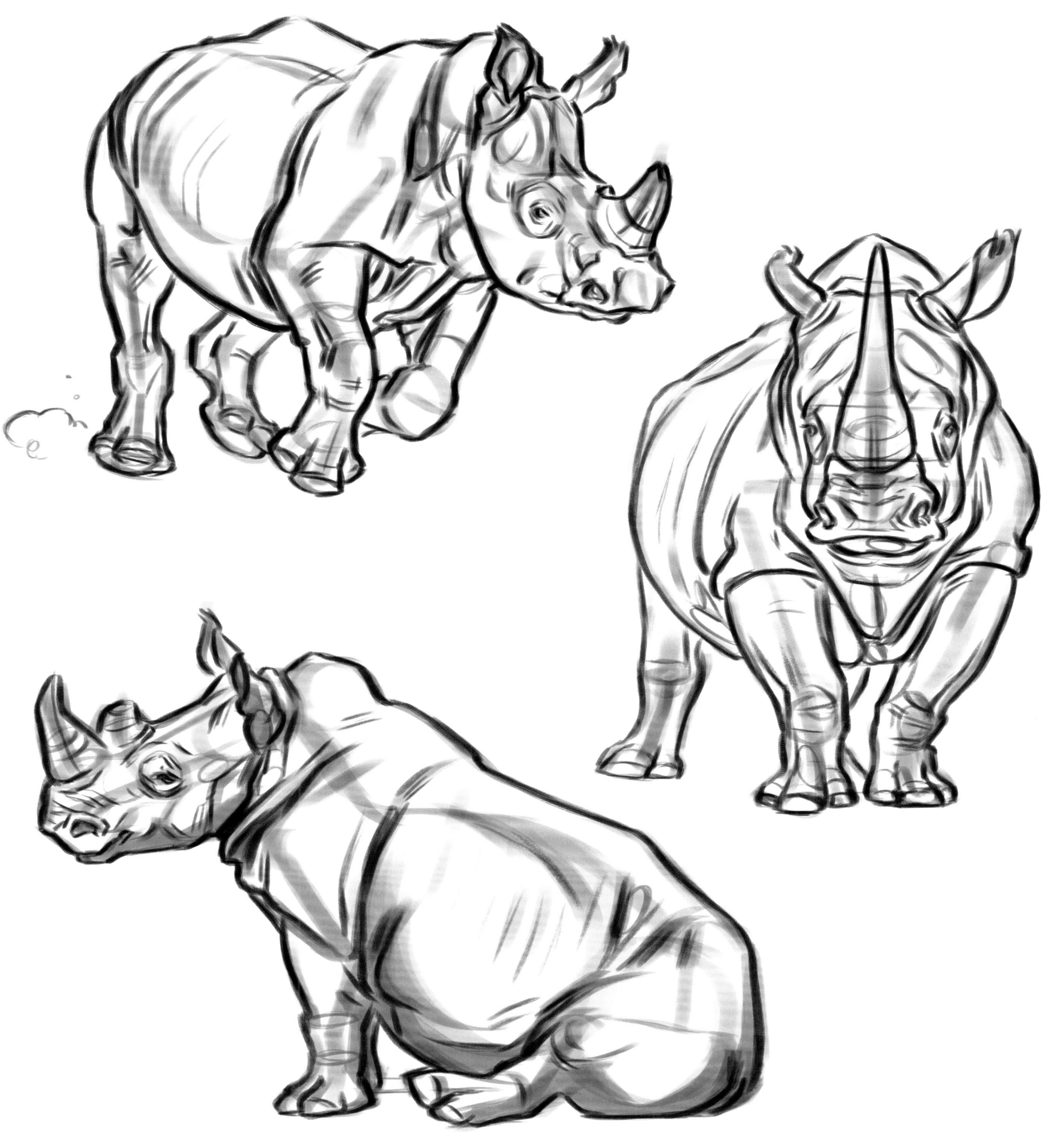

Tapir

South American tapir
(Tapirus terrestris)

CLASS: MAMMALIA
ORDER: PERISSODACTYLA
FAMILY: TAPIRIDAE

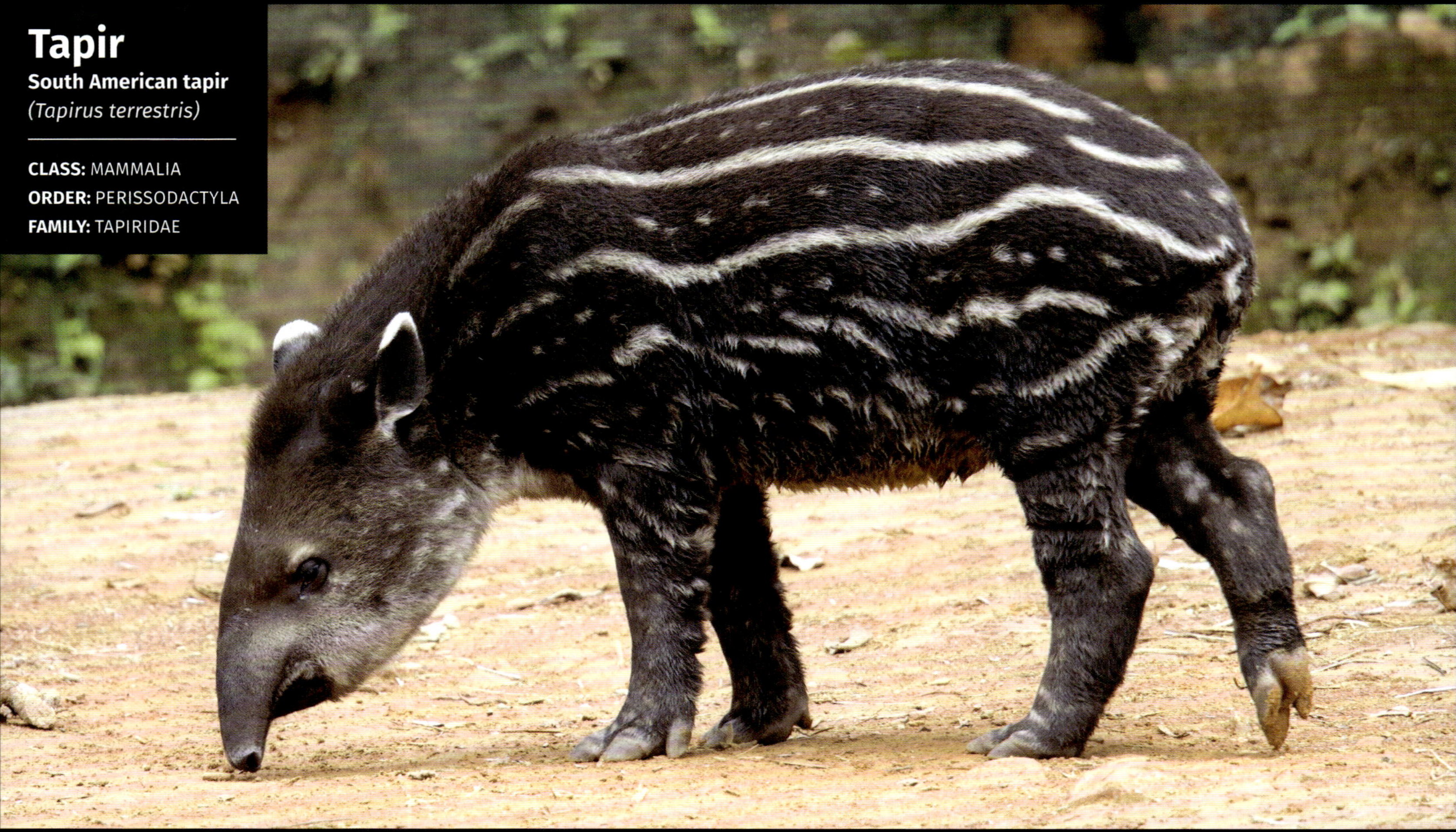

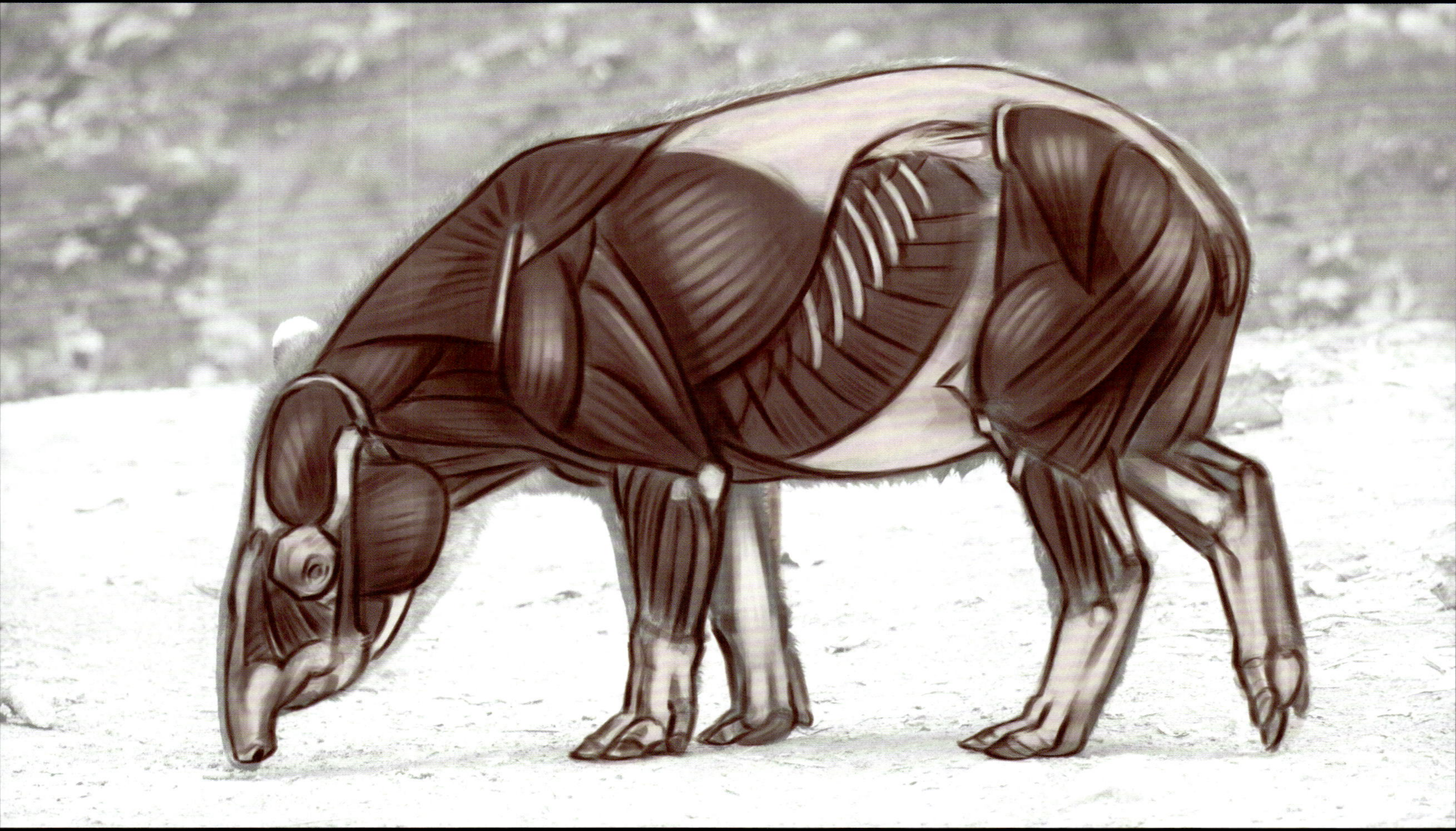

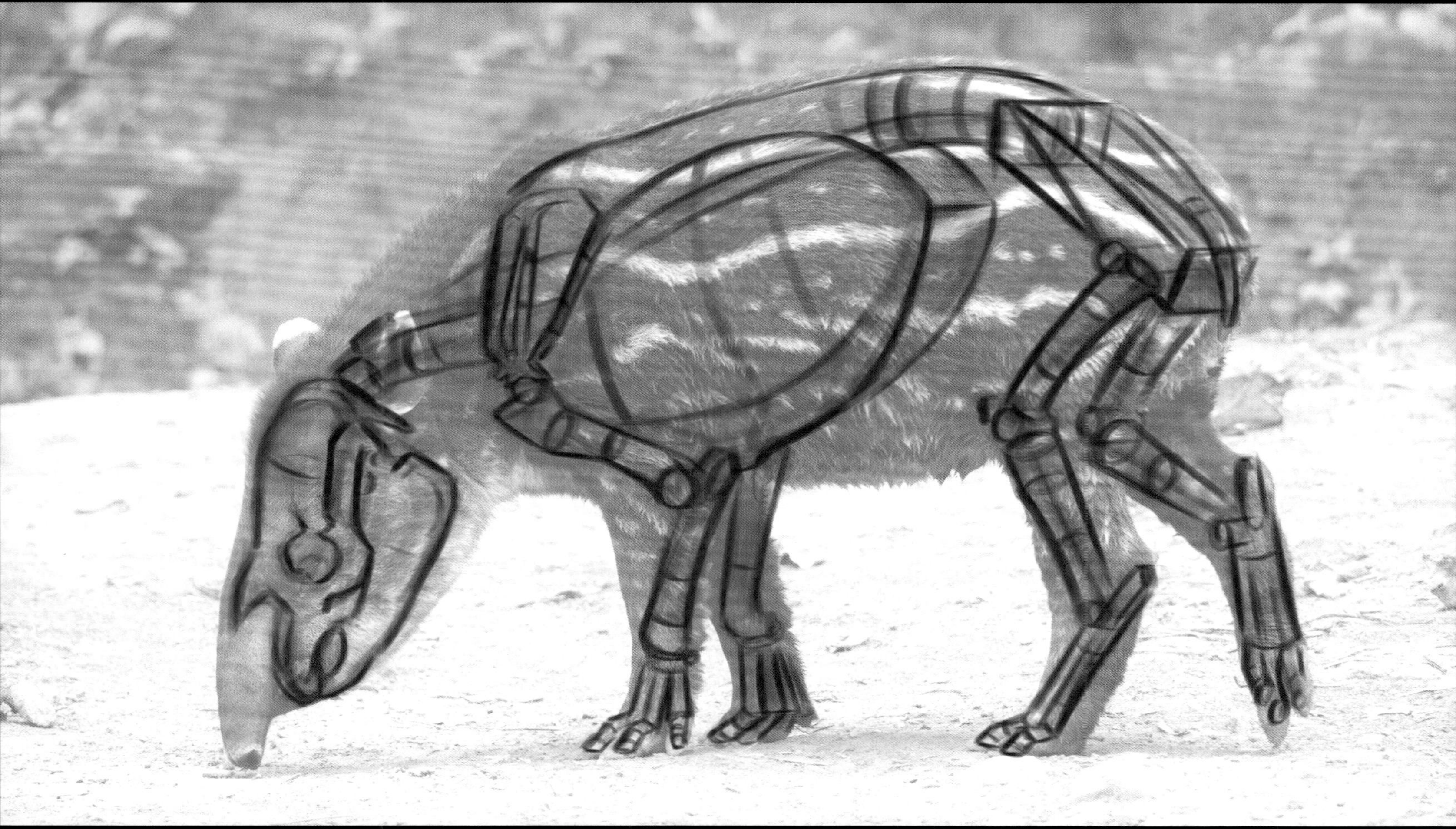

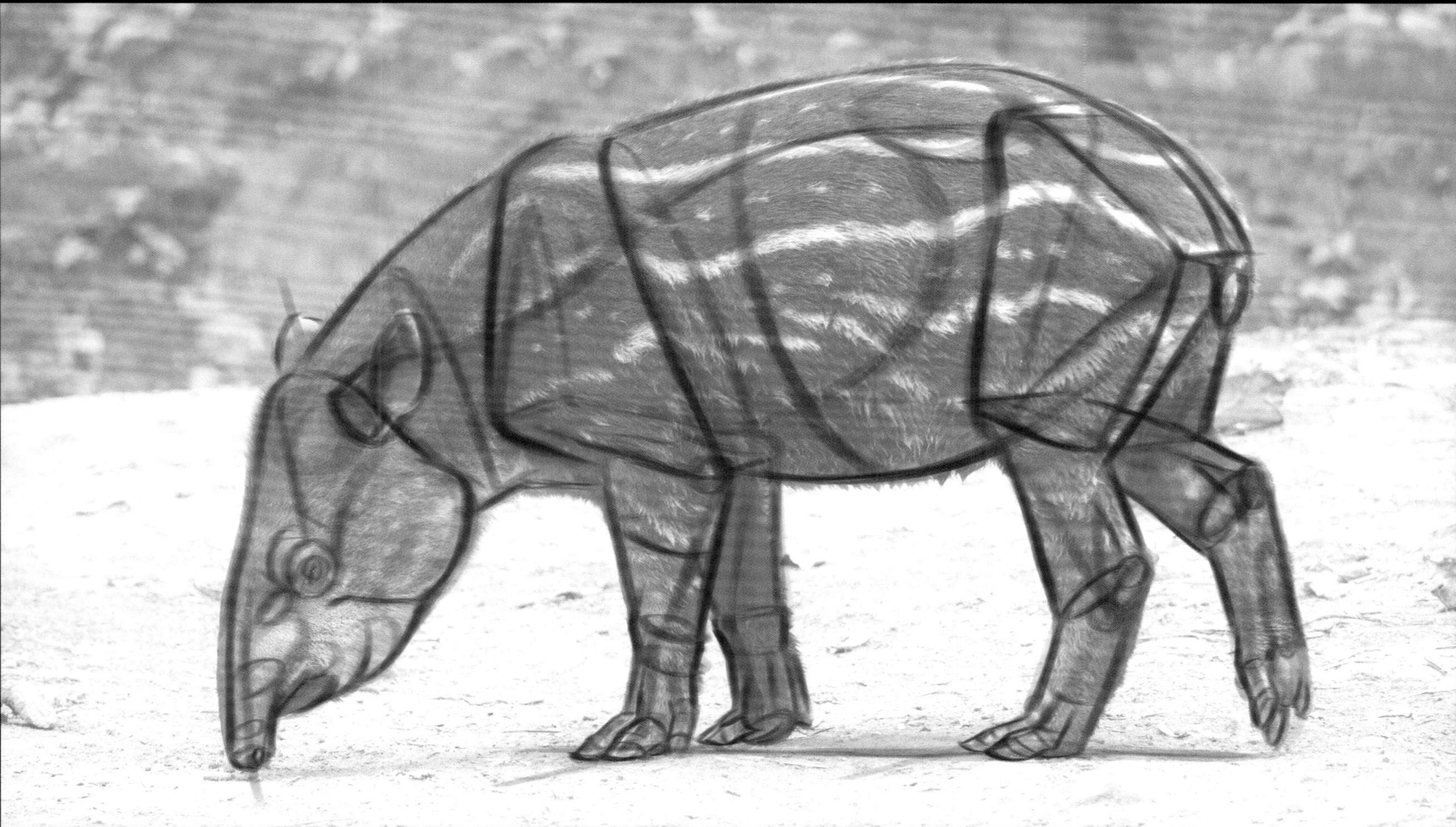

Photograph © Tom Friedel / Agami.nl

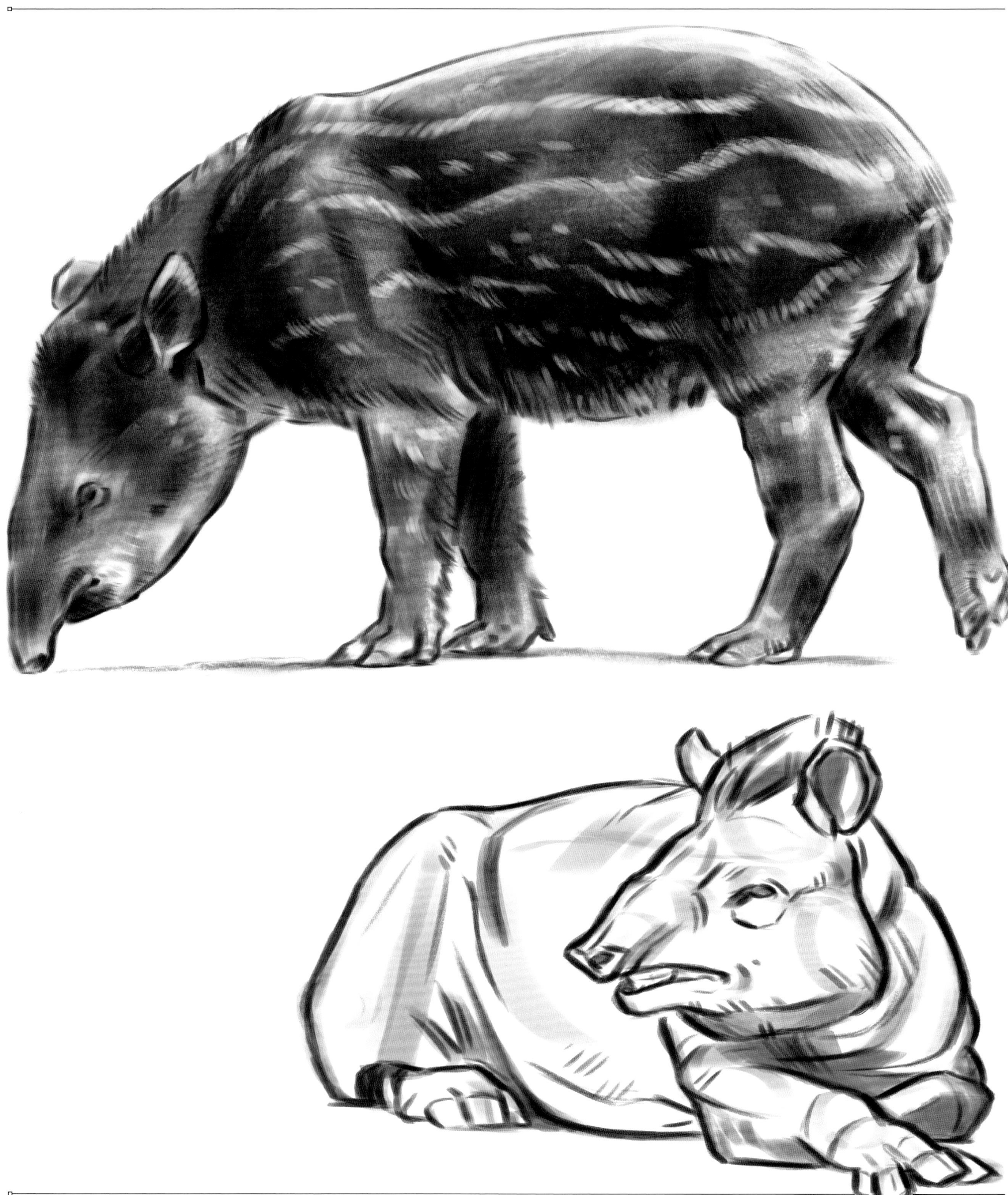

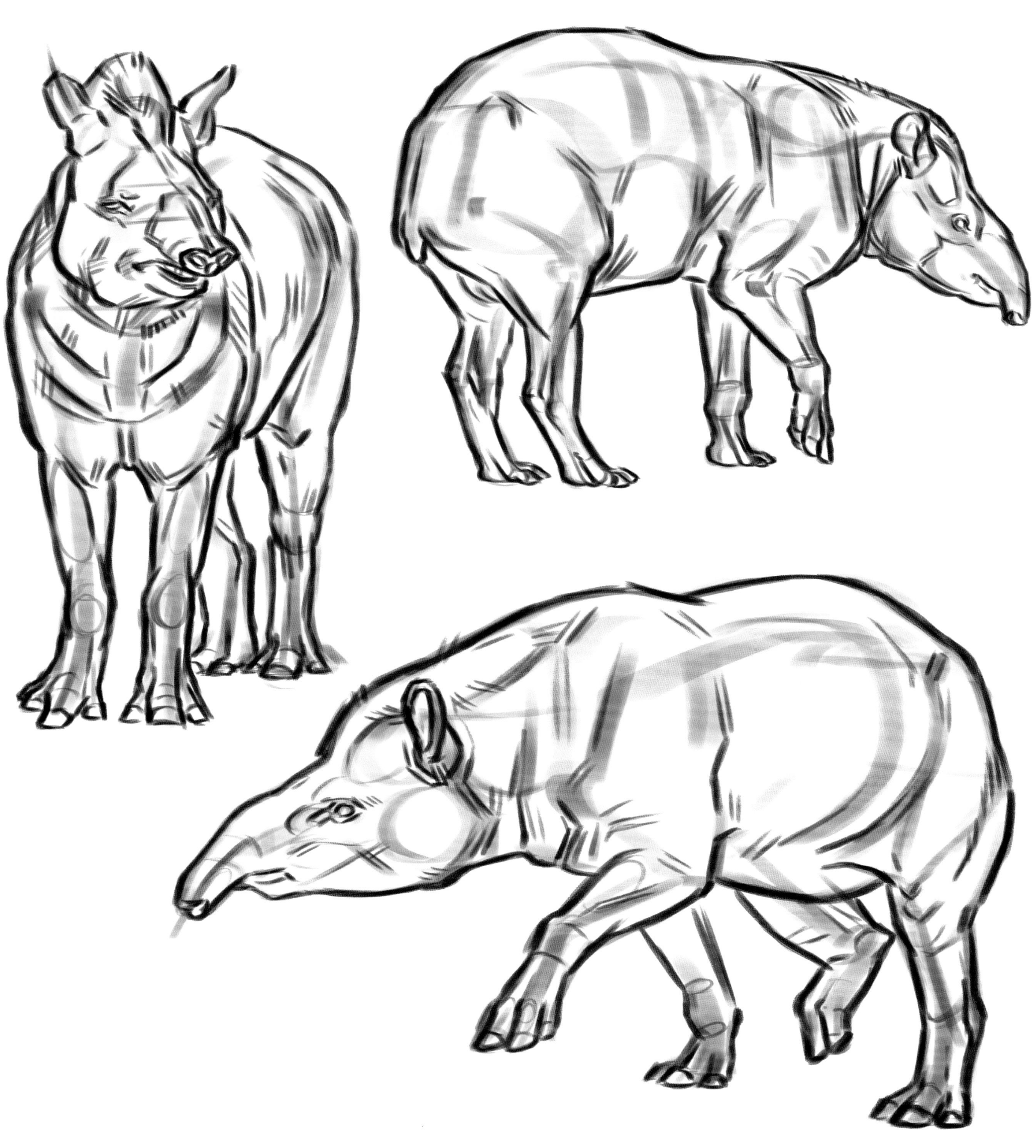

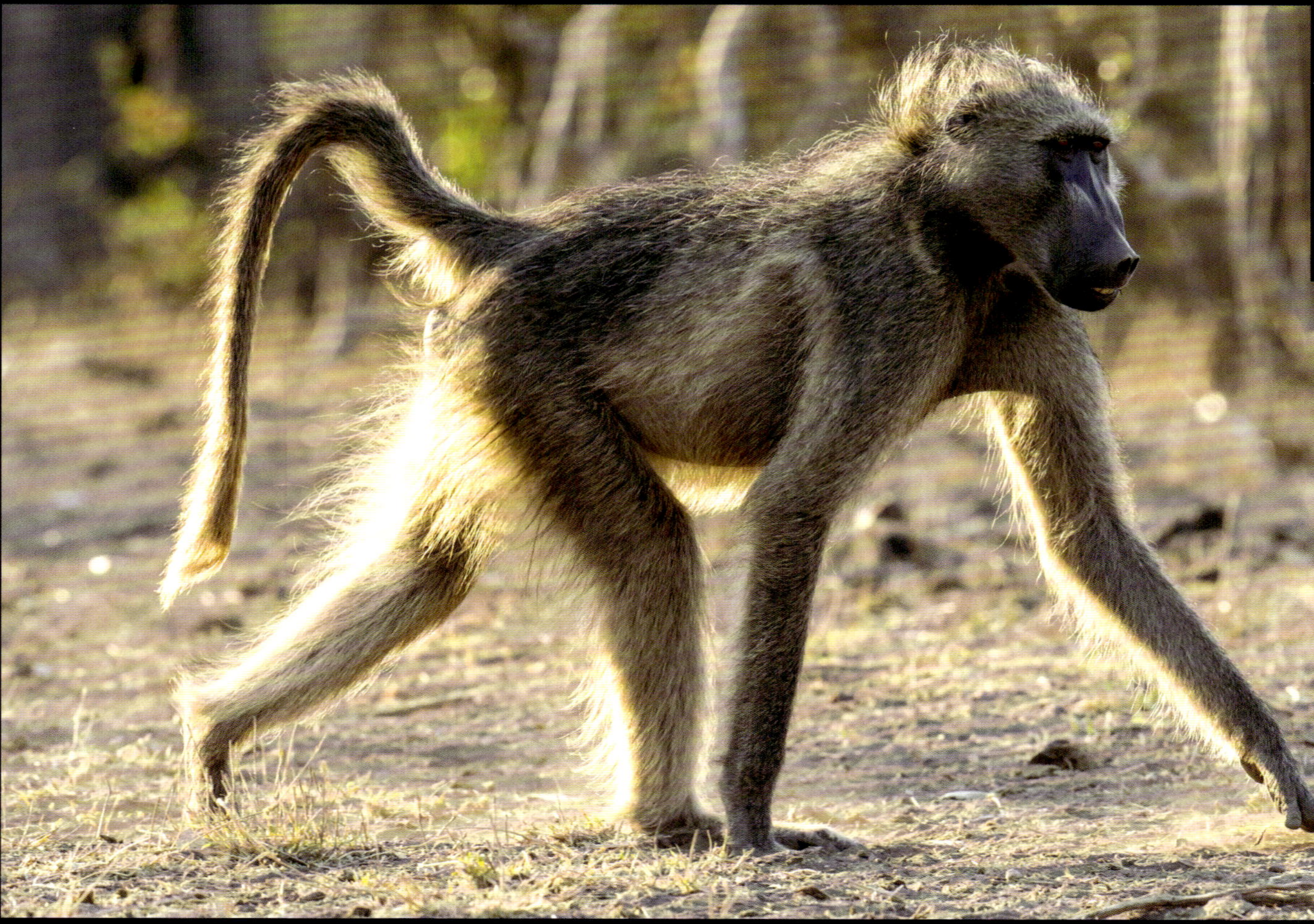

Baboon

Cape baboon
(Papio ursinus)

CLASS: MAMMALIA
ORDER: PRIMATES
FAMILY: CERCOPITHECIDAE

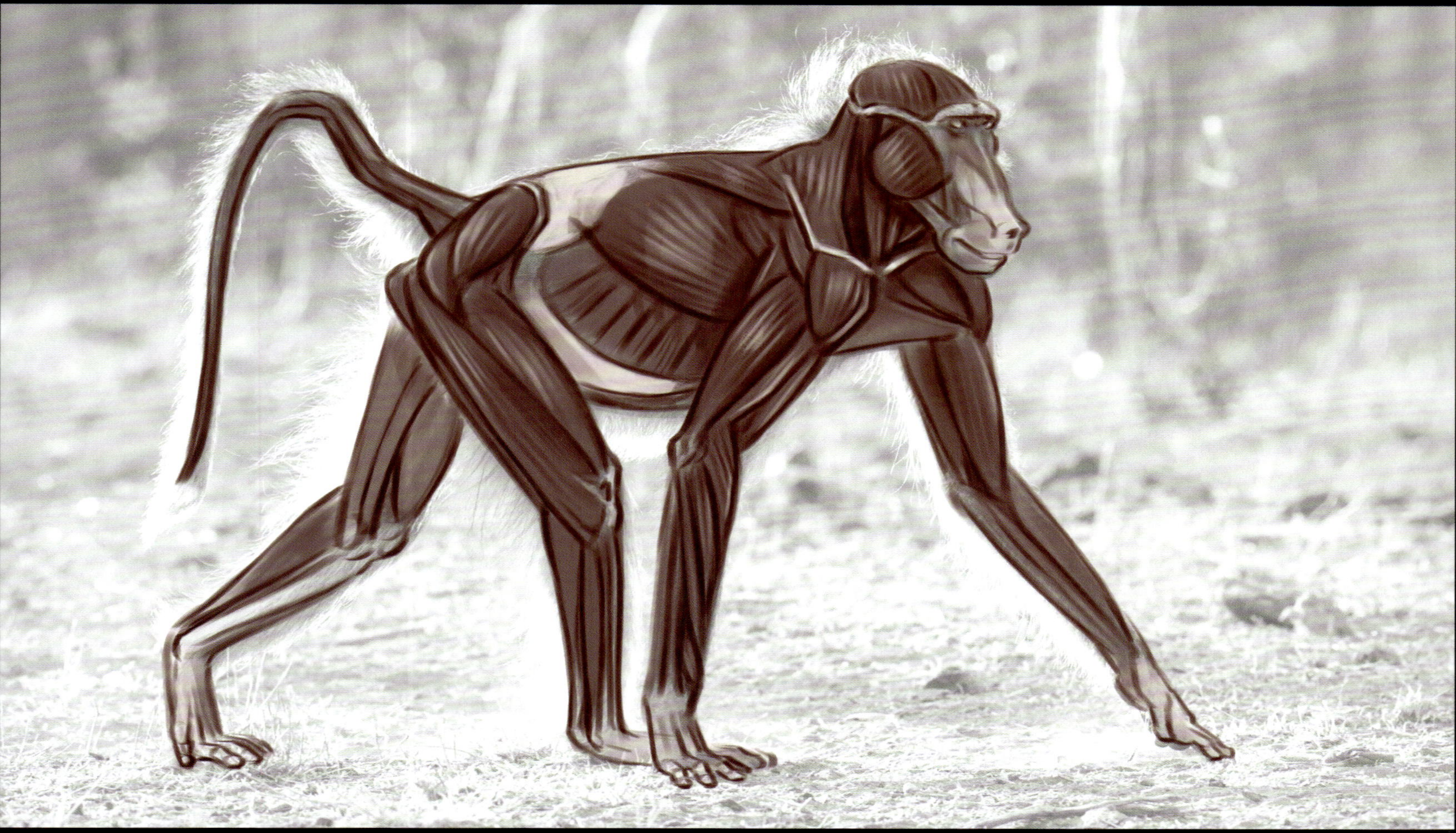

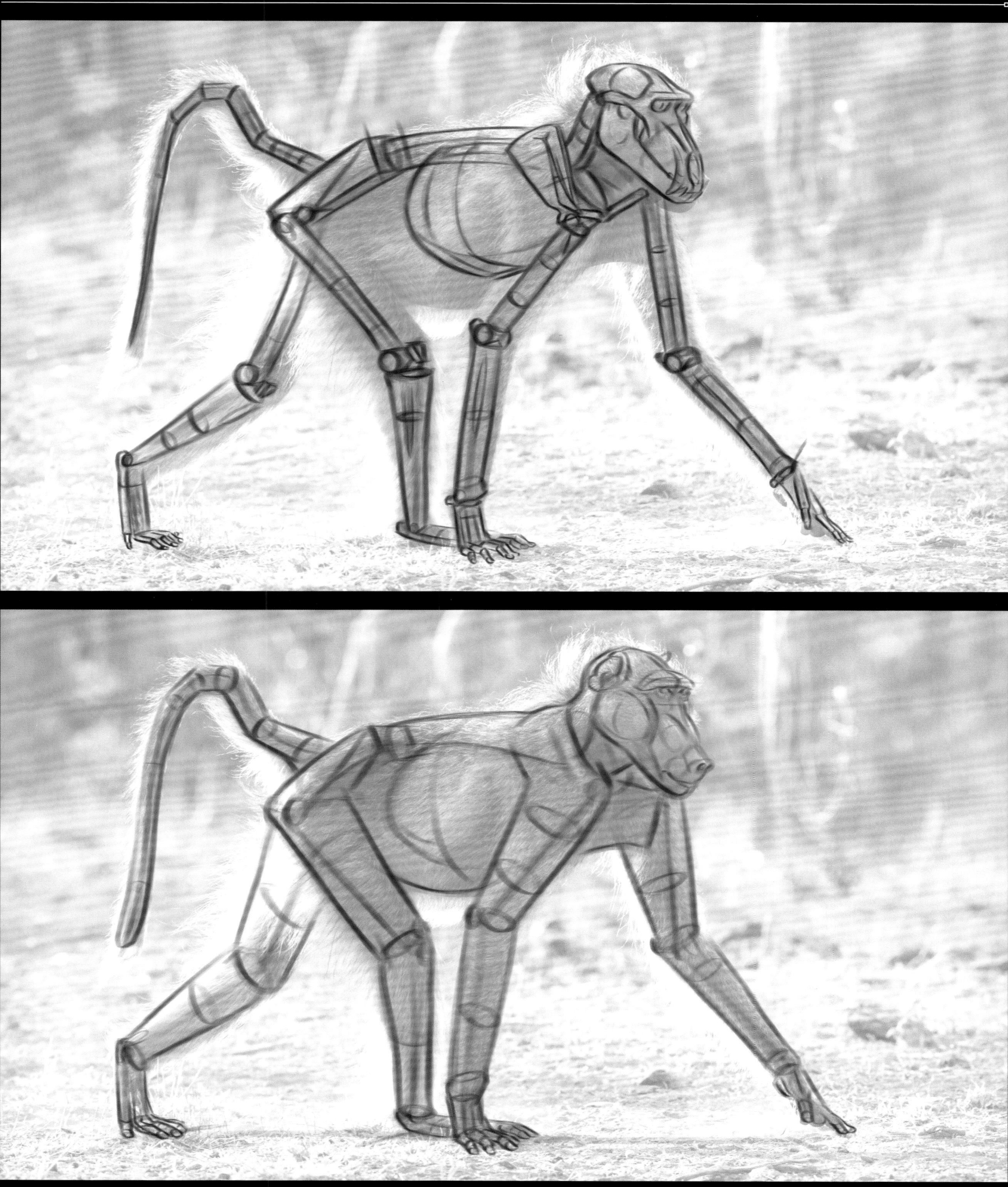

Photograph © Saverio Gatto/ Agami.nl

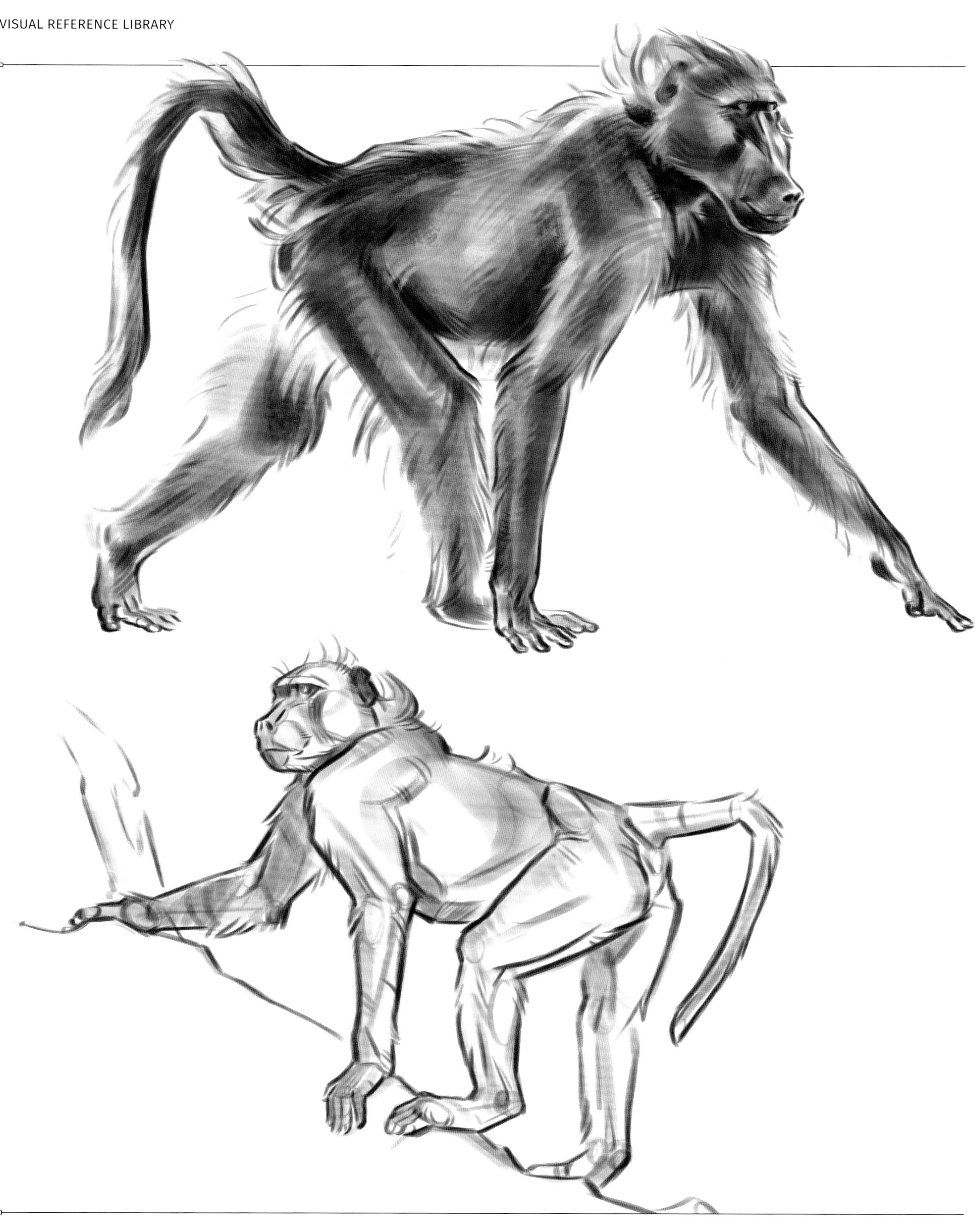

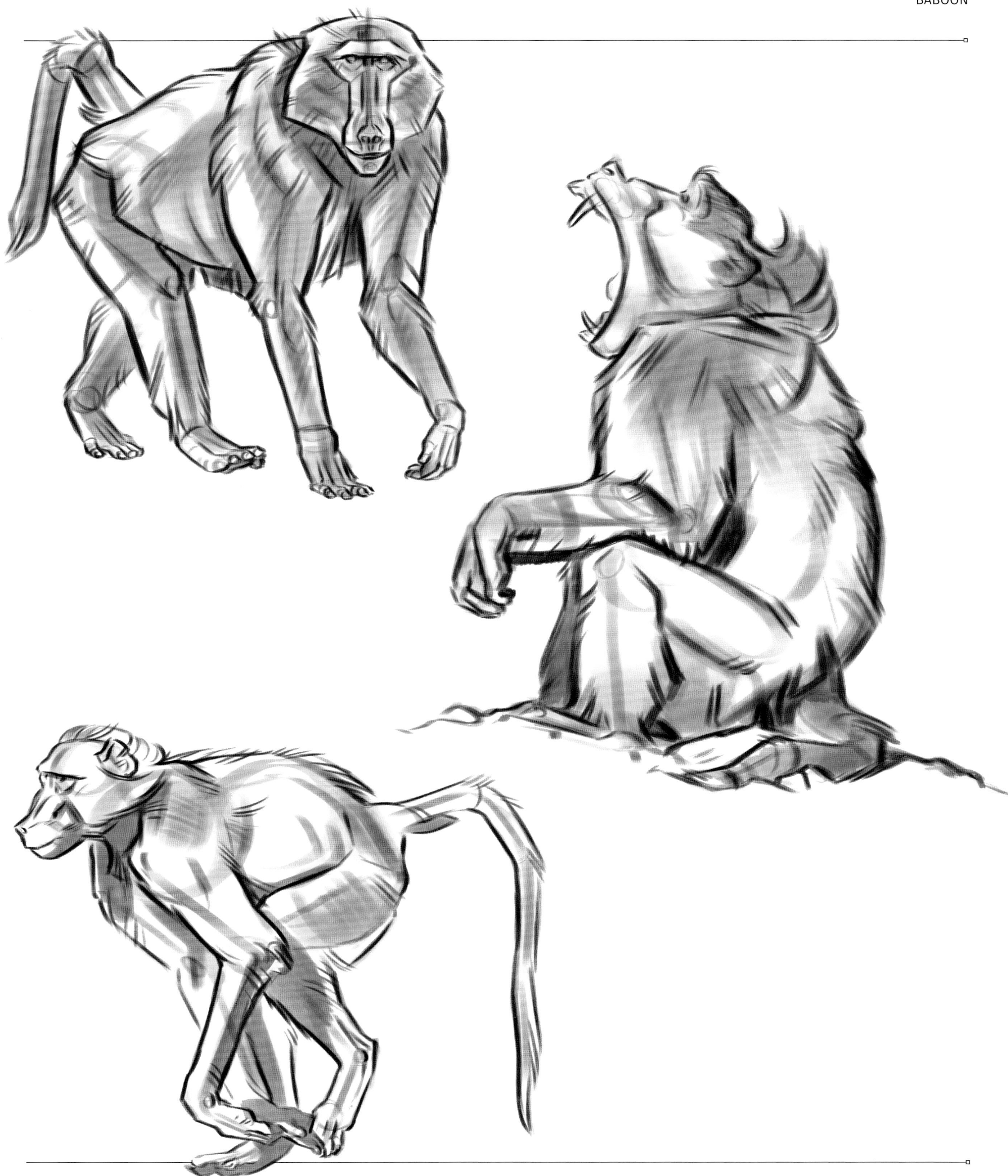

Rhesus macaque

Rhesus macaque *(Macaca mulatta)*

CLASS: MAMMALIA
ORDER: PRIMATES
FAMILY: CERCOPITHECIDAE

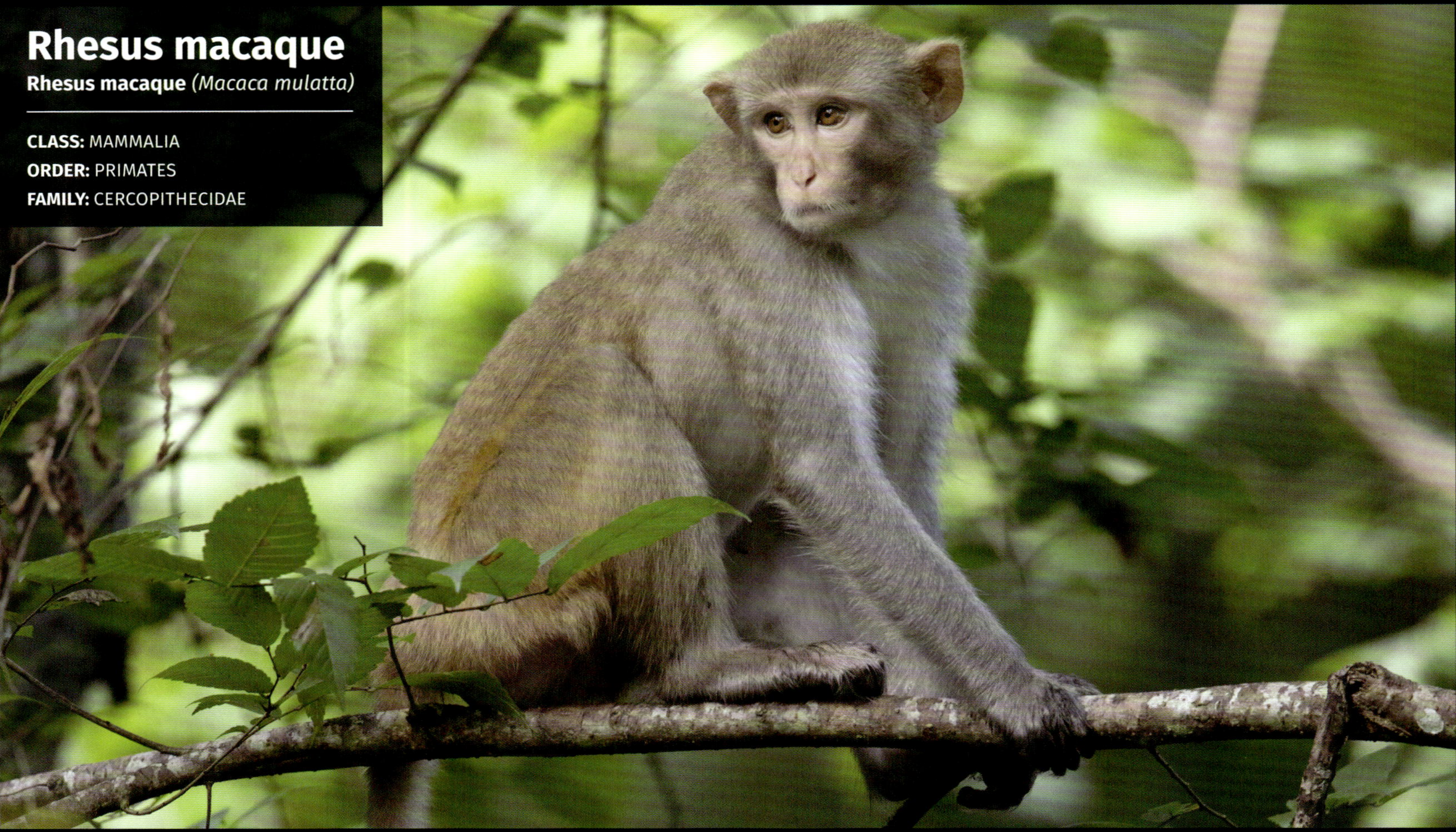

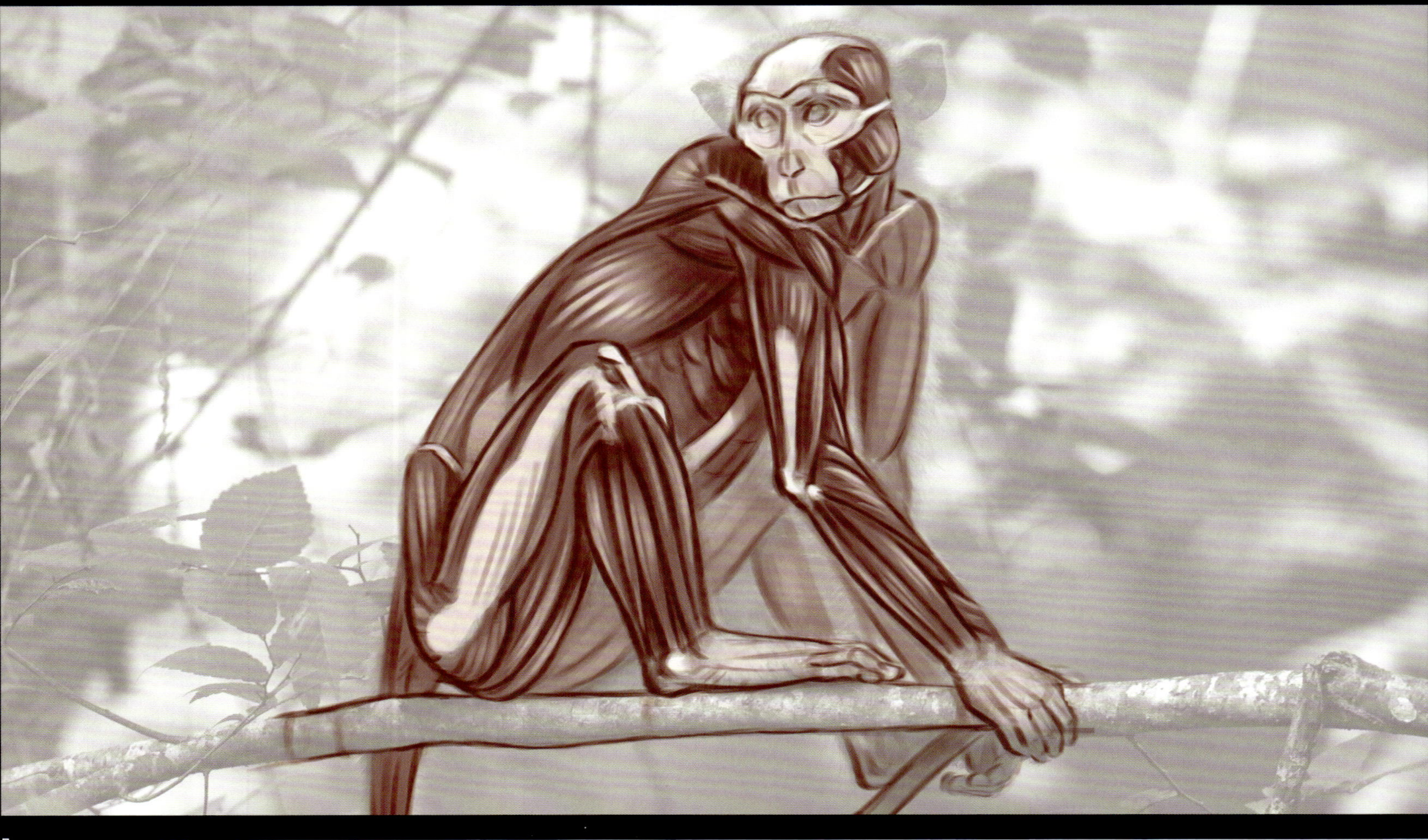

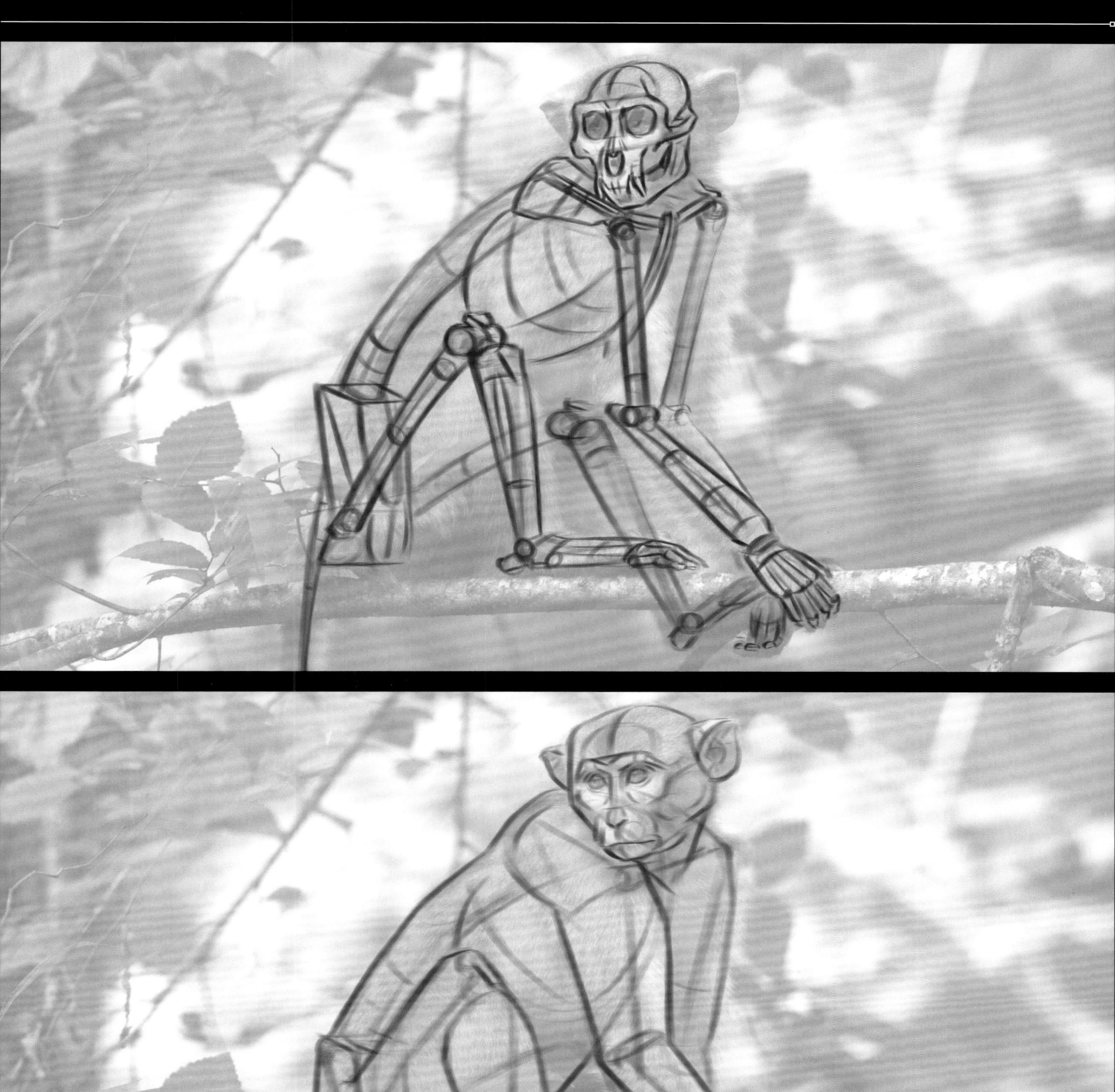

Photograph © Tom Friedel / Agami.nl

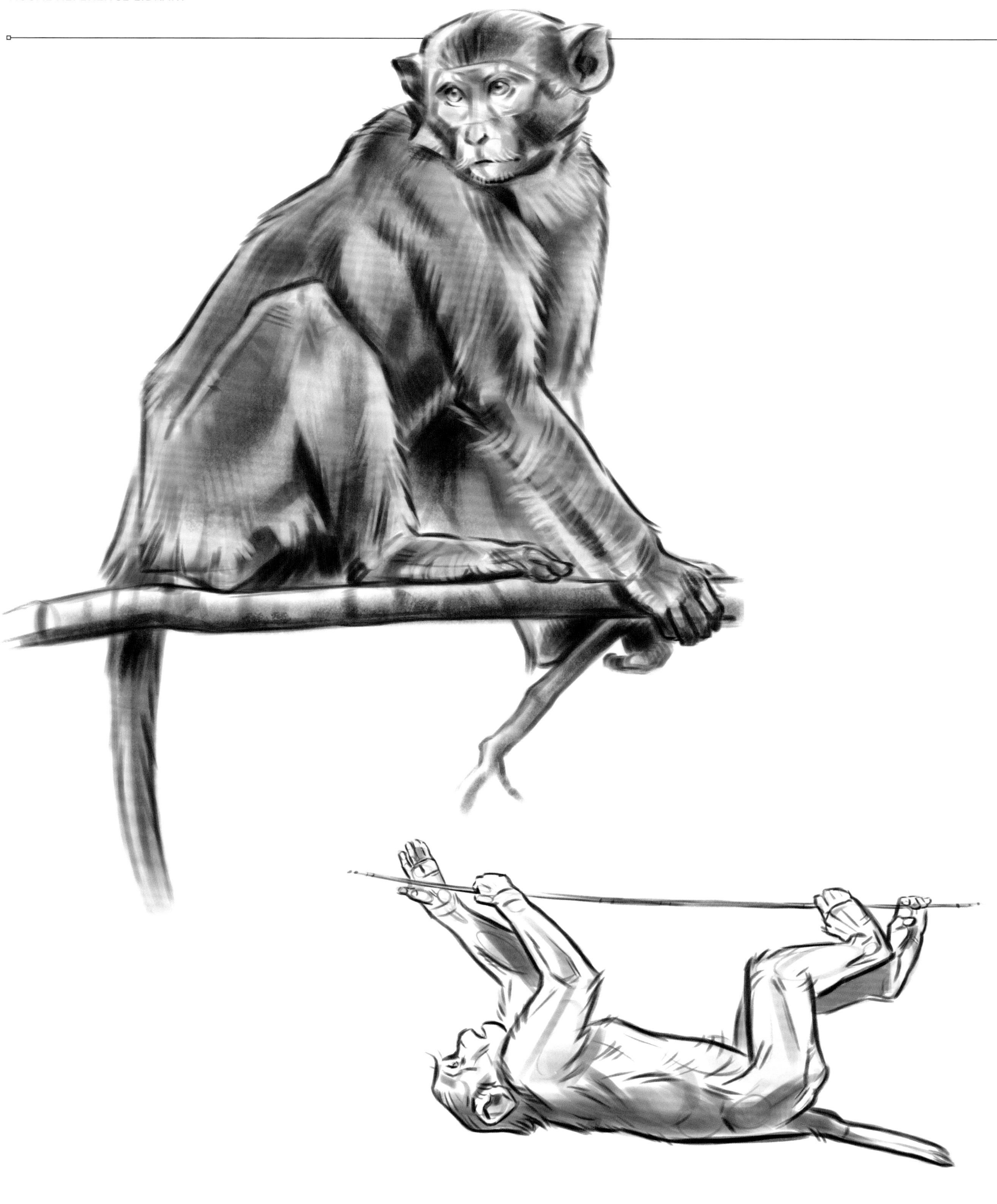

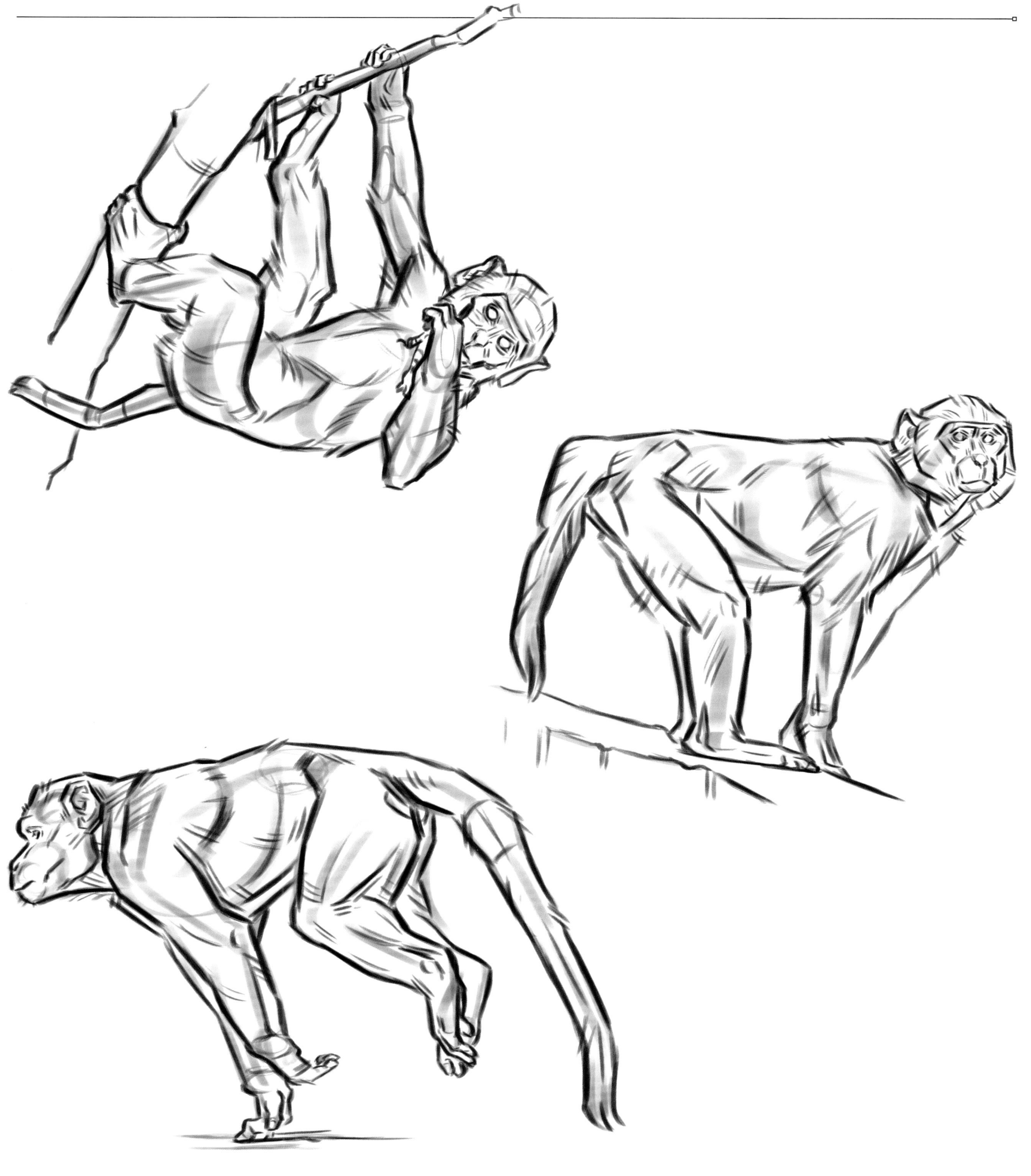

Chimpanzee

Chimpanzee *(Pan troglodytes)*

CLASS: MAMMALIA
ORDER: PRIMATES
FAMILY: CERCOPITHECIDAE

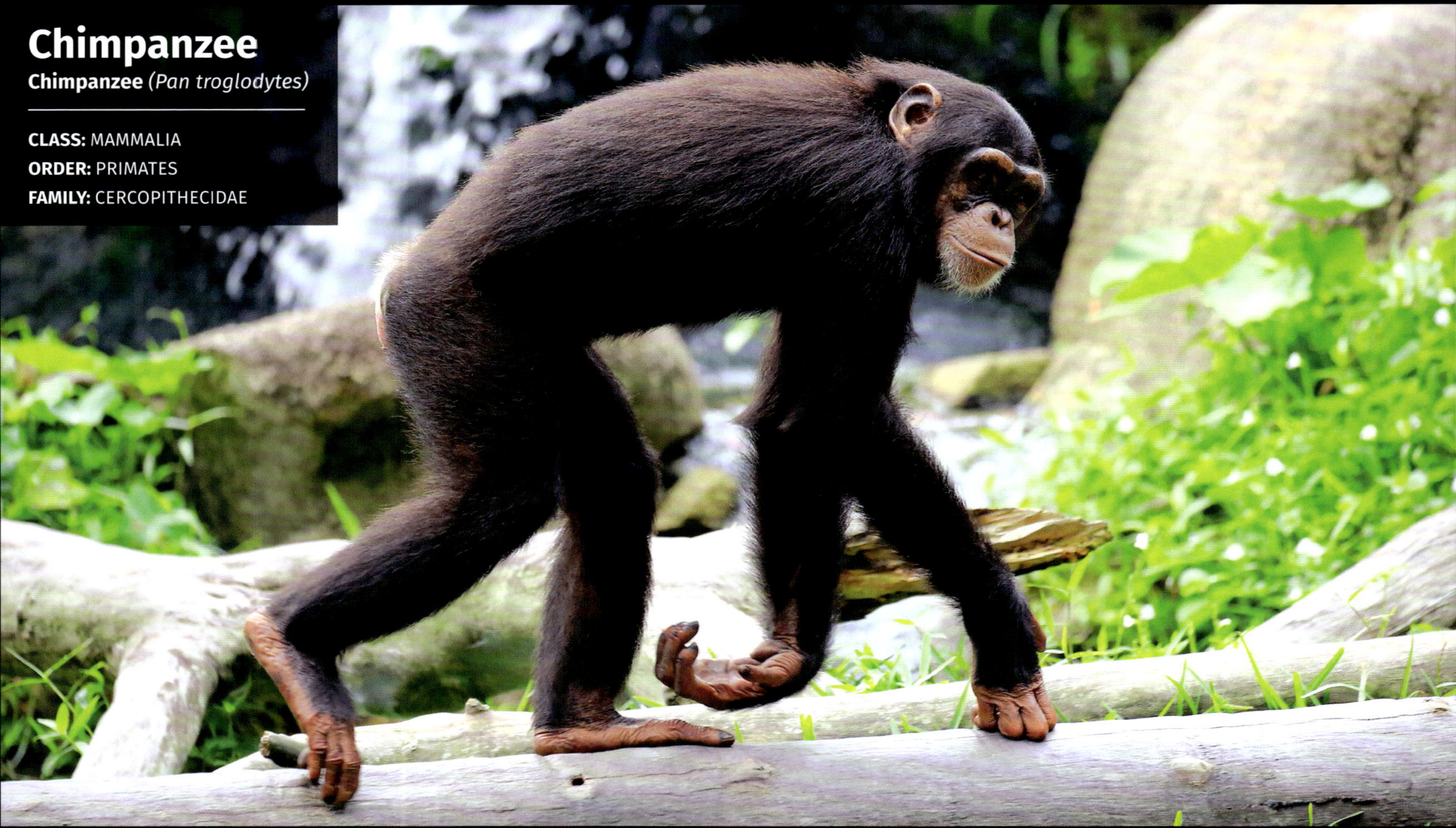

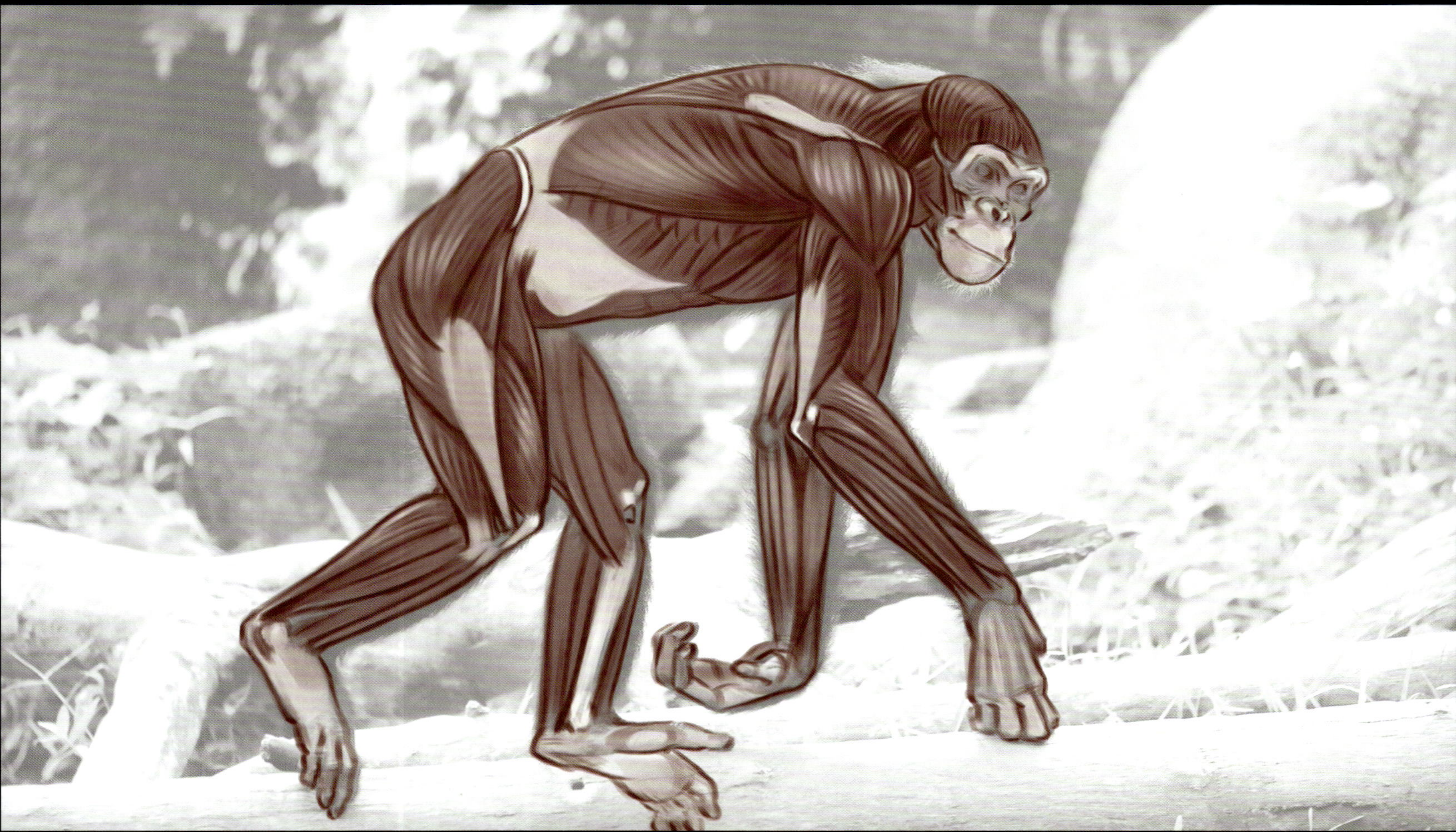

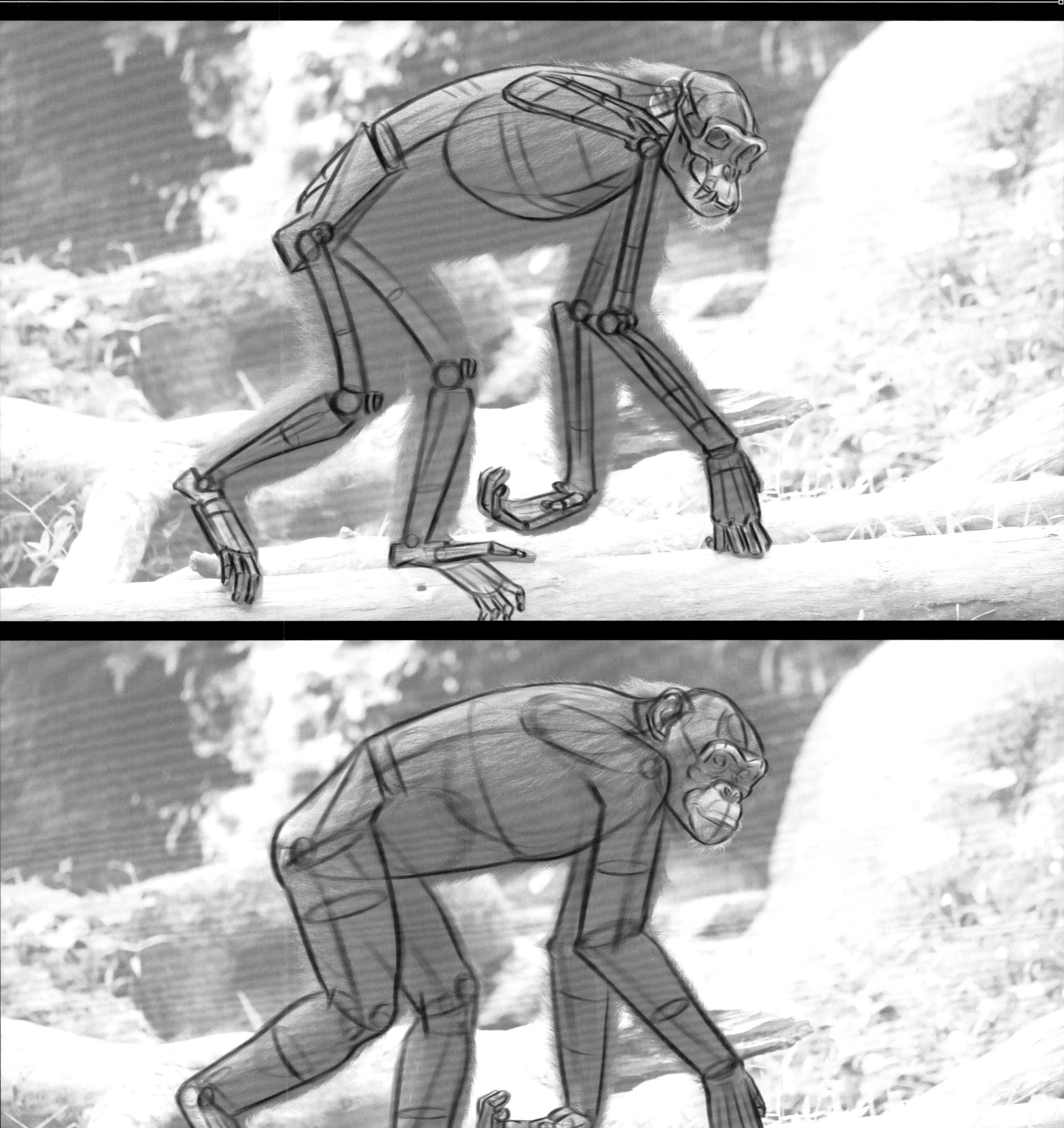

Photograph © imageBROKER.com / Jürgen & Christine Sohns

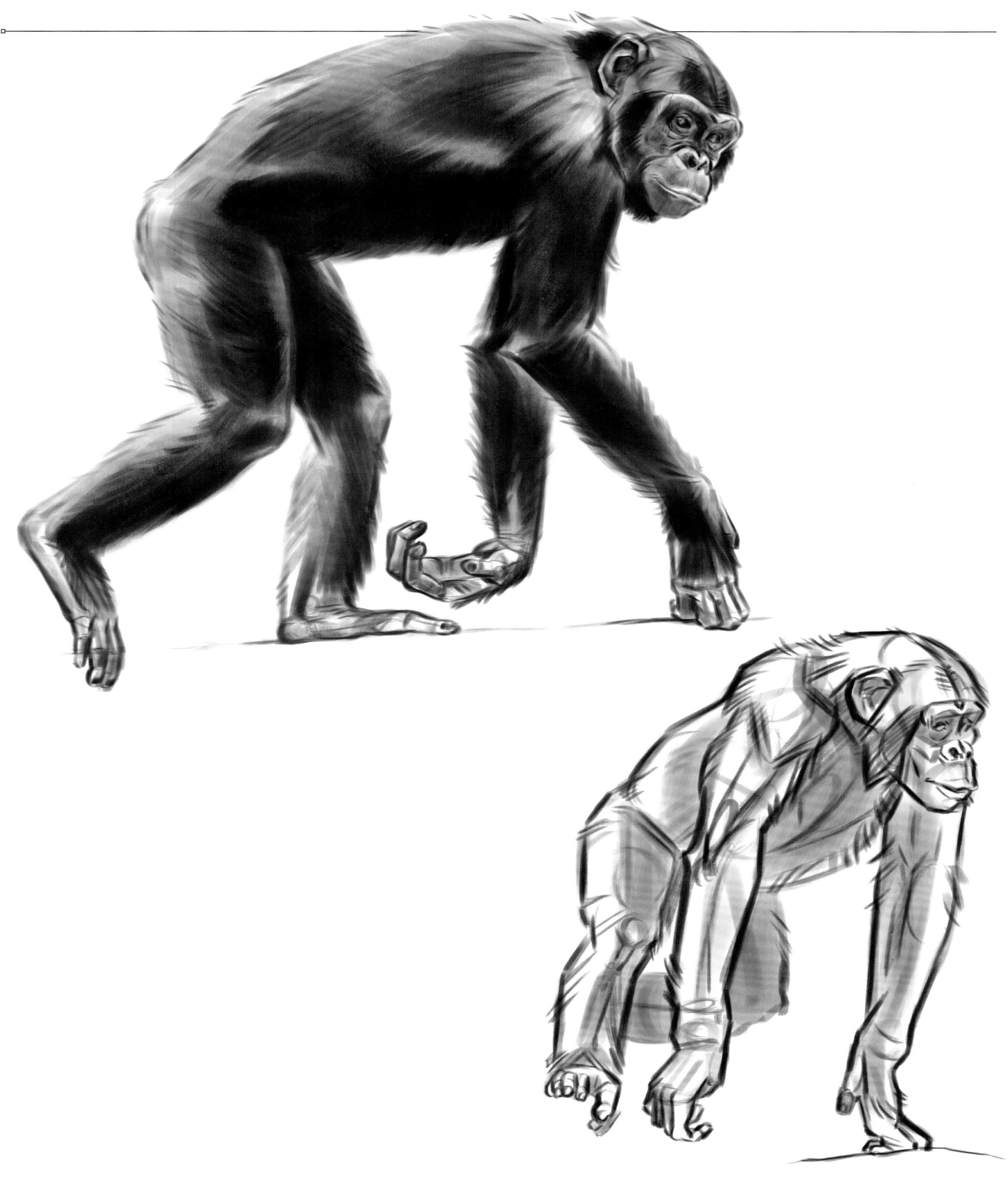

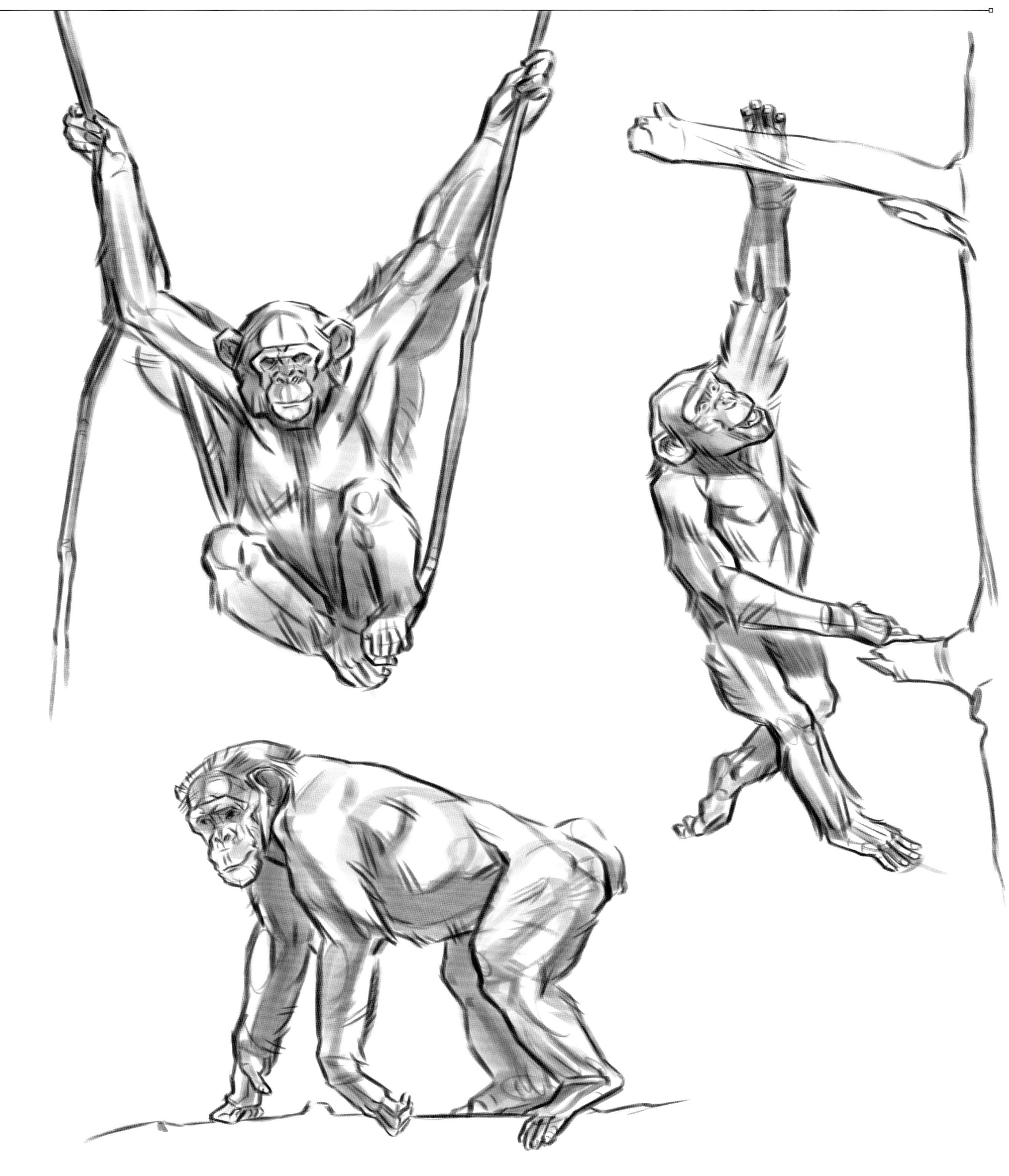

Gorilla

Eastern lowland gorilla
(Gorilla beringei graueri)

CLASS: MAMMALIA
ORDER: PRIMATES
FAMILY: HOMINIDAE

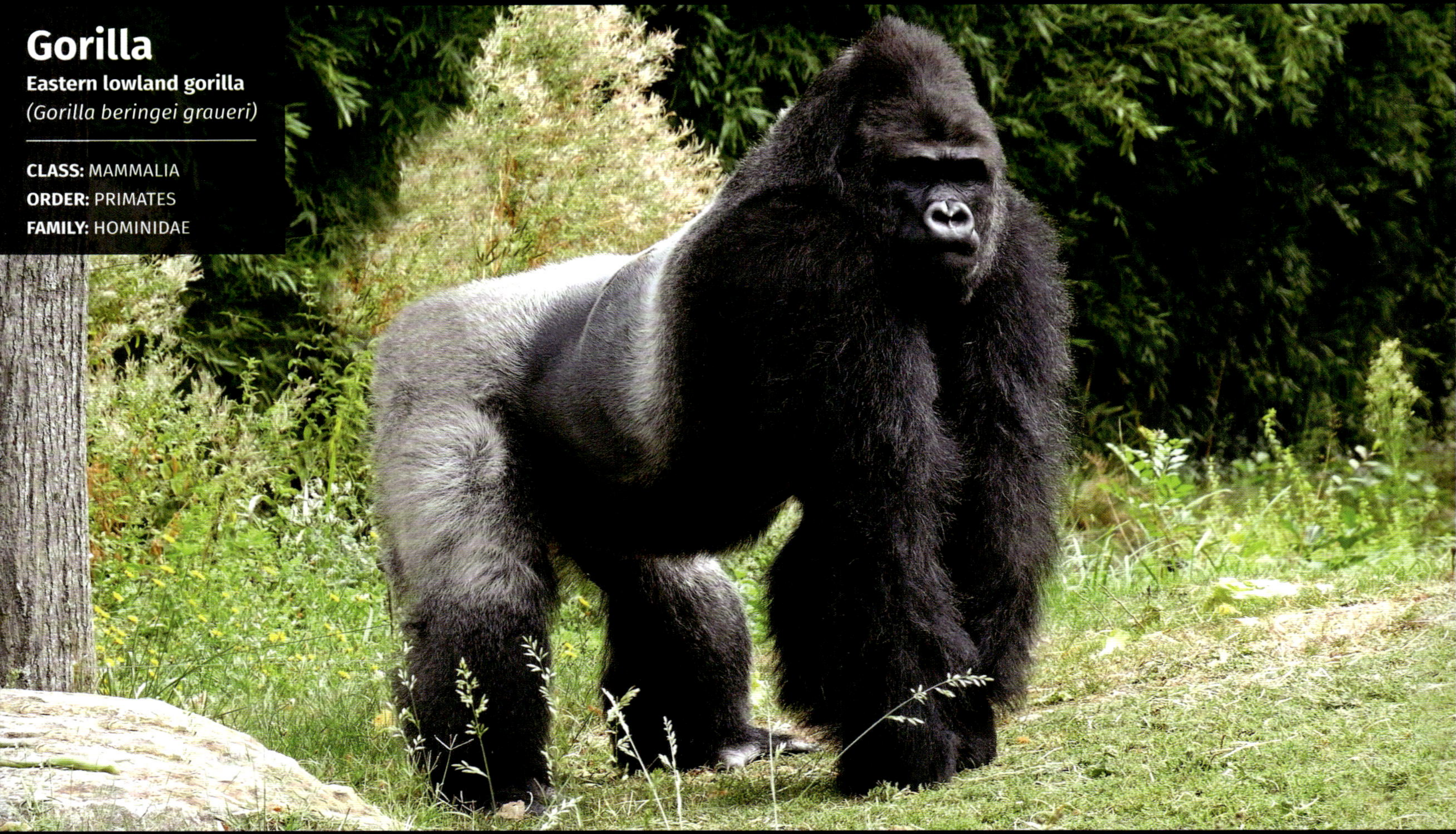

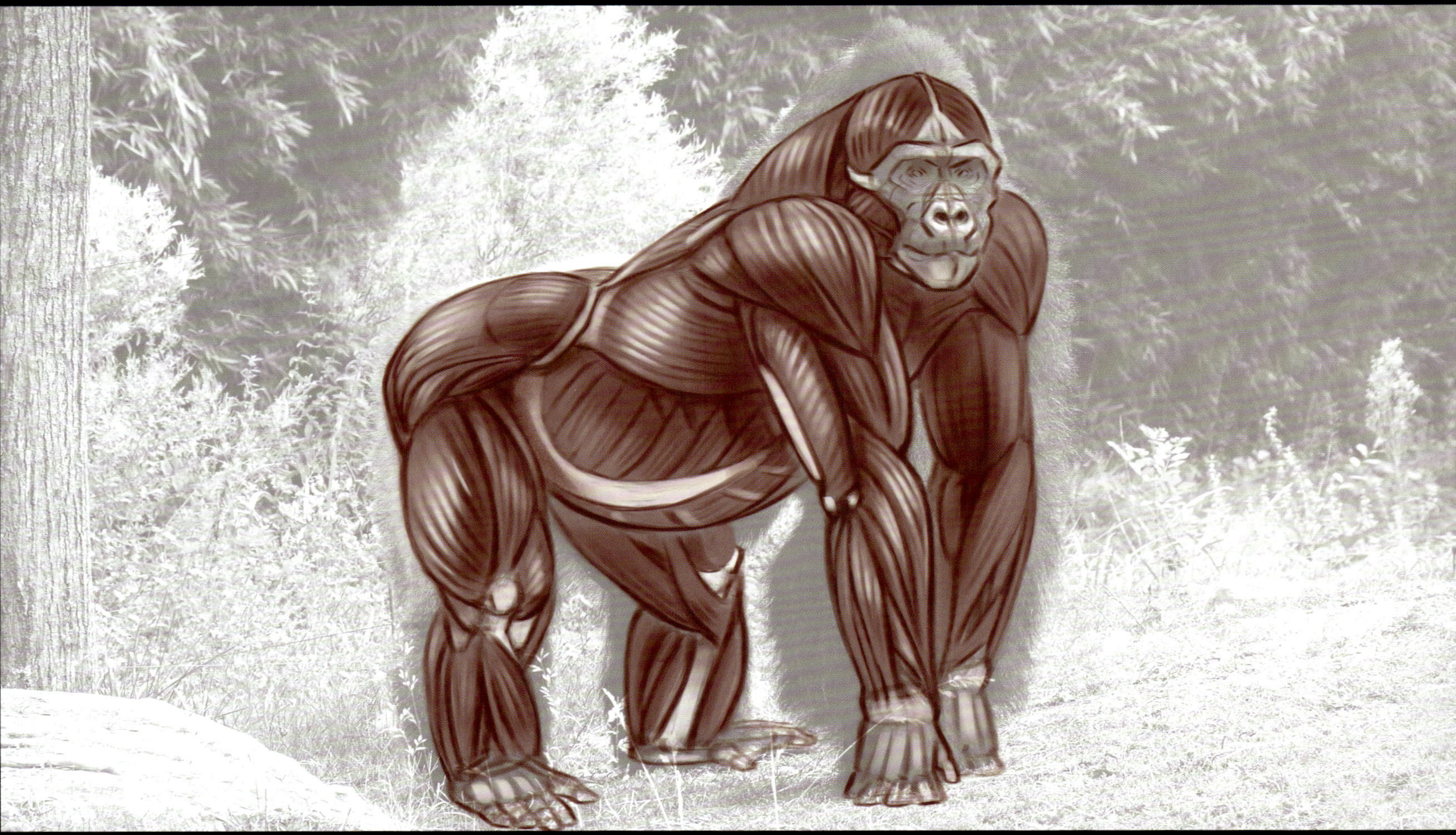

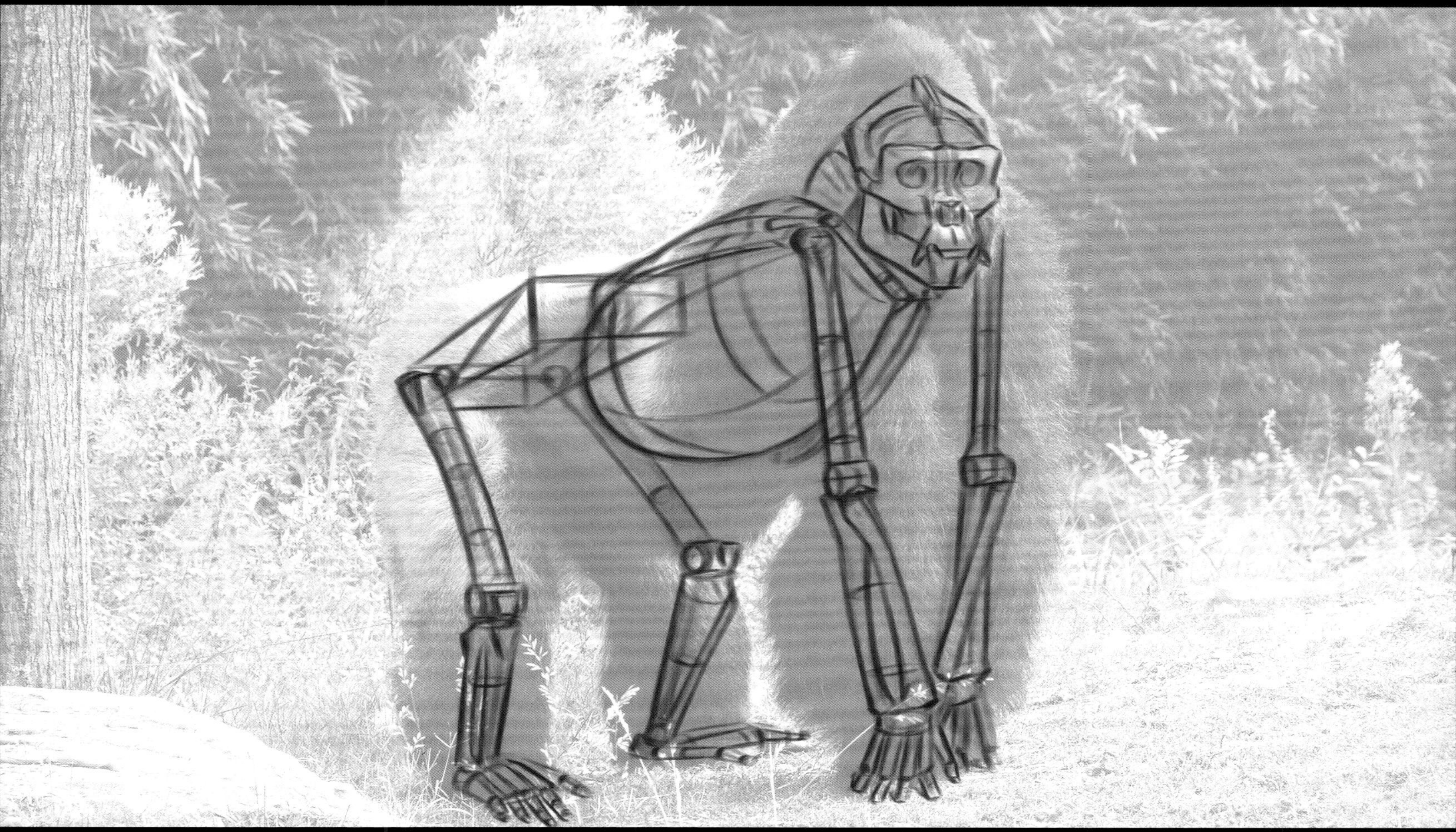

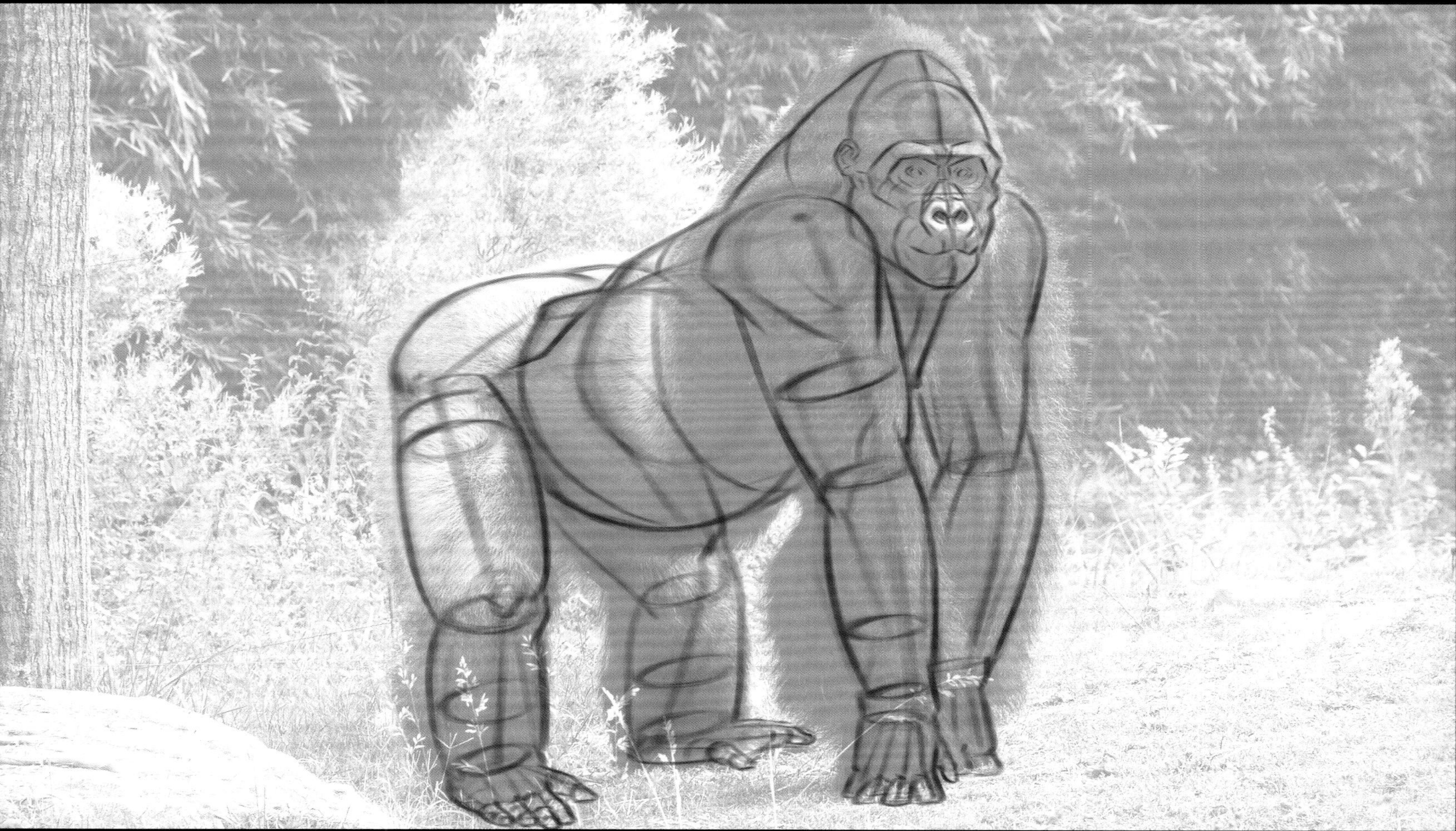

Photograph © imageBROKER.com / Lacz Gerard

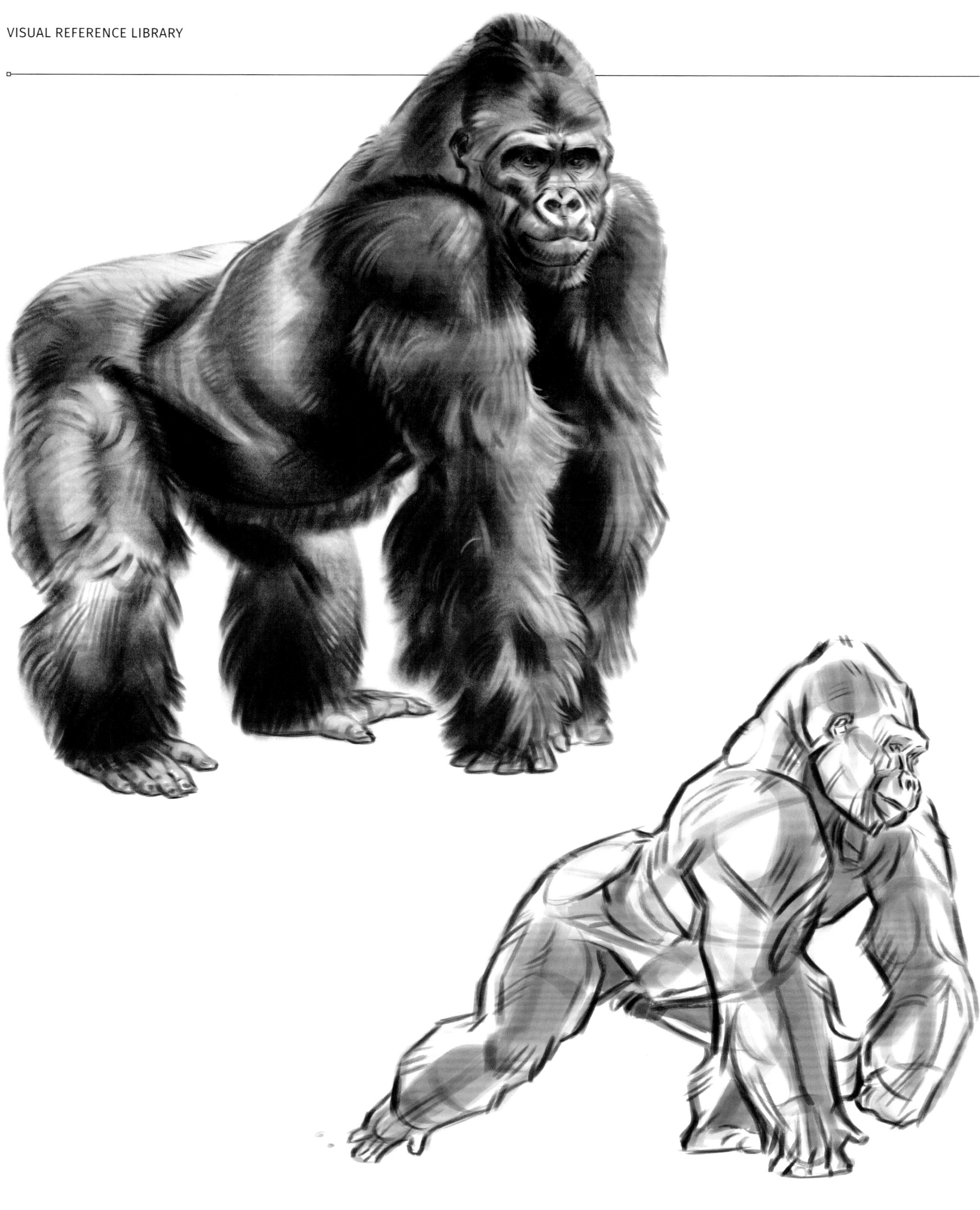

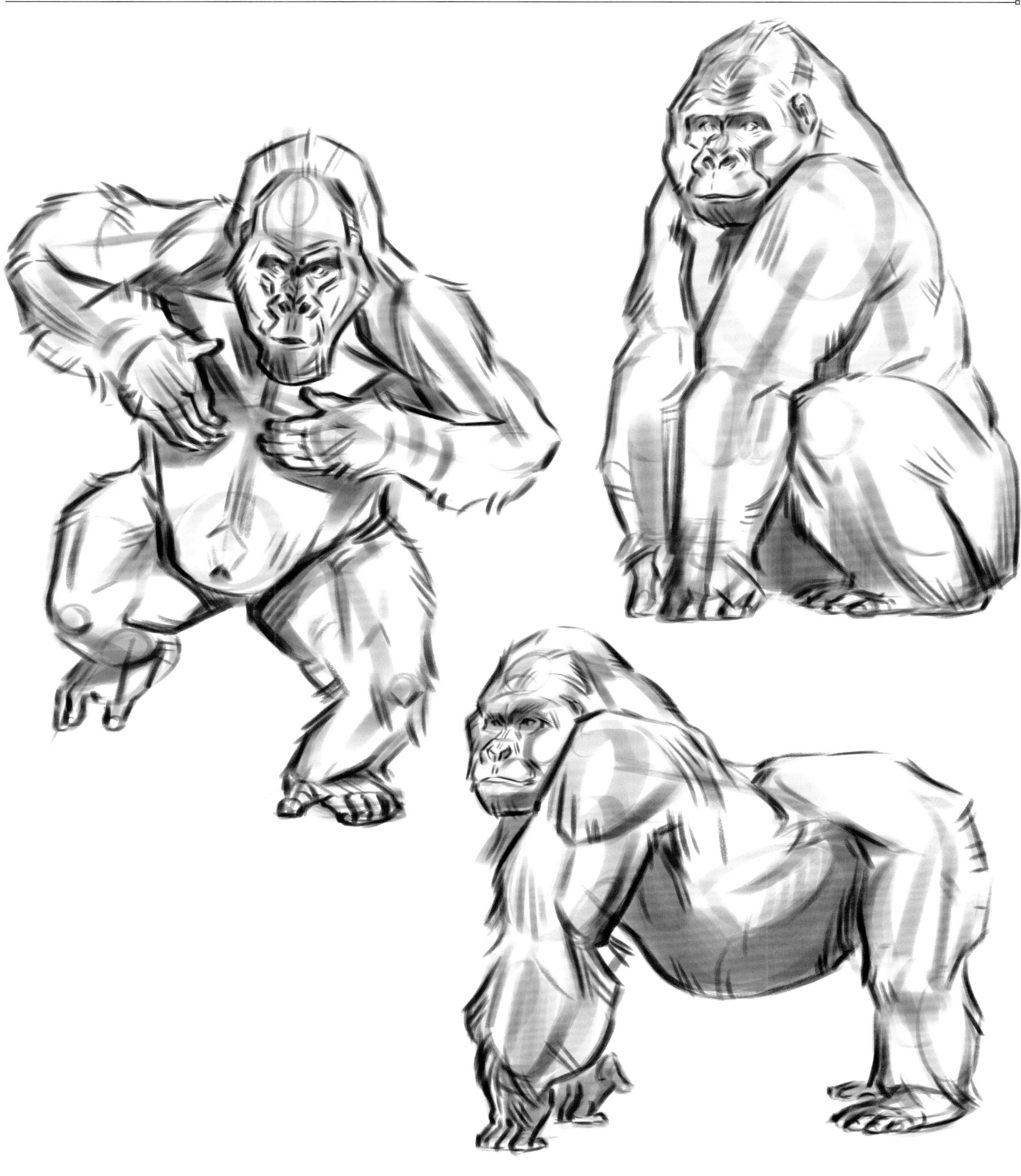

Elephant

African elephant

(Loxodonta africana)

CLASS: MAMMALIA

ORDER: PROBOSCIDEA

FAMILY: ELEPHANTIDAE

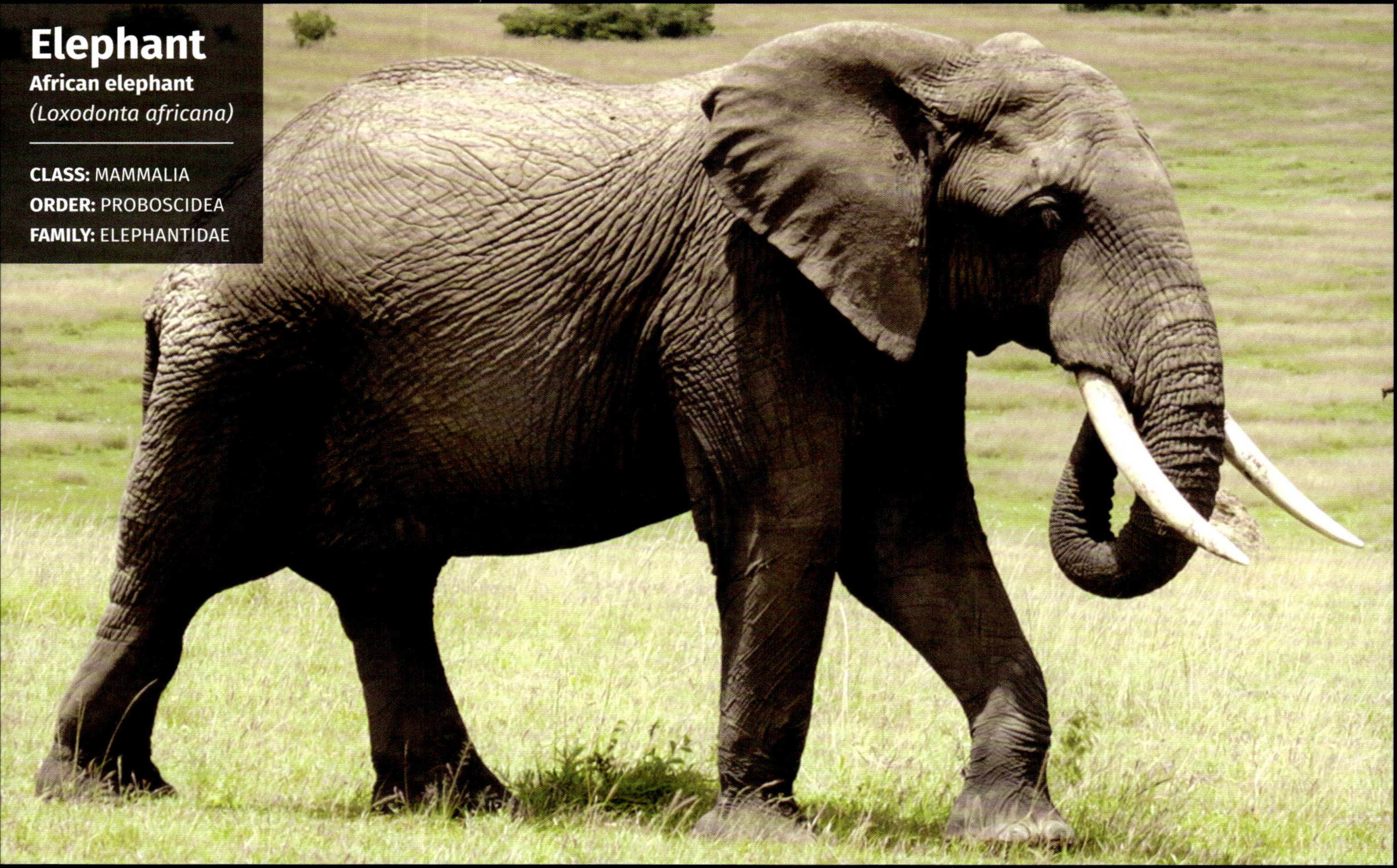

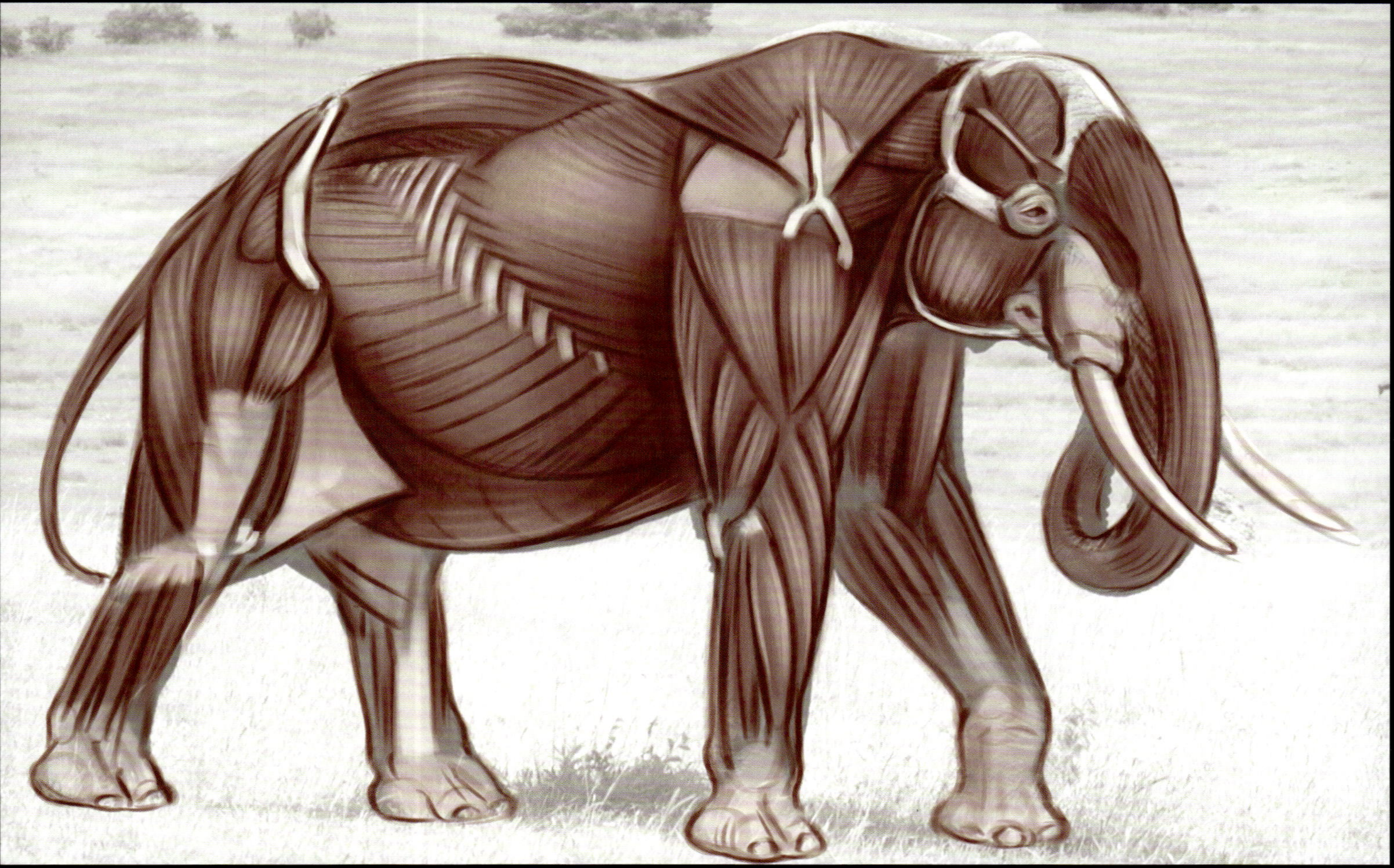

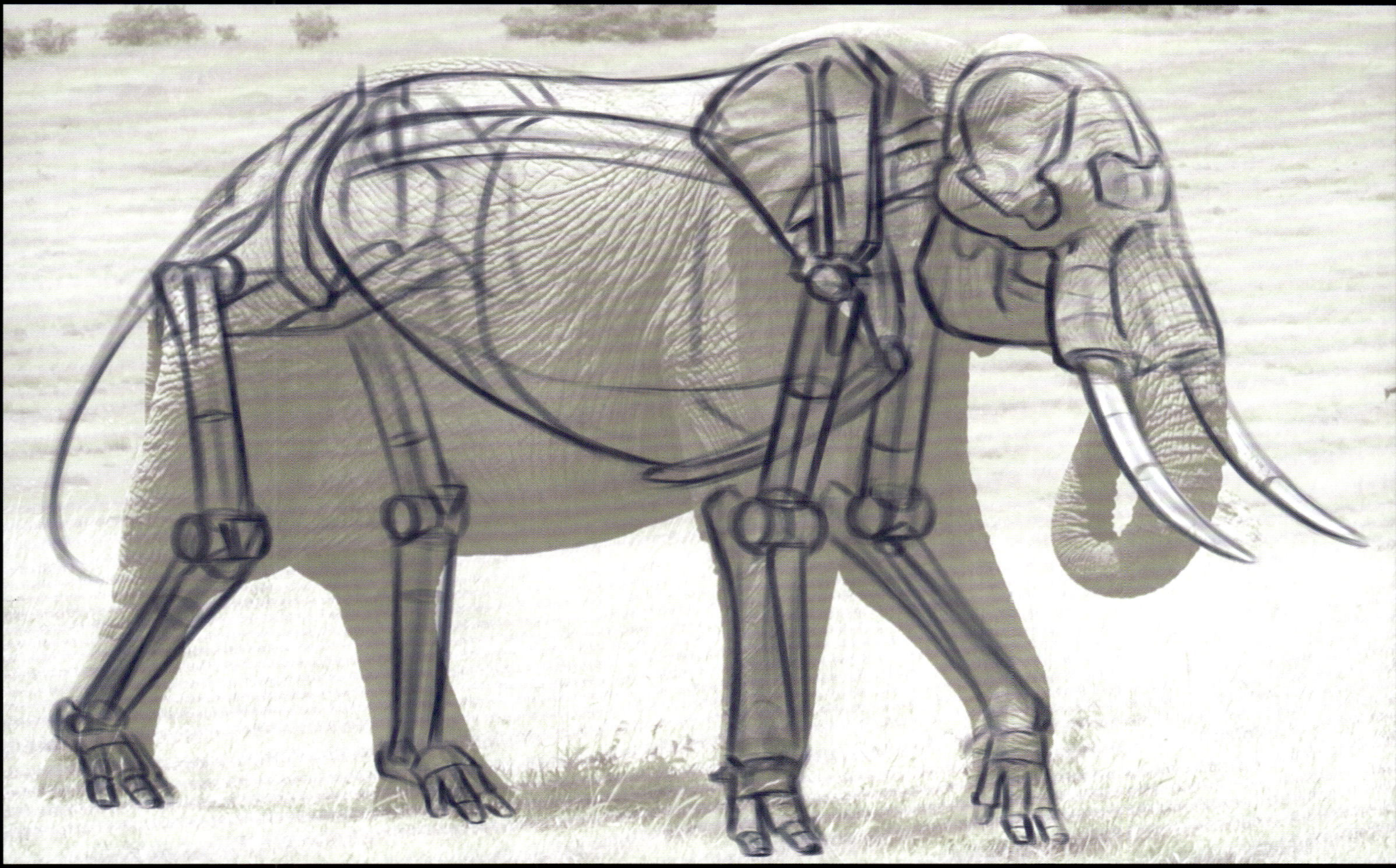

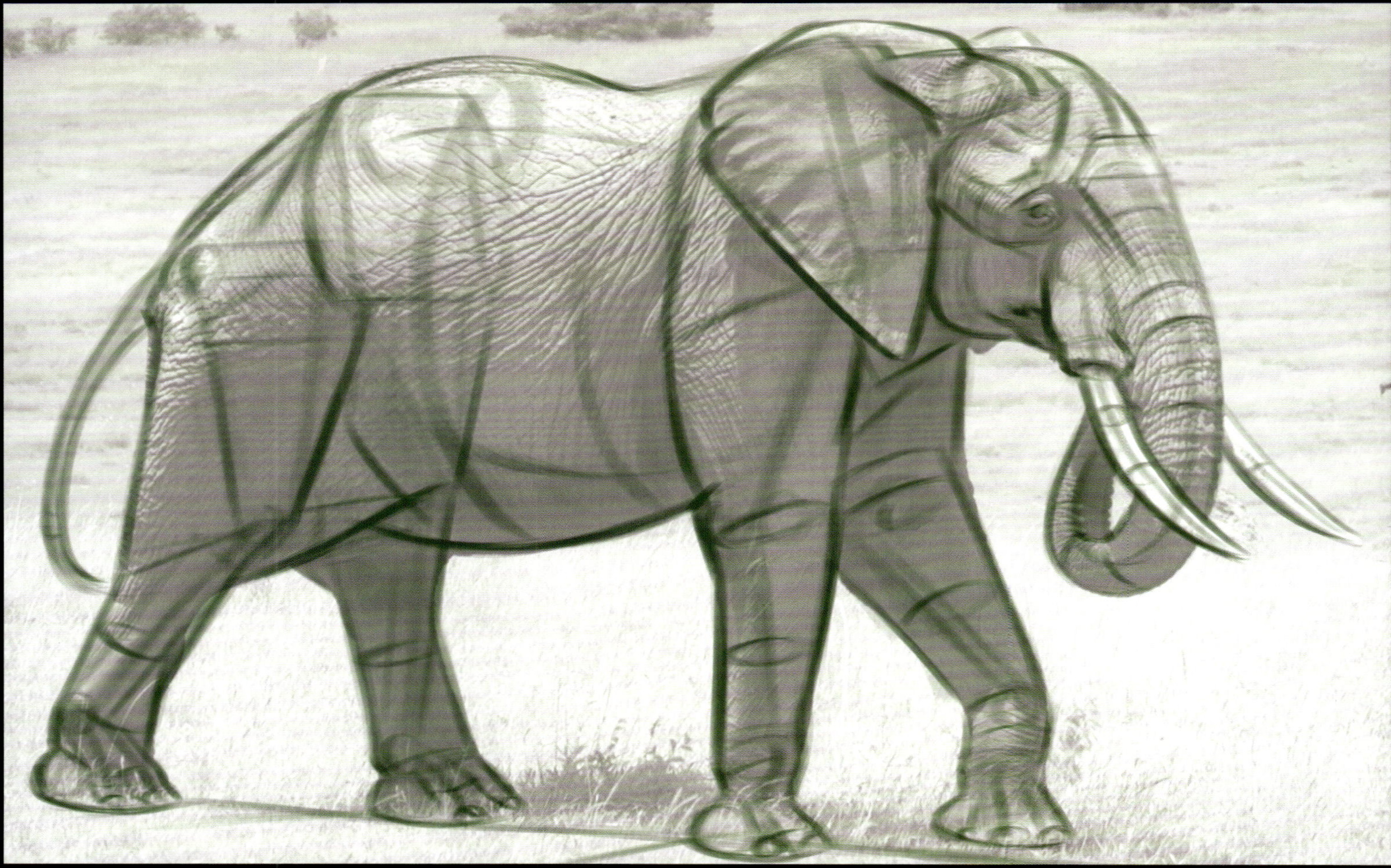

Photograph © Caroline Piek/ Agami.nl

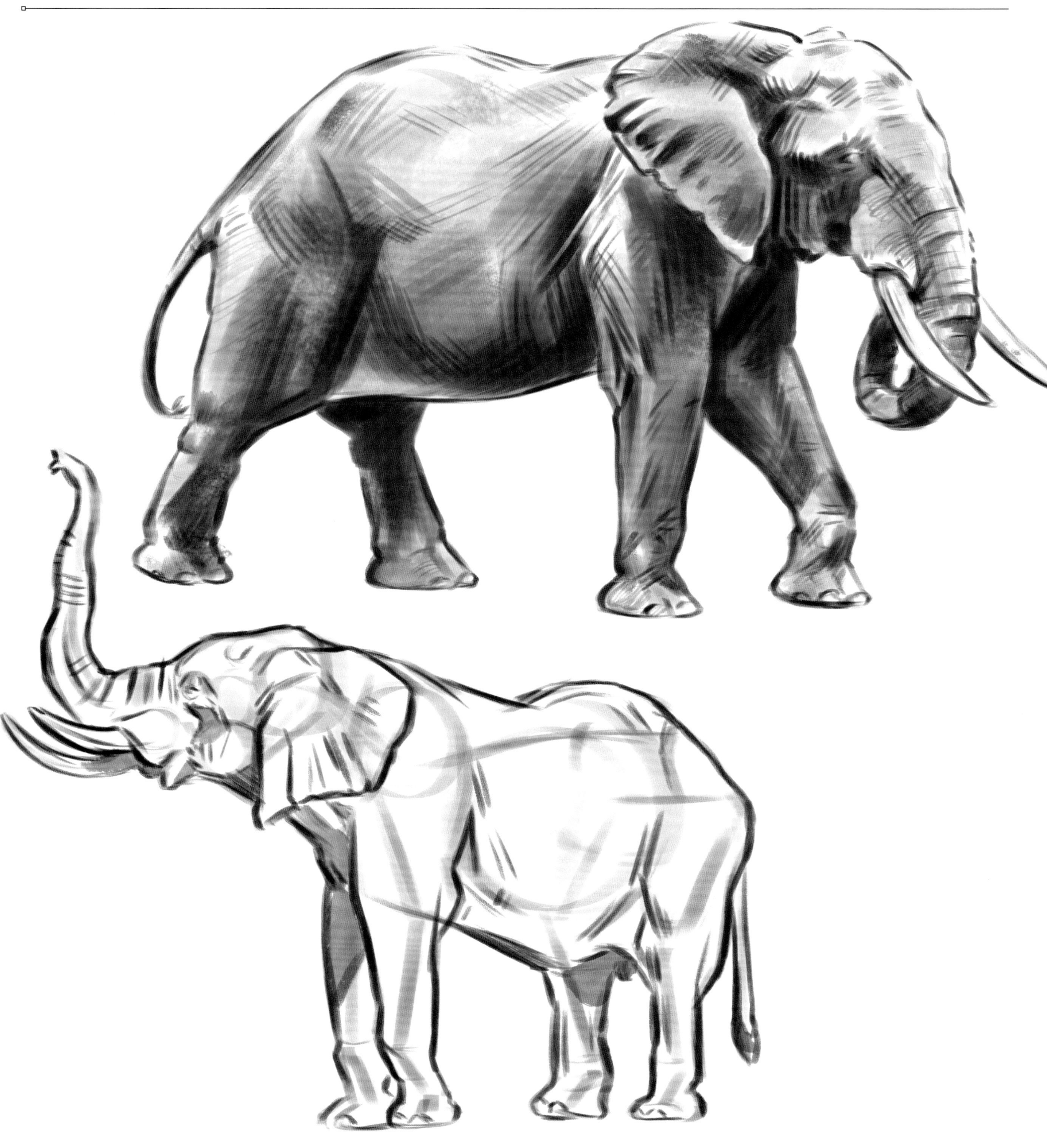

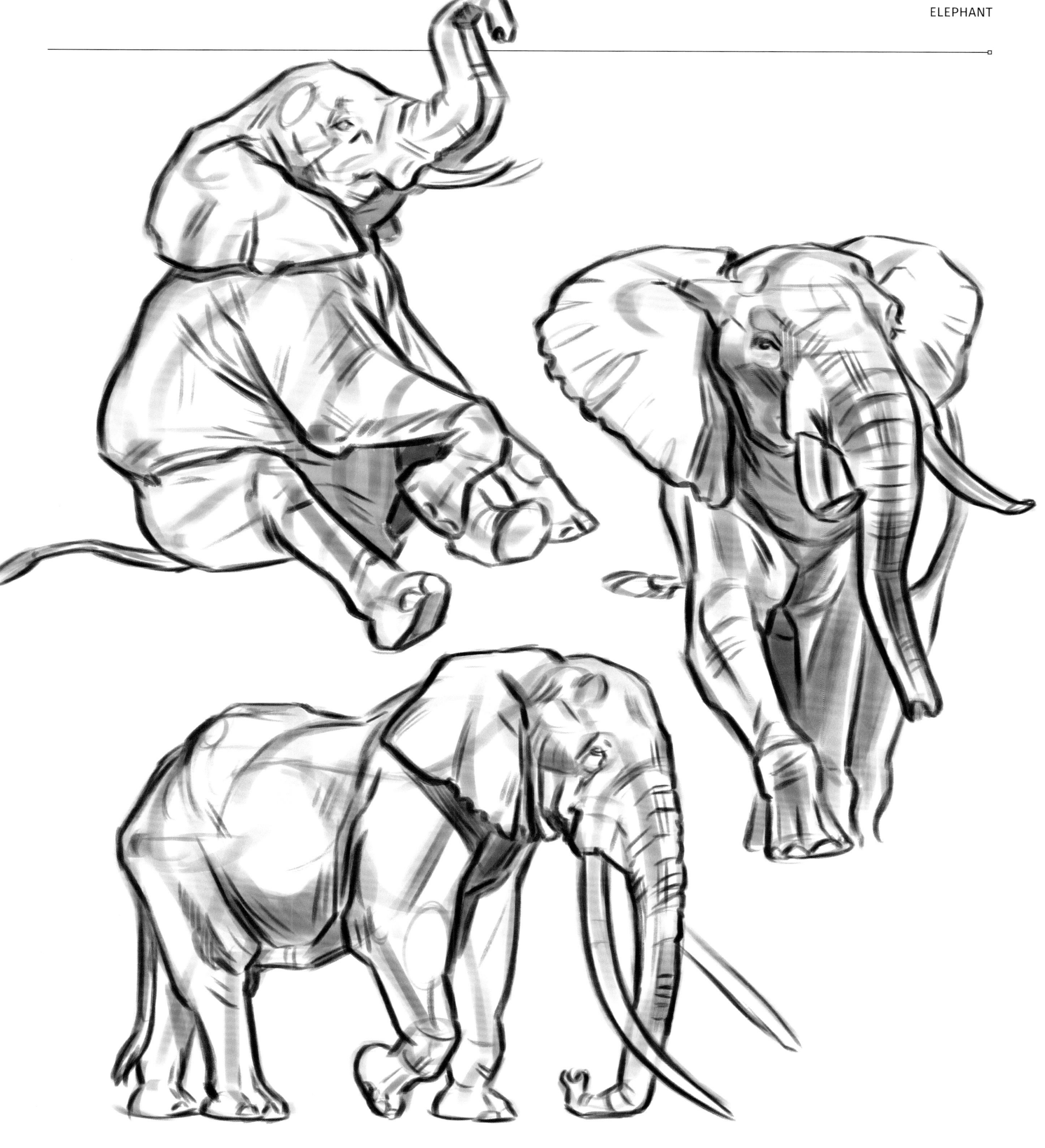

Beaver

European beaver
(Castor fiber)

CLASS: MAMMALIA
ORDER: RODENTIA
FAMILY: CASTORIDAE

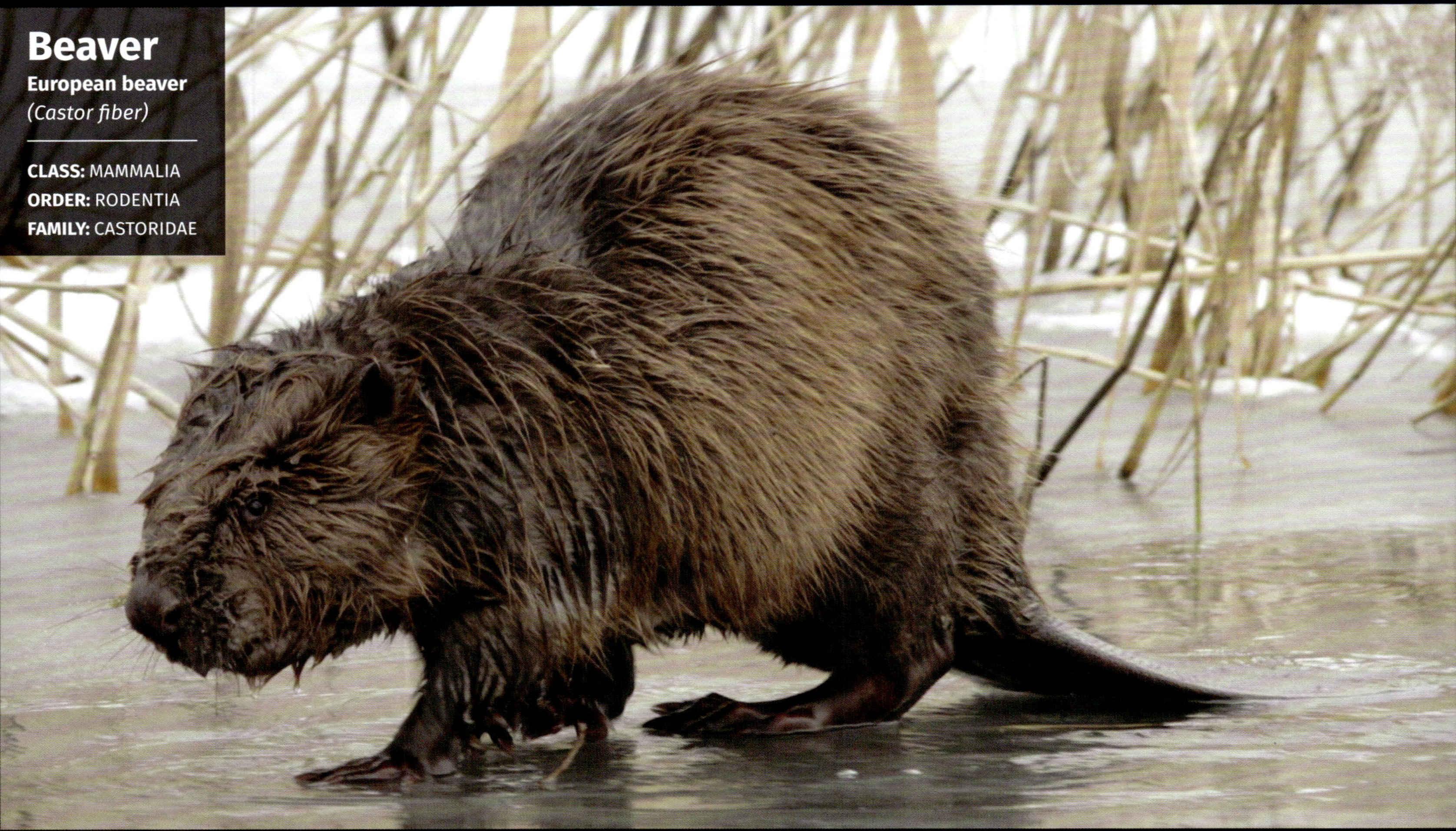

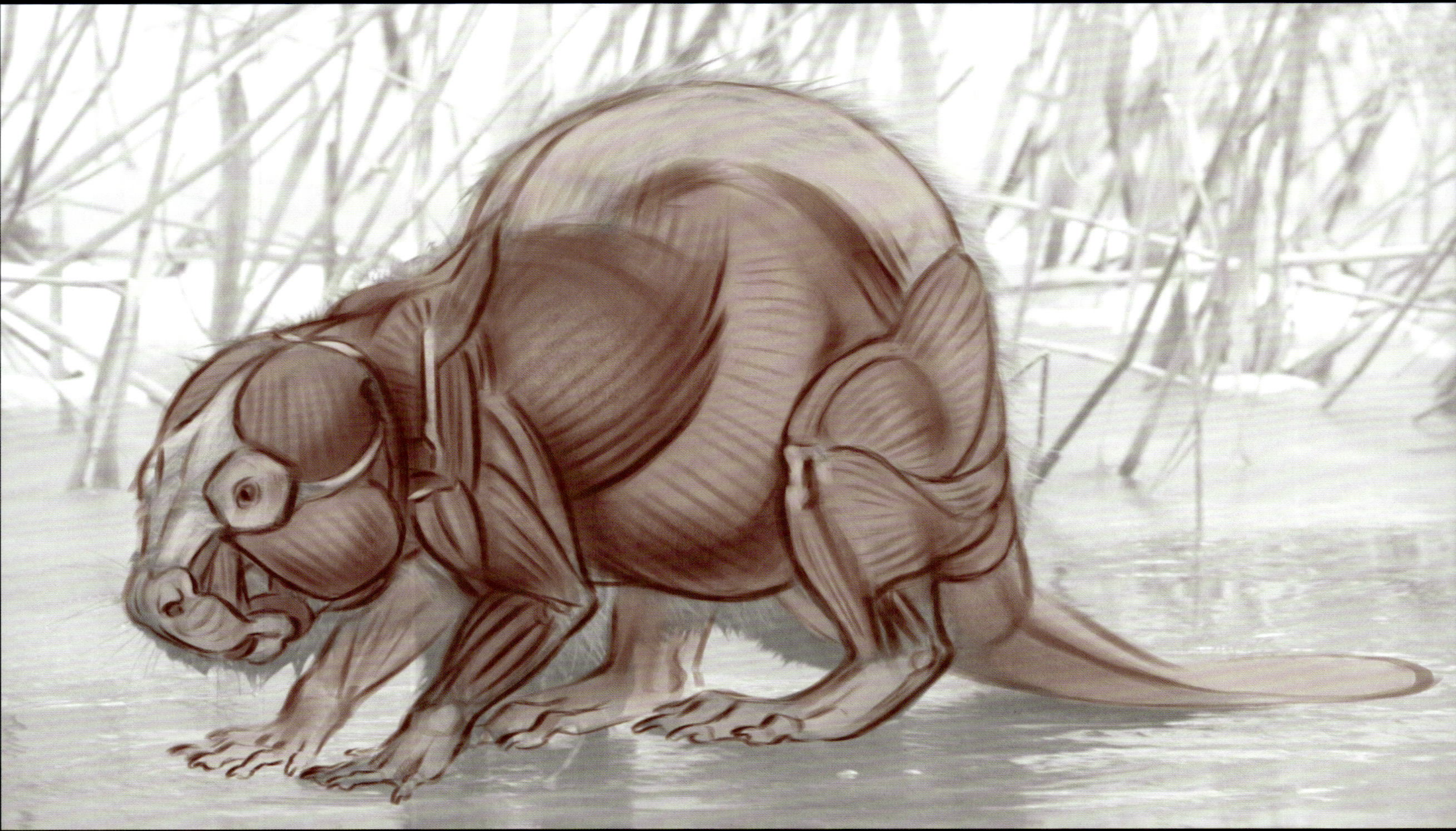

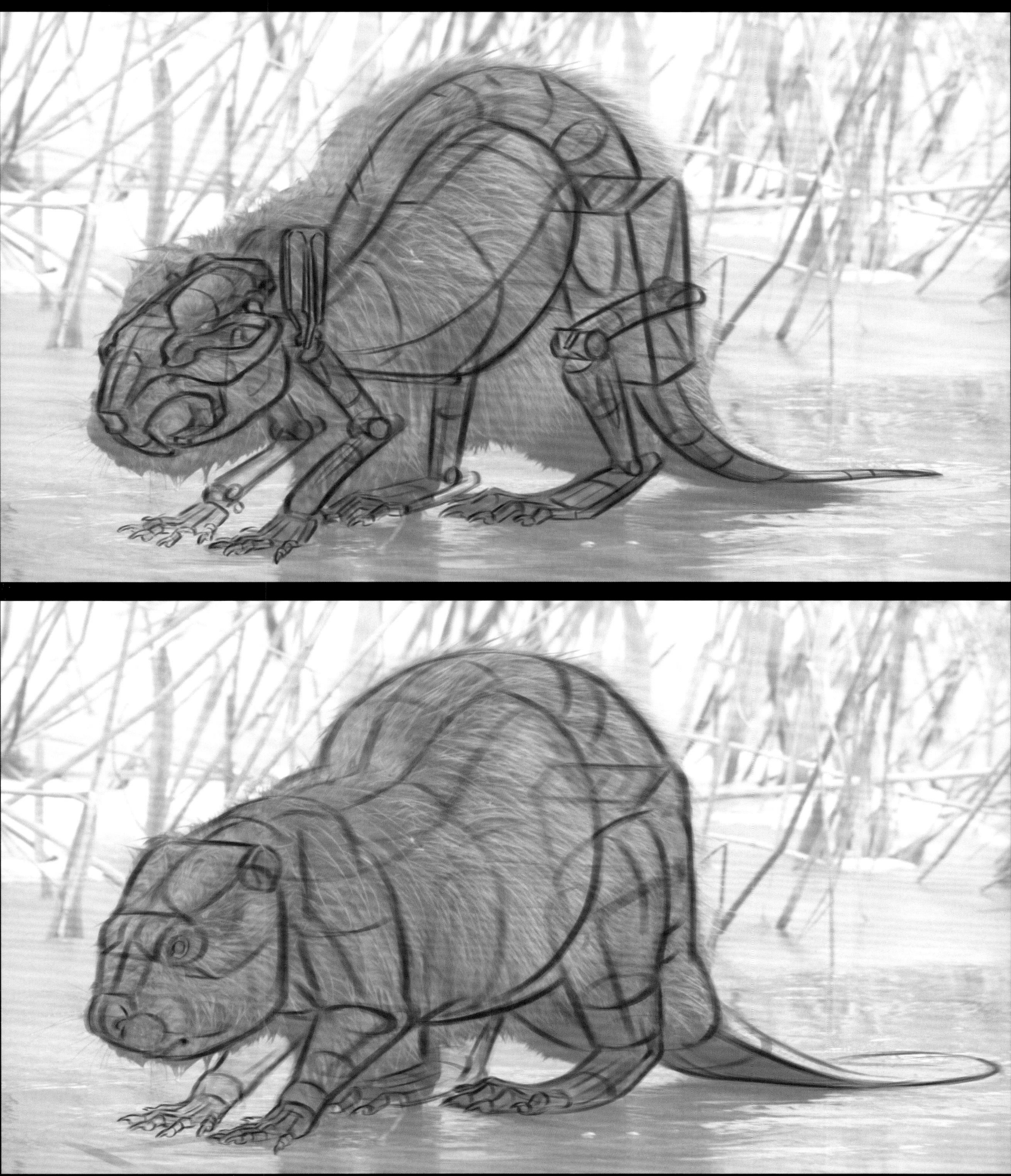

Photograph © Karel Mauer/ Agami.nl

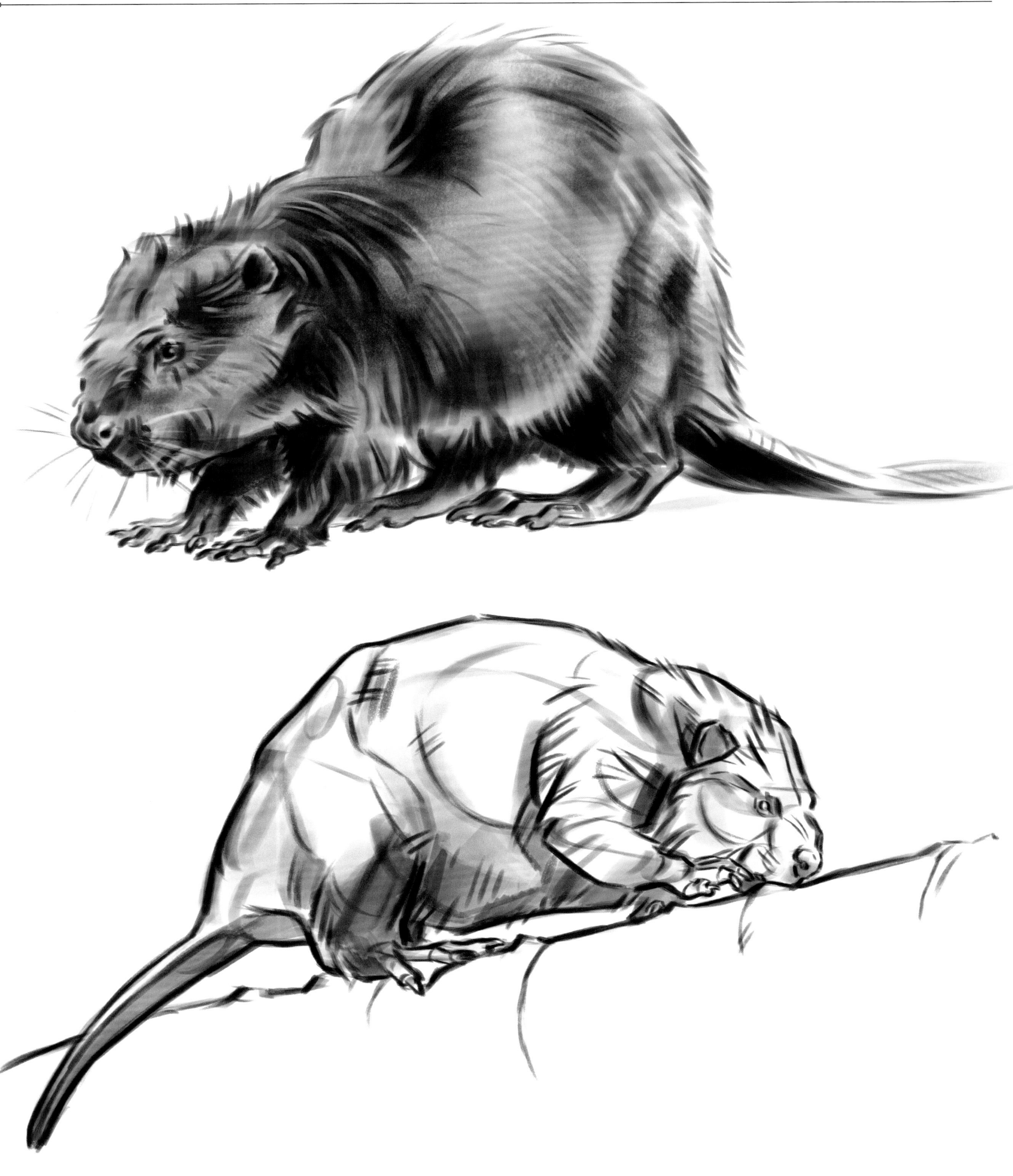

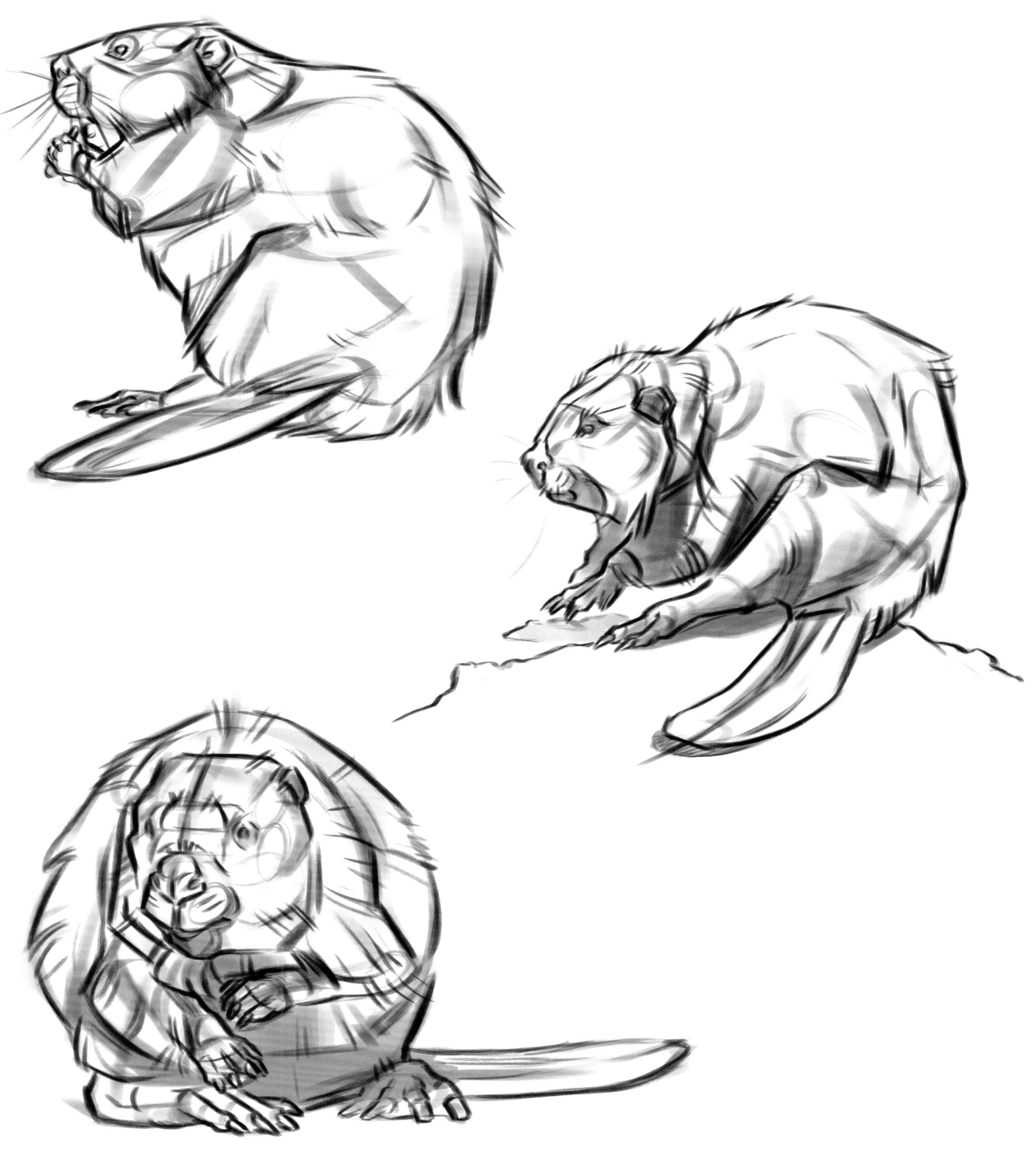

Mouse

Wood mouse
(Apodemus sylvaticus)

CLASS: MAMMALIA
ORDER: RODENTIA
FAMILY: MURIDAE

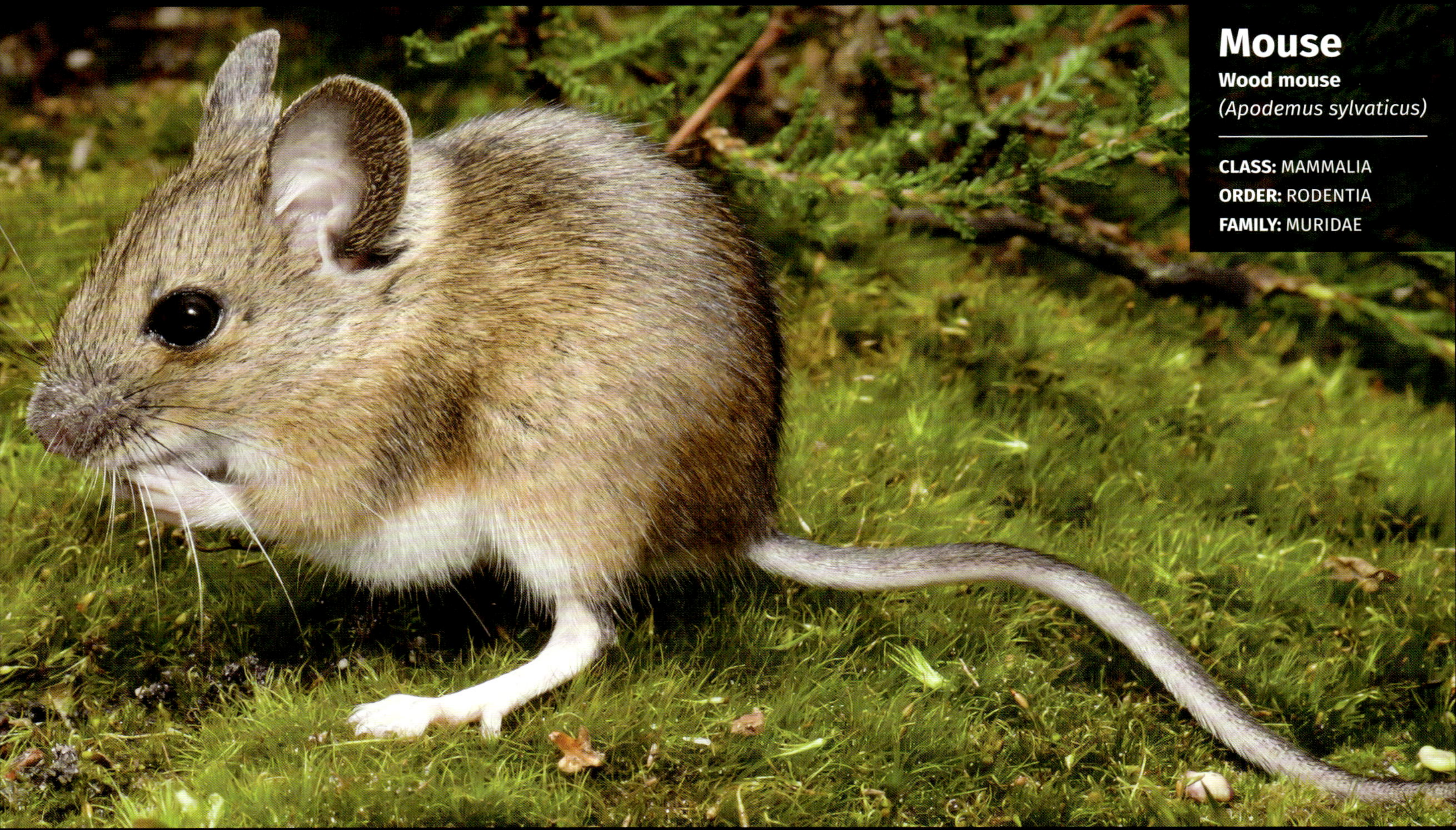

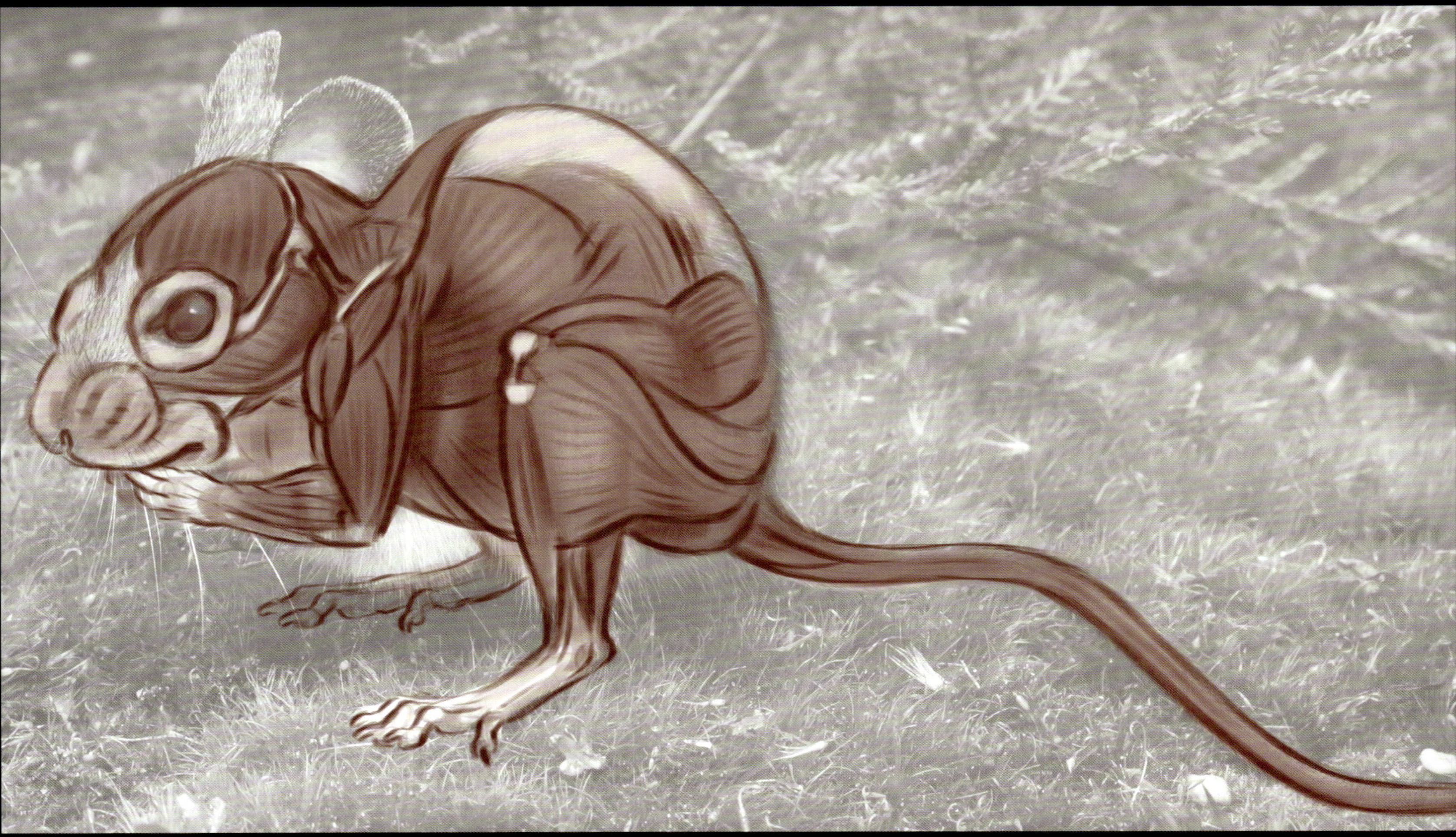

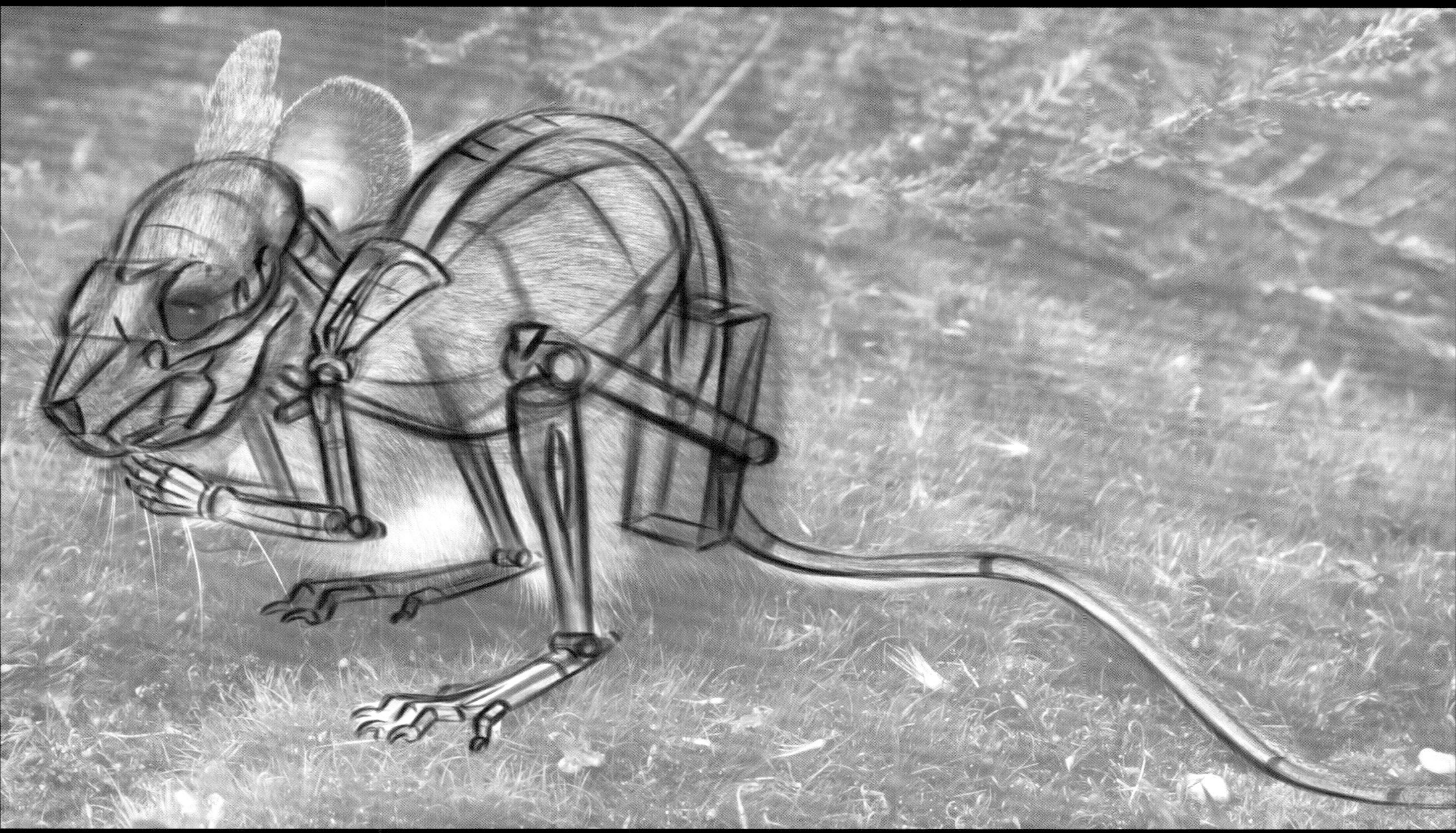

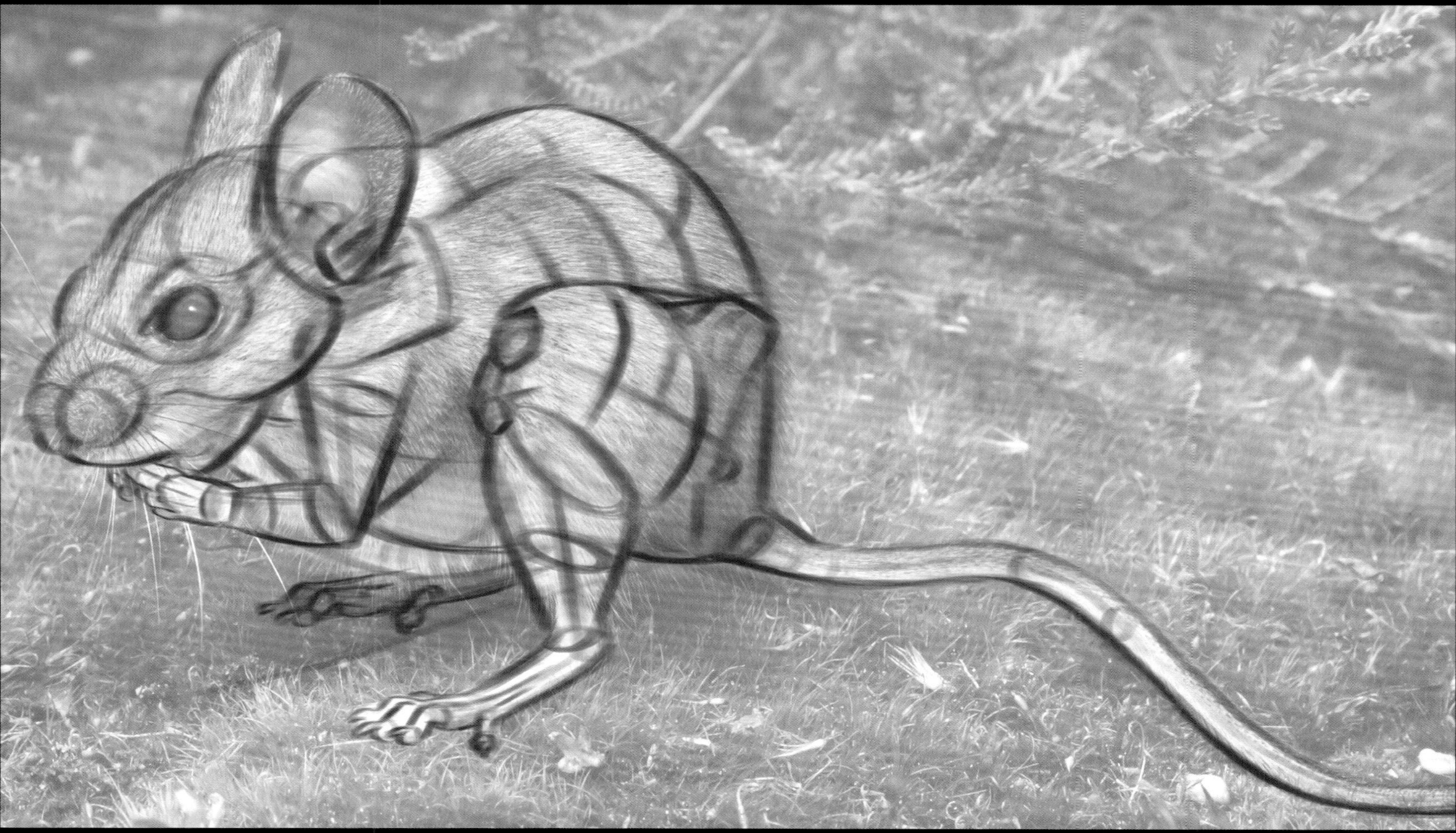

Photograph © Theo Douma/ Agami.nl

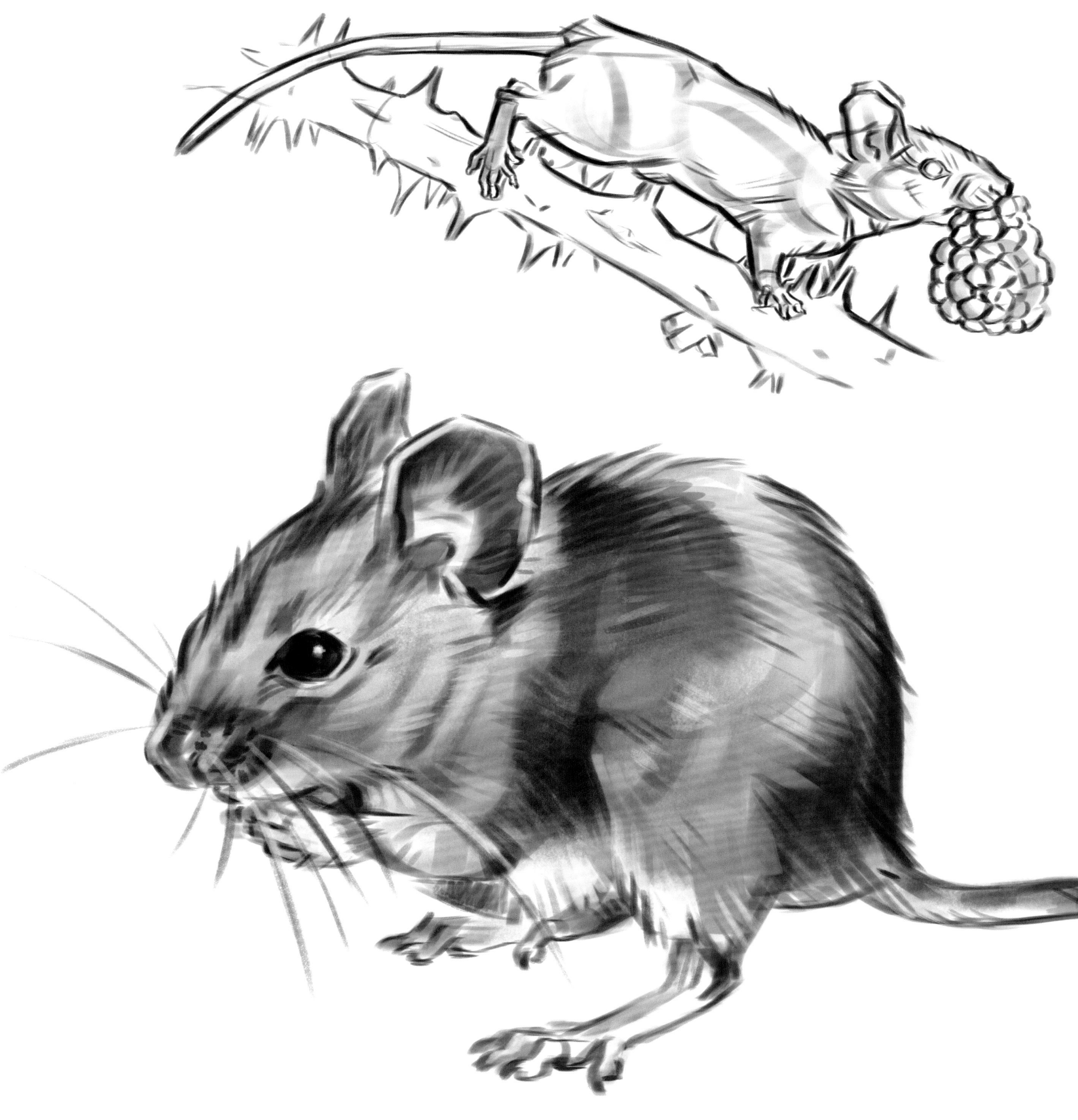

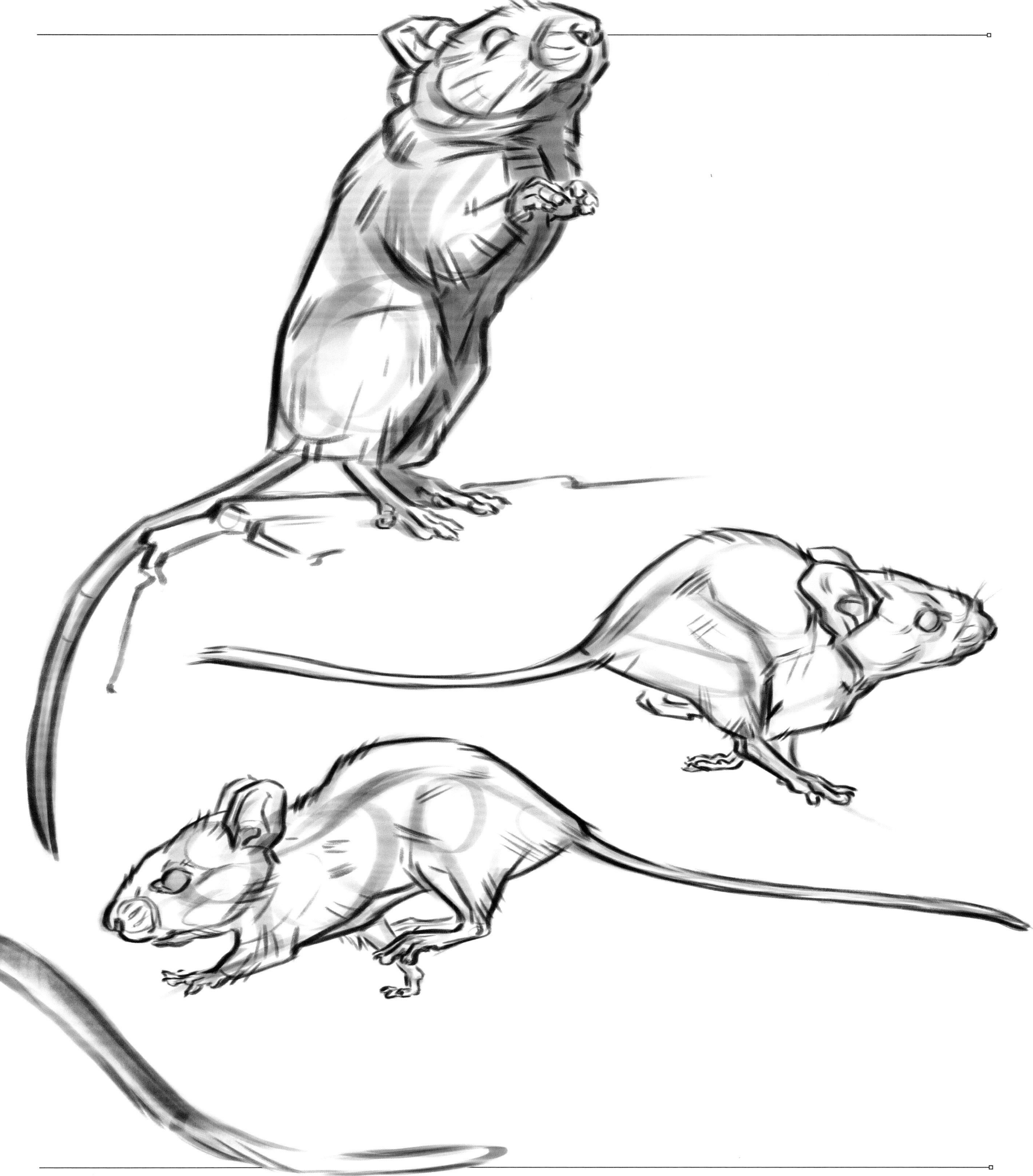

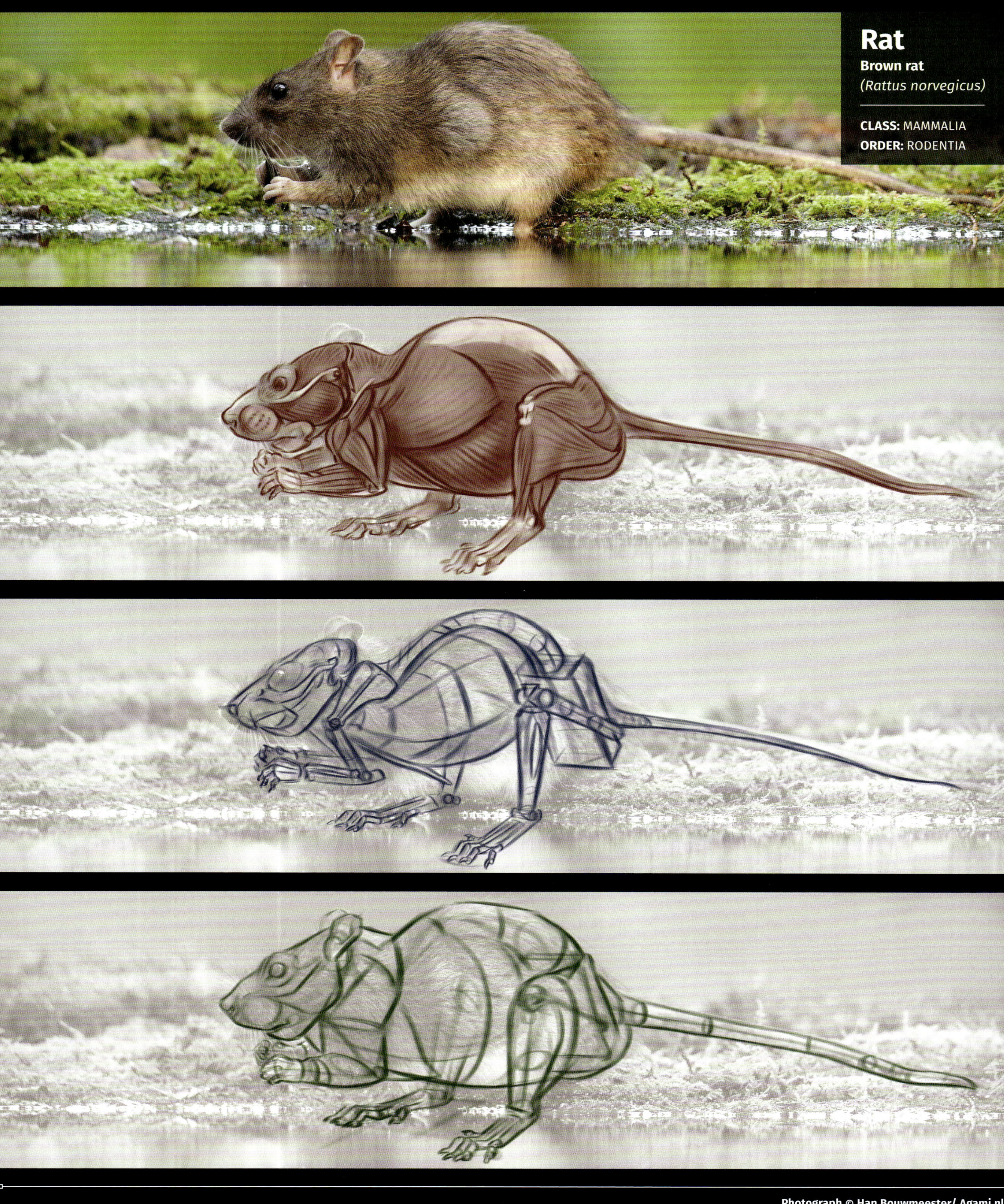

Photograph © Han Bouwmeester/ Agami.nl

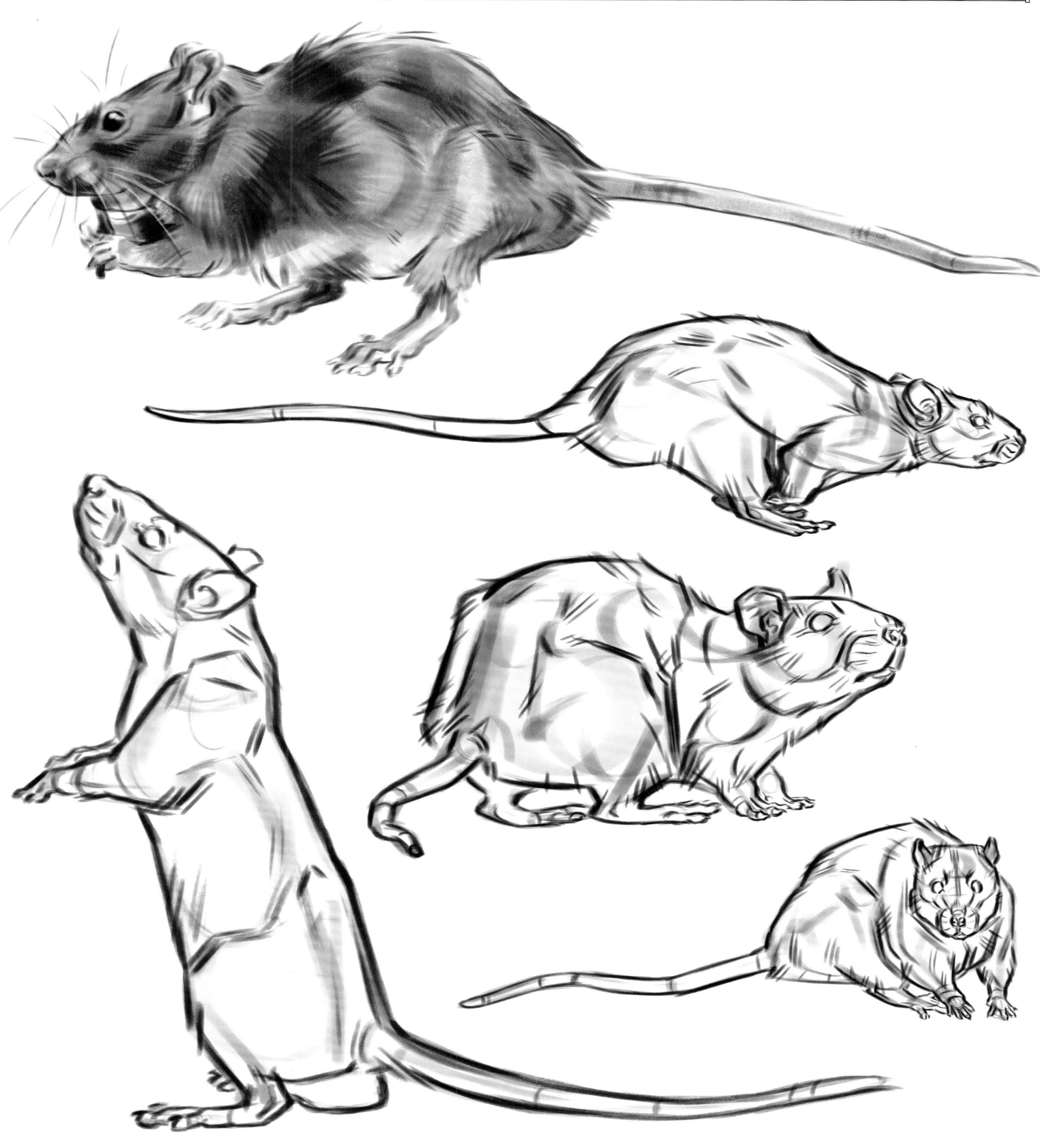

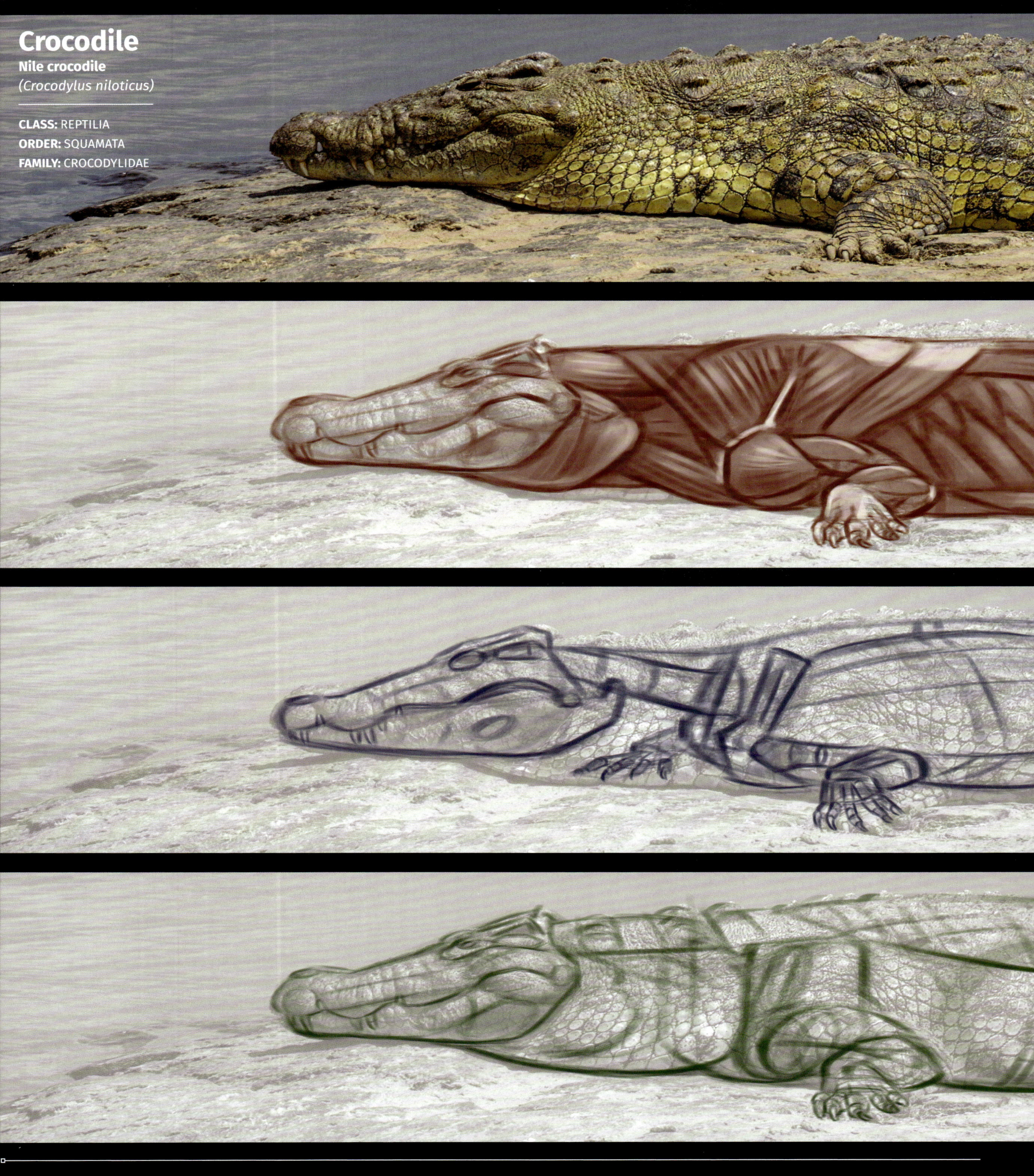
Crocodile
Nile crocodile
(Crocodylus niloticus)
CLASS: REPTILIA
ORDER: SQUAMATA
FAMILY: CROCODYLIDAE

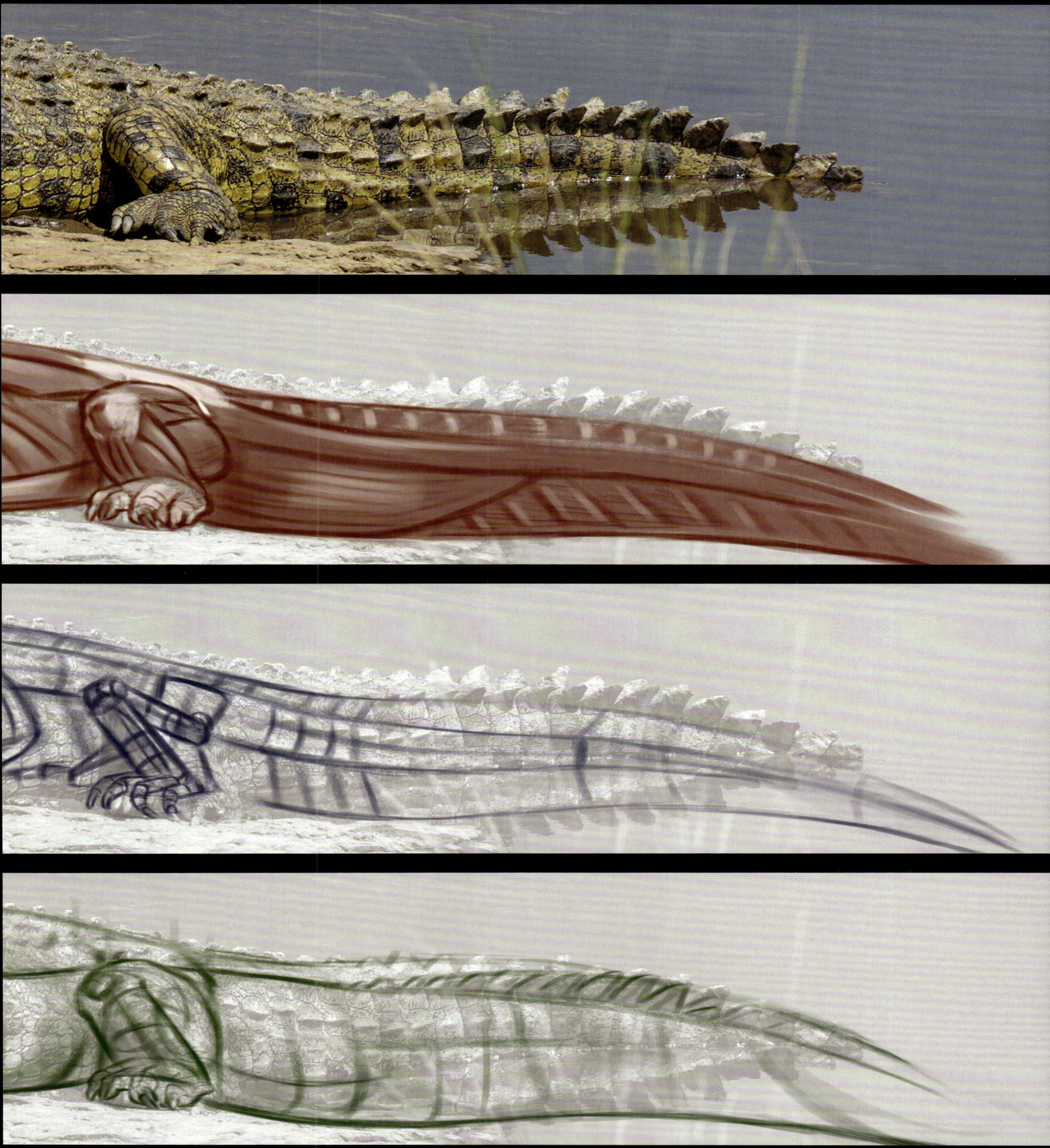

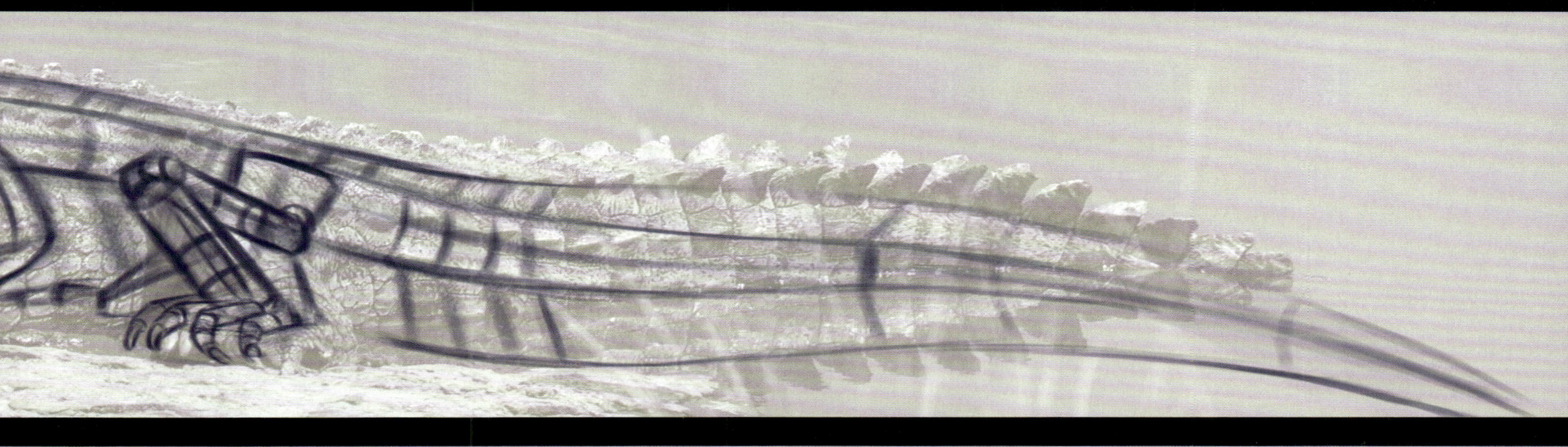

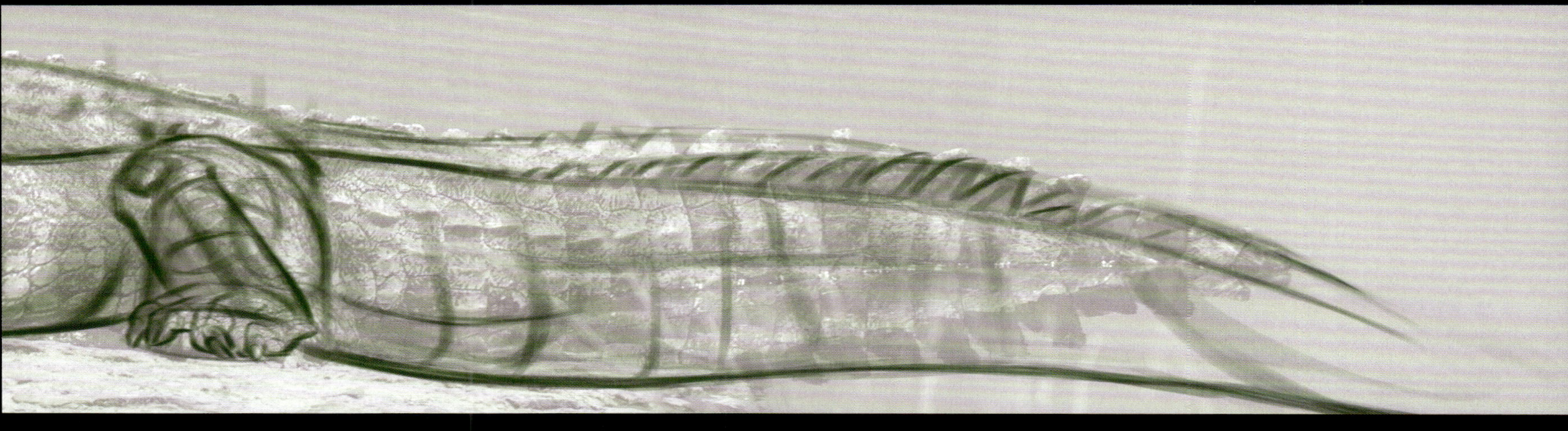

Photograph © Sergio Pitamitz/ Agami.nl

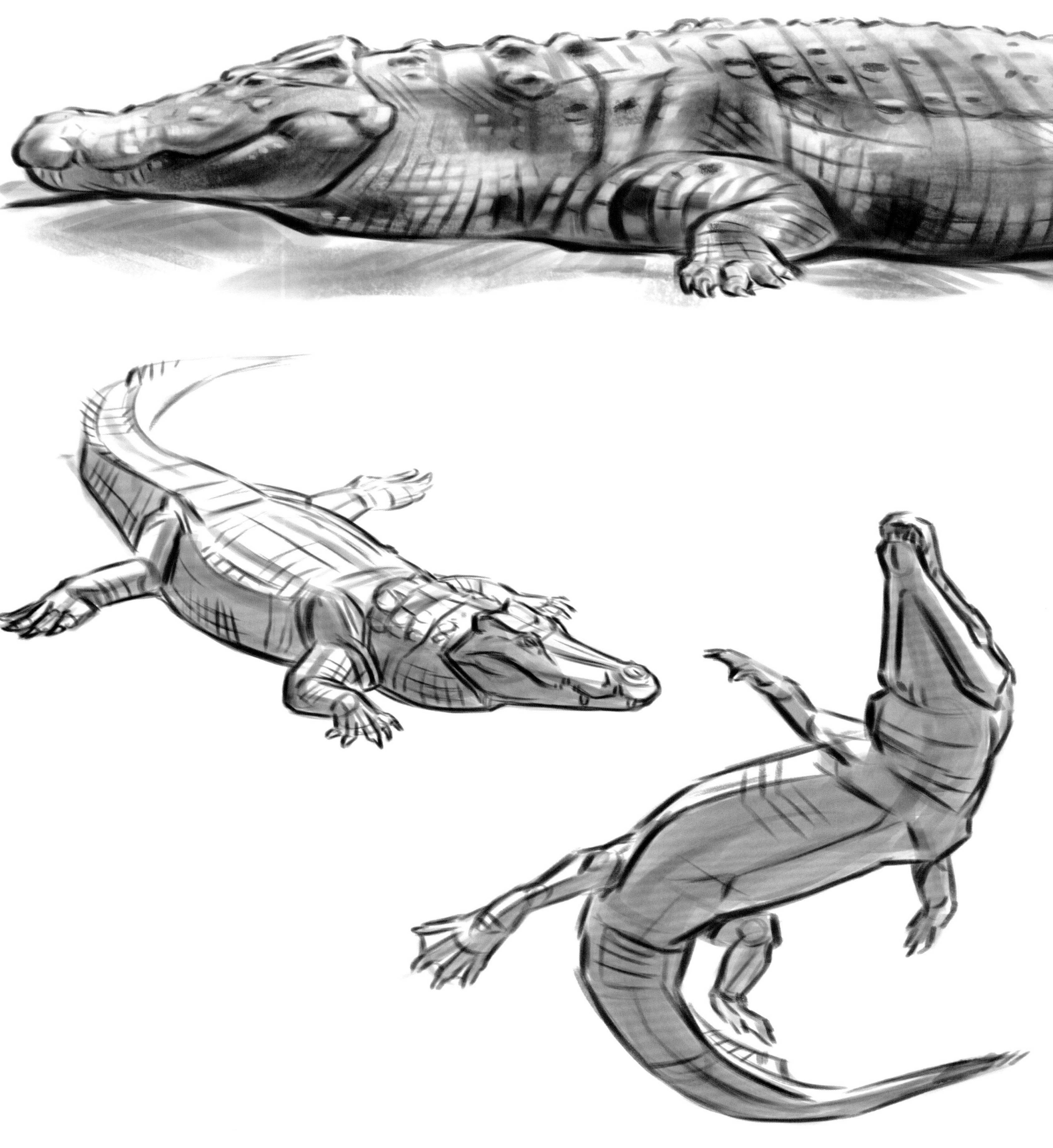

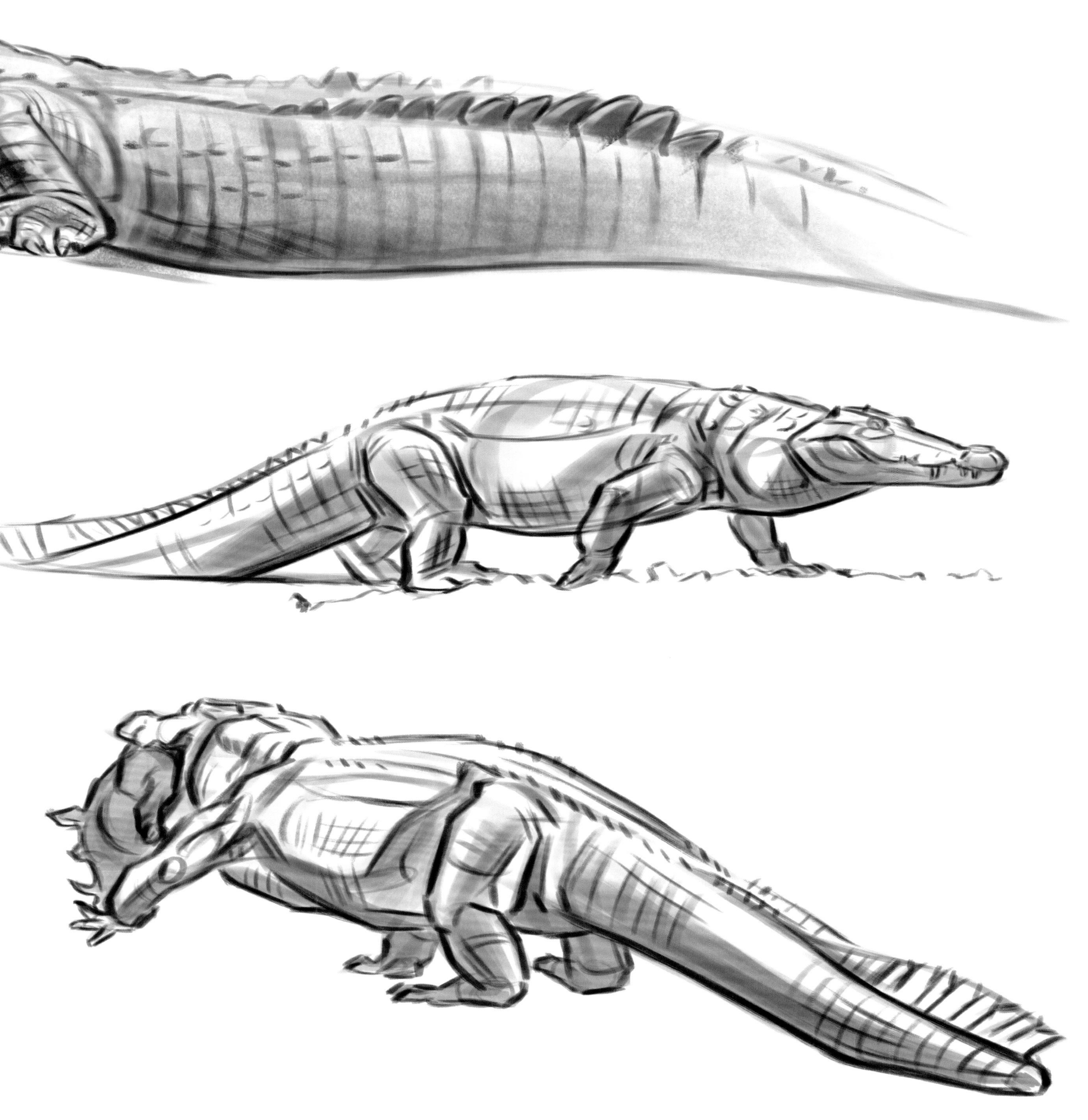

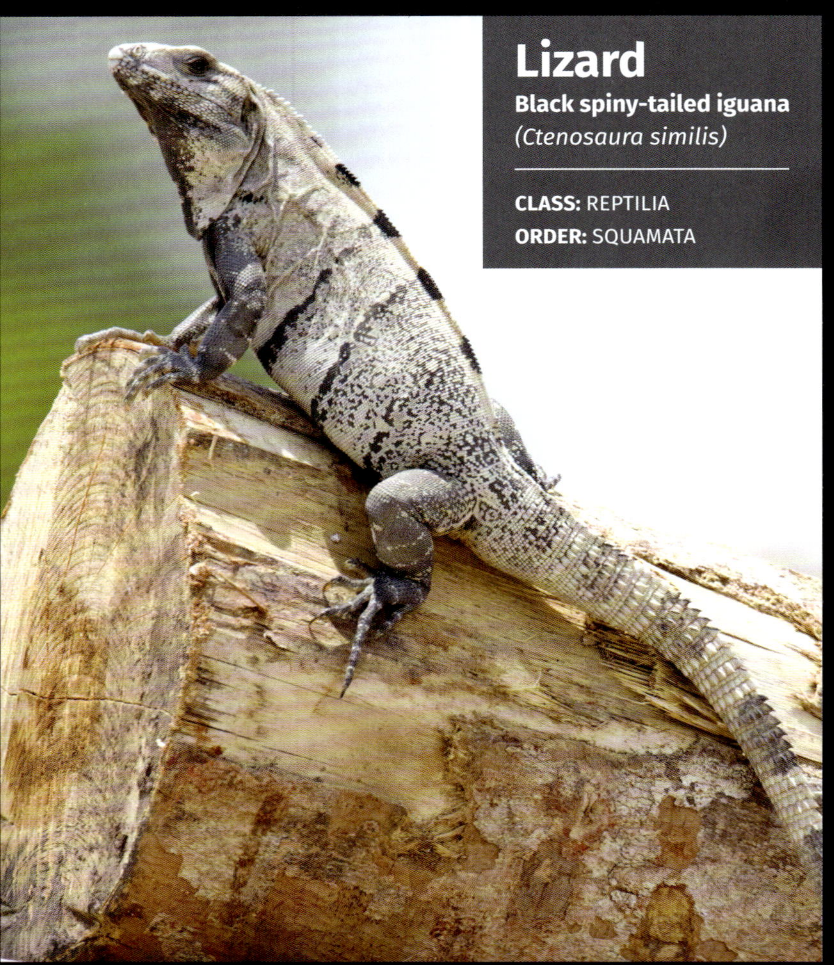

Lizard

Black spiny-tailed iguana
(Ctenosaura similis)

CLASS: REPTILIA
ORDER: SQUAMATA

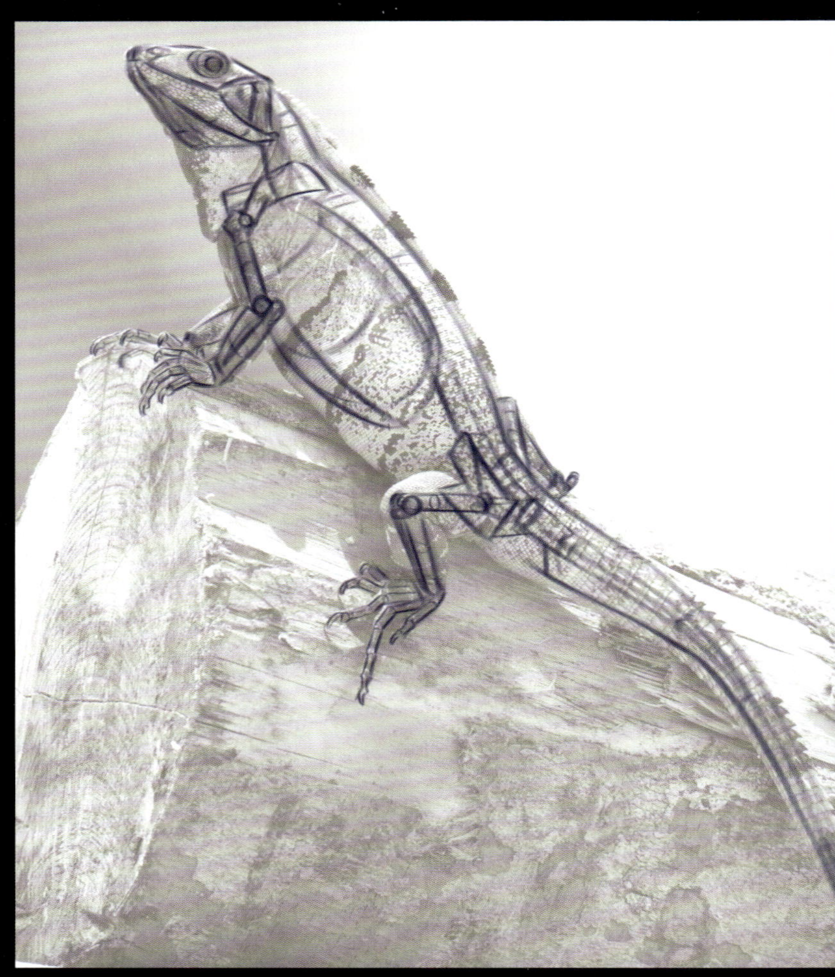

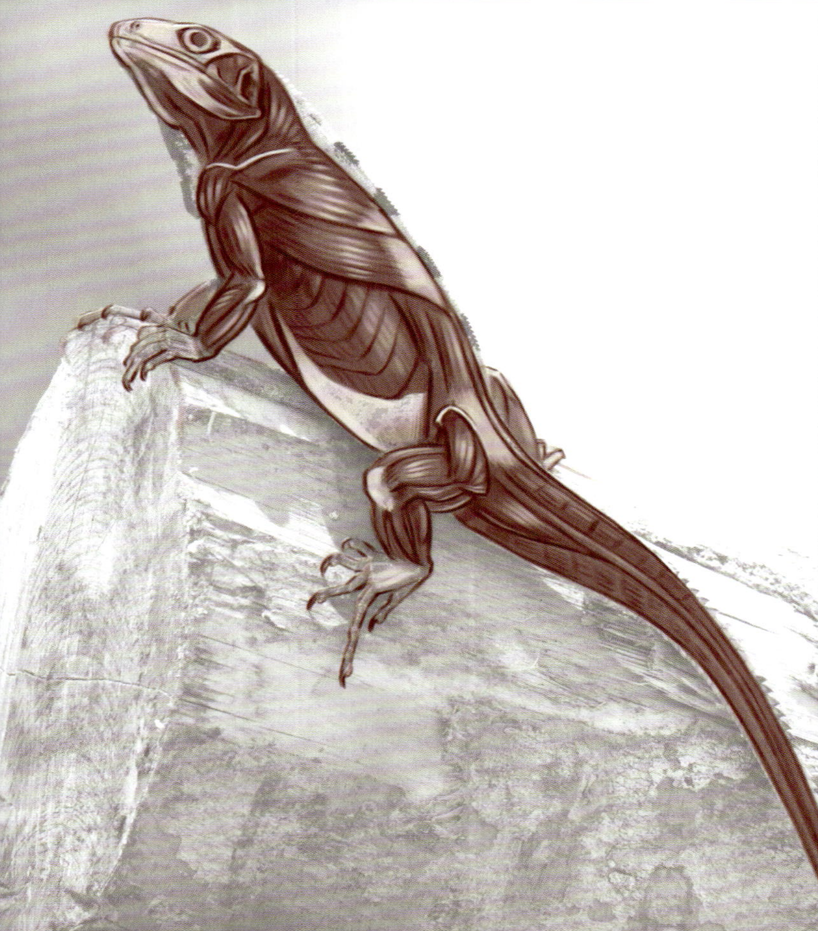

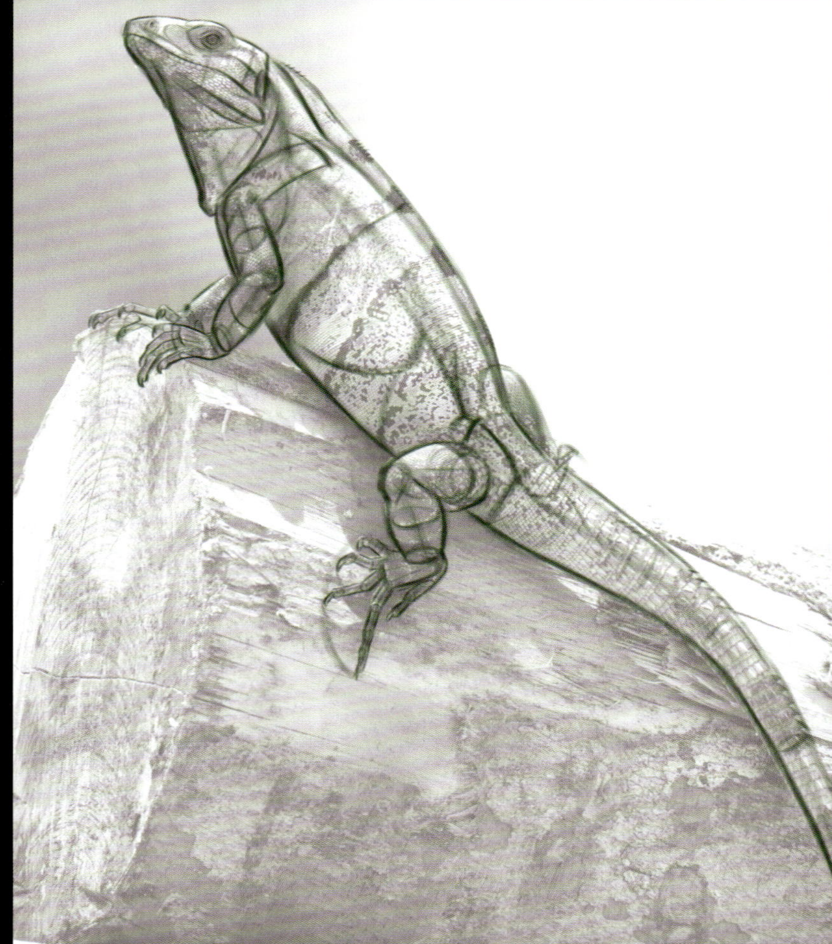

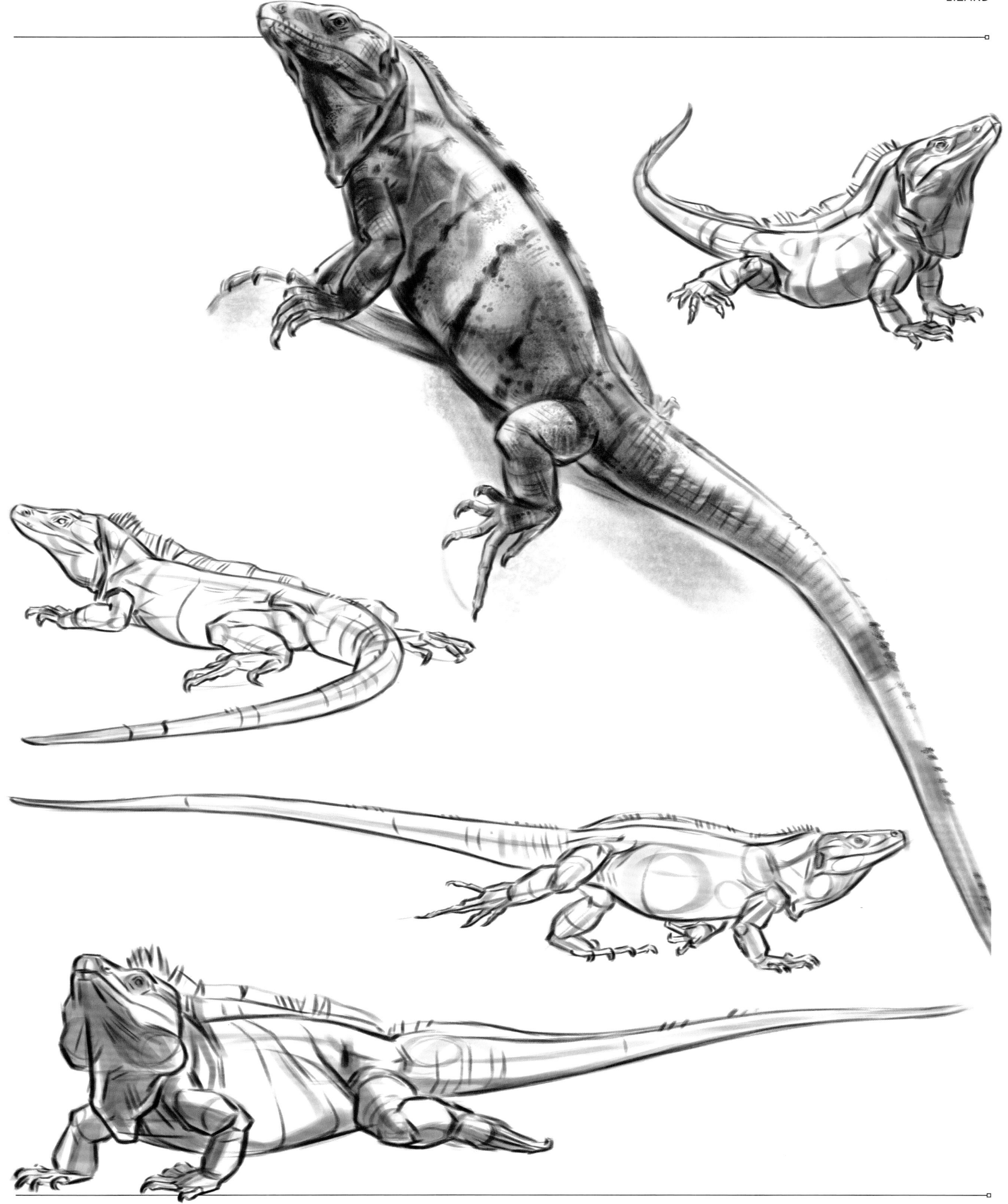

Hawk

Roadside hawk
(Rupornis magnirostris)

CLASS: AVES
ORDER: ACCIPITRIFORMES
FAMILY: ACCIPITRIDAE

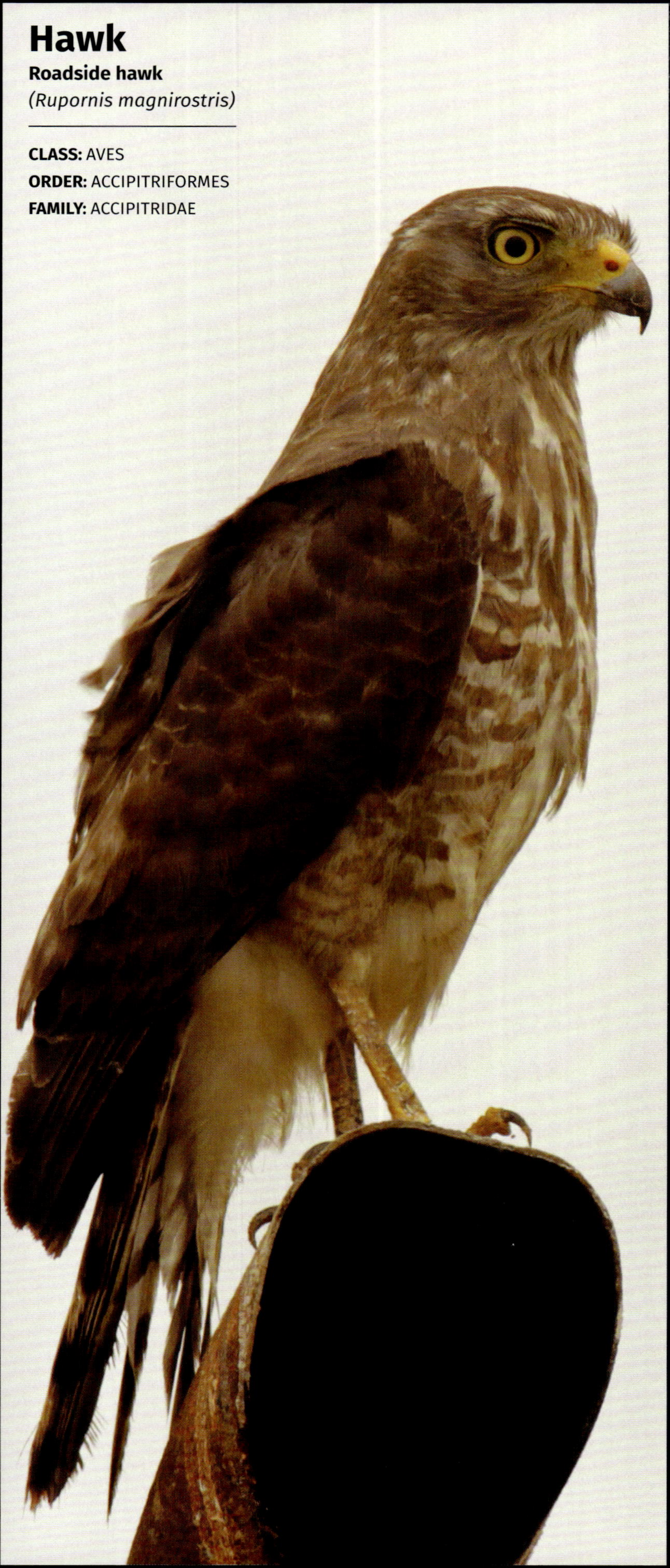

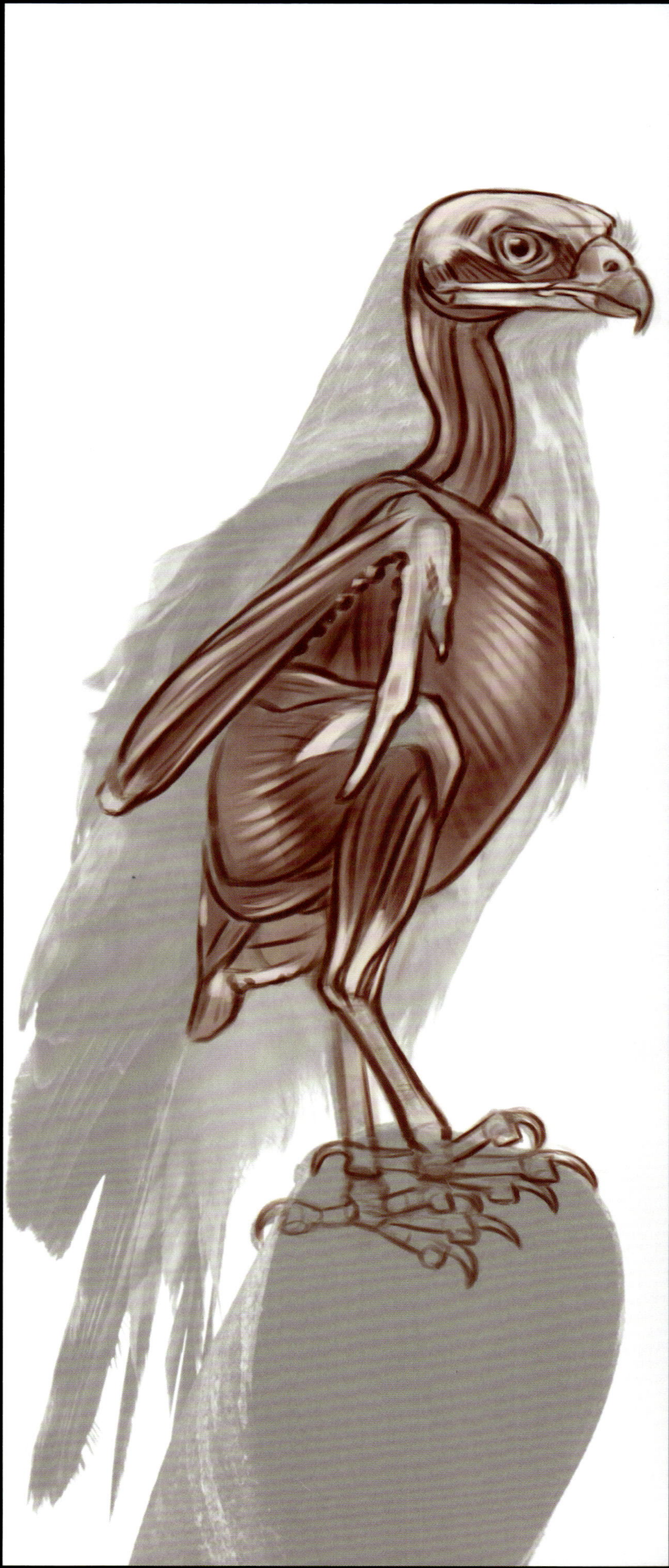

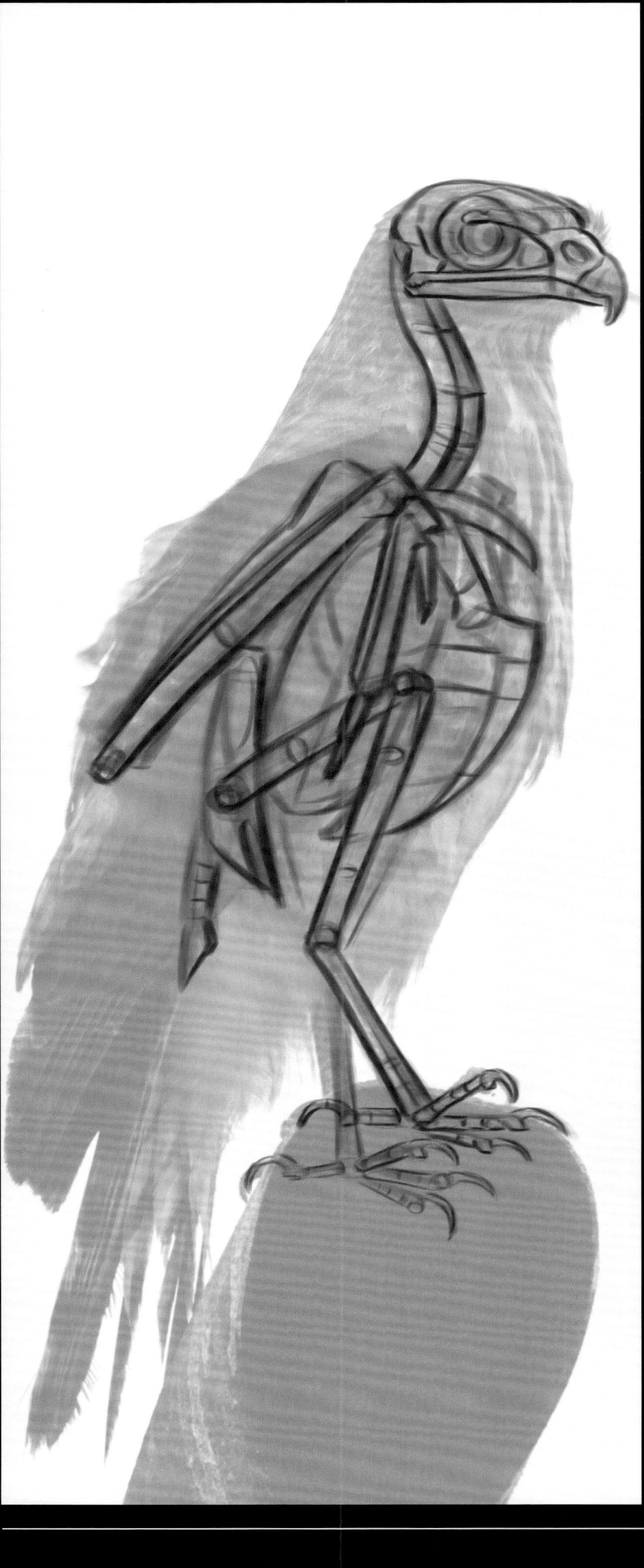

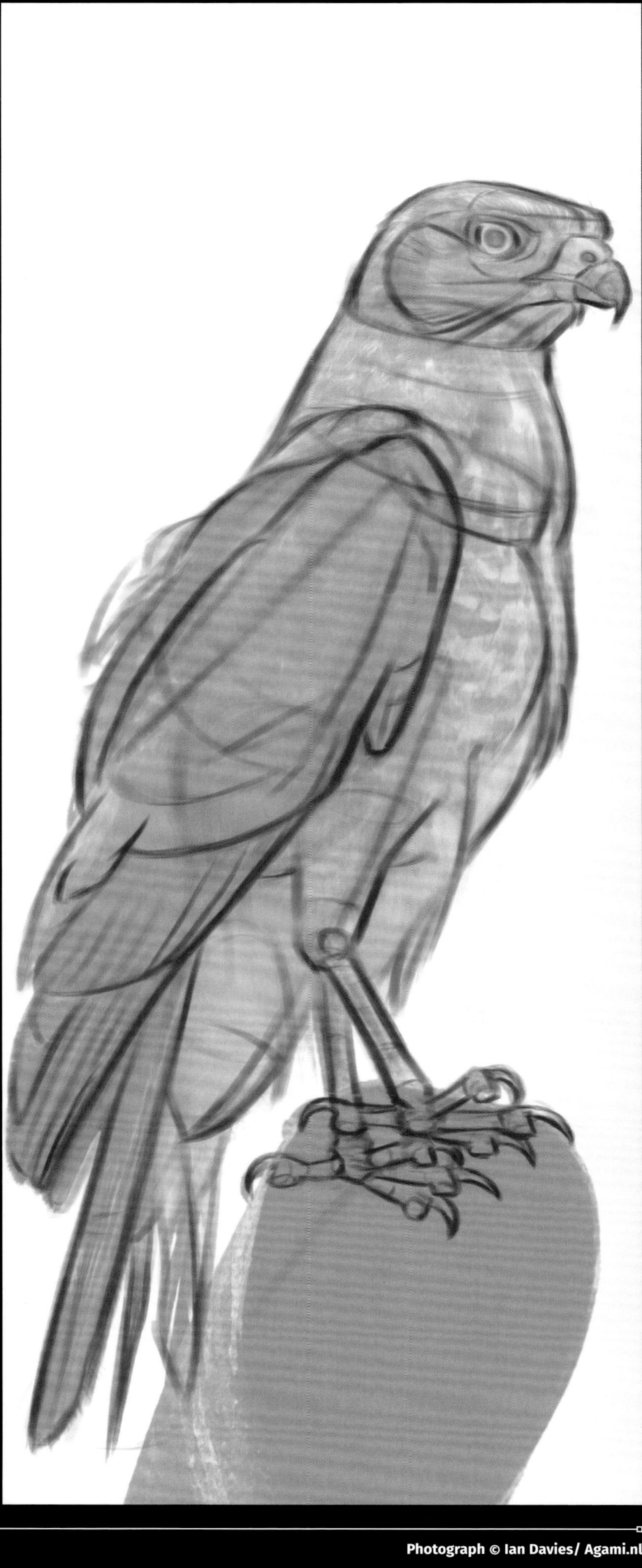

Photograph © Ian Davies/ Agami.nl

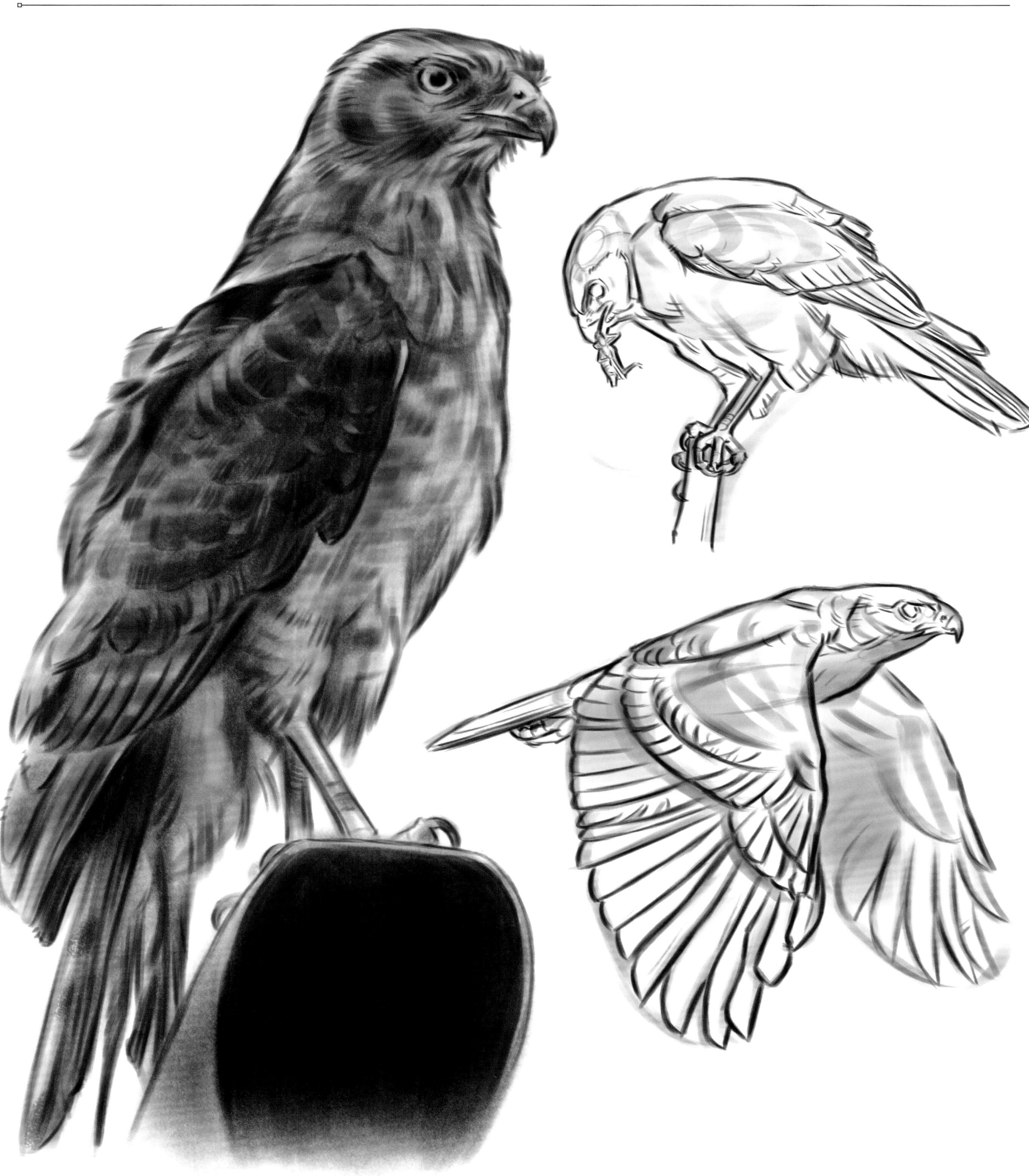

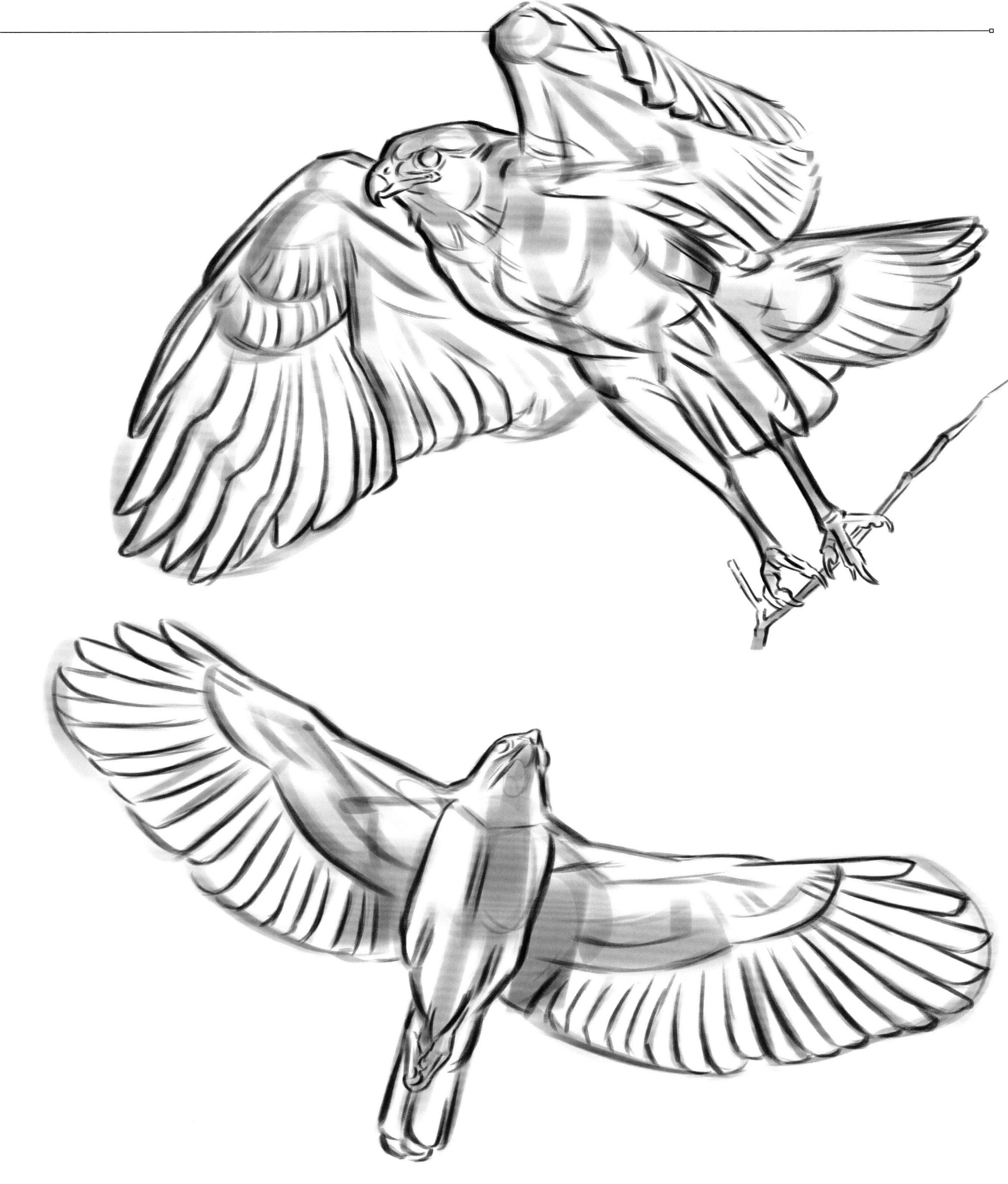

Contributors' Gallery

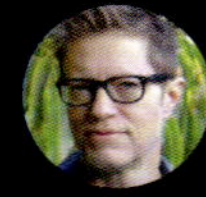

Joe Weatherly

Animal artist & professor of animal art

Based in Southern California, Joe Weatherly specializes in the drawing and painting of animals. His style is bold and vigorous, capturing the essence and drama of the subjects he draws and paints. His work aims to convey the attitude and expression of the animal's character, along with telling a visual story. Joe is passionate about the conservation of the natural world and hopes his work will motivate people to protect it and promote its survival.

joeweatherly.com

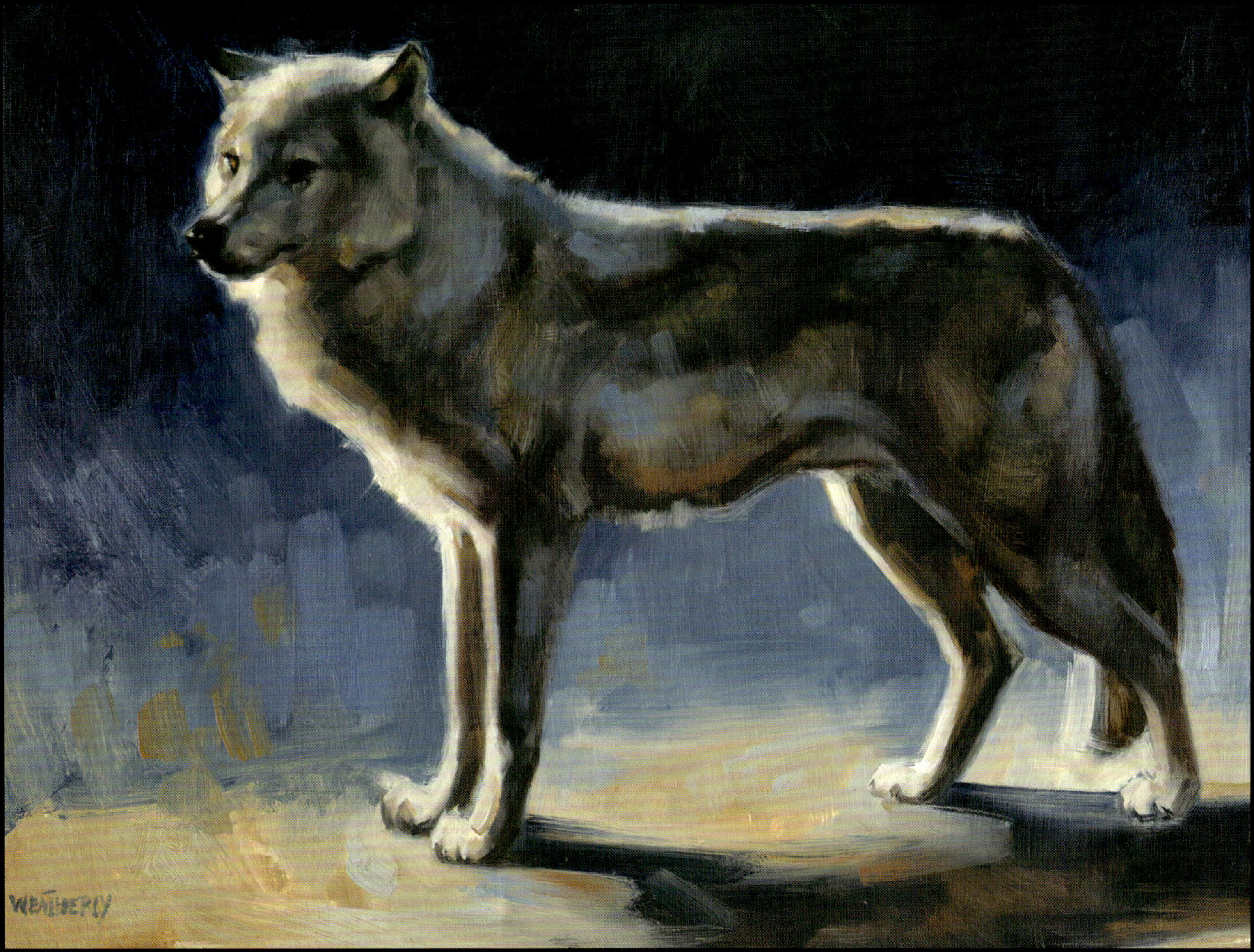

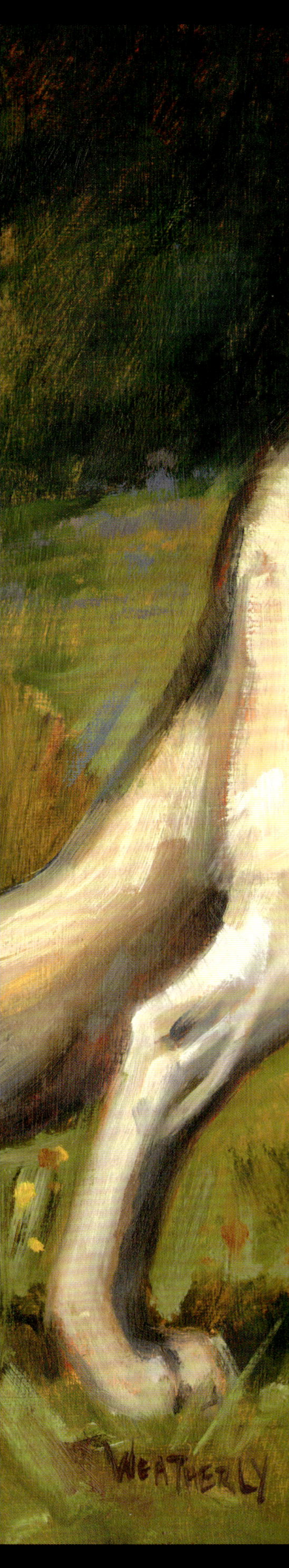

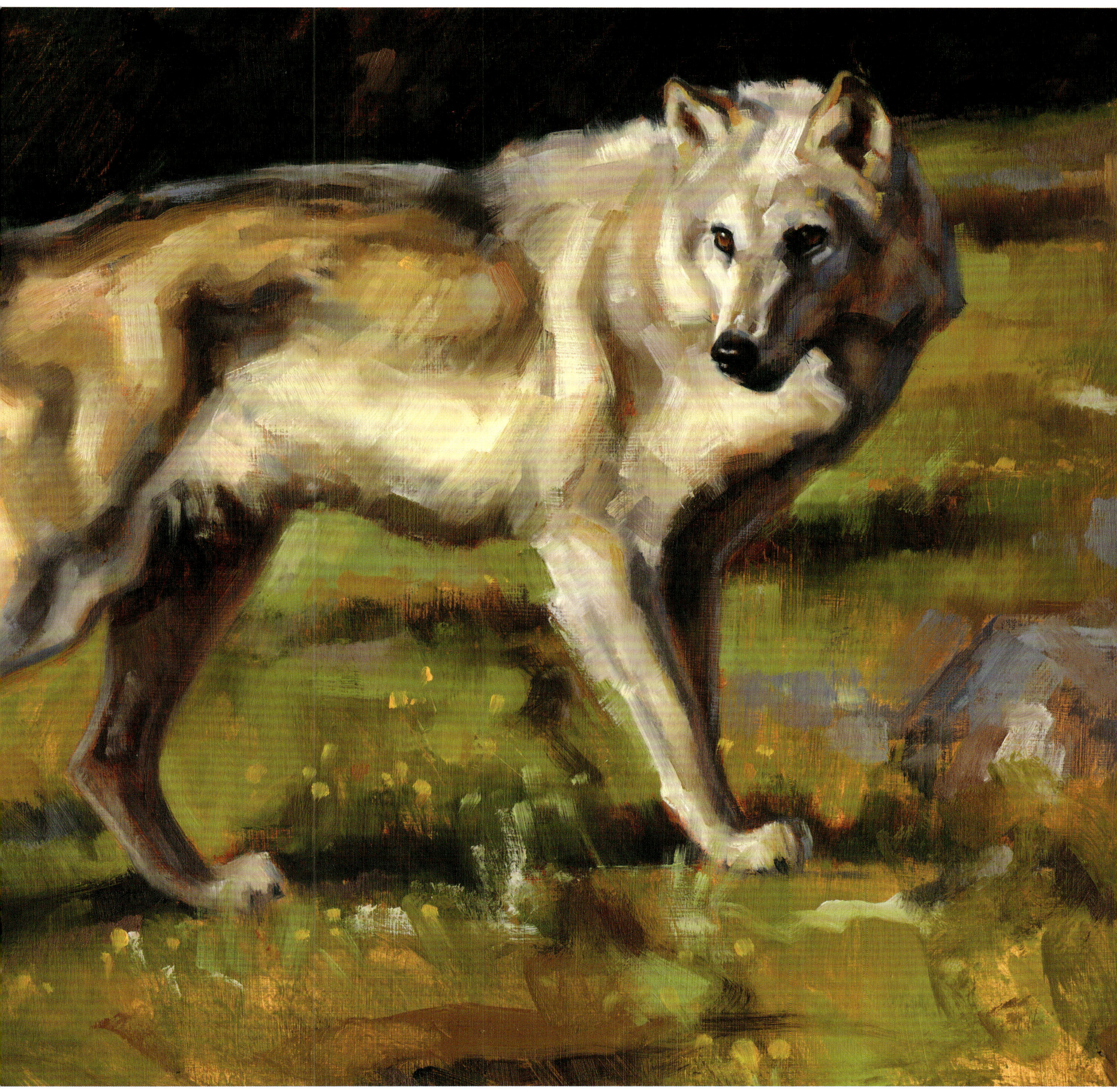

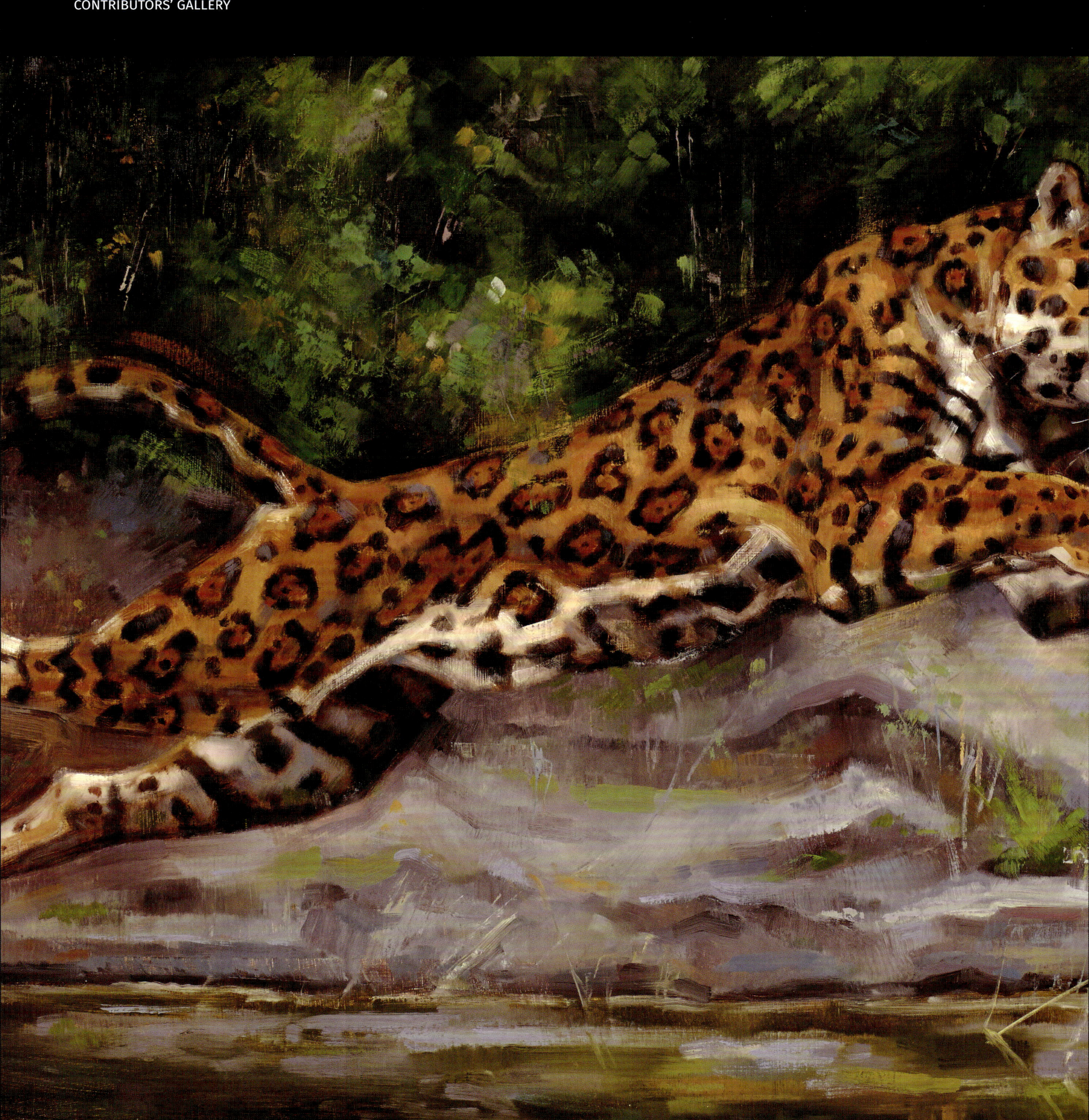

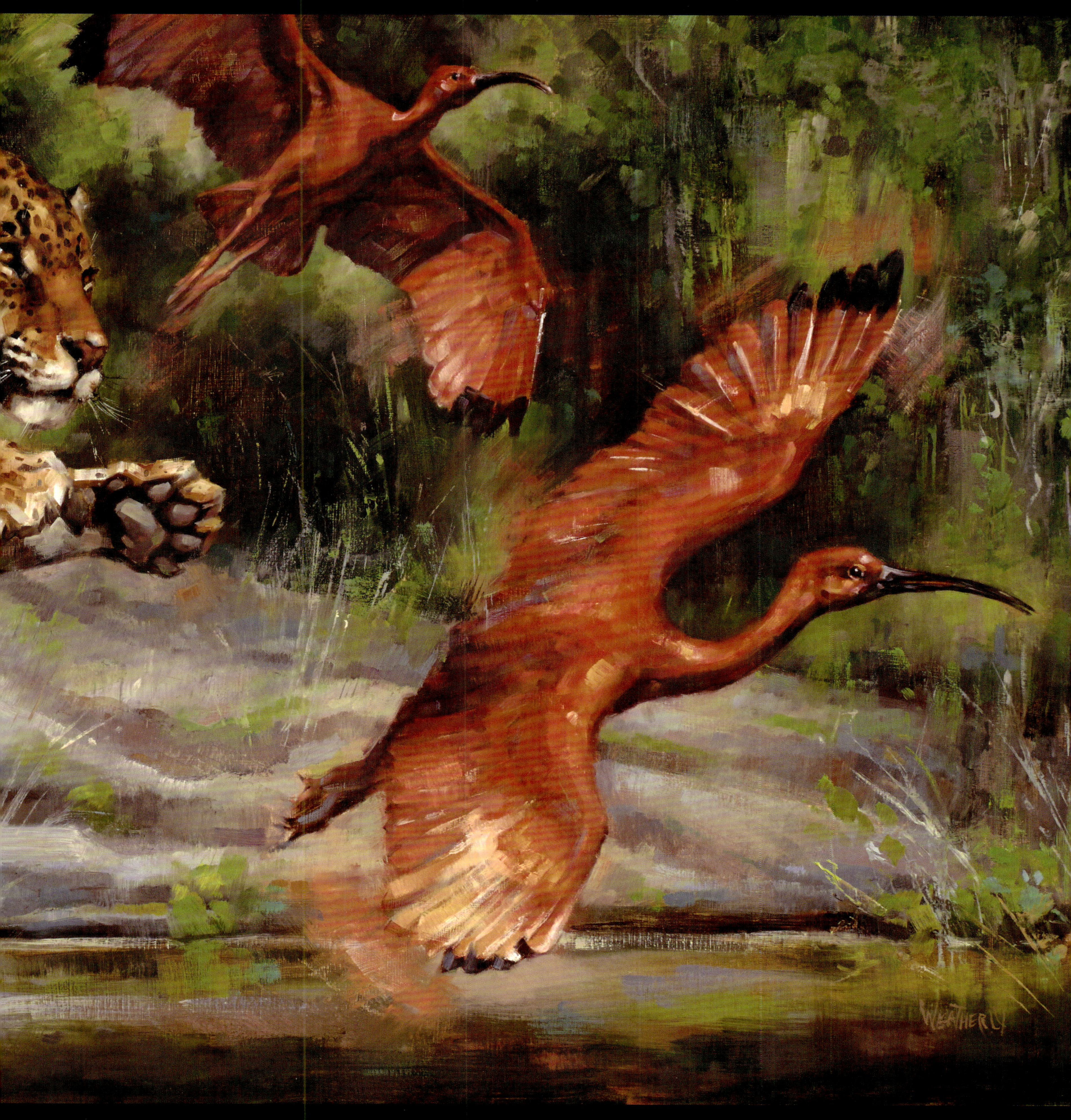

Artwork © Joe Weatherly

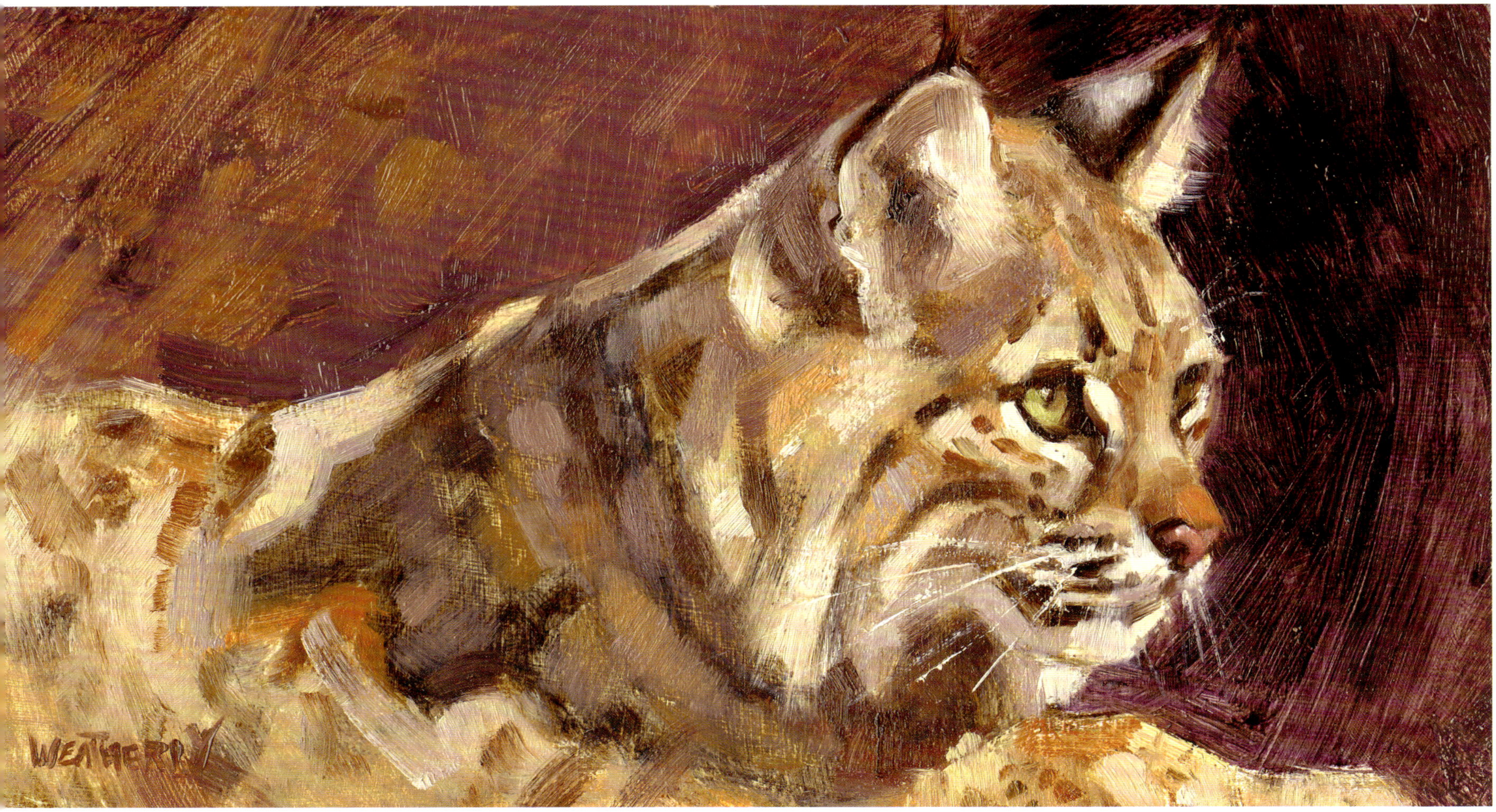

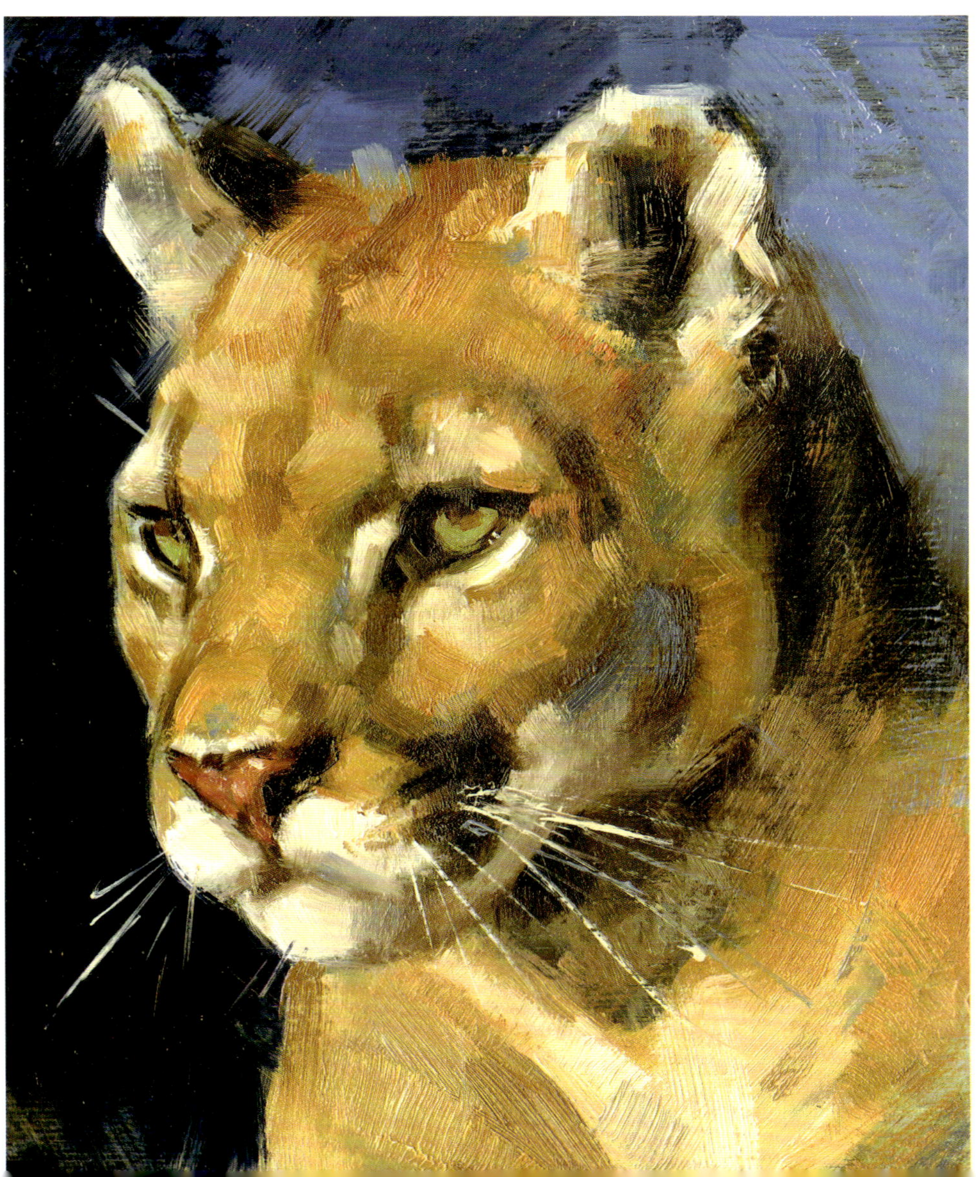

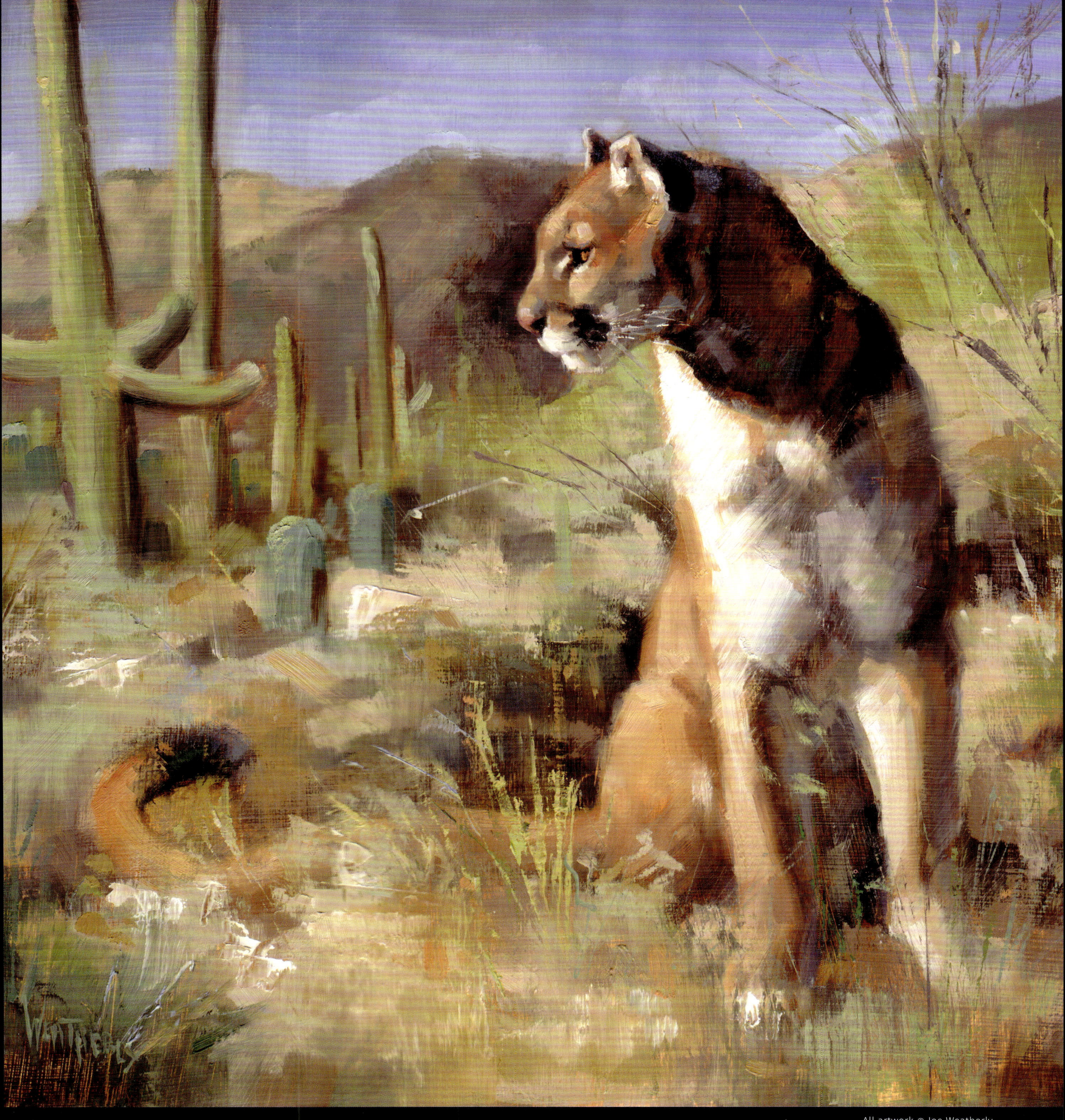

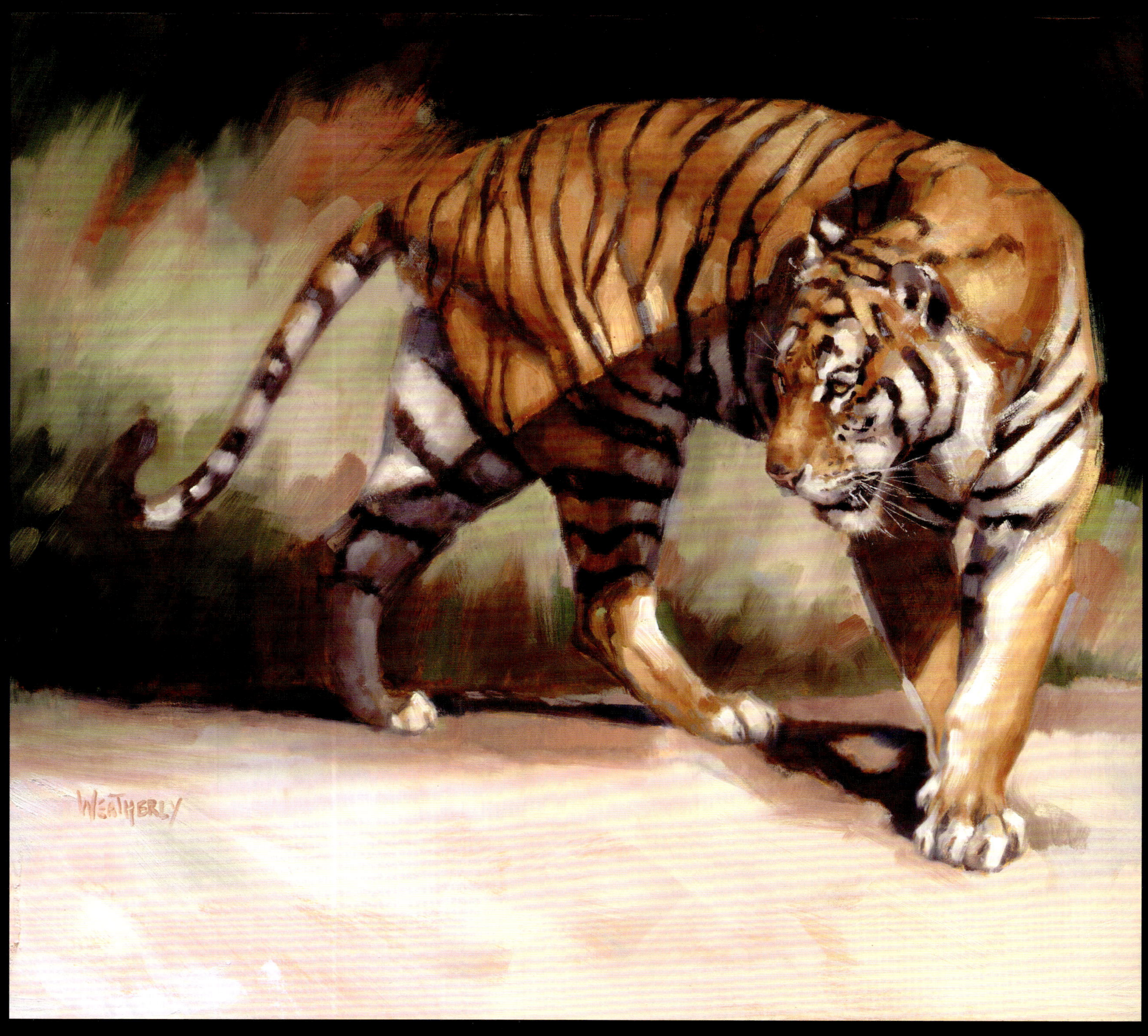
WEATHERLY

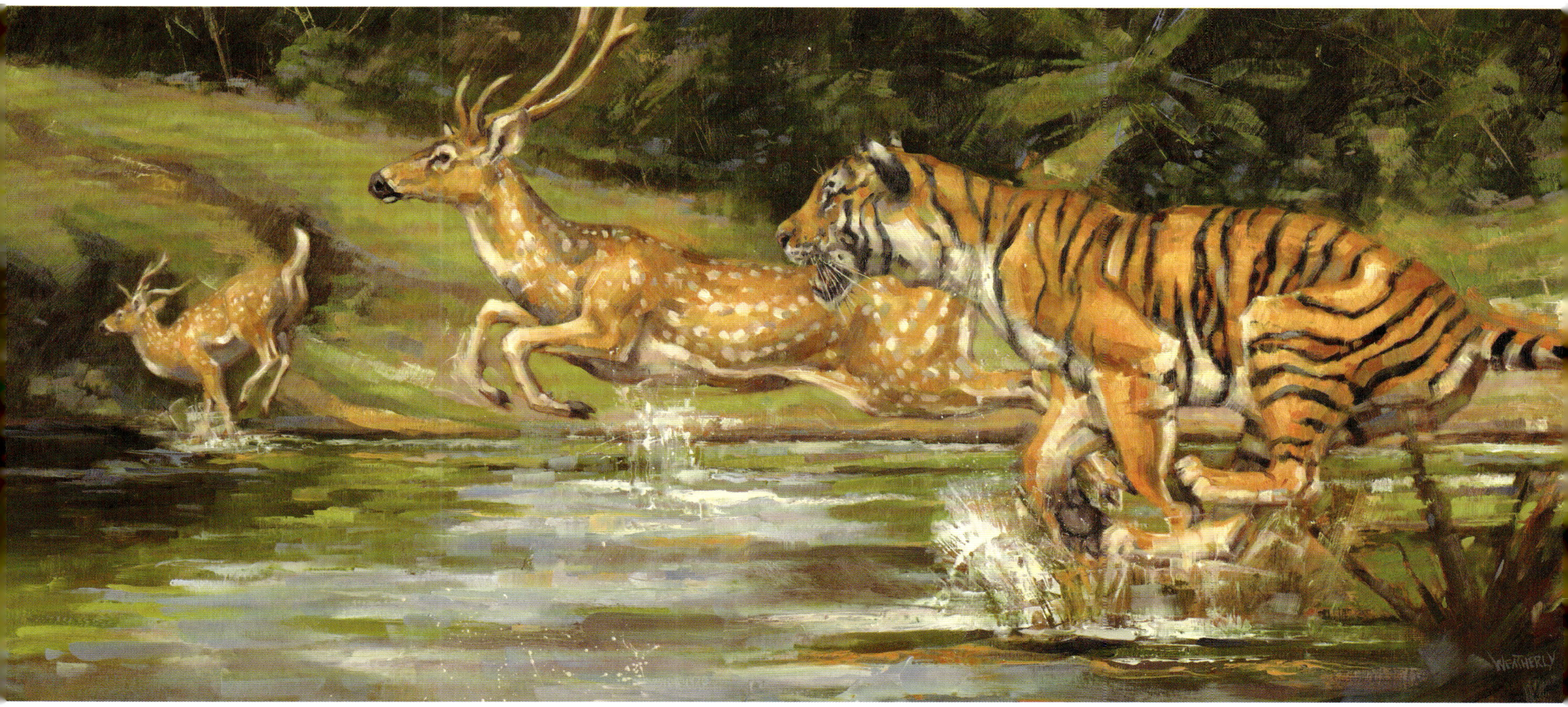
WEATHERLY

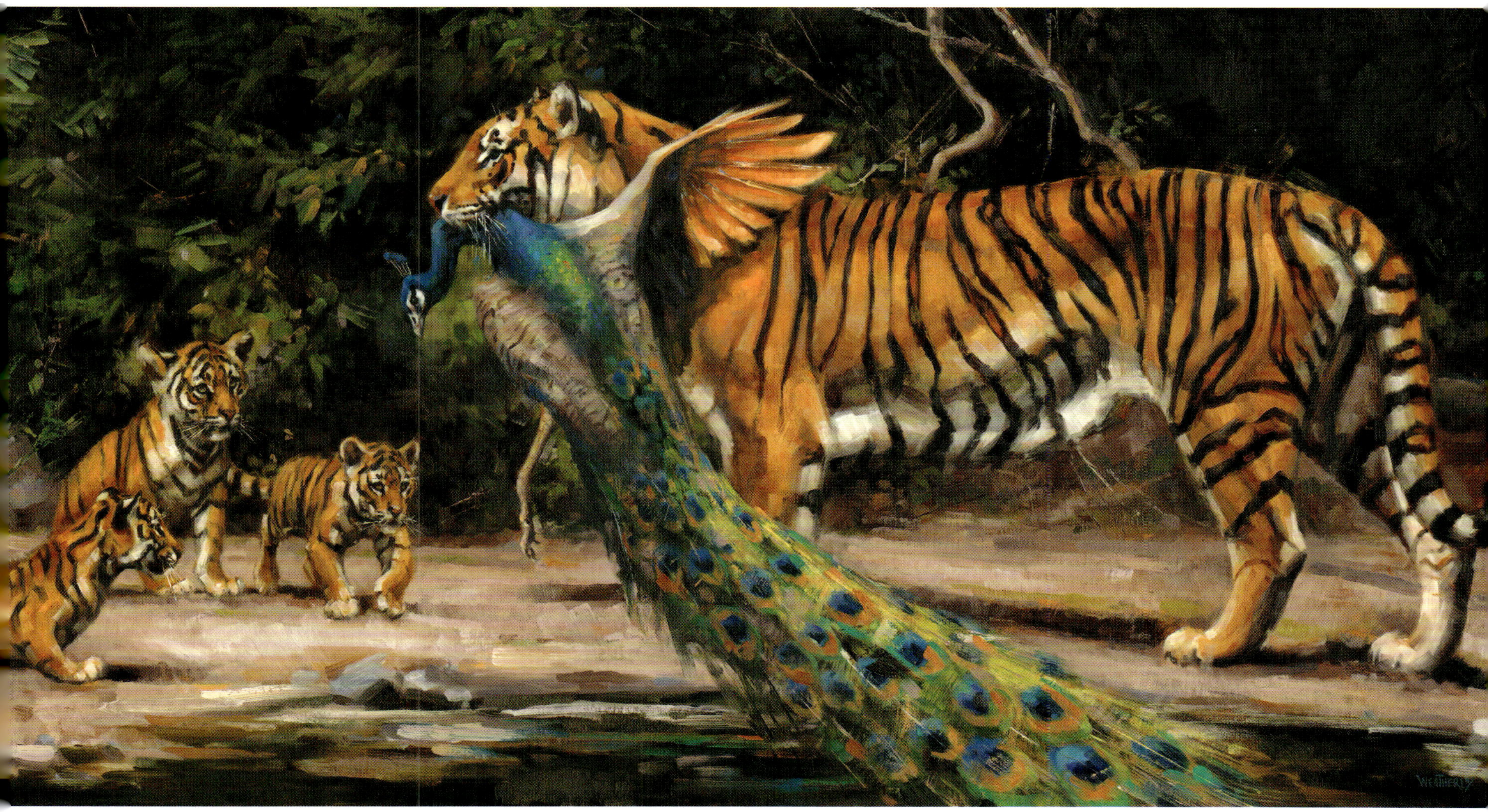
WEATHERLY

Artwork © Joe Weatherly

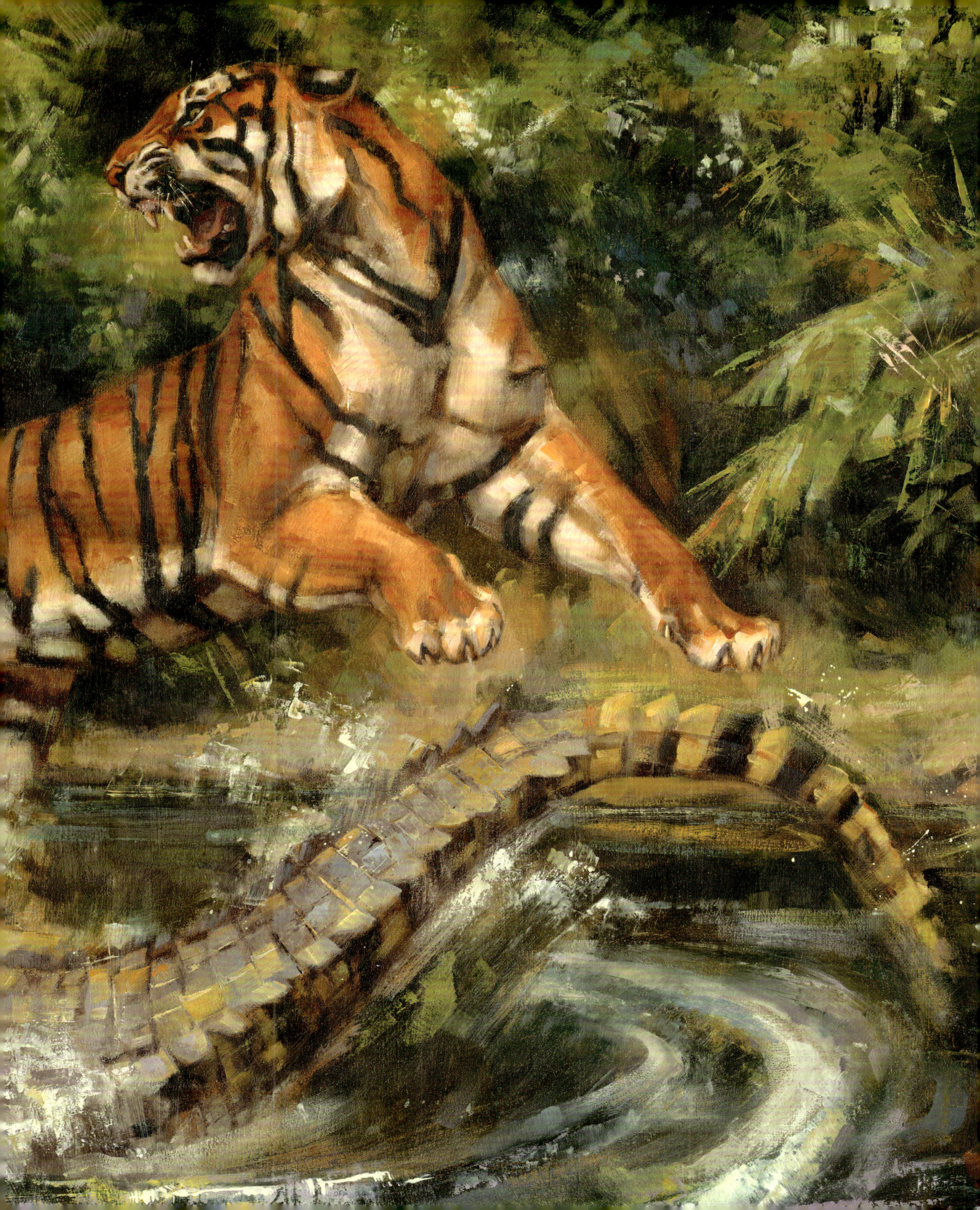

Contributors' Gallery

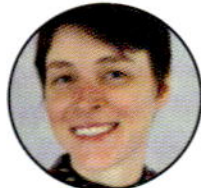

Shannon 'Alex' Beaumont

Freelance artist & illustrator

Originally from Missouri, USA, Shannon now lives and works as a freelance-independent artist in the quaint forest of Rheinland-Pfalz, Germany. Her clients include governmental institutions, zoos, toy companies, and higher education organizations, amongst others. She loves learning about the critters that inhabit or have inhabited planet Earth, being with the fellow humans she loves, and collecting (almost) anything and everything related to animals and her favourite characters.

shannonscribbles.com

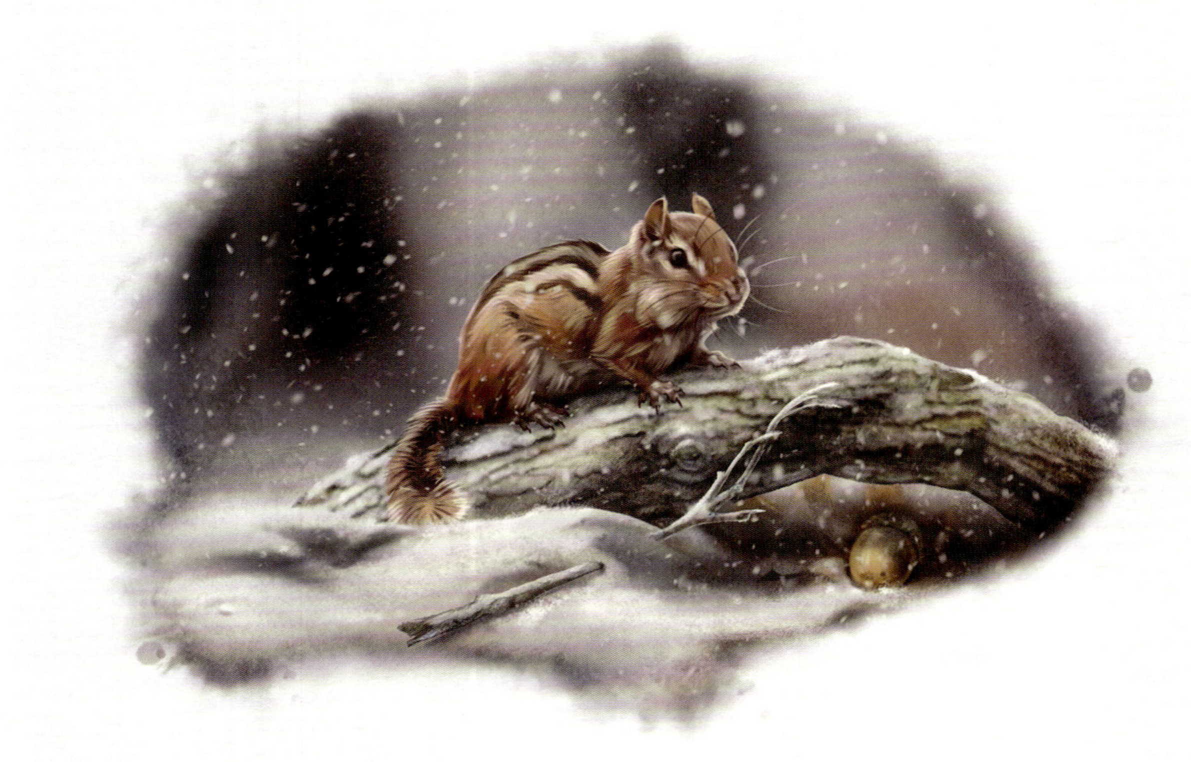

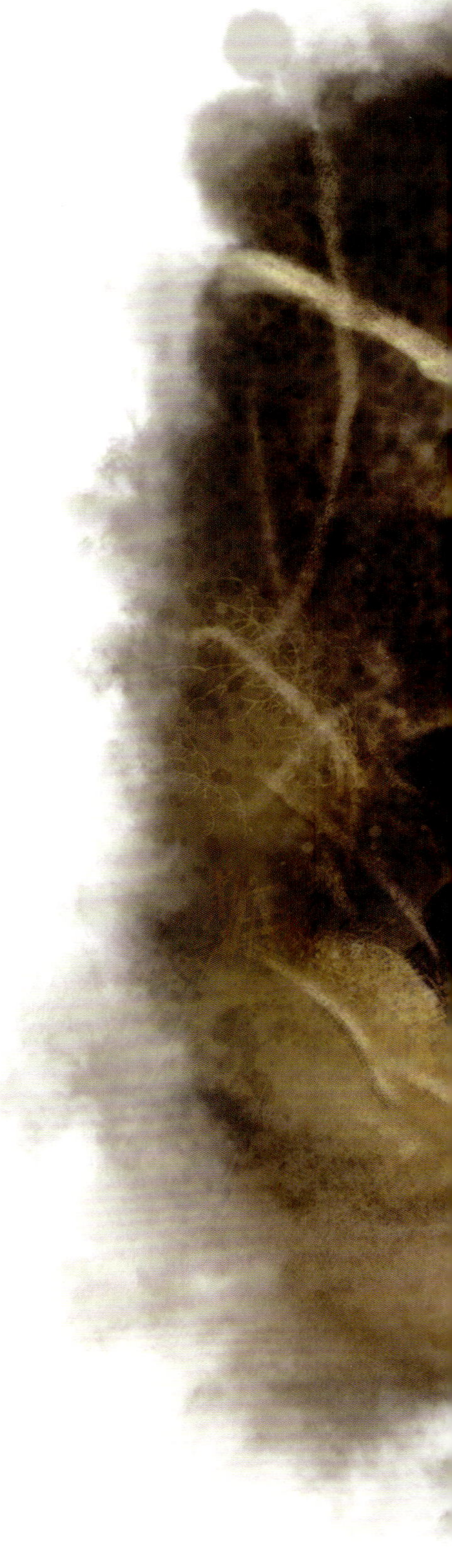

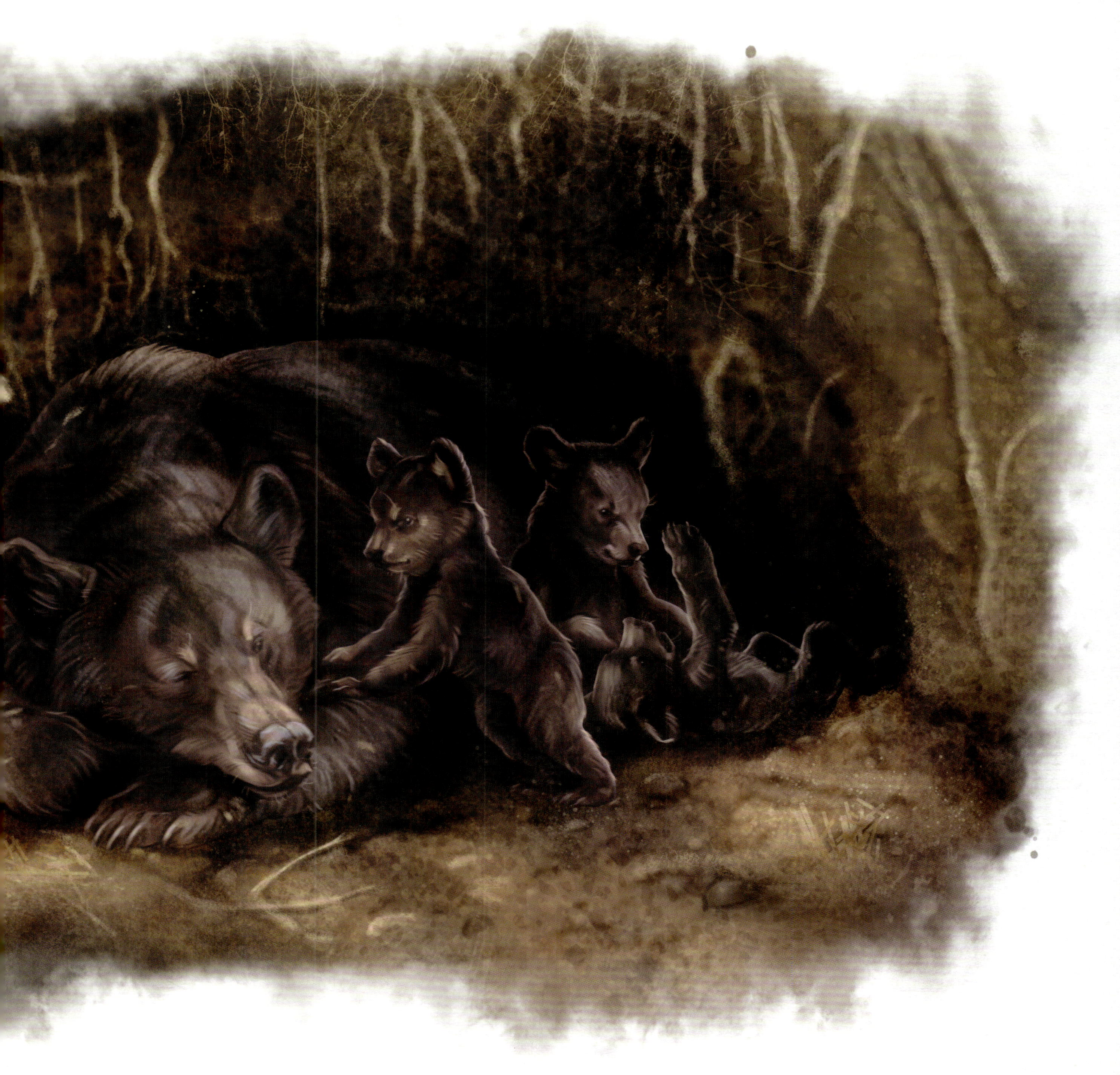

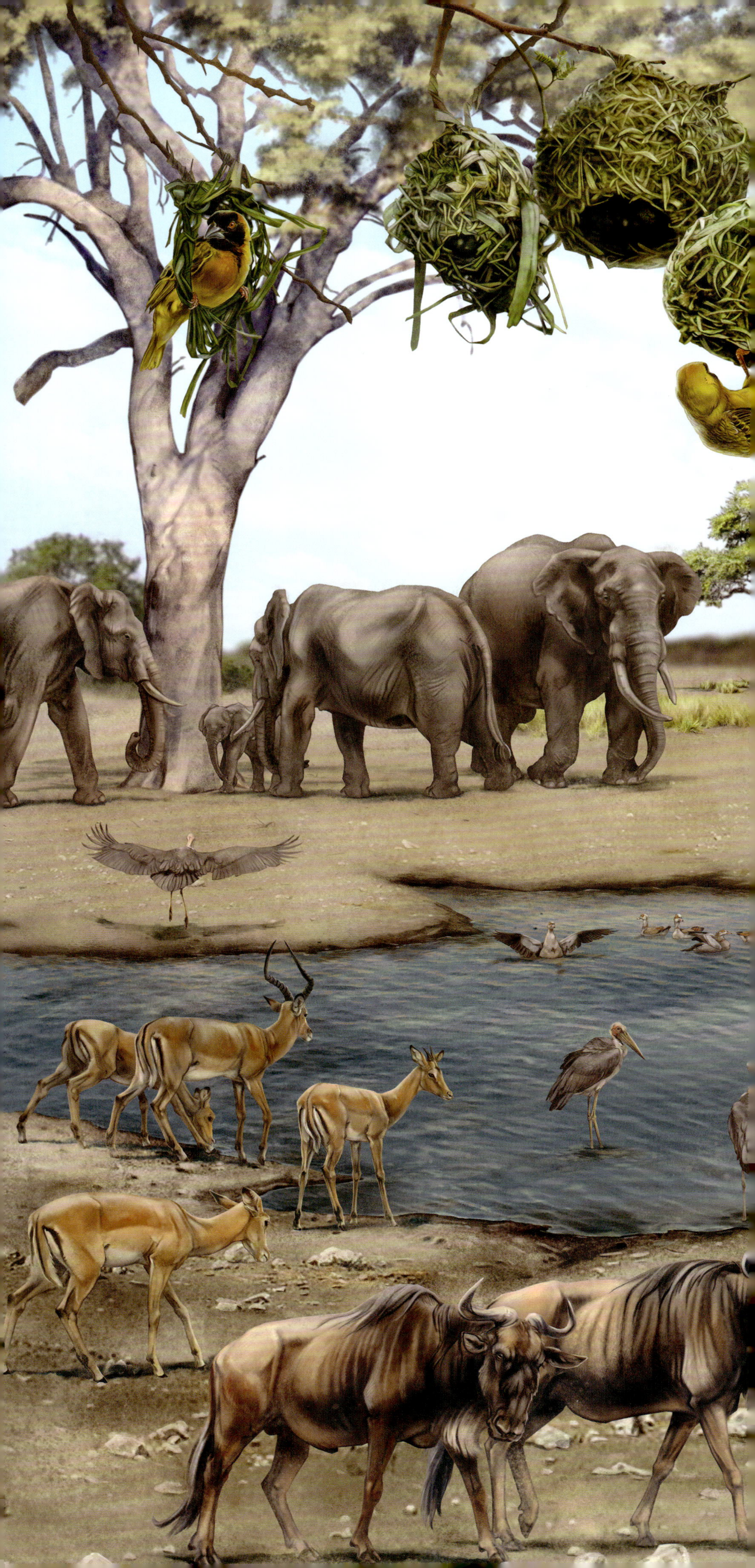

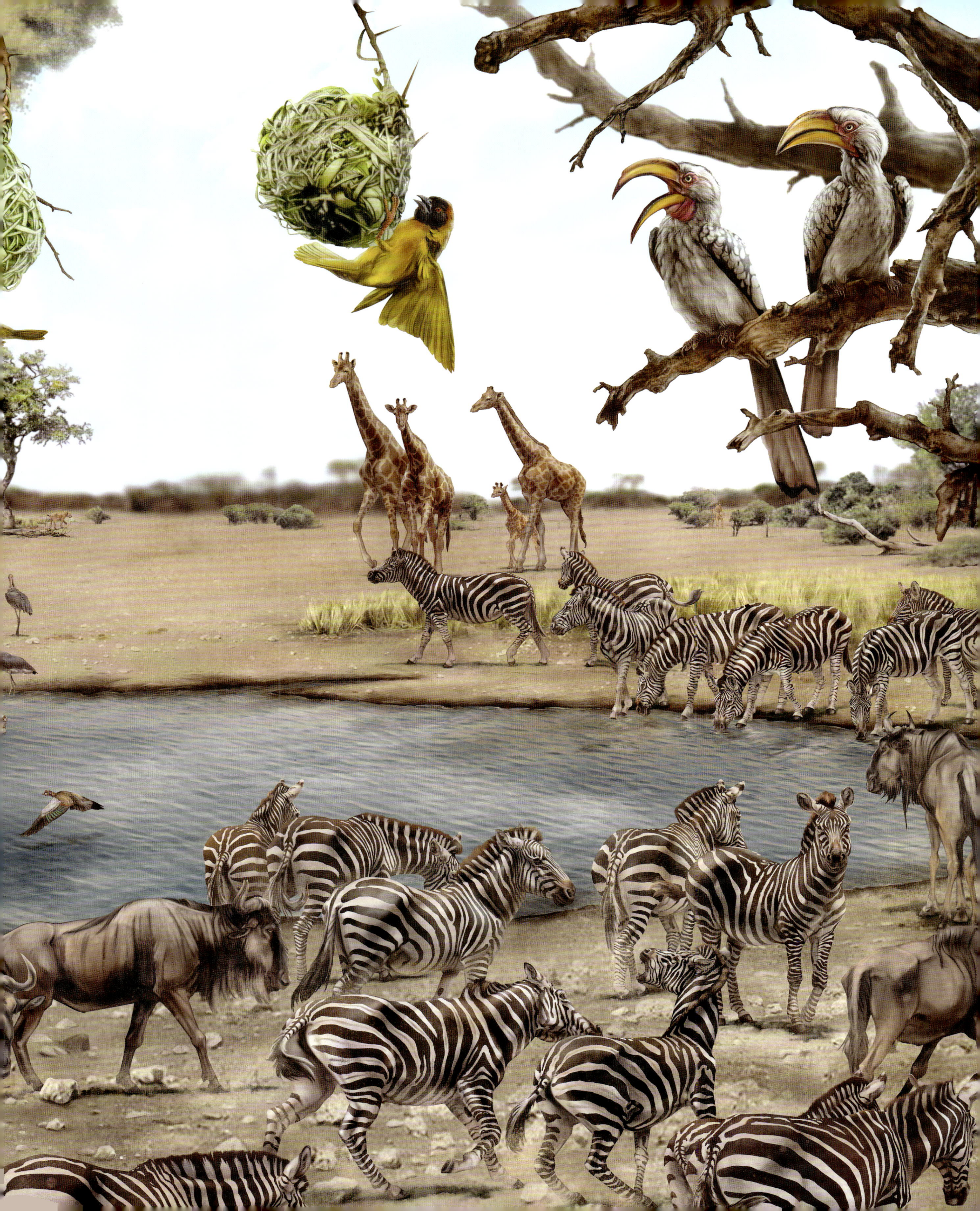

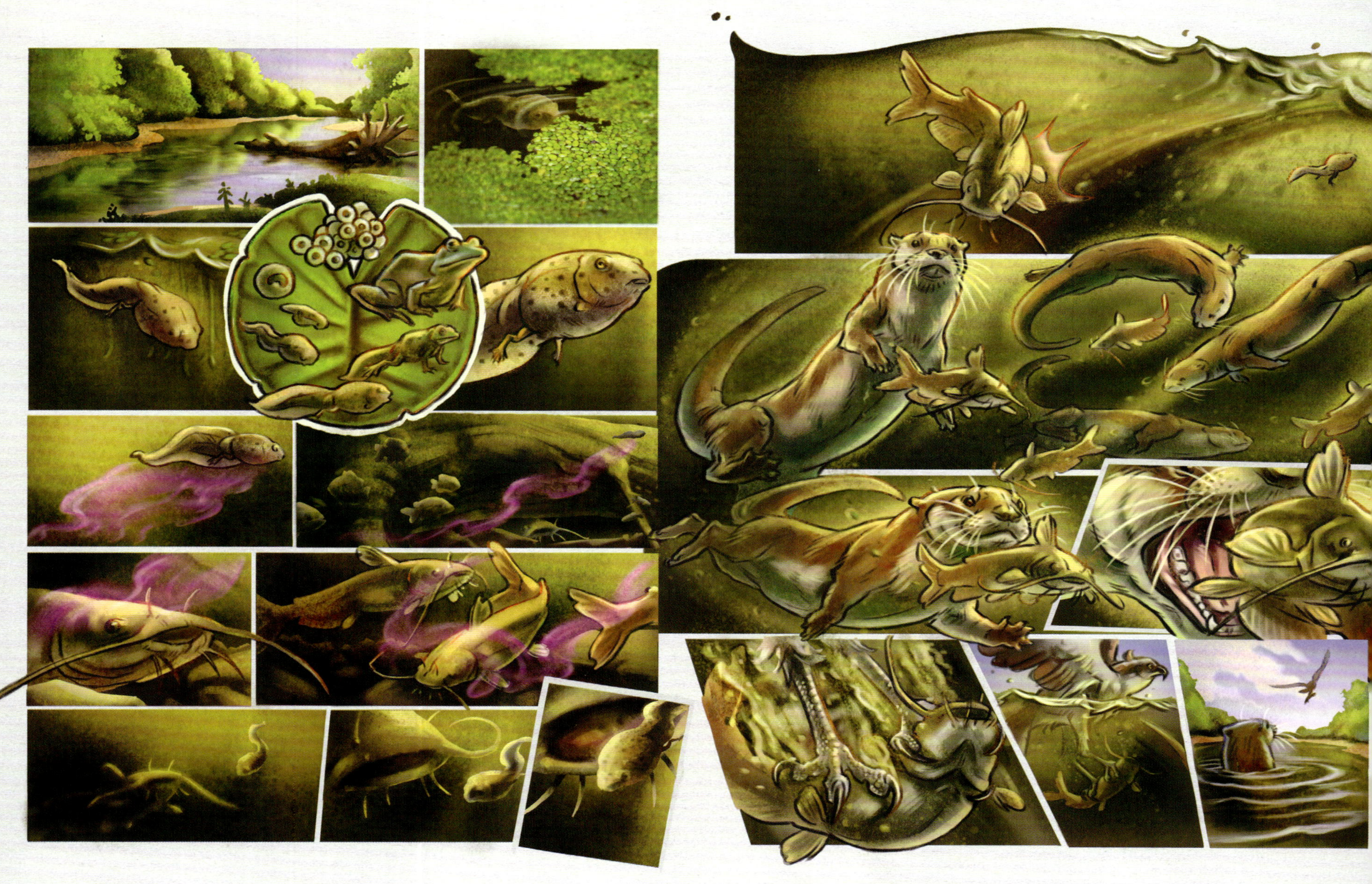

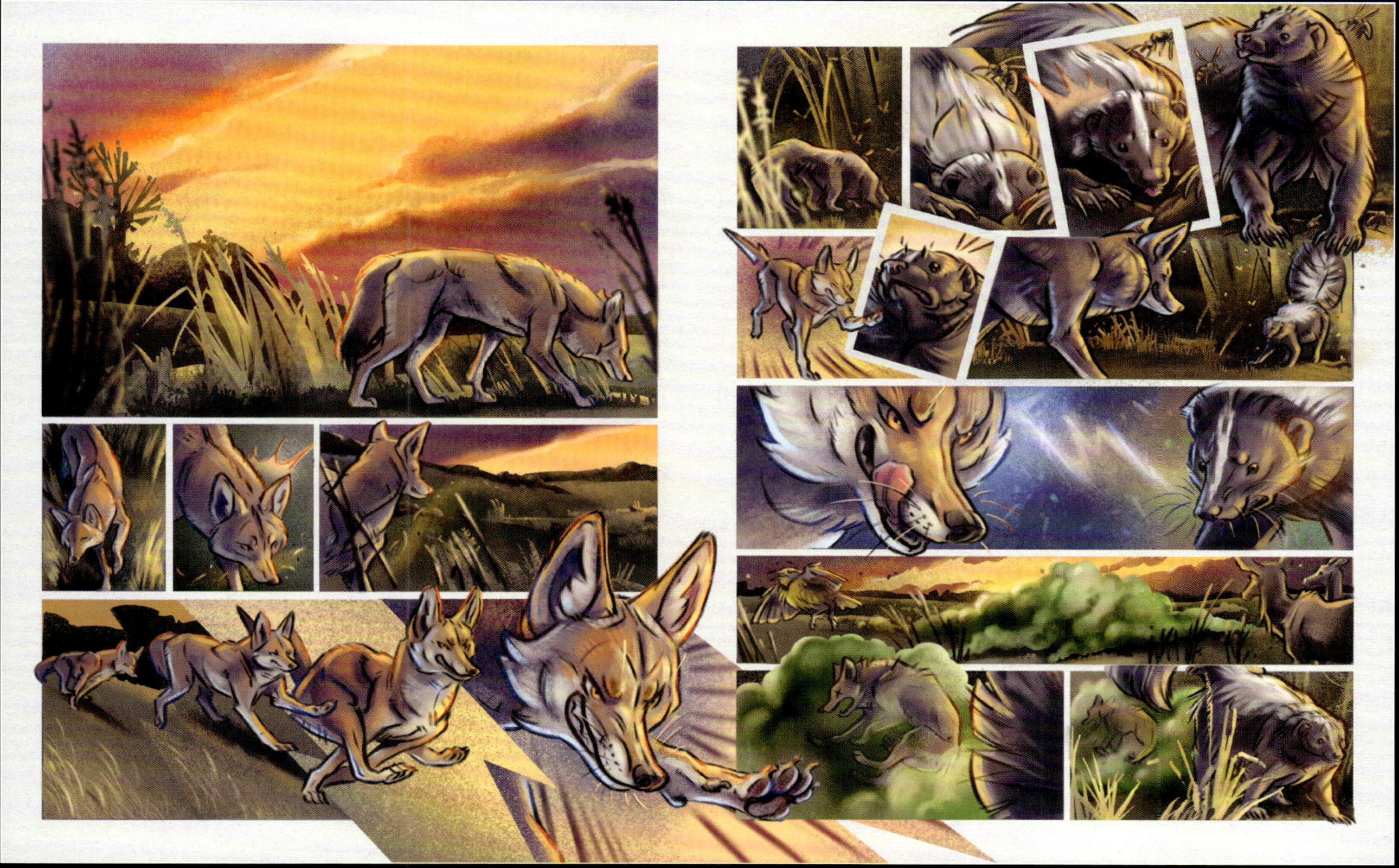

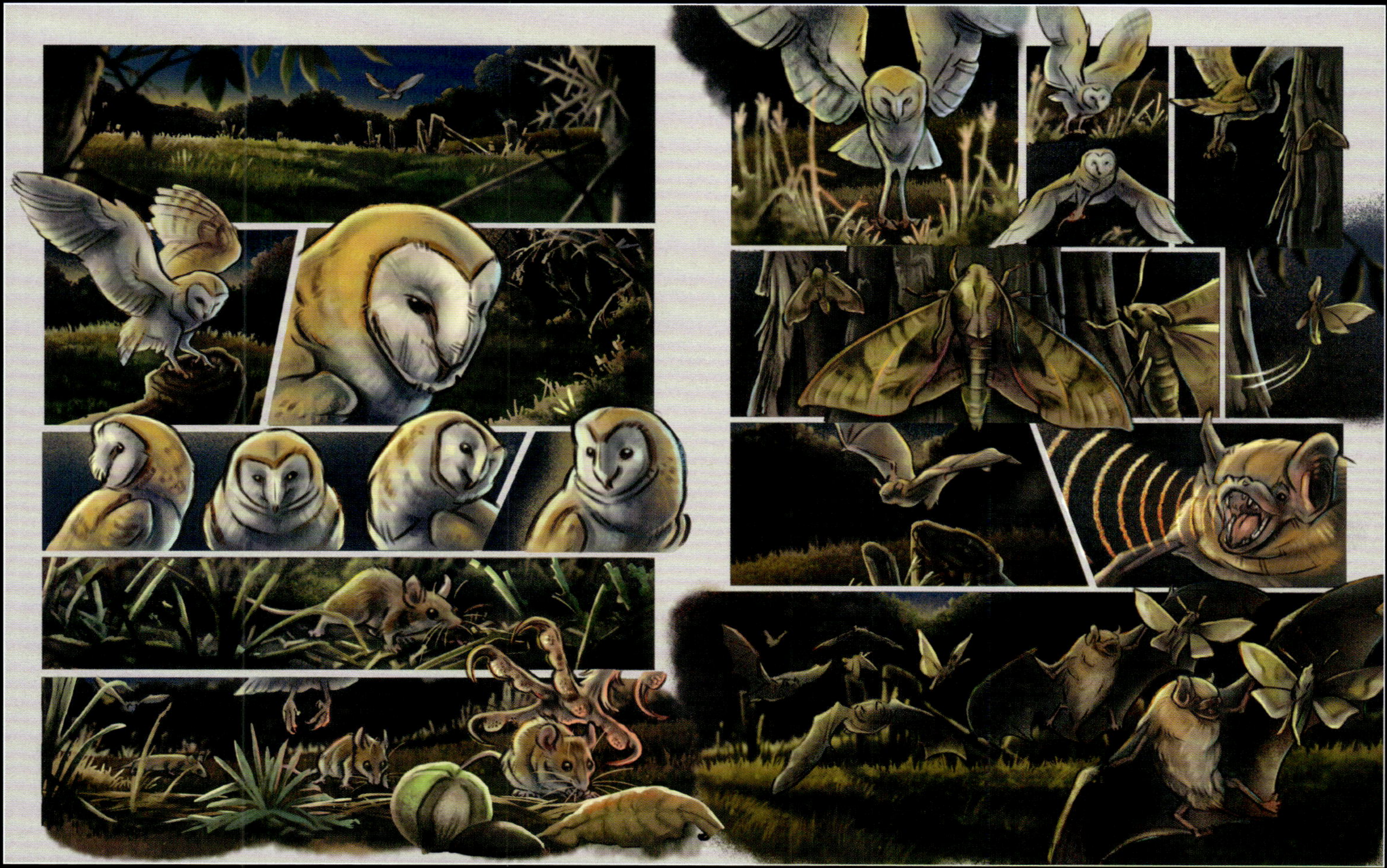

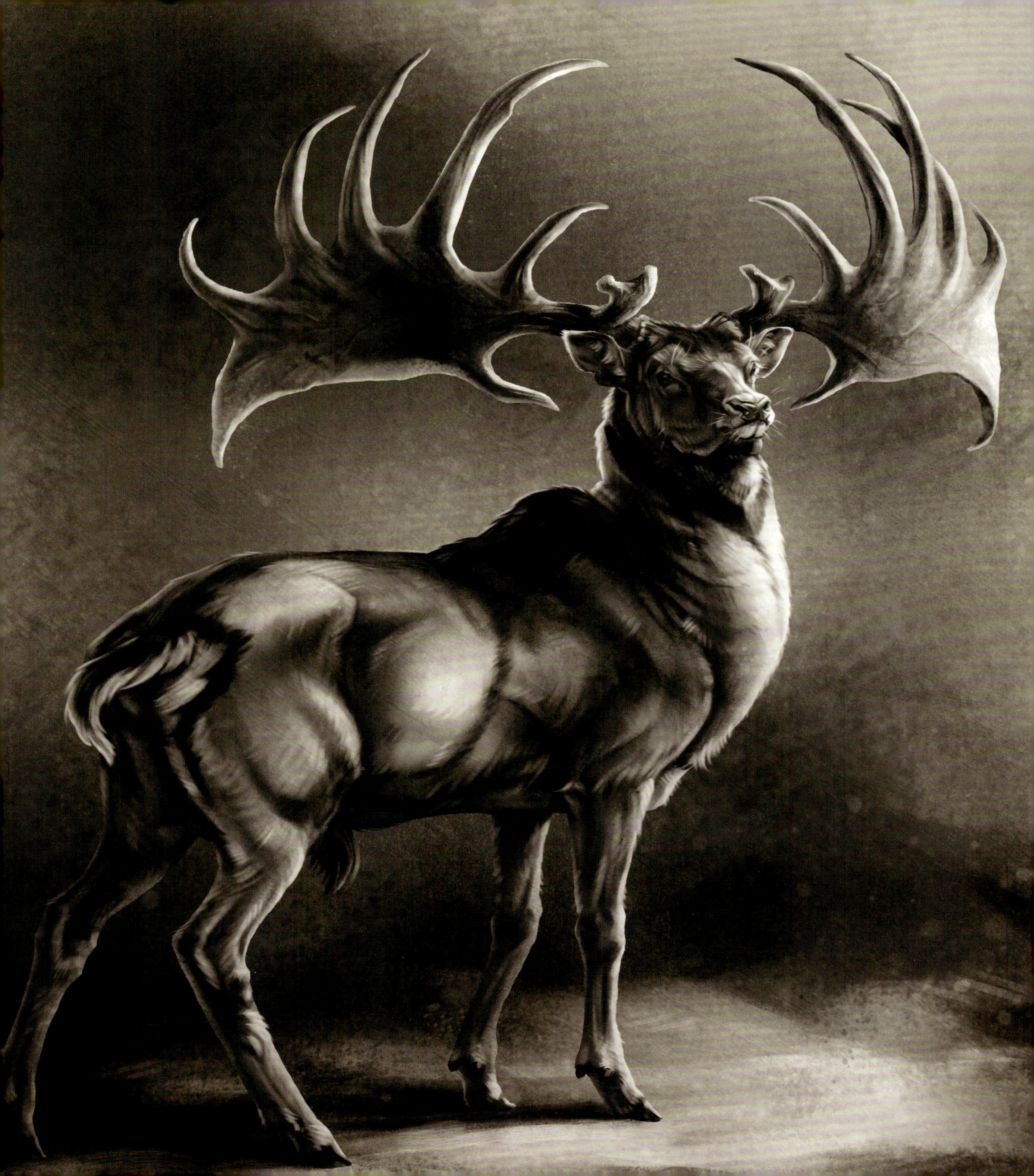

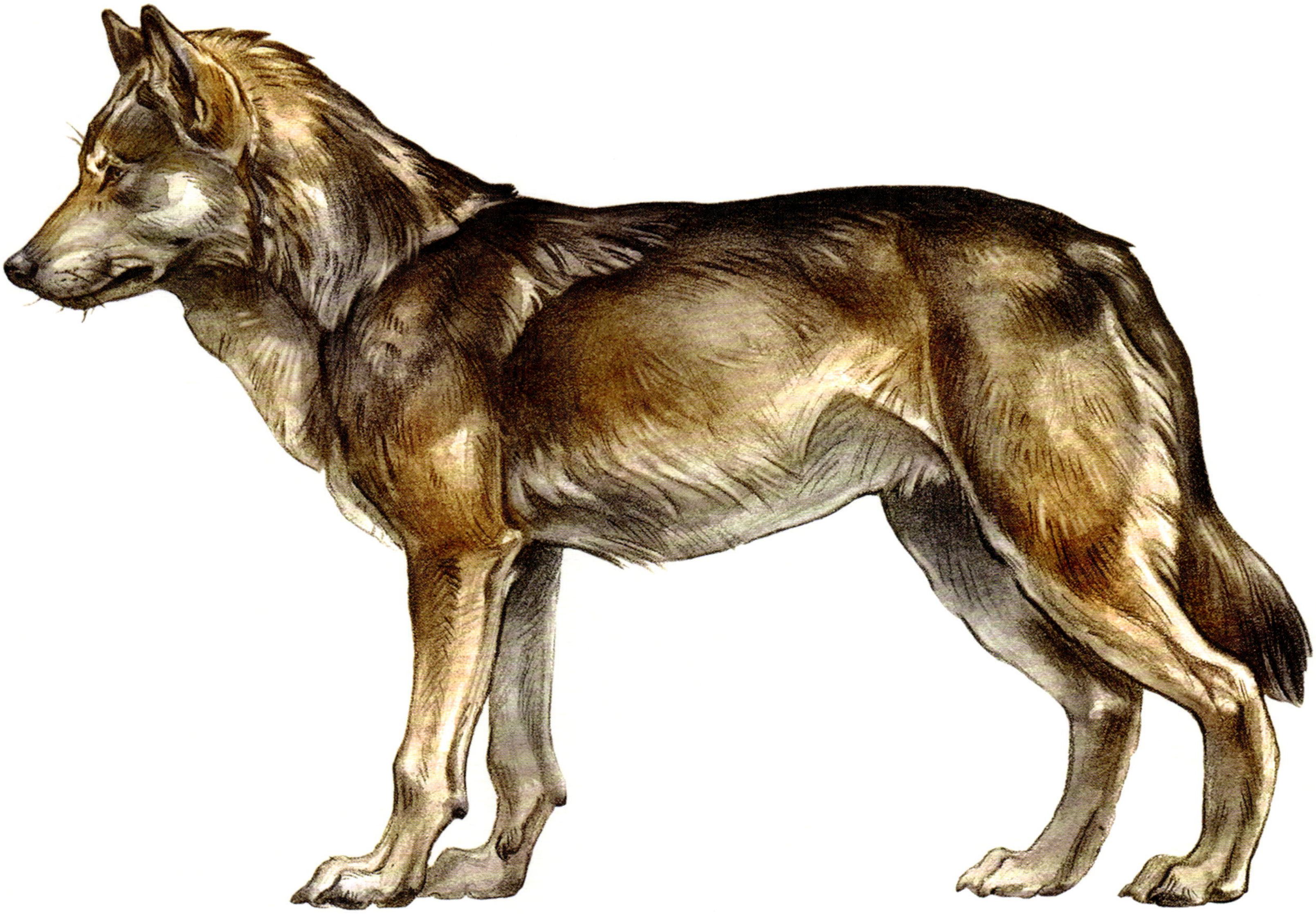

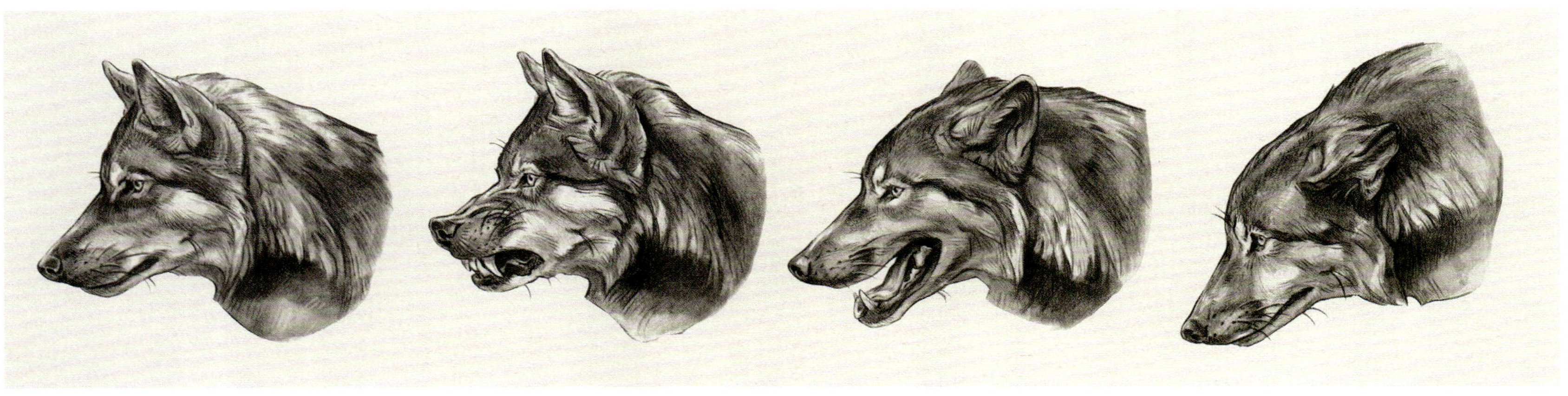

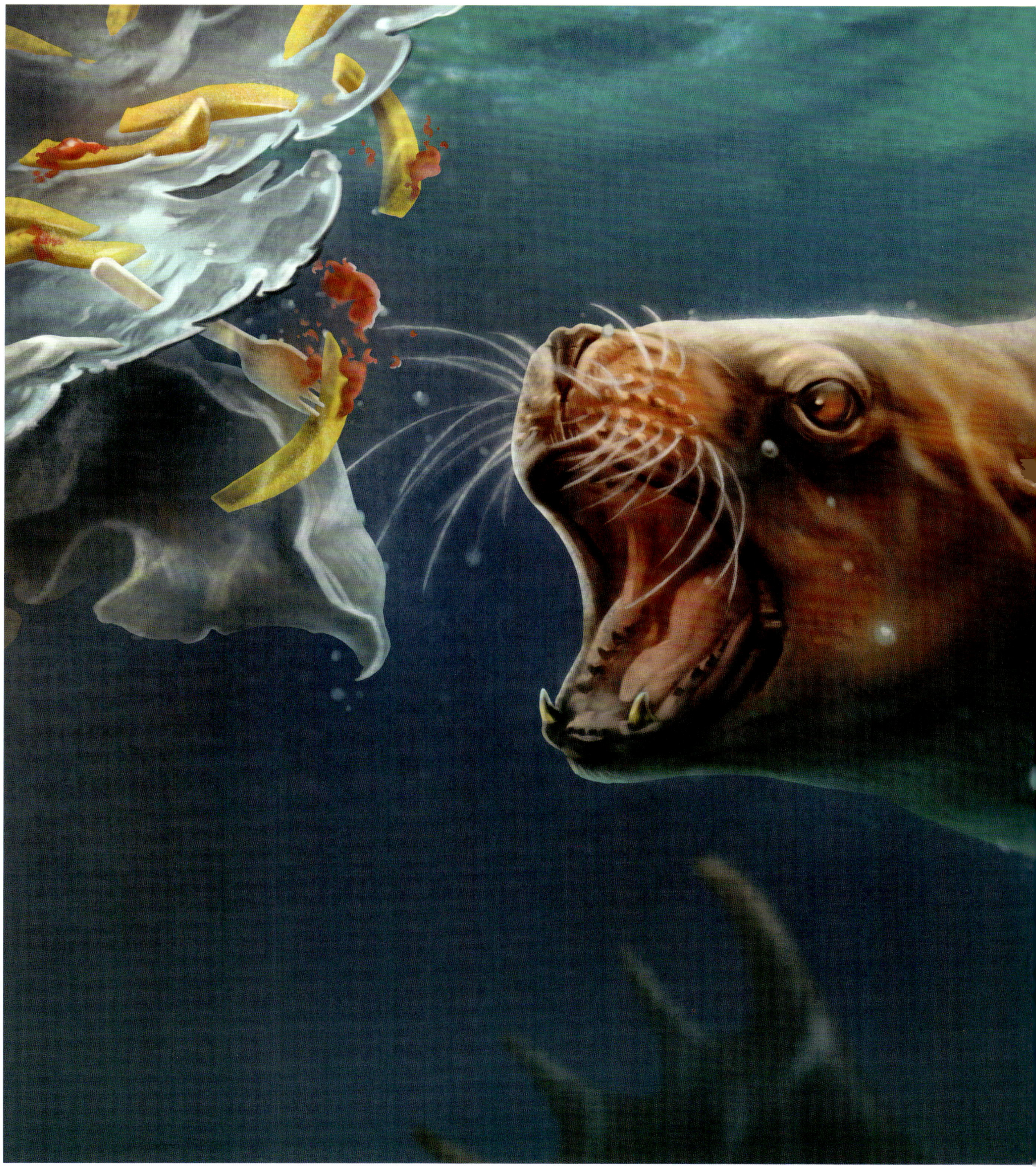

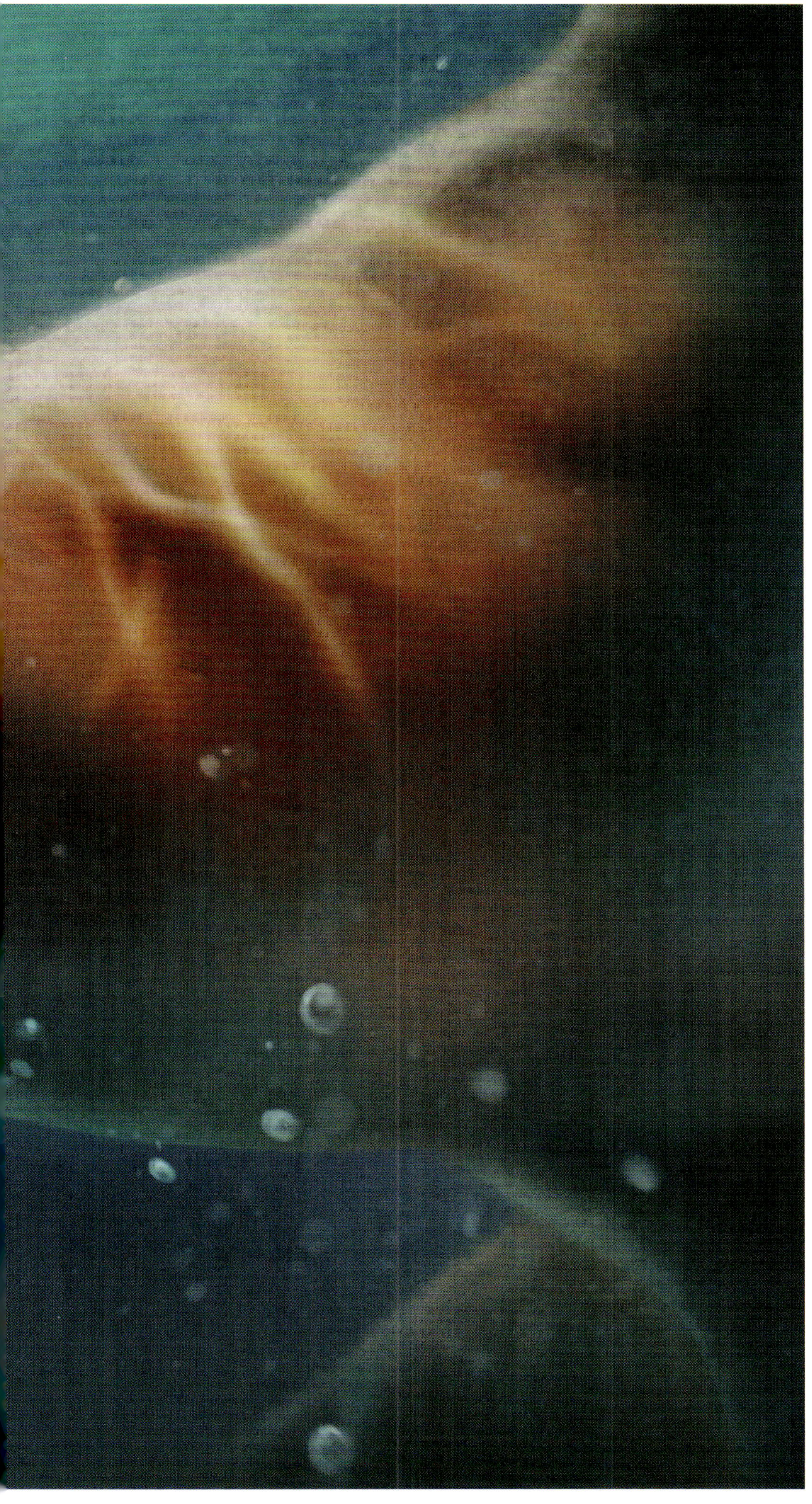

Glossary

Bipedalism
The ability to move upright on two legs, whether walking, striding, or running. This is a defining characteristic of humans, though primates possess a level of bipedal ability too.

Bird
Warm-blooded vertebrates with feathers, beaks, and wings, including hawks, penguins, hummingbirds, and flamingos. Birds reproduce by laying eggs, and most of them can fly.

Bony landmarks
The underlying structure of an animal's bones and joints, visible on their outward form. Including these in your animal drawings will prevent them from looking shapeless and 'stuffed'.

Bovine
A group of medium to large ungulates, including bison, cows, buffalo, and some antelope. They are herbivorous mammals and typically have cloven hooves.

Canine
Members of the dog family, which includes domestic dogs as well as wild relatives such as wolves and foxes.

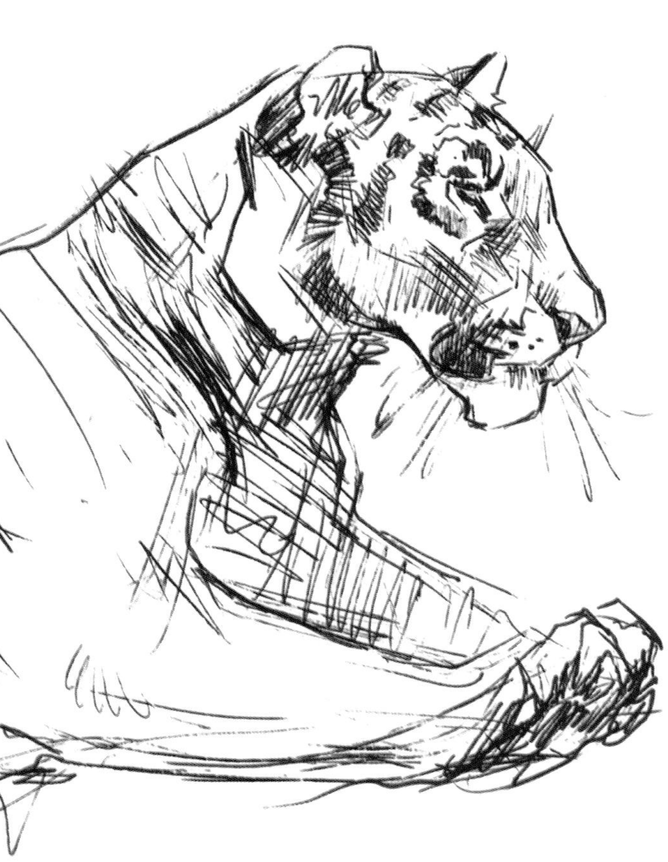

Comparative anatomy
The study of similarities and differences in the anatomy of different species.

Construction
A method of drawing using simplified forms. Linear construction uses lines to draw shapes and forms in a way that shows their three-dimensional structure by drawing 'through' everything as though it is transparent.

Contour lines
Lines used to define the edges of a form or shape, creating a two-dimensional representation of a three-dimensional object.

Cross-contour drawing
Drawing lines – often elliptical ones – around sections of forms or shapes to reveal their three-dimensional qualities.

Digitigrade
Animals that walk on their toes, such as cats and dogs.

Equine
Members of the horse family, including horses, zebras, and asses. They are herbivorous mammals with a single hoof, unlike cloven-hoofed bovines.

Feline
Members of the cat family, including lions, tigers, lynxes, and domestic cats. They are carnivorous mammals.

Fish
An aquatic, cold-blooded, vertebrate animal with fins and gills.

Foreshortening
Drawing an object that appears to be angled towards or away from the viewer, or objects that recede away from or advance towards the viewer. As forms recede in space, they get smaller and change shape.

Forms
Three-dimensional shapes – such as cylinders, spheres, and boxes – that can be combined or morphed to construct an animal drawing.

Gesture drawing
A way of capturing the life, character, or essence of what your subject is doing, either as a work of art on its own or a means of laying in a drawing. They are typically sketched quickly and composed of long, sweeping, and rhythmical lines.

Hind
A body part that is behind, such as hind legs or hind paws.

Line of action
A tool used by artists to make their subject matter, whether animal or human, more dramatic and dynamic. This is often the animal's spine, as it powers the body's movement, but any body part can be a point of departure.

Mammal
Vertebrate animals with fur or hair, where the females of the species have milk-producing mammary glands to feed their young. These range from whales and giraffes through to weasels and bats.

Phalangeal pads
The cushion-like part of an animal's paw or digit (toe).

Planar
A shape that is two-dimensional or formed from flat, geometric surfaces.

Plantigrade
Mammals that walk on the soles of their feet, such as humans and bears.

Quadrupedalism
The ability to walk on four feet, as opposed to upright on two.

Reference
Materials and resources – such as photographs, diagrams, or artwork – used to inform your drawing.

Reptile
Cold-blooded vertebrate animals, such as crocodiles, lizards, and snakes. They typically lay eggs and have scaly skin.

Rodent
Small mammals characterized by a single pair of continually growing incisors in the upper and lower jaws, including mice, squirrels, and beavers.

Twinning
When an animal's legs are drawn in the same position on both sides. This creates a dull, stiff, symmetrical image that does not reflect natural movement.

Unguligrade
Animals that walk on hooves, such as horses and cattle.

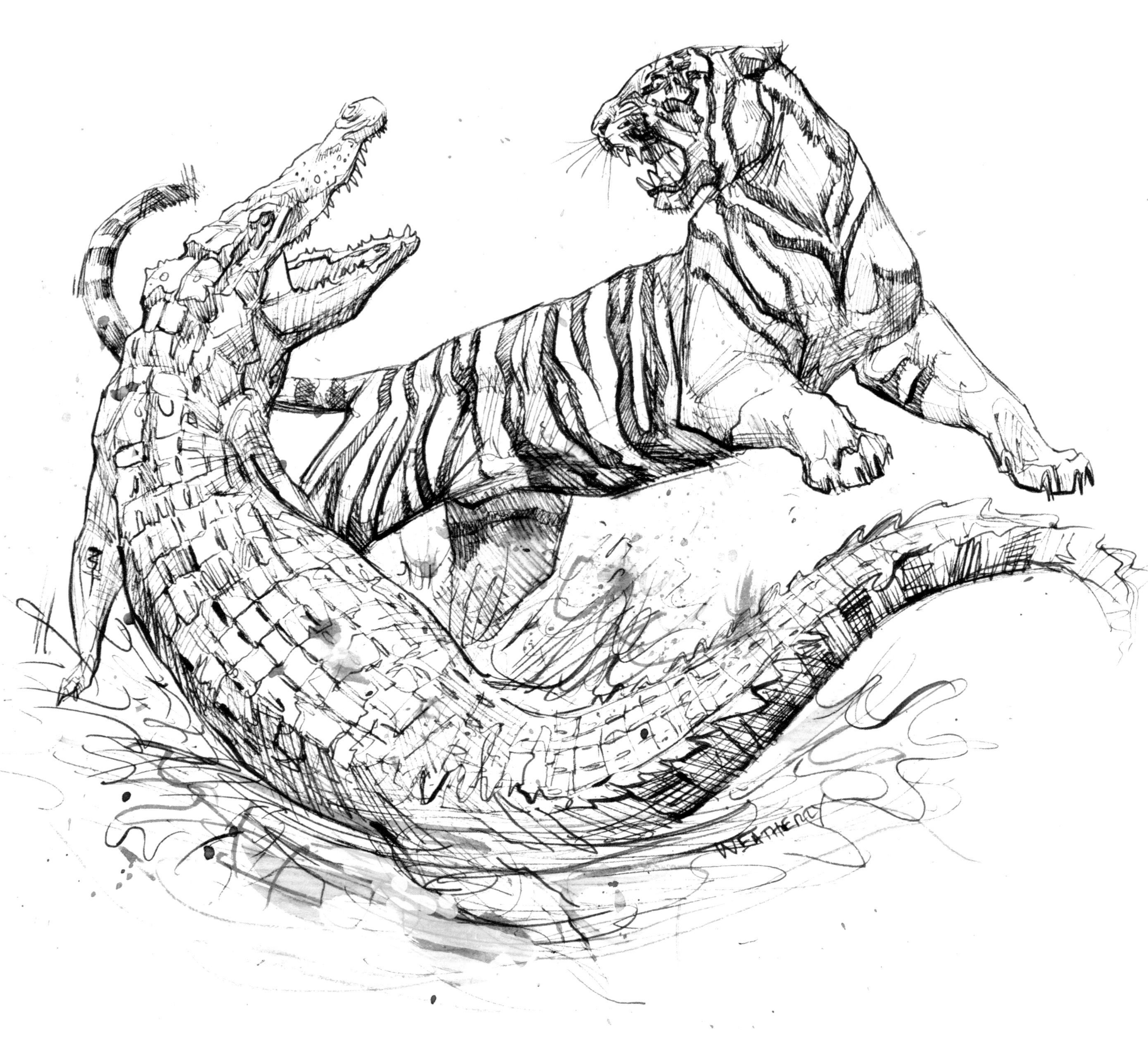
WEATHERLY

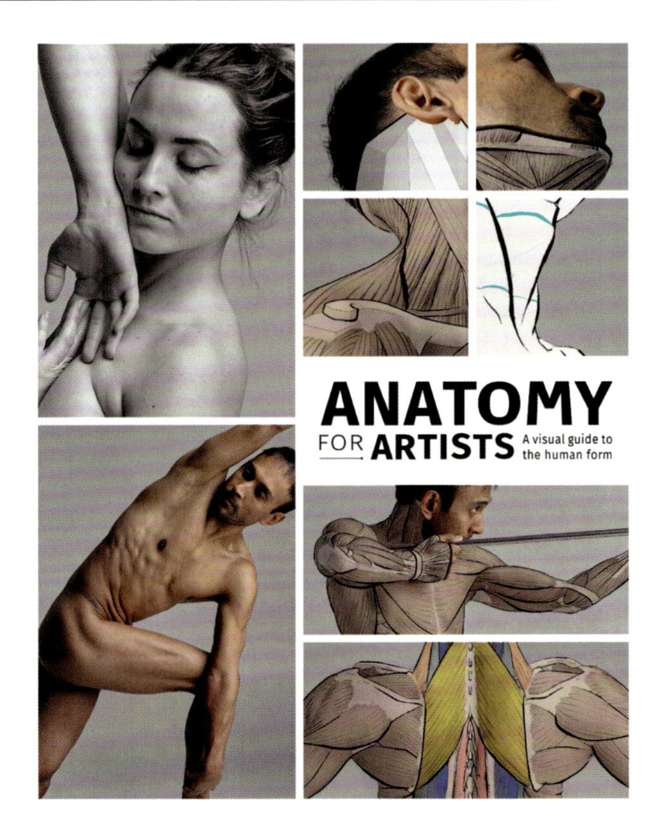

ANATOMY FOR ARTISTS

A visual guide to the human form

Anatomy for Artists is an extensive compendium of high-quality, detailed photography and drawings showing the human figure in a variety of shapes, sizes, and poses, which can be used as a solid foundation for all character art. This thorough and detailed library of visual resources consists of stunning photography and comprehensive drawings showing the muscular structure of figures of varying body types. These male and female references act as an invaluable starting point for artists trying to create art based on the human figure. Whether you're a traditional sculptor, oil painter, or 3D digital artist, the resources within this book will prove to be useful and informative and will help you improve the quality and accuracy of your own art.

ANATOMY IN MOTION

An artist's guide to capturing dynamic movement

Study the dynamic movements of the human figure with *Anatomy in Motion*, a huge collection of detailed photography and layered illustrations. Hundreds of shots capture professional models performing a wide range of actions, from walking and jumping to combat and dance. Explore each pose in depth with planar, contour, and muscle illustrations that provide an innovative visual resource for artists of any skill level or medium. Building on the success of 3dtotal Publishing's previous *Anatomy for Artists*, this volume is a must-have for anyone seeking to capture the beauty and complexity of humans in motion.

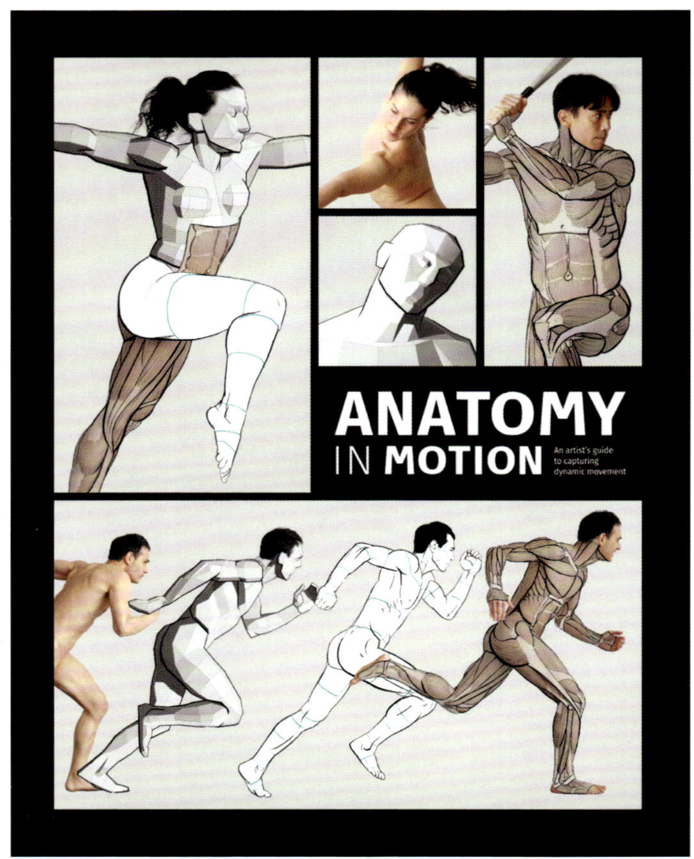

store.3dtotal.com

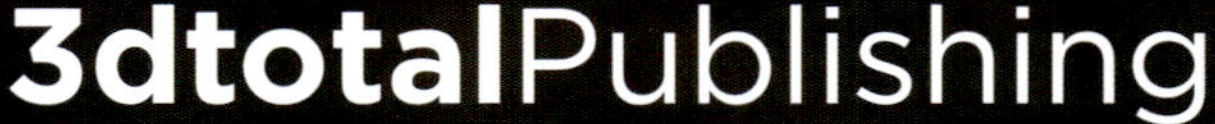

3dtotal Publishing is a trailblazing, creative publisher specializing in inspirational and educational resources for artists.

Our titles feature top industry professionals from around the globe who share their experience in skilfully written step-by-step tutorials and fascinating, detailed guides. Illustrated throughout with stunning artwork, these bestselling publications offer creative insight, expert advice, and essential motivation. Fans of digital art will enjoy our comprehensive volumes covering Adobe Photoshop, Procreate, and Blender, as well as our superb titles based around character design, including *Fundamentals of Character Design* and *Creating Characters for the Entertainment Industry*. The dedicated, high-quality blend of instruction and inspiration also extends to traditional art. Titles covering a range of techniques, genres, and abilities allow your creativity to flourish while building essential skills.

Well-established within the industry, we now offer over 100 titles and counting, many of which have been translated into multiple languages around the world. With something for every artist, we are proud to say that our books offer the 3dtotal package:

LEARN • CREATE • SHARE

Visit us at store.3dtotal.com

3dtotal Publishing is part of 3dtotal.com, a leading website for CG artists. founded by Tom Greenway in 1999.

Photograph © Markus Varesvuo / Agami.nl

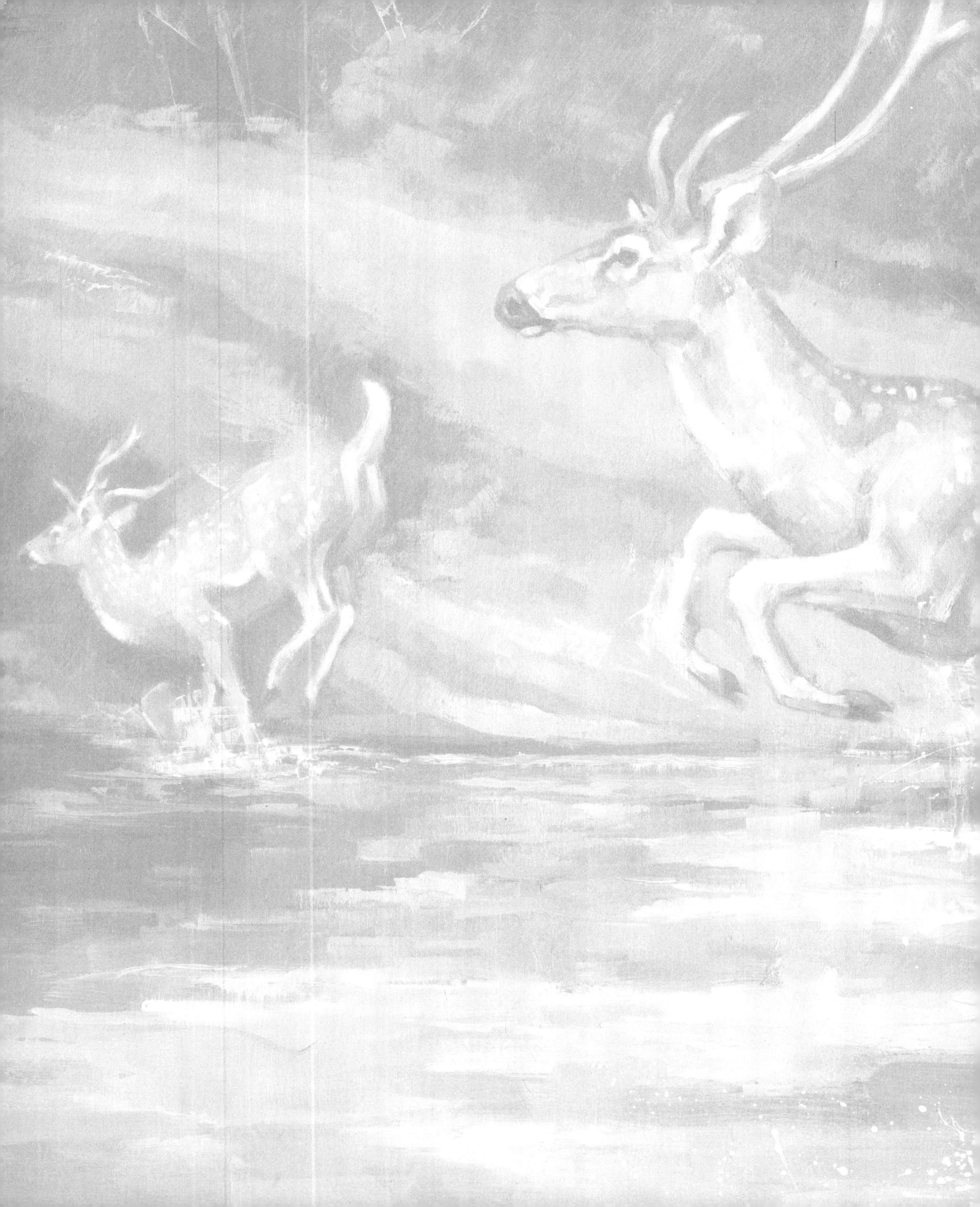